I0762220

BRUTALIST
KOREA

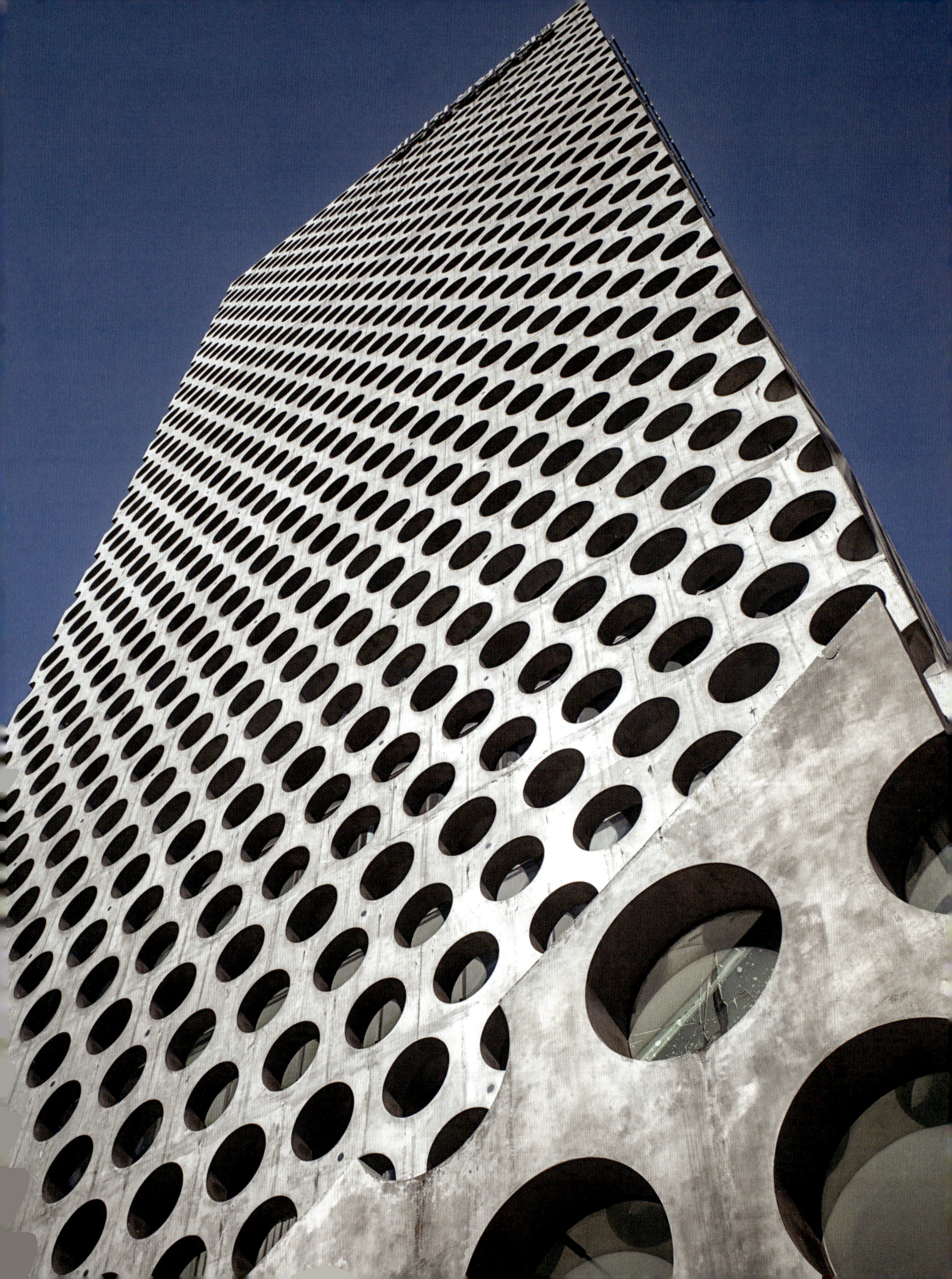

PAUL TULETT

BRUTALIST KOREA

PRESTEL

Munich · London · New York

CONTENTS

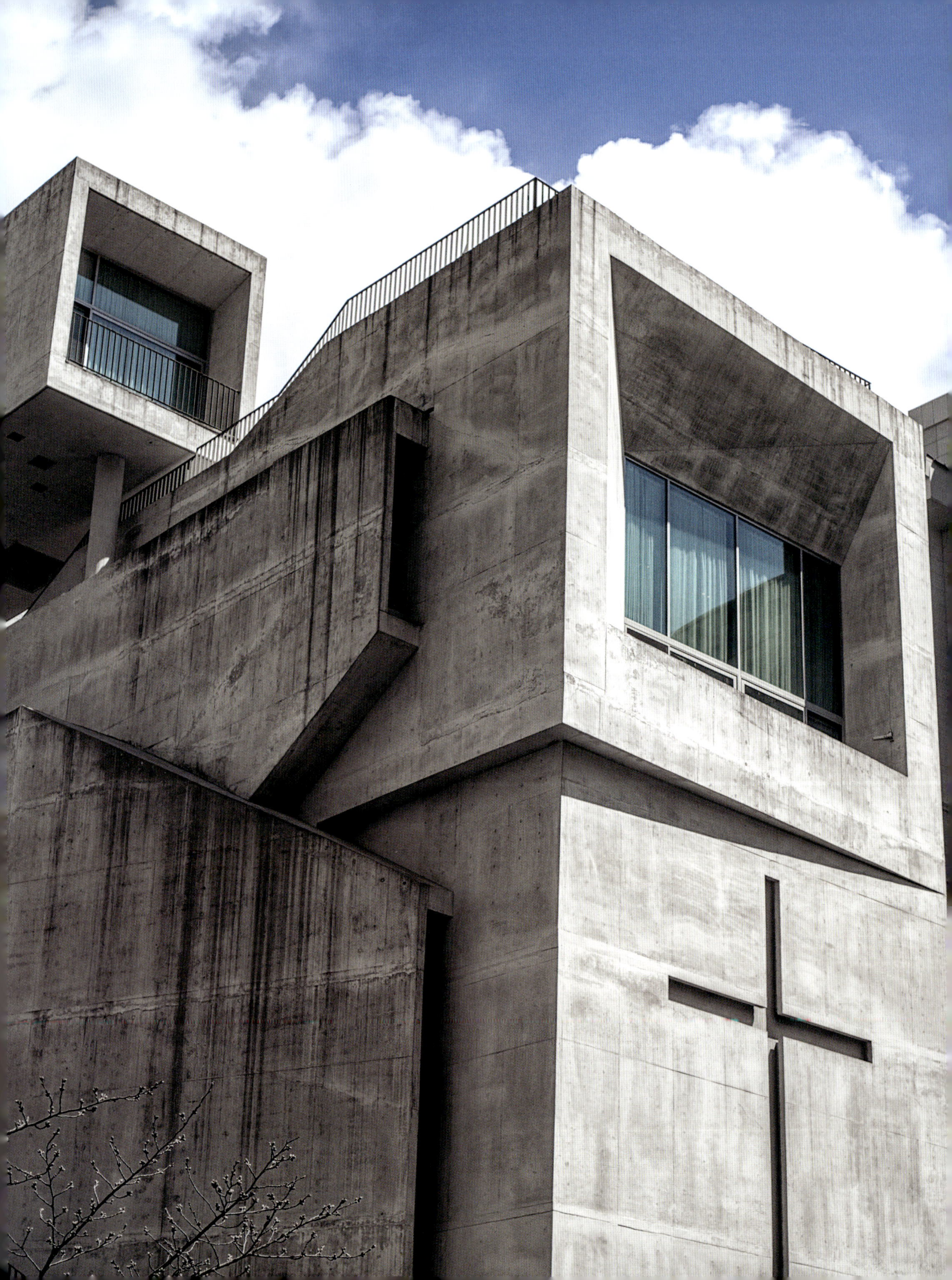

Nu-Bru is a term I've coined to partner with my more wanky *béton nécessaire*. The latter covers the necessity of concrete in typhoon-ravaged Okinawa. Nu-Bru placates the pedants that insist upon a certain Eurocentric timeline for Brutalist architecture and covers contemporary concrete constructions exemplified by South Korea. Essentially, this is what this book is about. But don't fret. I cover old-school examples.

Curt by name, curt by nature, my editor pinged me a short article on concrete architecture in Seoul and simply asked, "Is there a book in this?" "For sure. Pyongyang and that?" "Nah, we can't afford you getting arrested." Doubt it. Anyway, here we focus on Brutalist architecture south of the 38th parallel.

Béton Beyond Borders

When I first began photographing Brutalist architecture in Japan, I thought I'd already found my concrete Valhalla. But Korea, it turns out, wasn't merely waiting in the wings – it was quietly rebuilding the stage. If Japan's *béton nécessaire* spoke of refinement through adversity, Korea's concrete is a more impatient beast: raw, upright, hungry. Less Zen garden, more blast furnace. The Korean peninsula doesn't politely inherit modernism, it consumes it, metabolizes it, and spits it out with edge.

It's impossible to talk about Korean Brutalism without talking about trauma – war, division, and the breakneck sprint into modernity that followed. Concrete was the language of rebuilding, not ideology. In the West, Brutalism was a manifesto; in Korea, it was a method. Post-war necessity gave it traction; ambition gave it teeth. Architects like Kim Swoo-geun and Kim Chung-up conjured a modernism that didn't mimic Europe, but conversed with it – brusquely, perhaps, but on its own terms.

Kim Swoo-geun's Space Group Building (1971) remains an audacious act of architectural autobiography: part machine, part metaphor for national awakening. Its labyrinthine interior feels like a nation trying to remember how to breathe. Meanwhile, Kim Chung-up's French Embassy (1962) – that quietly evocative composition of concrete – distilled diplomacy into architecture. You can almost hear the conversations about independence, identity, and influence vibrating through the grain.

If Japan had folded its modernity into quiet refinement, Korea welded its own version into a skeleton of identifying necessity. These early Korean masters didn't seek beauty – they sought truth, and beauty arrived, reluctantly, as a by-product.

Raw Republic

By the late 1960s, Seoul was a city mid-explosion. The Olympic ambitions, the rise of education as a national faith, the sprawling dormitories of the middle class – all required architecture that could be built quickly, stand firmly, and symbolize modern life without apology. Concrete was not an aesthetic choice, it was an ethical one.

I've thought that old-school Korean Brutalism often feels more corporeal than cerebral. The concrete doesn't whisper of technique – it announces survival. You can sense the hands that poured it, the sweat that hardened into the aggregate. There's nothing reticent about Kim Chung-up's Dr Seo's Women's Clinic (1967). At the intersection of Eulji and Toegye roads, the building reads like a manifesto in curves – an architecture of anatomy over geometry. Its concrete skin bends and swells with purpose, its folds forming a consultation between protection and exposure. Light travels over its concave surfaces like breath, animating the façade as if the structure itself were inhaling the city's haste and exhaling calm. Inside, Kim traded efficiency for intimacy: walls and furniture entangled in sculptural conversation, a deliberate resistance to the sterile logic of medical space. He once described it as "an ode to newborn life", and that sense of renewal lingers. Set near Gwanghuimun, the former "gate of the dead", the clinic repositions the urban narrative – from passage to afterlife to threshold of beginning. In 1960s Korea, where concrete embodied both state ambition and personal modernity, Kim used it to craft a sanctuary that was neither purely functional nor purely symbolic. The result is an act of architectural tenderness in a time of industrial severity – a small, curved defiance against the straight lines of progress.

Aum Duck-moon's Sejong Center for the Performing Arts (1978) is more lineal: a cultural lung beating in theatrical concrete. Opposite sits the U.S. Embassy – sleek, smug, and sealed – while the Sejong brims with civic theatre and public noise. One trades in diplomacy, the other in drama, but both rely on performance. If concrete is the state's costume, Seoul wears it with complex pride.

To be honest, the Sejong Center has the totalitarian overtures of Brutalism I asked readers to expunge in *Brutalist Japan*. Bear in mind, though, that South Korea was a "developmental dictatorship" under Park Chung-hee (1961–79) and Chun Doo-hwan (1980–88).

This was the age when Brutalism wasn't yet retro – it was revolutionary, if also authoritarian.

Brutalist Balance

There's a particularly Korean way of making concrete personal. Where European Brutalism often alienates, Korean Brutalism invites. The rough textures, deep recesses, and sunken-ness are never simply visual. They're gestures towards empathy, towards creating pause in the rush.

For decades following the Second World War, East Asia remained deeply fragmented. The region's key nations and territories – China, Japan, South Korea, North Korea, Taiwan, and Hong Kong – existed in relative isolation from one another and from the wider world. This geopolitical separation profoundly shaped their architectural cultures and influenced how the ideas and aesthetics of Brutalism were received, adapted, and circulated within each society.

In South Korea, rising anti-Japanese sentiment after disputes over wartime reparations pressured Kim Swoo-geun – educated in architecture at the University of Tokyo – to abandon his earlier sculptural concrete style. His design for the Puyo National Museum (1965–71) was criticized as being "too Japanese", prompting a shift towards a Brutalist language of monumentality that embraced native materials, especially brick, and emphasized spatial experience as a means of expressing Korean identity. This complex interplay between Brutalist principles and regional expression has continued to shape East Asian architecture, fostering new interpretations of place amidst the dominance of global design trends.

Korean architectural writer Hyungmin Pai states that "Brutalism is a problematic idea for South Korea." Although numerous notable buildings from the 1960s and early 1970s display traits associated with the term, few within Korea's architectural community at the time were even aware it existed. While several factors contributed to the widespread use of concrete, the simplest explanation lies in the lack of viable alternatives: up until the 1980s, concrete and brick were virtually the only available construction materials in South Korea. Government emphasis on cement production and the promotion of construction as a national economic driver encouraged the rise of labour-intensive cast-in-place concrete structures. Simultaneously, whether through interpretations of traditional Korean motifs or expressive sculptural forms, concrete became the principal medium through which both state and private architects articulated their architectural identity.

Brick Benedictions

Then there is Kyungdong Presbyterian Church. The expanding Christian institutions in South Korea became a key source of commissions for architects pursuing a design language that could evoke poetic simplicity through unembellished spatial form.

In its structural essence, Kyungdong Church embodies many hallmarks typical of its era: the dense layering of functions within a complex section, a desire for expressive form, and an uneasy dialogue with Seoul's ever-shifting urban fabric. At the same time, it is a compelling example of how architecture absorbs social and technical realities, offering a distinct reflection of its moment and context. Completed in 1981, the project represents the culmination of Kim Swoo-geun's architectural philosophy and is one of the defining works by South Korea's foremost twentieth-century architects. Following his 1960s role as the de facto state architect for a rapidly industrializing nation, Kyungdong Church reveals his effort to fuse the monumental force of his earlier *béton brut* style with a new-found intimacy and sensitivity to material and identity.

Located on a compact, bustling site in Seoul, the church forms an enclosed inner world defined by conjoined towers that incline from their upper portions. Its exterior, clad in brick intentionally fractured for a rough texture, references the long association between brick and ecclesiastical architecture while reflecting the labour-intensive practicality of the material in early 1980s Korea. Inside, multiple programmes are deftly interwoven through a tightly composed sectional plan. What appears irregular follows a disciplined system of parallel walls, angled to shape and direct space. The main chapel's heavy concrete piers and beams define a rhythmic, enclosed volume, evoking spiritual depth. Despite later alterations, the church remains amongst the most intact examples of Kim's built legacy. Strikingly, it forgoes the rooftop cross typical of Korean churches.

In a nation known for its vast and fervent Christian movements, Kyungdong Church houses one of South Korea's most progressive congregations. Here, absence itself becomes a defining presence – an architectural expression of strength through restraint and quiet conviction.

Seoul Searching

Shooting Seoul, I sensed an architectural split personality: one half sprinting towards futurism, the other pausing to remember. Amidst the glass towers stand stubborn slabs of sincerity. Some have survived half a century of development pressures simply because they refuse to yield. Brutalism here is less movement than adaptation and resurfacing. I asked the editor if I should stick to the capital and call the book *Solid Seoul*. A big thanks to him for saying no.

North-west of the city lies Paju Book City, a utopian experiment in publishing and urban planning conceptually inspired by Hay-on-Wye in Wales – the small "town of books" famous for its second-hand shops and literary festivals. Where Hay-on-Wye grew organically, Paju was meticulously planned by the Korean Publishers Association and the national government as an integrated hub for every stage of book production – writing, printing, publishing, and distribution. It sought not tourism but coherence: a "city of books" unified through architectural restraint, high-quality materials, and the fusion of industry and artistry.

This framework produced one of the most distinctive architectural experiments in Asia – a landscape of Neo-Brutalism, or what might be called "new concrete humanism". From the outset, strict design guidelines banned visual noise: no billboards, no bright colours, no façades competing for attention. Exposed concrete became the unifying language – neutral, austere, and endlessly expressive through texture, light, and proportion. By the 1990s and early 2000s, Korean architects, influenced by Tadao Ando and the legacy of Kim Swoo-geun, had rediscovered concrete as both ethical and artistic – a material that conveyed permanence and intellect rather than spectacle.

Concrete's tactile honesty suits Korea's climate and the contemplative mission of Paju itself. It softens light, absorbs silence, and merges with the riverine landscape near the demilitarized zone (DMZ). Each building follows shared rules of modesty and clarity, yet the city's streets are alive with subtle variation – freedom thrives within discipline. For many architects, concrete here became the physical analogue of the printed page: plain, weighty, and enduring.

Digital fabrication and parametric tools haven't diluted Brutalism here; they've sharpened it. Lines are cleaner, junctions tighter, yet the material speaks with the same gravitas. Korea's contemporary architects seem to treat Brutalism as code: something that can be rewritten but never erased.

Sayuwon

"Say you won"? I'm always winning. Waking up with a hard hangover, I needed to get out of a concrete conundrum I had cornered myself into. Time to get out of my search for the solid. To the north of Daegu lies Sayuwon – a mountain arboretum and architecture garden that straddles the line between wilderness and built form. Spread across the ridges of Palgongsan, it hosts a constellation of architectural "interruptions" in raw concrete and steel rust – interventions by Álvaro Siza, Seung H-Sang, and others. Here the solid faced me again. No getaway.

Here, concrete is not spectacle. In Soyoheon, Siza frames voids and courtyards in rough, unadorned concrete, arranging fragments like islands of light and shadow. With his Sodae, a leaning 20.5-metre concrete tower, apertures open onto views, translating borrowed scenery (*chagyeong*) into architectural act.

Walking through Sayuwon is to step through a choreography of mass and void, light and texture. The concrete interventions often recede, become overgrown, or sit quietly in shadow – they do not shout. They escort your senses, rustle your mind. Some parts barely register until you become still. That tension – between presence and absence, between the raw geometry and the whisper of wind – is architecture as poetic pause.

In a place that deliberately blurs "nature first, then architecture", Sayuwon offers a counterpart to the urban Nu-Bru in Paju. Here, concrete is gentle insistence, not confrontation. It is silence shaped.

Brutalism's New Skin

There's a phrase I kept returning to as I travelled between Seoul, Busan, Daegu, and Jeju: "Brutalism reborn through precision, poise, and poetic concrete." It captures what I call Nu-Bru – the new Korean Brutalism that neither fetishizes nostalgia nor fears technology. Architects working in this style grew up in the shadow of steel and glass but rediscovered concrete's charisma. Their buildings are leaner, more measured, often polished smooth where their forebears were rough. Yet the intention remains the same: honesty, structure, truth.

Nu-Bru is Brutalism without the hangover. It doesn't beg to be loved or understood; it simply exists, comfortable in its weight. You can see it across the peninsula and on Jeju Island – where buildings wear concrete like a tailored suit: calm and utterly confident. Brutalist roots are evident in the massing and rhythm, but the tone is lyrical.

Throughout Korea, Nu-Bru appears less as revival than reincarnation. Architects embrace Brutalism's moral clarity but remix its tone – adding warmth, craft, and an almost cinematic composure.

So what exactly is Nu-Bru? It's not a movement – there's no manifesto, no clenched-fist rhetoric. It's an attitude. It's the realization that Brutalism's power does not lie in its age, but its ethics. These contemporary Korean buildings inherit the discipline of their predecessors but not the guilt. They're confident enough to use concrete without apology and humane enough to let light in.

The generally accepted time frame for "true" Brutalism – mid-1950s to late 1970s – is well represented here: Kim Swoo-geun's and Kim Chung-up's pioneering works, the Sejong Center, and others. But my lens extends beyond that horizon. Korea didn't stop making Brutalism when the world declared it passé. It just got better at it. This book, then, is less a retrospective than a revelation – recognition that the brutal can still be beautiful, that the honest can still be humane.

In these pages, you'll see the continuum: from raw civic concrete to polished digital mass, from weathered stoicism to sculptural grace. Nu-Bru is Brutalism after the apocalypse – architecture that remembers the past but faces forwards. Eyes on the horizon.

Concrete Confessions

As with Japan, my exploration of Brutalism in Korea began as curiosity and became confession. I came searching for relics and found relevance. Brutalism here never truly died

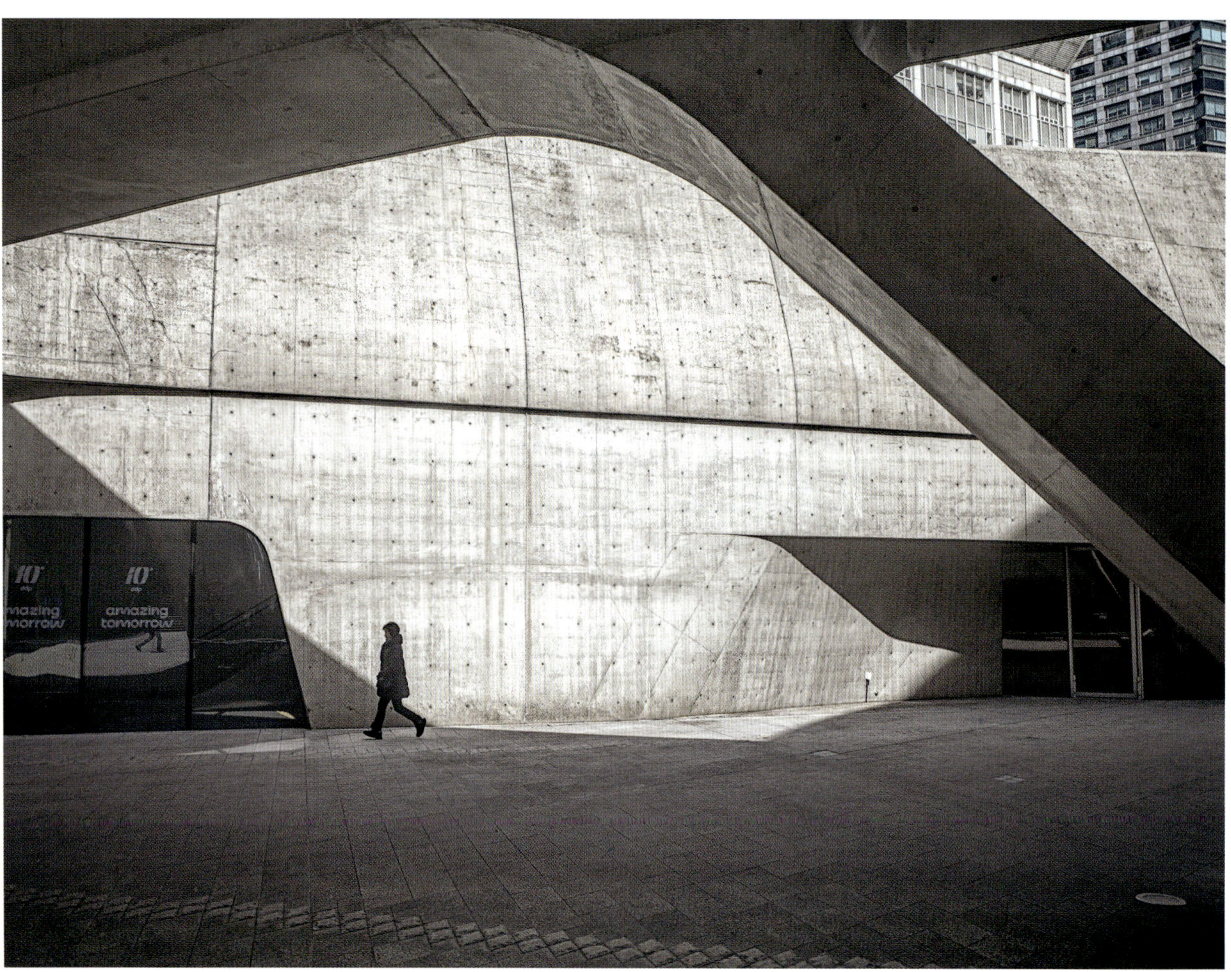

because it never became fashion – and thus could never go out of it. This challenges the notion that contemporary Korean concrete construction is the result of the nation's inherent faddishness or sheep-like nature. It is architecture as continuity, not commodity or fad.

Korea's relationship with concrete is less sentimental than Japan's and less cynical than the West's. It is pragmatic, born of willpower. This is a country where architecture still means work – physical, civic, and moral. Even when it flirts with aesthetics, there's always purpose beneath the polish.

When I shoot these buildings, I think less of preservation and more of persistence. The stains, the seams, the frost lines – they tell stories of survival, not decay. And while the Western debate around Brutalism obsesses over nostalgia, Korea just keeps building it.

Heavy Breathing

If Japan taught me that concrete could be spiritual, Korea taught me it could be stubbornly alive. These buildings breathe differently. They exhale confidence, scepticism, irony. They know that sincerity, like concrete, cracks under pressure but holds its shape. In a world distracted by lightness, Korea remains gloriously heavy.

The country's architects continue to refine the brutal impulse – to make it more precise, more performative, more human. From the solemn grace of Jeju's anonymous ecclesiastical works to the theatrical austerity of Seoul's civic blocks, Korea proves that Brutalism need not be frozen in the past. It can adapt, flirt, even smile.

Brutalism doesn't have to be cold, grey, or gone. In Korea, it's still breathing. And like the nation itself, it never really stopped building.

Solid Cyberscape

How is this aesthetic surviving?

Brutalism resonates with cyberpunk aesthetics both visually and ideologically. Its stark, utilitarian forms echo the dystopian urbanism, technological dominance, and industrial grit that define the genre. Exposed materials and monumental geometries evoke a world stripped of sentiment – an architecture of endurance that matches cyberpunk's hardened, hyper-mechanical cityscapes. In both, the built environment feels oppressive, indifferent, and inescapably real.

The vast, repetitive structures of Brutalism embody institutional power, reflecting cyberpunk's vision of humanity dwarfed by corporate and technological monoliths. Alienation becomes spatial: people rendered small within immense concrete labyrinths. Yet Brutalism's origins in social housing and civic idealism complicate this darkness – it once aimed for equality, just as cyberpunk heroes often fight for agency in dehumanized systems. Both Brutalism and cyberpunk reveal tension between collective aspiration and oppressive control.

Brutalism's credo of "form follows function" also aligns with cyberpunk's pragmatic worlds, where survival eclipses luxury and utility dictates form. This stripped-down honesty – raw concrete, exposed systems, visible mechanics – mirrors the genre's visual code: neon against decay, tech wired into flesh. Both share a fascination with the aesthetics of necessity, crafting beauty from what remains when comfort, polish, and illusion are gone. Functional realism becomes their common mantra. Perhaps Brutalism's aesthetic and moral overlap with cyberpunk explains its appeal amongst young gamers.

Cured Closure

Prior to putting this book together, I thought of Korea as a place of tentacled and existential drama, K-pop, fit female golfers, dead-eyed archers, and fermented cabbage. Now I know it punches above its weight in the Brutalist realm.

Following "Is there a book in this?", mass protest, physical assault, a car accident, and local kindness, here it is. *Gamsahabnida.*

DONGDAEMUN DESIGN PLAZA

SEOUL · Architect: Zaha HADID · Completed 2014

Brutalist Korea? So why start with architecture designed by Iraq-born and UK-based Hadid? Because it's brutally bloody brilliant. And it's ultra Nu-Bru.

Rising from the historical heart of Seoul like a colossal spacecraft crash-landed on centuries of memory, the Dongdaemun Design Plaza (DDP) is a monument to audacity. It is often read as fluid, futuristic, and post-structural – yet beneath the curvature lies a deeply Brutalist soul, one forged in concrete, complexity, and confrontation.

Though cloaked in aluminium skin, the structure is undergirded by an immense concrete skeleton – its flowing interior voids, cantilevered volumes, and massive spans recall the muscular confidence of old-school Brutalism. The vast underground galleries, poured-in-place concrete stairwells, and fortress-like substructure create a visceral, bodily experience: the architecture surrounds, dwarfs, and absorbs the visitor. Where classic Brutalism wore its concrete on the surface, the DDP sublimates it into experience – oppressive in scale, unapologetically raw beneath the sheen.

This is Brutalism reimagined as topography. The DDP's sinuous form subsumes the city's previous geometries – markets, walls, ruins – into one continuous architectural event. It rejects the grid, mocks the rectangle, and in doing so reflects Seoul's own rebellious, recursive growth. The plaza doesn't merely house design, it enacts it. Every fold, void, and ramp is a declaration that architecture can provoke, not just serve.

Yet for all its spectacle, the DDP carries cultural weight. It occupies the site of a former Japanese military facility and sits beside excavated Joseon relics. Like Korea itself, the DDP is built on the past but refuses to be defined by it. It vaults forwards, concrete lungs beneath a polished skin, brutal in ambition and execution.

In this light, the DDP is not an alien imposition, but a new Korean monument: a Brutalist phoenix, hatched from history, soaring towards futures yet unimagined.

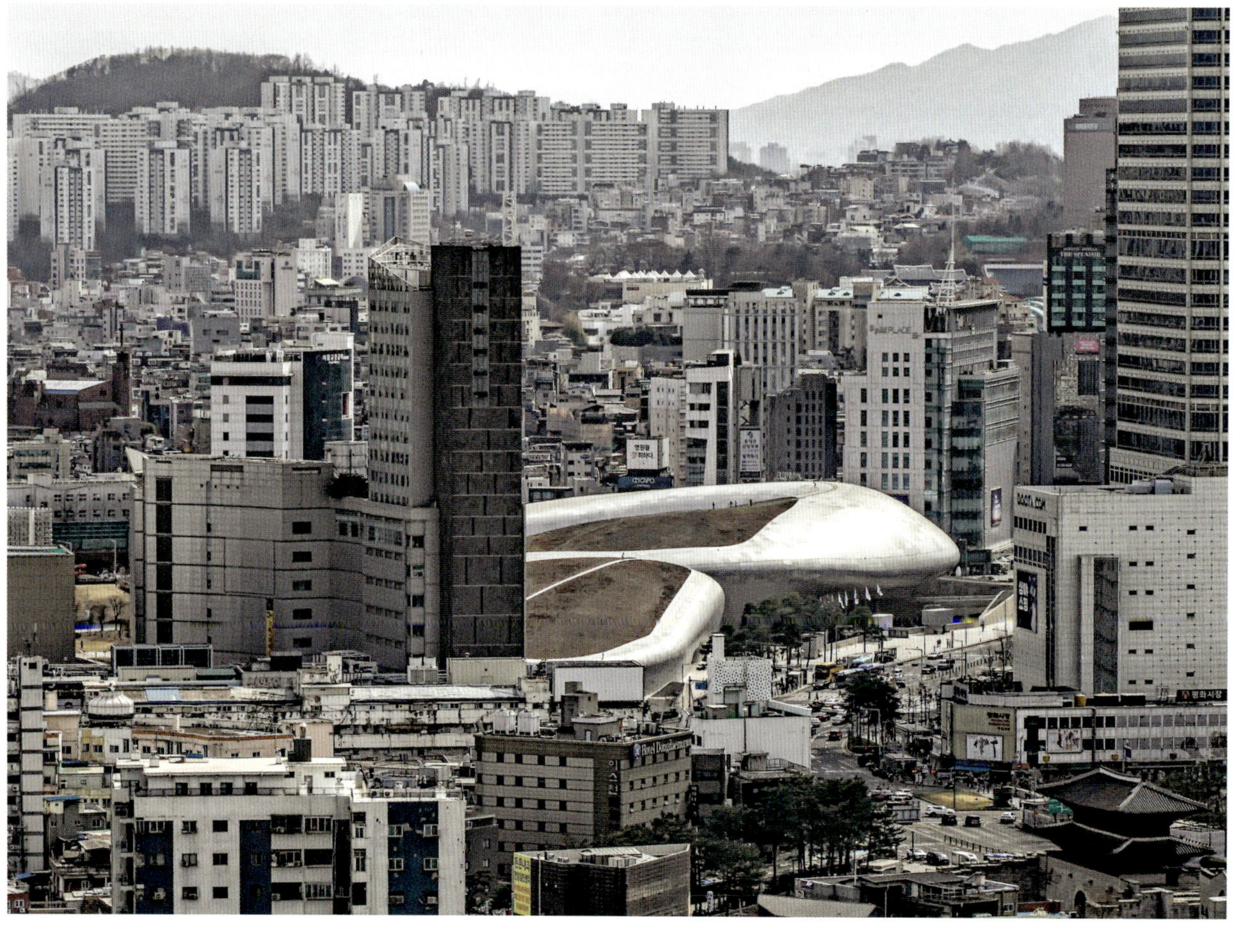

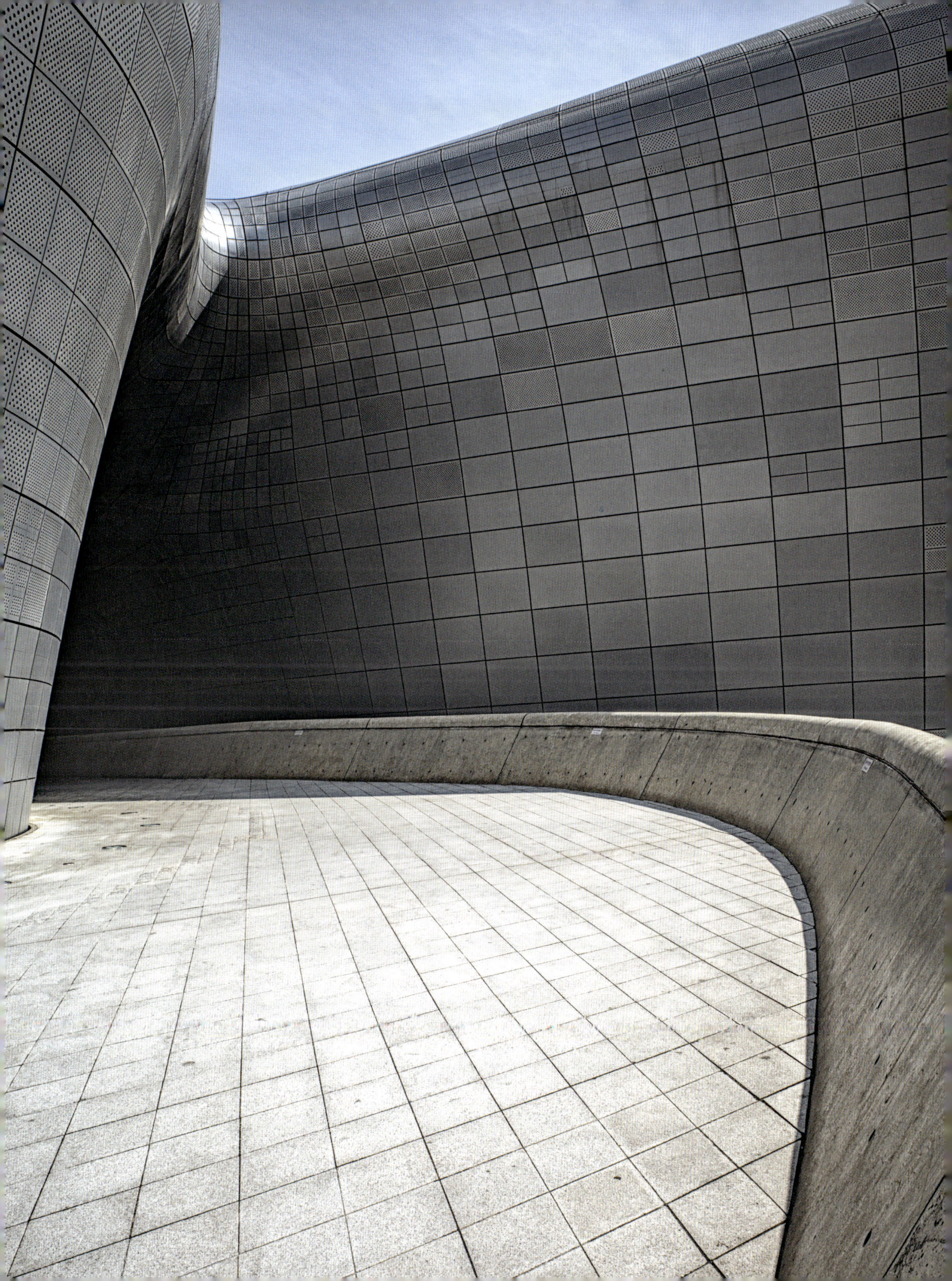

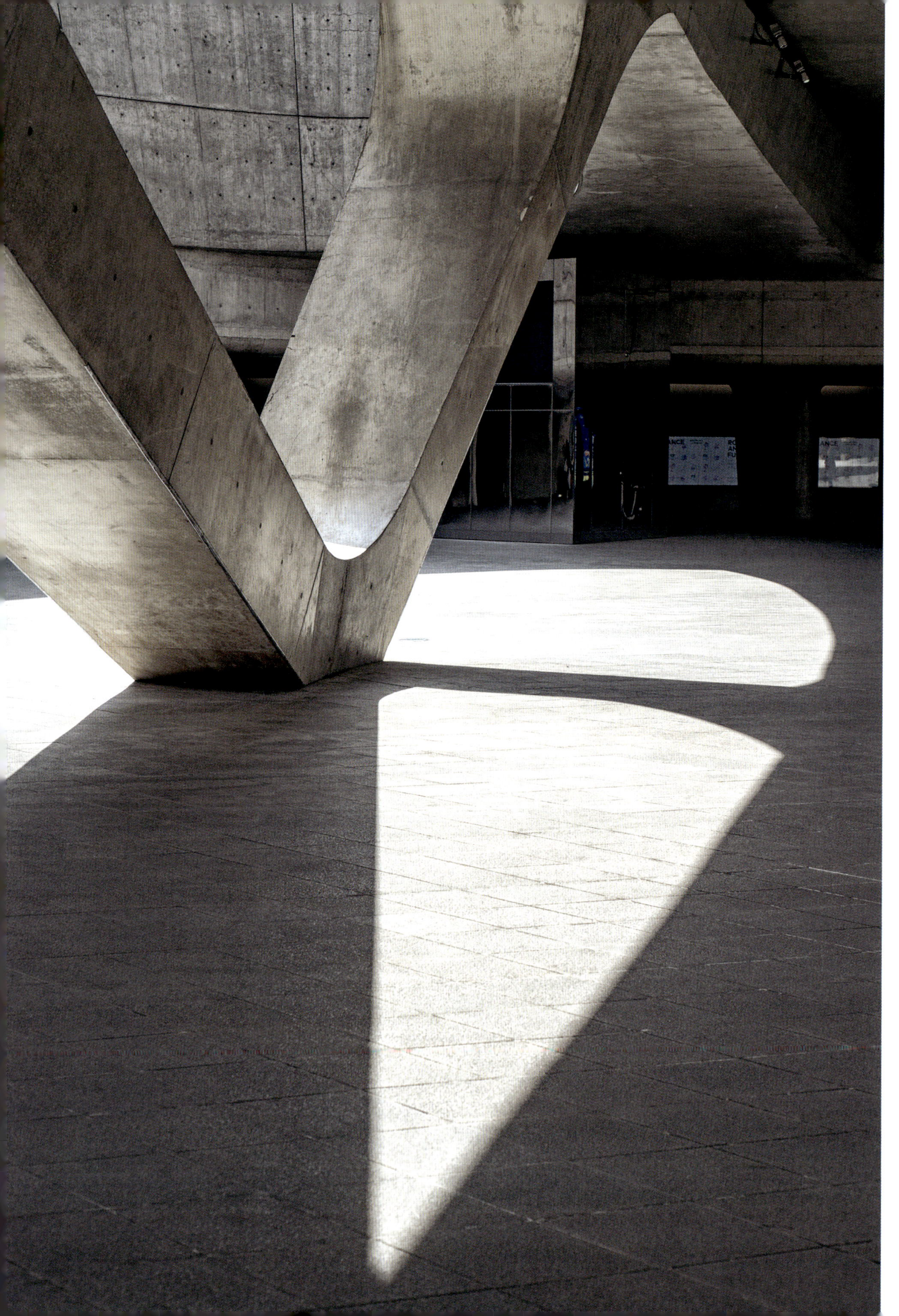

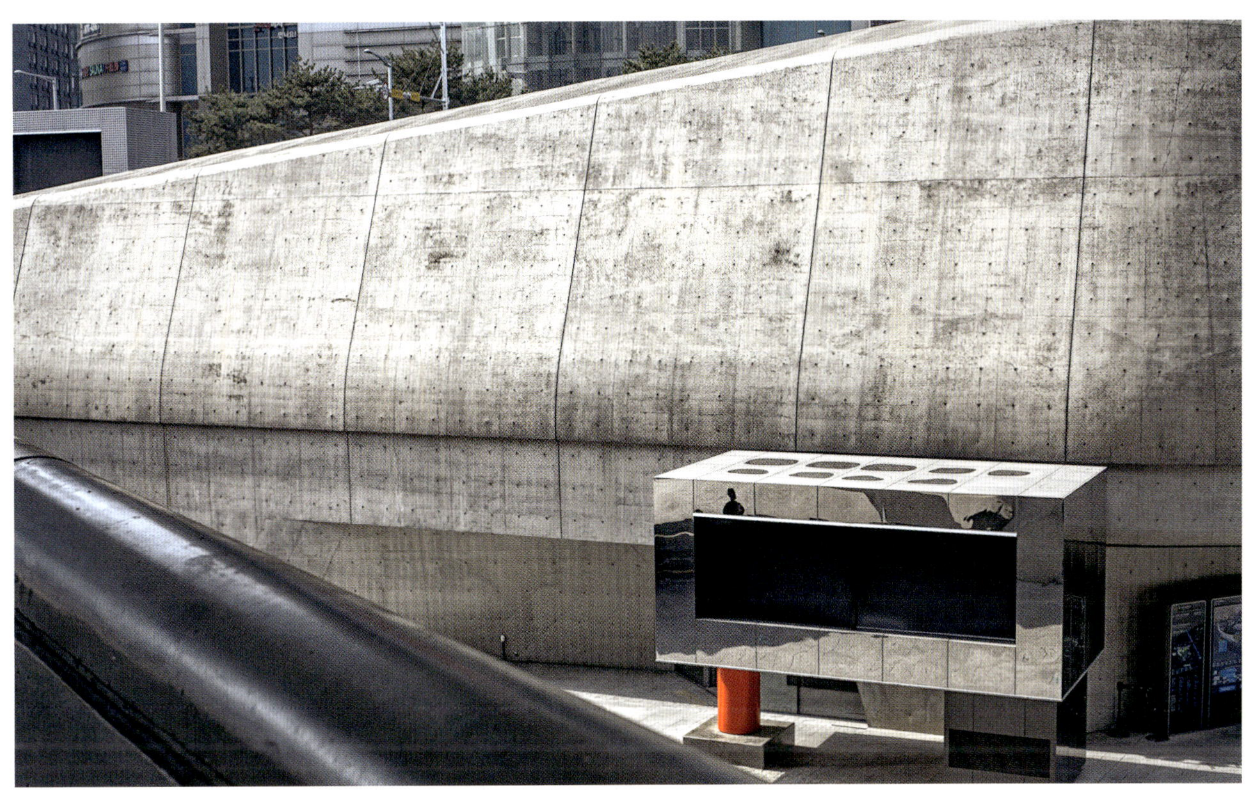

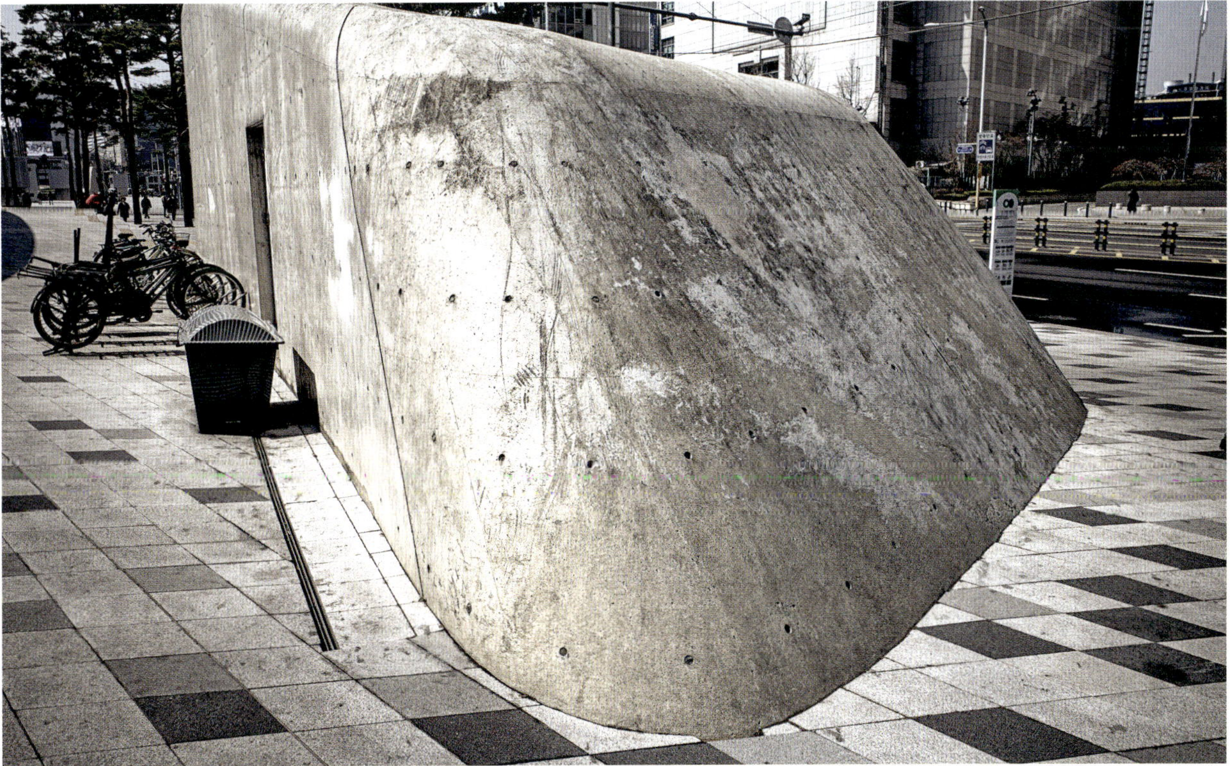

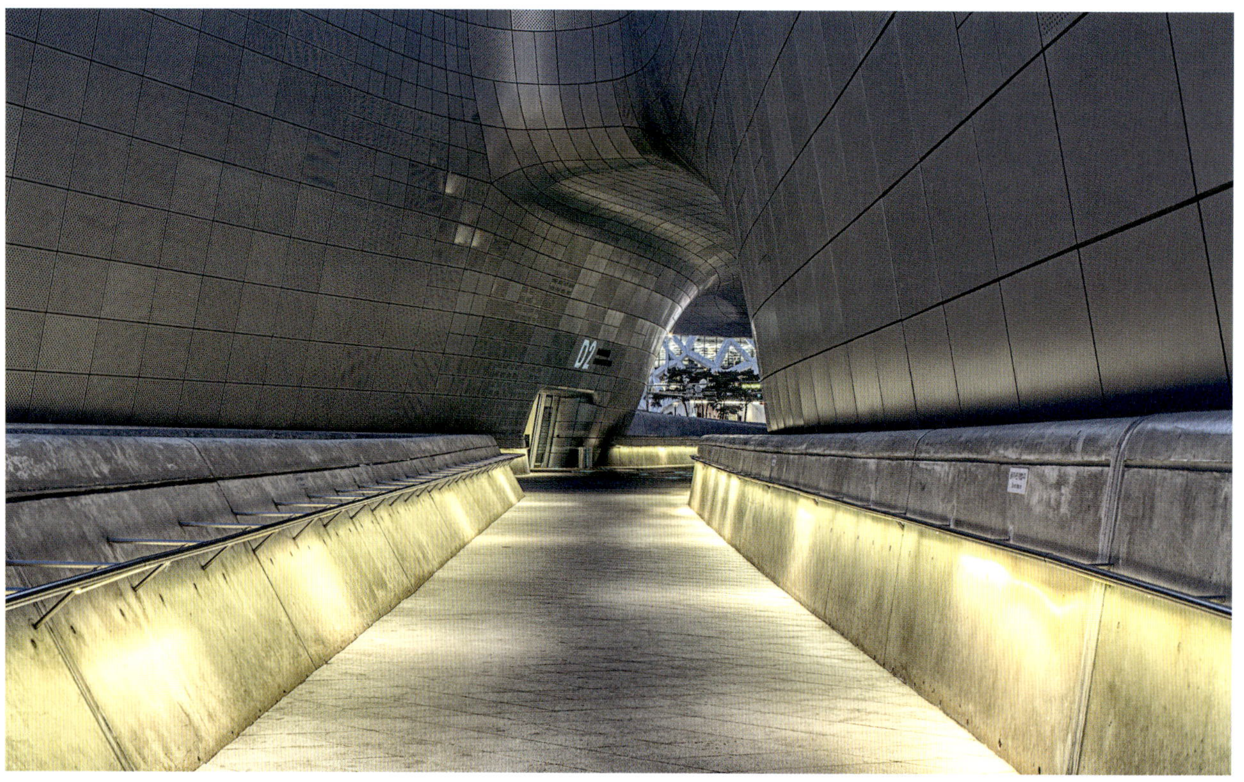
D2

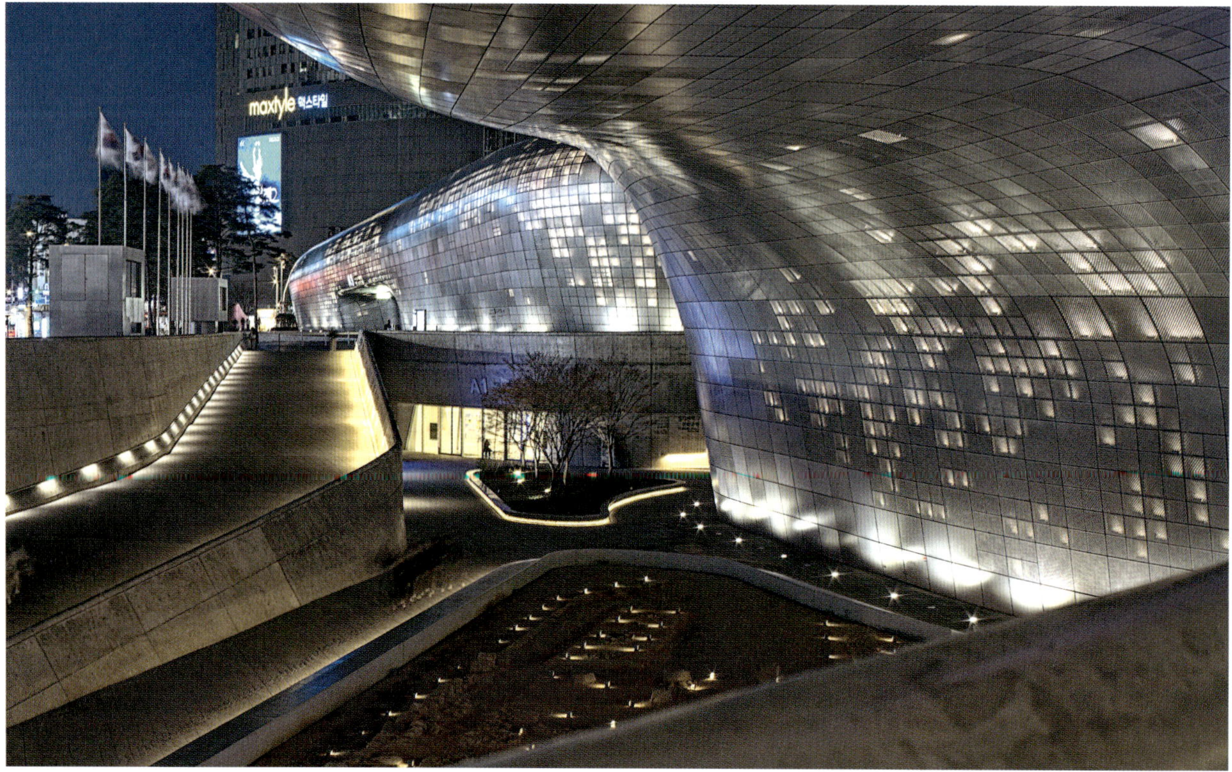
maxtyle 맥스타일
A1

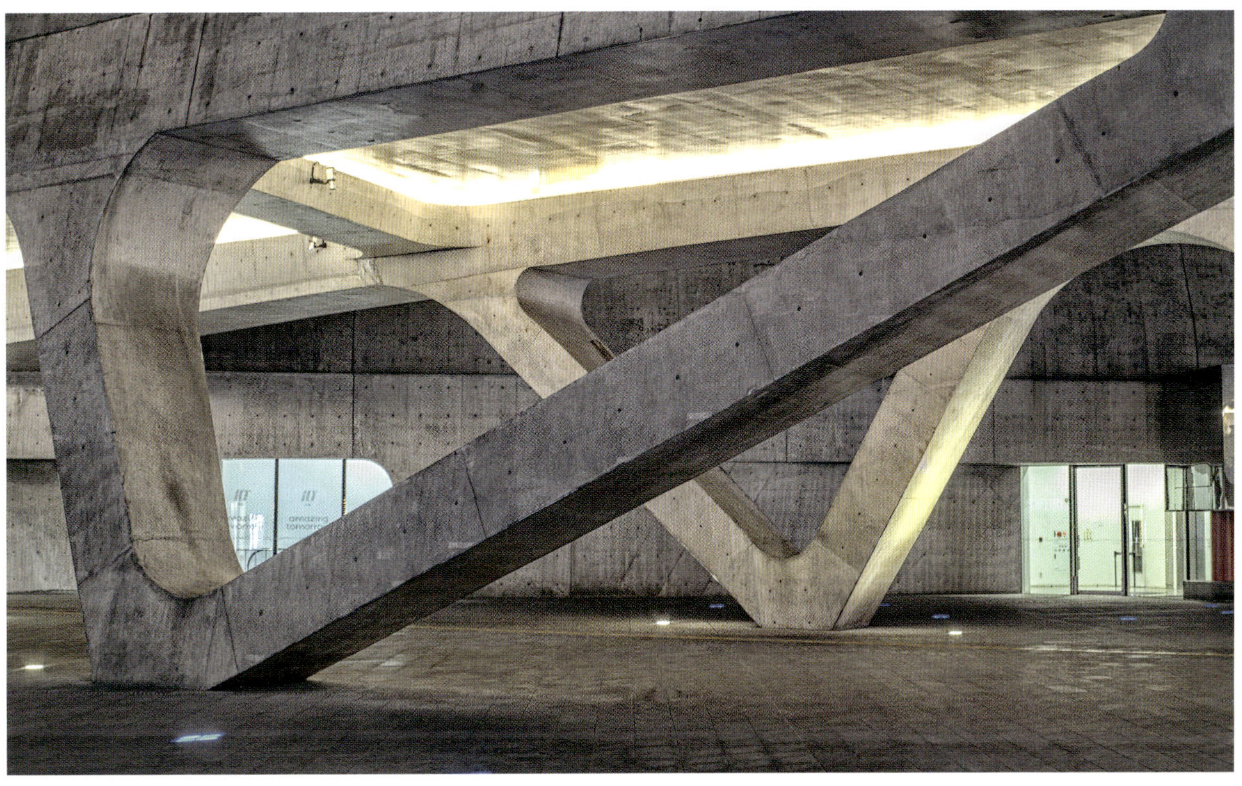

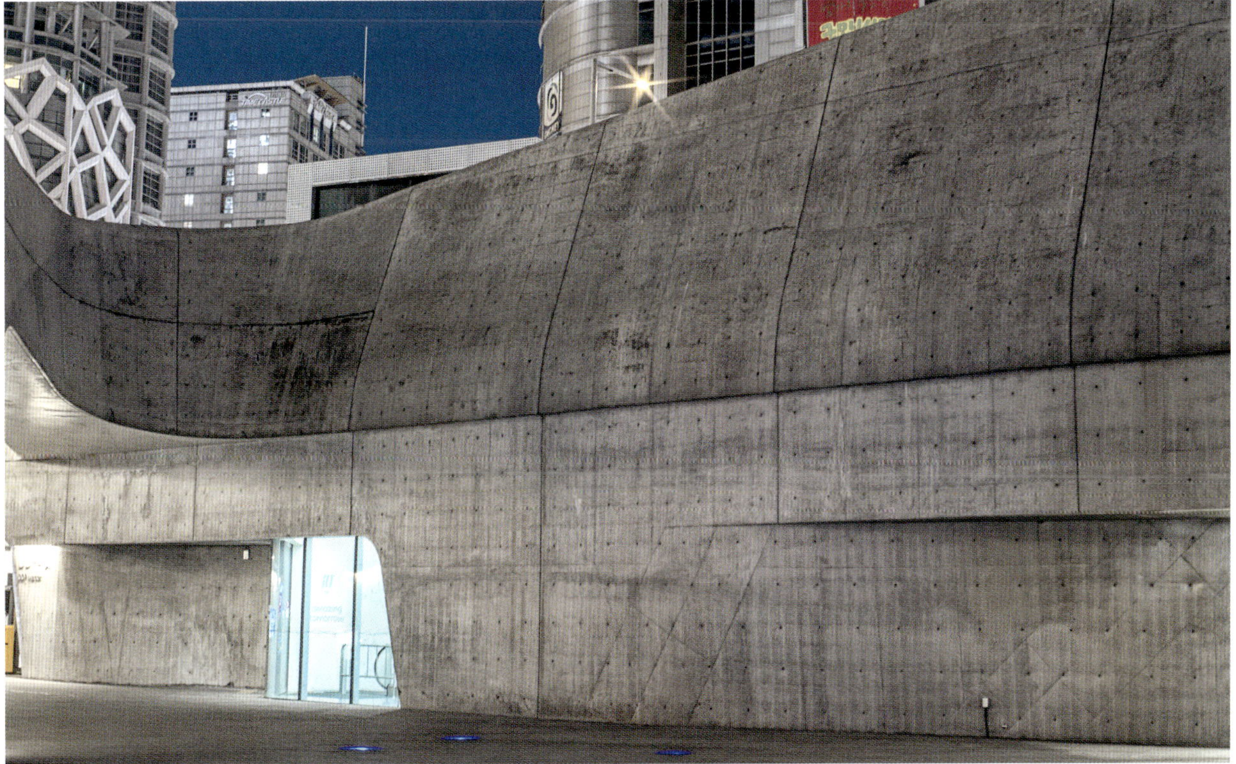

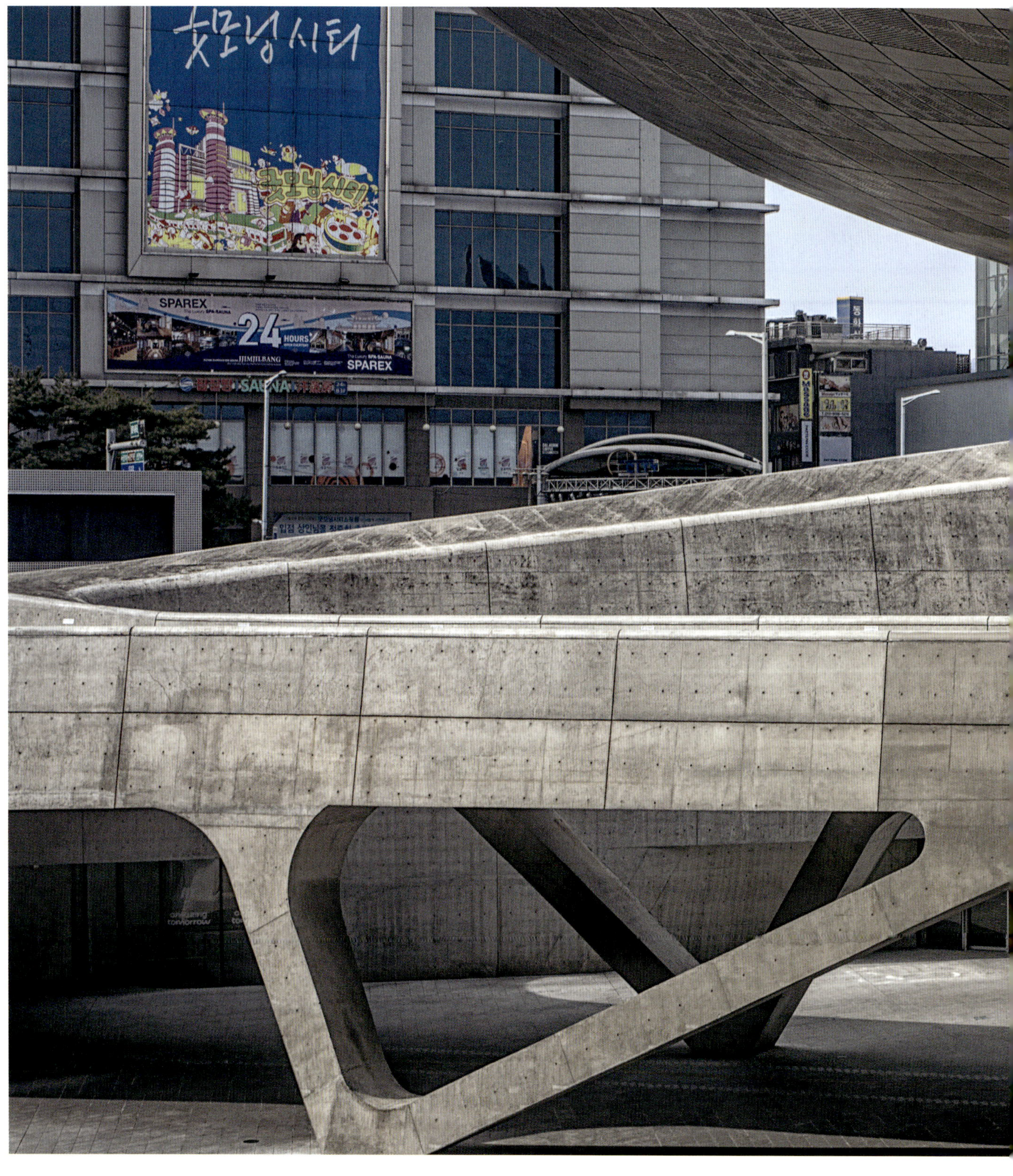
굿모닝시티
SPAREX
24
HOURS
JJIMJILBANG
SPAREX
SAUNA

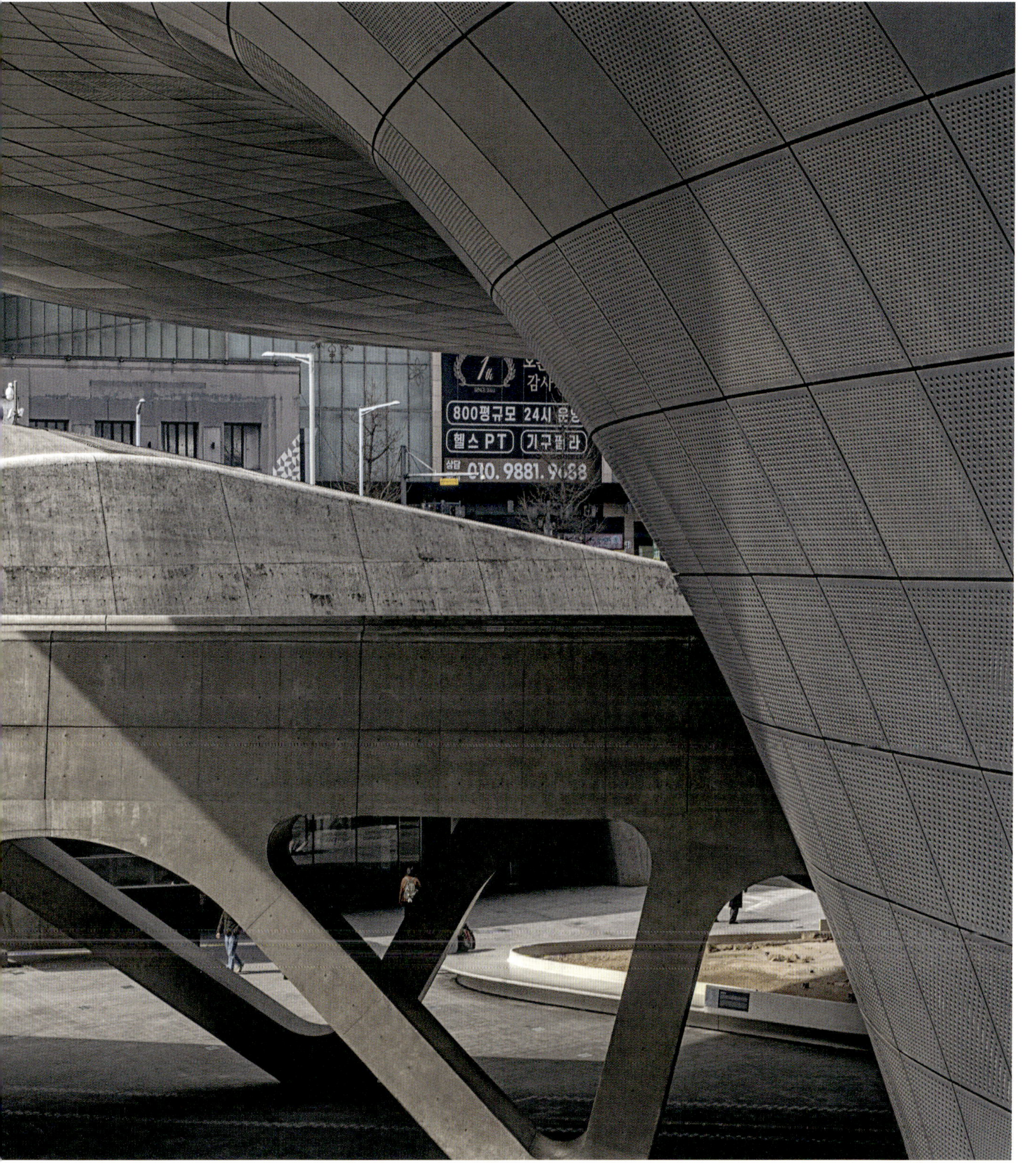
800평규모 24시
헬스 PT
상담

EMBASSY OF FRANCE

SEOUL · Architect: KIM Chung-up · Completed 1962

Steps from Chungjeongno Station, Seoul's French Embassy may not wear a beret, but it does speak fluent *béton*. Designed by Kim Chung-up in 1962, this low-slung slab marries Corbusian modernism with Korean sensibility – *hanok*-like eaves stretching over a forest of pilotis. It is France meets Far East, not in pomp, but in poise.

Forget marble grandeur: Kim delivered concrete restraint, diplomacy lifted above the ground as if floating over bureaucracy itself. A coup d'état against the drab chancery box, the building whispers authority in raw, textured tones – ageing like Bordeaux, not crumbling like a stale baguette.

Inside the courtyard, solid walls spar with sheets of glass, a well-timed metaphor for Franco-Korean relations – anchored but open to change. Though the embassy has since moved, Kim's *béton* classic remains in service as the Institut Français. And unlike croissants, whose fate is to go stale, these crisp concrete lines only grow sharper with age.

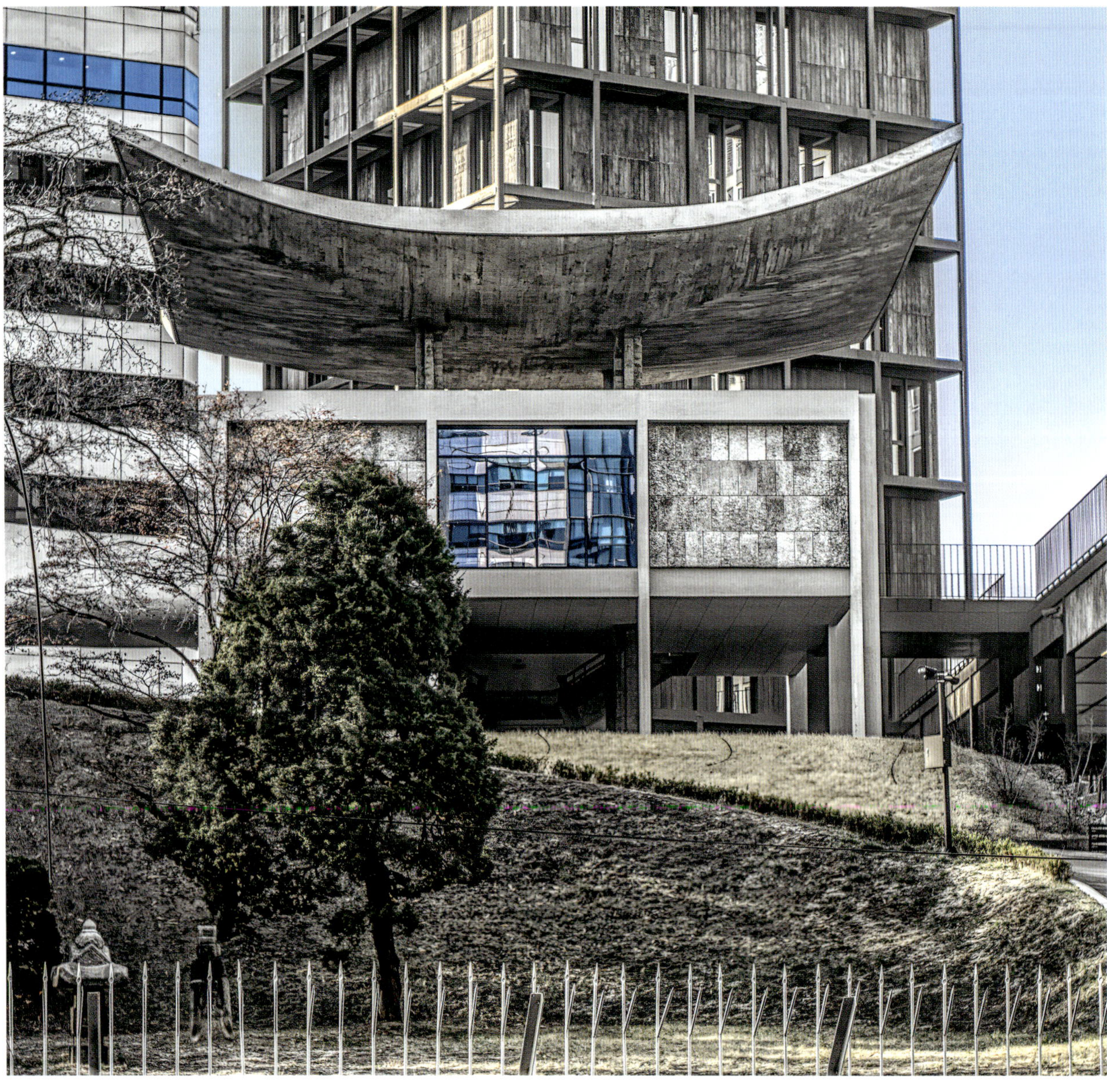

CHANGSIN SUNGIN QUARRY OBSERVATORY

SEOUL · Architect: JO Jin-man · Completed 2020

Dramatically piercing the sky from a hillside in Seoul, this striking café exemplifies a seamless blend of Brutalist structure and modern transparency. A robust concrete core anchors the building to the ground, supporting a cantilevered glass volume that projects boldly into space. The contrast between the raw concrete and sleek glazing creates a powerful brew of heaviness and lightness – a recurring theme in post-war Korean architecture influenced by both functionality and poetic minimalism. Inside, coffee sippers are suspended and offered panoramic views of the surrounding landscape while remaining connected to the city below. The linear, bridge-like form not only responds to the steep topography but also symbolizes transition – a place between nature and urbanity. This architectural composition transforms a simple café into an elevated experience, merging material honesty with a sense of levitation that encapsulates the contemporary Korean reinterpretation of modernist ideals.

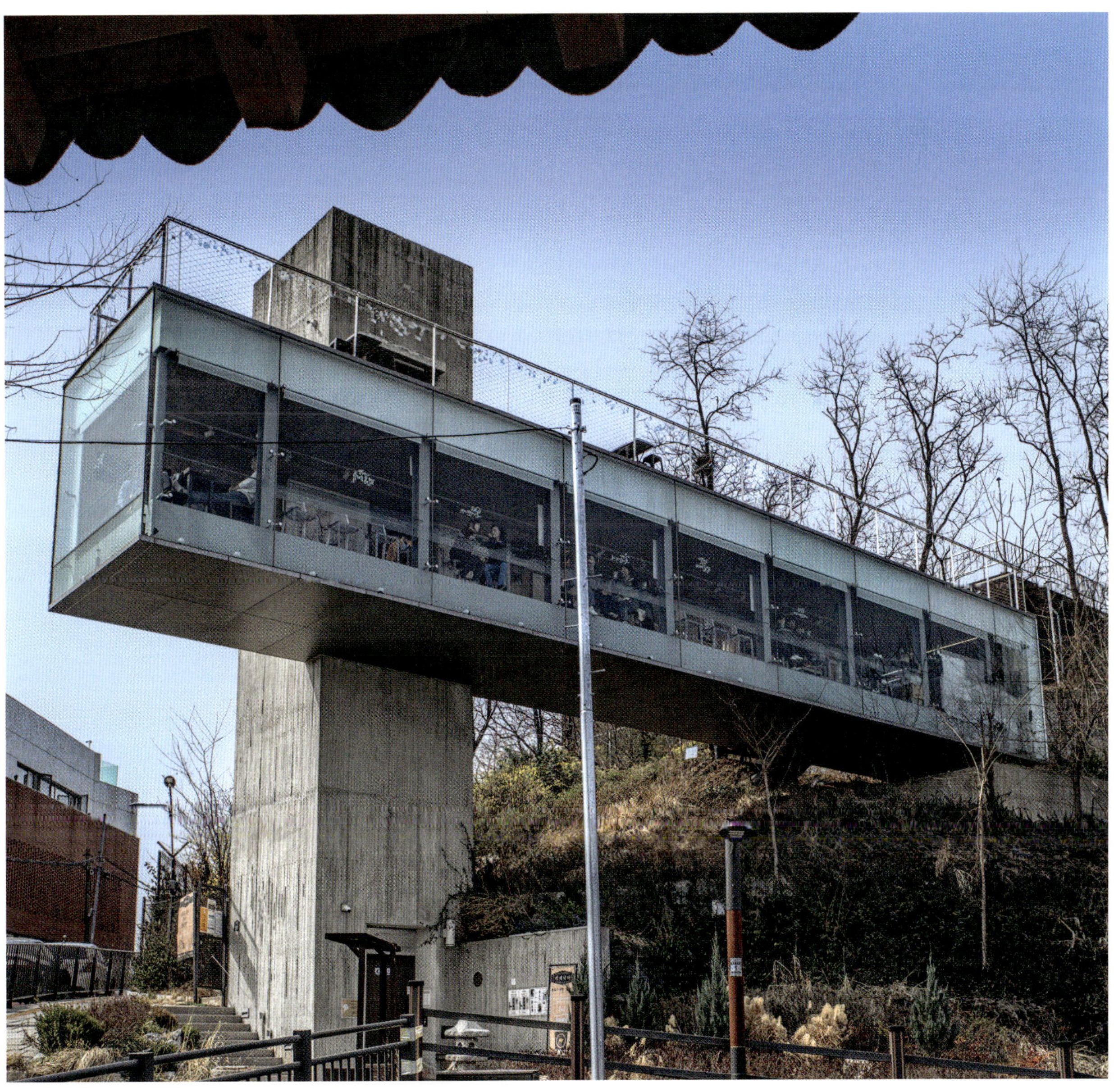

WASA

SAYUWON · Architect: SEUNG H-Sang / IROJE Architects & Planners · Completed 2019

Wasa is a meditation hall that replaces spectacle with stillness. Set beside the reflective Odang Pond – its name meaning "temple along water" – the building seems to flow with the landscape, not rise above it. Folded red-tinted iron plates trace the terrain's descent, their origami-like geometry appearing more placed than constructed. Brutalist in spirit yet serene in effect, its weathering steel cladding and pared-back form convey discipline and restraint. As the metal rusts, it blends into the soil and stone, allowing time to become texture. Inside, a single quiet chamber offers reflection through filtered light. Heavy in material yet light in intent, Wasa embodies the paradox of solidity serving transcendence. It is architecture as meditation – contextually attuned, stoic, and quietly profound, a space where thought slows to the rhythm of water and even the structure itself seems to pause and breathe.

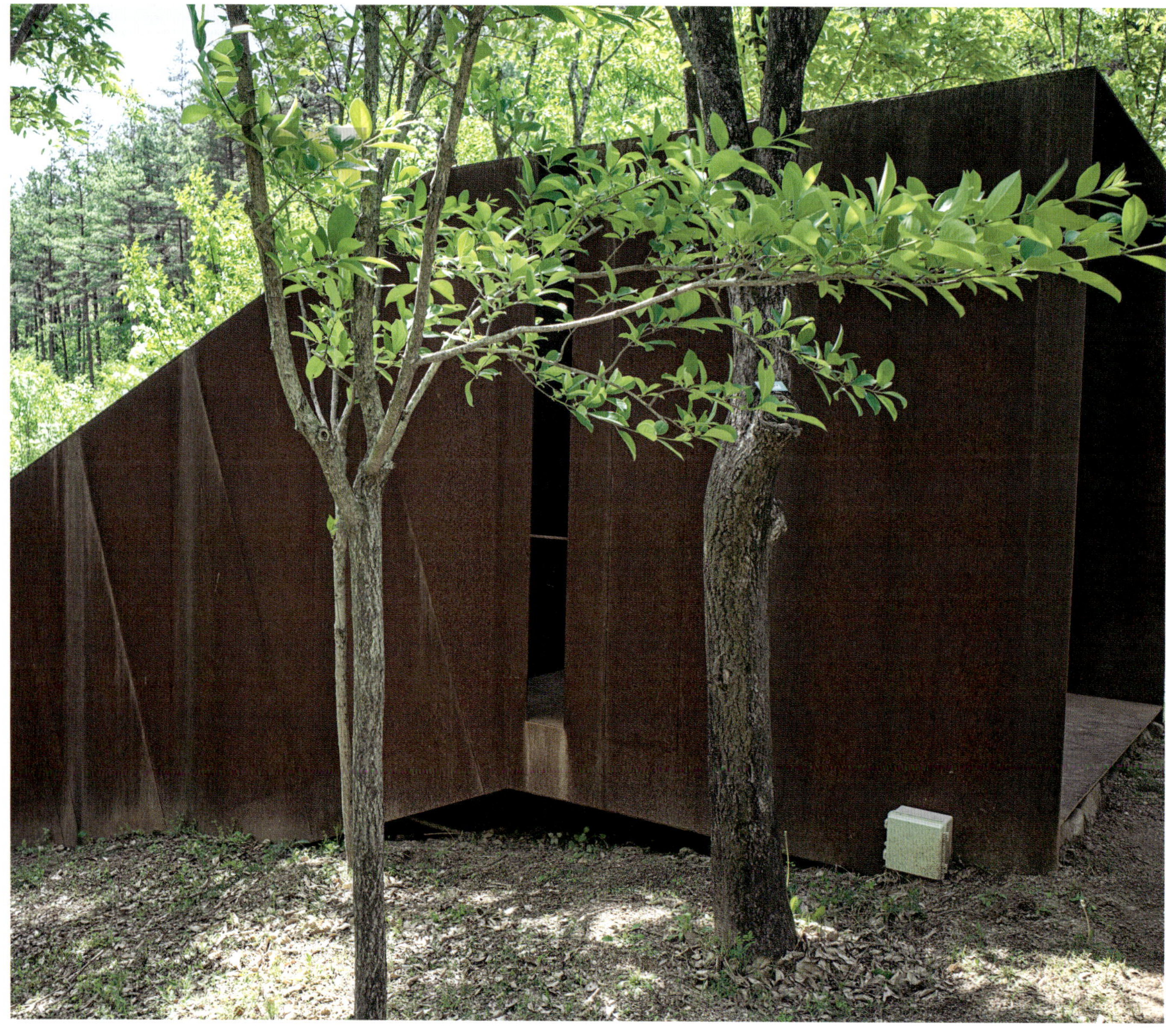

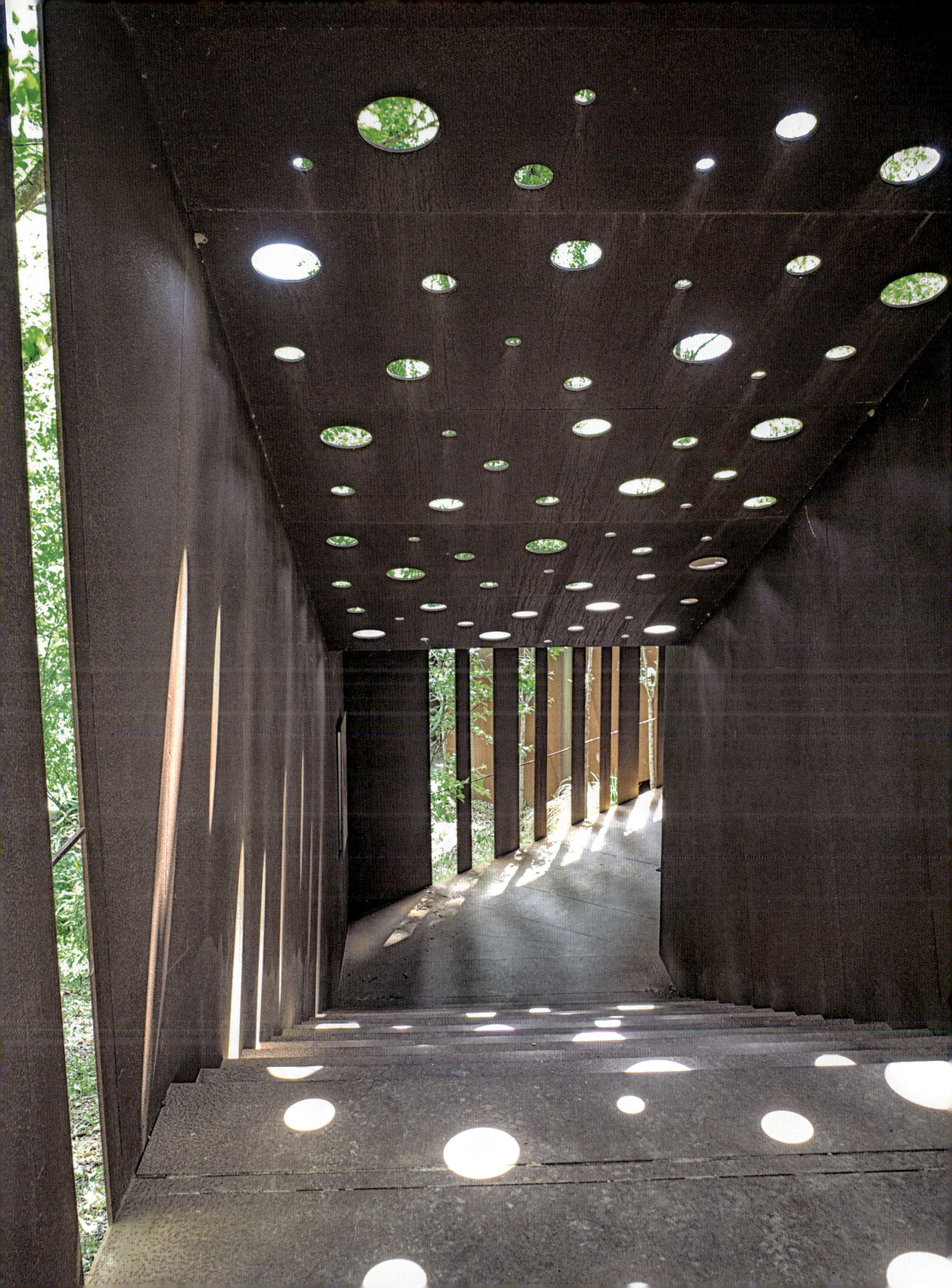

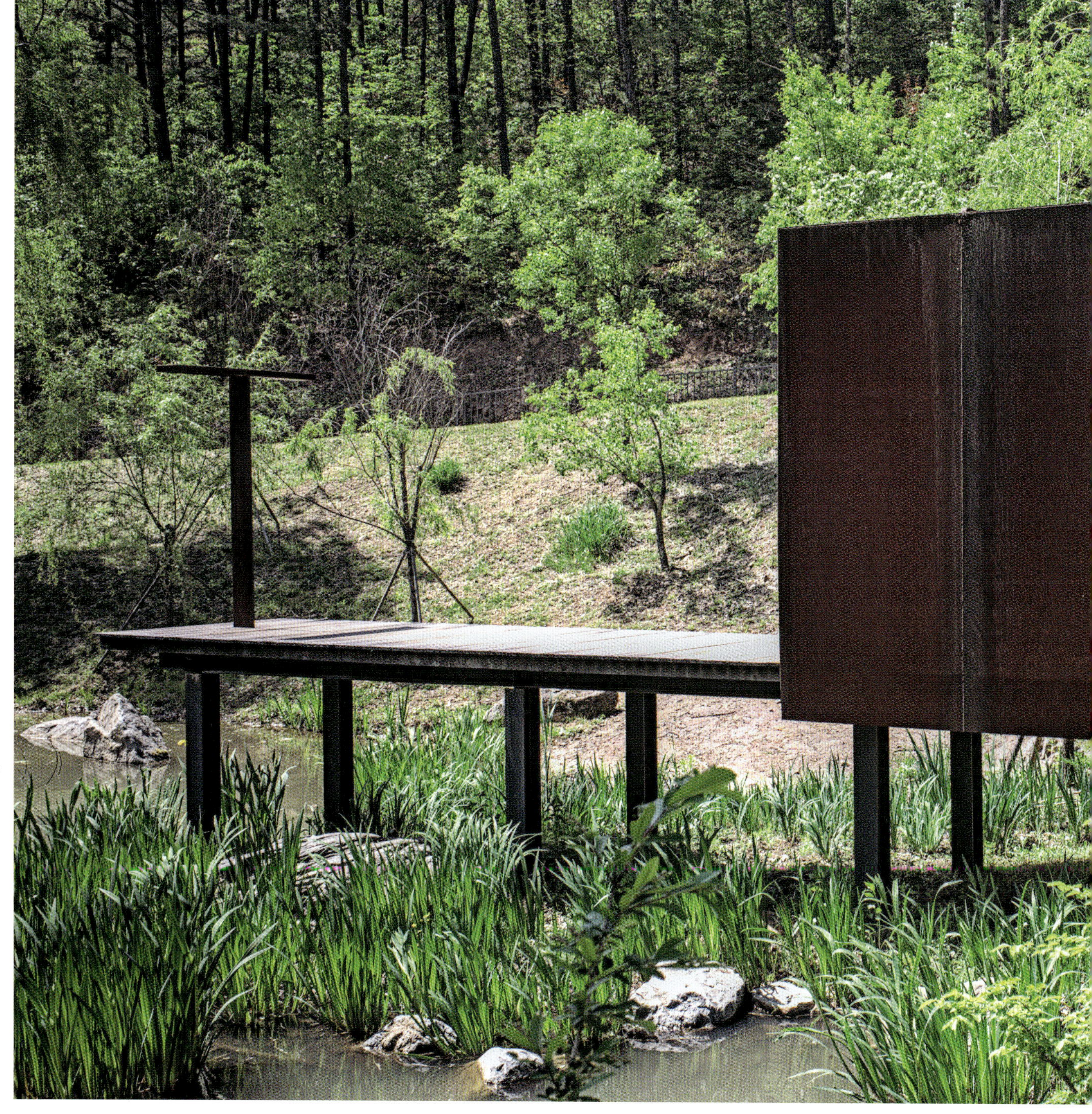

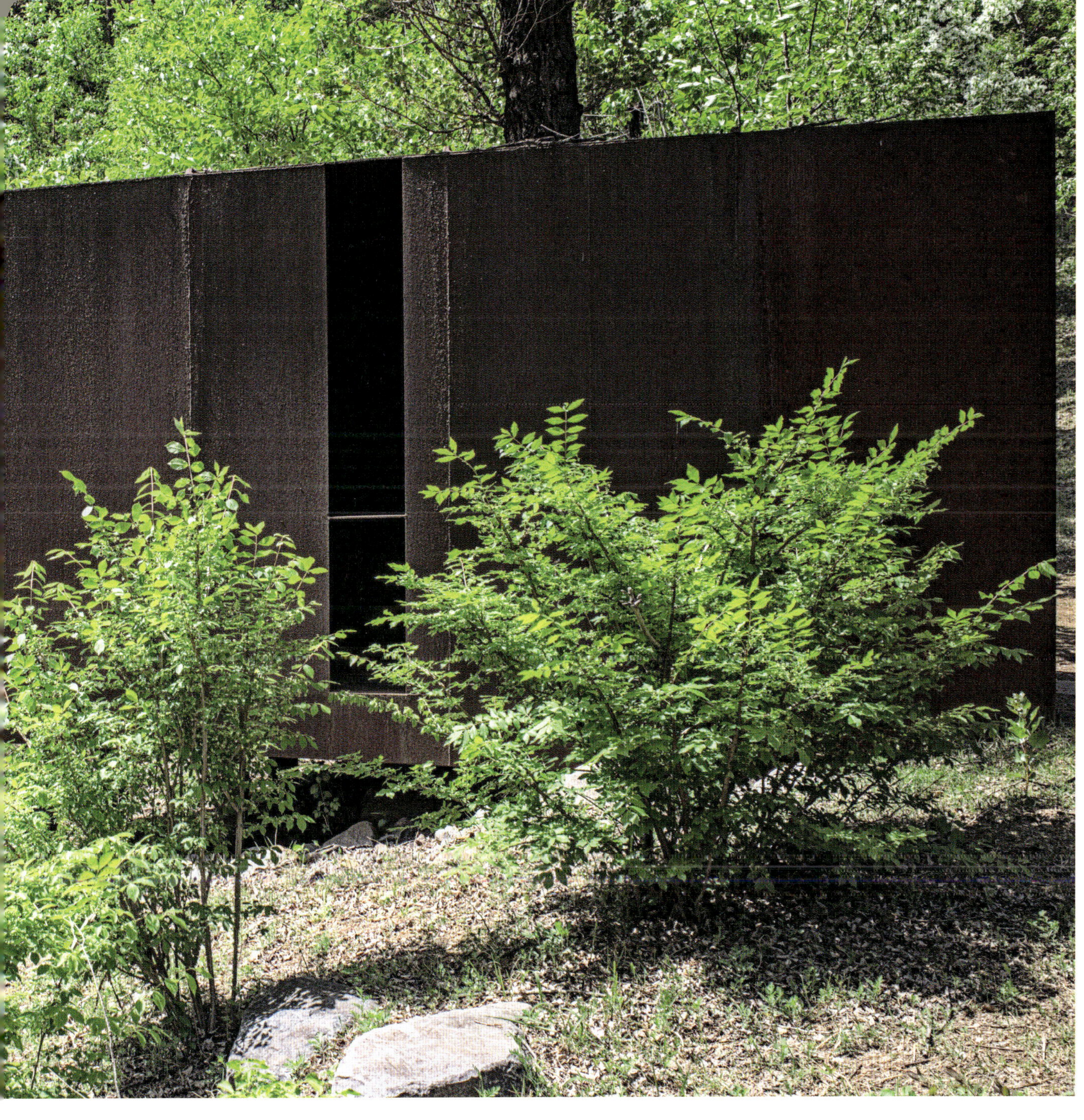

BOSAN CLINIC

DONGDUCHEON · Opened 1974

This "clinic" emerged in the late decades of South Korea's military rule as part of a network of facilities used to detain and "rehabilitate" prostitutes, particularly those operating near military bases and border zones. Officially designated as a medical inspection site, its true purpose blurred the line between public health and punitive control. Women were arrested during vice raids and brought for medical examinations – primarily for venereal disease testing – and held for days or weeks under quasi-legal authority. The government justified these measures as protecting public morality and the health of soldiers, yet conditions were harsh and rights virtually non-existent.

These institutions reflected a wider authoritarian apparatus that conflated sexuality, poverty, and social order. By classifying sex workers as both moral deviants and health risks, the state exercised disciplinary power disguised as medical care.

As South Korea transitioned to democracy in the late 1980s and human rights norms evolved through the 1990s, facilities like this gradually fell out of use. The rise of NGOs and legal reforms targeting police abuse led to the closure or repurposing of such centres. This site was eventually abandoned – its records fragmentary, its history largely unacknowledged.

Today, the remaining structure persists as a rare physical trace of that system – a stark witness to the period when control of women's bodies intersected with public health policy and state ideology. Though officially forgotten, its existence speaks to the uneasy legacy of governance through confinement, and to the ways architecture once served as an instrument of both discipline and erasure.

Big thanks to the freelance writer I call "Struggle Sleuth" for getting me in here. Some sneaky moves involved.

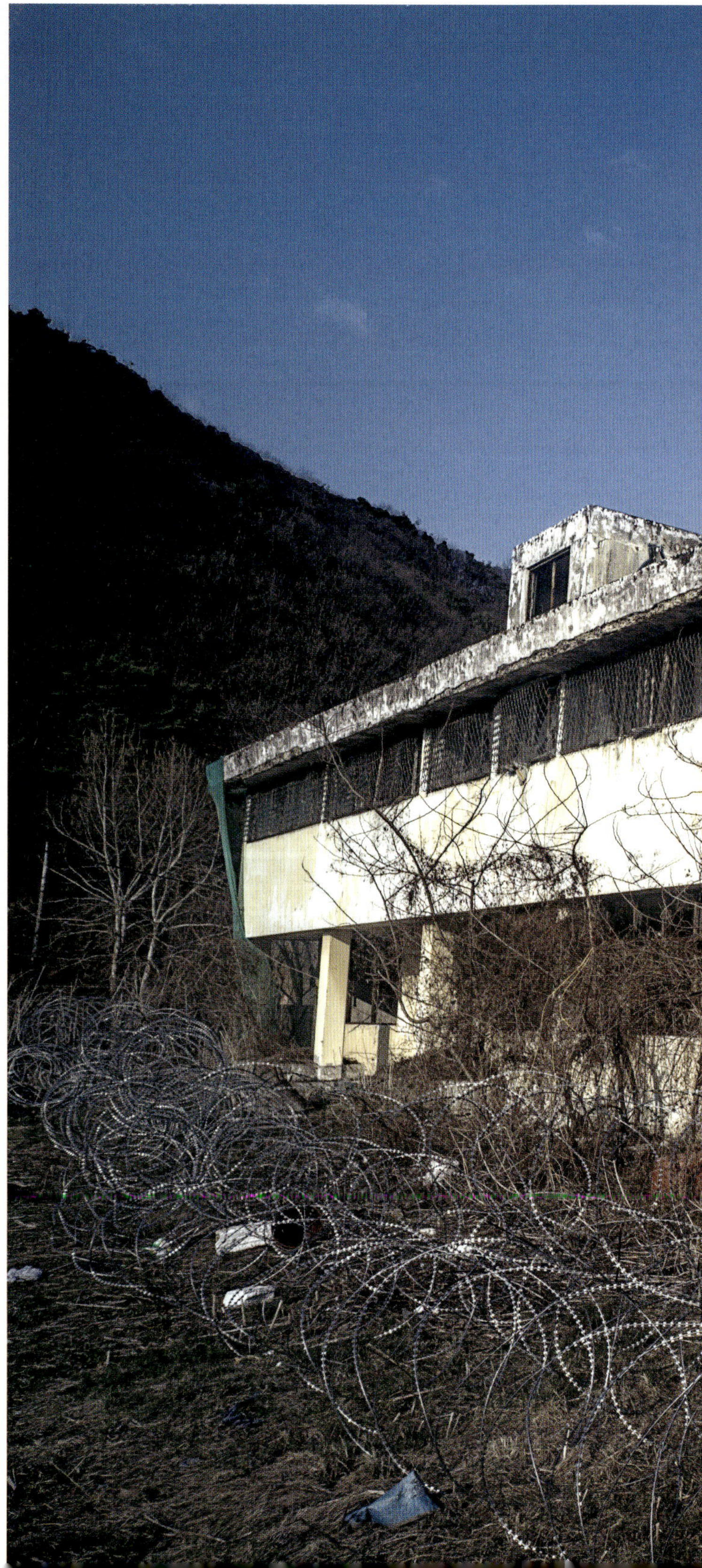

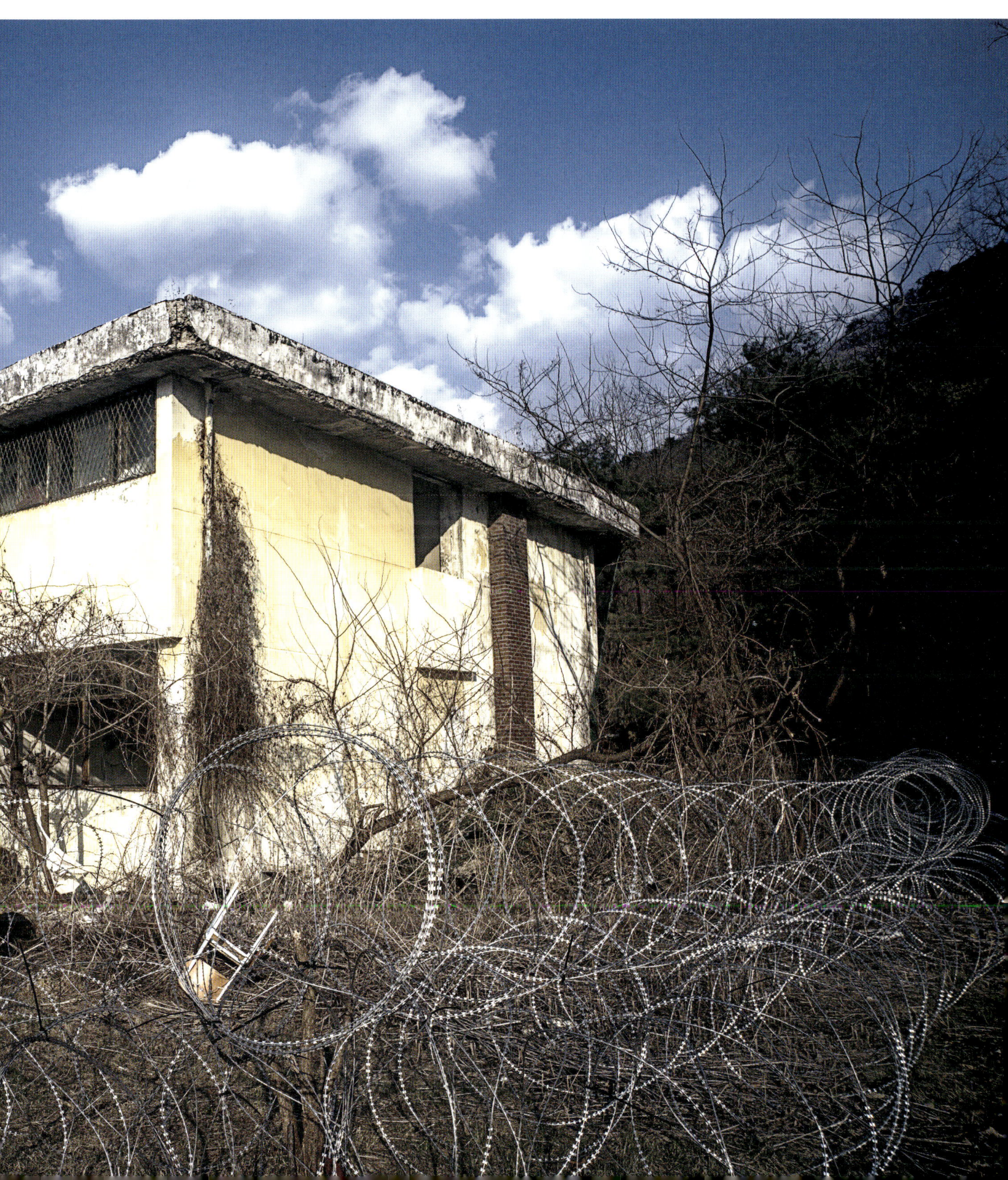

DONGDAEMUN HISTORY MUSEUM

SEOUL · Architect: Samoo Architects & Engineers · Completed 2009

The Dongdaemun History Museum anchors the historical core of Seoul's Dongdaemun History and Culture Park. Conceived as the first phase of the site's transformation from the former Dongdaemun Stadium into a cultural precinct, the museum was built to safeguard and interpret the archaeological relics uncovered during the site's excavation – foundations, fortress walls, wells, and the historic Yigansumun Water Gate, all dating back to the Joseon Dynasty.

Architecturally, the museum is a study in restraint. Its low, elongated form is partially embedded in the landscape, merging seamlessly with the park's gentle topography. Clad in muted stone and concrete, it avoids any gesture of monumentality, acting instead as a respectful frame for the heritage it protects. This subdued material palette and the horizontal emphasis humbly combine to create a visual and conceptual counterpoint to Zaha Hadid's Dongdaemun Design Plaza (DDP), which rises nearby in fluid metallic contrast. Where Hadid's work looks to the future, Samoo's looks quietly to the past.

Inside, the museum unfolds as a spatial narrative. Visitors move through dimly lit corridors into sunken galleries where the excavated remains are preserved in situ. Carefully calibrated lighting – filtered through skylights and concealed sources – highlights textures of stone and earth, emphasizing the tactility of Seoul's buried history. The design invites reflection, foregrounding the relationship between architecture and archaeology.

Externally, the museum connects seamlessly with open-air exhibition zones and landscaped walkways that link the Relic Exhibition Hall, Yigansumun Water Gate, and the DDP beyond. This network of paths and views situates the museum within a continuum of time and space, fusing ancient infrastructure with contemporary civic life.

More than a building, the Dongdaemun History Museum is an act of urban archaeology – a measured architectural gesture that turns discovery into memory, and memory into place.

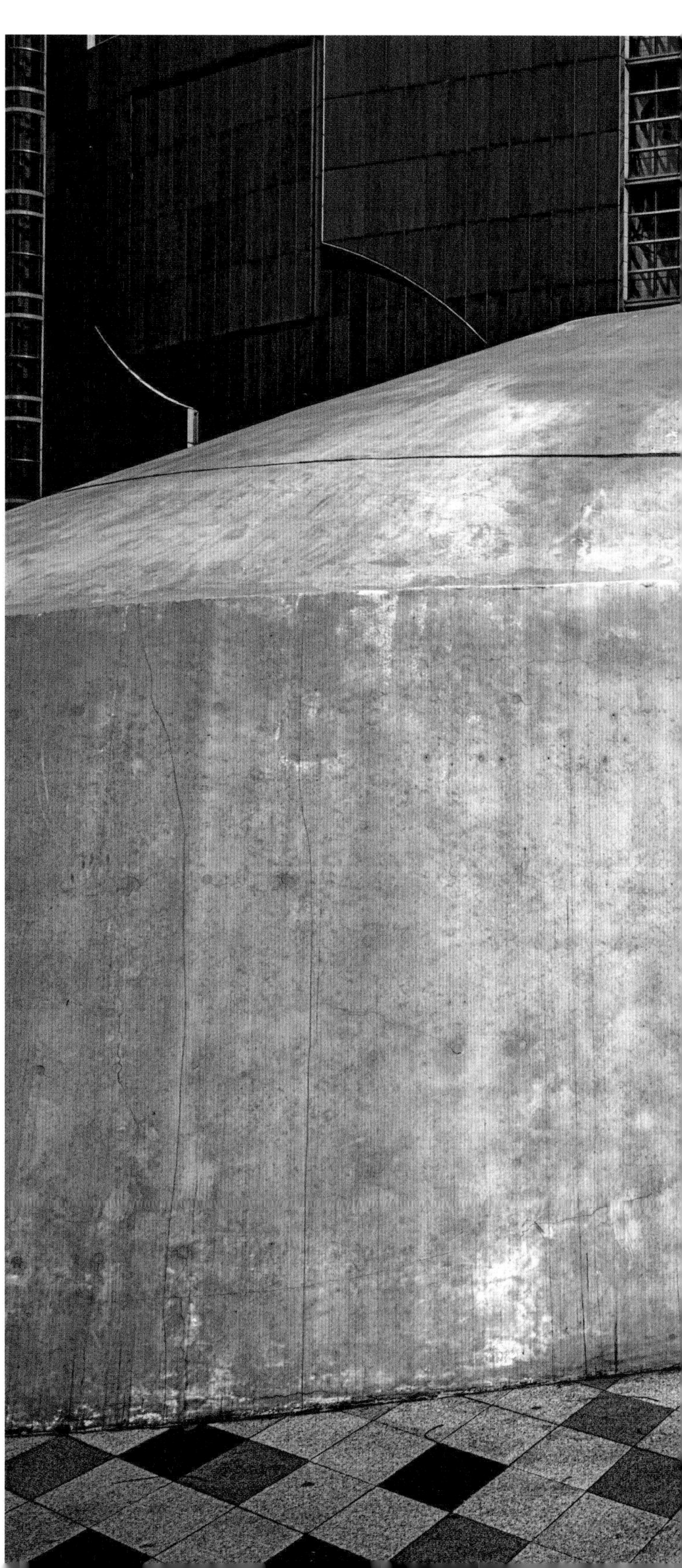

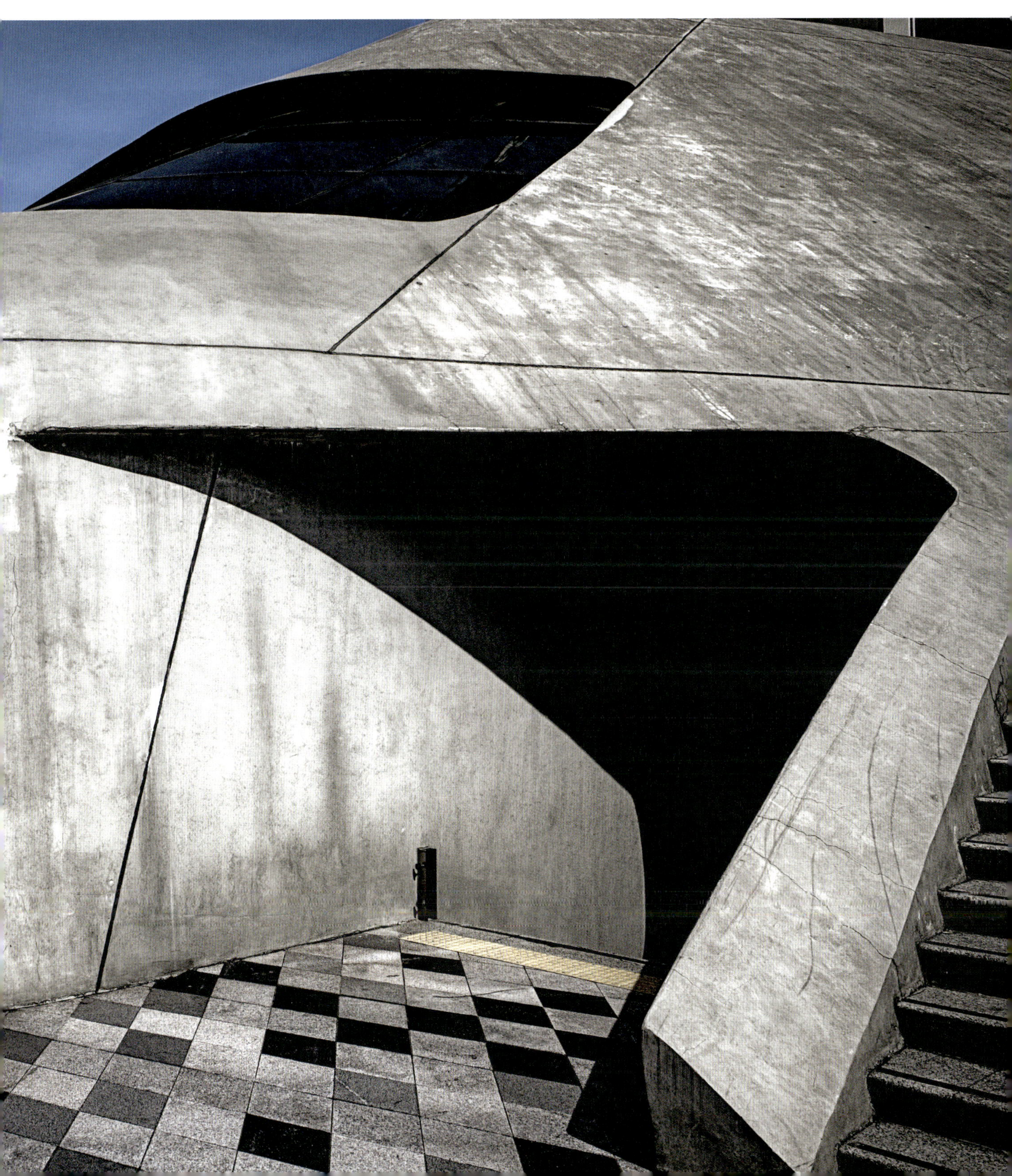

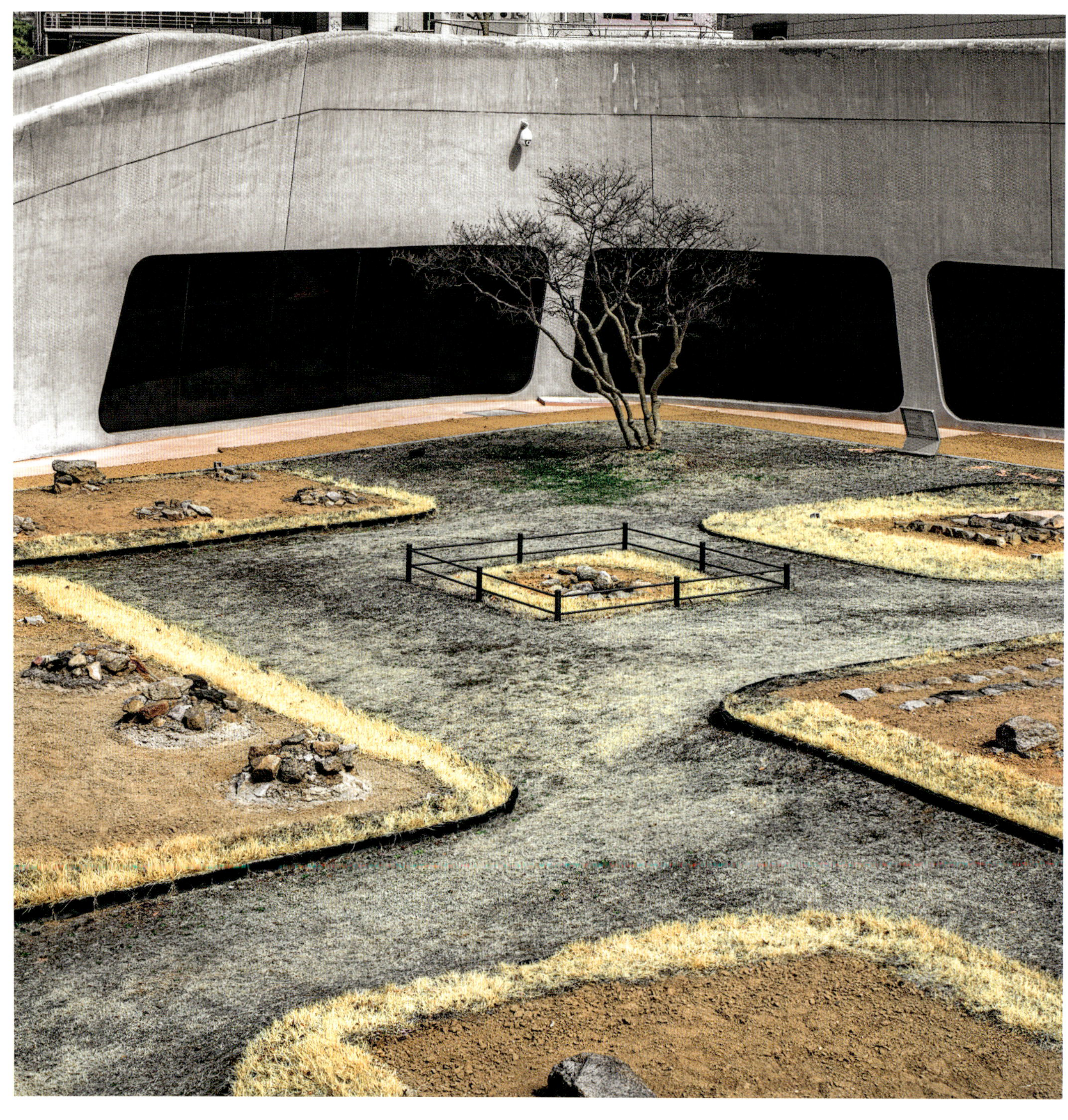

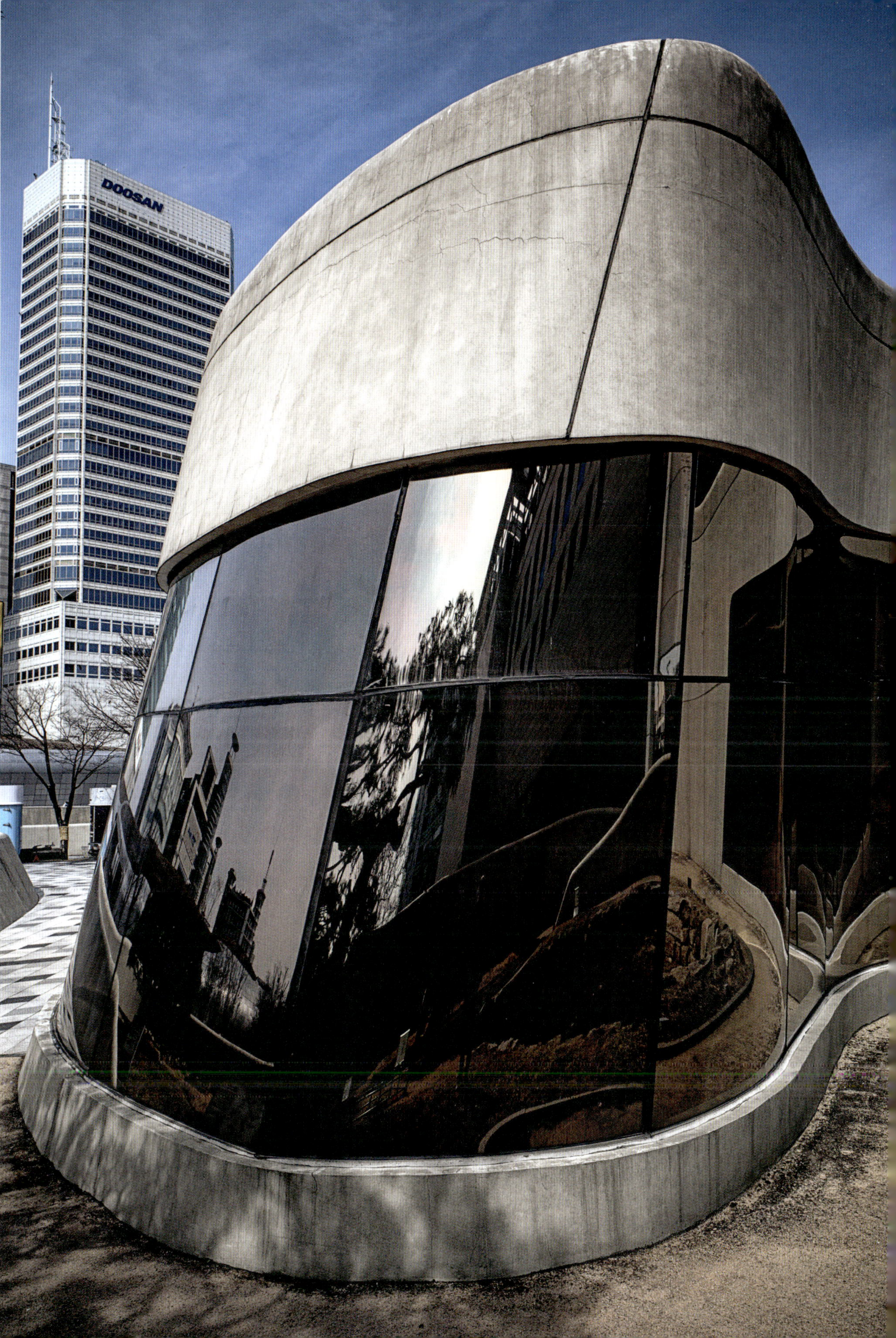
DOOSAN

BUCHEON ART BUNKER B39

BUCHEON · Architect: KIM Kwang-soo · Completed 1995

Bucheon Art Bunker B39 is a rare example of industrial architecture reborn without losing its scars. Originally constructed in 1995 as a municipal incineration plant in Buncheon's Samjeong-dong neighbourhood, the facility burned waste for over a decade before closing in 2010 amidst rising environmental standards. In June 2018, after a sensitive conversion by architect Kim Kwang-soo, it reopened as a multidisciplinary cultural complex – a space where concrete, rust, and memory coexist with performance, art, and civic life.

Kim's renovation retained the plant's original anatomy: the thirty-nine-metre-tall bunker, ash chambers, fan rooms, and control booths were all preserved, transformed into a raw architectural narrative of combustion and renewal. The Air Gallery, once the furnace's core, now hosts performances and installations within a vast vertical void that feels more cathedral than factory. Overhead catwalks and steel stairways traverse the concrete shell, offering both drama and perspective.

Visitors trace the building's former operational flow – from refuse intake to filtration – through corridors now converted into studios, laboratories, and rehearsal spaces. The preserved Induced Draft Fan Room and the old control booth stand as functional relics, lending authenticity and grit. At ground level, the former machinery chamber houses Café B39, where minimal wood furnishings soften the concrete backdrop, transforming industry into intimacy.

The architecture celebrates what it once contained. Weld seams, soot stains, and formwork impressions are left visible, embodying a Brutalist honesty that feels both monumental and human. B39's name itself honours the bunker's thirty-nine-metre height, a measure of its physical and symbolic weight.

Today, the complex operates as Bucheon's creative furnace – a civic engine powered not by waste, but by imagination. In Kim Kwang-soo's hands, the building's transformation is both poetic and practical: a resurrection through reuse, proving that even ashes can become art.

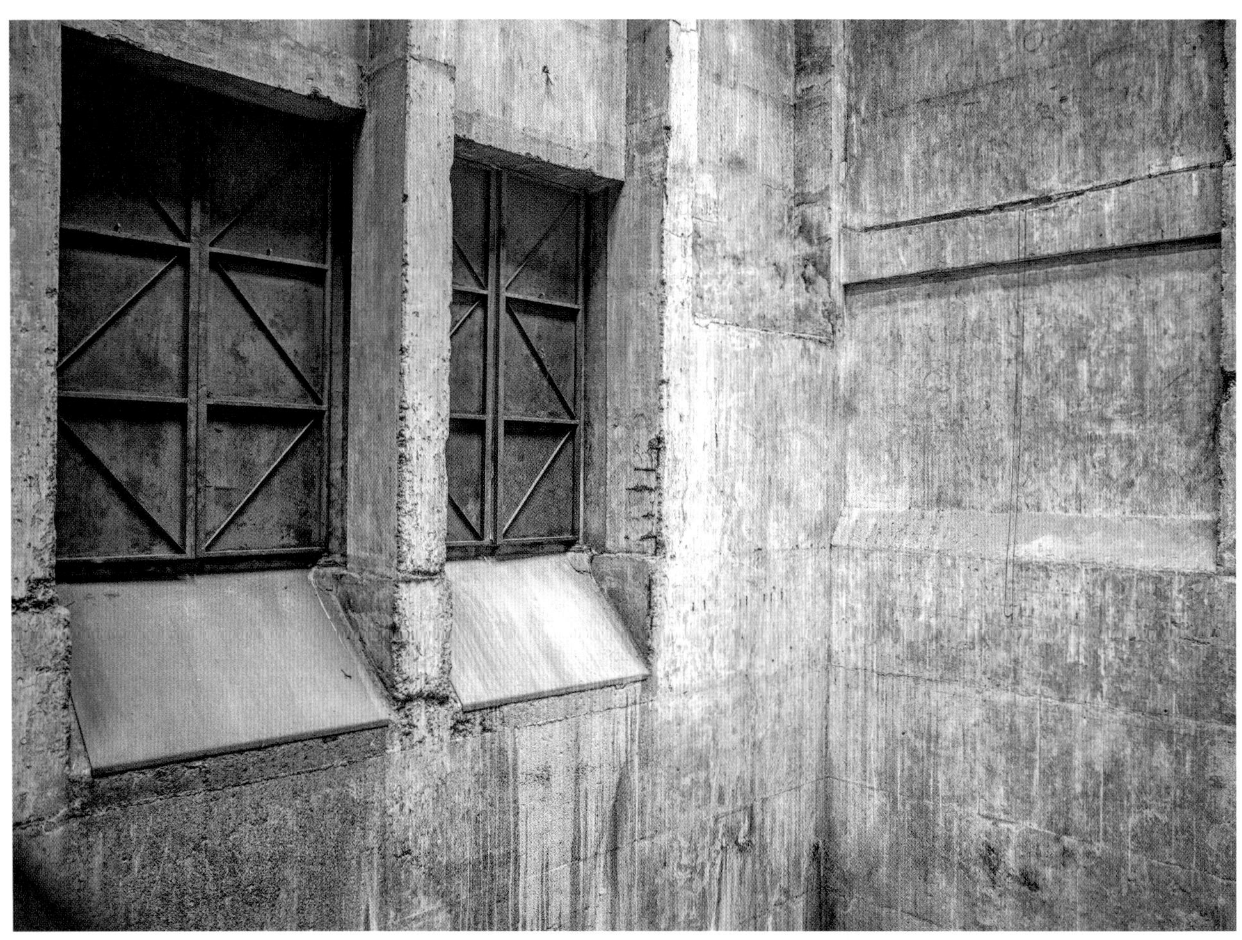

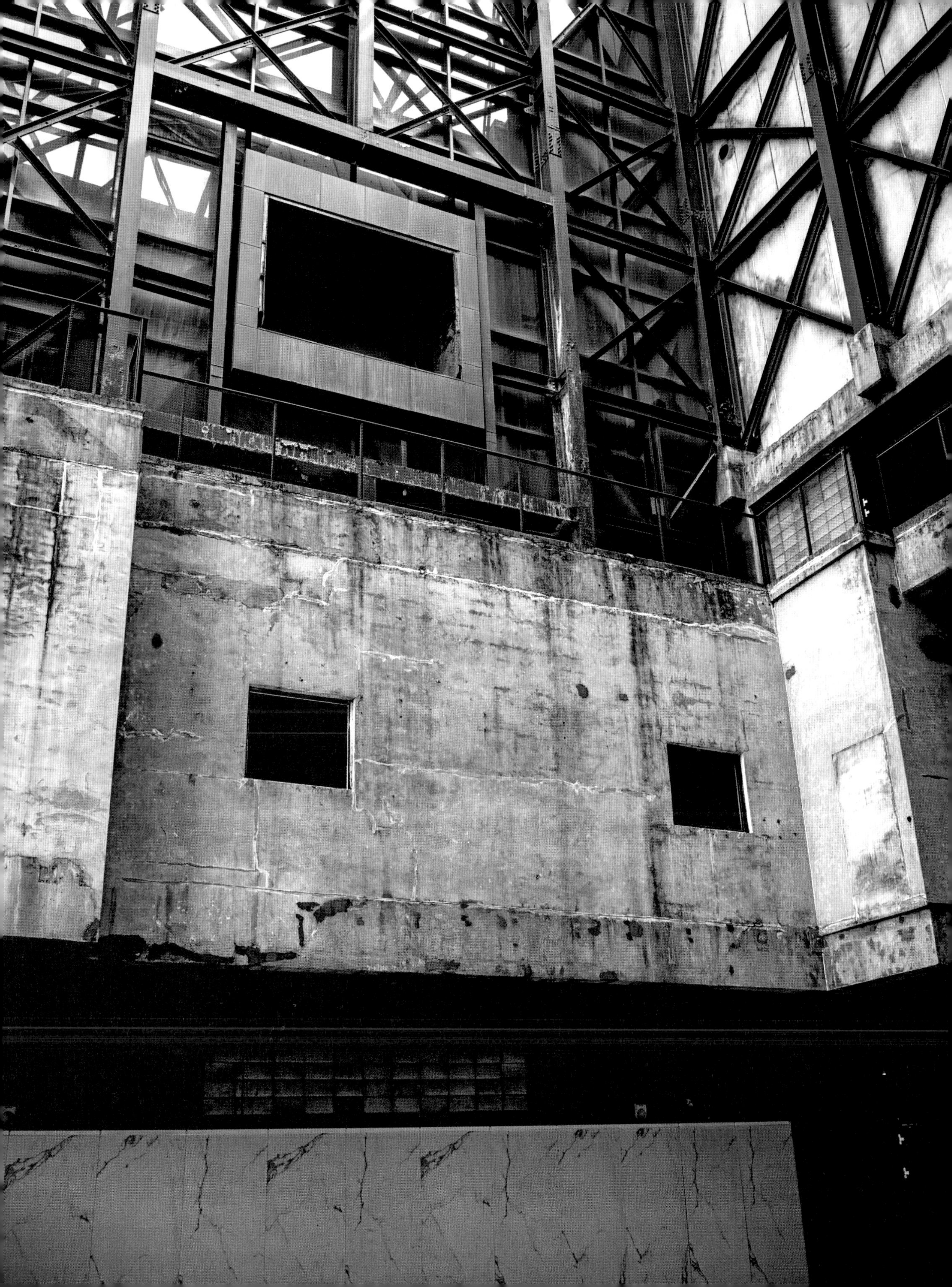

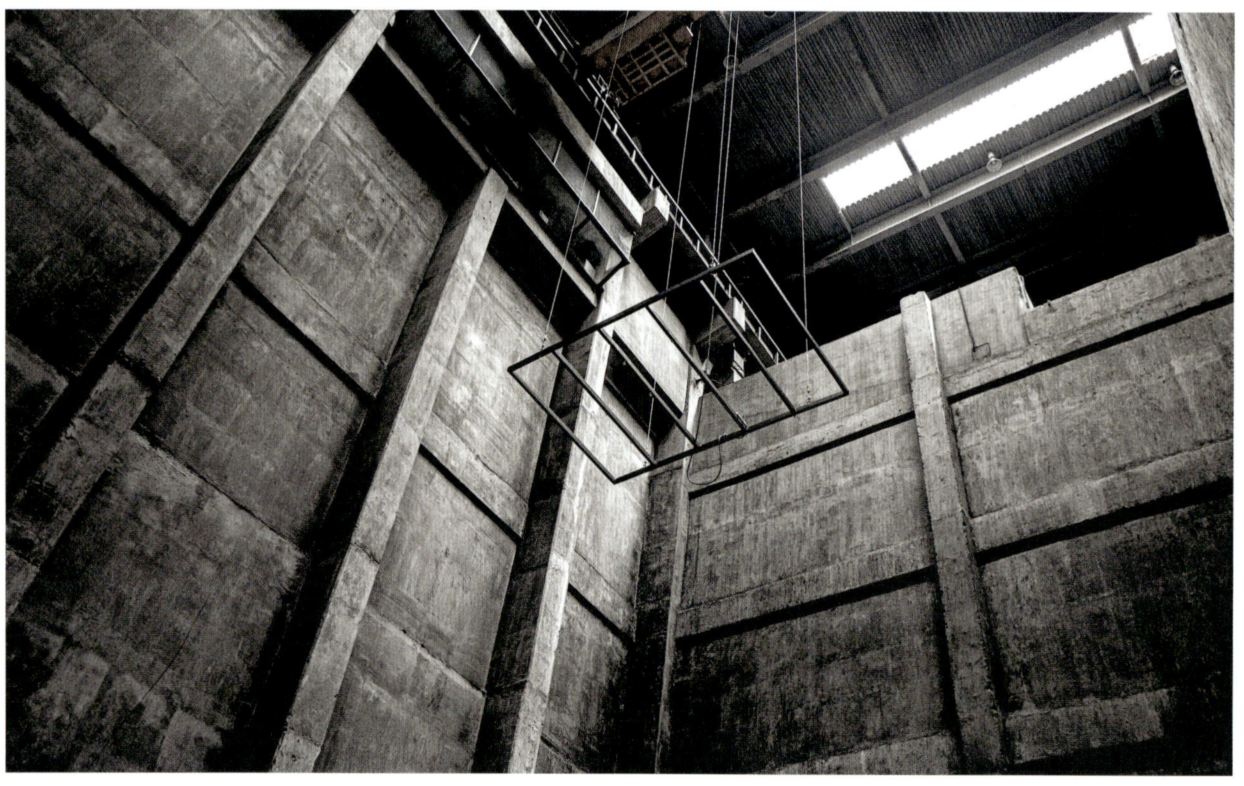

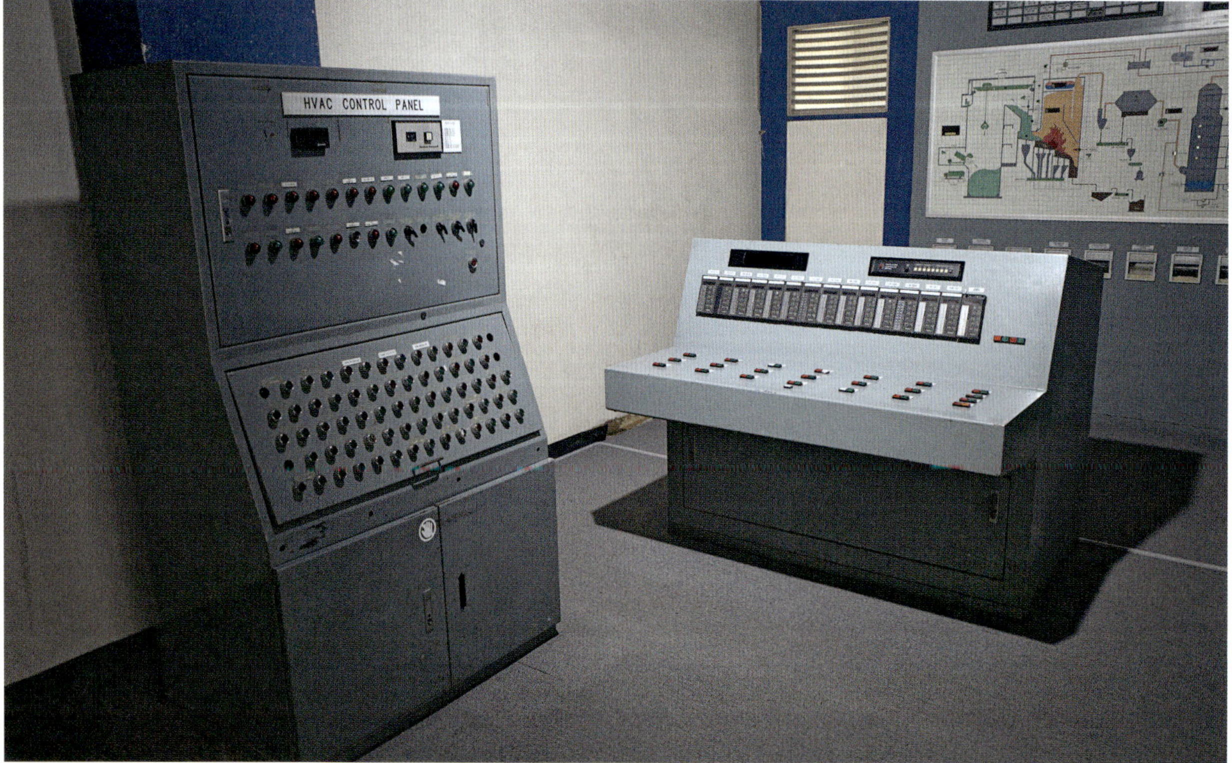
HVAC CONTROL PANEL

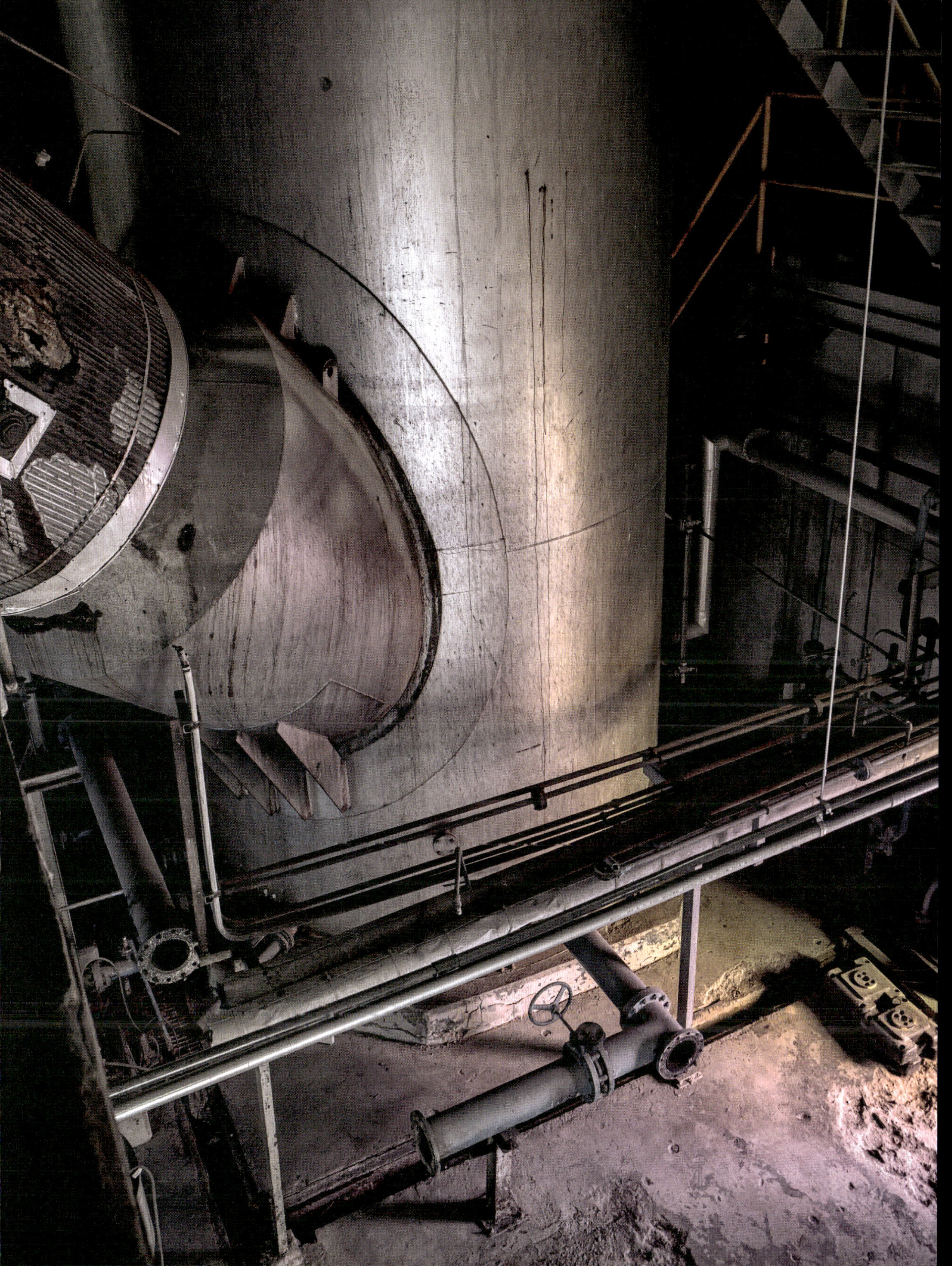

GENIUS LOCI: YUMIN ART NOUVEAU COLLECTION

JEJU ISLAND · Architect: ANDO Tadao · Completed 2008

Tadao Ando's pair of pavilions for the Art Nouveau Collection on Jeju Island are quiet, concentrated studies in control – of light, movement, and material. Set amidst the windswept volcanic terrain of Seopjikoji, they resist spectacle and instead retreat into a language of restraint, carving spatial drama from seemingly mute concrete volumes.

The horizontal building stretches low and lean, defined by a long blind façade that reads more like a retaining wall than an invitation. Only once inside does the plan reveal itself, unfolding a carefully measured sequence of spaces, each diffusing light with solemn precision – well-suited to the delicacy of the French Art Nouveau glassware on display.

Nearby, the vertical pavilion rises not so much as a tower, but as a compact cruciform of mass and void. Its defining feature is an open courtyard cut into its core, shifting the weight of the structure inwards. Visitors move between periphery and centre, passing along concrete corridors that conceal more than they reveal. The architecture tightens and releases like breath.

There's a sense of near-monastic focus here. Ando's trademark use of concrete – cool, grey, and methodically scored – finds sympathetic resonance with Jeju's lava rock and low skies. And rather than emulate the flowing lines of the works within, the architecture offers an ascetic counterpoint: where the glassware curls and coils, the buildings remain rigid, almost stoic.

This is architecture as pause – drawn neither to the horizon nor the heavens, but to the act of slowing down. The buildings don't demand attention; they lower the register, dial the volume, and stage a contemplative encounter between nature, craft, and shadow. In a landscape of volcanic drama, Ando's intervention is anything but loud – its confidence lies in understatement, and in knowing when not to perform.

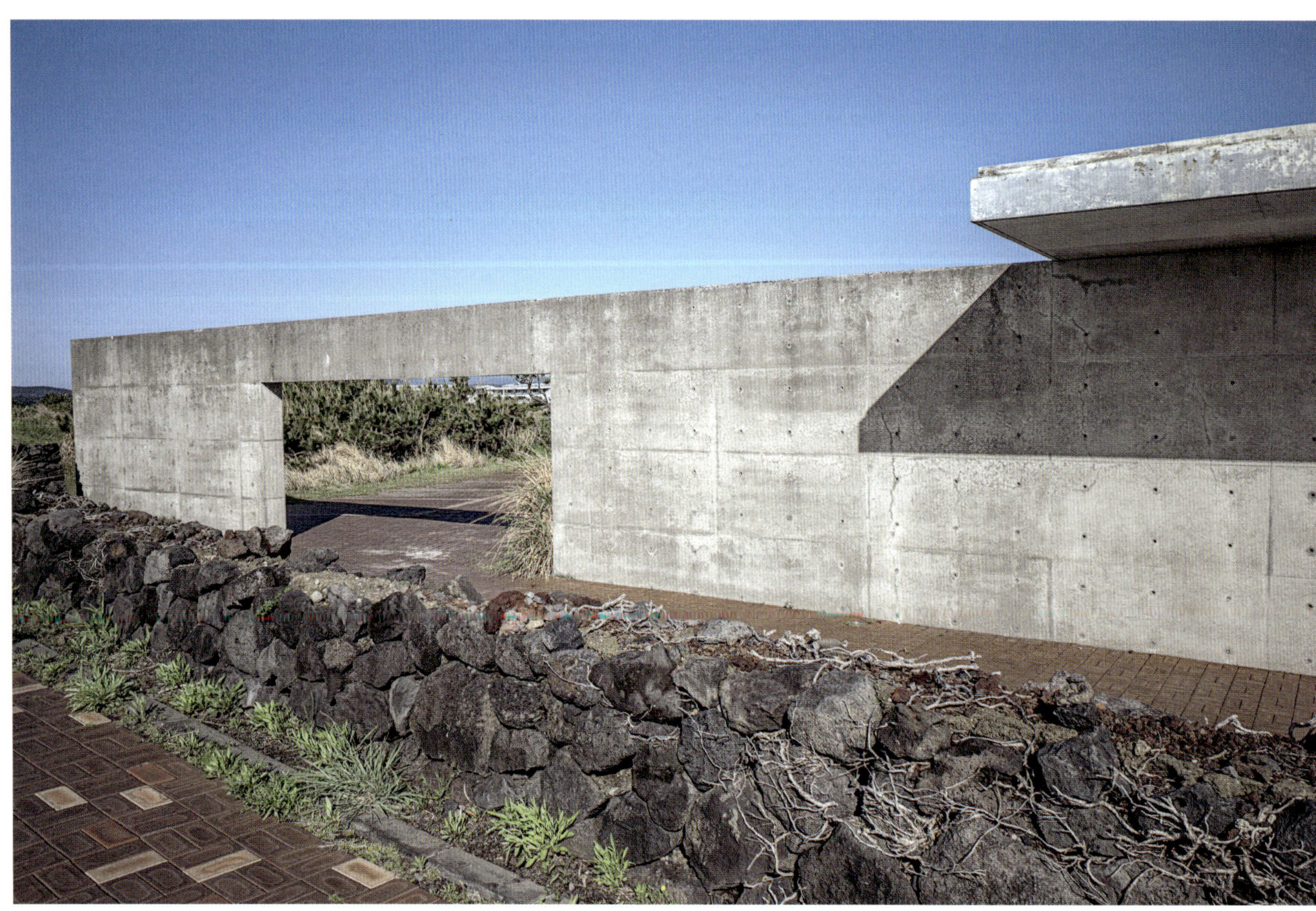

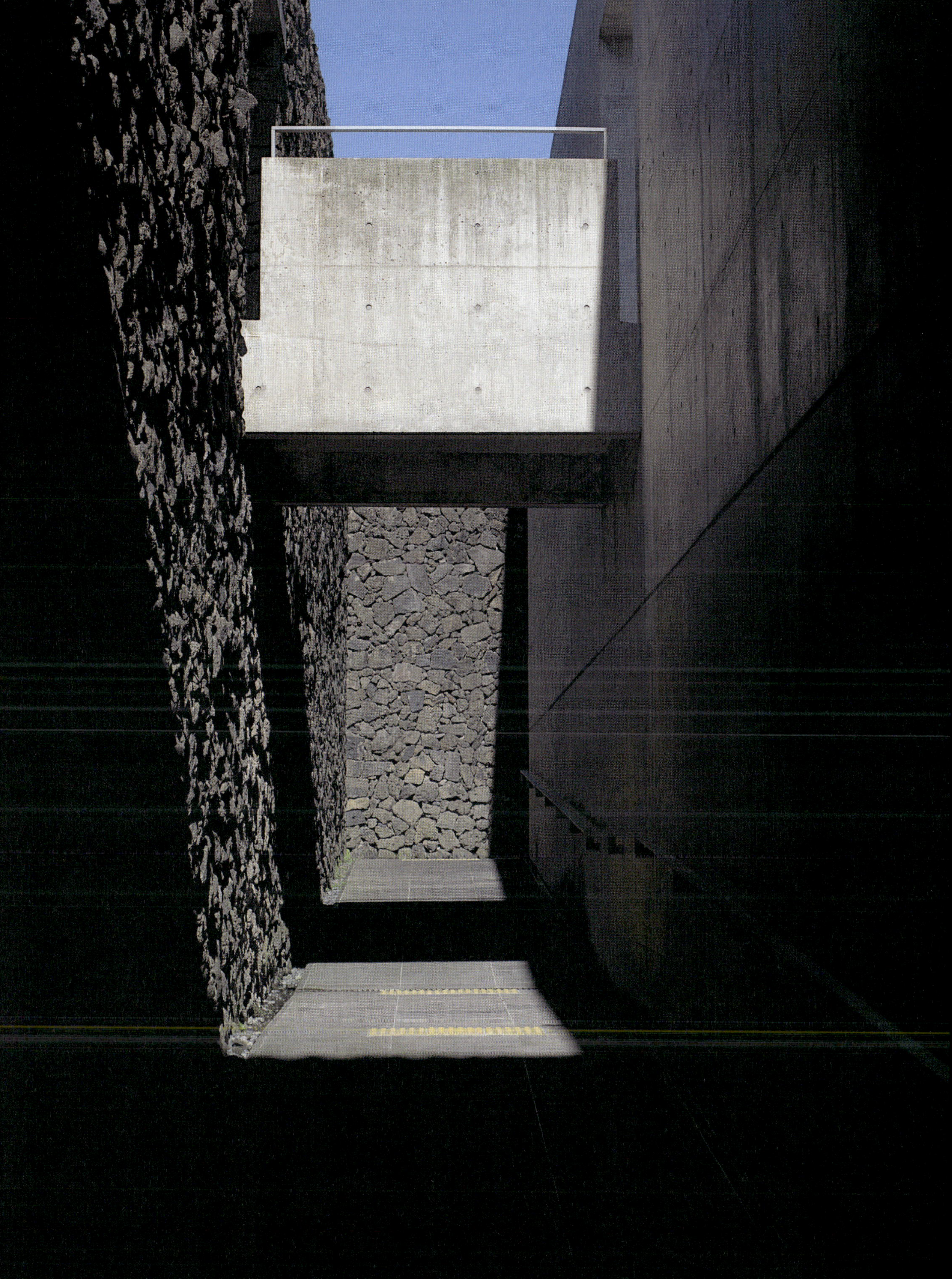

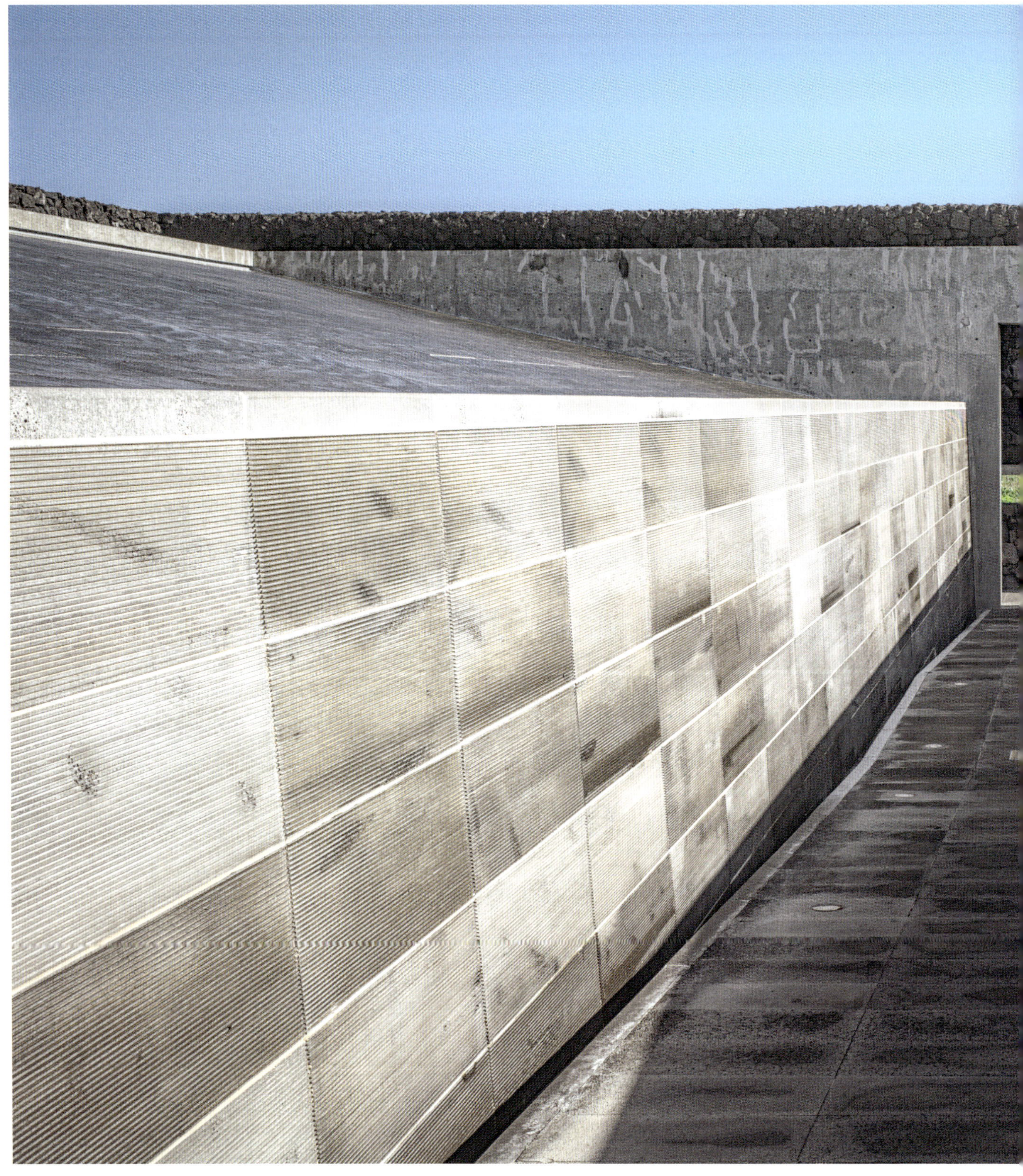

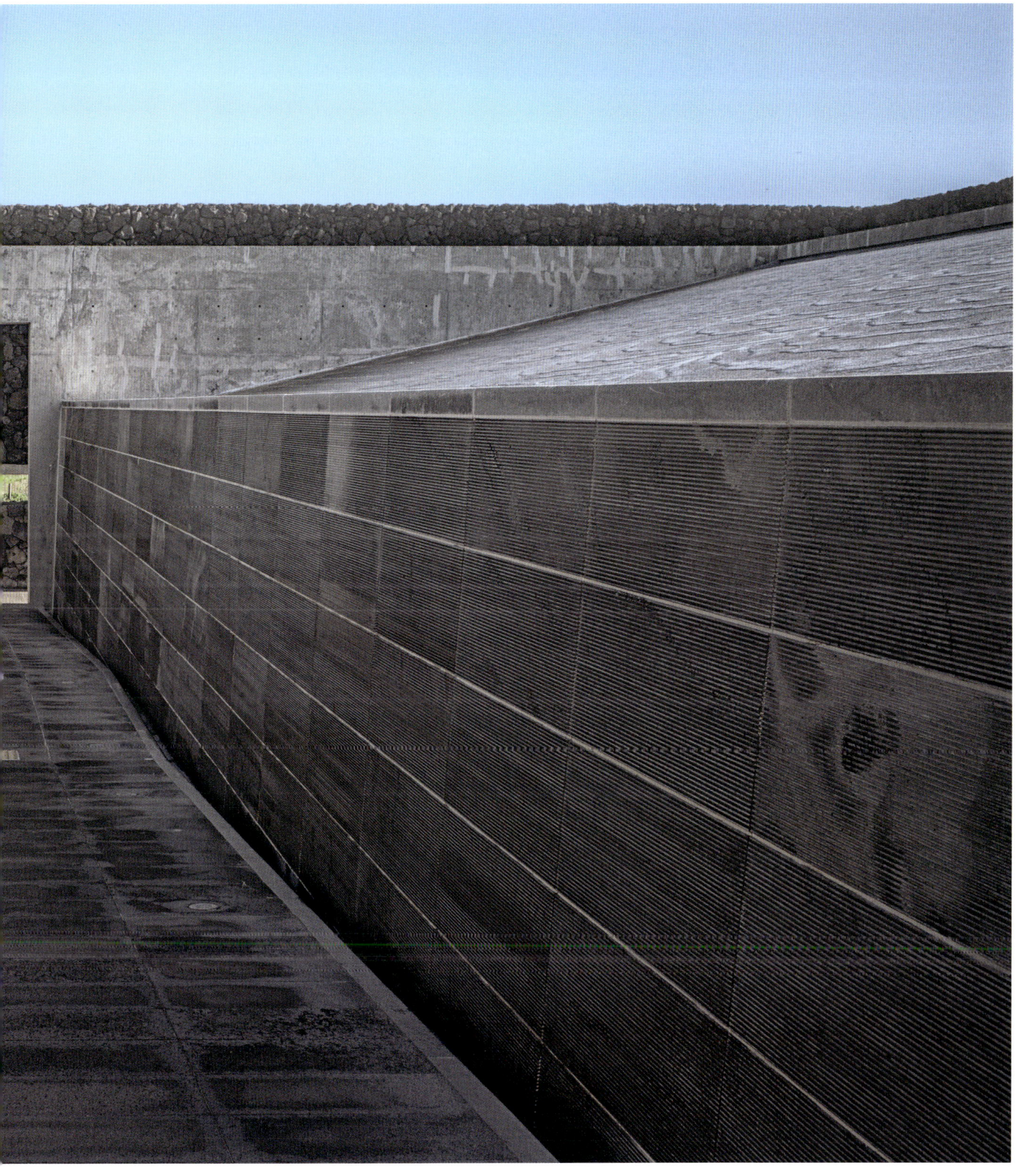

GEUMO YUHYEONDAE

SAYUWON · Architect: SEUNG H-Sang · Completed 2017

In the wooded calm of Sayuwon, Seung H-Sang's Geumo Yuhyeondae is less a lookout than a pause made physical – a rusted comma facing Mount Geumo. Formed from weathered steel, its walls bleed into the forest, oxidizing into burnt oranges and earthy reds. There's no glass, no theatrical flourish, just a slanted metal plane inviting both body and thought to lean towards the ridgeline.

Avoiding assertion, it disappears into place, a gesture expressed in metallic purpose: honesty, utility, and the refusal to embellish. Its corroding surface speaks of impermanence; its geometry, of restraint.

Among meditative interventions at Sayuwon, this is not quite the quietest – but still a low murmur of architecture that asks for nothing but attention. Yuhyeondae: a platform to wander, to look, to reconsider. Nothing more than rust, air, and stillness, and nothing less.

The quietest intervention is a platform of a different type that sits below Gaga Binbin, a building at Sayuwon's highest point. It is a sparse Zen garden comprised of a concrete plane, two shallow reflecting pools, and a deep void. Vegetation is within the frame it guides you to set. It complements Choi Wook's Gaga Binbin above with contemplative stillness below – a literal grounding of Seung's philosophy. A boulder interrupts the plane's surface like a thought breaking meditation. Both of these works that encourage observation form a conversation between gravity and grace: one rusted and metallic, one of smooth concrete, both engendering a sense of transience. Here, architecture breathes in sync with nature – every reflection, rust stain, and shadow part of an evolving script of soaring stillness.

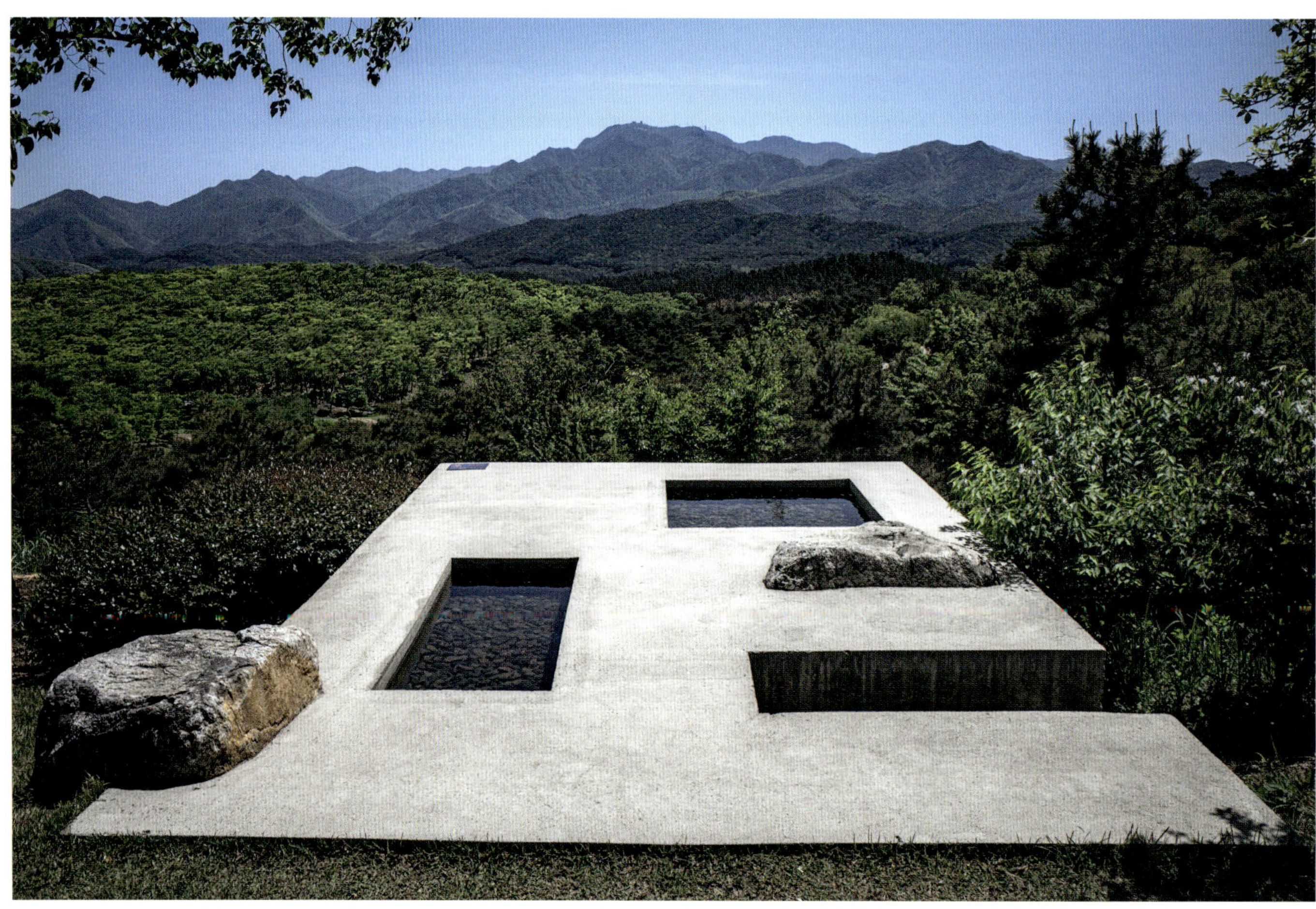

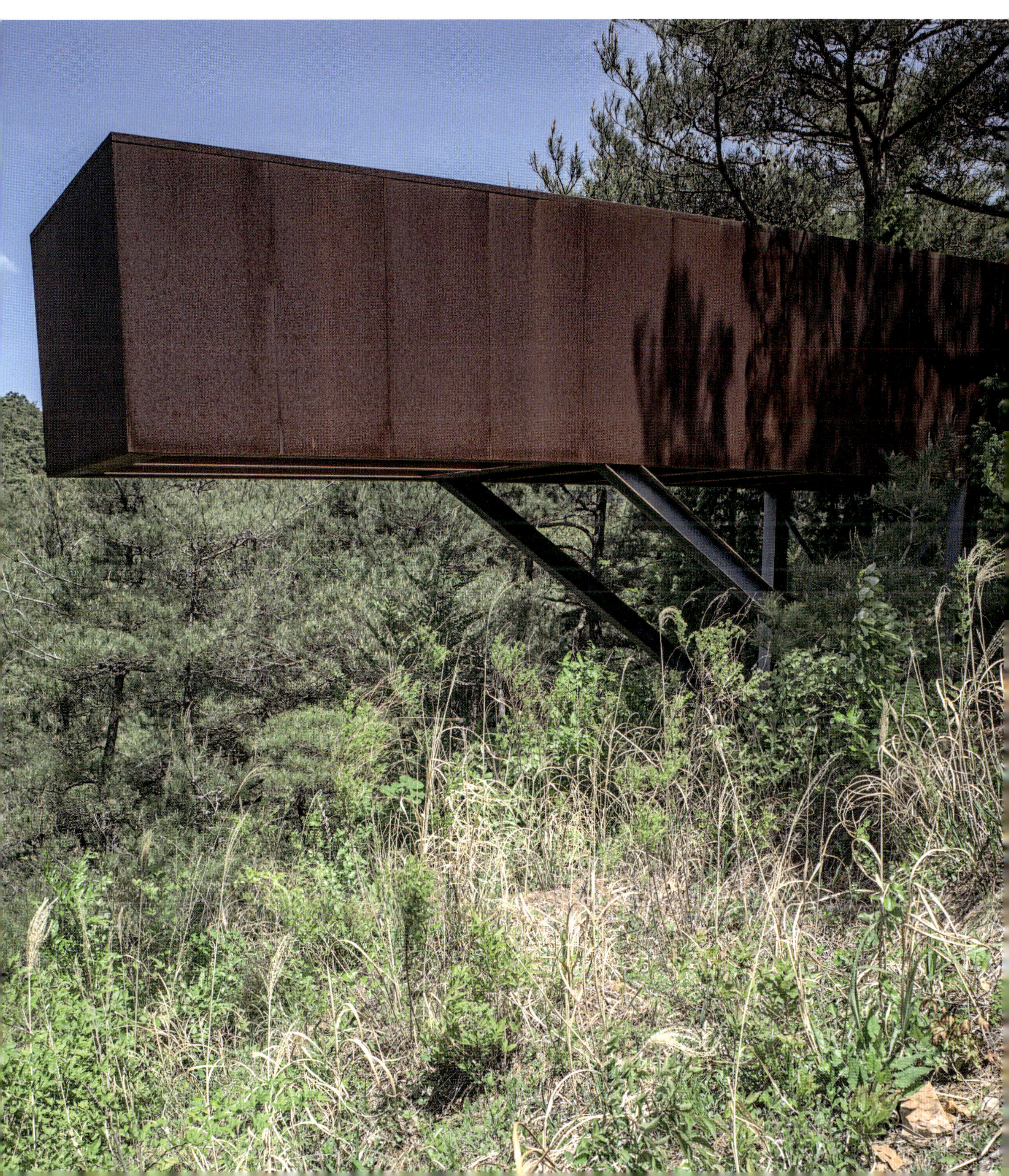

WHITE CUBE MATRIX – PAJU KINDERGARTEN

PAJU BOOK CITY · Architect: UnSangDong Architects · Completed 2014

The White Cube Matrix Kindergarten in Paju looks less like a cradle of play and more like a monument to geometry's stern authority. Designed by UnSangDong Architects in 2014, it reimagines childhood within a concrete labyrinth of cubes and apertures – each window a porthole to imagination, or perhaps confinement, depending on one's bent. The façade reads like an architectural toy box, where mass and void have been arranged with childlike daring and adult precision. Its stack of solid forms evokes building blocks left behind by a particularly austere toddler, one who grew up to lecture in urban minimalism. Inside, light filters through square punctures like a cautious parent – never overbearing, but always supervising. There's humour in the contrast: a fortress built for finger paint and nap time, a Brutalist bunker reinterpreted as playground. In this improbable paradox, architecture learns to smile when recognizing we don't need no education.

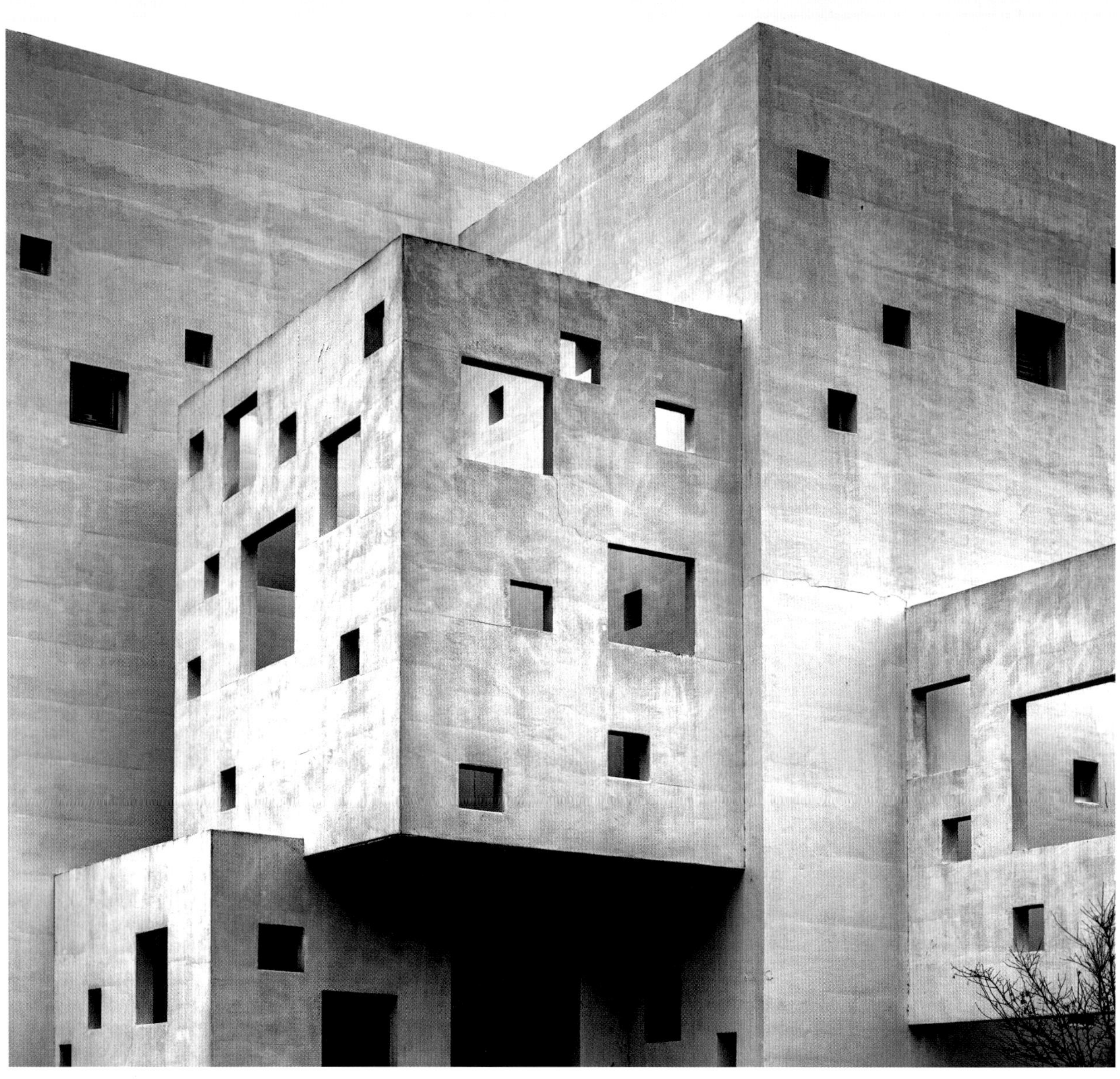

SCULPTURE AT GALLERY BAKYOUNG

PAJU BOOK CITY · Sculptor: KIM Won-geun · Completed 2008

Kim Won-geun's *Man Series* may not be cast in concrete, but it shares Brutalism's aesthetic and emotional DNA. Both emerge from a philosophy of unvarnished honesty – where surface, structure, and imperfection are exposed, not concealed. Like a Brutalist façade, Kim's figures, whilst colourful, are blunt, unashamed forms revealing their materiality with disarming directness. Their exaggerated massing and tactile surfaces echo the weight and gravity of architectural concrete.

Old-school Brutalism often sought to humanize modernism through texture and scale. Kim monumentalizes the modern human condition through the same lens of truth to form. His men – solid, static, and vulnerable beneath their bravado – are emotional equivalents of Brutalist architecture: awkward, dignified, unpretentious, and vulnerable.

Fittingly placed outside Gallery Bakyoung, the first gallery in the concrete constellation of Nu-Bru that is Paju Book City, the sculpture becomes a human proxy for the building itself – a concrete soul in polyester skin. Both stand unguarded against judgement, offering sincerity over polish. Honesty over bullshit.

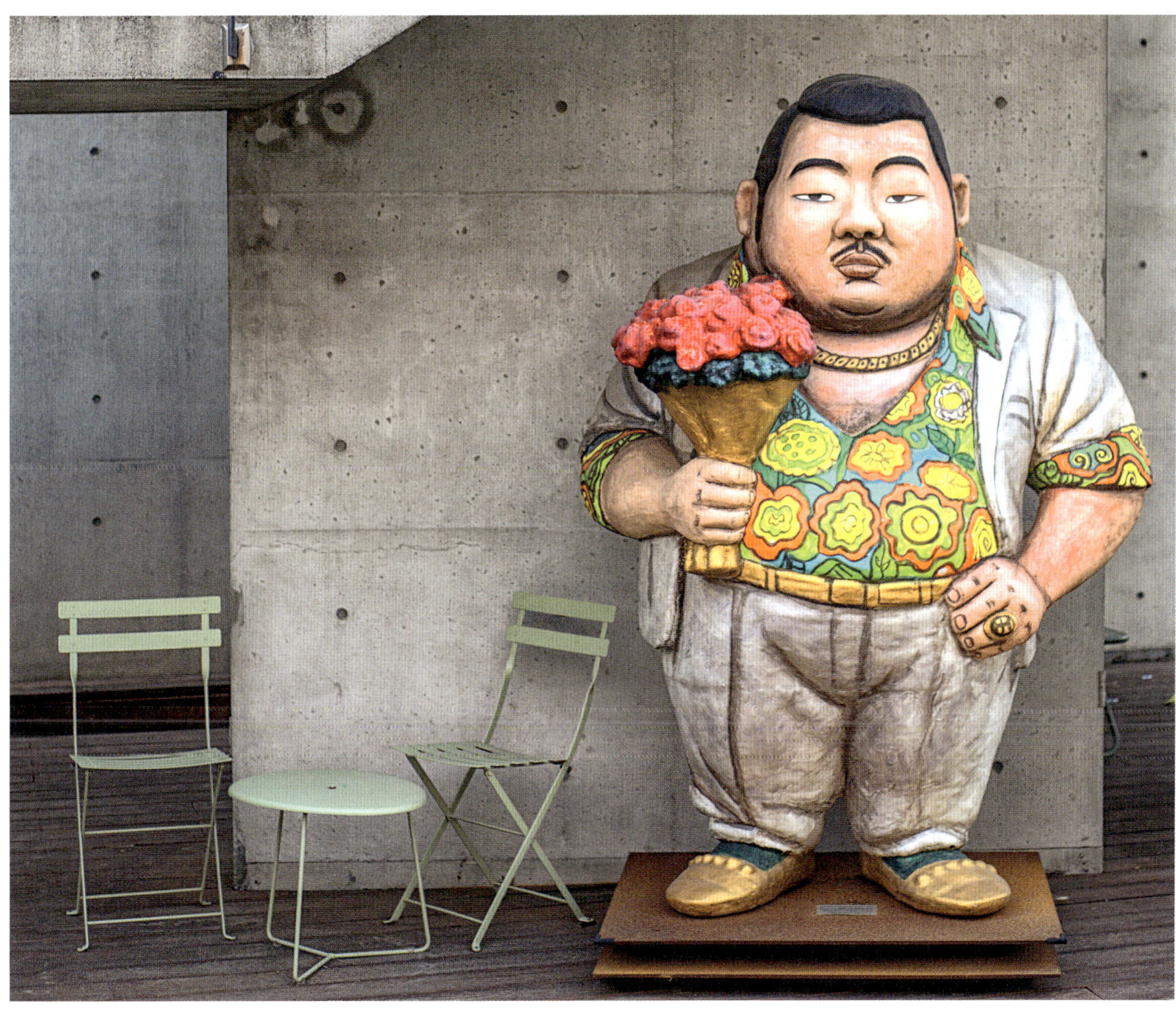

WELCOMM CITY

Seoul · Architect: SEUNG H-Sang · Completed 2000

Designed by Seung H-Sang of IROJE Architects and completed in 2000, Welcomm City reimagines the office complex as a living fragment of Seoul's urban fabric. Instead of a single tower, Seung composed four rust-toned Corten steel boxes atop a light-toned concrete podium, each distinct yet unified in plan. Between them, three deliberate voids invite air, light, and movement – transforming what could have been a wall into a porous frame for city life.

The contrast of materials defines its quiet power: the concrete base provides civic stability, while the weathering steel above evolves with time, its patina marking the passage of seasons. These textures embody Seung's philosophy of "erasing the box" to reveal connections between architecture and its surroundings. Within the courtyard, shifting shadows and glimpses of neighbouring life turn the complex into a micro-city – a place where structure, community, and time converge in modest, enduring harmony.

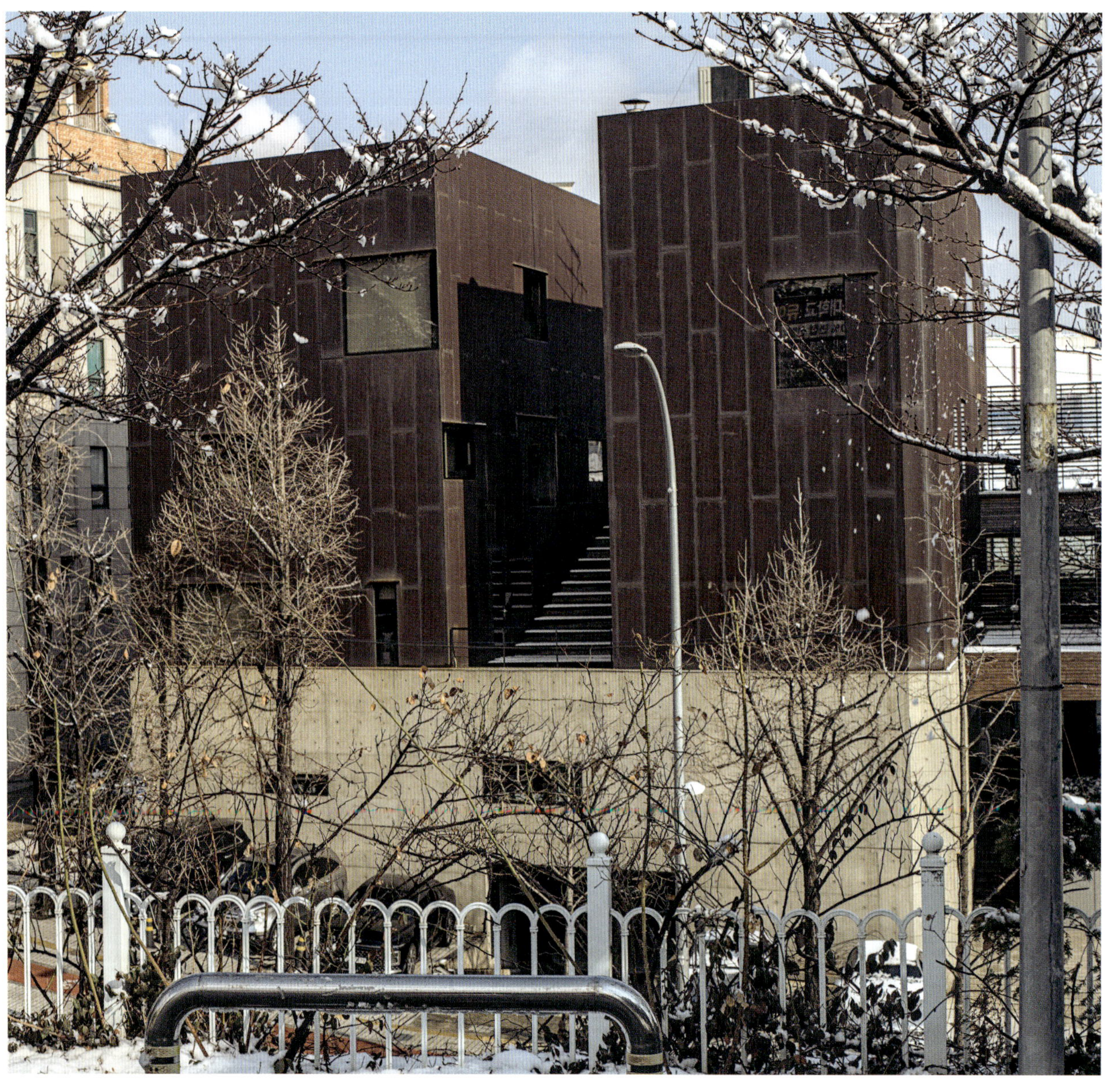

INTERROBANG

SEOUL · Architect: OH Sae-min · Completed 2014

Lurking like a concrete kaiju caught mid-sentence, Interrobang by Oh Sae-min refuses to sit – it prowls. A ribbed, writhing mass of grey muscle, it is part dinosaur, part question mark, part architectural tantrum. Brutalism here goes full B-movie, and the spectacle is gloriously unashamed.

Forget symmetry or solemnity – this is Brutalism with a grin. Its scaly concrete skin ripples and buckles like tectonic plates mid-roar. Moon Hoon doesn't flirt with fantasy, he marries it. The building more than suggests a creature – it *is* one: a hulking, stair-spined beast with an appetite for attention.

Yet amidst the chaos lies brutal honesty. No gloss, no disguise – just form, force, and faith in its own weirdness. Inside, spaces twist and compress like the bowels of a mythic monster, an apt metaphor for Seoul's urban churn. Interrobang isn't polite, pretty, or apologetic – it is a concrete punctuation mark roaring "What if architecture had teeth?"

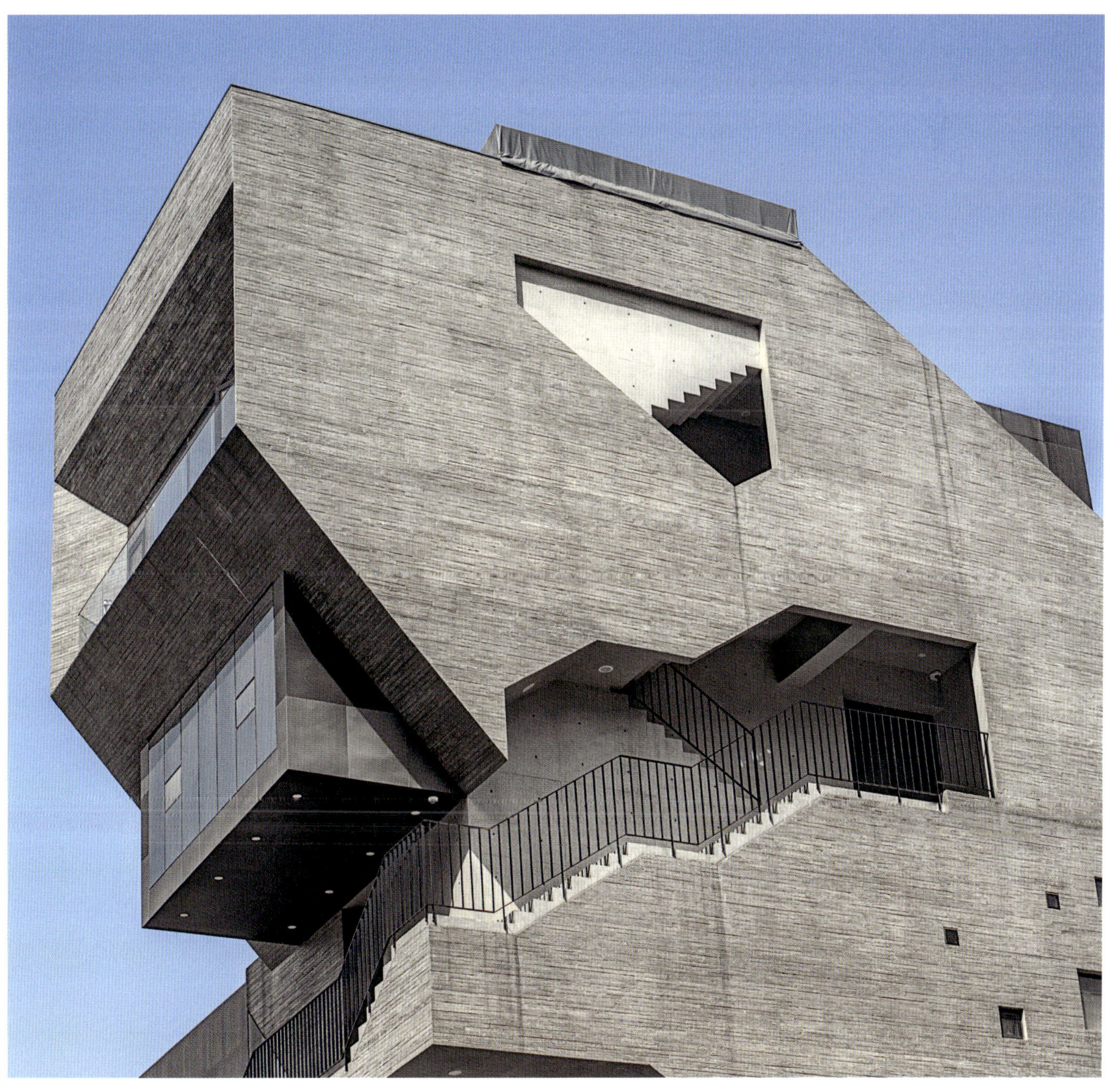

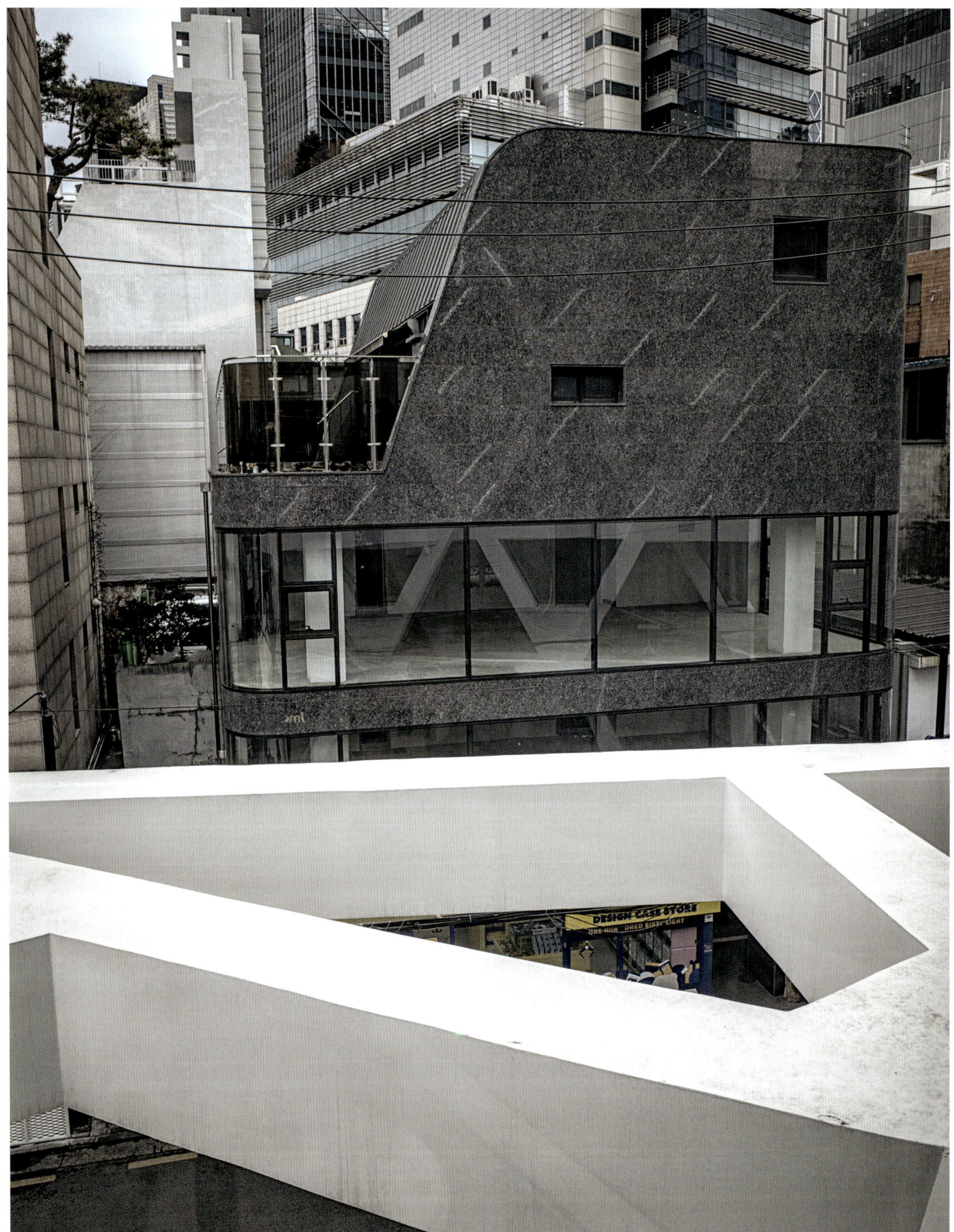
DESIGN CASE STORE

COFFEE PERFORMANCE HALL / URBAN PERFORMANCE HALL

SEOUL · Architects: KIM Seong-min and RYU Sam-yeol · Completed 2025

Defining a corner within the district of Gangnam, this building leaves a striking visual mark on the street with its powerful presence. This architecture aggressively embraces geometric repetition: clusters of triangular modules stack and offset to form a lattice-like façade. Each triangular cell becomes a framed chamber – window, balcony, or void – to turn the envelope into a three-dimensional play of light and depth. White-painted concrete gives the structure a crisp sculptural presence. Glazed infills contrast the solidity of the frame, permitting transparency and view corridors. The massing steps and shifts vertically, with upper volumes cantilevered over lower levels, producing a cascade of overlapping rooflines.

Functionally, the building's dual identity is mirrored in its architecture. The dynamic façade takes on a theatrical life of its own, while its layered geometry conceals private recesses within. The lattice mediates between communal and secluded areas, turning the exterior into both spectacle and shelter. Form, structure, and interior flow are interwoven, creating a sense of architectural harmony. Most striking is the way its corners are hollowed out, reimagined as open urban voids that invite public presence. It is a bold architectural voice that refuses to play background music.

However, the building's dramatic sculptural ambition earned it both admiration and critique. Its striking exterior form impressed the judges enough to merit an Excellence Award at the 43rd Seoul Architecture Awards, yet that same boldness ultimately worked against it. The spatial constraints created by its complex geometry limited interior adaptability and everyday practicality. Reviewers praised its presence as a commanding urban landmark – an artwork in concrete and steel – but noted that its interior programme struggled to match the versatility its outward form promised. In the end, the jury deemed it visually and conceptually exceptional, but functionally rigid – a triumph of expression over flexibility. Hence, while it deserved recognition for elevating architectural discourse in the city, it stopped just short of the Grand Prize, its sculptural bravado both its strength and its stumbling block.

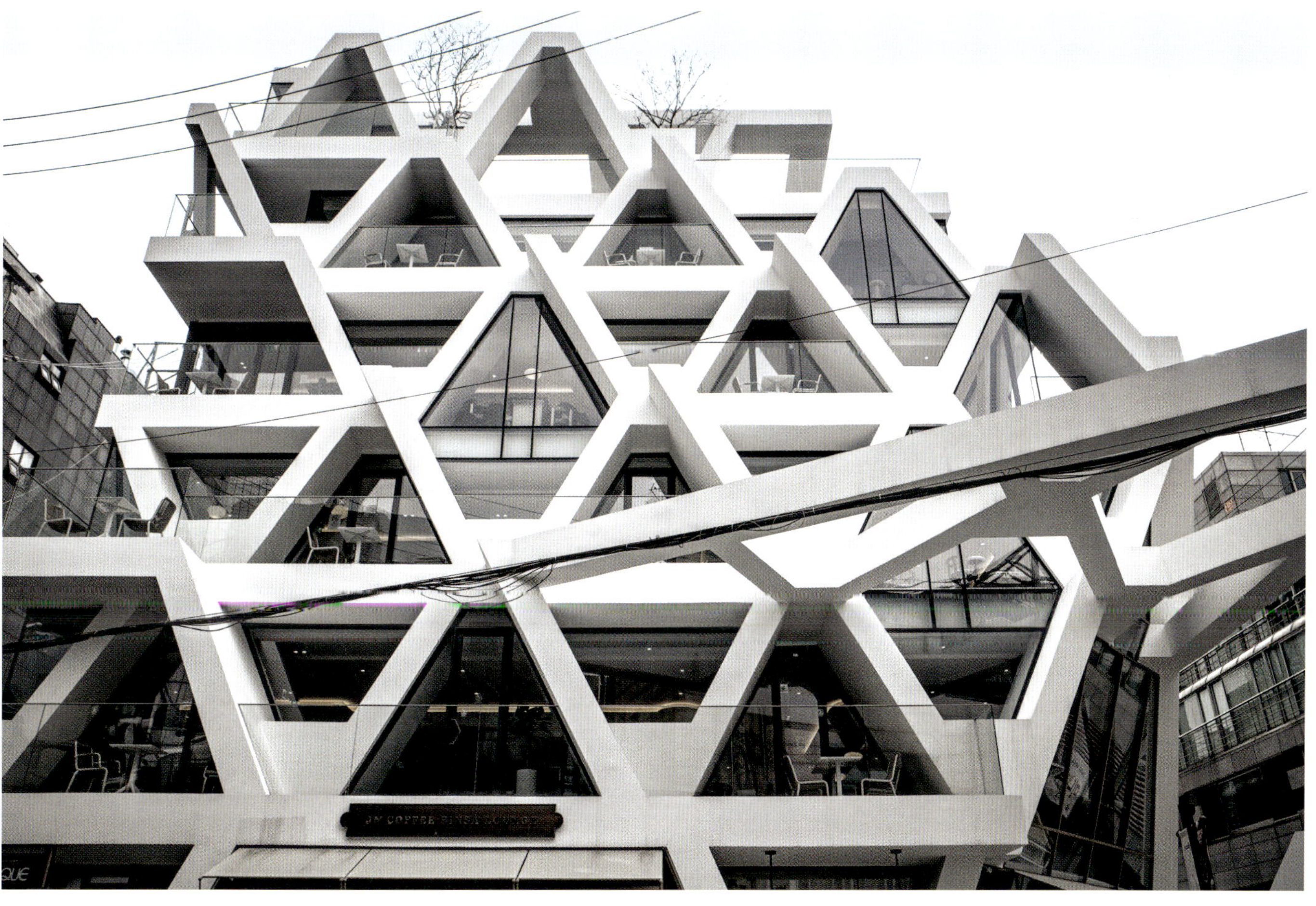

DR SEO'S WOMEN'S CLINIC BUILDING

SEOUL · Architect: KIM Chung-up · Completed 1967

The Kim Chung-up Women's Clinic (now the Arium Office Building), conceived in 1965 and completed in 1967, cradles the junction of Eulji-ro and Toegye-ro in Seoul's Jung-gu district. Designed by the pioneering modernist Kim Chung-up, this four-storey concrete sculpture embraces abstraction and anatomical allegory – embodying both chamber and womb in its sweeping curves.

Its fluid concrete shell refuses rigid box logic. The façade's curved geometry captures light and shadow like a visual heartbeat, while concave folds invite introspection and enclose interior life with grace. Interiors were intentionally labyrinthine – furniture didn't simply fit, it conversed with the walls – an architectural echo of Kim's remark that the building is "an ode to newborn life".

In 1960s Korea, concrete symbolized progress and modern identity – and here Kim wielded it with poetic courage. Its sculptural language was daringly expressive at a time when practicality dominated architectural discourse.

Culturally, the clinic occupies a potent urban moment. Situated near the historic Gwanghuimun gate – once the "death gate" through which the deceased passed – Kim's design seems to diffuse that sombre legacy with its emphasis on birth and renewal. In its curves, it balances dualities: creation and loss, shelter and exposure, function and metaphor.

Now repurposed for studio and chicken shop use, its narrative remains readable. The building stands as a testament to modern architecture's sculptural potential and to Kim Chung-up's unique voice – a creator who treated concrete like clay, shaping civic symbolism and personal memory into one fluid form. A medical office transformed into concrete myth. Concrete rendered tender.

A real highlight whilst shooting for this book was being invited inside this building by the kind owner – hence the interior and balcony shots you won't find elsewhere of this icon. An extra bonus was getting to view the original architectural drawings by Kim Chung-up.

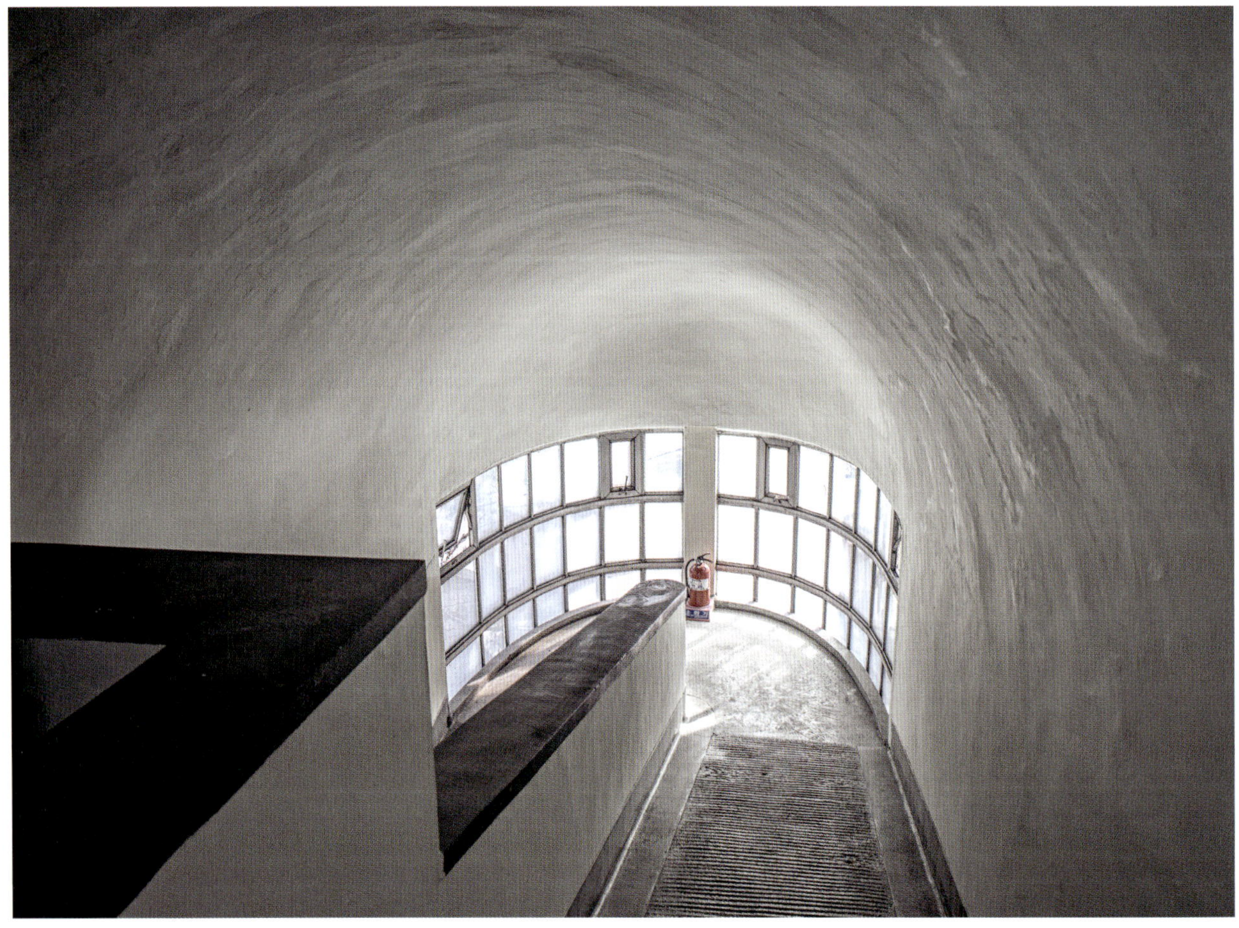

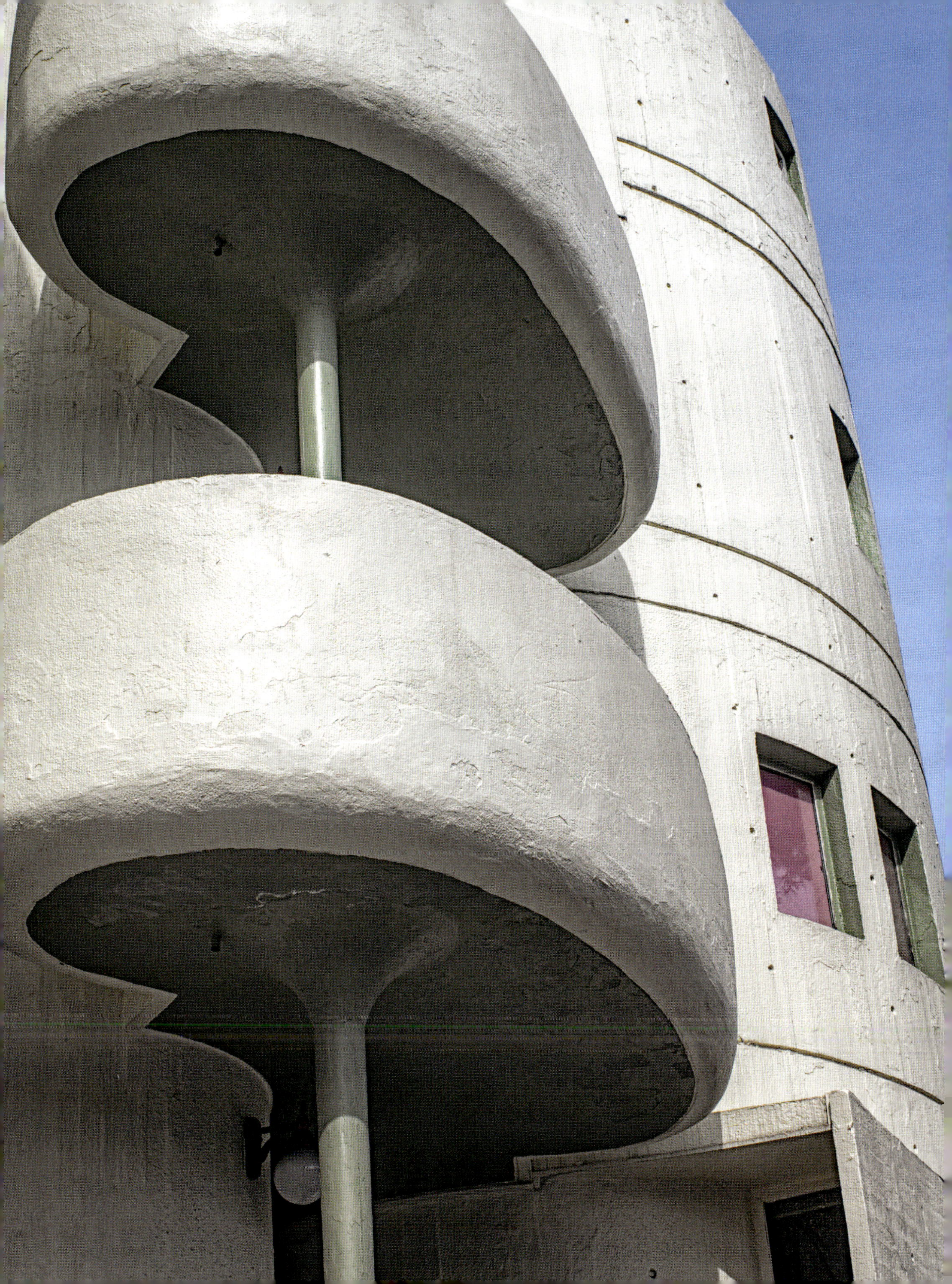

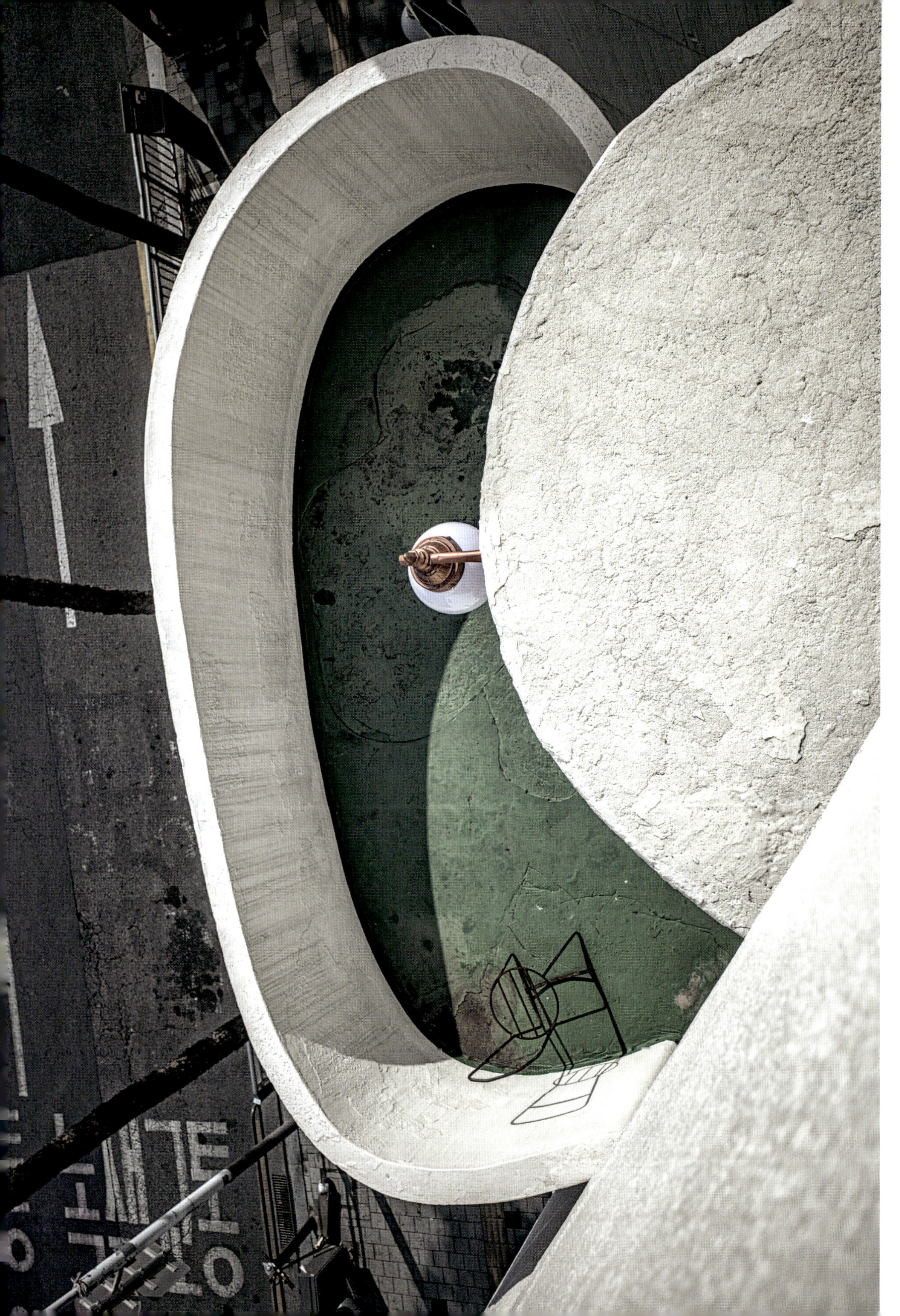

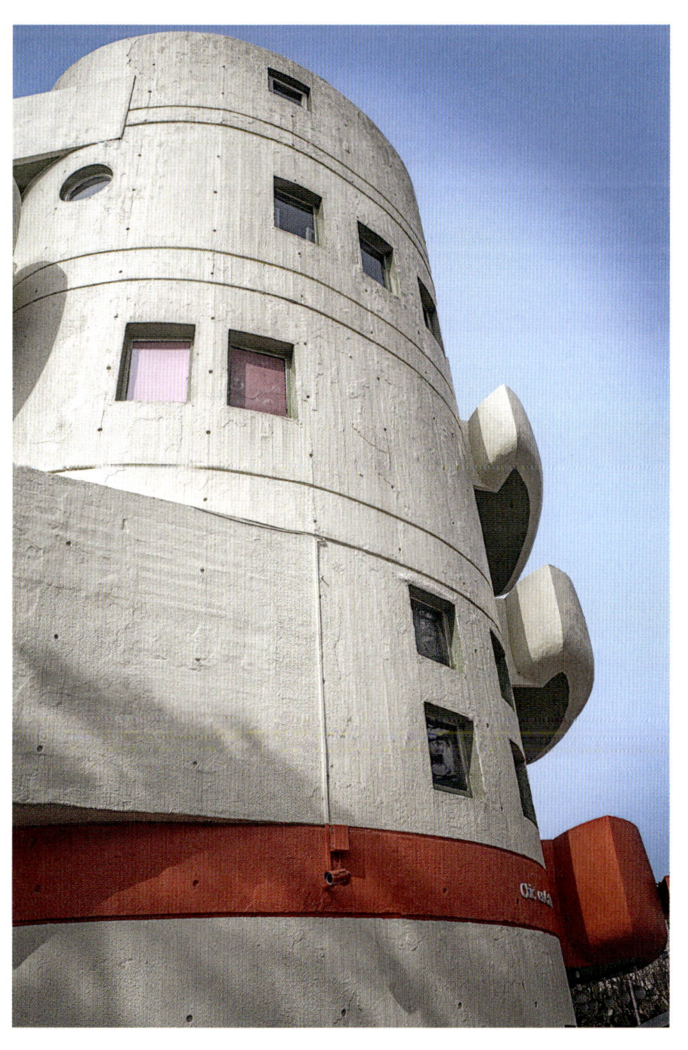

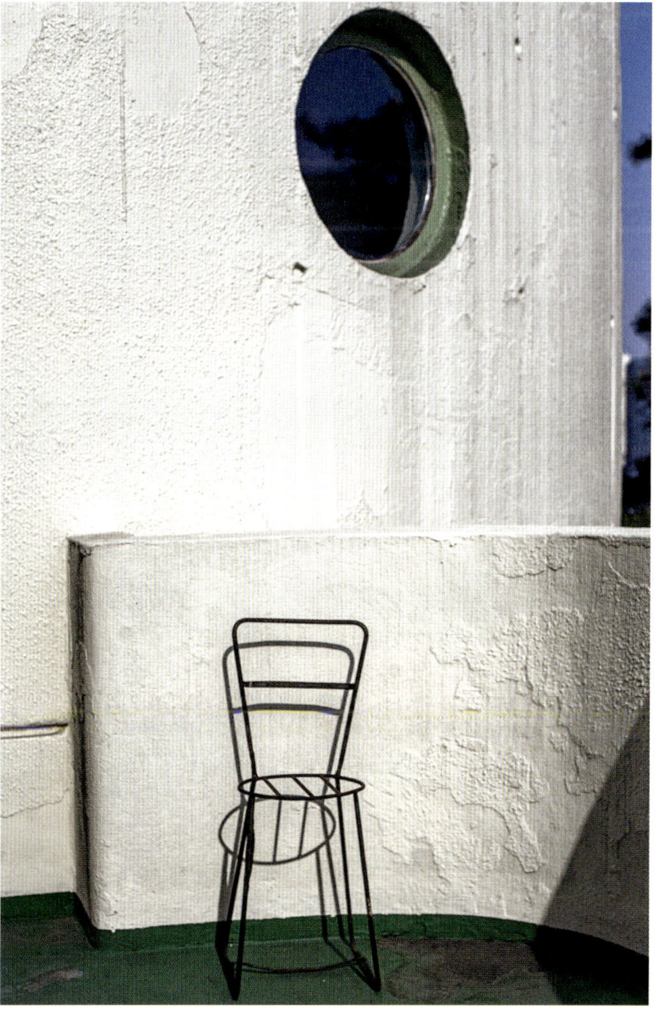

DAEYANG GALLERY AND HOUSE

SEOUL · Architect: Steven HOLL · Completed 2012

This gallery/home hybrid seems forever undecided about whether to host a cocktail party or a symposium. Steven Holl's composition folds concrete, glass, and copper into a kind of architectural sonata – measured, precise, yet faintly improvisational. The upper volumes, clad in burnished metal, catch the afternoon light, while the ribbed concrete base hums with quiet restraint. Beneath a reflecting pool, the gallery floats in a cool hush, as though the building's subconscious were tucked underwater. It's a rare residence where you could live upstairs and curate your own existence below, each room a movement in an ongoing composition. The copper skin will age; the concrete will bloom with time. Yet the tension between domesticity and display remains its central refrain – a house that occasionally forgets it's not an exhibition, and a gallery that can't quite stop feeling lived in.

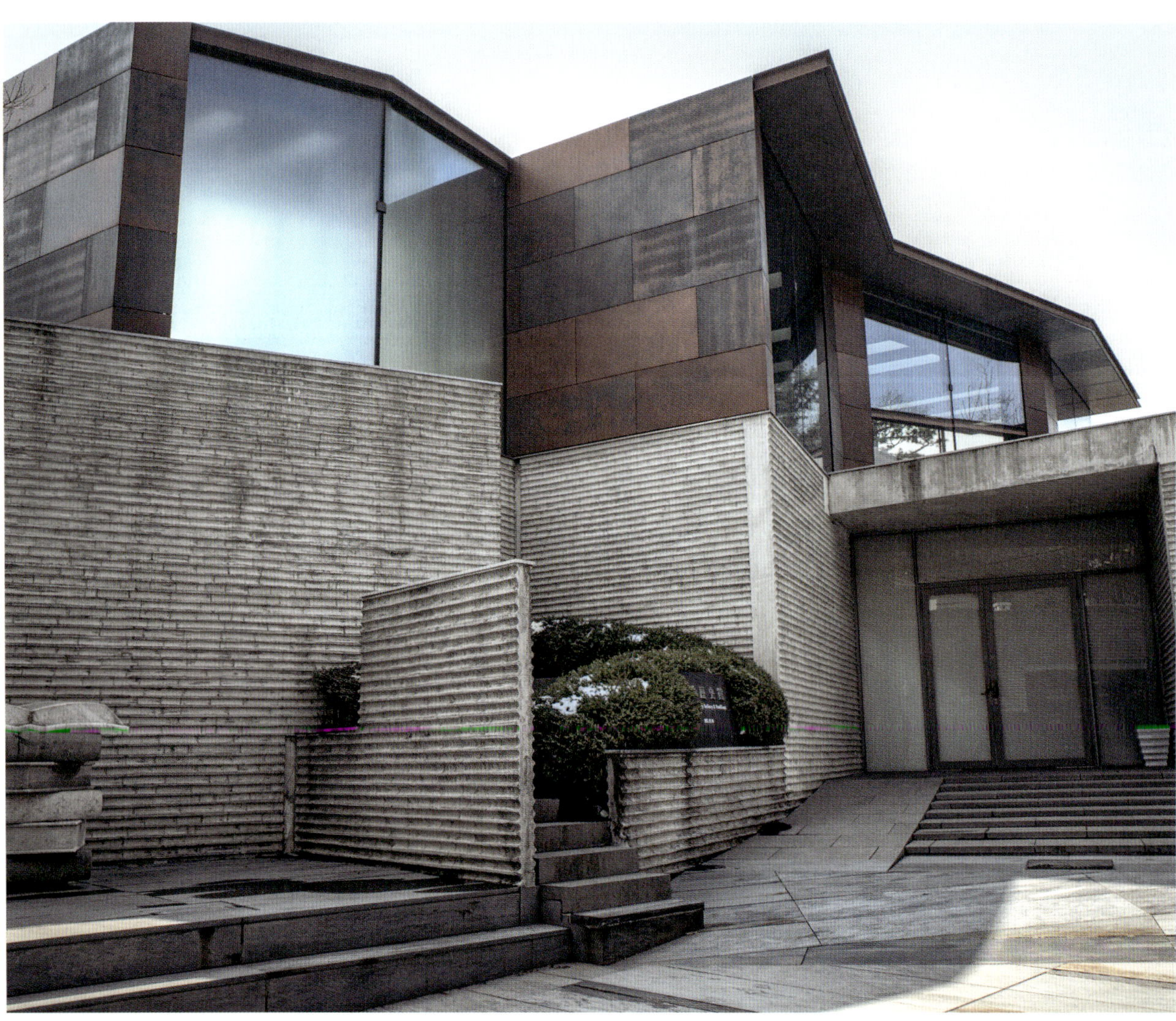

BUSAN POST LAB

BUSAN · Architects: JEONG Tae-bok and LEE Chae-geun · Completed 2009

It's an unlikely duet – a sound studio sharing its wall with a mail depot. The Busan Post Lab presents a precise concrete punctuation. The glazed façade reflects the city's hum, but tucked beneath it an austere utility box seems to hum a quieter frequency. Poured with near-clinical control, its surface is studded with tie-hole dots that resemble the perforations on a postage stamp. This tactile detail gives the structure rhythm, echoing both the cadence of recorded sound and the mechanical tempo of mail-sorting next door. There's an odd harmony in that pairing: sound and post, both dealing in transmission. The building feels like a broadcast frozen mid-wave – an architectural pause between dispatch and delivery, where concrete becomes its own kind of static.

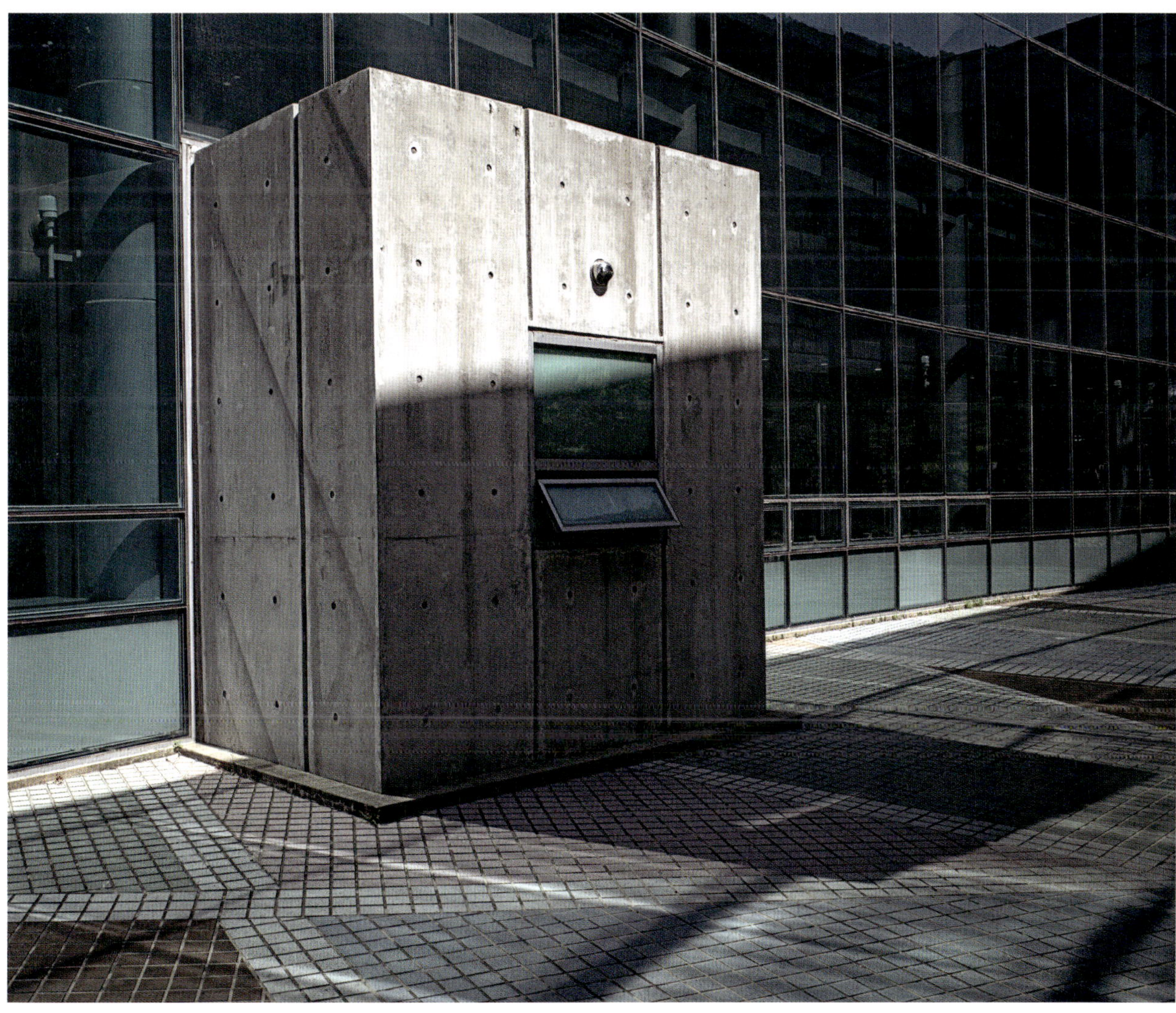

WAVEON COFFEE

BUSAN · Architect: KWAK Hee-soo (IDMM Architects) · Completed 2016

Straddling a rocky bluff in Gijang, the Waveon Coffee café by Kwak Hee-soo of IDMM Architects is a sculptural ode to sea and light. It deftly stacks cantilevered concrete volumes, each angled towards a different slice of horizon. The building feels both anchored and adrift – Brutalist in material, lyrical in intent. Inside, ocean views change with the tide. The cantilevered section steps outwards like the deck of a ship, blurring boundary between coast and construction. Light bounces through the angled planes, turning shadow into geometry and coffee into ritual. Waveon isn't a café that overlooks the sea – it's a café that *becomes* the sea's extension: fluid, layered, and perpetually in motion. Here, Kwak proves that concrete can float, and that architecture, when tuned to landscape, can feel as alive and restless as the waves themselves.

It is an effort to get to, so I was somewhat perplexed when told by a staff member I could not shoot from where I had sneaked into. All that changed when I told him to tell the boss the building would feature in this book. I should have asked for a free mocha!

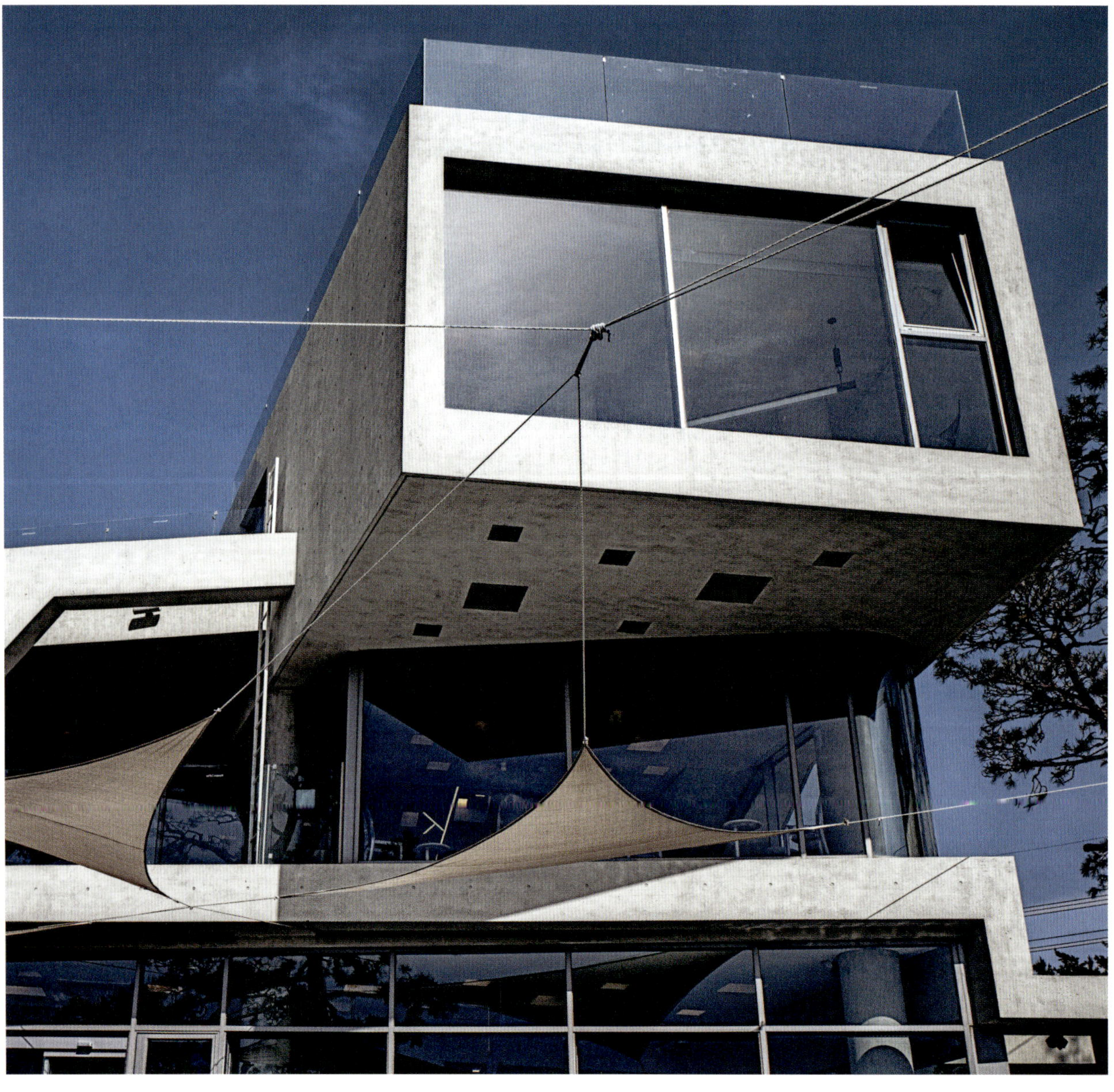

SANGSANG PORTRAIT

SEOUL · Architect: MOON Hoon · Completed 2004

Sangsang Portrait by Moon Hoon is what happens when a camera grows walls. Framed in Seoul's Mapo-gu district, it is a concrete self-portrait of a photographer – part house, part studio, part exhibition in perpetual exposure. The building behaves like a camera obscura turned inside out: solid mass sculpted by light leaks and apertures.

Concrete is exposed like high-ISO film grain, while windows act as viewfinders, framing Seoul in ready-made compositions. By night, its circular openings glow like red-eyed film reels – Moon's playful nod to both Dracula and the sleepless photographer.

Two façades shoot in different styles: one wood-clad and composed, the other raw and chaotic – a perfect double exposure of public and private lives. Inside, light slices through the concrete like shutter bursts, revealing moments, not just rooms. Sangsang Portrait isn't just architecture; it's a slow-developing image – one that keeps its subject perfectly, provocatively out of focus.

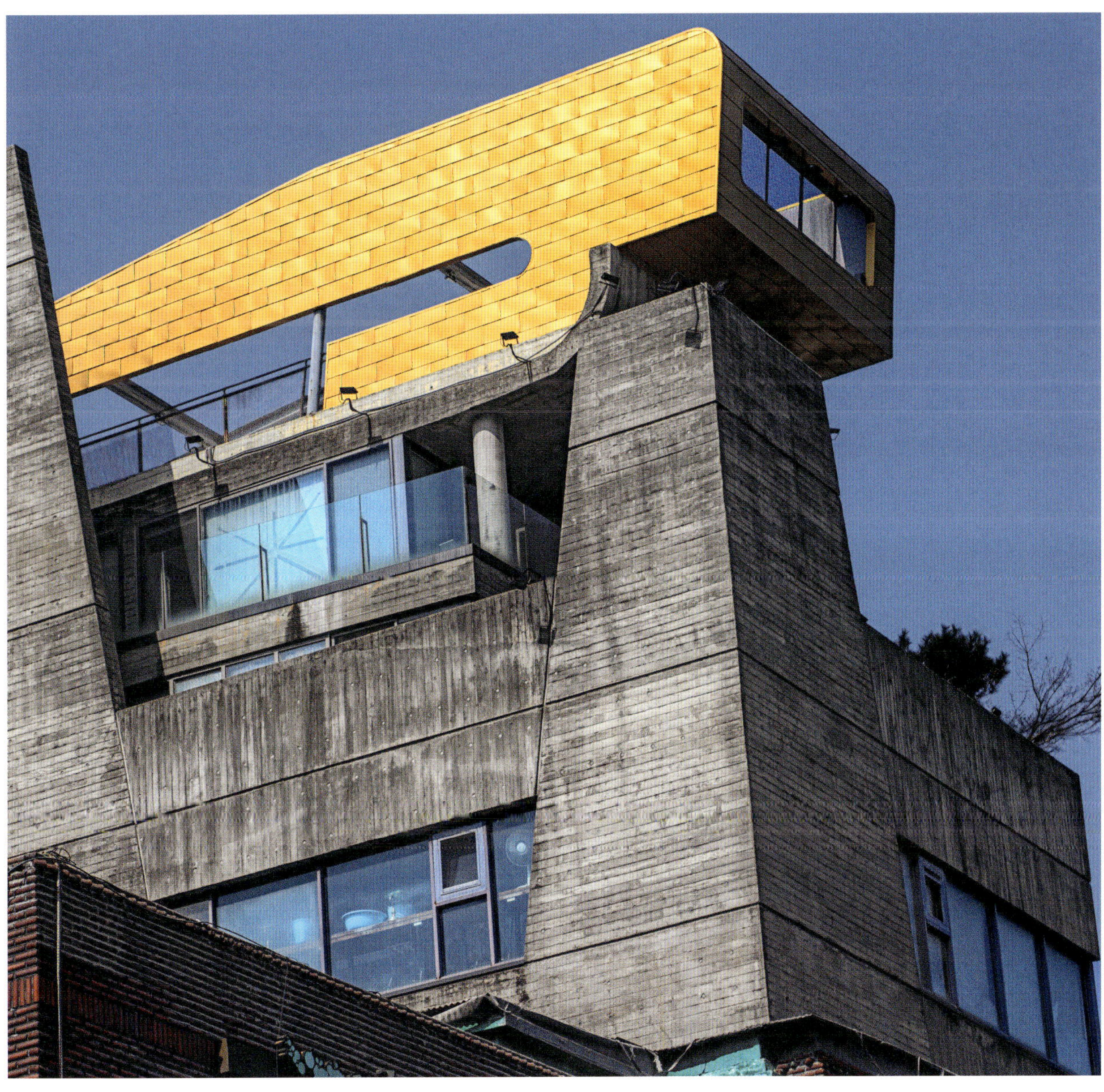

KYOBO BOOK CENTRE HQ

PAJU BOOK CITY · Architect: IROJE Architects & Planners · Completed 2008

Like a shelf of oversized hardbacks, the Kyobo Book Center in Paju Book City presents a sequence of blocky, matt-grey volumes that seem stacked with editorial precision. Each cuboid "chapter" projects slightly from the next, creating a visual rhythm of margins and indentations that reads like a text in relief. The building's massing suggests both the permanence of print and the discipline of layout. Its dark ceramic skin, gridded like pages under pressure, gives the structure a tactile gravity – less a façade than a cover. Strip windows and protruding frames break the surface like marginal notes, offering moments of clarity amid the density. Despite its weight, there's an underlying order here, a sense of paragraphs arranged and aligned. It is Brutalism with editorial restraint – an architecture not of narrative flourish, but of binding, composition, and enduring structure.

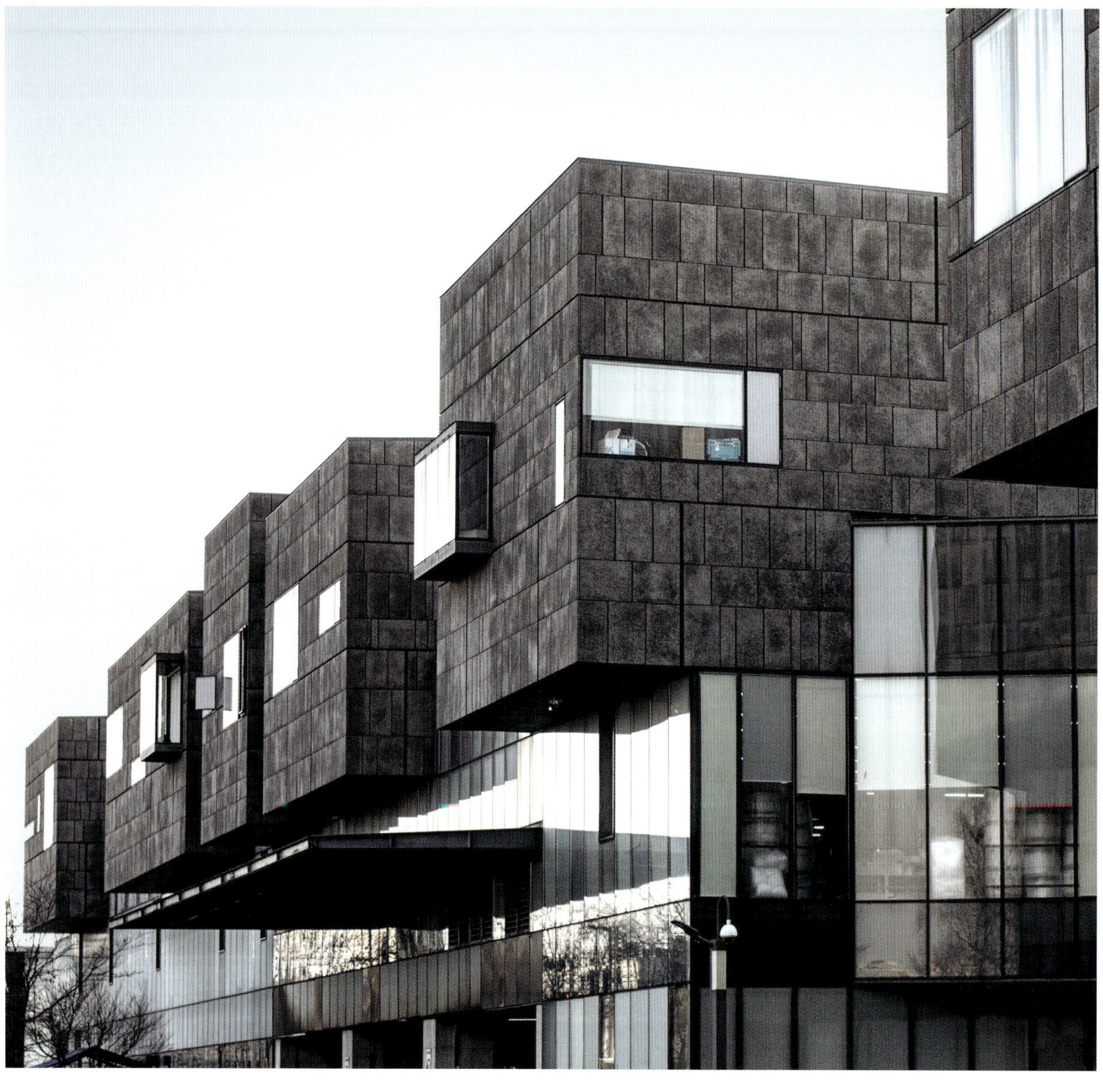

CHEONGLIM PUBLISHING BUILDING

PAJU BOOK CITY · Architect: KIM Heon (STUDIO ASYLUM) · Completed 2006

It may house a publisher, but its architect seems to have attempted leaving the manuscript uncredited. In short, it was hard to find the creator behind the story. This concrete composition in Paju Book City is a Brutalist statement with the gravity of a first edition that nearly never saw print. Angular slabs fold over one another like stiff, unbound pages, their margins defined by the sharp geometry of shadow and light. The exterior bears the patina of weather and time – water stains, streaks, and tonal variations forming a kind of accidental calligraphy. A cantilevered chapter juts out like a sentence in mid-thought, unfinished yet deliberate. Here, the raw honesty of exposed concrete reads as the building's only text – dense, uncompromising, and devoid of ornament. While most of Book City's architecture whispers of calm intellect, this structure prefers to declaim in block capitals, its presence as heavy and declarative as a concrete colophon – despite the apparent attempt at architectural anonymity.

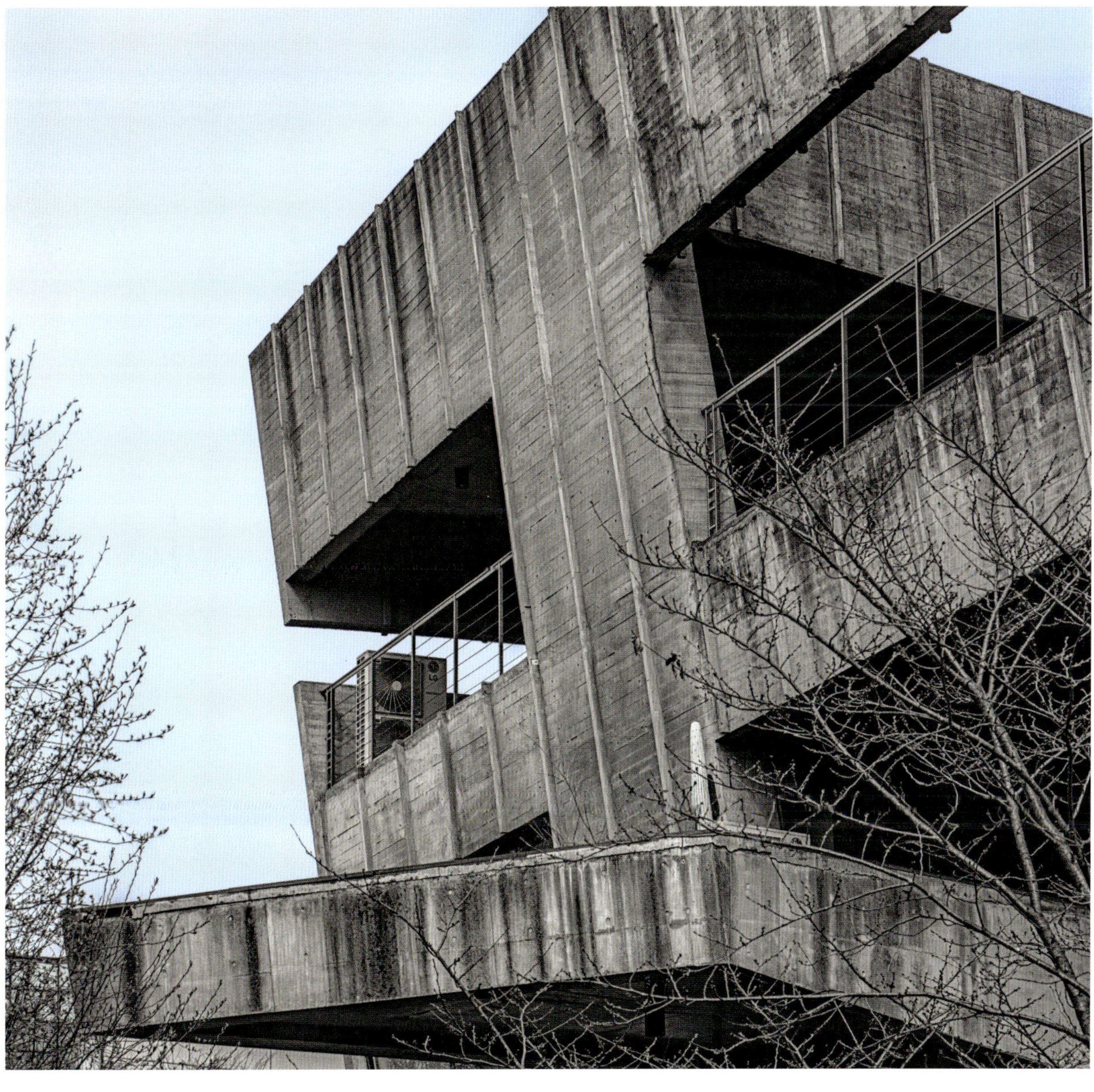

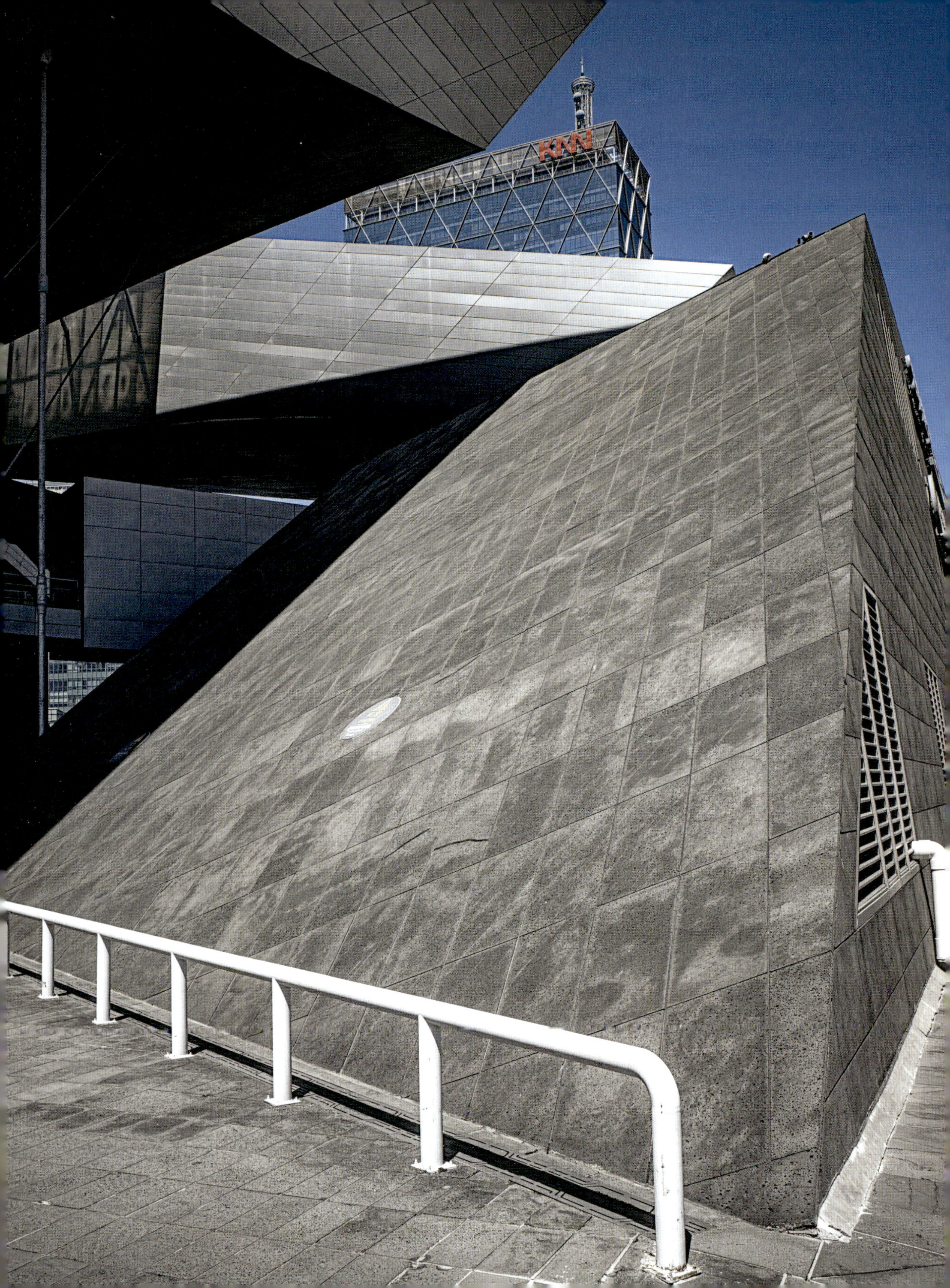
KNN

BUSAN CINEMA CENTER

BUSAN · Architect: Coop Himmelb(l)au · Completed 2011

The Busan Cinema Center straddles the banks of the Suyeong River like a colossal piece of infrastructure turned cultural machine. Its eighty-five-metre cantilevered roof – a slab of steel and concrete mass suspended in mid-air – defines the complex, a gesture of raw confidence that borders on the impossible. Brutal in scale and materiality, the structure wears its weight proudly and forms a visible anatomy of tension and compression.

This is architecture as engineered spectacle. The Double Cone, a sculptural steel lattice supporting the vast canopy, stands like a spinal column – part tower, part anchor. Around it, the complex unfolds as a stacked terrain of concrete volumes: Cinema Mountain, BIFF Hill, and the Urban Valley. Each mass interlocks through ramps and bridges, producing an experience that feels more infrastructural than decorative.

The building's material language is unvarnished. Concrete, stone, metal, and taut surfaces amplify the sensation of physical gravity. The immense roof, studded with thousands of LED points, refuses to hide its brute structure behind technology; rather, light becomes another layer – a synthetic skin stretched over bone.

What distinguishes the Cinema Center's Brutalism is its theatricality. Space is not framed so much as staged, with voids and shadows performing like actors under the hovering canopy. The plaza beneath – once pure emptiness – has been made monumental by the sheer presence above it.

Power lies in presence and exposure – a cue that both cinema and architecture are founded on light, shadow, and the framing of form.

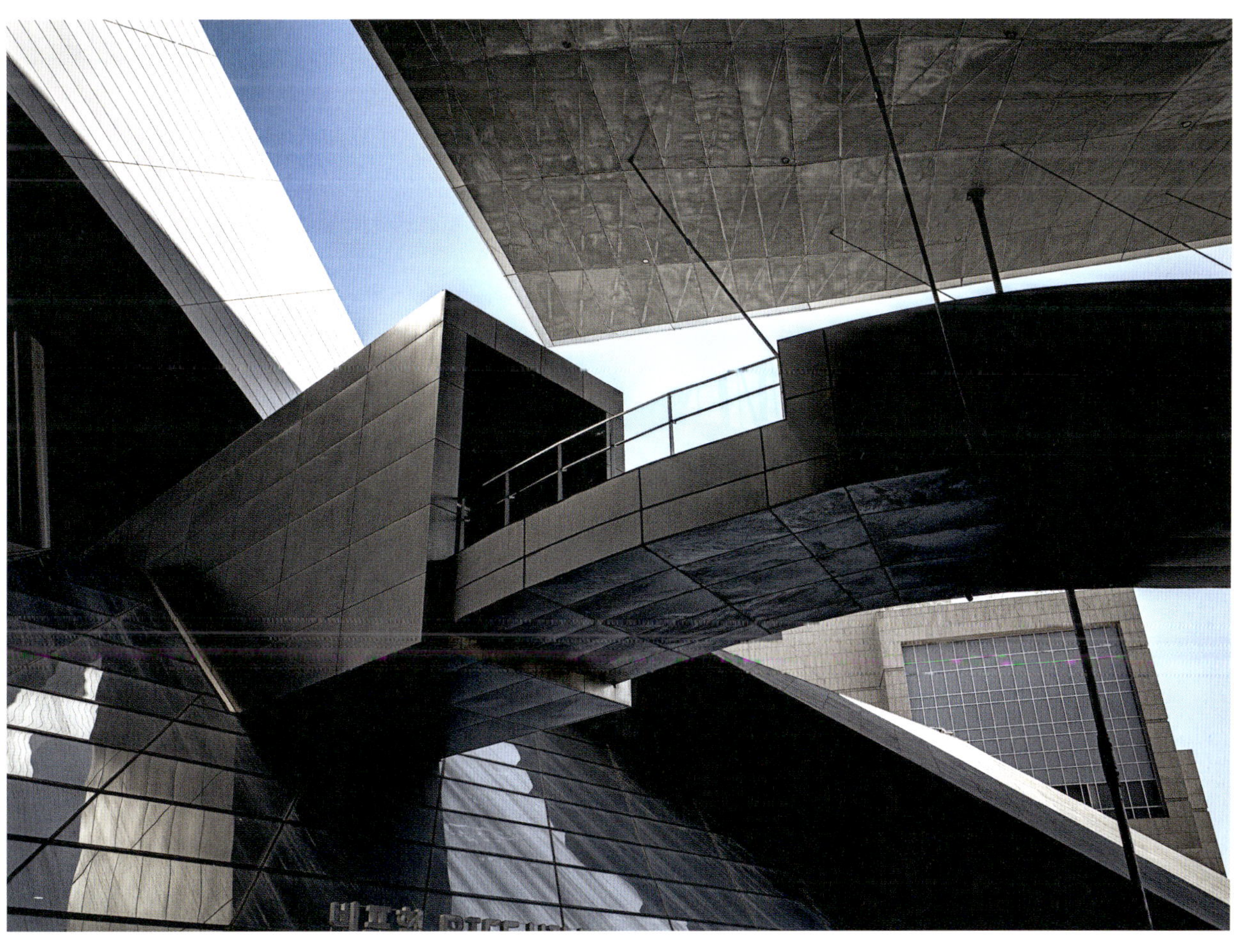

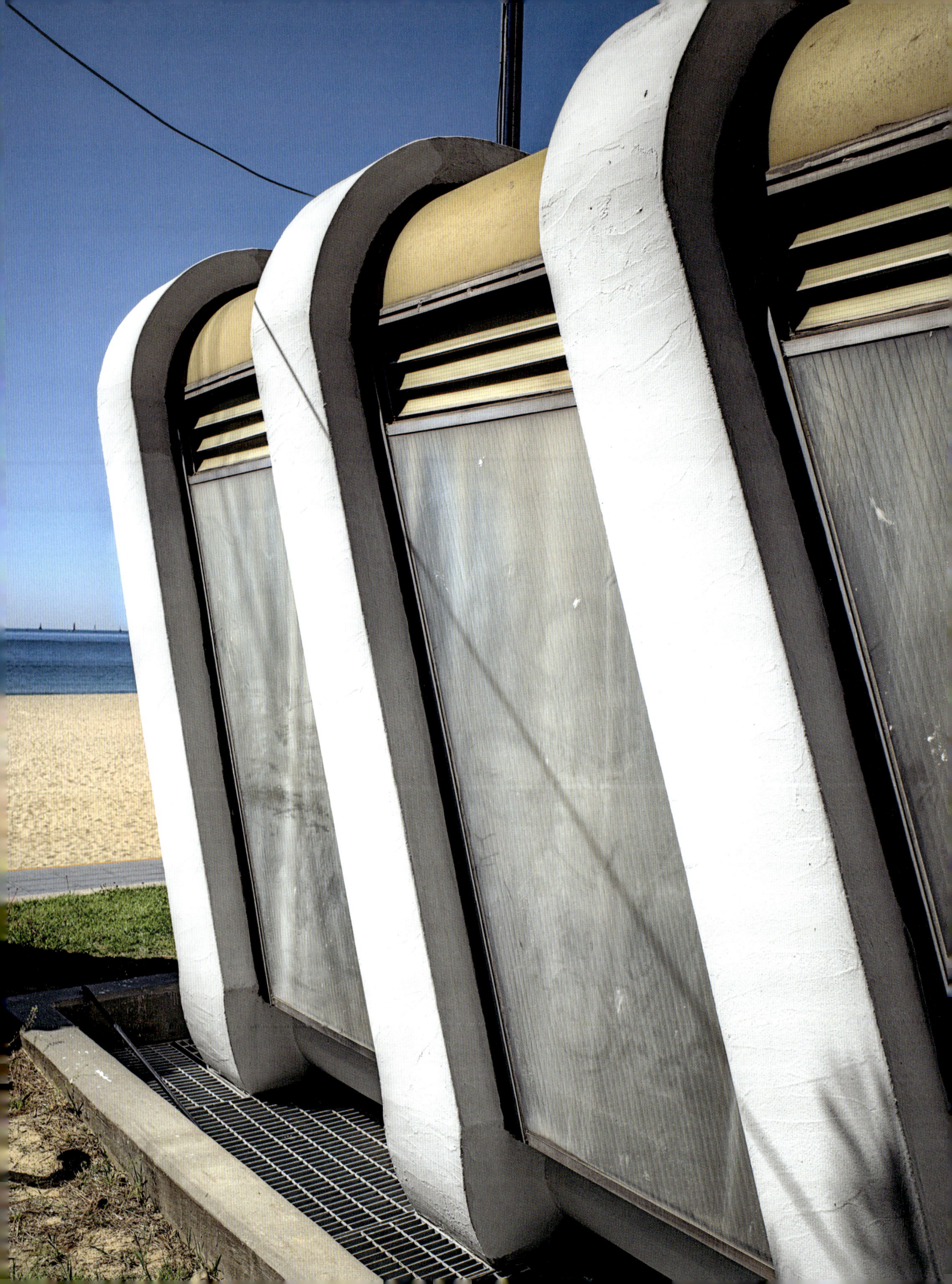

HAEUNDAE BEACH PUBLIC TOILETS & SHOWERS

BUSAN

Along Busan's Haeundae Beach, the public restroom and shower pavilions turn necessity into sculptural expression. Their ribbed white frames, tilted like breaking waves, form a rhythm of curves and shadows that speak more to modernist confidence than municipal modesty. The frosted panels glow with seaside light, filtering the glare of sun and surf into a diffused shimmer that feels almost luxurious for a space devoted to sand removal. Every detail seems to echo motion – the lean of each rib, the sweep of the form, the sense of wash and flow embedded in concrete. It's a refreshingly literal kind of architecture: you rinse, the building breathes; you exit, the façade gleams anew. Part shelter, part sculpture, it straddles that fine line between brutal function and coastal elegance. Few beachside conveniences make such a strong case that cleanliness has always been next to good design.

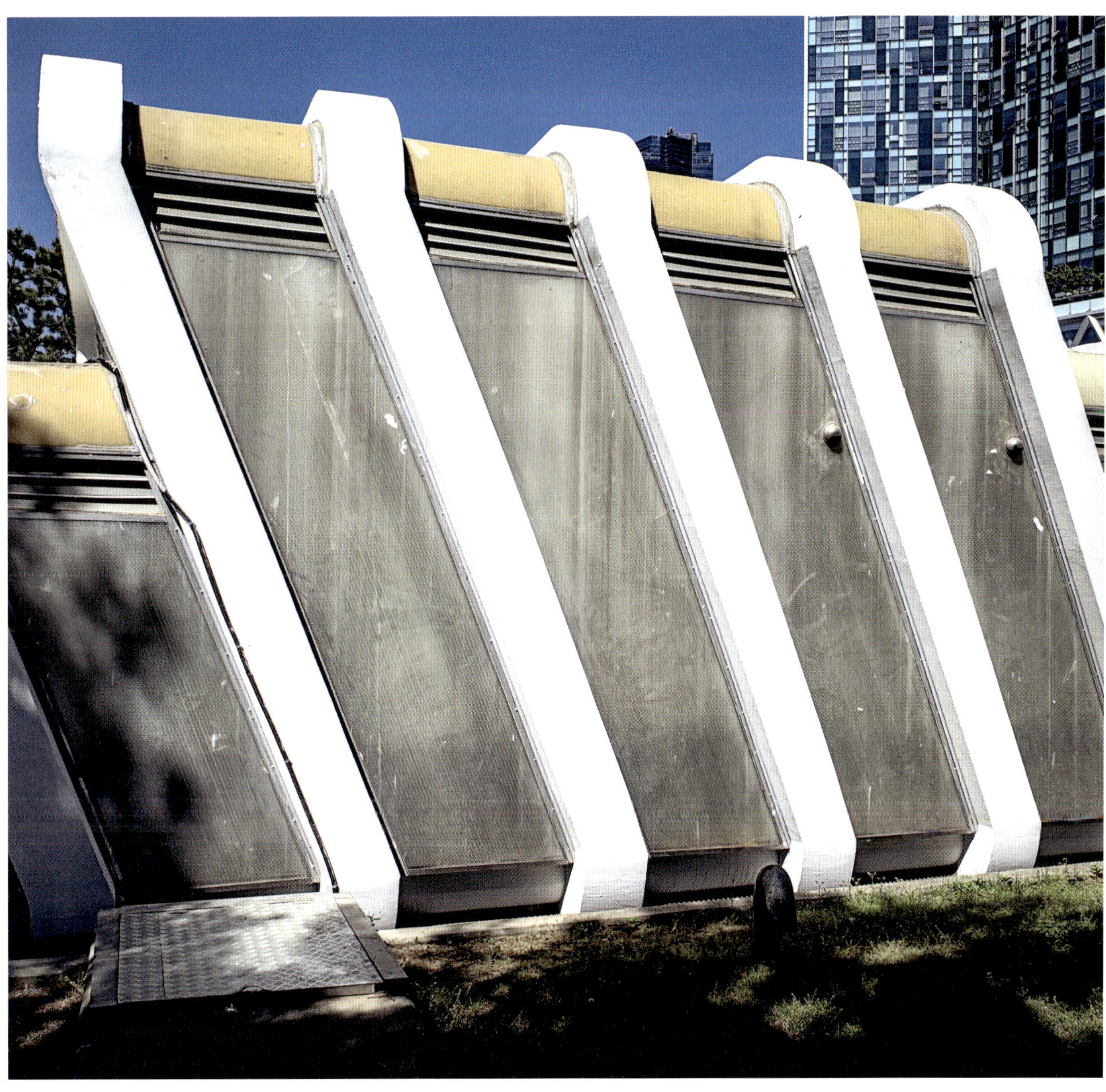

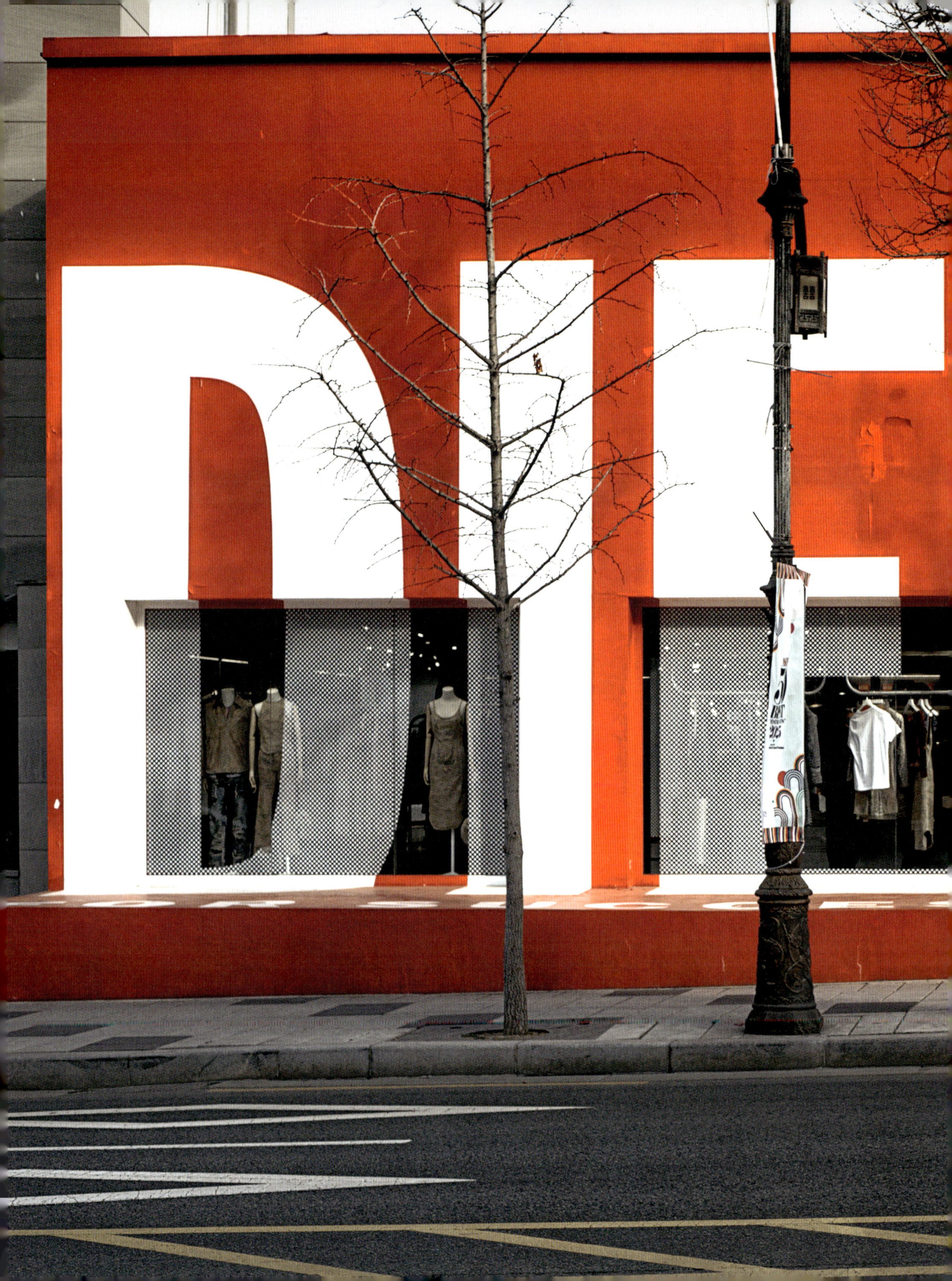

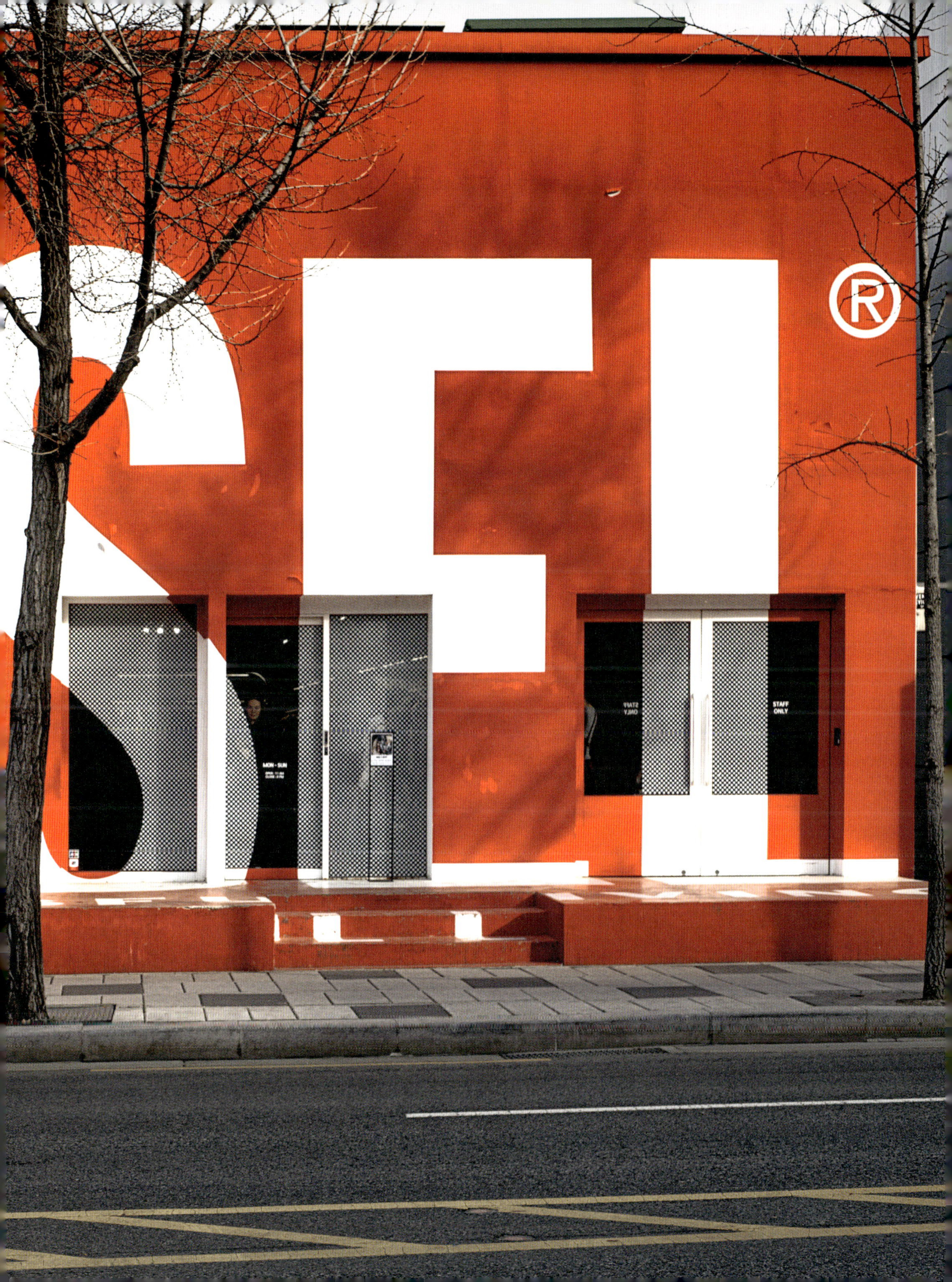

MON - SUN
STAFF
ONLY

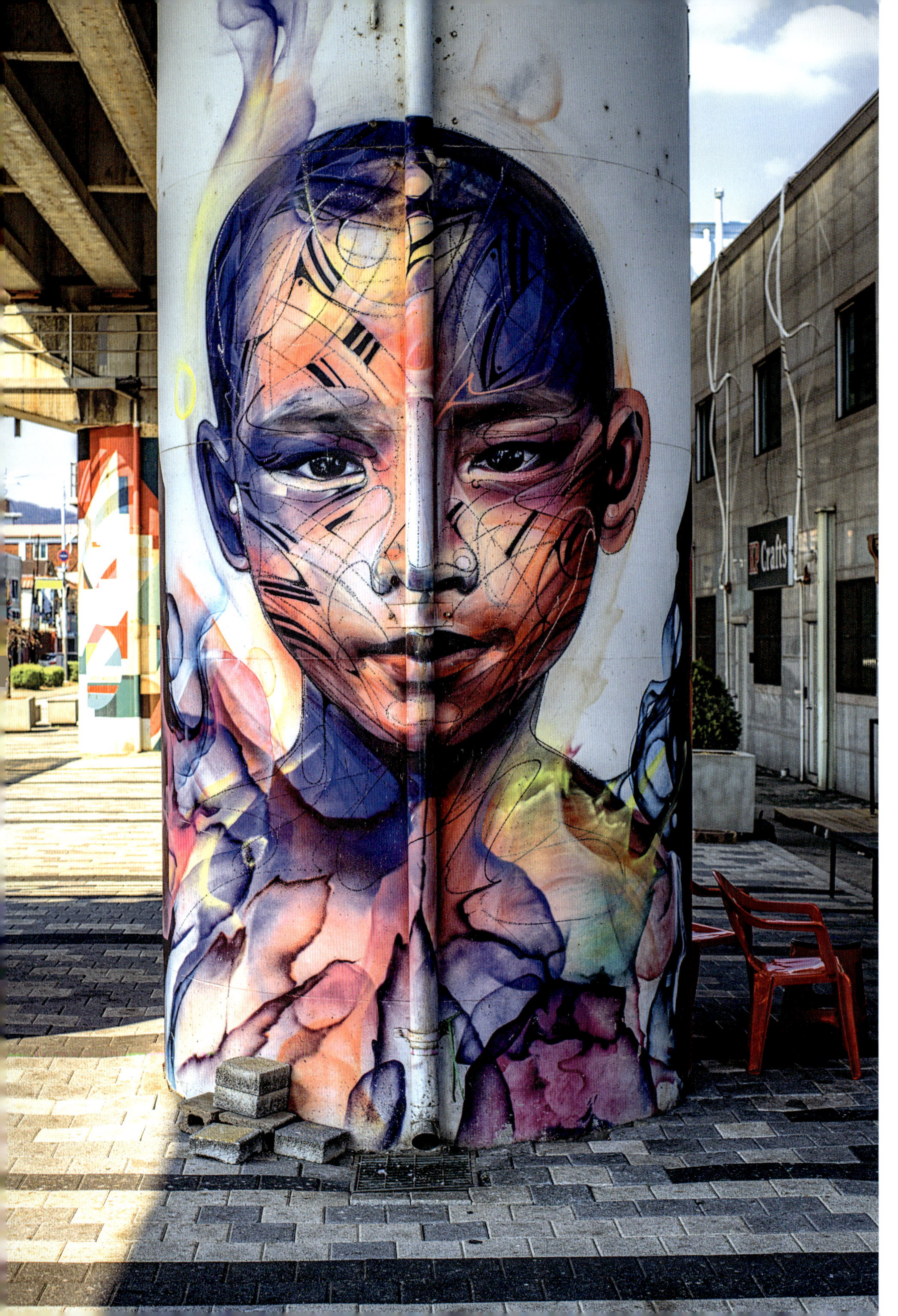
Crafts

BOSAN

DONGDUCHEON (near Camp Casey)

Bosan, an area housing the U.S. military's Camp Casey, remains a living artefact of Korea's uneasy alliance urbanism. The U.S. base is still active, yet the streets around it have begun to evolve – slowly, unevenly – from a service strip catering to soldiers into a hybrid district of cafés, studios, and small businesses run by locals and returning Koreans. Ageing bar façades and motels now share space with galleries and coffee shops, hinting at renewal fighting rupture. The area's regeneration isn't state-led but organic, shaped by shifting demographics and the gradual cultural thinning of the military presence. There's tension here: fenced order beside spontaneous urban life, foreign infrastructure beside Korean reinvention. Bosan's transformation isn't about erasure – it's about coexistence. The base still hums, but around it a new civic rhythm is trying to emerge, one beat at a time, in the shadow of barbed wire and concrete.

I generally grimace in the face of painted concrete in Okinawa, but Korea somehow does a fine job of it. No complaints here.

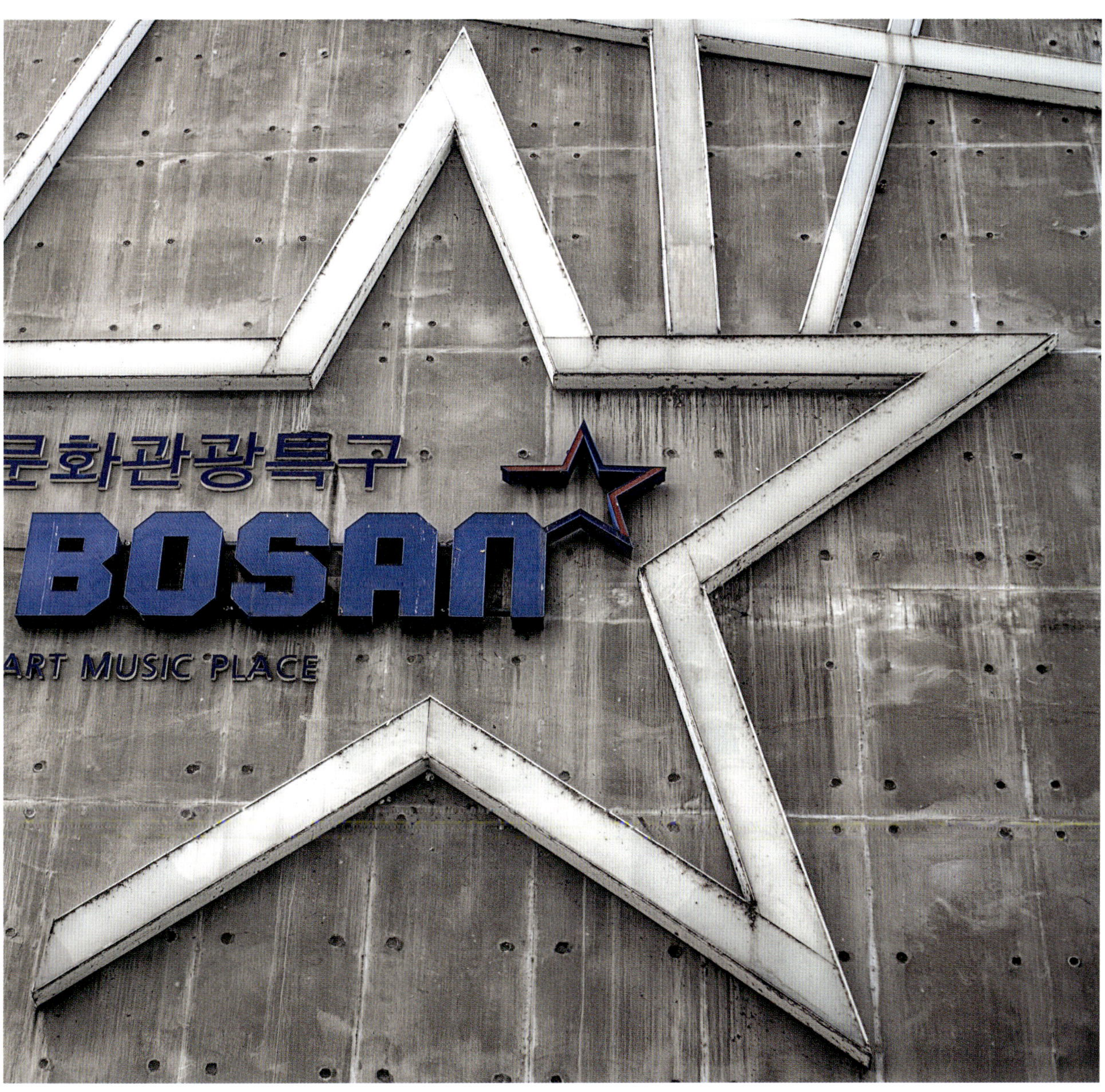

HALLA GYMNASIUM

JEJU ISLAND · Architect: Jeju City Architectural Office (presumedly) · Completed 1983

Halla Gymnasium is a confident relic of the island's civic and sporting ambition – a Brutalist-leaning colossus of concrete girders and angular geometry that still manages to look ready for take-off. Its rhythmic white ribs, pitched at expressive diagonals, form a sculptural exoskeleton around a broad domed hall capable of hosting everything from volleyball to billiards to mixed martial arts – activities whose physical intensity finds a fitting echo in the building's dynamic form.

The design captures a moment when Korean public architecture was eager to announce modernity through structure: beams are not hidden but flung outwards like a taekwondo kick, supporting deep canopies and casting theatrical shadows across the stepped forecourt. Yet despite its brawny silhouette, the gymnasium also possesses a curious lightness – part spacecraft, part seaside pavilion – with the blue roof glinting like a pool under Jeju's fierce sun.

Four decades on, Halla Gymnasium has outlasted the optimism of its making. Talks of demolition and redevelopment, wrapped into Jeju's larger "Sports Town" modernization plan, have placed it on uncertain footing. Critics point to its ageing facilities and poor energy efficiency; defenders note that few newer arenas carry such sculptural conviction. For now, the gym still resounds with the thud of a volleyball serve or the slap of an MMA glove. Architecture, like a seasoned fighter, can keep taking hits long after its prime. Whether it is finally counted out or granted a reprieve, Halla remains one of Jeju's most distinctive pieces of civic concrete – equal parts gym, sculpture, and time capsule.

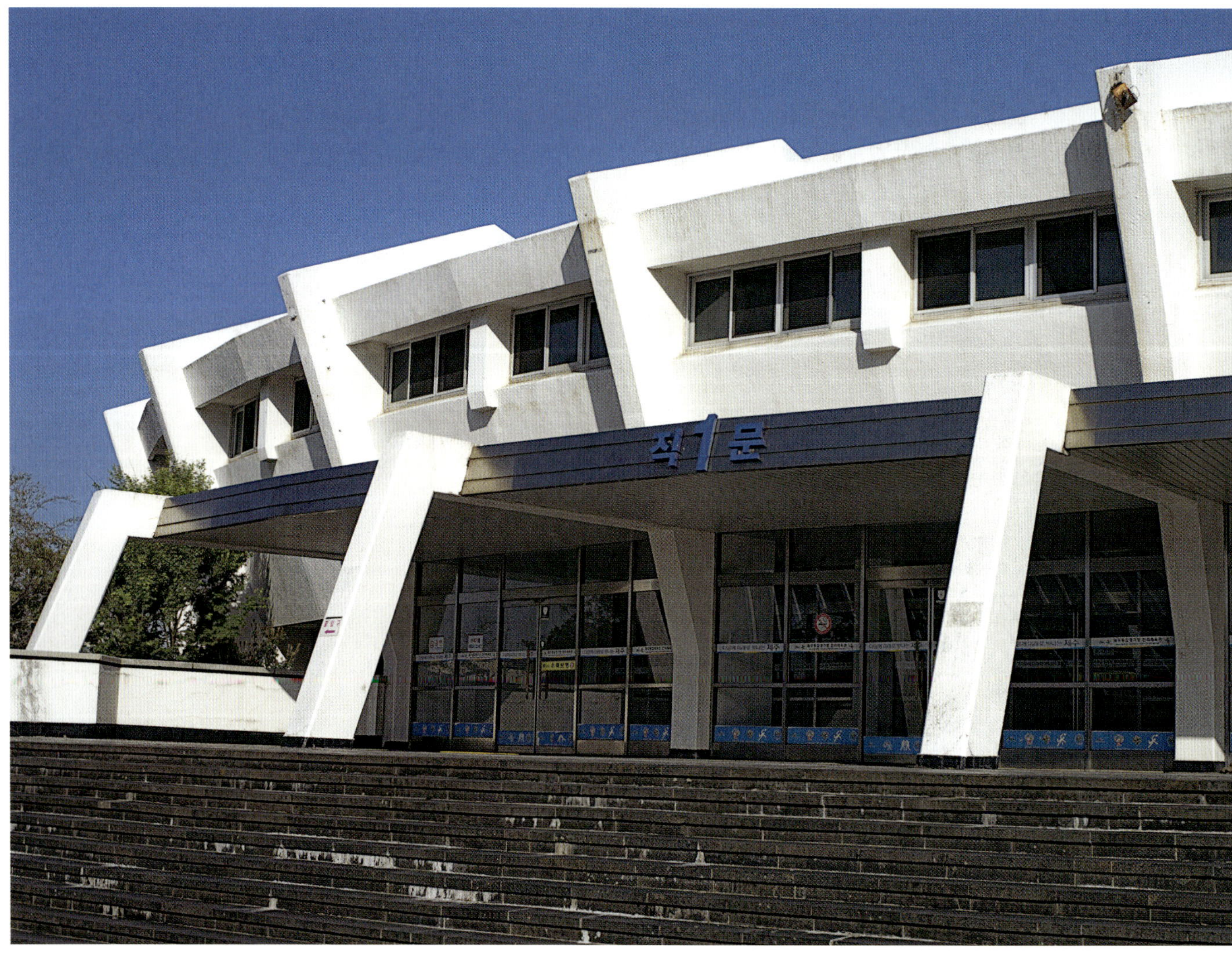

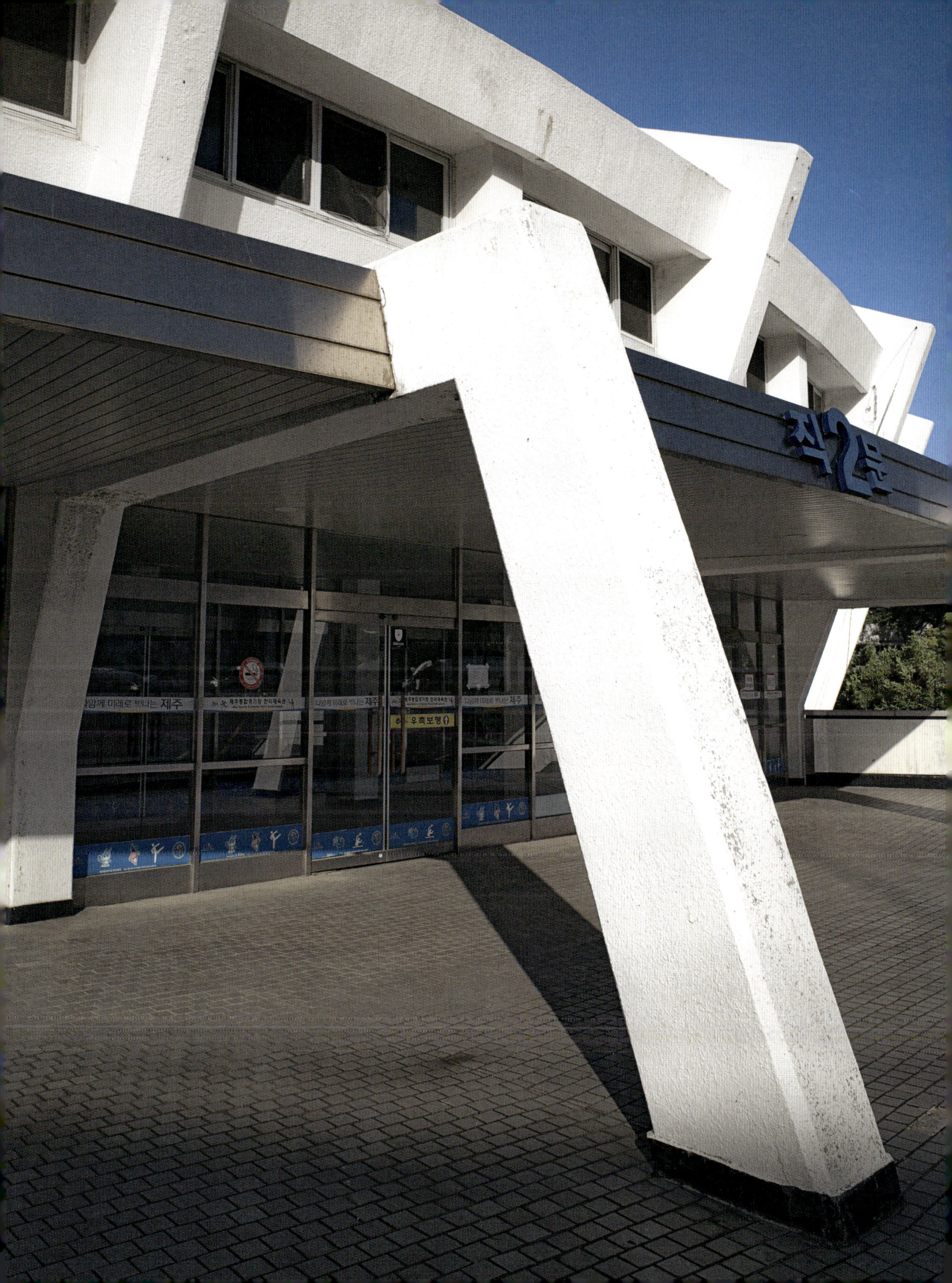
제2문
우측보행

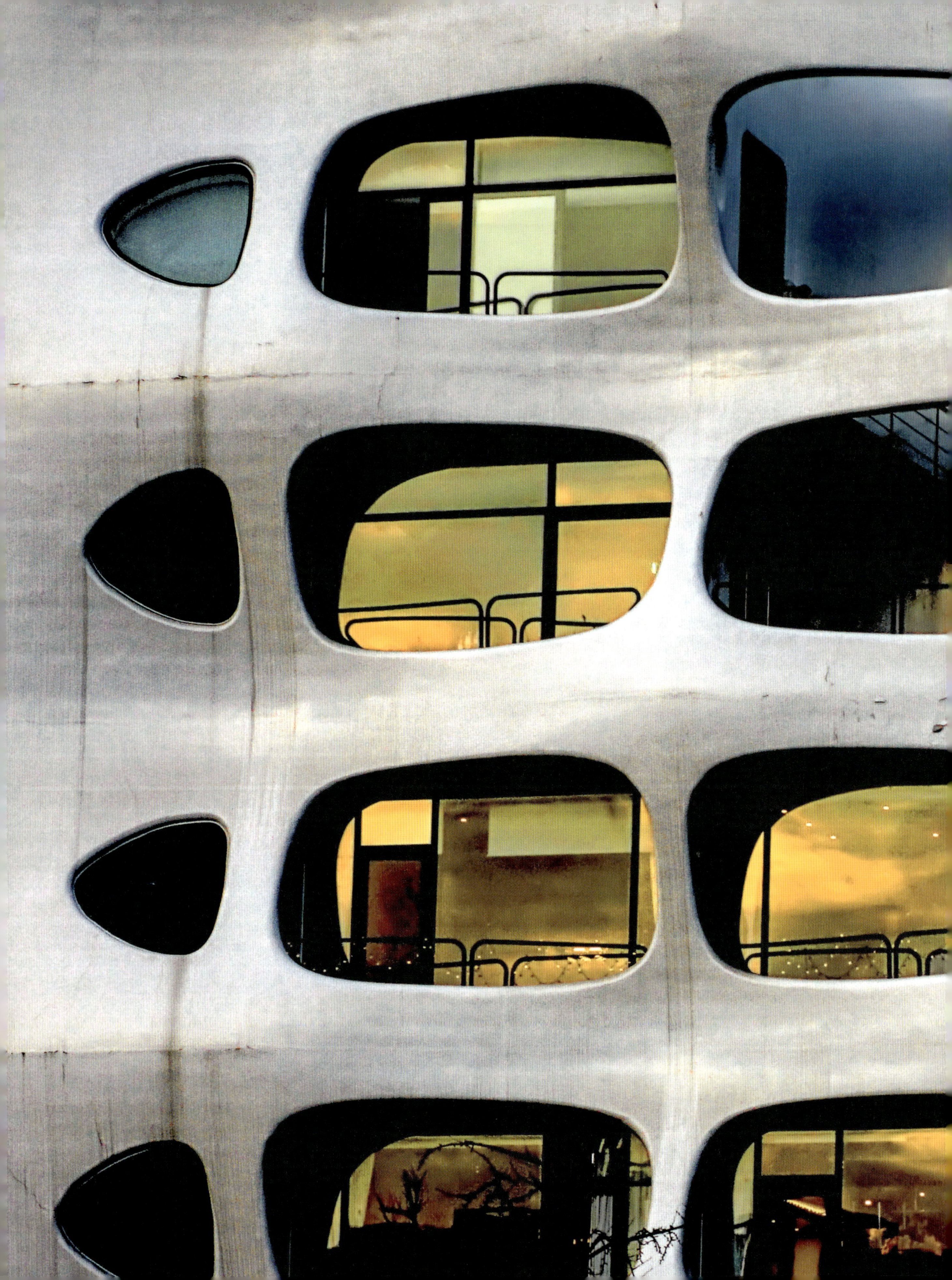

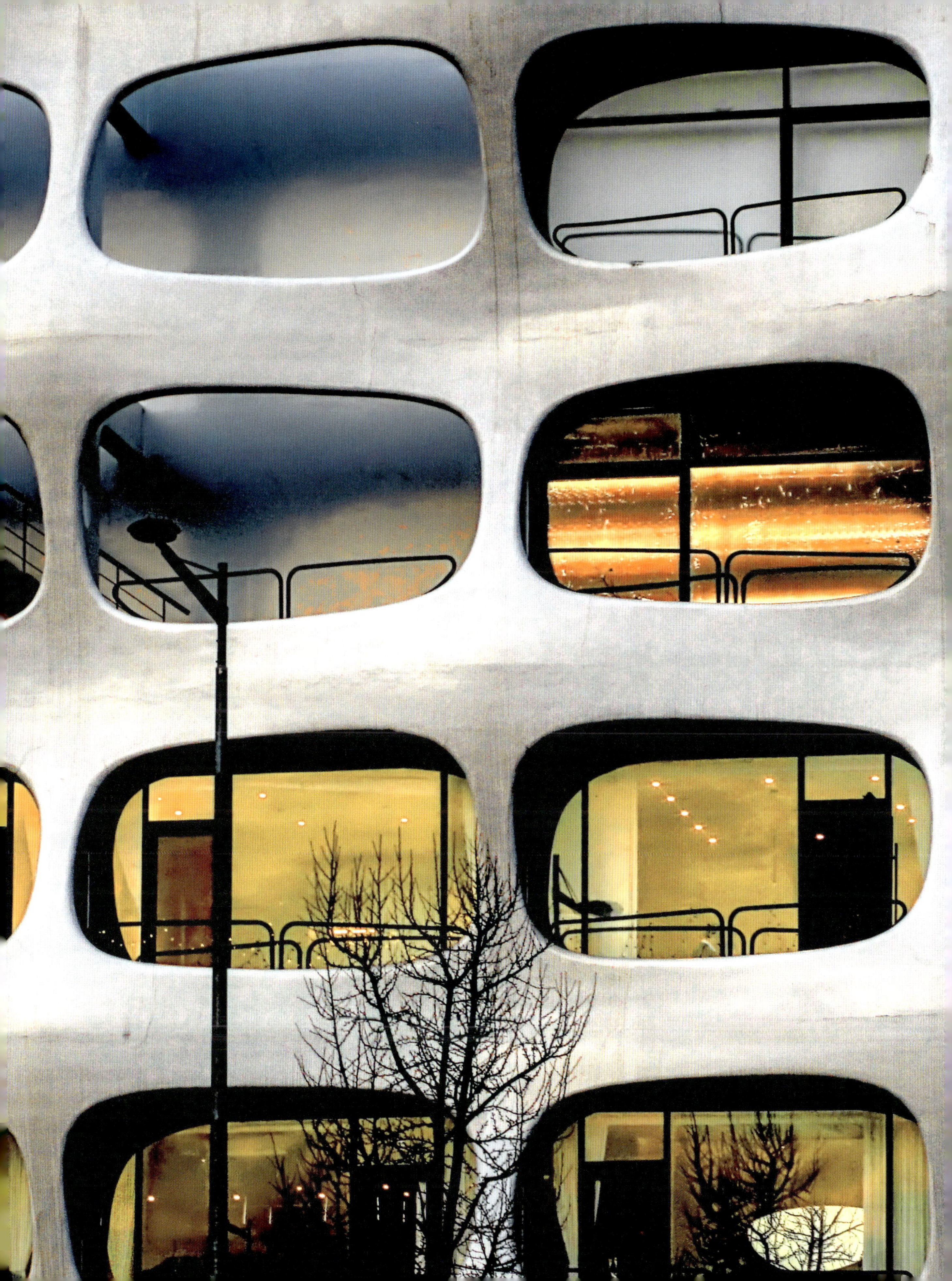

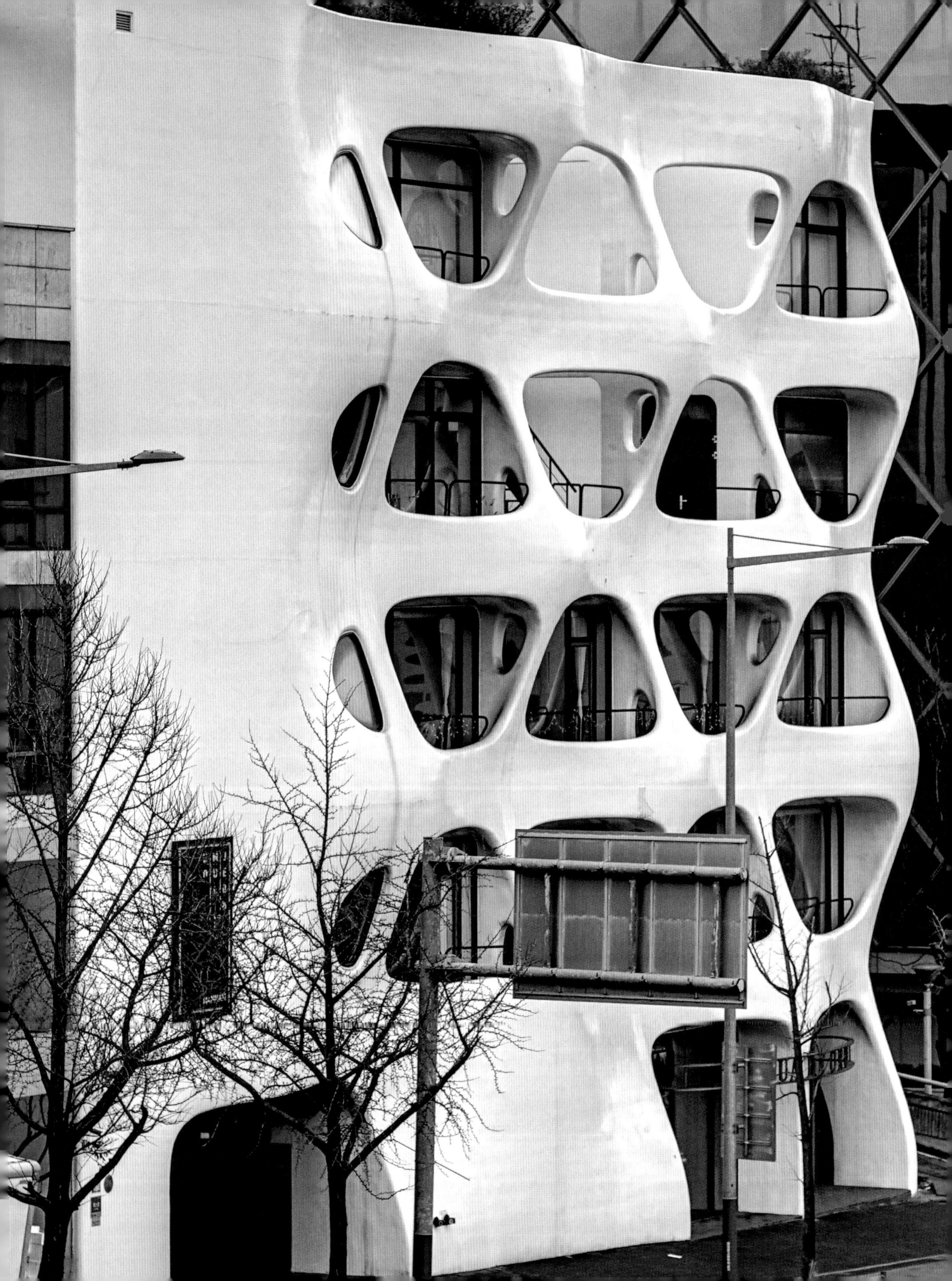

HANDS CORPORATION

SEOUL · Architect: KIM Chanjoong (THE_SYSTEM LAB) · Completed 2014

On Seoul's frantic Hannam-daero, the HANDS Corporation Headquarters by Kim Chanjoong of THE_SYSTEM LAB looks like a concrete organism flexing its muscles. This is Brutalism with charm – a sculpted exoskeleton that invites a hug. The building's curving concrete shell ripples with ribs and folds, as if cast from motion itself, turning structure into performance.

Each protrusion doubles as a balcony, those shallow recesses giving workers brief escapes into open air above the roar of traffic. The seven-storey mass hums with tactile rhythm – more body than building. From a distance, the façade reads as a single sculptural sweep; up close, it breaks into convex pockets and concave shadows, a modulation of light that changes by the minute.

Technically, the shell is a feat of patience. Cast in place using split steel moulds, each section was poured and peeled with surgical precision. The resulting texture carries the memory of process – the concrete's grain and curvature exposing the craftsmanship that birthed it.

Seen from the street, the building plays tricks on the eye. One angle flattens its surface into a graphic pattern; another reveals its depth, a visual pulse that animates the corridor of cars. Kim's approach transforms concrete from mute mass into voice: the façade acknowledges the drivers who stare at it daily, returning their gaze with sculptural empathy.

In a city defined by vertical glass and noise, HANDS feels startlingly humane. Its curved shell converses rather than dominates. It is Brutalism reimagined for Seoul's modern condition: dense, restless, and yearning for texture. Kim Chan-joong turns concrete into language, tension into rhythm, and the everyday commute into a fleeting architectural encounter – a high-rise handshake between building and passer-by, showing how even mass can have warmth.

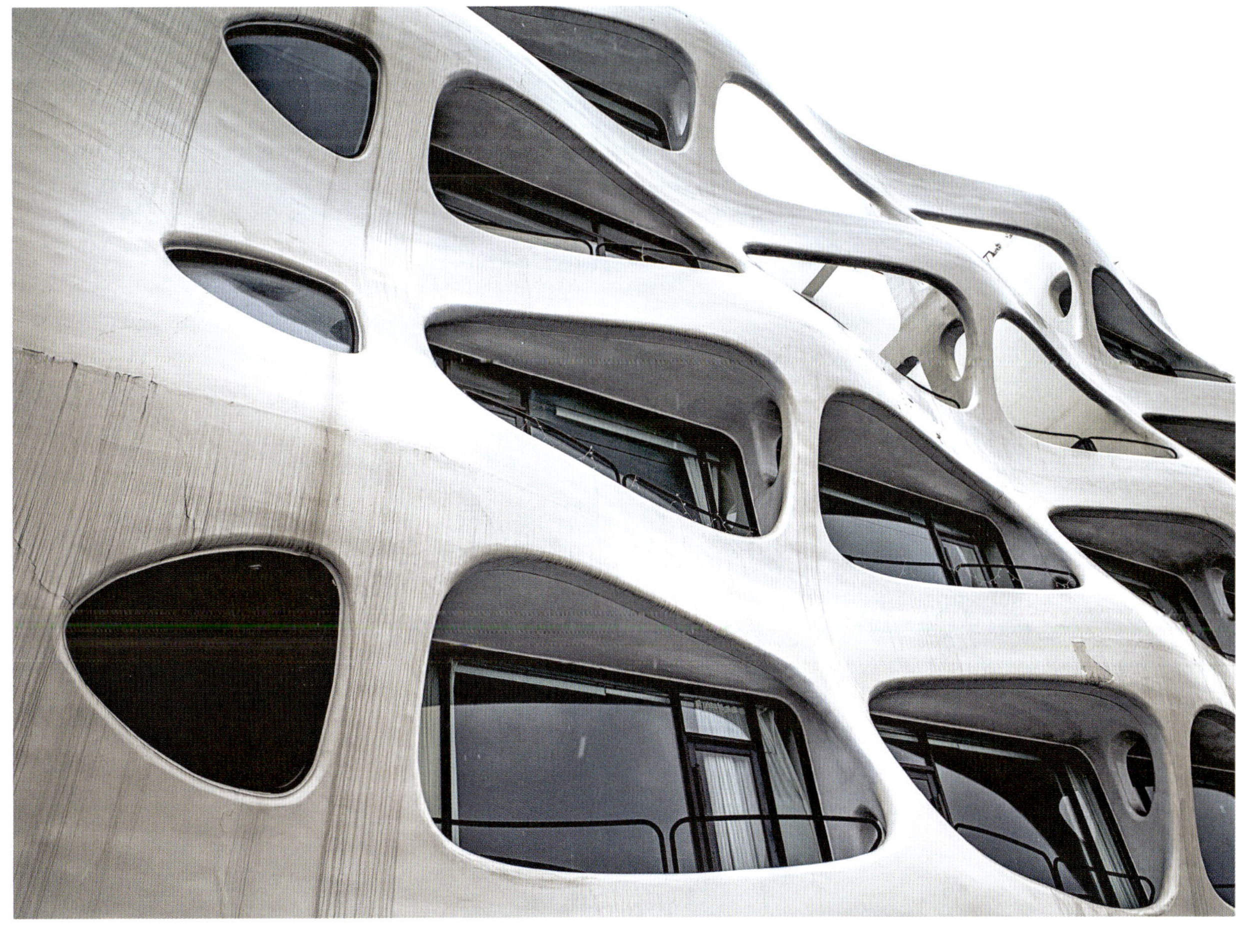

UNITED STATES EMBASSY

SEOUL · Architect: Alfred GERHARDT · Completed 1965

The U.S. Embassy in Seoul is a steadfast relic of mid-century diplomatic Brutalism. Squatting along the thoroughfare Sejong-daero amidst the glassy skyline of the main gate Gwanghwamun, its rectilinear concrete mass projects authority over allure. The façade – punctuated by deep horizontal bands and narrow window slots – embodies the security-driven logic of the Cold War era, where transparency was a liability and solidity a statement. Minimal ornament gives the building an austere dignity. It is both fortress and bureaucratic machine. Yet in its weight and rhythm lies a strange honesty: this was architecture built to endure, not to charm. Now dwarfed by Seoul's vertical optimism, the embassy remains a stubborn monument to another time – when diplomacy was built like defence, and concrete served as both shelter and symbol of American permanence abroad. Note its difference to the French Embassy on page 20.

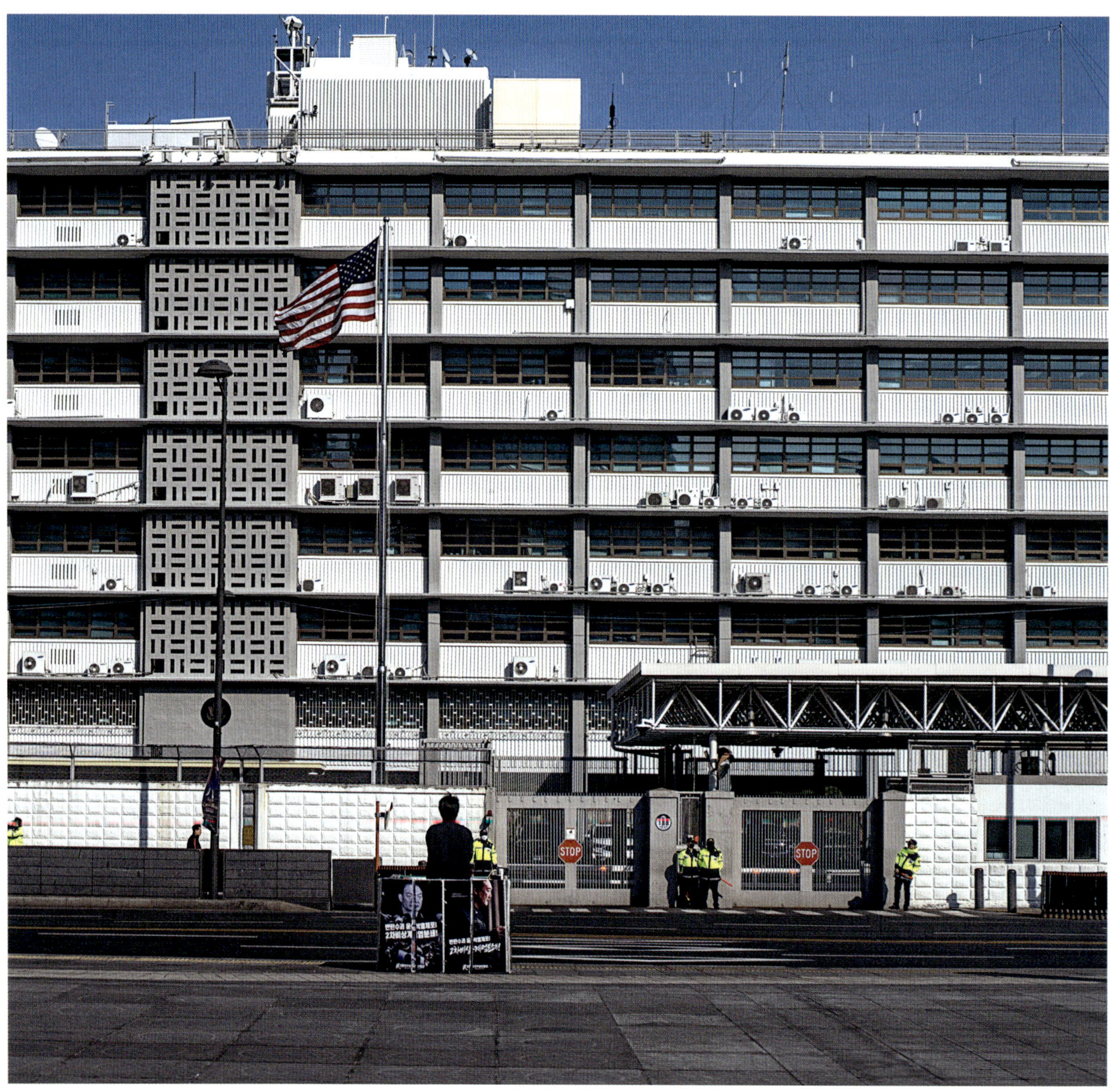

RAW RANDOM

SEOUL

This random find exemplifies Seoul's evolving Brutalist sensibility, reinterpreted through a contemporary lens. Its exposed concrete shell, unflinchingly raw and weathered, conveys both permanence and vulnerability. Angular geometries fracture the façade, with diagonal glazing slicing through the mass like fissures of light, while metal panels interrupt the concrete rhythm with a cooler industrial sheen. This tri-material mix – concrete, glass, and metal – creates a tension between opacity and reflection, structure and skin. The result is neither sleek nor chaotic, but a precisely orchestrated ruggedness. Brutalism's honesty is present here not only in the material expression but also in its refusal to flatter the viewer; beauty emerges from the grit, from the visible bolts and stains that chart time's passage. It is architecture as palimpsest – an urban composition that resists polish yet achieves elegance through proportion, craft, and the friction of contrasts.

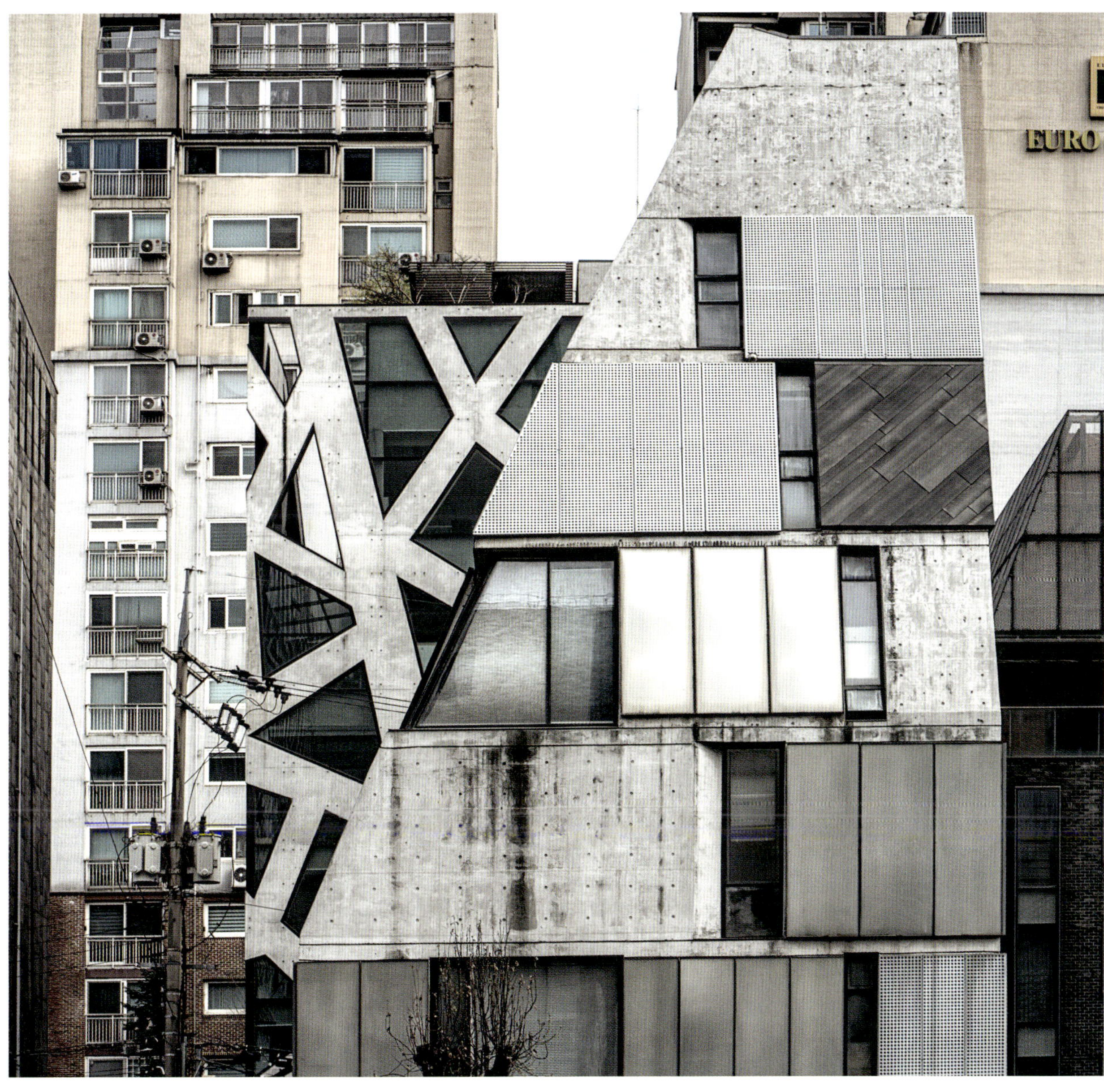

KB CHEONGCHUN MARU

SEOUL · Architect: KIM Swoo-geun · Constructed 1960s / Renovated 2017

Standing at 18 Hongik-ro, the building on this page, now known as KB Cheongchun Maru, began life as a modest branch of Kookmin Bank, designed under the Space Architecture lineage founded by Kim Swoo-geun – whose legacy of civic minimalism shaped 1960s Seoul. The structure's bones still carry his influence: an honest concrete frame, recessed glazing, and an emphasis on rhythm. In 2017, a young team of architects from Hongik University and Kim Si-won's Sidam group reimagined the ageing bank as a cultural platform for Seoul's restless youth, replacing tellers' desks with coworking tables and terrace steps. The renovation preserved the structural austerity while softening its edges – introducing timber screens, street-facing glass, and the now-iconic yellow stair that spills towards the pavement. The result is part bank, part bleacher, part public living room – a thoughtful retrofit that bridges Korea's modernist past with its participatory urban present, where concrete heritage and communal energy share the same account.

The following page presents a building in the neighbourhood of Hyehwa-dong. Restraint defines the architecture, despite a recent tangy paint job. Completed in 2001, its four-storey reinforced-concrete frame offers calm precision. With just 259 square metres of floor area, each level is compact, leaving the façades to shoulder the task of expression. Their language is one of clean horizontals and verticals, a sober composition that aligns with the street edge while acknowledging the human scale of Jongno district's layered urban fabric. Inside, the plan favours open spans and adaptable partitions, supporting its use as a jewellery store. The building sits stylistically between Korea's late-modern pragmatism and early-2000s minimalism – a period when honest materials, unadorned concrete, and quiet craftsmanship spoke louder than ornament. Its modesty, in context, becomes its distinction. As with the yellow stair of KB Cheongchun Maru, I actually don't mind the lick of paint.

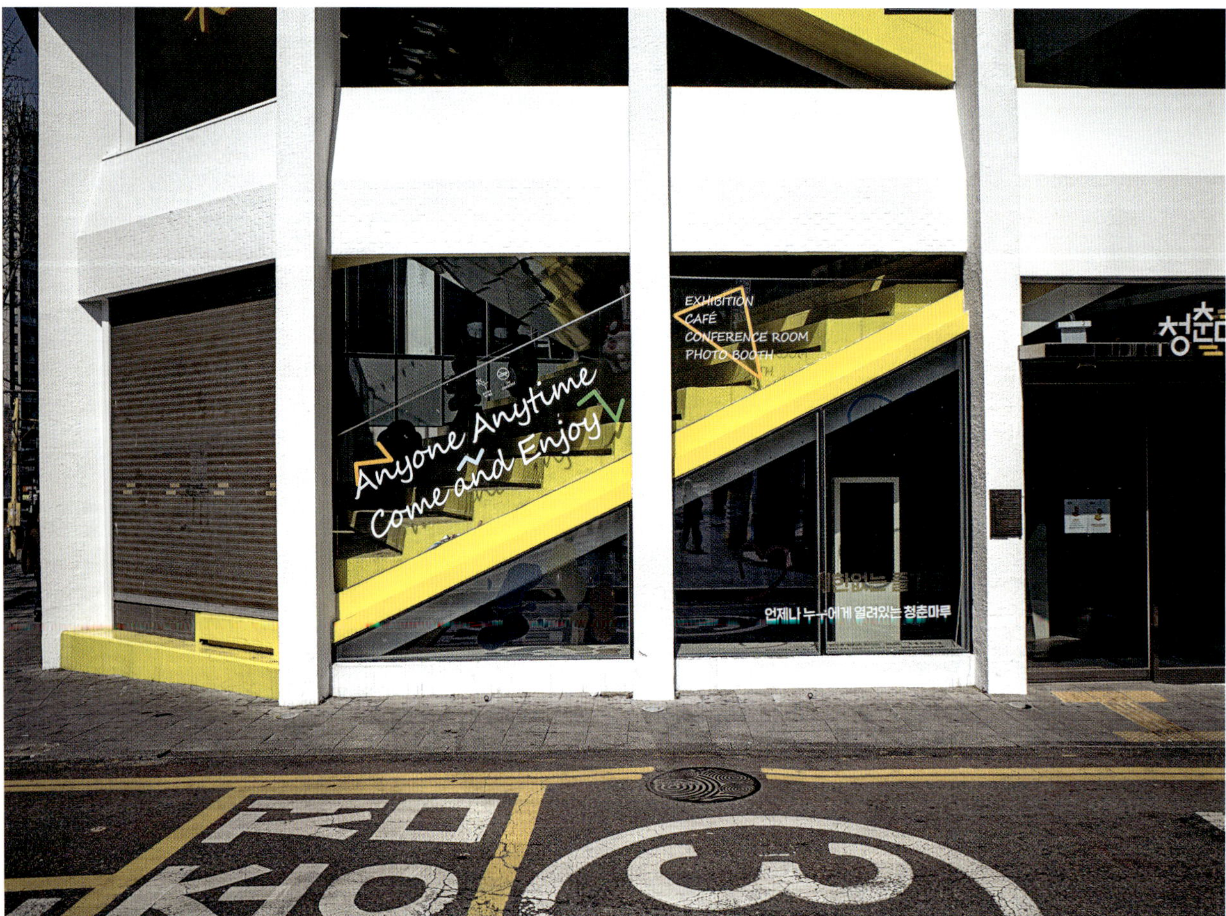

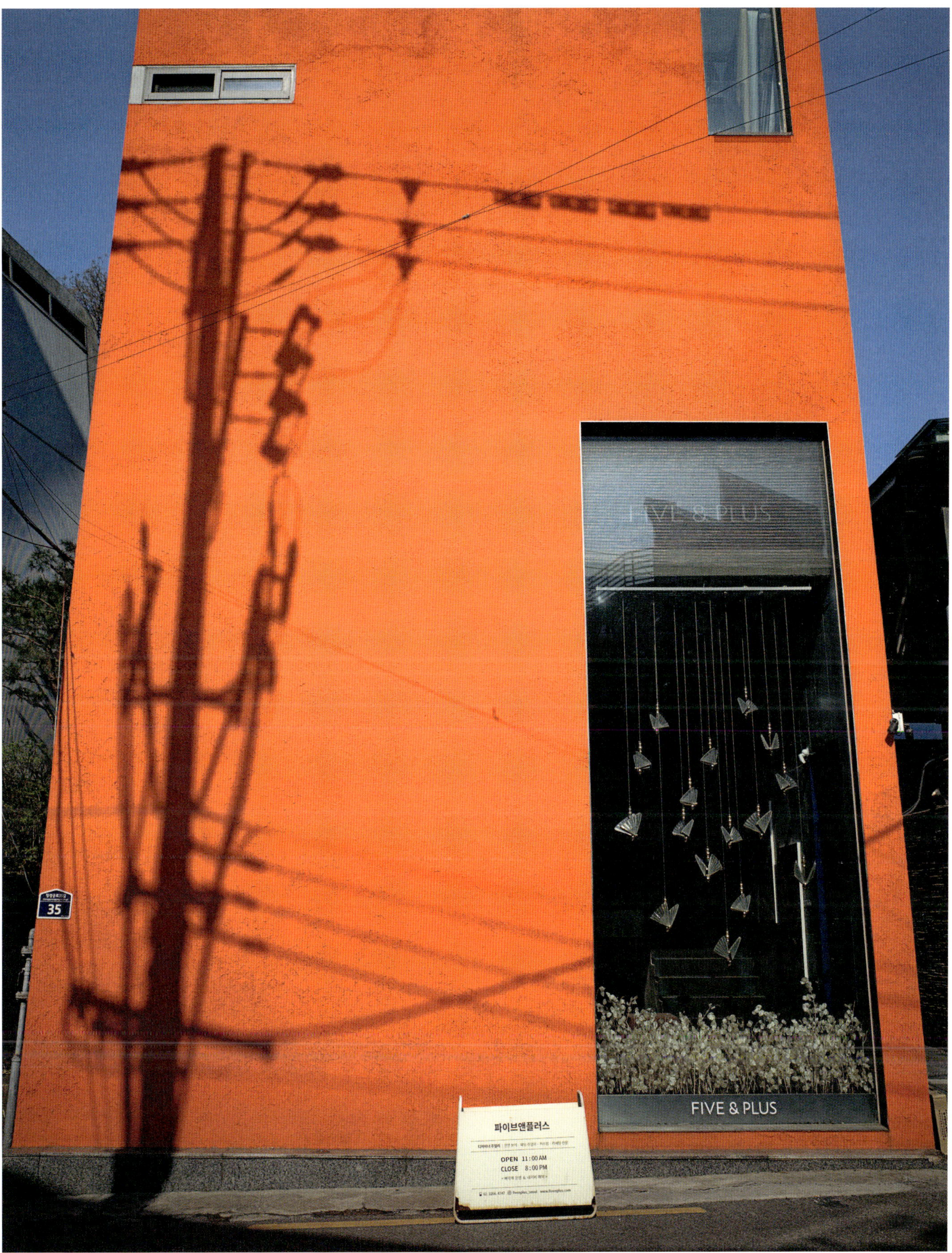
FIVE & PLUS
FIVE & PLUS
파이브앤플러스
OPEN 11:00 AM
CLOSE 8:00 PM
35

MRNW DAEGU CULTURAL CENTER

DAEGU · Architect: Society of Architecture and Yerin KANG · Completed 2022

MRNW Daegu Cultural Center, now home to the Mr. Womack café, serves up a bold blend of concrete grit and spatial rhythm. The building's raw concrete surfaces feel like a strong espresso – robust, textured, and full-bodied.

The façade's grid of concrete columns set at a 45-degree angle jitter like the crema ripples atop a freshly poured cup, adding a playful energy to the building's sturdy frame. These angled pillars create a visual percolation, breaking up the mass with architectural espresso shots that keep the eye engaged.

Inside, the elliptical courtyard softens the heavy concrete with gentle curves, like a swirl of steamed milk folding into a bitter brew. Reflective water pools add a shimmering contrast, echoing coffee steam's delicate dance in morning light.

The split volumes frame a clear path through the centre, guiding visitors from the busy street to a quieter refuge, much like a perfectly crafted pour-over – methodical, smooth, and satisfying. Glass panels mingle with concrete walls, balancing transparency with solidity as deftly as cream balances a dark roast.

Exposed concrete throughout feels honest and raw – a true architectural roast where form follows function with bold clarity. The interplay of angles and textures nods to Brutalism's celebration of material strength, while the layered spatial experience offers a welcoming escape from the city's buzz – the architectural equivalent of savouring that first calming sip.

MRNW is a strong, structured blend of cultural space and urban design, inviting visitors to pause, enjoy, and come back for another shot. Hard to get to? Yes. Worth the hassle? For sure, for it's a great example of the Nu-Bru iteration that Korea excels in. Sip it up, but be patient if you visit and want shots devoid of people.

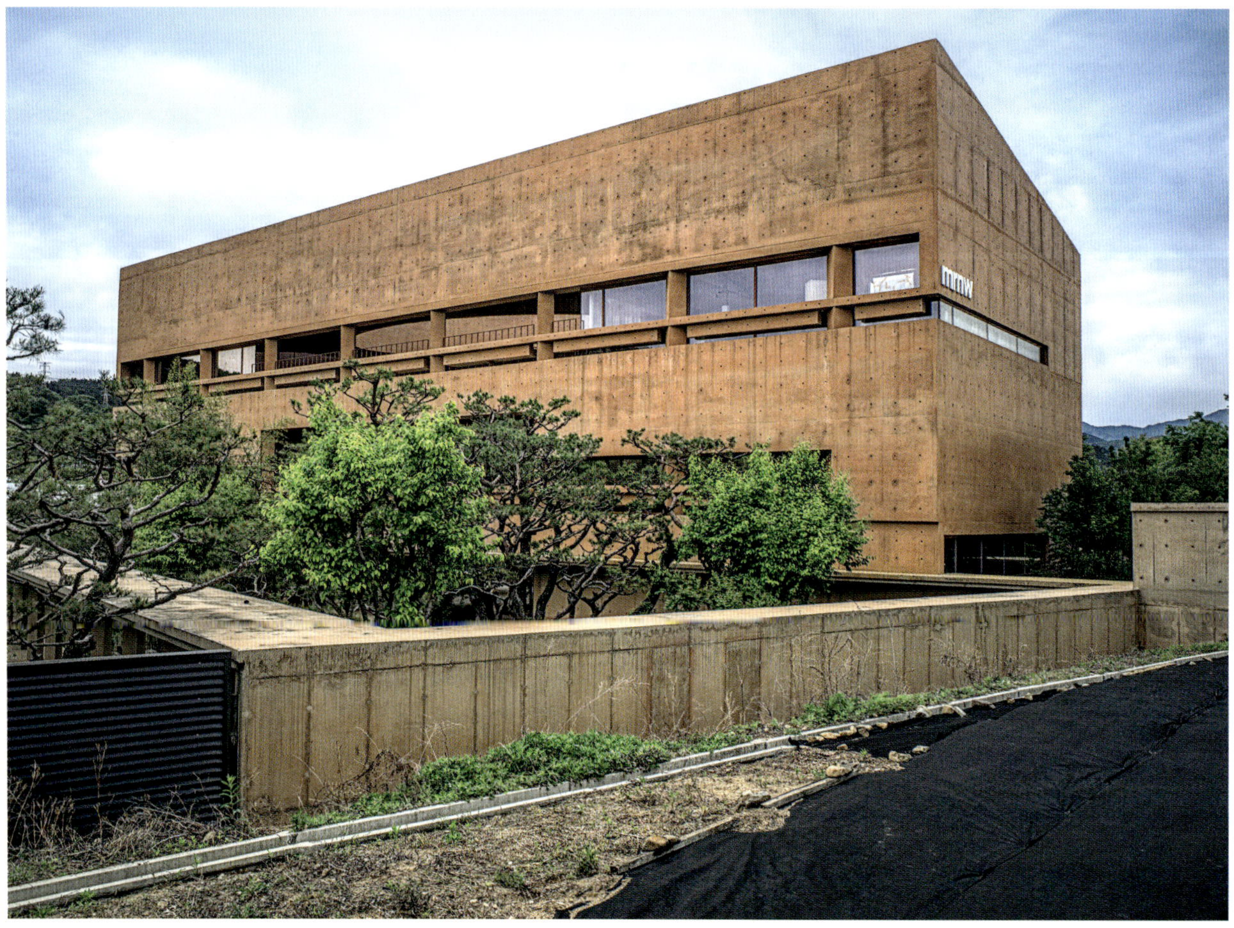

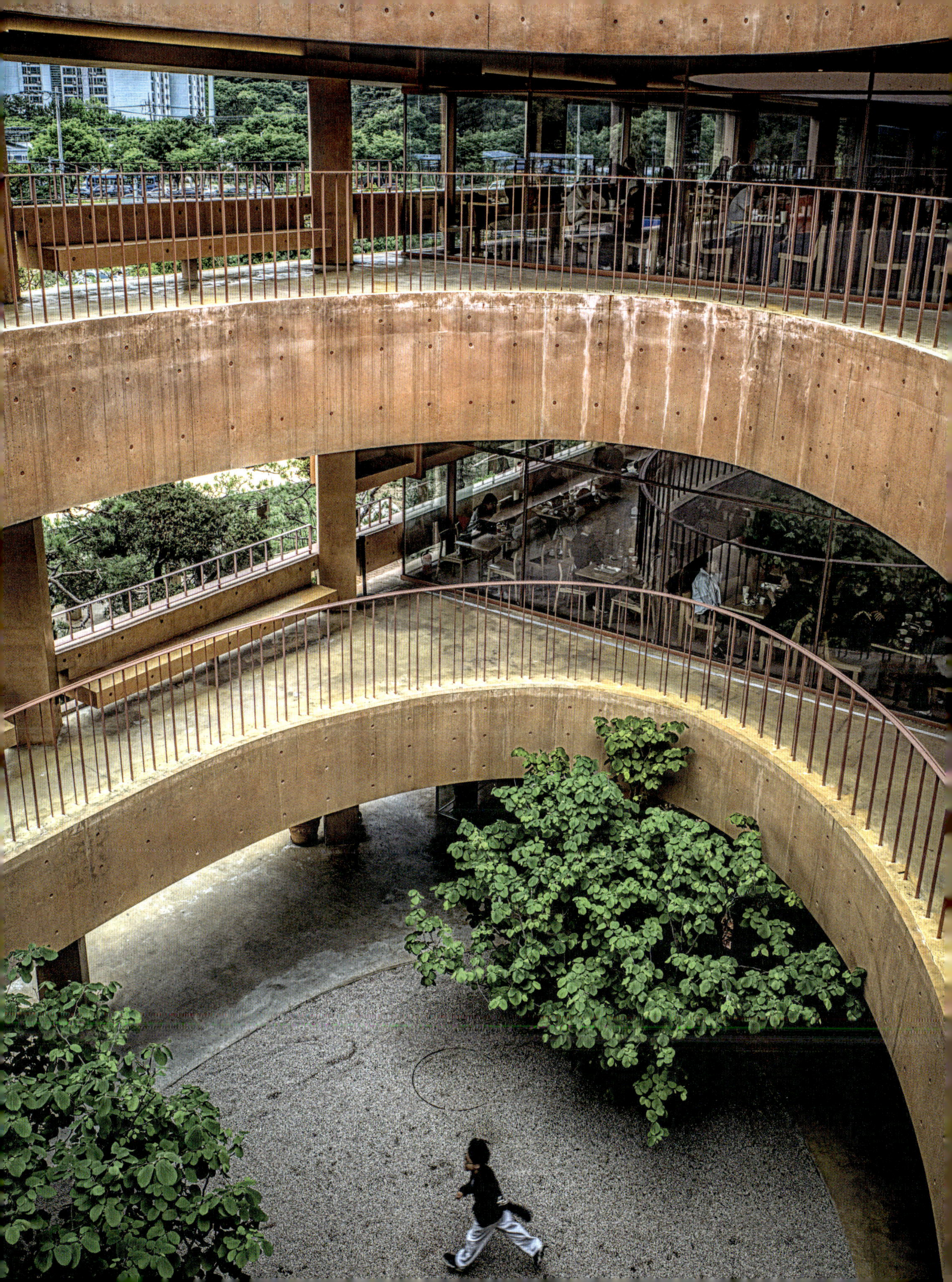

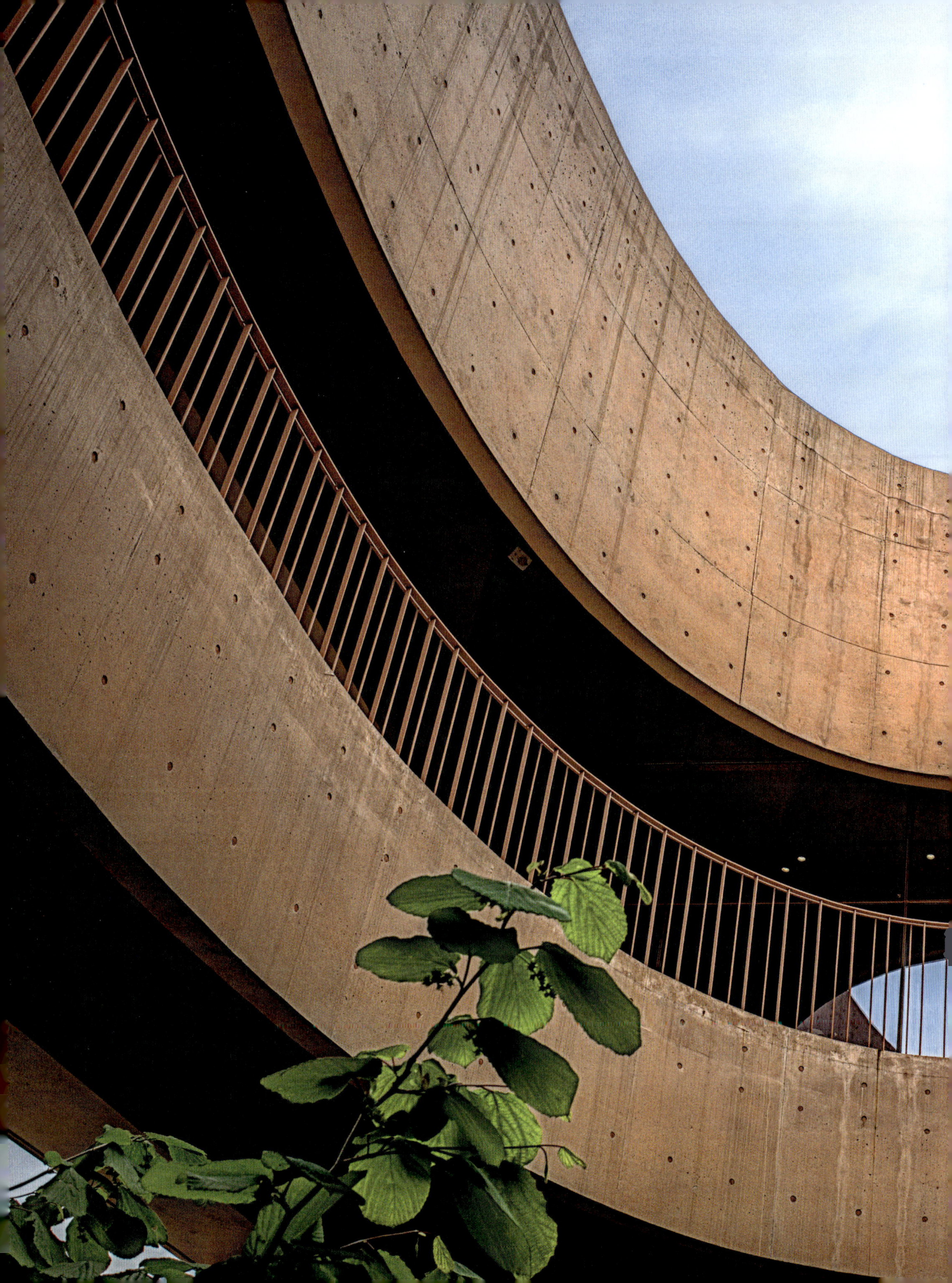

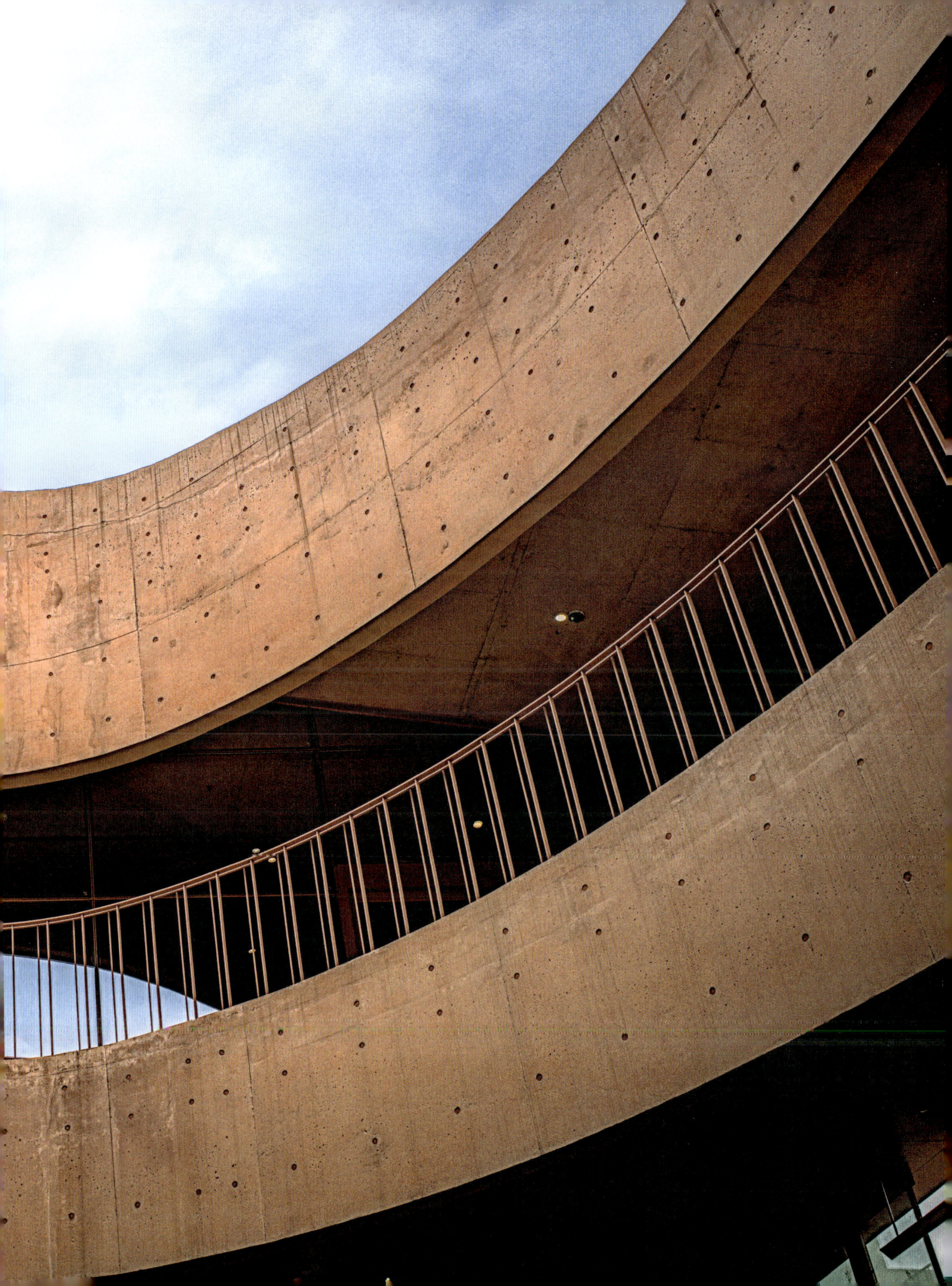

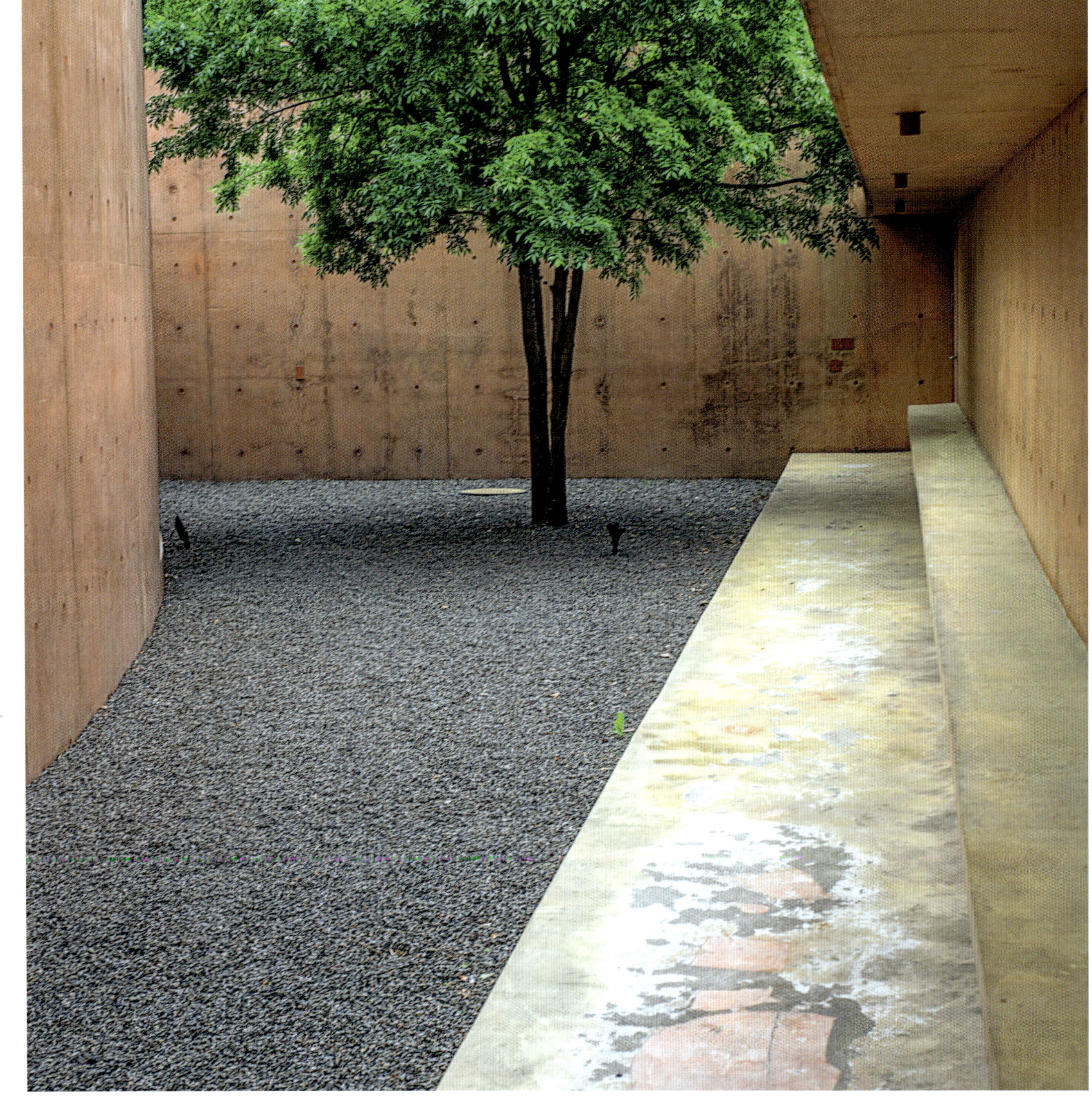

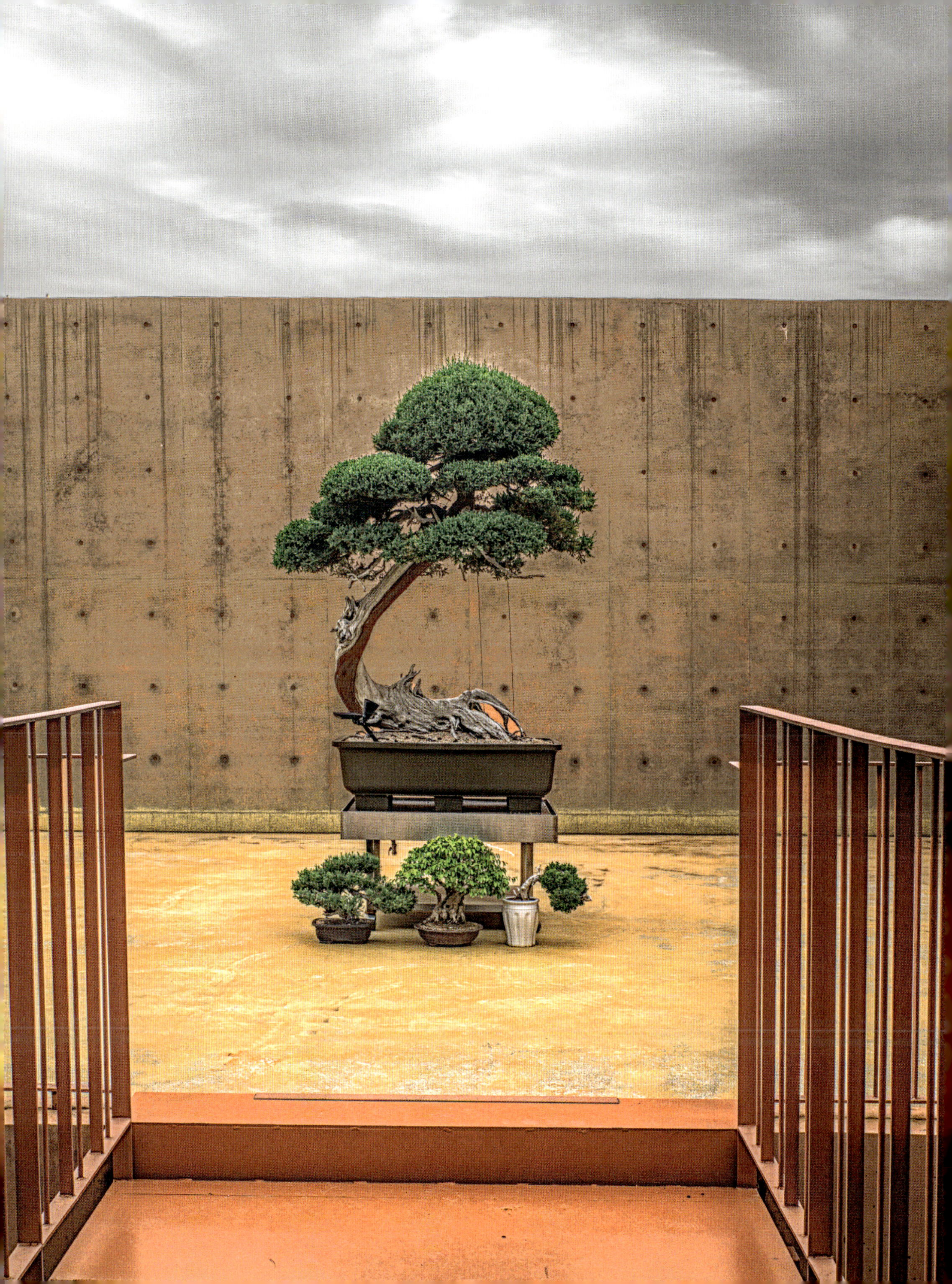

HYEONAM

SAYUWON · Architect: SEUNG H-Sang · Completed 2013

Hyeonam, meaning "black rock cottage", is Seung H-Sang's 2013 meditation on weight, weather, and humility – an elemental pavilion at the edge of Sayuwon's botanical gardens in Gunwi, near Daegu. The building sits low and deliberate, composed of two horizontal strata that converse: a board-formed concrete base pressed into the earth, and a Corten steel crown that appears to rise naturally from the hillside like oxidized soil made sentient.

The concrete lower level is grounded, its timber-imprinted surface recalling Korea's volcanic stone and traditional carpentry alike. Above it, the weathering steel shifts hue with time – glowing ember red at sunset, matt brown under rain, a living skin that blurs the line between architecture and landscape. The contrast is intentional: Seung wields materials not for ornament, but for mediation, translating geological process into architectural language.

A sloping green roof slices across the steel volume, merging structure and terrain. A discreet stair rises gently to a lookout bench framed by Corten panels – a serene cantilevered eyrie for viewing the valley below. This slight ascent transforms the house into a miniature pilgrimage: from the heavy realm of earth to the open clarity of air.

Inside, floor-to-ceiling glass introduces light like a controlled leak, filtering reflections of sky and foliage into the interior. The transparency acts as a counterweight to the building's density, allowing visitors to feel enclosed yet connected – part of the landscape, not above it.

Hyeonam distils Seung H-Sang's architectural philosophy: restraint over excess, silence over spectacle. Concrete grounds, steel breathes, glass reveals. In its modest scale and material confidence, the building becomes both retreat and revelation – a shelter that seems to exhale, quietly bridging the human and the elemental.

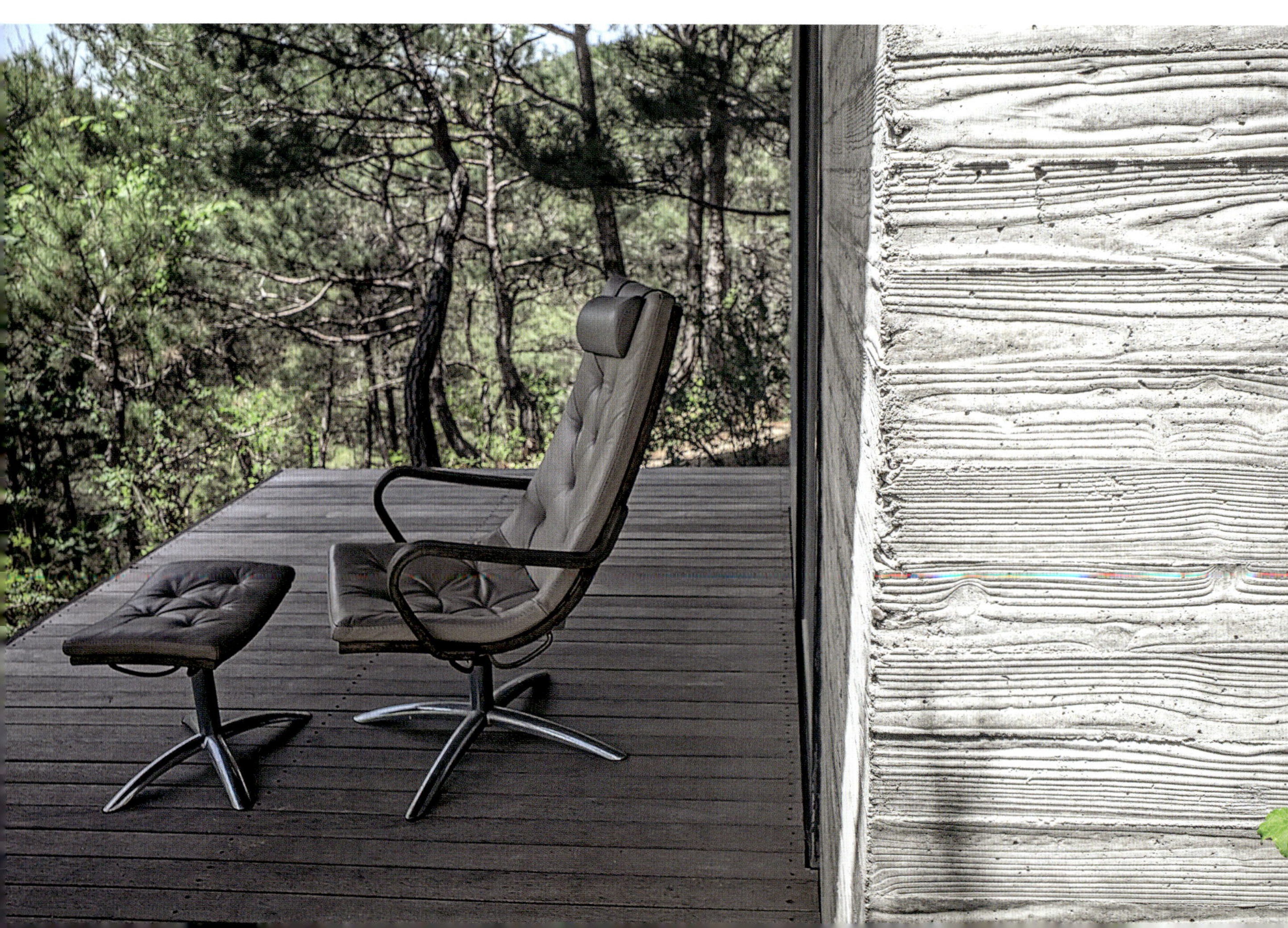

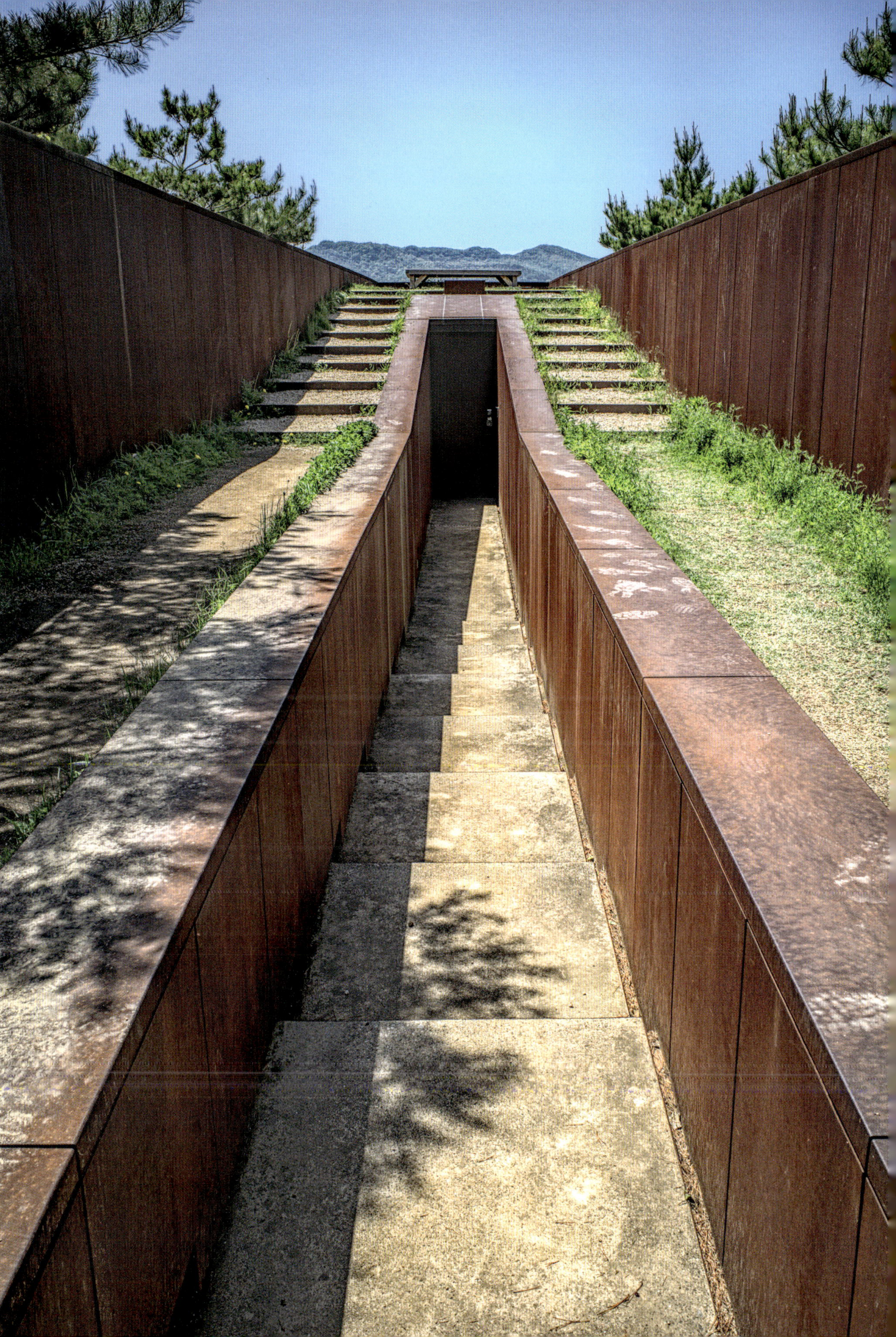

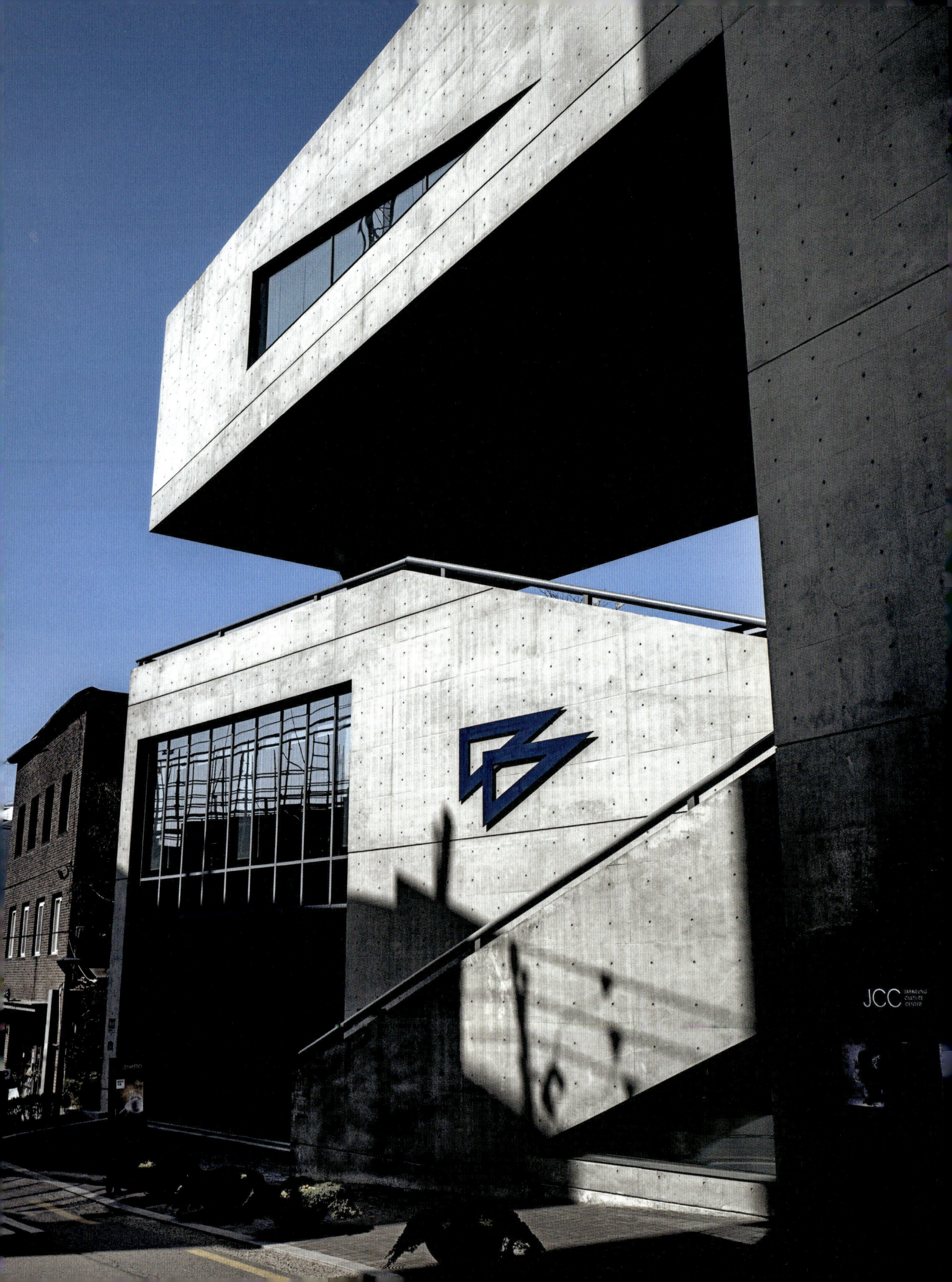
JCC

JAENEUNG CULTURE CENTER

SEOUL · Architect: ANDO Tadao · Completed 2015

The Jaeneung Culture Center (JCC) embodies Ando's lifelong pursuit of serenity through structure. Located in Hyehwa-dong, a district dense with cultural institutions and narrow streets, the building acts as both sanctuary and stage – a minimalist intervention that distils urban noise into architectural calm.

Composed of two volumes – the Art Center and the Creative Center – the complex is bound together by a shared language of exposed concrete, void, and light. Ando's trademark sublime concrete is rendered with monastic precision: smooth yet tactile, cool yet expressive. Every wall and plane is choreographed for light, which cuts across stairwells and washes surfaces like passing time. Shadows here are not by-products; they are the architecture itself.

The Art Center houses a performance hall lined with pale timber that softens the concrete's gravitas. The Creative Center introduces classrooms, studios, and informal gathering areas – spaces for exchange within Ando's meditative discipline. Circulation moves diagonally and obliquely, revealing framed glimpses of the city beyond. Each turn feels deliberate, an act of spatial editing.

Outside, the building engages its compact site with quiet force. The angled volumes and elevated sections create a subtle levitation, separating the centre from its surroundings while maintaining engagement with the Hyehwa district streetscape. Courtyards and narrow entry paths compress and release, transforming arrival into experience.

In true Ando fashion, JCC balances weight and lightness, introversion and outreach. It's a Brutalist symphony rewritten in lowercase – a concrete monologue softened by craft and proportion. Here, form becomes philosophy: simplicity as resistance, silence as invitation. Amidst Seoul's cluttered skyline, the JCC posits a pause, affirming architecture can whisper and still be heard.

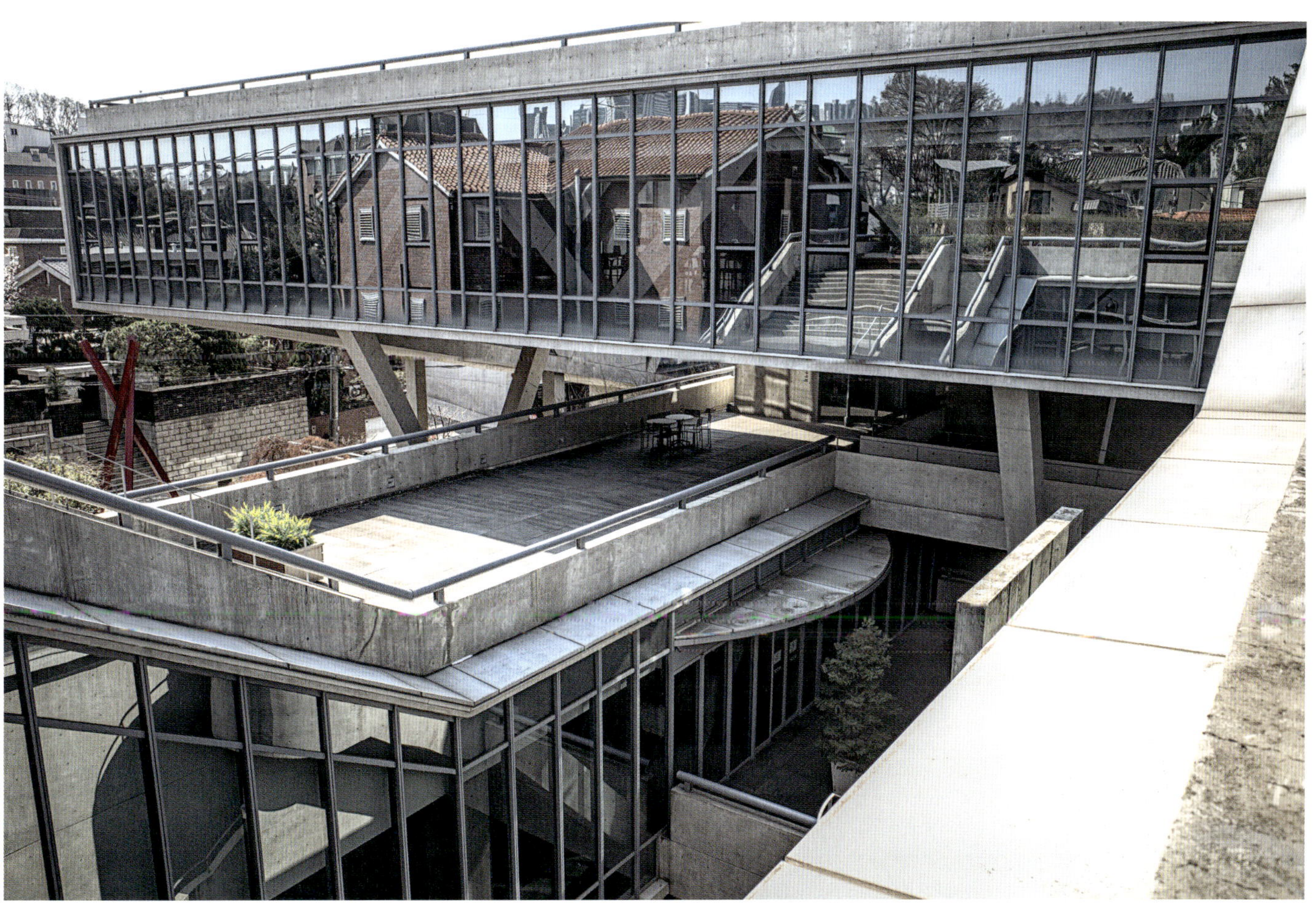

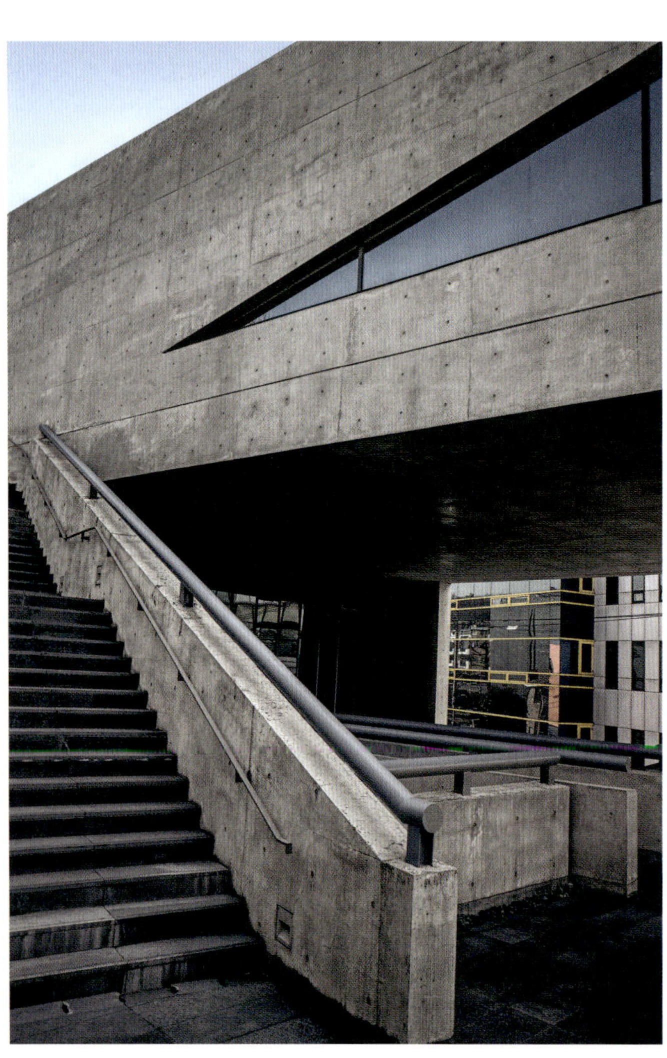

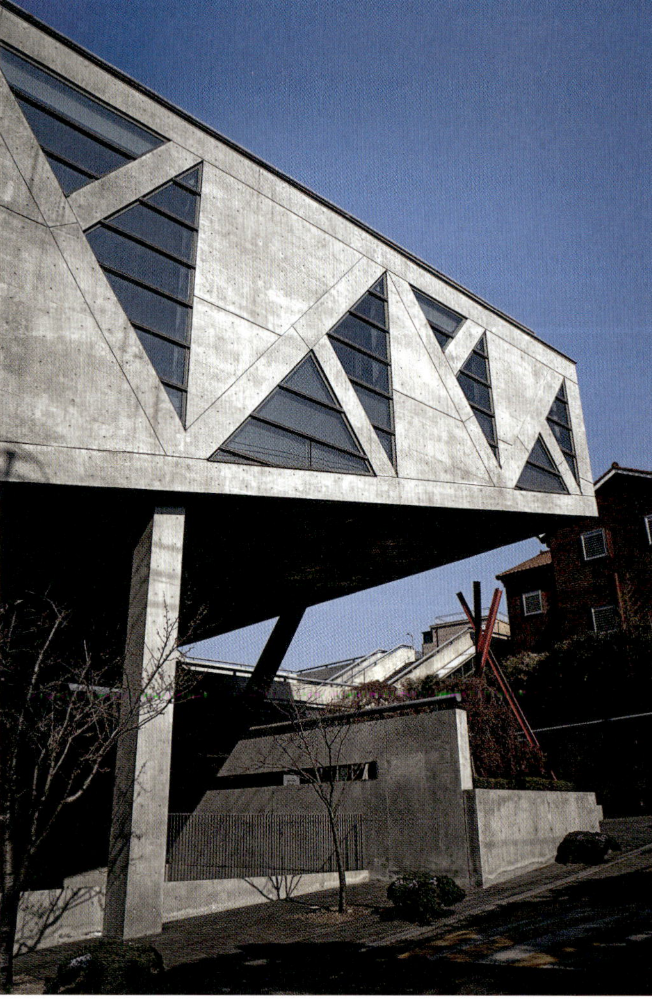

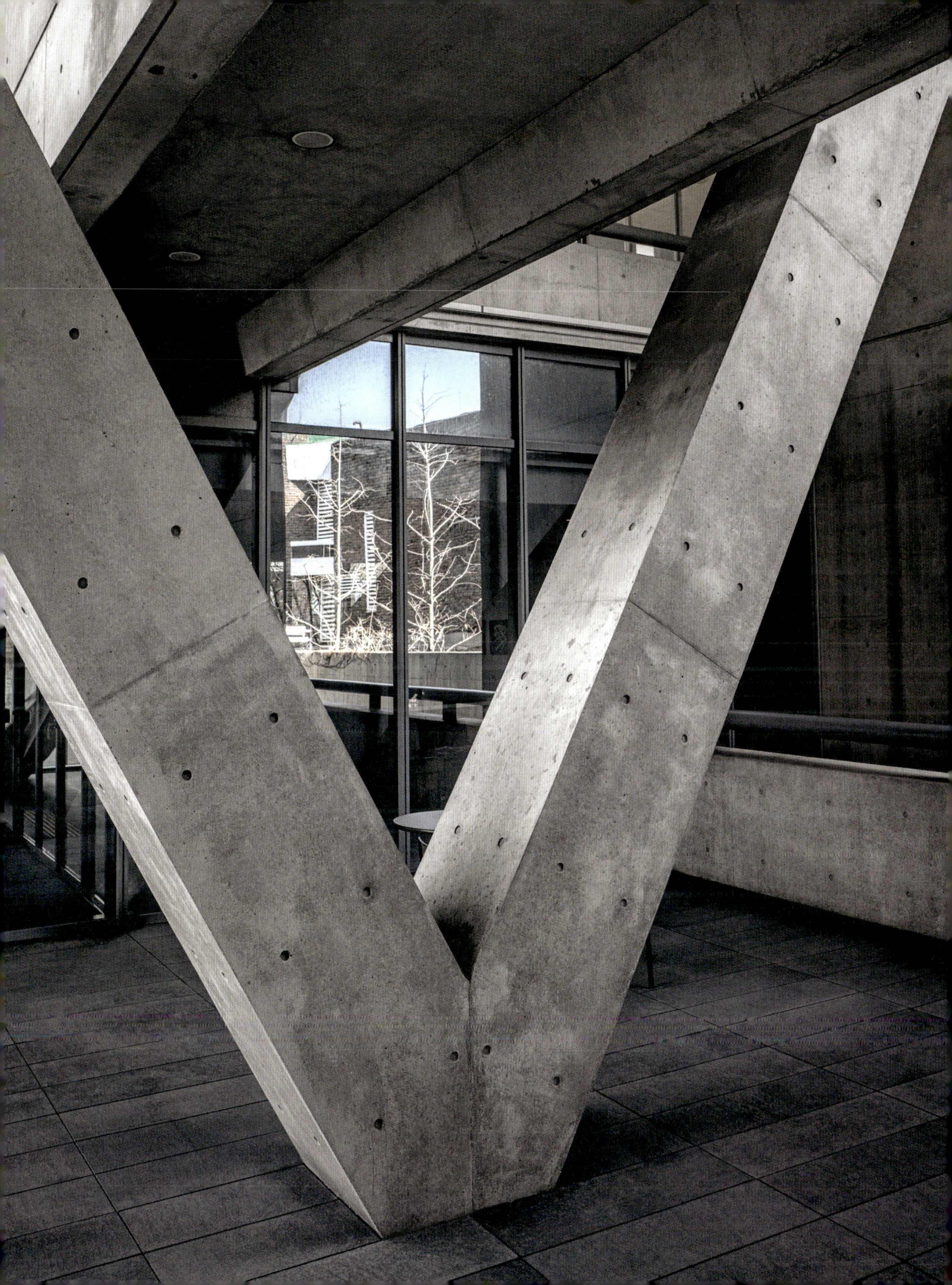

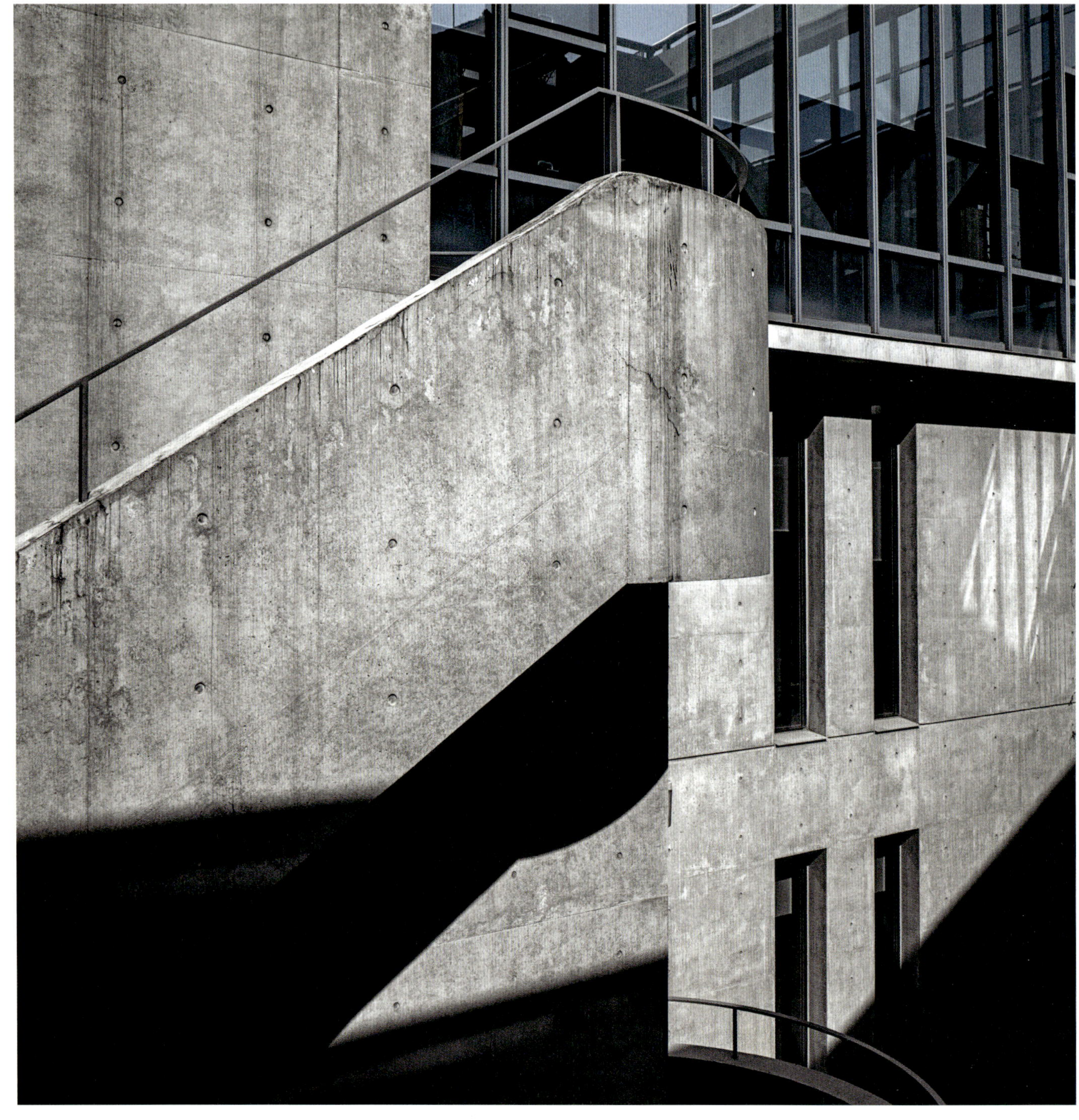

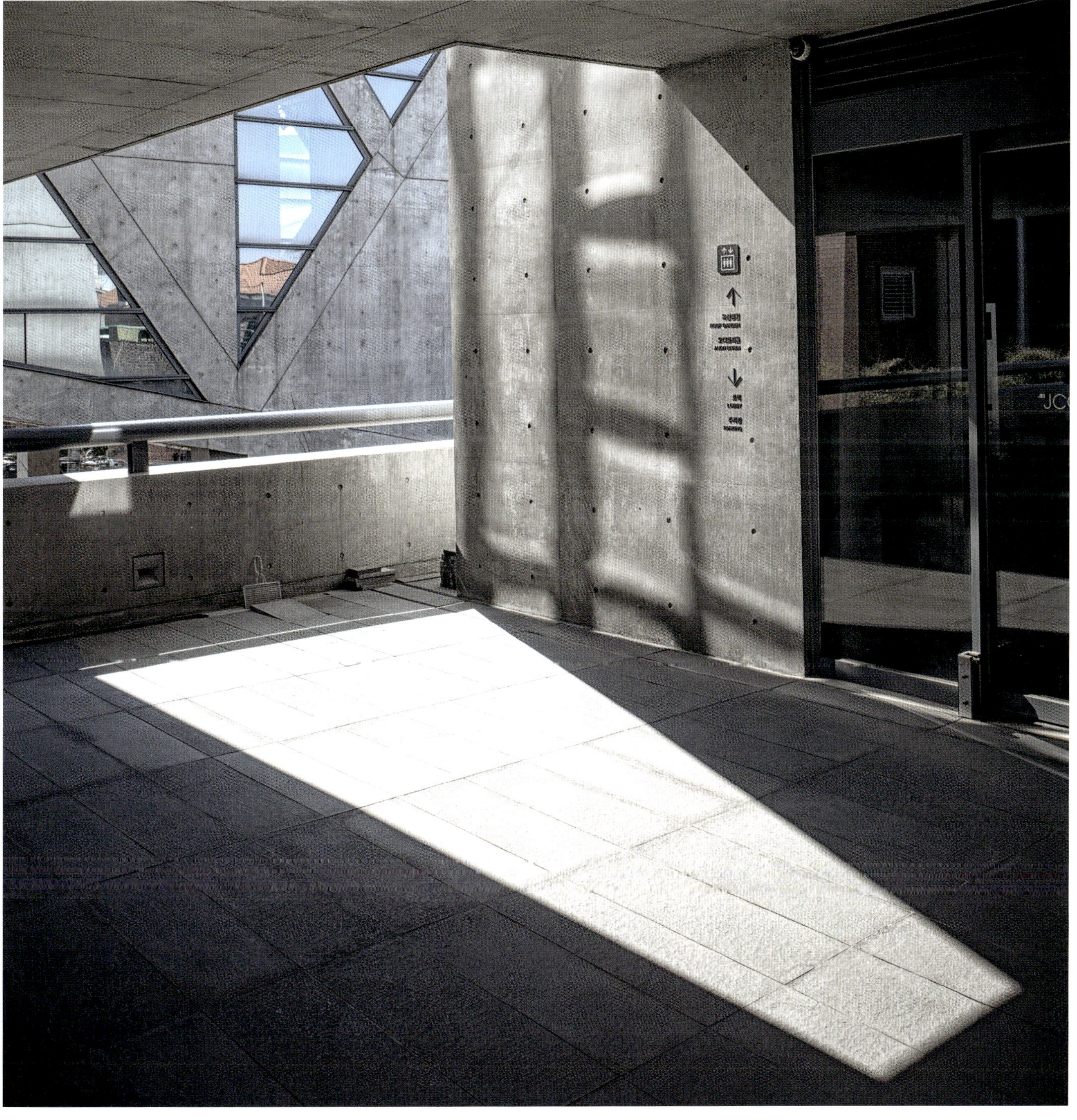

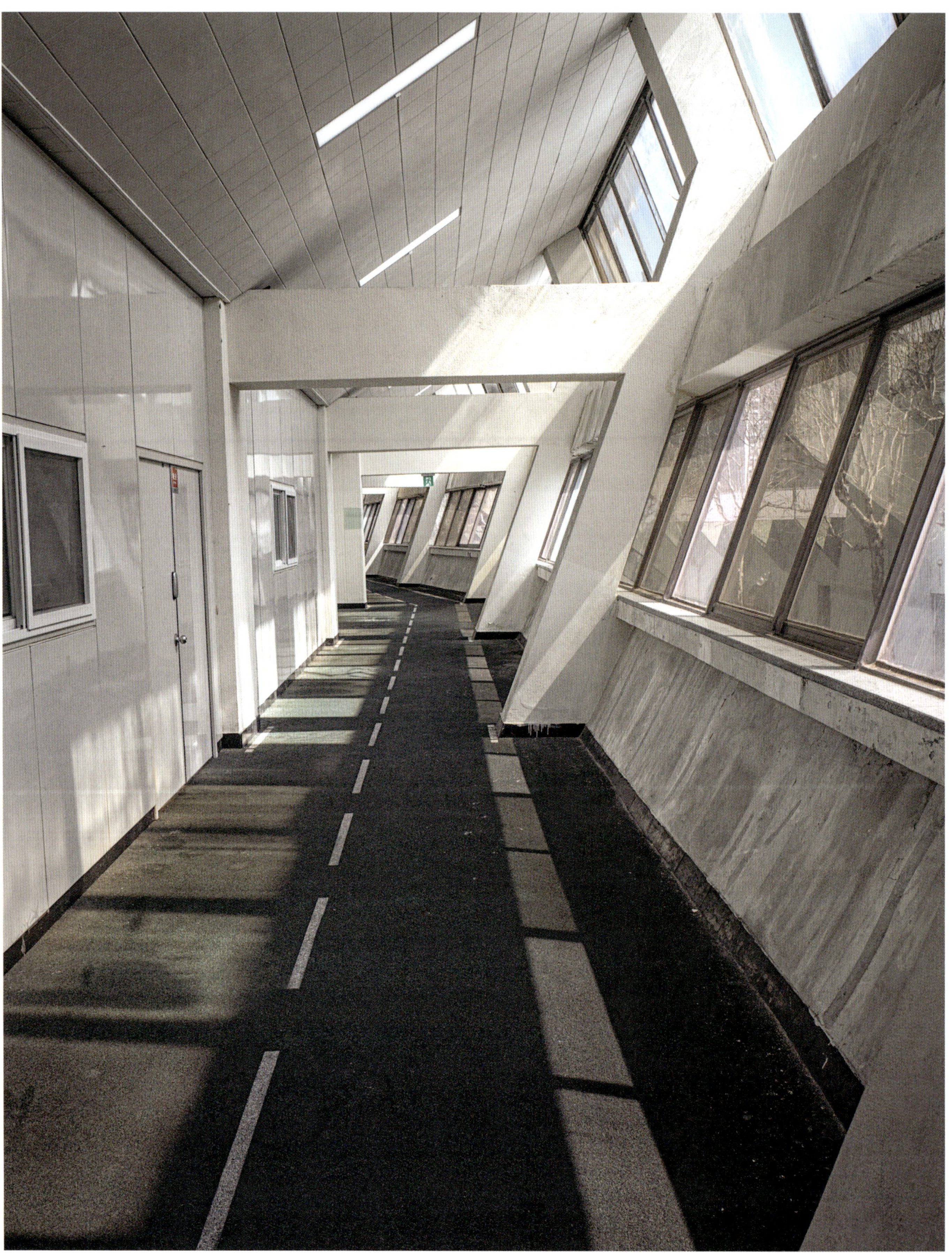

JAMSIL INDOOR SWIMMING POOL

SEOUL · Architect: HEO Pil-jeong · Completed 1983

Completed in 1980 as part of Seoul's Jamsil Sports Complex, the Jamsil Indoor Swimming Pool remains one of South Korea's most striking relics of late-modernist ambition. Designed under the guidance of Heo Pil-jeong, the building translates the streamlined optimism of pre-Olympic Korea into reinforced concrete, poured thick and sharp enough to anchor an entire generation of sports dreams.

Its exterior reads like a swimmer's dive caught mid-motion: a long slanted hull of concrete and glass slicing forwards, ribs exposed, balance impeccable. The massing leans outwards as if in perpetual readiness for take-off – or perhaps a butterfly stroke through time. Ribbon windows wrap the volume in long laps of transparency, punctuated by deep reveals that double as gills, ventilating both light and myth.

Inside, diagonal corridors and narrow light slots lend the sensation of being within a vessel, not a building. Shafts of sunlight glide across the angled walls like reflections across pool water, creating rhythms of illumination and shadow that move as fluidly as the athletes once did below.

Brutalism here isn't simply a matter of material, it's an ethos. Every beam is no-nonsense and structural, every panel a statement of force and endurance. The ageing patina of the façade – streaked, stained, and solemn – only heightens its aquatic drama.

If Olympic glory has faded, the architecture has not. It is dealing with retirement like an old champion: battered but proud, concrete muscles still flexed, ready for its next event – perhaps not a freestyle final, but the slow, meditative sport of architectural photography. Indeed, the interior is somewhat dilapidated and underutilized – particularly the upper floors that are inaccessible if you're not a dedicated concrete-sniffing beagle. Although sheltering dead rodents and birds, these afforded the shots of the neighbouring Olympic Stadium (pp. 150–153) – ground-level captures were hindered by works and tarpaulin.

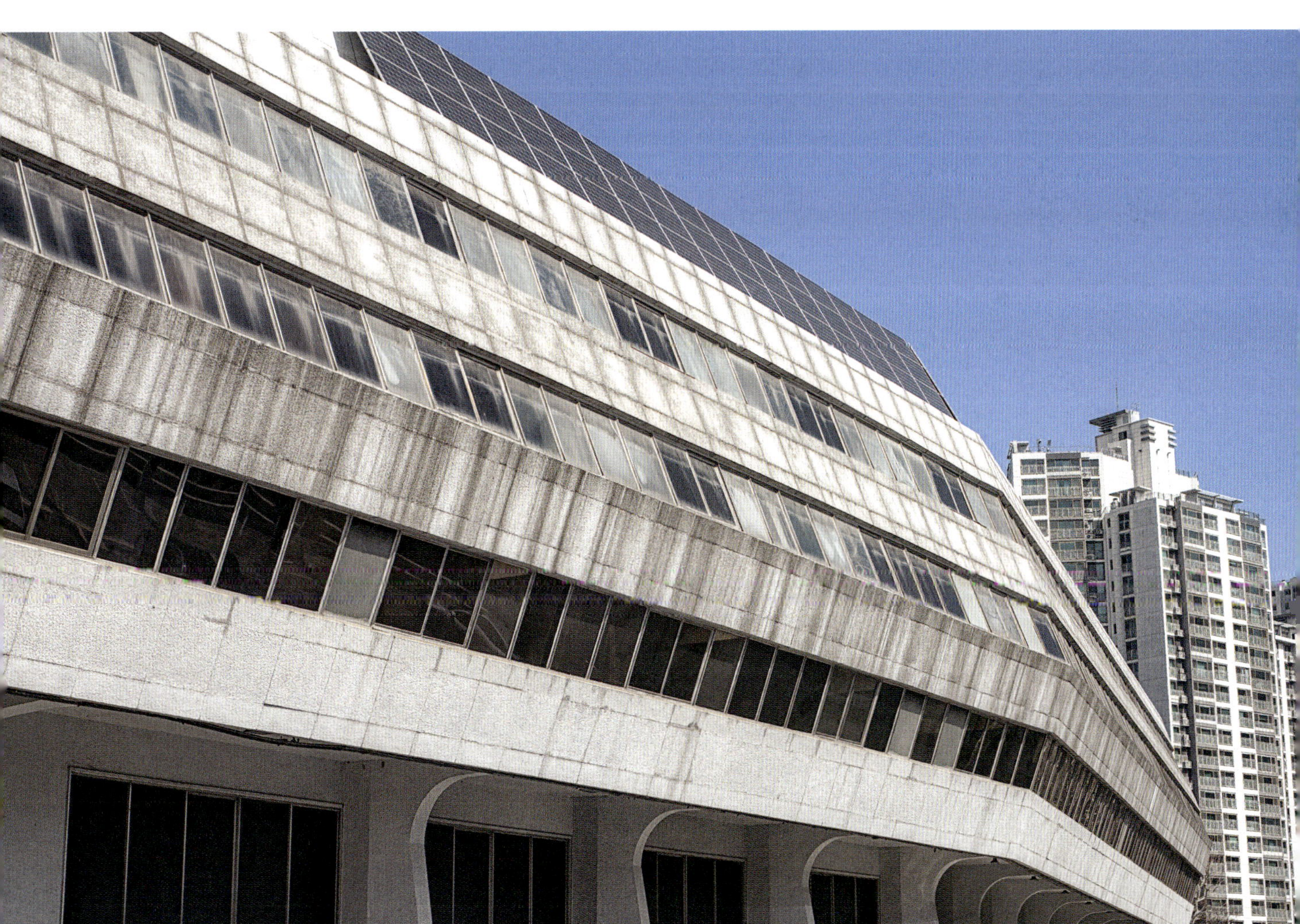

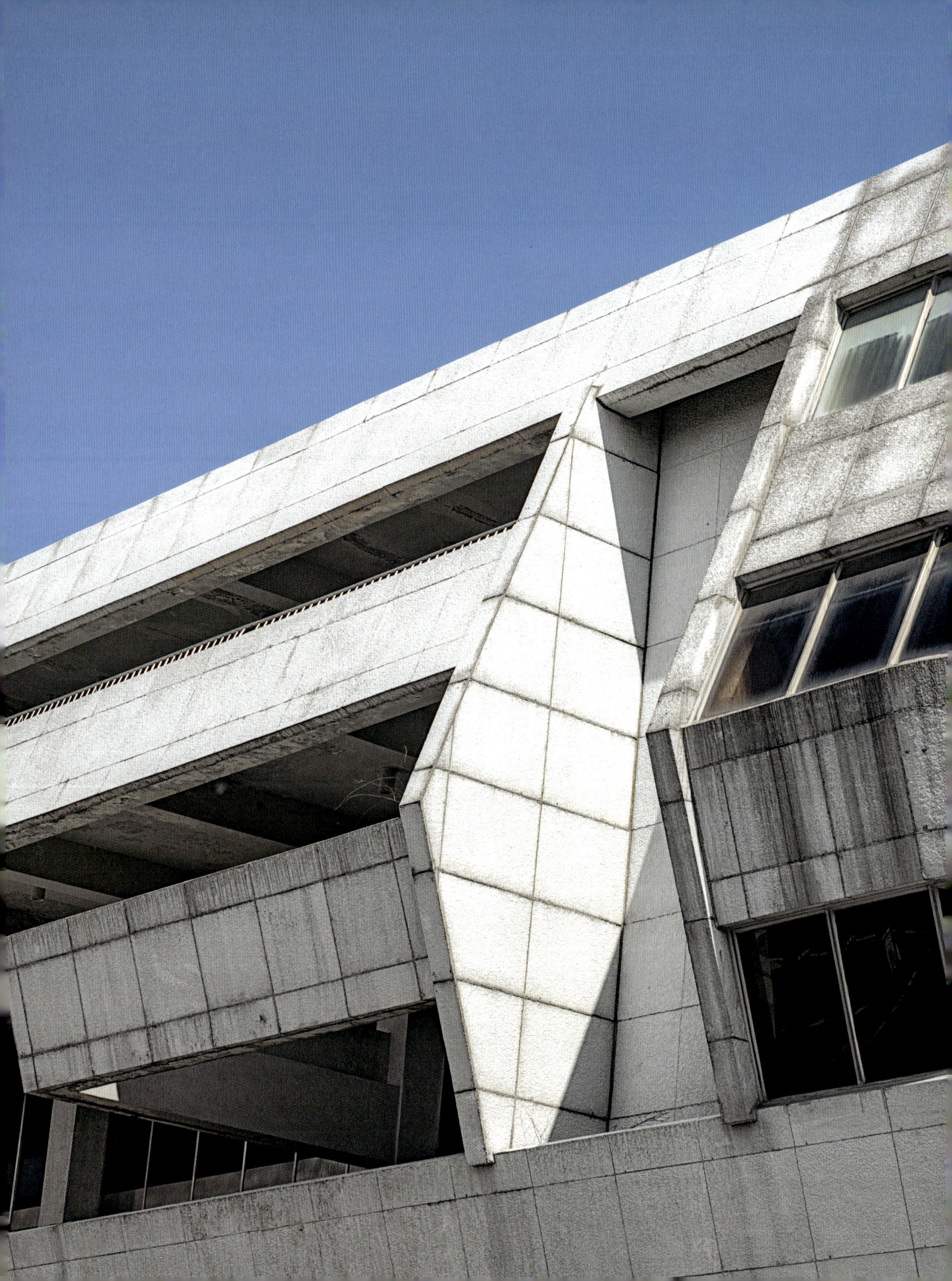

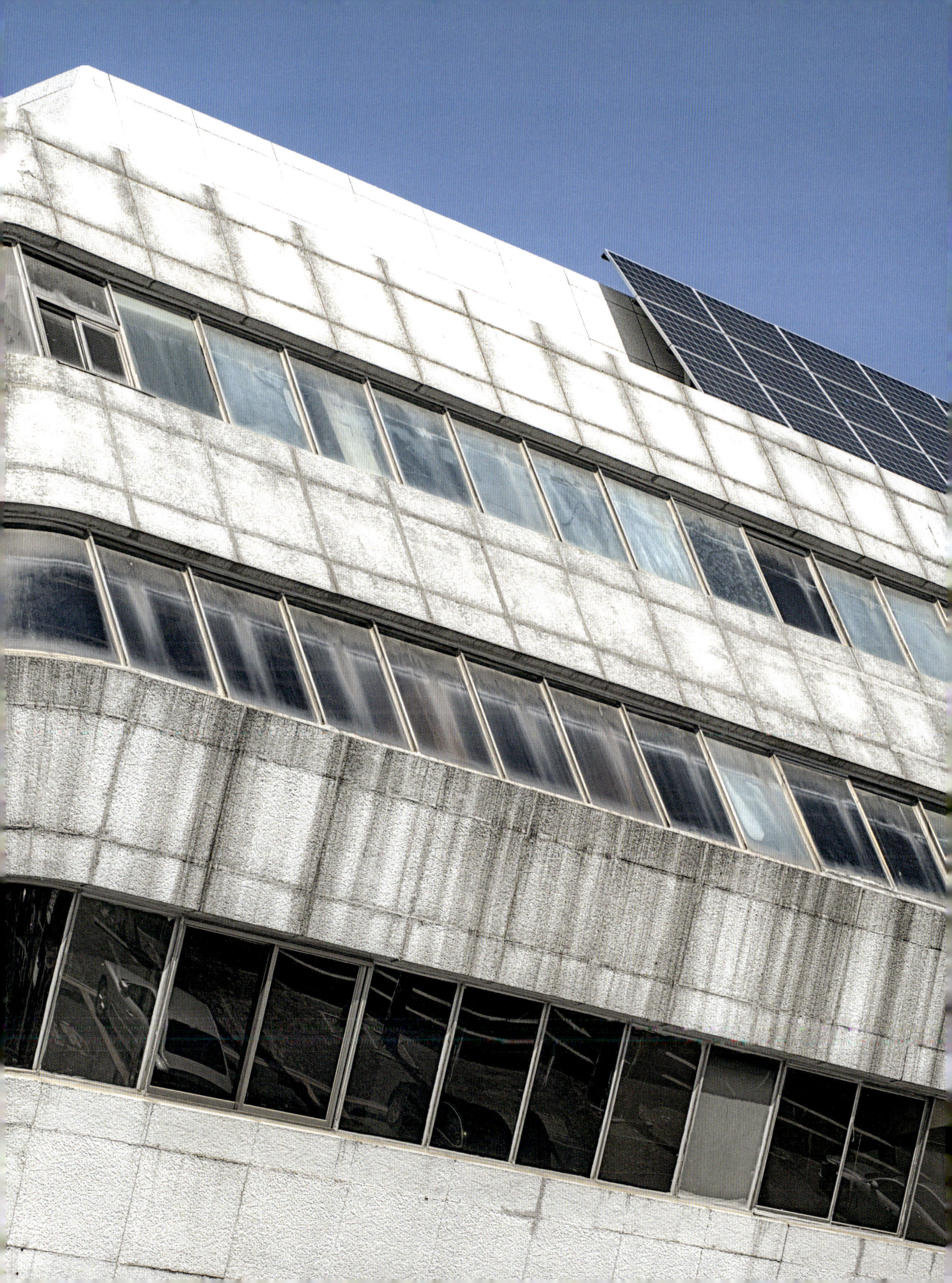

KYUNGDONG PRESBYTERIAN CHURCH

SEOUL · Architect: KIM Swoo-geun · Completed 1981

At first glance, this church might appear too pious in its brickwork to earn a seat at the Brutalist table. But step inside and the sceptic is swiftly converted. Designed by Kim Swoo-geun and completed in 1981, this ecclesiastical oddity is a cathedral of contradiction – part chapel, part bunker, and entirely in your face. Its exterior, a serrated silhouette of brick, evokes both fortress and furnace, rising like a defiant psalm in solid form. But it's the concrete interior where the Brutalist sermon truly begins.

This is not the church of stained glass and soaring spires – it's the church of shadow and silence, of God in the grain of poured concrete. The interior is cavernous, angular, and raw, like the Old Testament rendered in structural form. The sanctuary is less about glory and more about gravity – the weight of faith, the burden of reflection, all anchored in concrete so honest it might confess before you do.

Critics might question its Brutalist credentials because of the brick façade – but brick, in Korea, is no stranger to Brutalism. It's not the material that defines the movement, but the ethos: truth in structure, minimal adornment, emotional intensity. Here, the jagged brick is as much part of the Brutalist vocabulary as the concrete it shields – a kind of ecclesiastical exfoliation.

There's wit in this too: a church that looks medieval outside and post-apocalyptic within – as if the Second Coming arrived early and brought an architect. This church converts not through beauty, but through brutal clarity. In a city of megachurches with LED crosses and shopping mall sanctuaries, this one simply says: sit down, be silent, and listen. God is in the formwork and bricklaying.

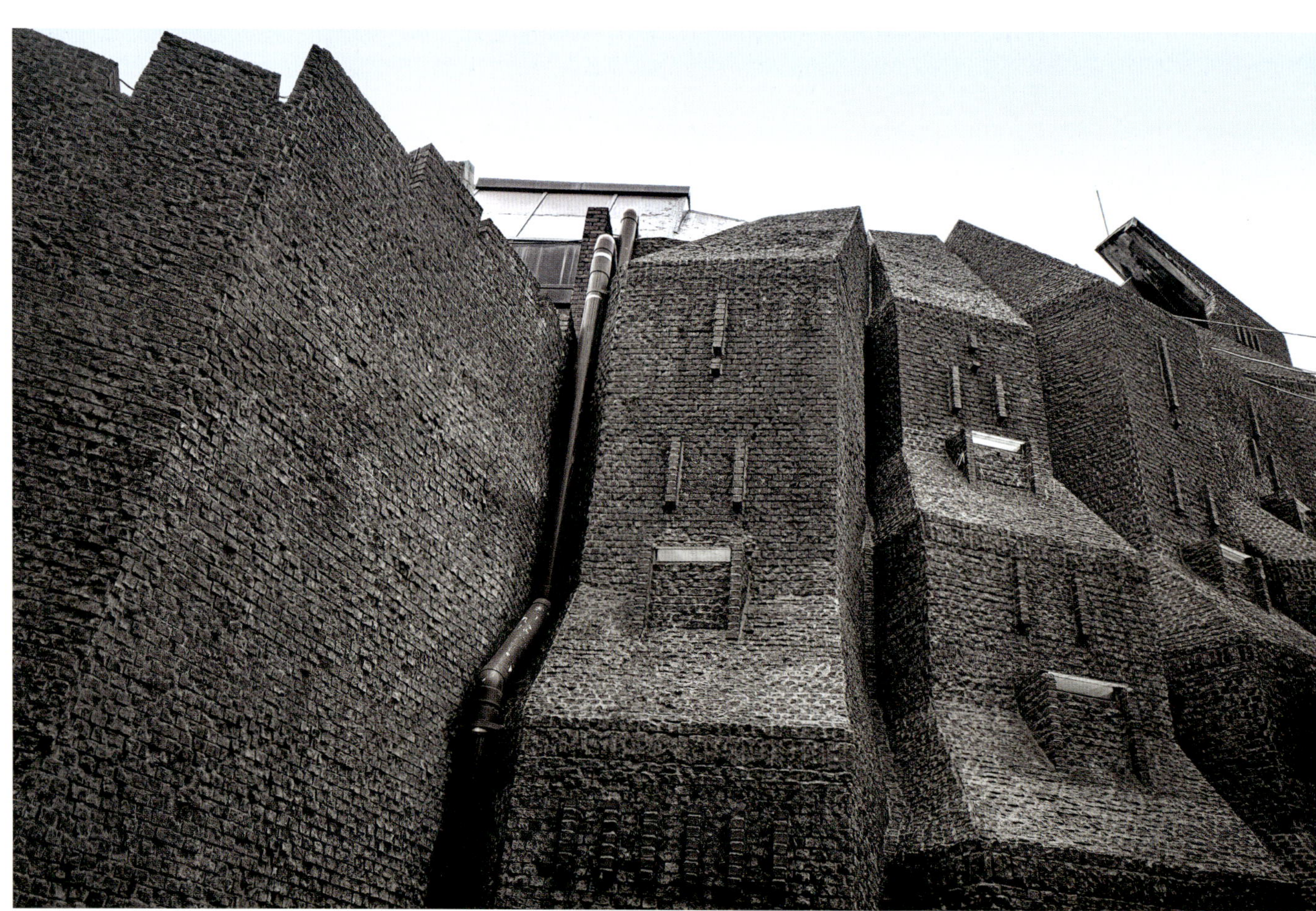

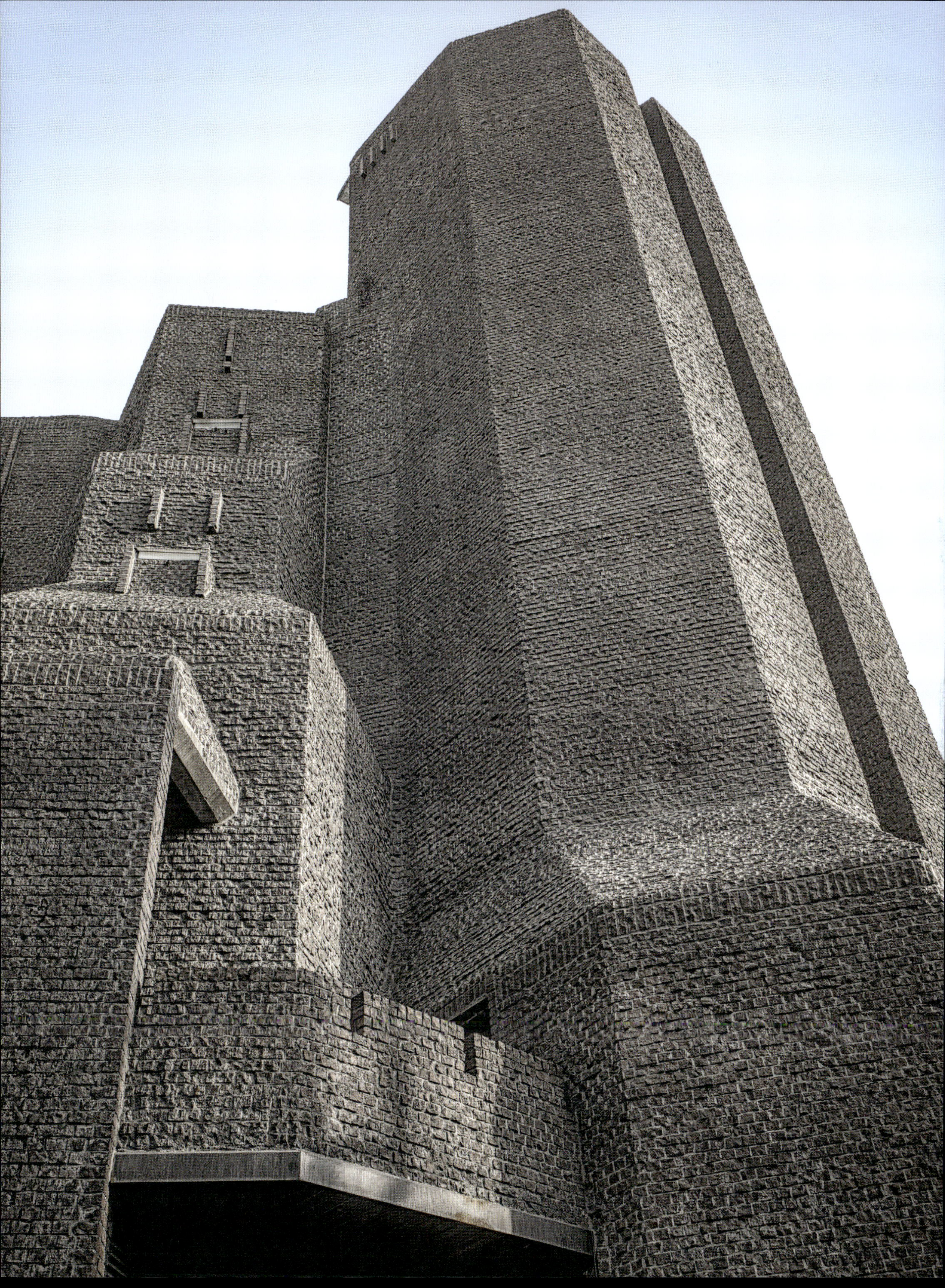

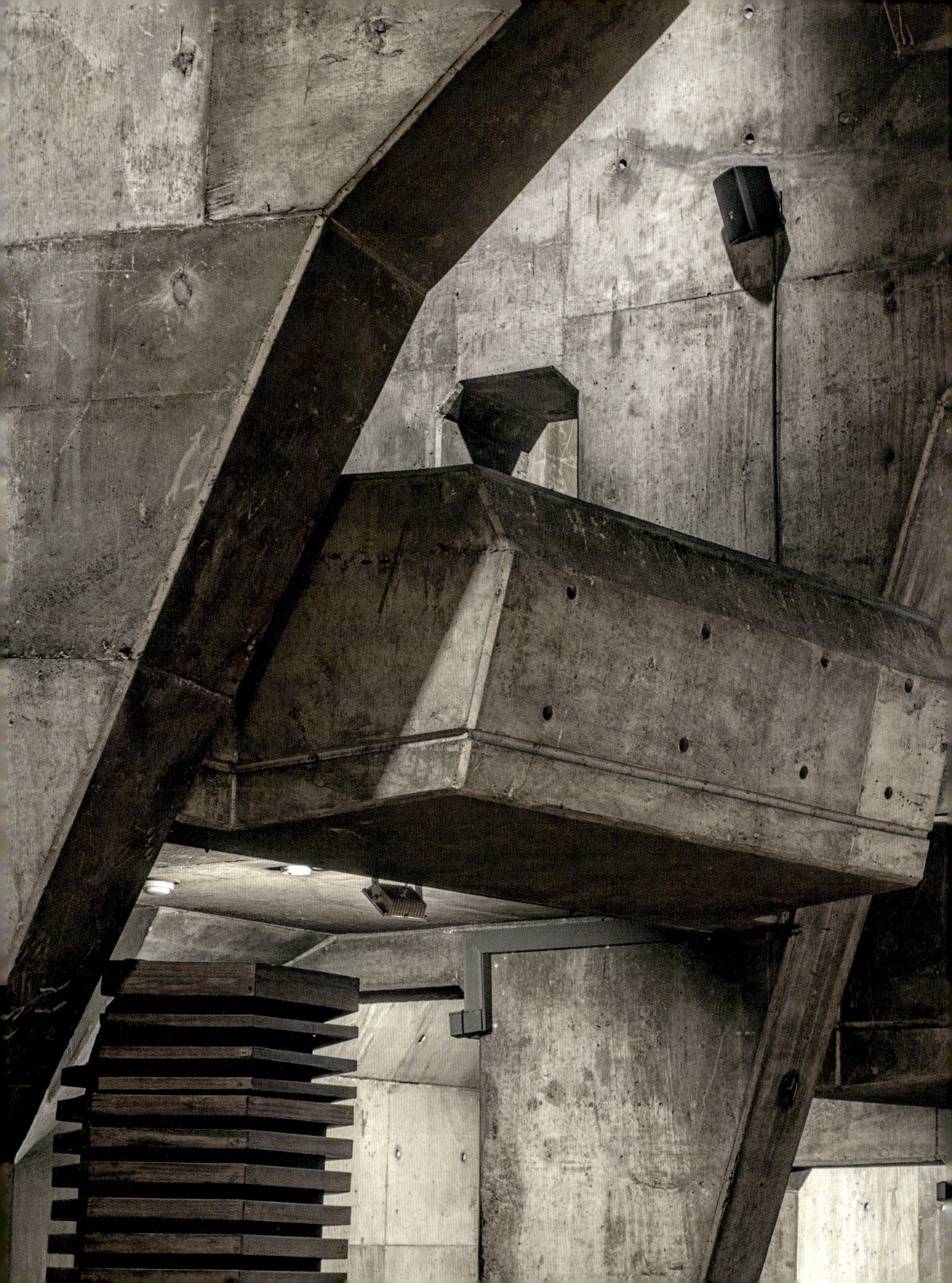

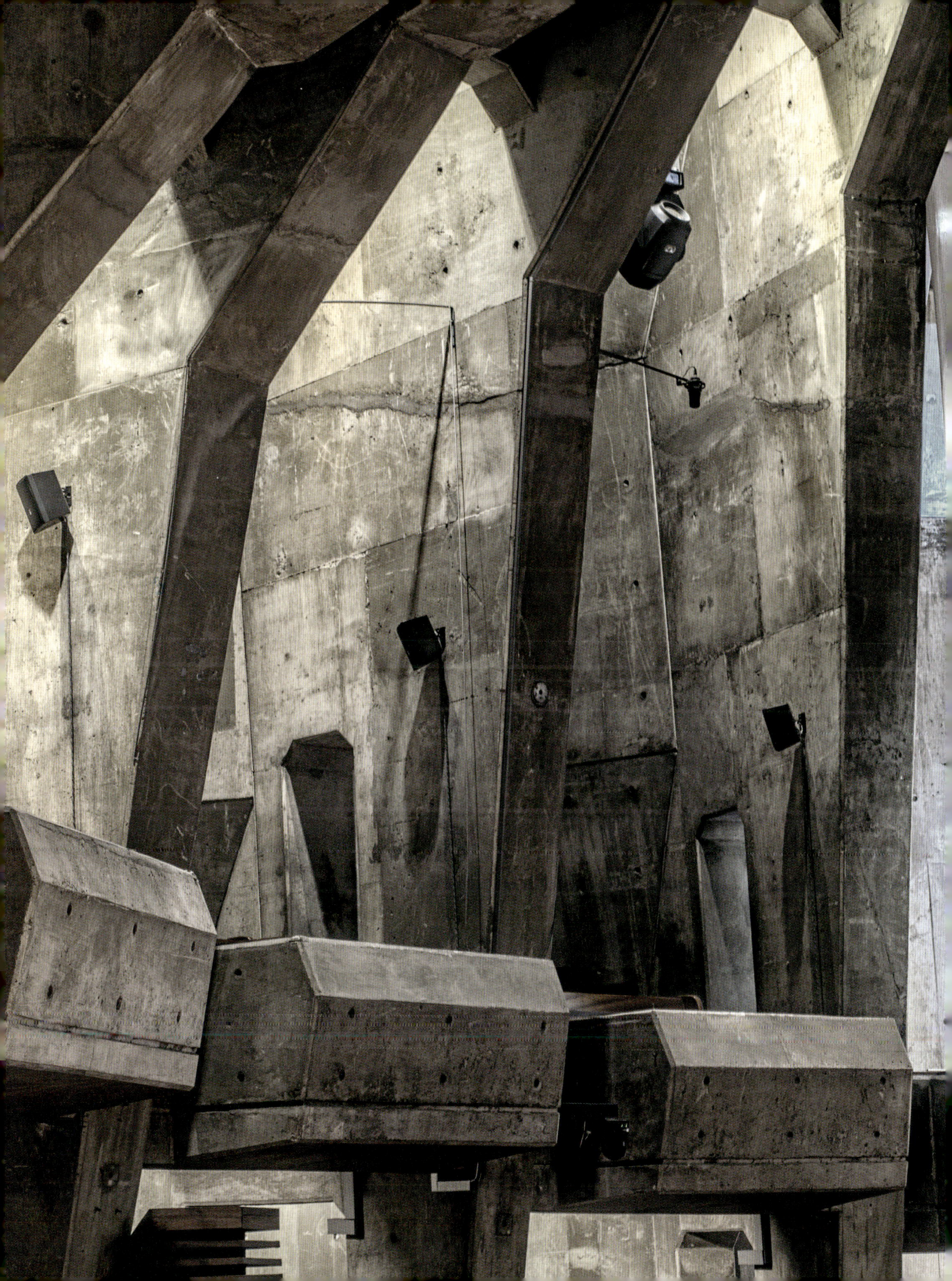

"QUEENS" DEVELOPMENT

JEJU ISLAND

On the way to Ando's Jeju Glass House, I managed to make rather dramatic contact with a volcanic rock. A tyre exploded and I performed an involuntary two-lane waltz before coming to rest. The misfortune, however, delivered a surprise detour. While sharing a consolatory cigarette with the recovery bloke, and given the height advantage of his truck, I noticed intriguing skeletal concrete forms rising from a barren site. Once my rental was re-shoed and roadworthy, I couldn't resist circling back. There they stood: silent, unfinished compositions of raw concrete and abandoned ambition. For once, I didn't have to wait for tourists to clear the frame. I had the large site entirely to myself. Misfortune, it turned out, makes an excellent location scout.

In the past decade, Jeju Island has lured an extraordinary number of developers chasing the dream of luxury resorts and high-end housing. Yet many of these ventures have ground to a halt, leaving behind half-finished structures scattered across the landscape. The reasons are less mysterious than the ruins themselves: an oversaturated property market, climbing construction costs, and a cooling appetite for investment have made many schemes financially untenable.

Adding to the strain, numerous construction companies on the island have folded under mounting debt, labour shortages, and escalating material prices. Environmental restrictions and tighter scrutiny of foreign-backed projects – especially those tied to Chinese capital – have further slowed momentum. In one high-profile case, a Malaysian developer even threatened international arbitration after a planned resort collapsed under regulatory friction. And when labour disputes or concrete delivery stand-offs erupt, the cranes simply stop turning – leaving an ever-growing open-air gallery of arrested ambition. For a photographer of concrete, that's pure gold – a stage set of unspoken architecture, waiting for its closeup.

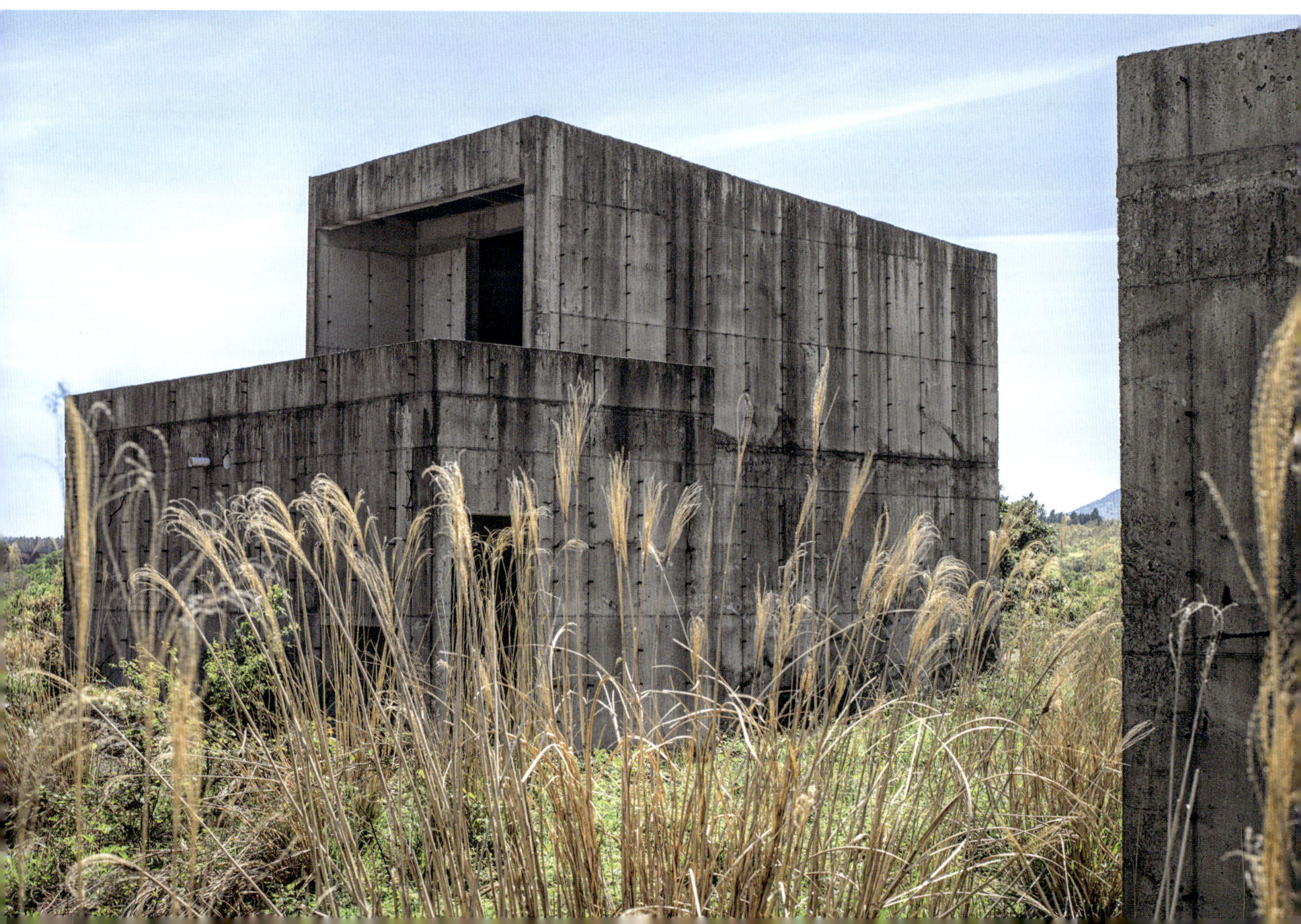

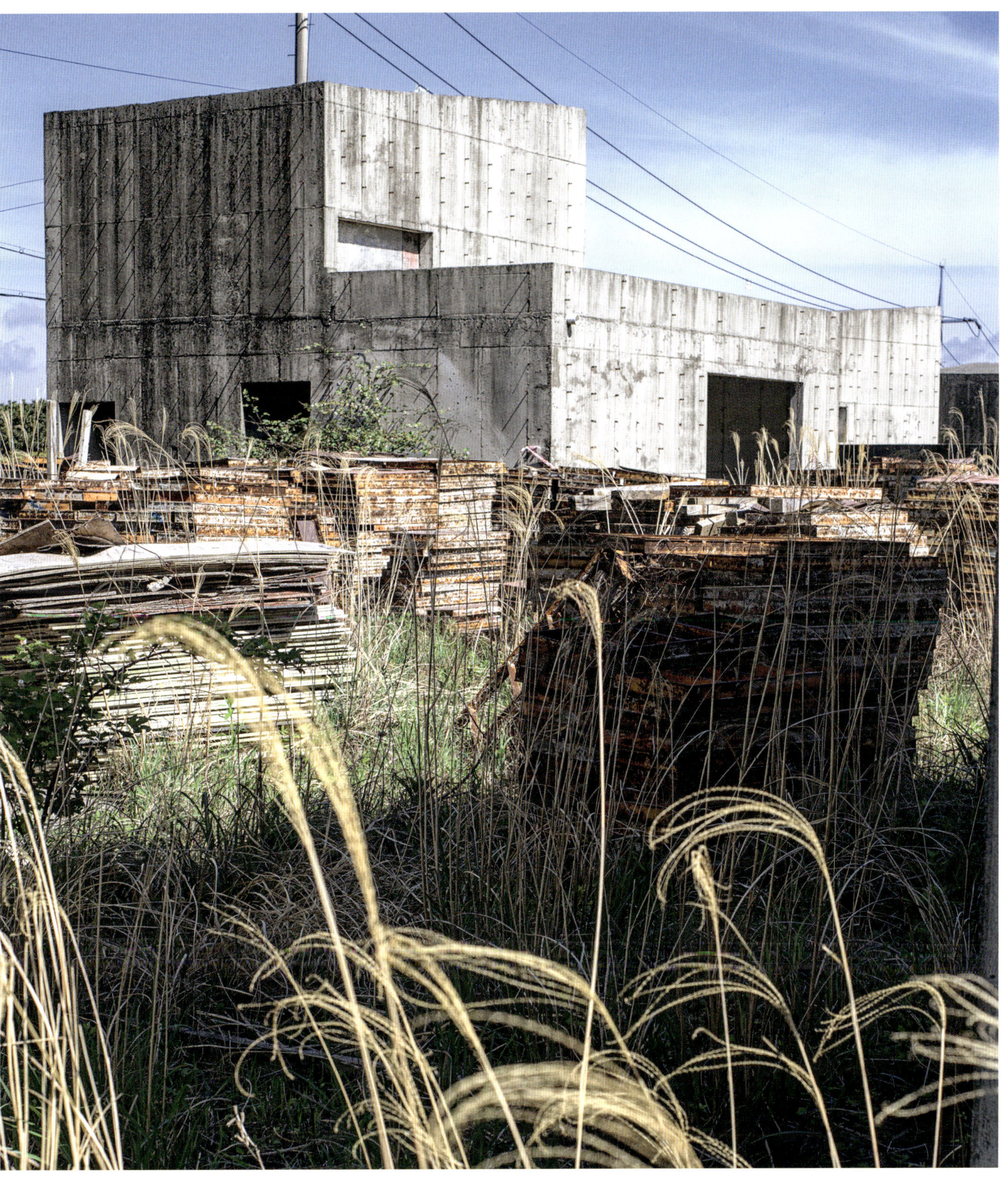

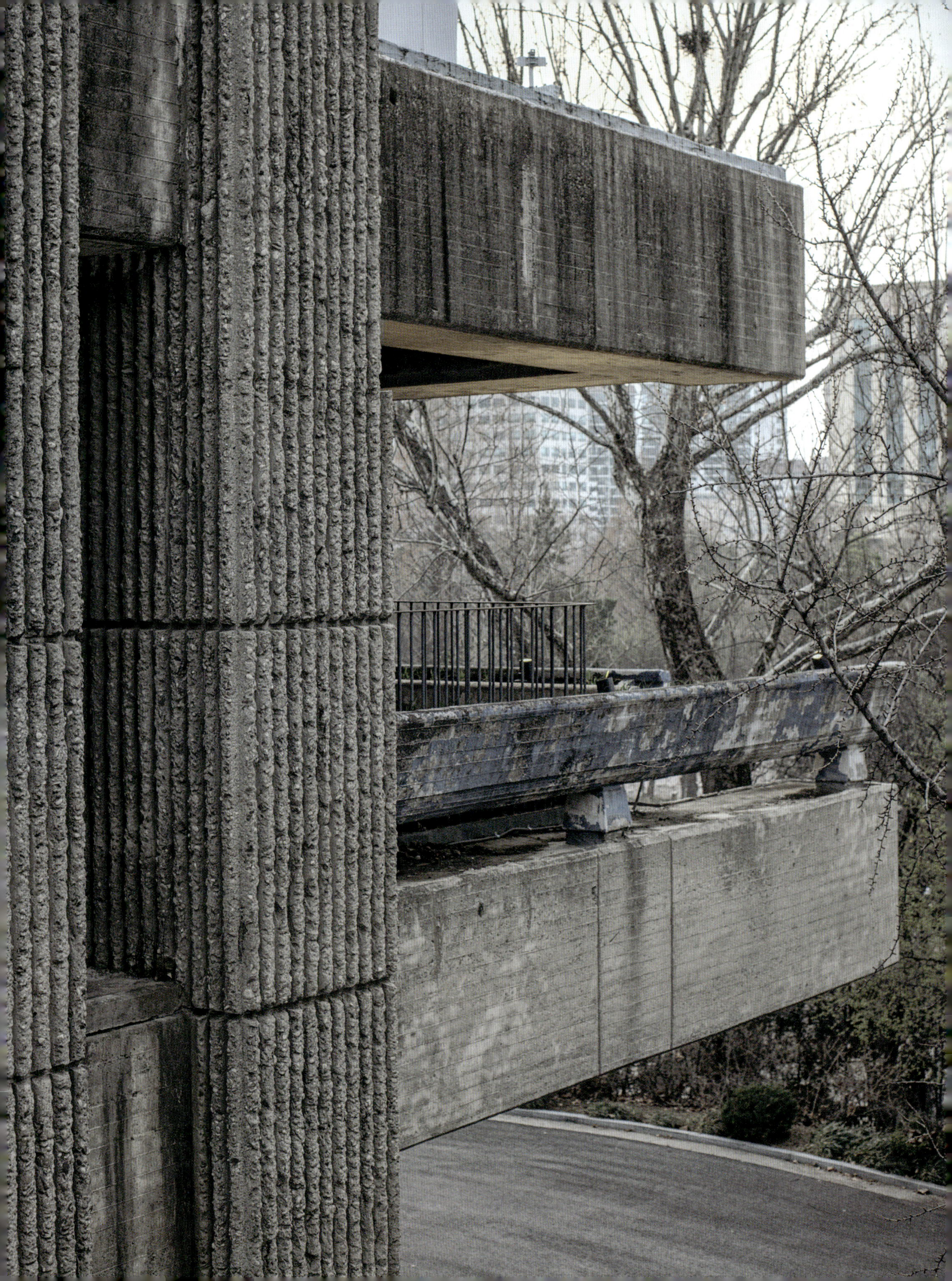

KKUMMARU AT SEOUL CHILDREN'S GRAND PARK

SEOUL · Architect: RA Sang-jin · Completed 1970 / Renovated 2011 by JOH Sung-yong and CHOI Choon

The Children's Grand Park main building in Seoul is what happens when Brutalism discovers a jungle gym – all chunky concrete limbs and heroic forms, but with just enough whimsy to keep it from collapsing under its own seriousness. Completed in 1970 when Korea was eager to build big and think bold, it's a rare case of a government structure that looks like it was made from oversized toy blocks left behind by a concrete-loving giant.

The building flexes Brutalist credentials with pride: *béton brut*, rigid geometries, and a kind of stern monumentality you might expect from a national archive – if that archive also handed out balloon animals and candy floss. It's a space built to impress small humans and bemuse large ones, where the scale is grand but the atmosphere remains oddly playful.

Vaulted corridors echo with the sound of shrieking glee. Staircases zigzag like giant slides that someone forgot to smooth out. There's a comic-book quality to the proportions – wide openings, deep shadows, and playful voids that could double as hideouts in a postmodern game of tag. Brutalism rarely smiles, but here the edges have softened just enough to allow mischief through the cracks.

Yet beneath the playful veneer lies a serious civic gesture: this is public architecture that dares to be both monumental and generous. In a city racing upwards, this broad-shouldered concrete creature reminds us that children deserve grandeur too – not just soft plastic and pastels, but bold forms and lasting materials.

It's a place where childhood meets concrete and wins – not by softening it, but by climbing all over it. A Brutalist playground for the imagination, and a lesson that even architecture with a heavy brow can still remember how to play.

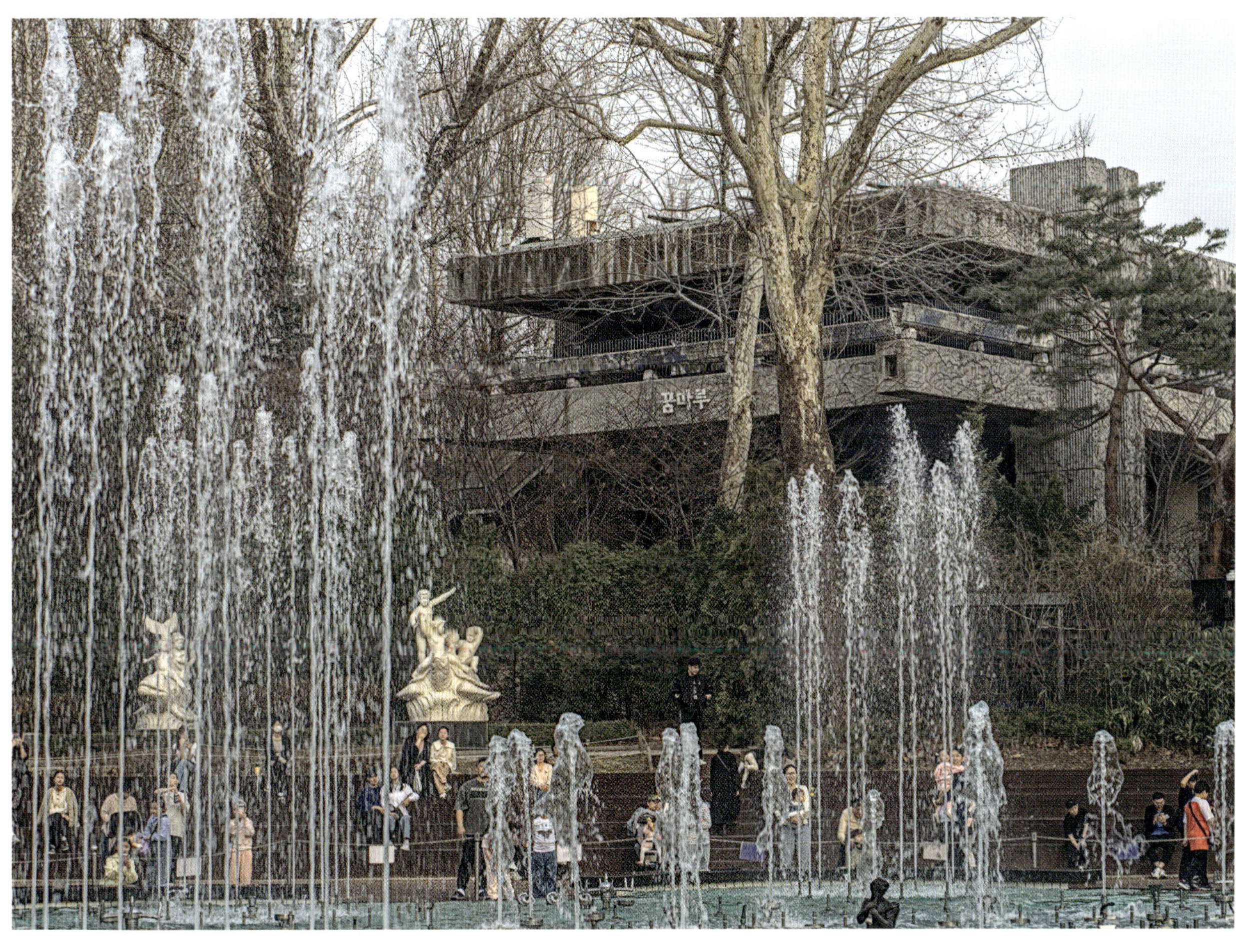

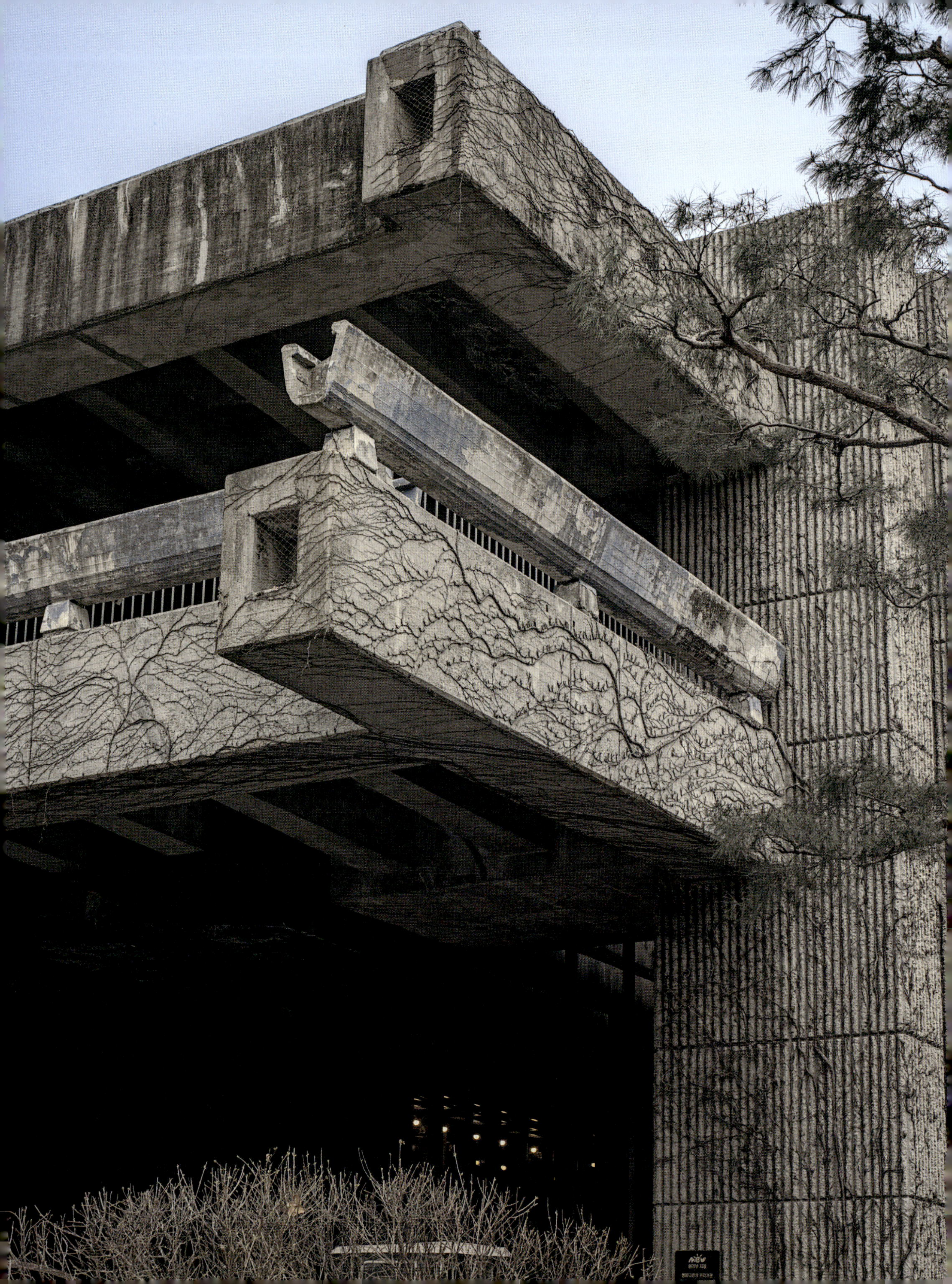

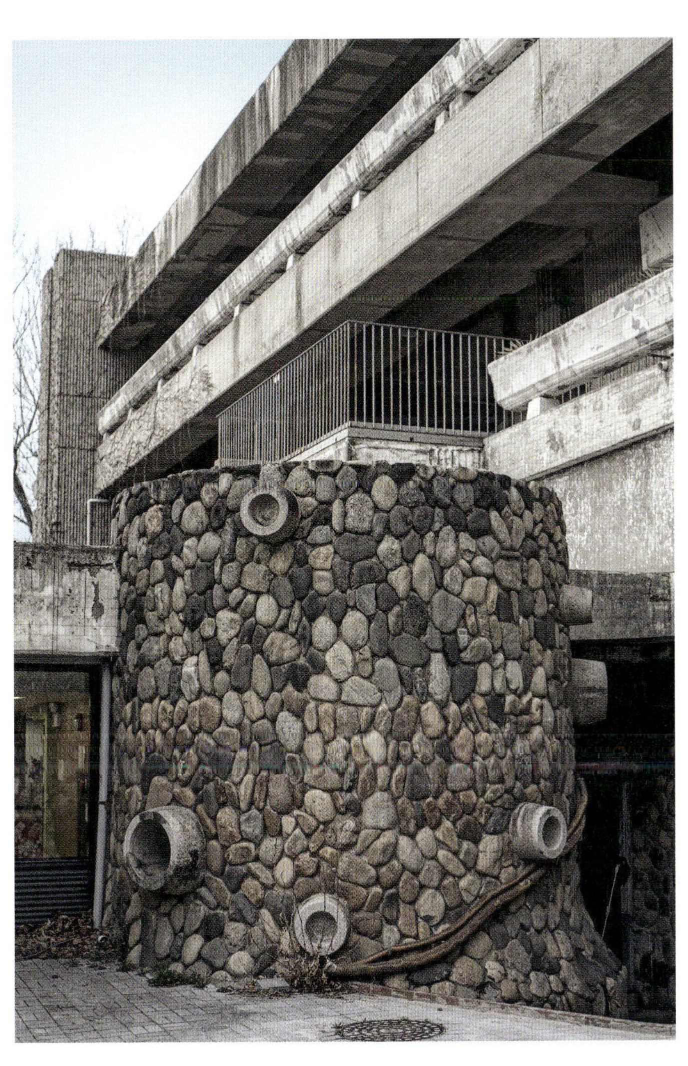

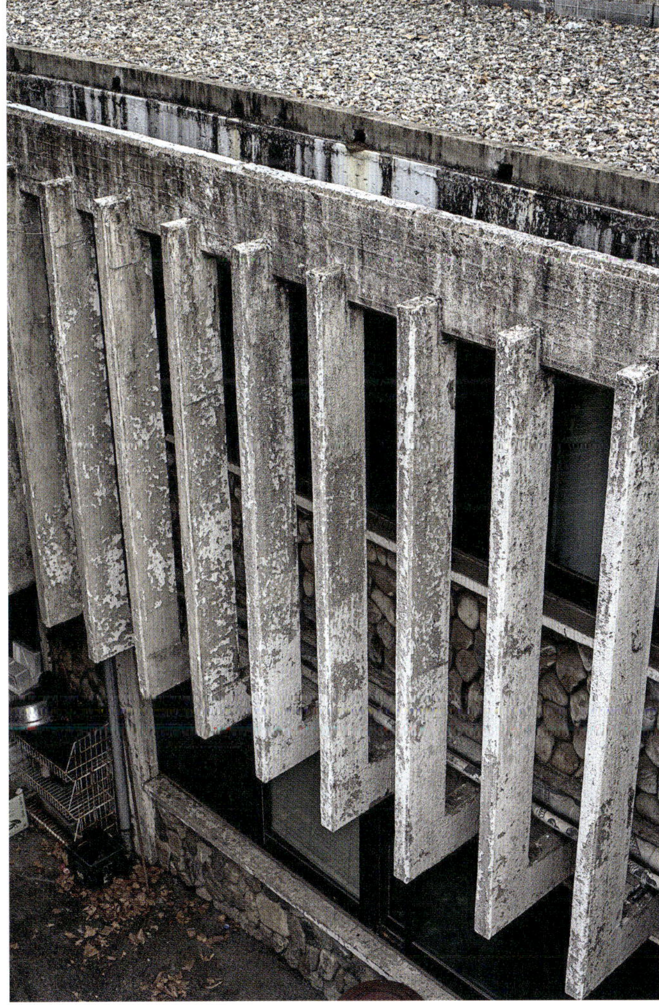

CÉLINE FLAGSHIP STORE

SEOUL · Architect: Casper Mueller Kneer Architects · Completed 2017

Céline's flagship in Cheongdam-dong rises like a bastion draped in a brick veil – a contemporary expression of Seoul's evolving Nu-Bru aesthetic. Designed by Casper Mueller Kneer Architects, the seven-storey structure embodies restraint and raw precision: a Brutalist language reimagined through couture discipline. Its stepped massing is wrapped in pale custom-made terracotta bricks, laid in a staggered rhythm that alternates between opacity and light. The surface becomes a tactile skin – part armour, part lace – filtering sunlight much like fabric modulates the body beneath.

A Braille-like array of long bricks – some recessed, others omitted to form slender apertures – is bound by deep flush joints, the façade draping the structure like a woven fabric. Yet beneath this elegance lies the Brutalist ethos of truth to material – structure exposed, craft revealed, and repetition celebrated. Hand-laid by Korean masons without digital assistance, the façade reads as both pattern and process: a handmade manifesto for Seoul's Nu-Bru minimalism – severe, sensual, and unmistakably modern.

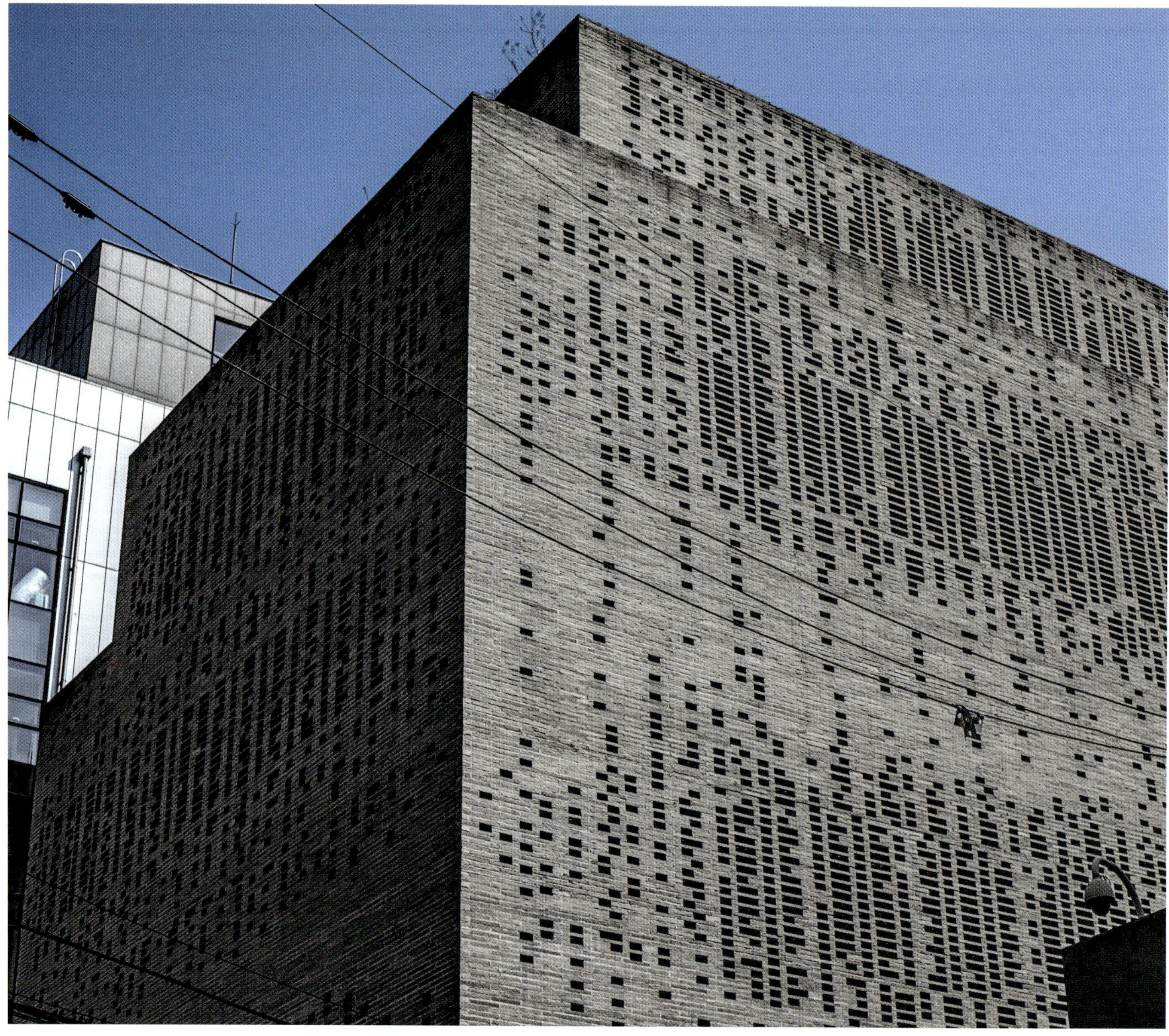

RAIVE FLAGSHIP STORE

SEOUL

This flagship store embodies the sartorial equivalent of concrete couture – another example of what I have coined Nu-Bru: a movement where current taste and fashion can meet formwork. Its façade, a grid of sculpted panels, drapes across the building like an architectural pleat – rigid yet rhythmic, structured yet sensuous. Beneath this skin, the store reveals glass transparency and steel precision, a runway of material honesty. Where Brutalism once wore its raw concrete proudly, Seoul's new iteration tailors the same ethos for the now – textured, photogenic, and perfectly cut.

The building is a store that smacks of a garment in mid-movement, frozen at the moment of a designer's fold. It sews together decoration and discipline, surface and substance – echoing the quiet confidence of Korean minimalism. This architecture models attitude – a new urban chic that struts, and shows that contemporary Brutalism can dress to impress.

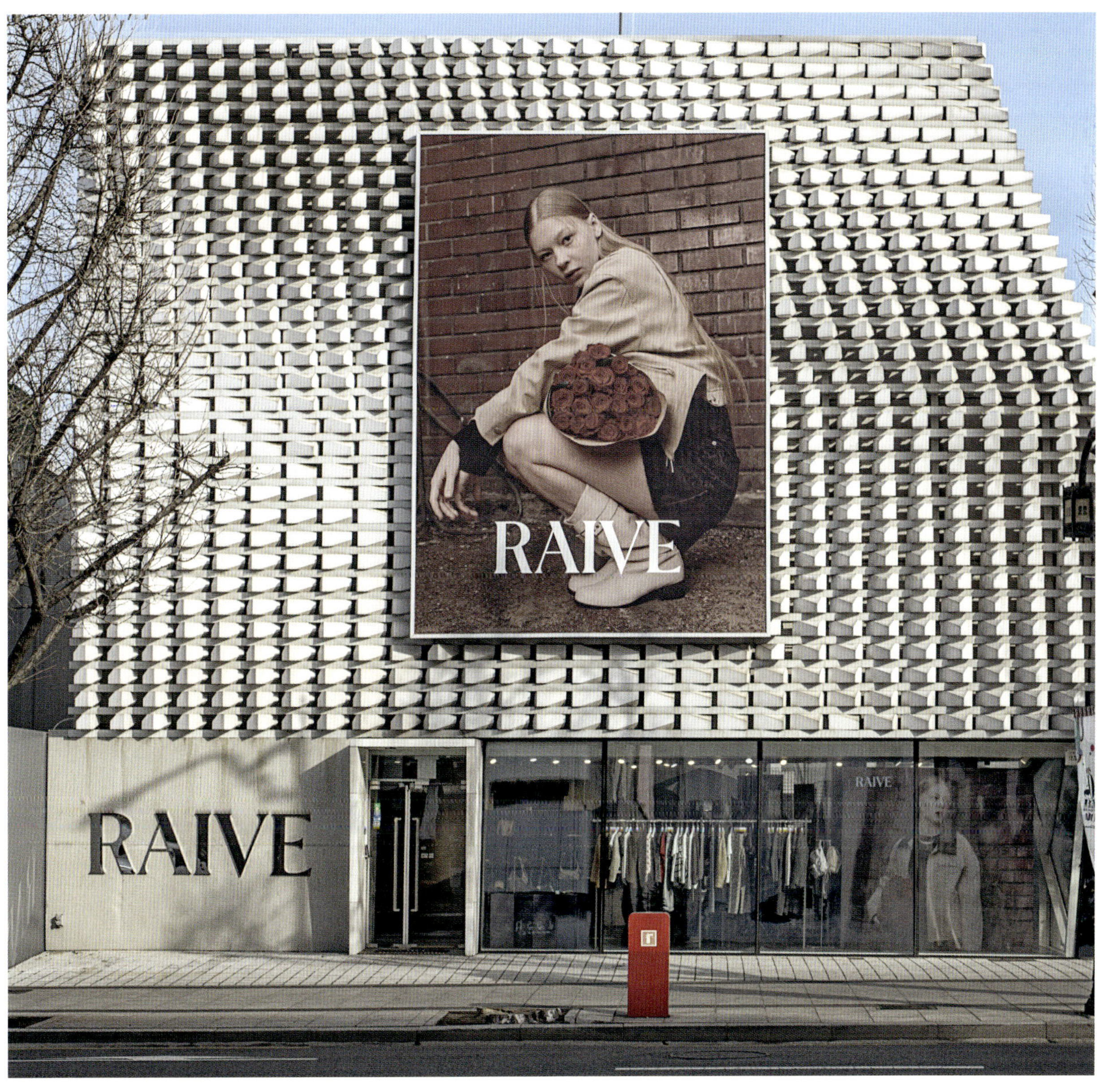

SOBAEK SESIMDAE

SAYUWON · Architect: SEUNG H-Sang · Completed 2016

The garden Pungseolgicheonnyeon (meaning "weathered for thousands of years") provides a silent hymn to endurance. Its entrance is Sobaek Sesimdae ("viewpoint for cleansing the heart and mind"). Tucked within Sayuwon's core grove of 108 ancient quince trees – the arboretum's original heart – the design doesn't build, it *completes*. The modest interventions are landscape gestures: low berms, cut-stone seating, and shallow ponds that cradle and frame the venerable trunks.

No monumentality here – only the hushed presence of history. Paths trace gentle arcs, guiding visitors past trees three to six hundred years old, connecting core memory with contemporary ritual. Subtle stone thresholds let people circle, sit, and listen: water ripples, leaves tremble, and the quince trees themselves become spatial markers.

The interventions employ local stone – granular, grey, unpolished – laid in imperfect patterns that echo the bark texture of the trees. Concrete appears only as narrow edging, its raw surfaces matching the weathered timber's grain. These minimal additions resist hierarchy, instead orchestrating quiet movement and focused attention on the living matter at the garden's centre.

Light here is a variable dimension, not a material. Over seasons, shadows from the pine-and-quince canopy trace new patterns; frost and snow accentuate the granite's relief. The garden frames not a view, but duration – slow time, deep roots, repeated seasons.

Pungseolgicheonnyeon isn't architecture in the usual sense. It is a *poetic infrastructure* – landscape as memory keeper, design as slow ritual. In a garden that began with rescued trees, the built elements exist only to amplify what was already there. It's a testament to patience: to *sit* amongst history, to breathe beside it, to recognize that some presences need no spotlight – just room to grow. Room for relief is shown on pages 107 to 109. The toilet block!

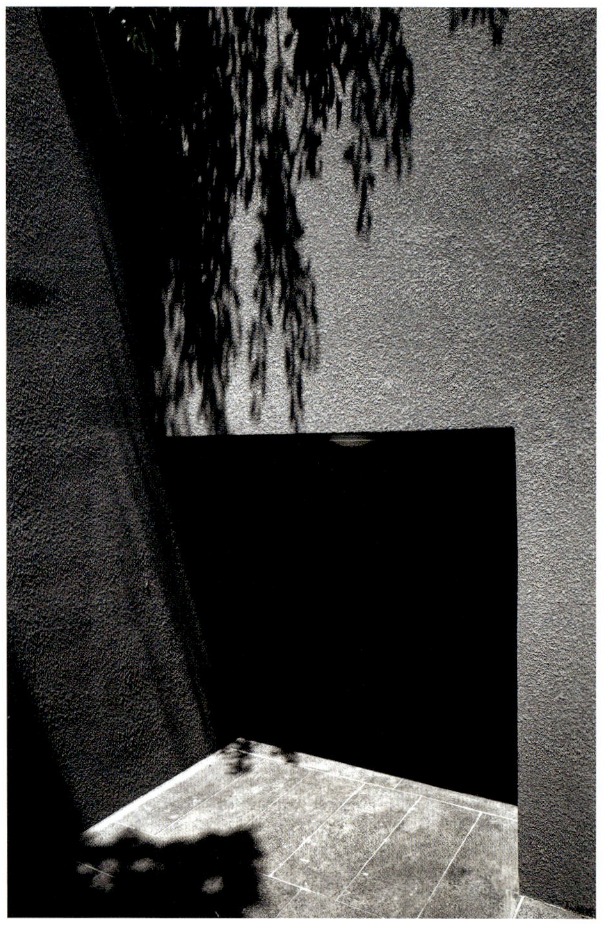

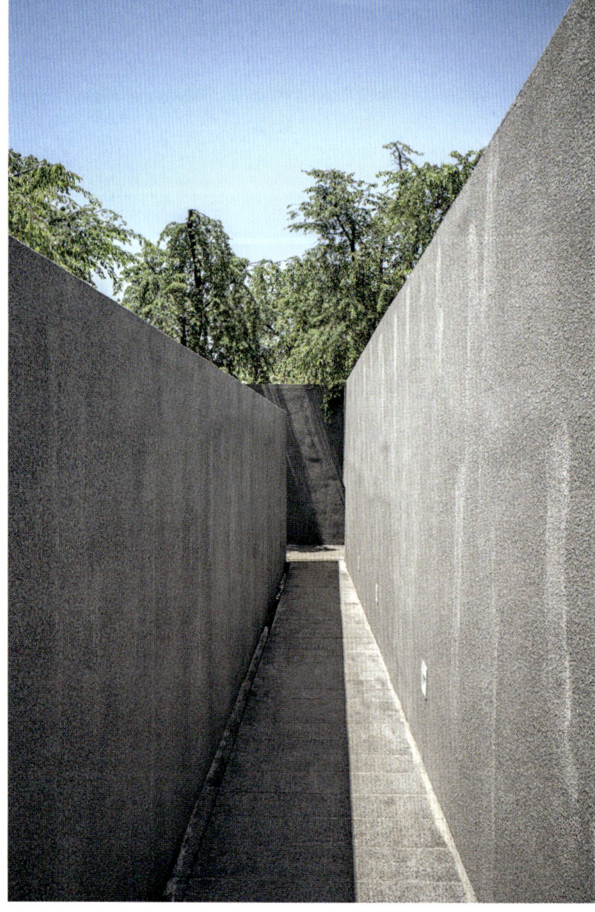

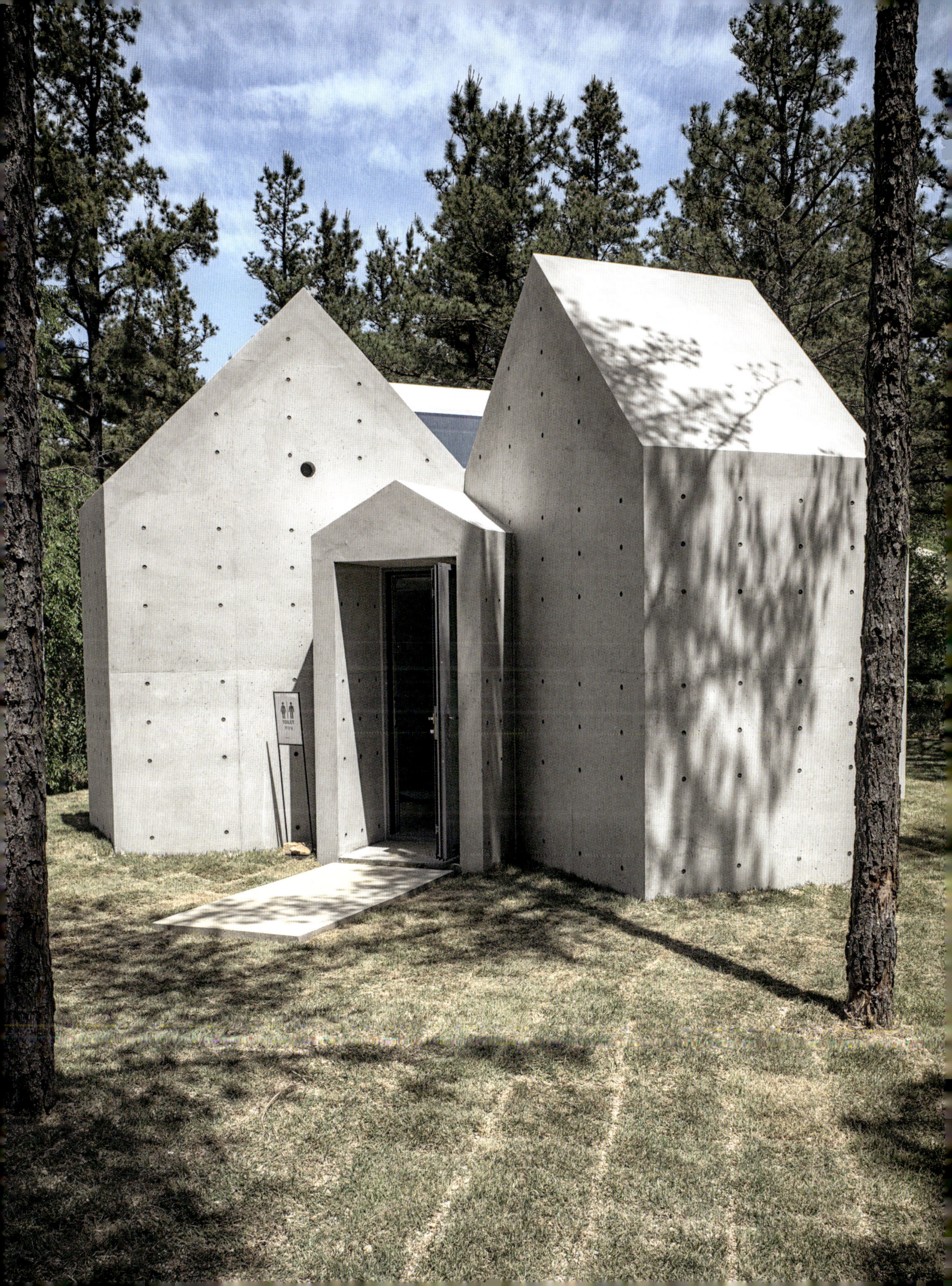
TOILET

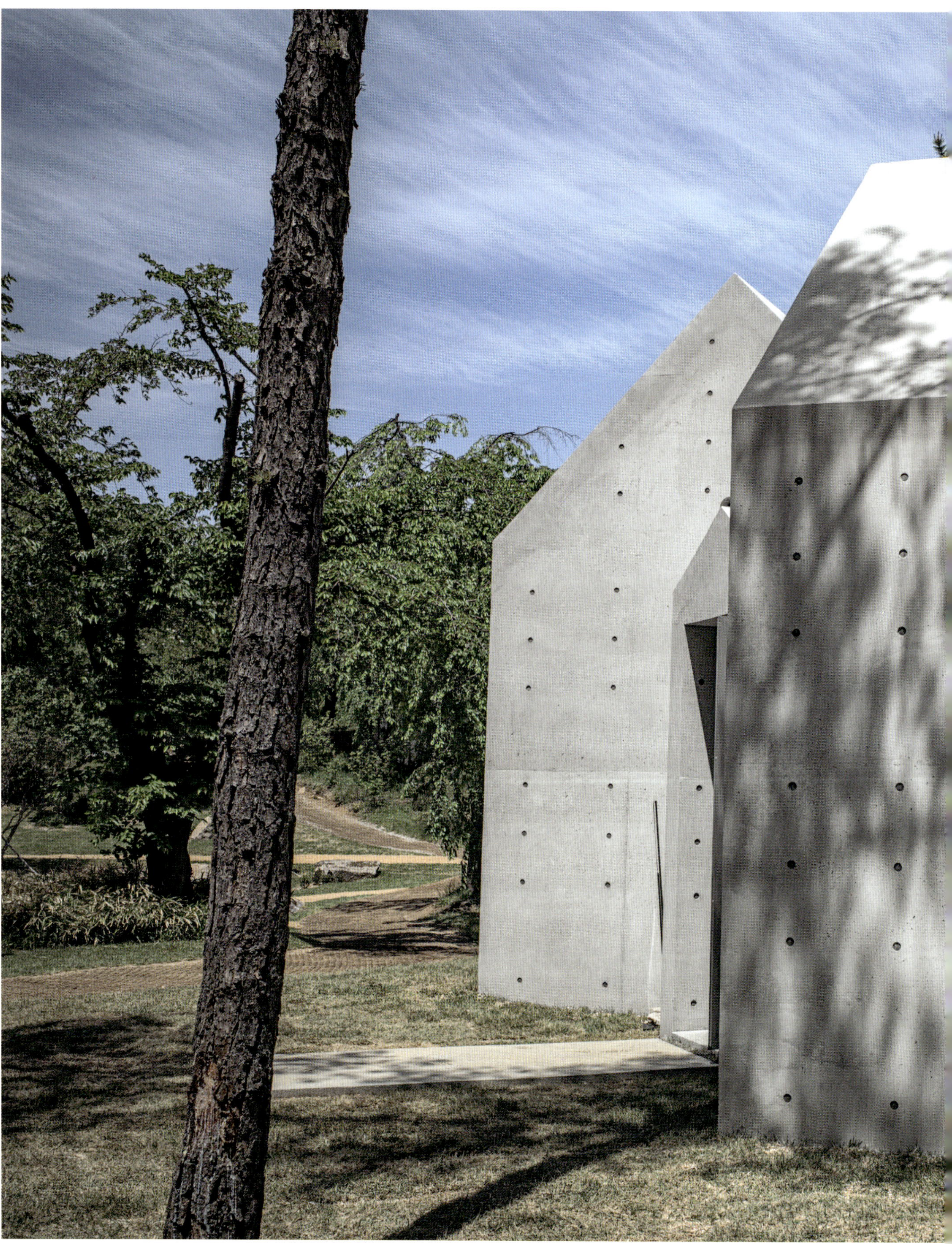

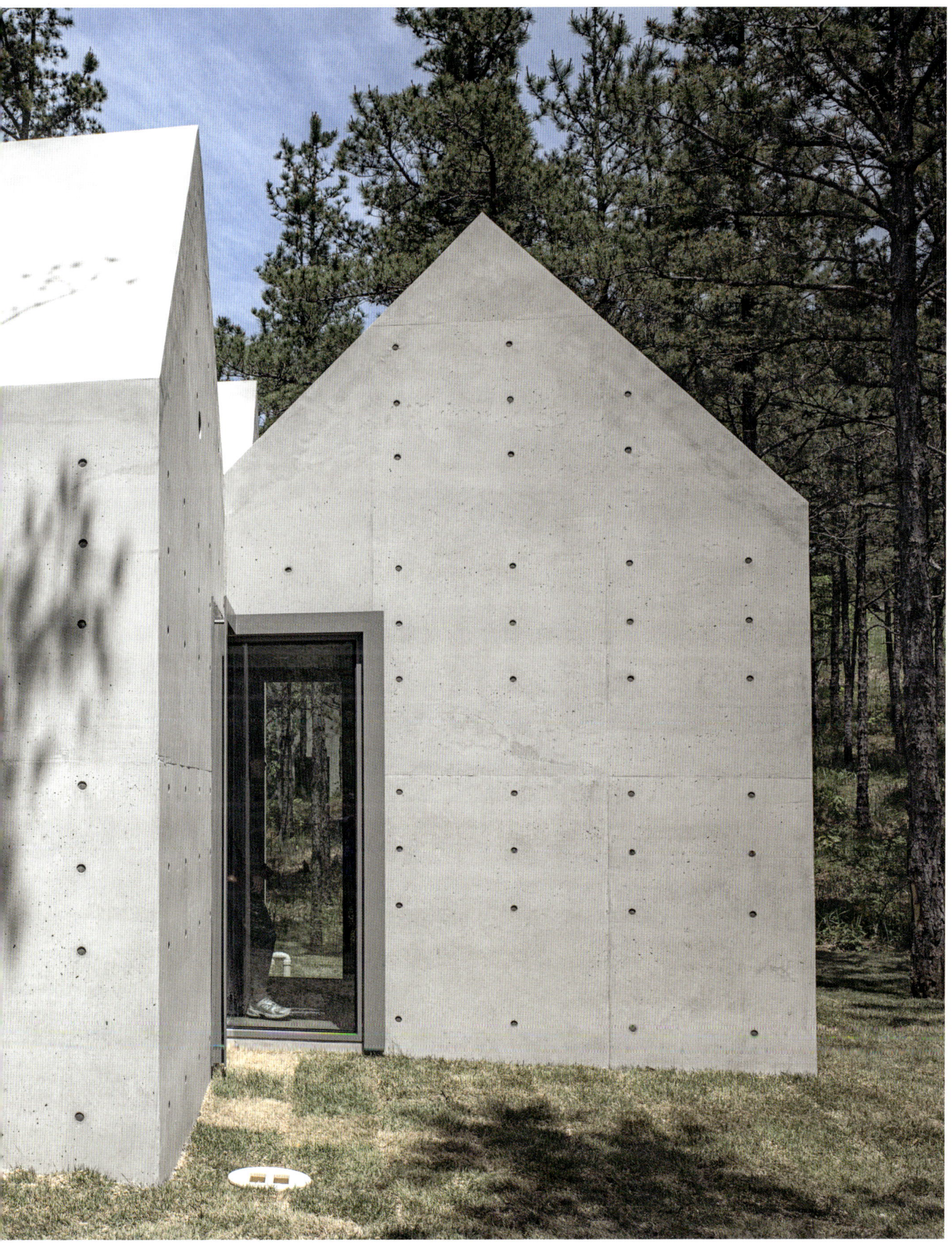

MIMESIS ART MUSEUM

PAJU BOOK CITY · Architects: Álvaro SIZA VIEIRA and KIM Jun-sung · Completed 2009

The Mimesis Art Museum is Brutalism seen through a painter's eye – all brushstroke curves in poured concrete, as though Le Corbusier swapped his T-square for a calligraphy brush. This is not Brutalism with clenched fists, but with a sculptor's poise – rigorous, yes, but sensual in its formal expression, like a concrete pirouette.

From the exterior, the museum reads like an architectural palimpsest: parts of it rectilinear and grounded, others swooping in unexpected arcs – a symphony of planar and organic geometries. The exposed concrete is superbly finished, but not fussy. It glows with a quiet precision, retaining the material honesty of Brutalism without the self-serious gloom. The building is monolithic, yet never oppressive; it broods with elegance.

But this is Brutalism for the aesthete. The museum refuses to shout; instead, it hums with the energy of containment, like a blank canvas just before the first stroke. Its spaces unfold slowly – long ramps, controlled light, tight apertures opening into sudden volumes. The plan is nearly choreographic: a concrete mise en scène where art is the protagonist but the architecture is the stage whisper that steals the show.

The name "Mimesis" suggests imitation – but Siza's concrete is no mimicry. Rather, it draws from memory, from classical restraint, from Korean naturalism and modernist rigour alike. Even the surrounding landscape is echoed in the building's form, with curves that feel like the wind's path traced in mass.

The Mimesis Museum makes a case for Brutalism as grace – where weight bends gently and permanence takes on poise. It's not just a gallery; it's a manifesto in material, a concrete brushstroke across the skyline that proves Brutalism doesn't always have to shout to be sublime.

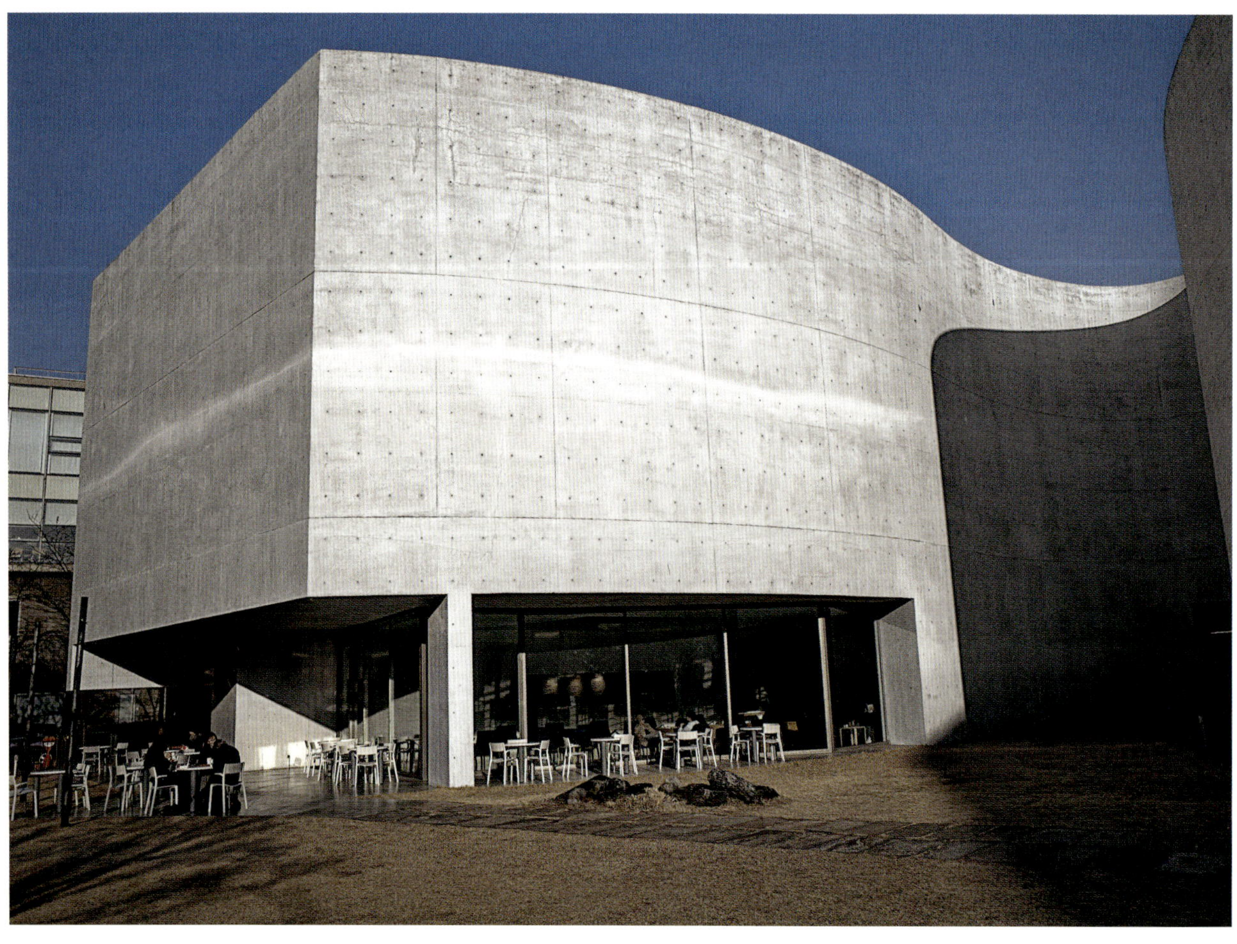

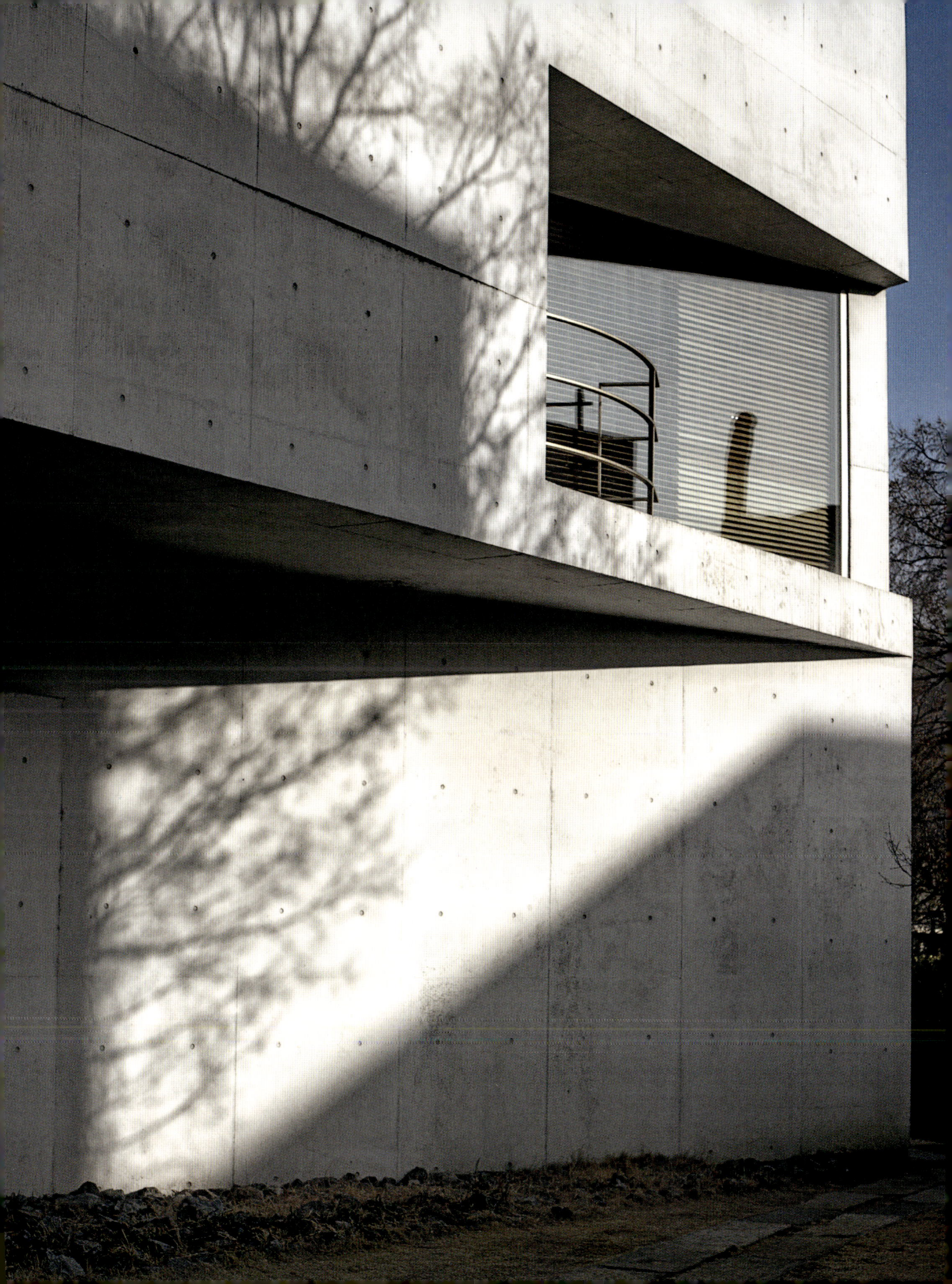

F1963 ART LIBRARY WATER GARDEN

BUSAN · Completed 1963 / Re-imagined 2016

Once home to the clatter of industry, the F1963 complex now whispers – through pages, light, and water. What began life as a wire factory in 1963 was sensitively reimagined in 2016 into a dynamic cultural destination.

At the heart of this contemplative campus lies the F1963 Art Library, a place where literary curiosity meets Brutalist zen. The concrete water garden outside steals the show – an elegantly raw expanse of poured planes, shallow pools, and mossy tactility that somehow evokes both Le Corbusier and a monastic retreat. It is sculpture by way of serenity: a reflecting space that reflects more than just the sky.

The geometry is minimal but never sterile. Slabs hover just above the waterline, inviting unhurried navigation, both physical and mental. Concrete ledges double as benches for reading, daydreaming, or dodging existential spirals after reading too much.

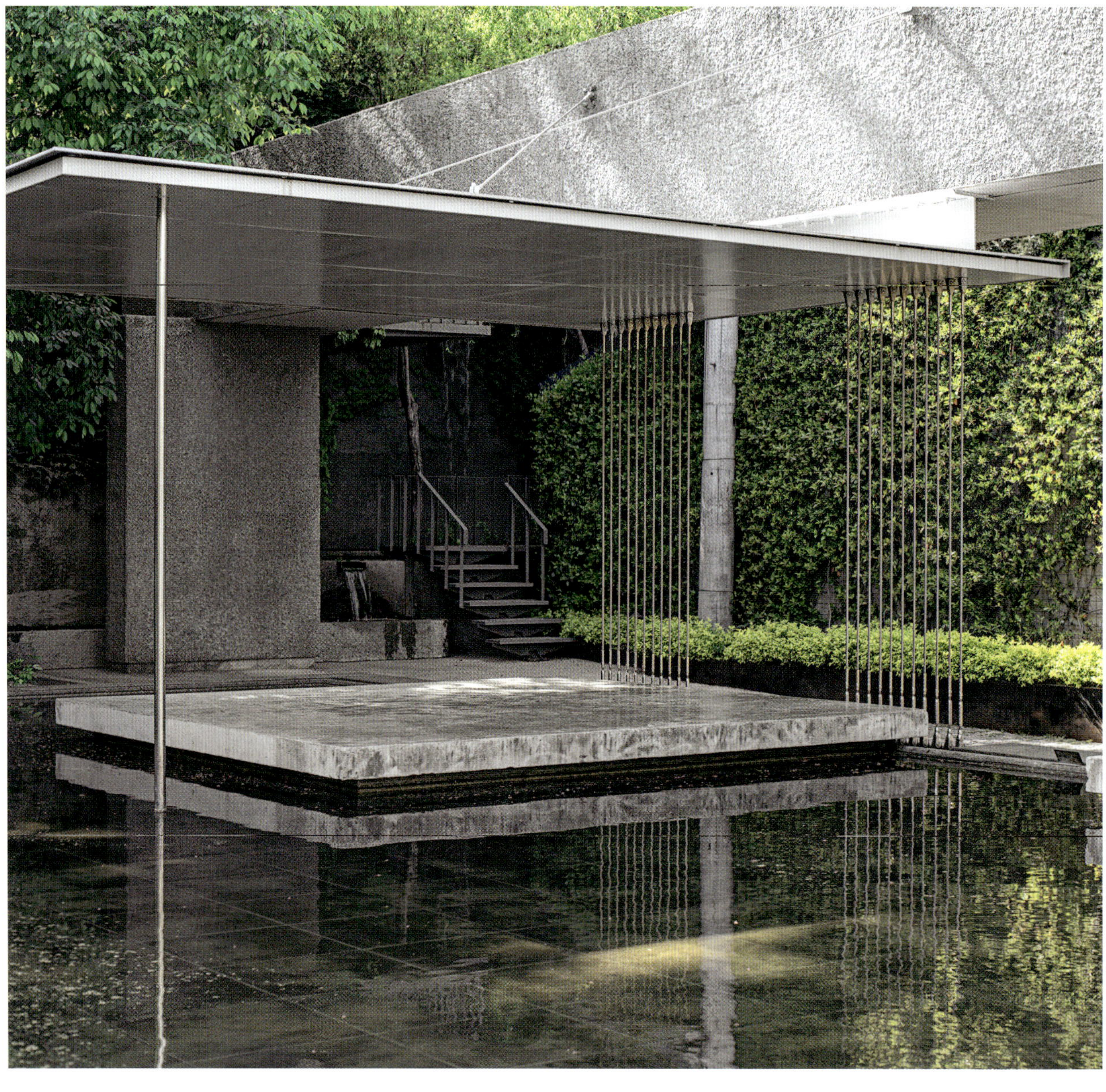

ASIA PUBLISHING CULTURE AND INFORMATION CENTER

PAJU BOOK CITY · Architect: KIM Byung-yoon · Completed 2004

This is a study in material eloquence – where weathering steel, concrete, and glass compose an architecture that feels both raw and refined. The oxidized steel clads the exterior like a well-aged book jacket, its shifting tones recording time and weather. Concrete provides the structural grammar – deliberate, weighty, and deeply rhythmic – while glass inserts offer punctuation marks of transparency, allowing light to read across its surfaces. Inside, timber shelving and flooring lend a quieter warmth, grounding the space in the tactile familiarity of the printed page. Together, these materials create a building that feels edited, not decorated: a precise balance between permanence and passage. Like a library without a cover, it opens onto the landscape, binding Paju's publishing dream into a durable, physical text – one written in steel, concrete, and silence.

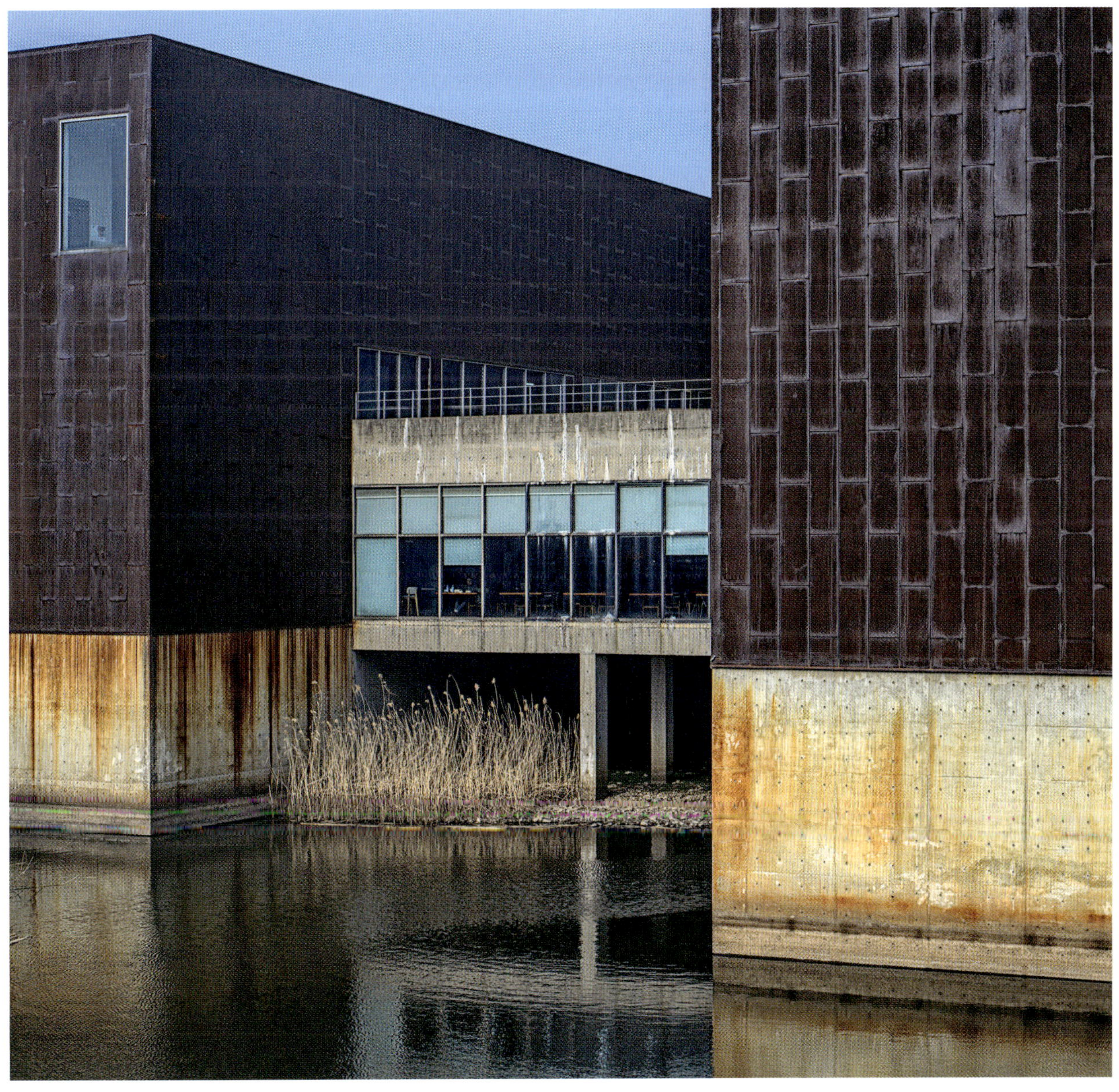

CHUNGHA BUILDING

SEOUL · Architect: MVRDV (remodelling) · Completed 1980s / Remodelled 2013

The Chungha Building in Seoul underwent a radical reinvention in 2013 by MVRDV, transforming a once-dated mid-century block on Apgujeong Street into a striking urban statement. Once derided as a "rotten tooth" in the Gangnam streetscape, it has been reborn as a sculptural, light-catching presence.

Intead of demolishing it, MVRDV treated the existing frame as an open canvas. They stripped away chaotic signage and wrapped the façade in curvaceous white frames, giving each level its own stage-like identity. The new skin shifts from tactile texture up close to smooth clarity from afar – a poetic riff on Seoul's obsession with surface and image.

Despite its tight dimensions, the redesign added a new top floor and generous terraces, bringing light and air into the vertical plan. The result turns commerce into street theatre: a Brutalist skeleton dressed for contemporary life, part glass billboard, part building, entirely reborn.

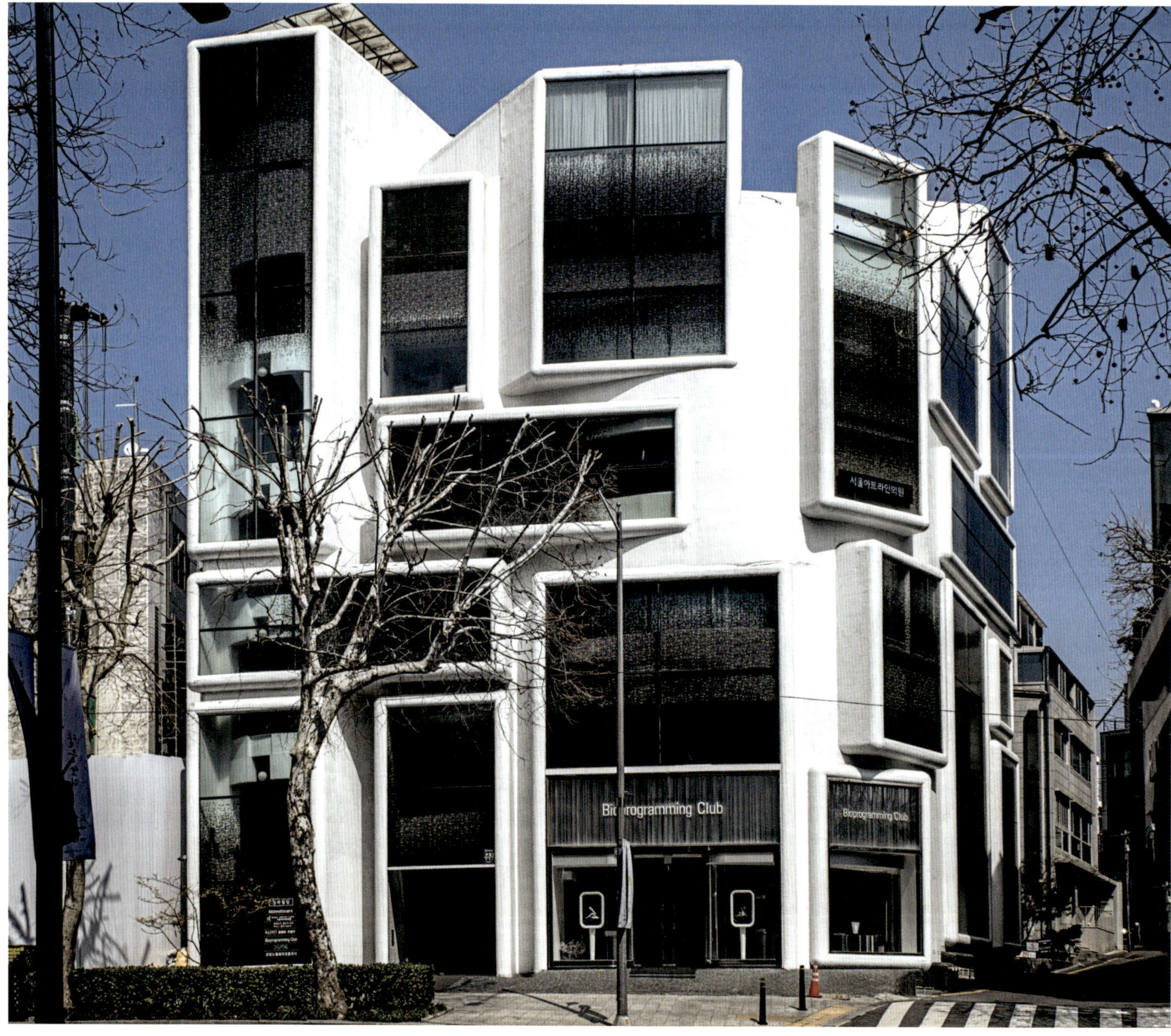

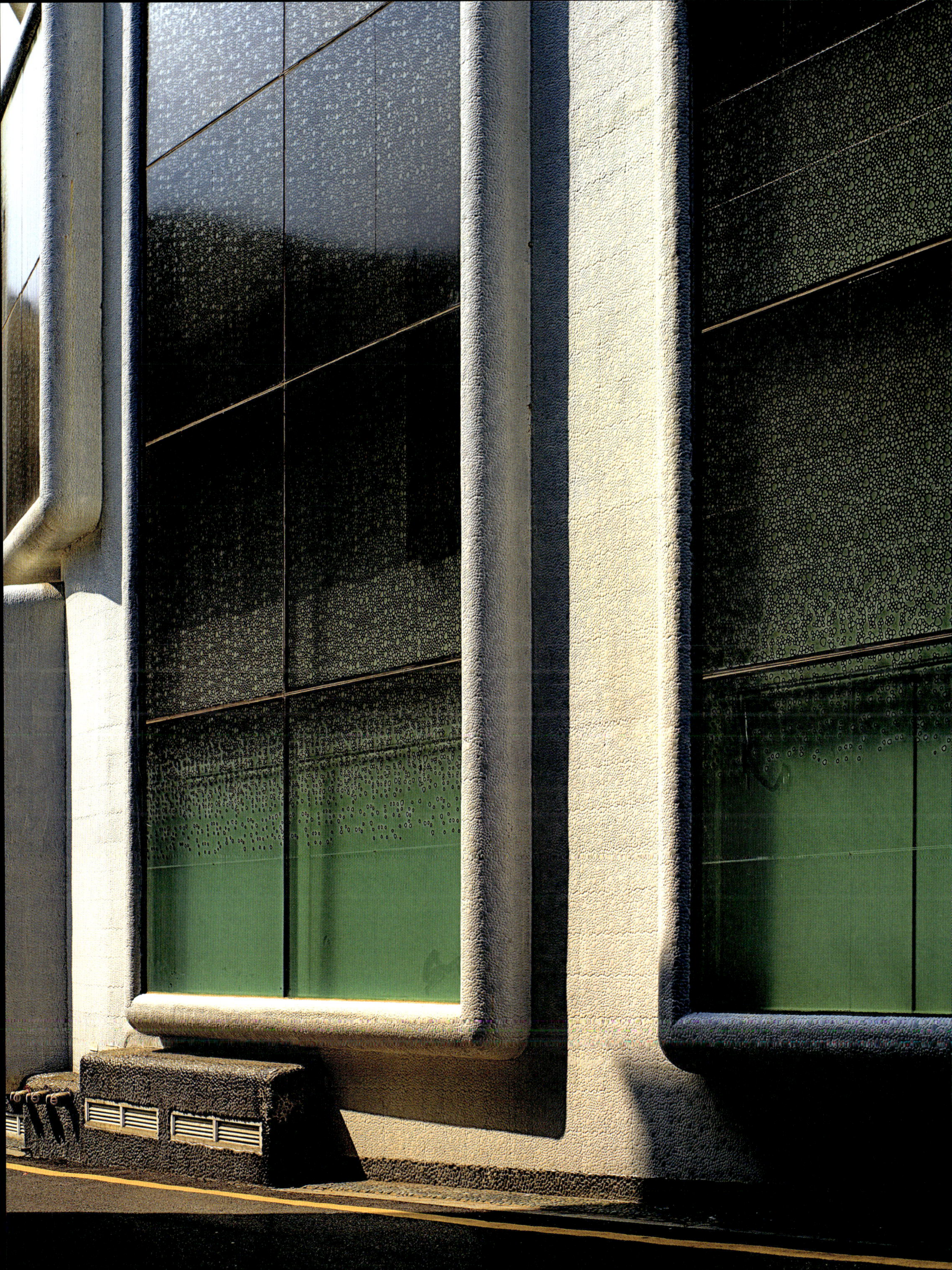

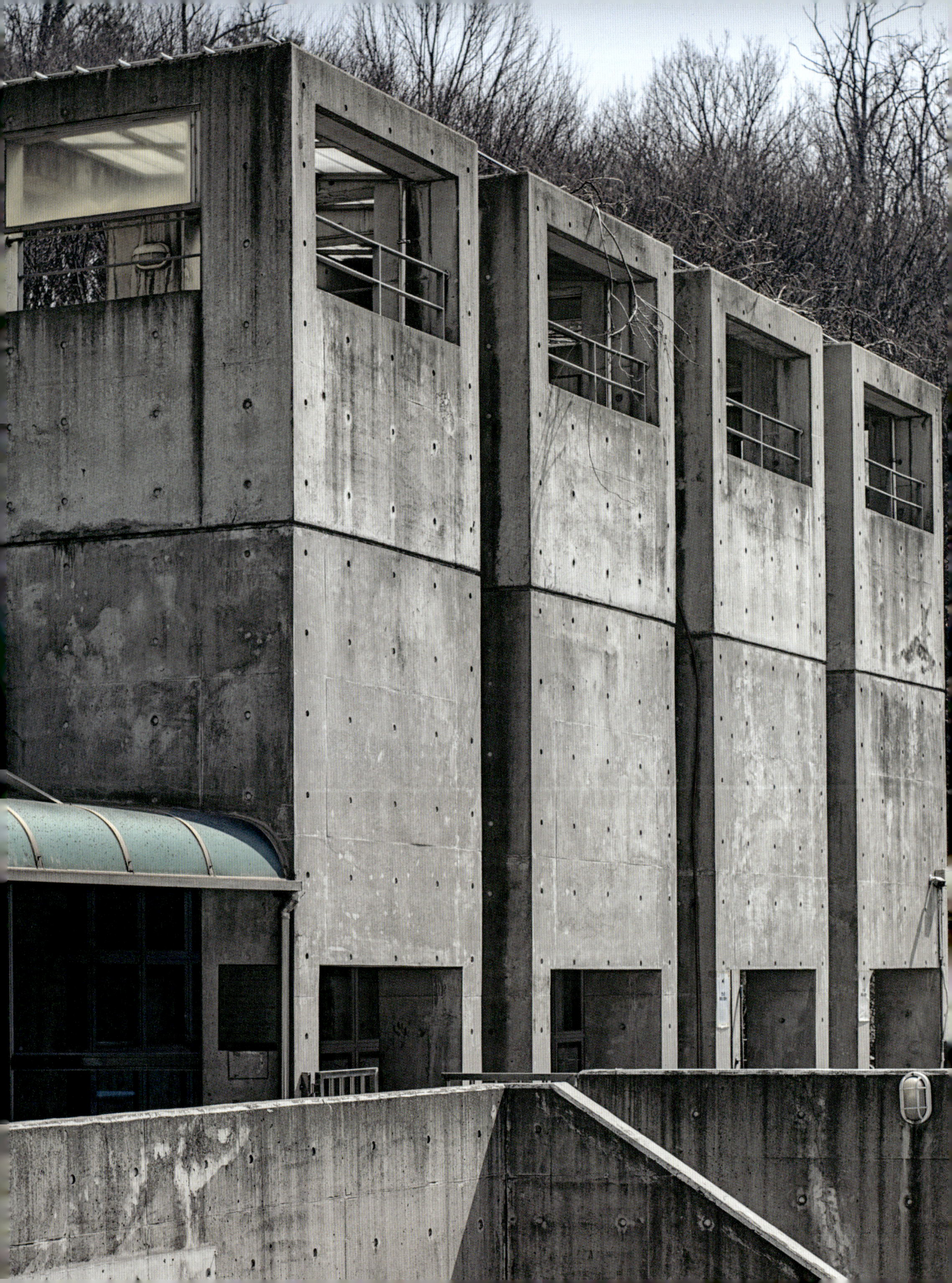

EUNPYEONG LIBRARY

SEOUL · Architect: KWAK Jae-hwan · Completed 2001

At the foot of Bukhansan's granite flanks, the Eunpyeong Public Library by Kwak Jae-hwan sits like a scholarly sentinel – a concrete bookmark lodged in the pages of Seoul's urban sprawl. Far from the hushed reverence of dusty bibliothèques, this is a library that shouts its presence in stacked slabs of rough-textured *béton brut*, as if declaring that knowledge, like architecture, should be public, weighty, and materially honest.

Its Brutalist credentials are robust and unmistakable: heavy cantilevers, monolithic massing, and a preference for expression over decoration. Yet the mood here isn't sombre; it's studious with a touch of swagger. The façade, rhythmically notched and layered, resembles an open folio – the concrete strata evoking both the geology of nearby mountains and the sediment of accumulated learning. It's as if the building itself is a fossilized archive, a literal volume of volumes.

Inside, light slices through apertures like insight breaking through dense prose. Reading rooms are quietly theatrical – spaces of contemplation framed by angular geometries and textural contrast. There's a spatial clarity here that feels editorial: no fluff, no footnotes. Just pure linear intent.

Wittily, the building flips the old notion of libraries as "temples of knowledge" – this one feels more like a fortress of thought. A place where ideas bunker down and books stand their ground. And in a society that is increasingly digital and dematerialized, this concrete structure reminds us: information still needs walls, weight, and weathering.

Kwak's design manages to be both cerebral and civic – a library you don't tiptoe into, but stride towards like a manifesto. It is Brutalism as bibliography, cast in the concrete certainty that literacy, like architecture, is a form of resistance – and this building, in all its textured gravity, is ready for a very long read.

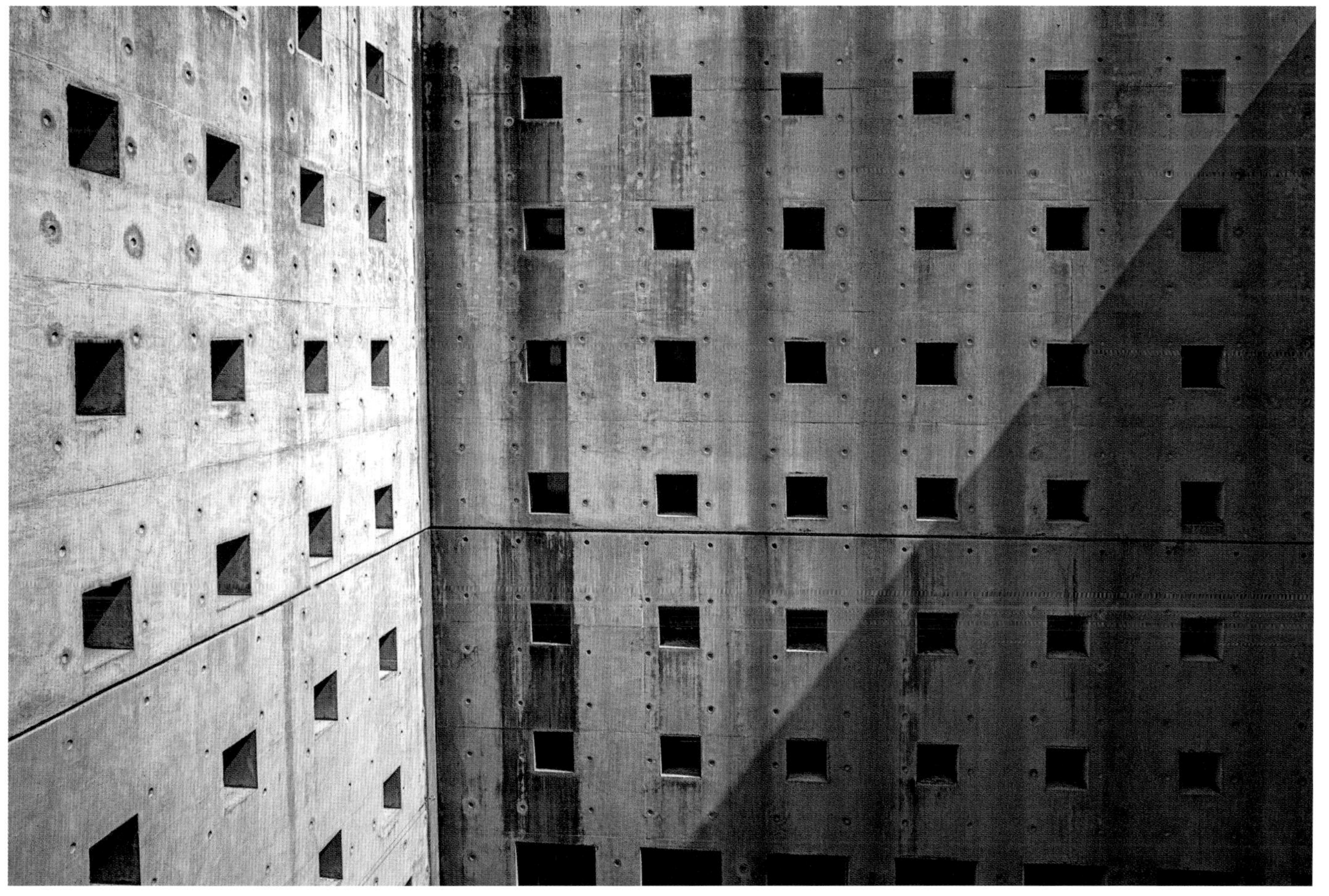

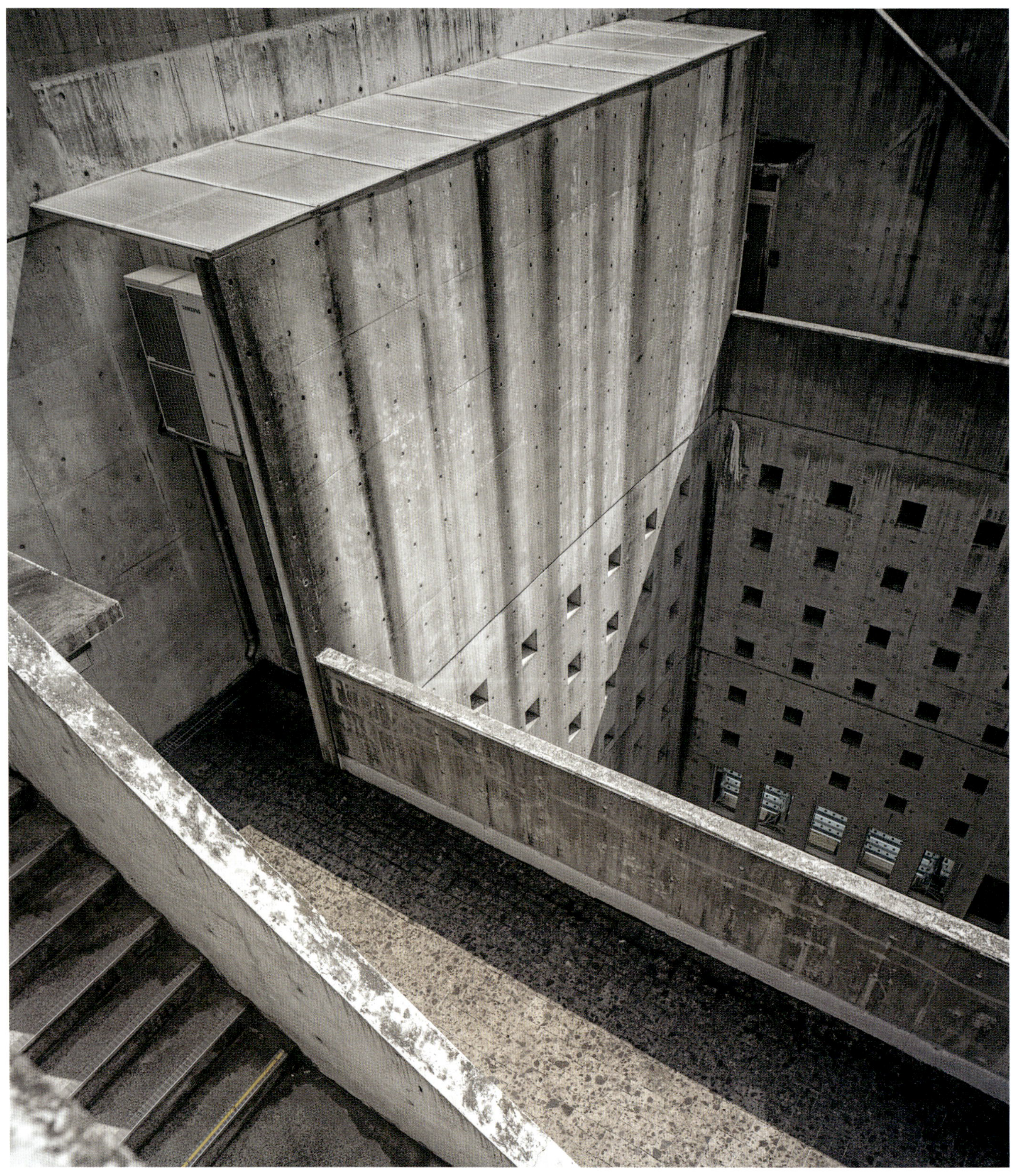

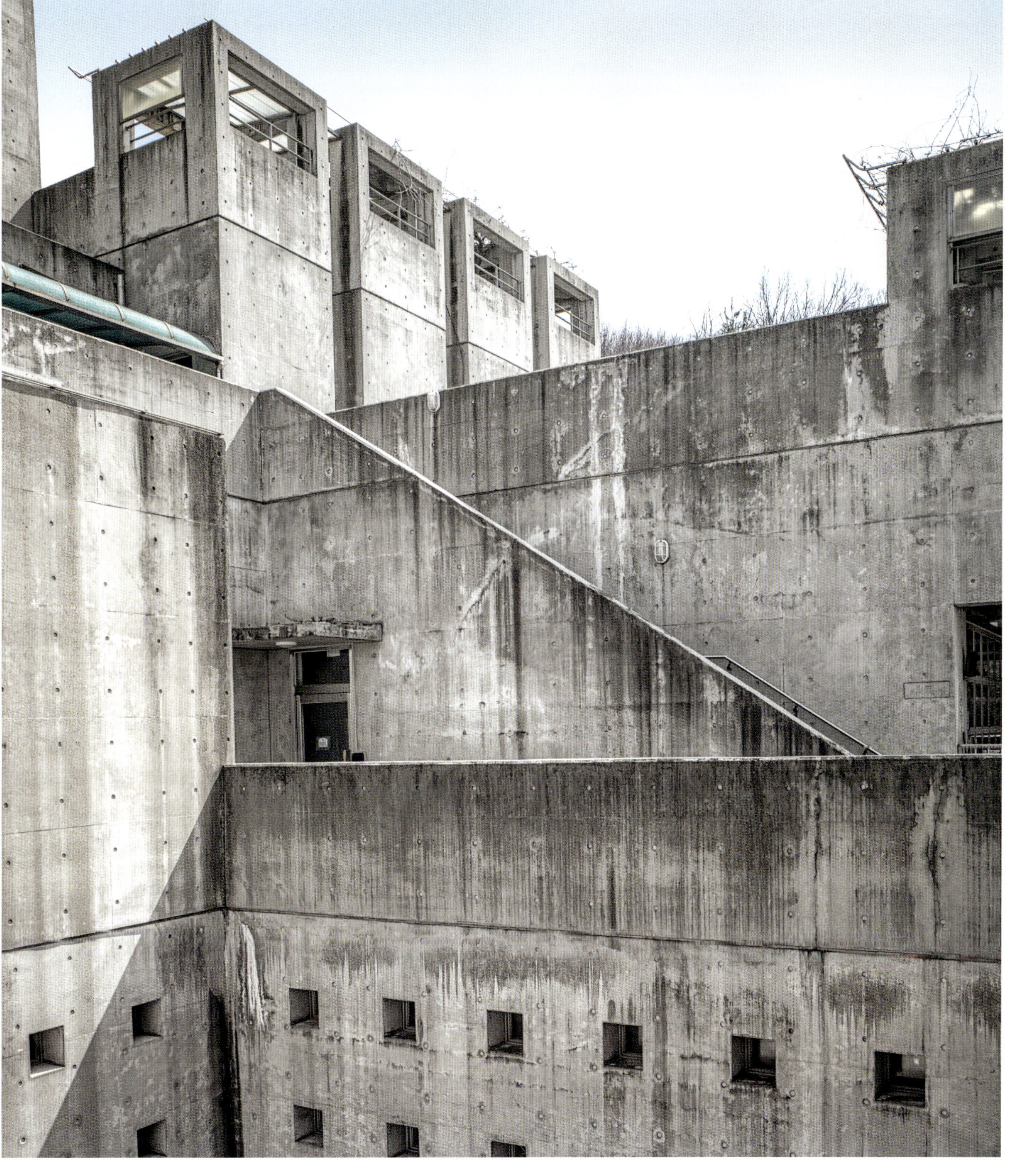

SOYOHEON & YOYO BINBIN (ART PAVILION)

SAYUWON · Architects: Álvaro SIZA VIEIRA and Carlos CASTANHEIRA · Completed 2017

In a landscape where the eaves of the *hanok* once brushed the forest canopy, Soyoheon proposes an entirely new kind of conversation between nature and structure. Set on a key battle site of the Korean War within the Sayuwon Arboretum in Gunwi, this austere pavilion – commissioned by Seung H-Sang – stands less as a building than as an architectural incision in the landscape.

Formed wholly from exposed concrete, Soyoheon carries the tactile honesty of mid-century modernism yet resonates with an unmistakably Korean sensibility. Its name, roughly meaning "a place for quiet reflection", conceals the severity of its form. The Y-shaped plan, shared with its companion structure Yoyo Binbin, slices through the wooded slope like a tectonic hinge. Towering slabs recall the defensive walls of Korea's ancient fortresses – not in imitation, but in spirit, embodying endurance and solitude.

Soyoheon's origins lie in an unrealized ambition: it was once intended to house Pablo Picasso's *Guernica*. That unfulfilled purpose still seems to echo through the material itself. The concrete is deeply expressive – its board-marked grain, streaks, and blemishes exposing every act of its making. This is not Brutalism as aesthetic posture but as philosophical truth: concrete revealing, not concealing.

Against this rawness, the surrounding forest asserts its quiet resistance. Pines edge close to its planes, creating a tension between organic growth and geometric will. Apertures and controlled sightlines recall the framed perspectives of traditional Korean gardens – moments of focus within vastness.

Soyoheon and Yoyo Binbin together form a duet of restraint and presence. They do not seduce with warmth but compel through stillness, demanding contemplation. If the *hanok* once murmured in timber tones, here concrete articulates the Korean spirit anew – measured, stoic, and utterly contemporary.

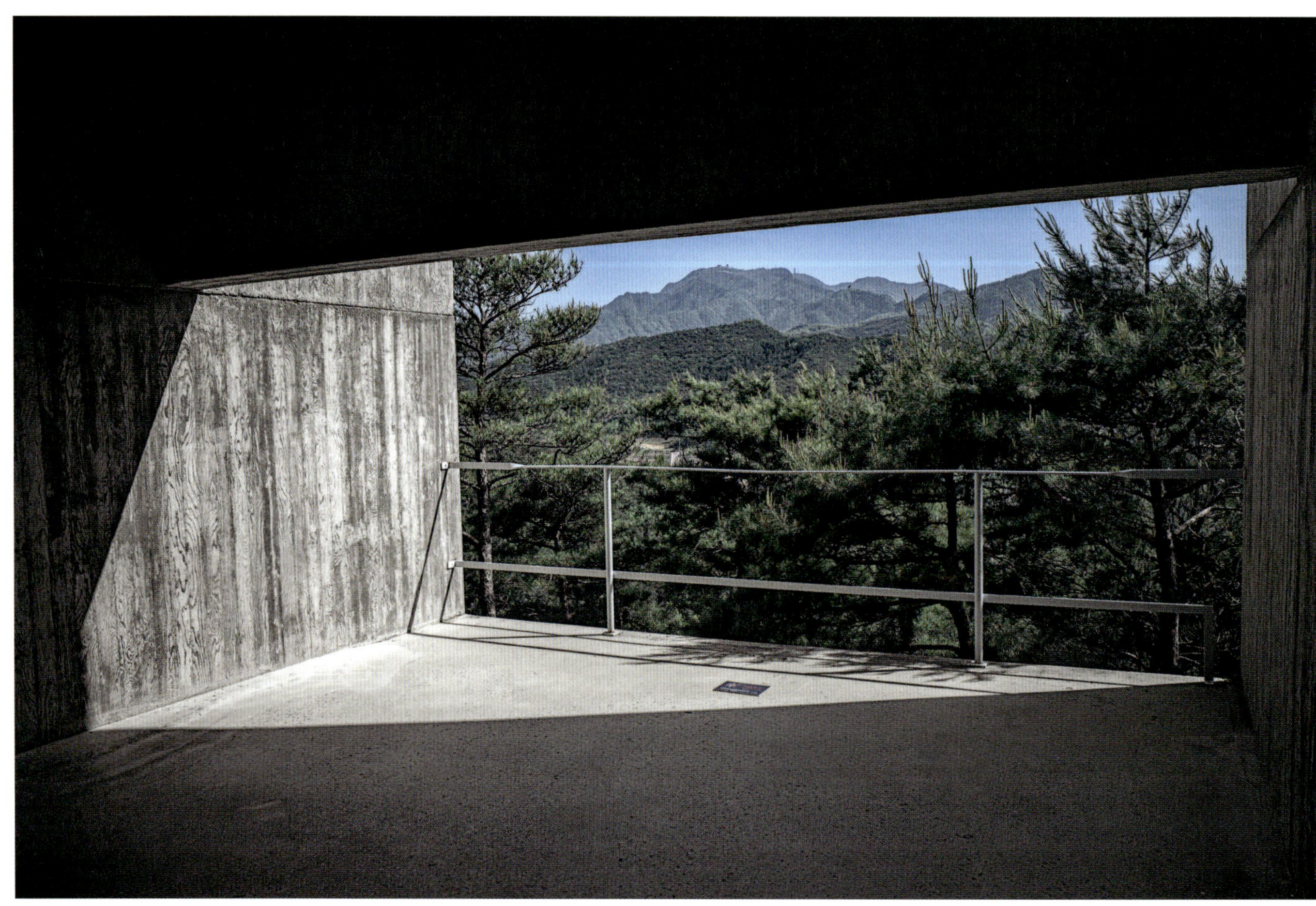

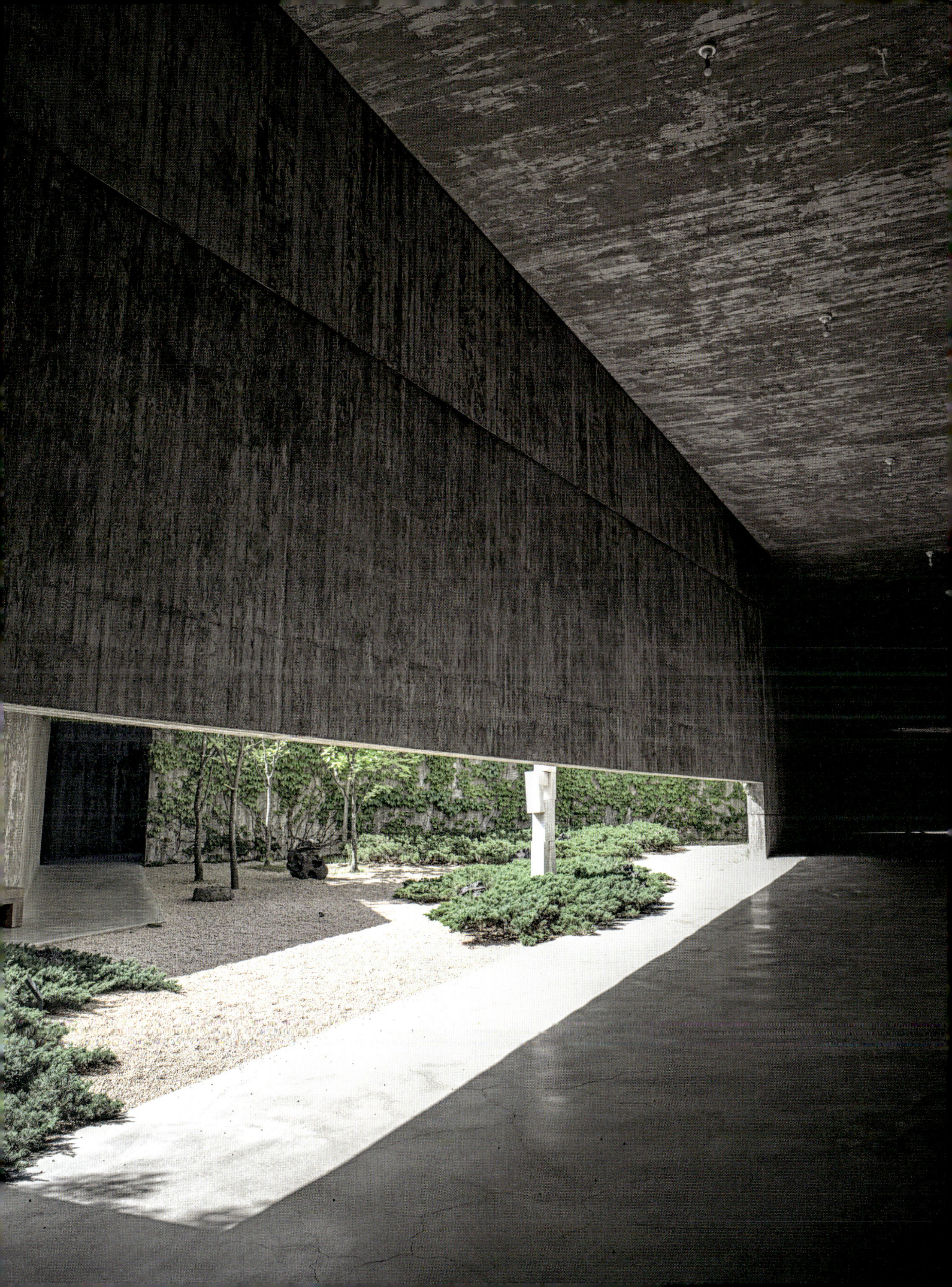

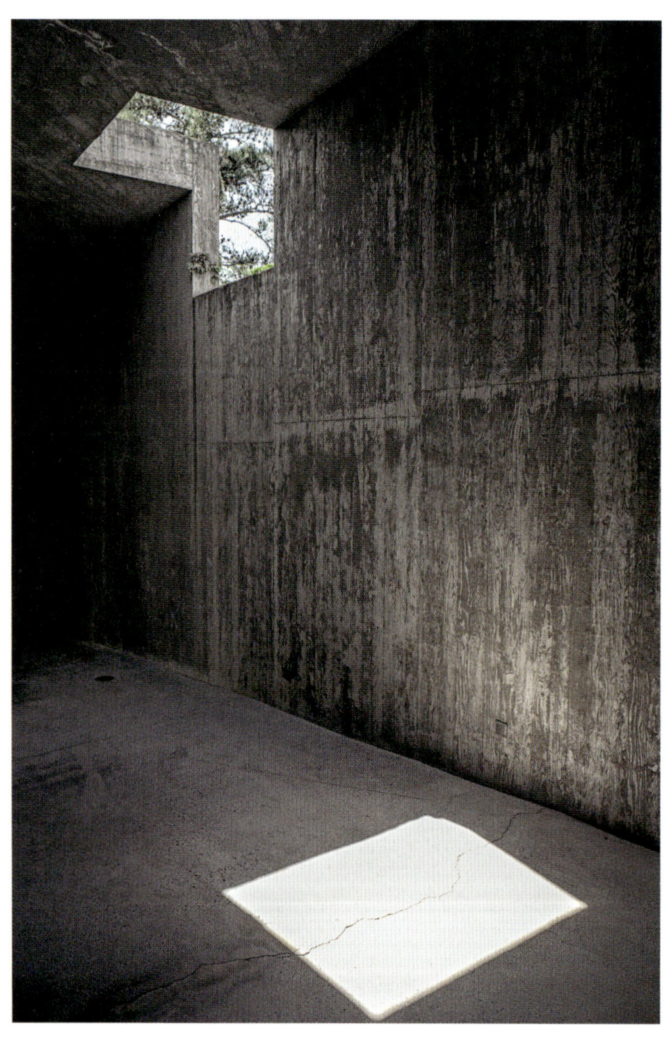

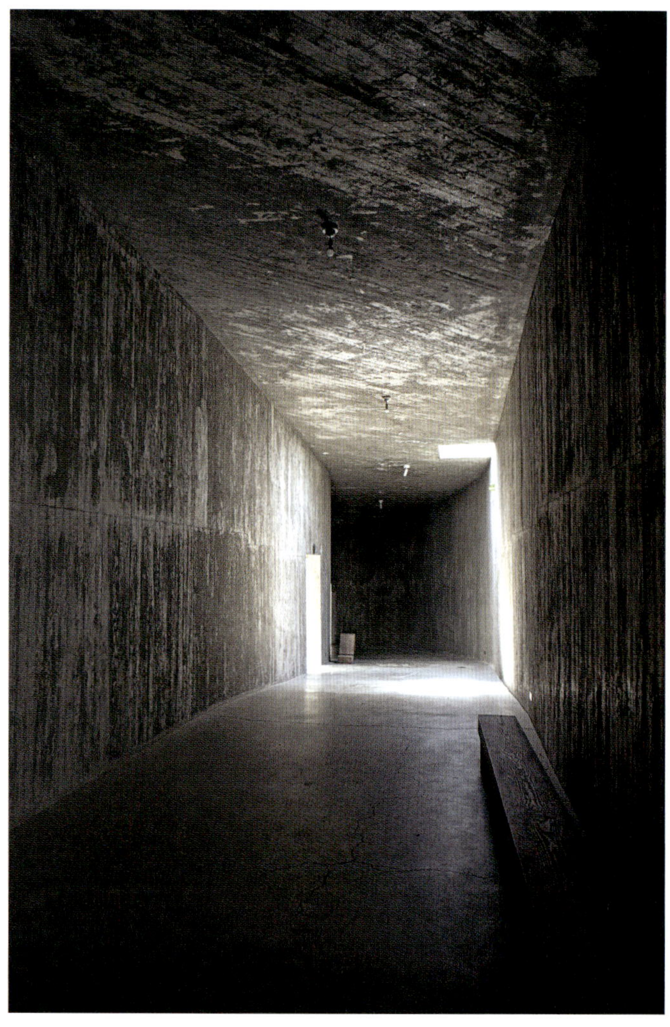

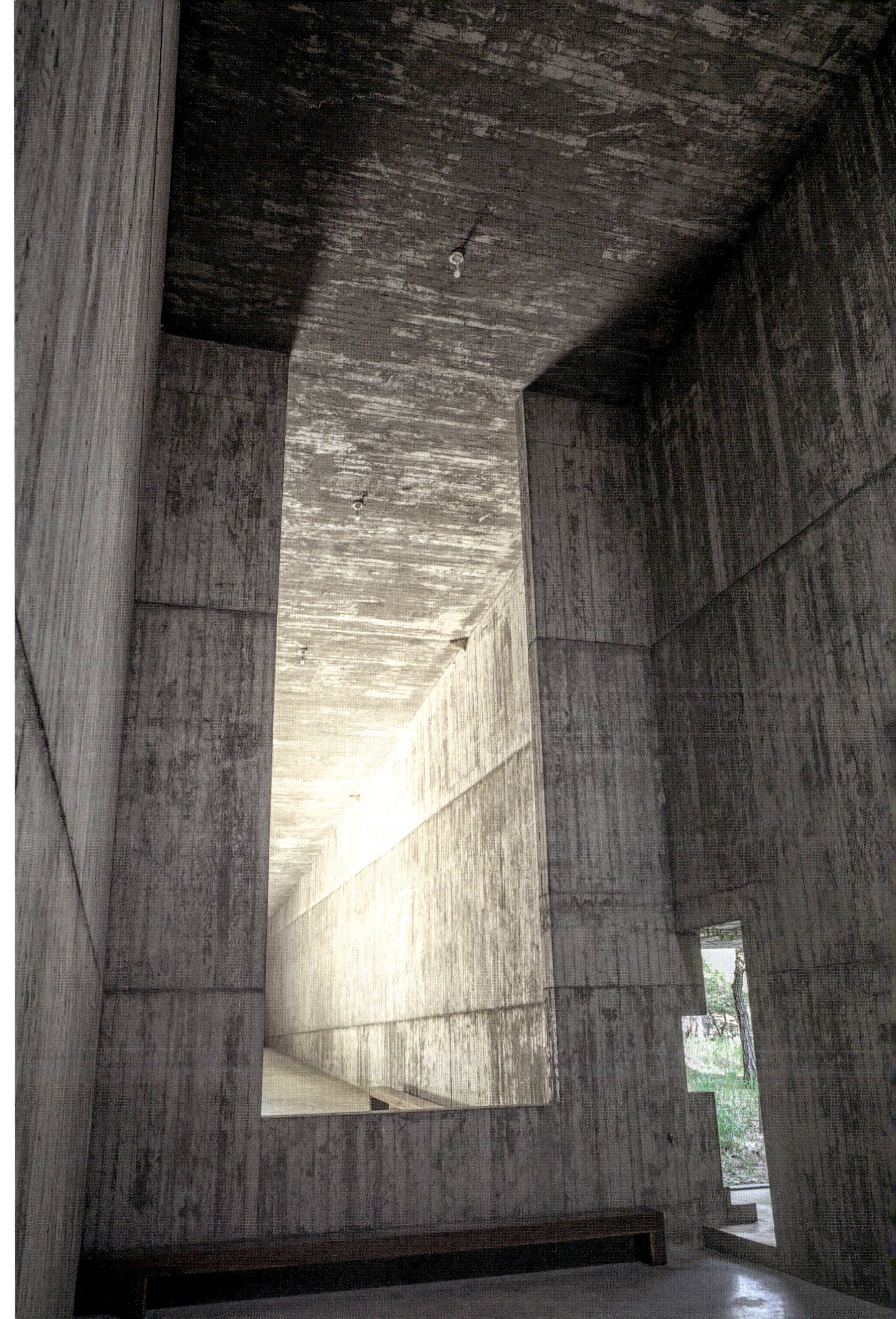

SUNGNYEMUN / NAMDAEMUN (SOUTH GREAT GATE)

SEOUL – Originally constructed 1398 / Reconstructed 1447 / Restored 2013

Architecturally, Sungnyemun represents classic Joseon-era wooden pavilion design, elevated atop a robust granite base. The intricate eaves, bracket systems (*gongpo*), and painted *dancheong* motifs embody Confucian ideals of harmony, order, and dignity. Its curved roof and monumental arched stone gate once formed the symbolic southern entry to the capital.

By day or night, it remains a deeply iconic structure – Seoul's literal and cultural threshold between past and present. Yet beyond its historic majesty lies a subtle continuity that helps explain why modern movements such as Brutalism have found an unusually warm reception in Korea. Traditional Korean architecture has long celebrated structural honesty – an admiration for exposed material, rhythmic geometry, and elemental balance. The raw timber frames and granite foundations of Joseon gates, in their candour and restraint, share an ancestral logic with the board-formed concrete and geometry of the twentieth century. Both speak of permanence, of architecture as moral weight.

In contemporary Seoul, Brutalism's revival is no nostalgic gesture; it is a negotiation with identity. The city's new generation of architects and citizens alike see in its concrete heft not austerity, but integrity – a tactile palimpsest of Korea's architectural DNA. As glass towers and LED façades now define the skyline, this reverence for concrete has acquired a new relevance. It reflects a yearning to root the hyper-modern within something enduring, to reconcile algorithmic cities with ancestral craft.

This synthesis of old and new – of granite thresholds and digital skylines – echoes a distinctly cyberpunk sensibility: layered timelines, where past and future coexist in the same streetlight's glow. In Seoul, a gate like Sungnyemun does not simply mark an entrance; it anchors a civilization that continues to rebuild, reimagine, and reassert itself – one concrete form and one illuminated eave at a time.

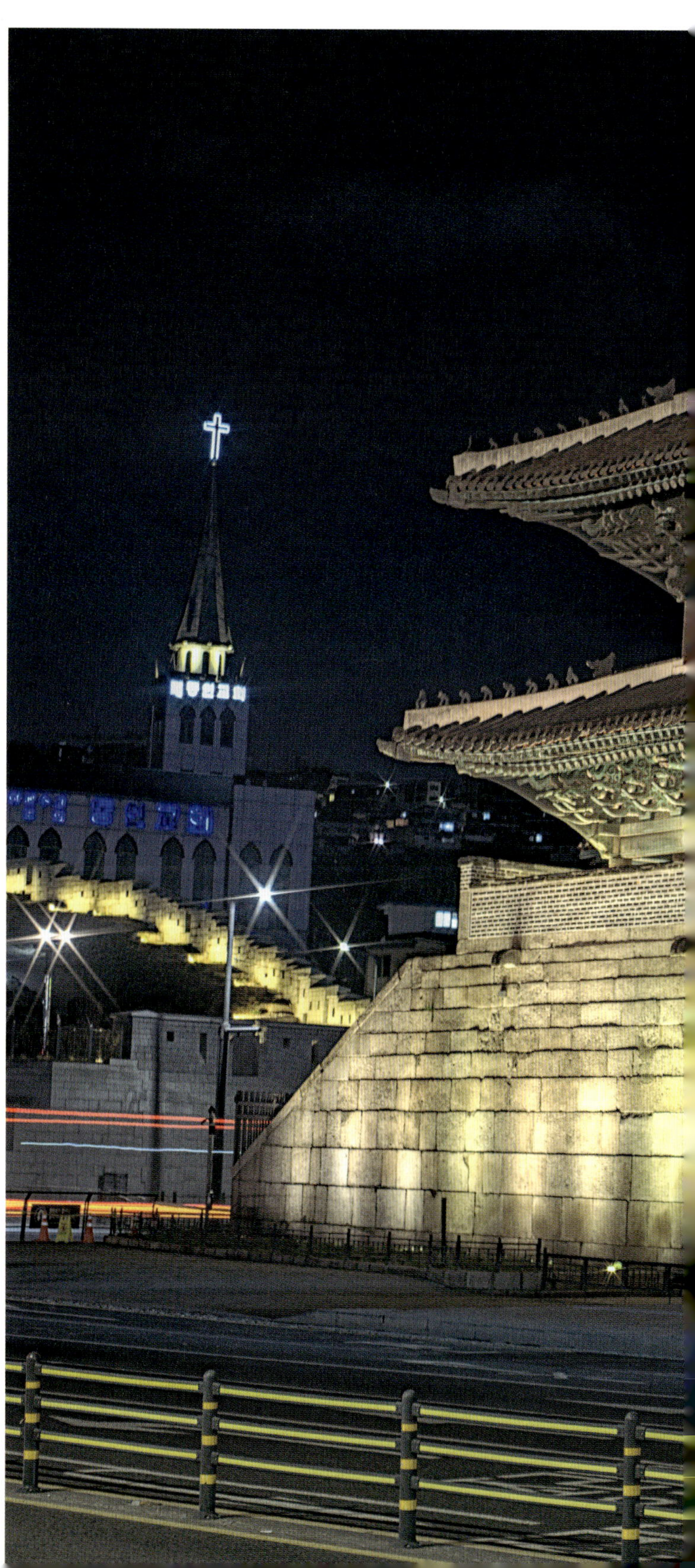

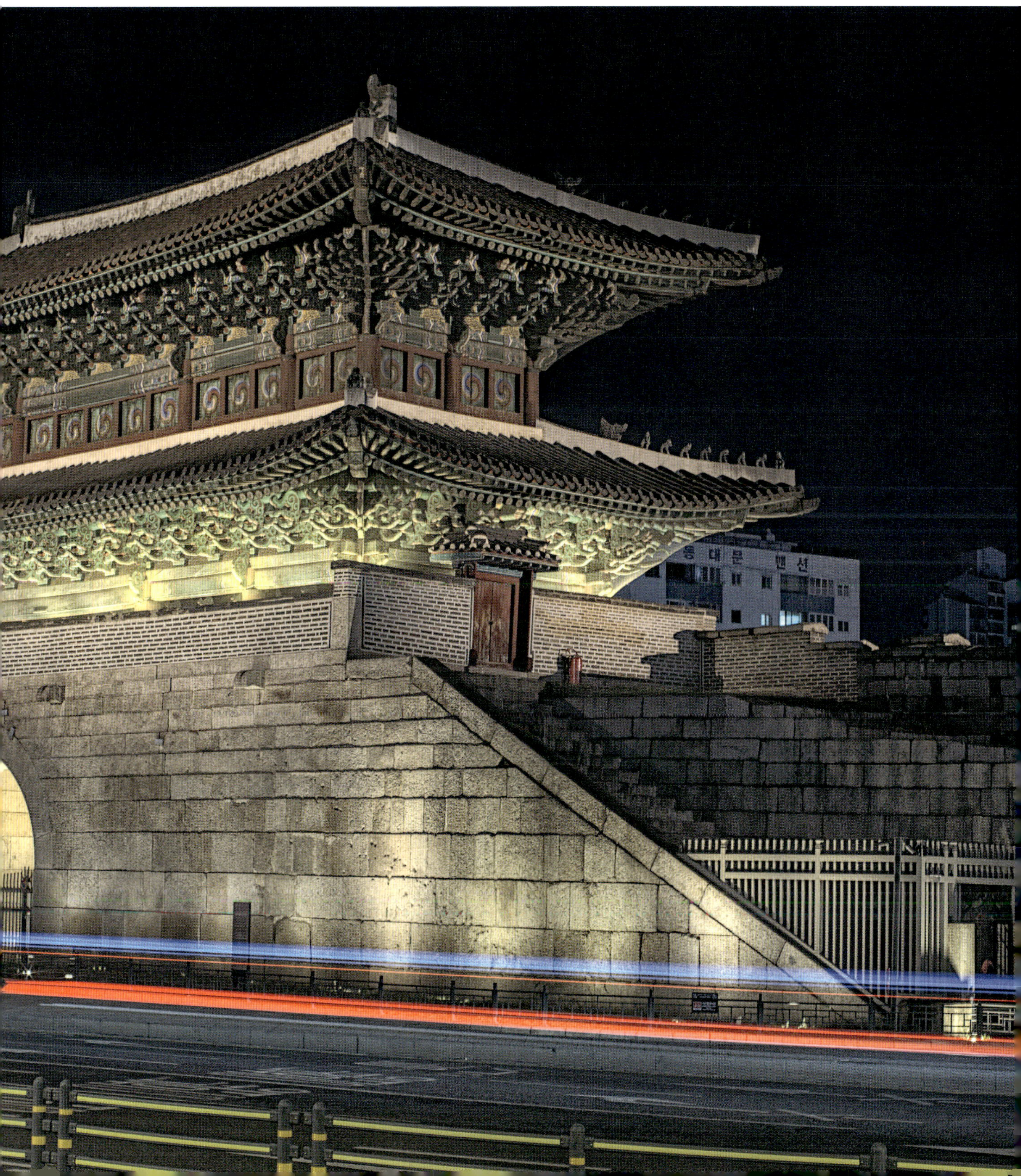
대문 맨션

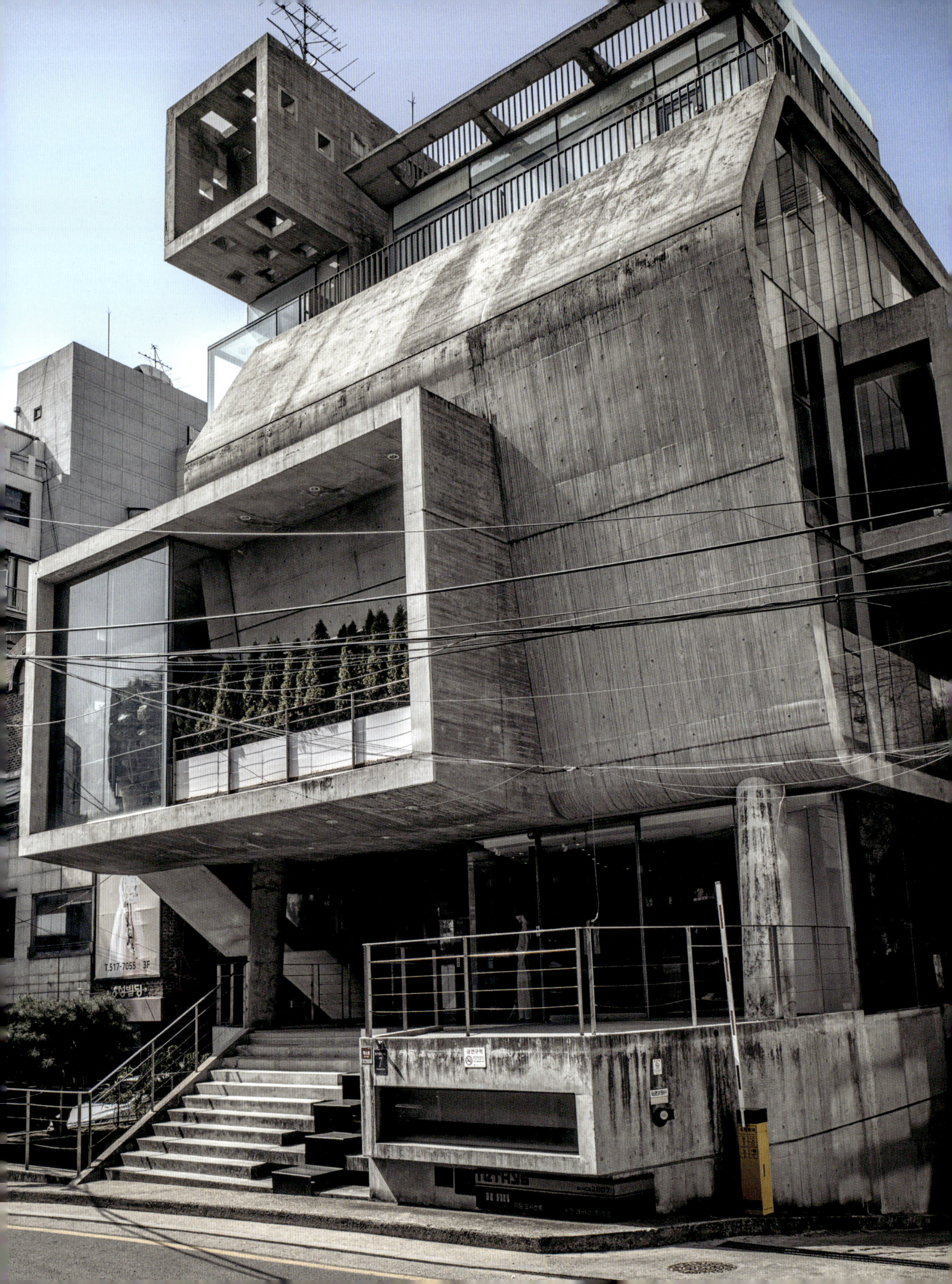
T.517-7055 3F

TETHYS

SEOUL · Architect: KWAK Hee-soo · Completed 2007

At once enigmatic and expressive, Tethys rises from Seoul's Gangnam district like a Brutalist enigma dropped into the folds of haute couture. This seven-storey hybrid of concrete and glass is less goddess-of-the-sea, more shape-shifting robot caught mid-transformation – part gallery, part office, part architectural interrogation of the city itself.

Its function is plural, and so is its form. No two elevations are alike: the front sports a bold, oversized square aperture; the flanks bristle with scattered portholes; the rear is a geometric remix. Like the district it inhabits – a dense weave of luxury storefronts and meandering backstreets – the building never settles on a single identity. It performs multiplicity, not symmetry.

A key flourish is the ground-floor piloti space: raised on slender columns, it floats above the tight plot with all the confidence of a structure that knows breathing room is a luxury in Gangnam. It's a clever inversion – a Brutalist bunker with a public pulse – inviting foot traffic, light, and the ambient energy of the street to flow beneath and through it.

Above, concrete asserts itself with material candour, interrupted by irregular glass voids that scatter daylight across interior surfaces like digital noise. These are not windows so much as code fragments, letting in just enough light to animate the mass while maintaining a fortress-like opacity.

Kwak described the building as an architectural response to "confusion and incongruity" – and it wears that tension beautifully. This is Brutalism not as dogma, but as urban dialect, speaking in mismatched façades and unexpected voids. A building as jarring, layered, and compelling as the Cheongam district itself – and one that earned it a Seoul Architecture Award, no less.

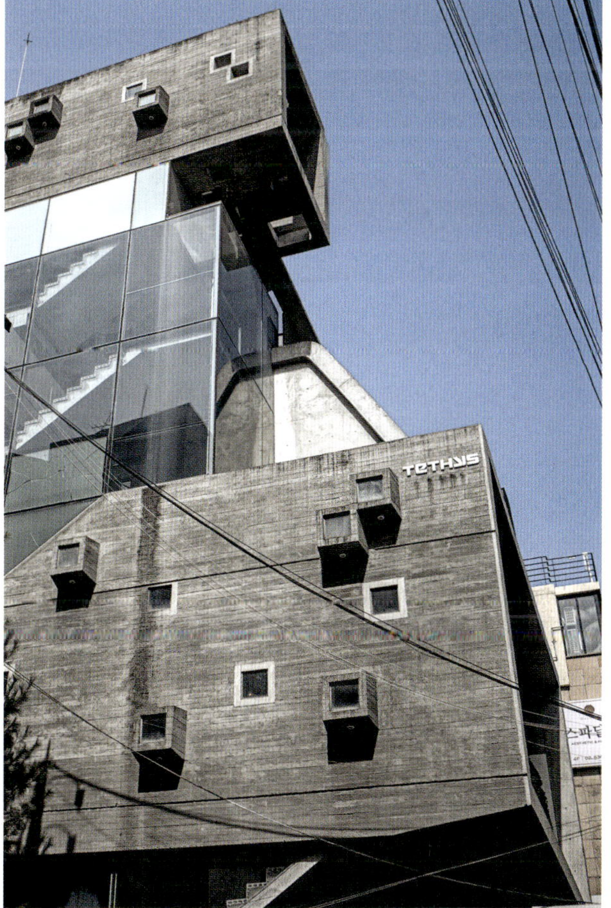

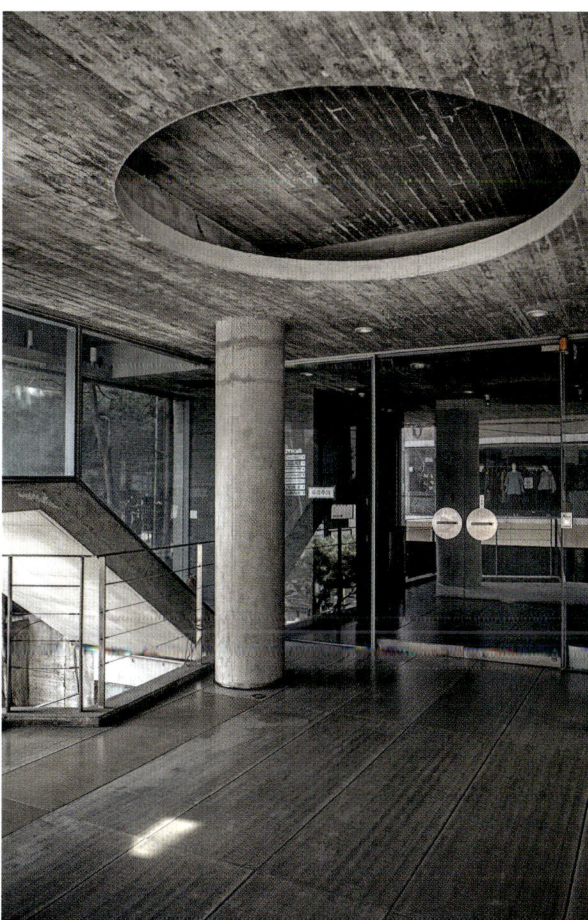

HOUSE OF OPEN BOOKS

PAJU BOOK CITY · Architect: Himma Studio · Completed 2005

Where publishing houses line the streets like well-thumbed volumes, the House of Open Books is one of Paju Book City's most sculptural tomes. Designed by Himma Studio, the building is a concrete meditation on language, translation, and the layered act of reading itself. Its folded planes and slanted lines conjure the image of an open book mid-turn – caught between comprehension and possibility.

The structure comprises two elongated "bars" set parallel like linguistic threads – languages running side by side, converging in intent yet never quite meeting. Between them, space becomes syntax: interstitial voids, slanted walls, and ramped circulation form the grammar through which movement reads as meaning. From the Han River to Simhak Mountain, the building's orientation and sectional play create a narrative of continuity, a sentence that bends but never breaks.

Externally, the board-formed concrete – striated, weathered, and exact – serves as both façade and metaphor, its grain recalling the pages of a heavy-bound text. Sunlight rakes across the surface like marginalia, drawing attention to detail only visible upon close reading. The building's folded envelope wraps its contents as a cover would protect a story, hinting at the depth within while maintaining a solemn restraint.

Inside, ramps replace conventional stairs, creating a gentle rhythm of ascent and descent – a spatial editing that feels less like circulation and more like interpretation. It is a building designed not for speed, but for slow comprehension, where architectural language mirrors the act of reading, translating, and rereading.

A concrete novel in spatial form, the House of Open Books transforms architectural mass into metaphor, reminding visitors that great buildings – like great literature – are not meant to be skimmed, but savoured.

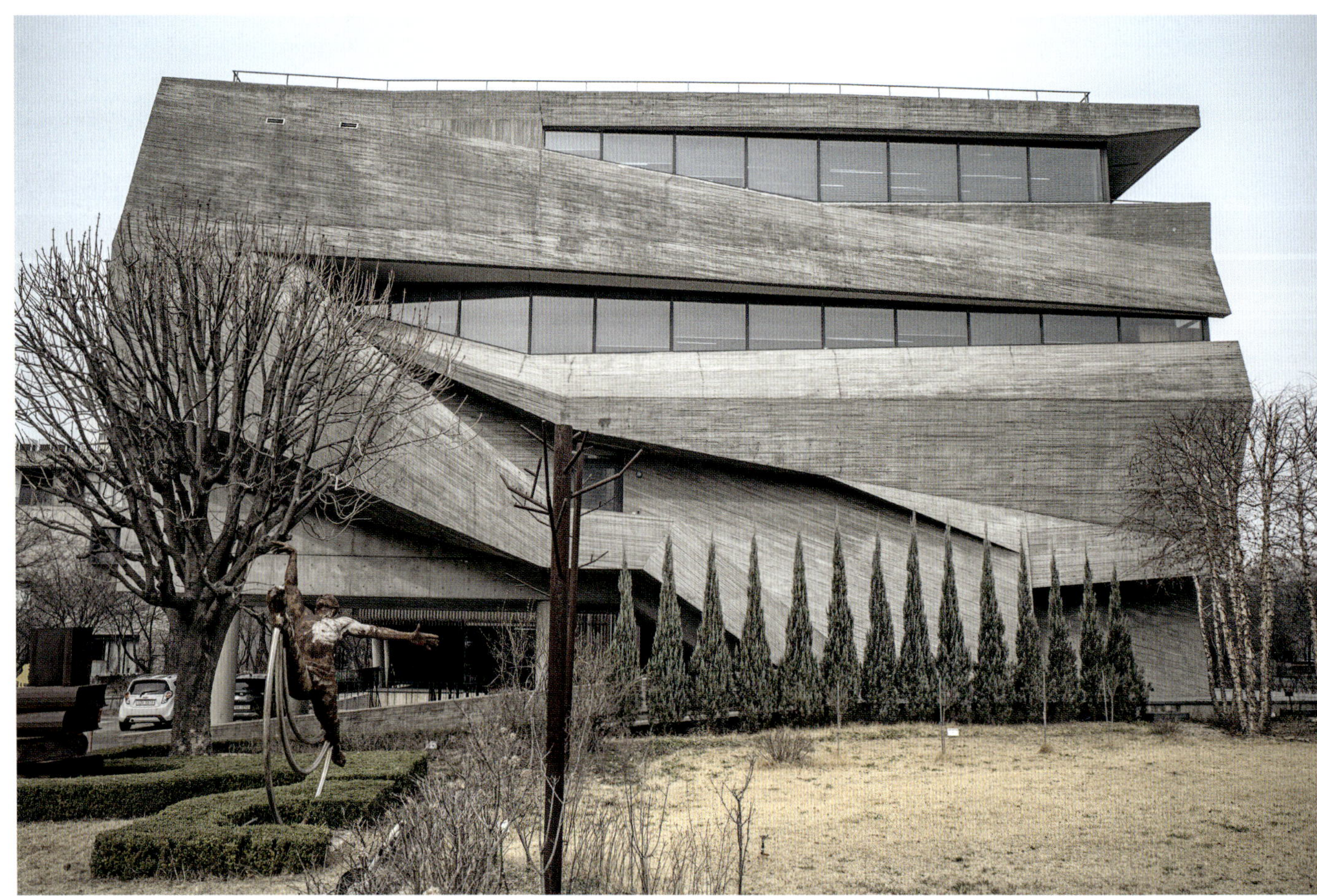

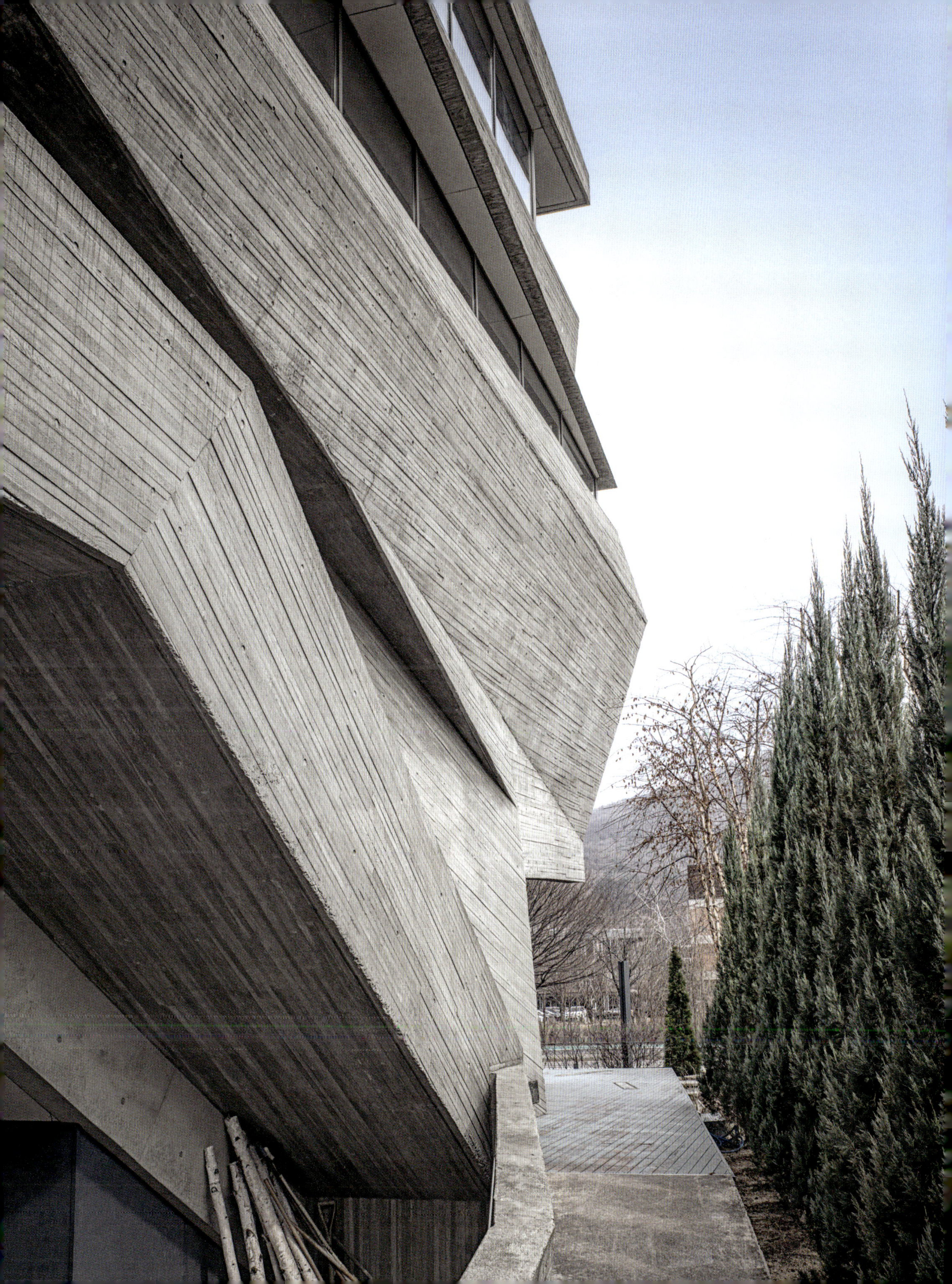

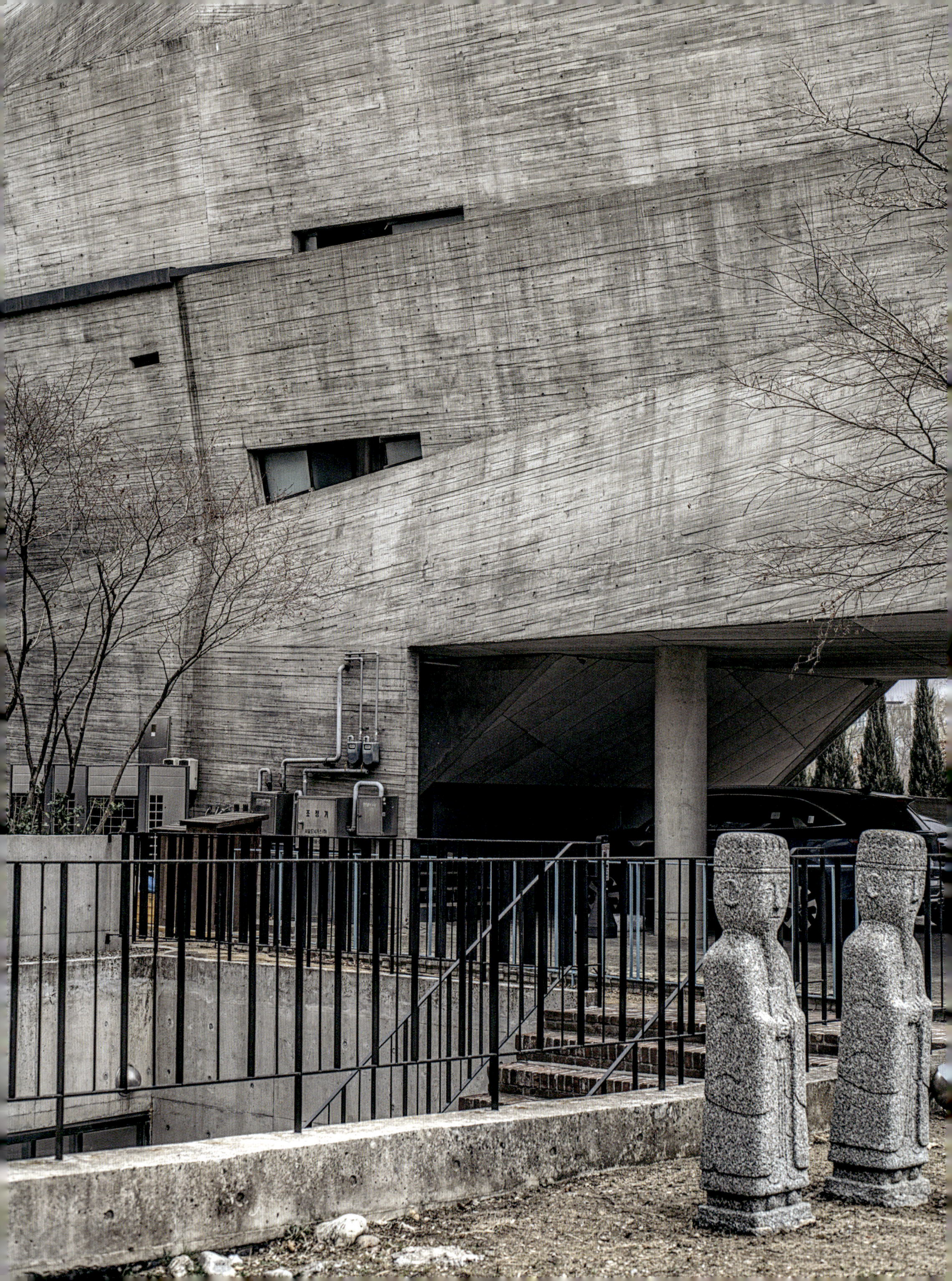

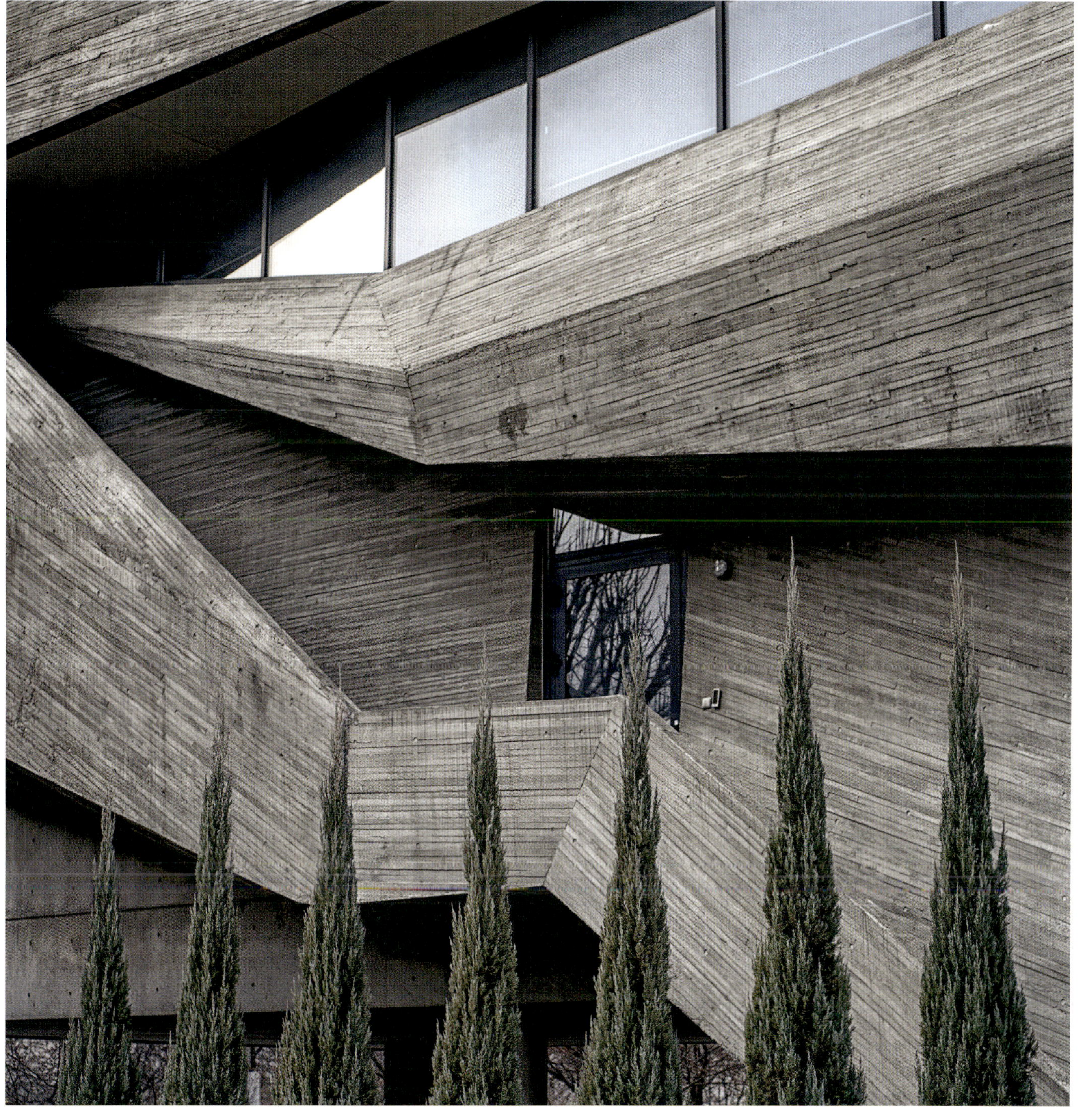

JEOLDUSAN MARTYRS' SHRINE

SEOUL · Architect: LEE Hee-tae · Completed 1967

Above the Han River, Jeoldusan Martyrs' Shrine feels less like a sanctuary and more like a fortress remembering the fallen. Completed in 1967 by Lee Hee-tae, it commemorates the Catholic martyrs executed during the 1866 Joseon persecution. The structure's blocky concrete mass and austere geometry channel both defiance and grief – a modernist echo of medieval endurance.

The shrine's bare walls and sharply cut voids create a sculptural solemnity. There's no ornament, no gesture towards comfort – only form, weight, and purpose. Its name, Jeoldusan ("Beheading Mountain"), deepens the building's severity, grounding its architecture in place and history.

From certain angles, it resembles a cracked sarcophagus: a vessel for collective memory split open to light. Inside, relics and exhibition halls extend that tension between brutality and belief. Amidst Seoul's glassy futurism, Jeoldusan postures unyielding – a Brutalist hymn of concrete conviction and enduring faith.

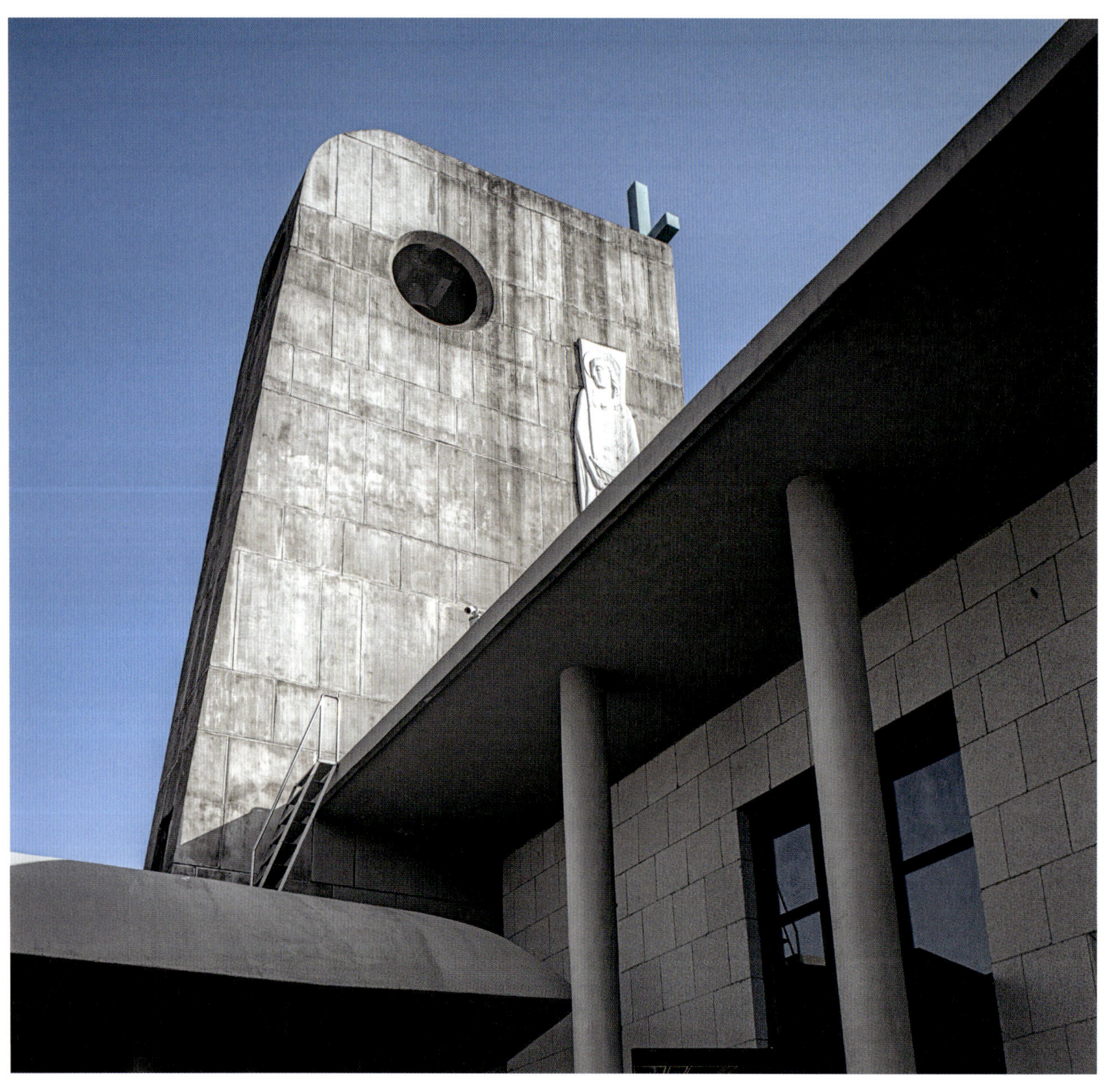

BANYAN TREE CLUB & SPA ANNEX BUILDING

SEOUL · Architect: KIM Swoo-geun · Completed 1969

The former Tower Hotel – now the Banyan Tree Club & Spa Seoul – proves that concrete can age with surprising sophistication. Originally built as an executive hotel, its form nonetheless exudes the calm solemnity of a place that might once have hosted prayer instead of power lunches. Kim's vertical recesses and deeply shadowed apertures lend the façade a quiet authority, as if the building itself were meditating on Seoul's transformation below. The structure's rigorous symmetry and sculptural massing suggest restraint over opulence, yet within those geometric walls now lie saunas, cocktails, and views of Namsan Mountain's greenery. There's a dry irony in watching a onetime symbol of corporate ambition reborn as a wellness retreat – a building that once promised prestige now dispensing serenity. The concrete remains stoic, but the clientele has learned to breathe.

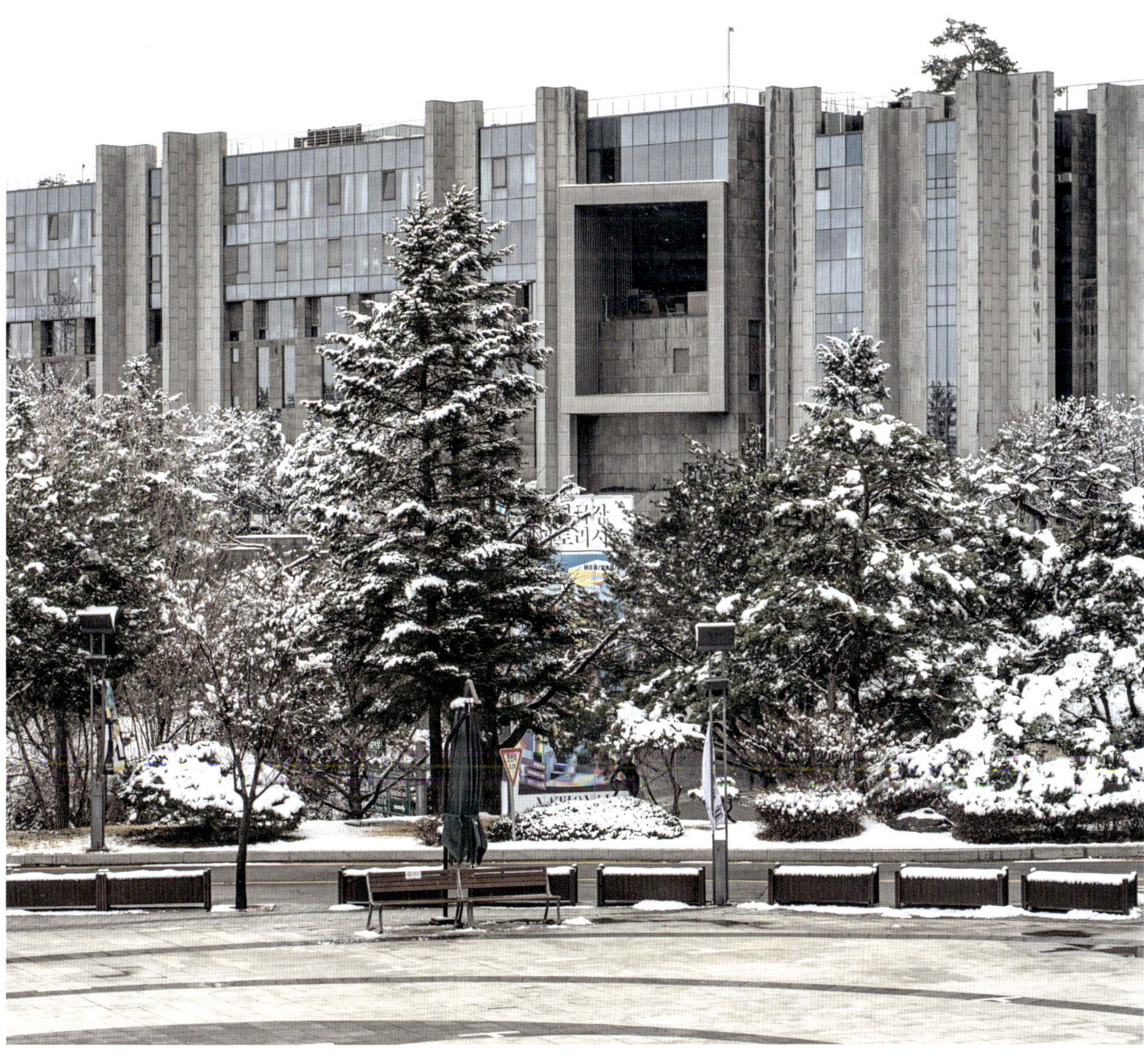

SSAMZIGIL

SEOUL · Architect: CHOI Moon-gyu · Completed 2004

Designed by Choi Moon-gyu of Ga.A Architects with early input from Gabriel Kroiz, Ssamzigil opened in 2004 as a vertical reinterpretation of Insa-dong's craft alleys – a spiralling street in the sky. The four-storey brick and concrete complex organizes around a continuous five-hundred-metre ramp that threads through some seventy tiny shops, galleries, and cafés. The ascent recalls the flow of traditional *hanok* courtyards but reimagined mid-air, forming a gentle urban spiral, not a rigid block.

Materials speak quietly but honestly: concrete and steel railings offer modern pragmatism. Its open courtyard thrums with market chatter, street food, and impromptu performances, while the rooftop garden offers calm.

Ssamzigil's unvarnished textures and visible structure nod to Brutalist ideals – community and craft over gloss. It's not an icon shouting for attention, but a civic spiral designed for movement, memory, and creative exchange.

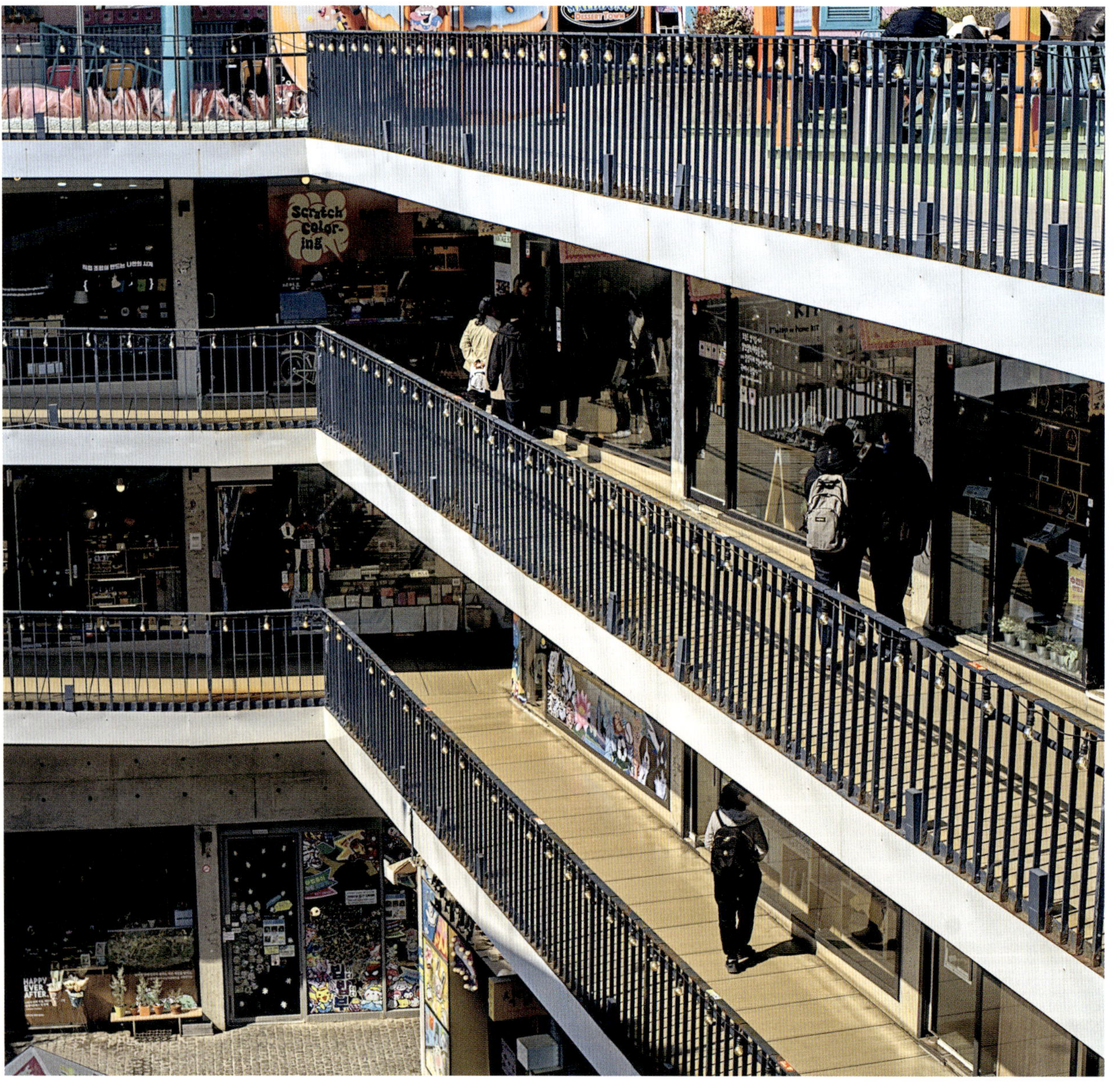

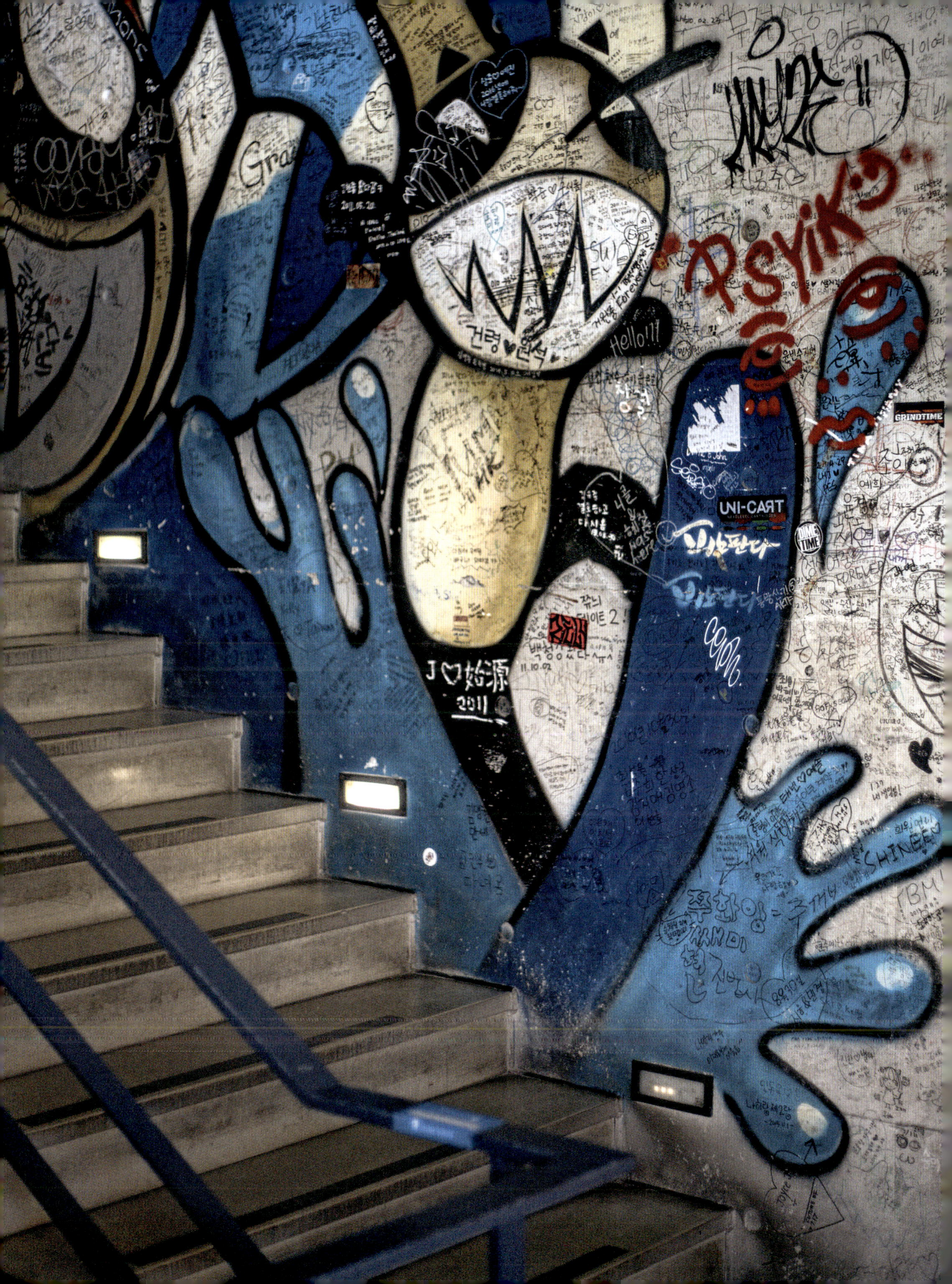
PSYK
Hello!!!
UNI-CART
GRINDTIME
J♡始源
2011
SHINEE

MYEONGJEONG

SAYUWON · Architect: SEUNG H-Sang · Completed 2019

Myeongjeong – or Meditation Garden – is less a building than an act of disappearance. Designed by Seung H-Sang, it sits within the Sayuwon complex in Daegu as a subterranean meditation chamber that seems to grow out of the earth, not rest upon it. Seung has long spoken of "the beauty of poverty" – an architecture stripped to essence – and here that philosophy finds its purest form.

Half-buried in the hillside, only a single concrete wall hints at what lies beneath. Behind it, a quiet corridor slopes downwards, drawing visitors into shadow and stillness. The descent becomes a ritual, each turn revealing slivers of sky, trees, and light. This play of concealment and revelation – void and illumination – is Seung's signature: architecture as movement of spirit, not form.

At the centre lies a shallow channel of water, threading through the stone floor like a thought made visible. Its sound replaces decoration; its reflection replaces ornament. Openings and chambers branch subtly from this spine, each space offering a fragment of solitude.

Myeongjeong's concrete surfaces bear their texture proudly – poured, marked, imperfect. Nothing here is polished for spectacle. The walls breathe with the imprint of their making, their simplicity achieving a solemn power.

It's not a structure designed to be seen but to be felt. Seung forges a monument to built silence. Myeongjeong is one such silence – an underground sanctum where architecture, landscape, and contemplation meet. In an age of noise and display, it exists as an architectural whisper: humble, elemental, and profoundly human.

Within its walls, the outside world falls away. What remains is rhythm – the rhythm of footsteps, of water, of breath. A space not for looking, but for listening – to the land, to light, and to the self.

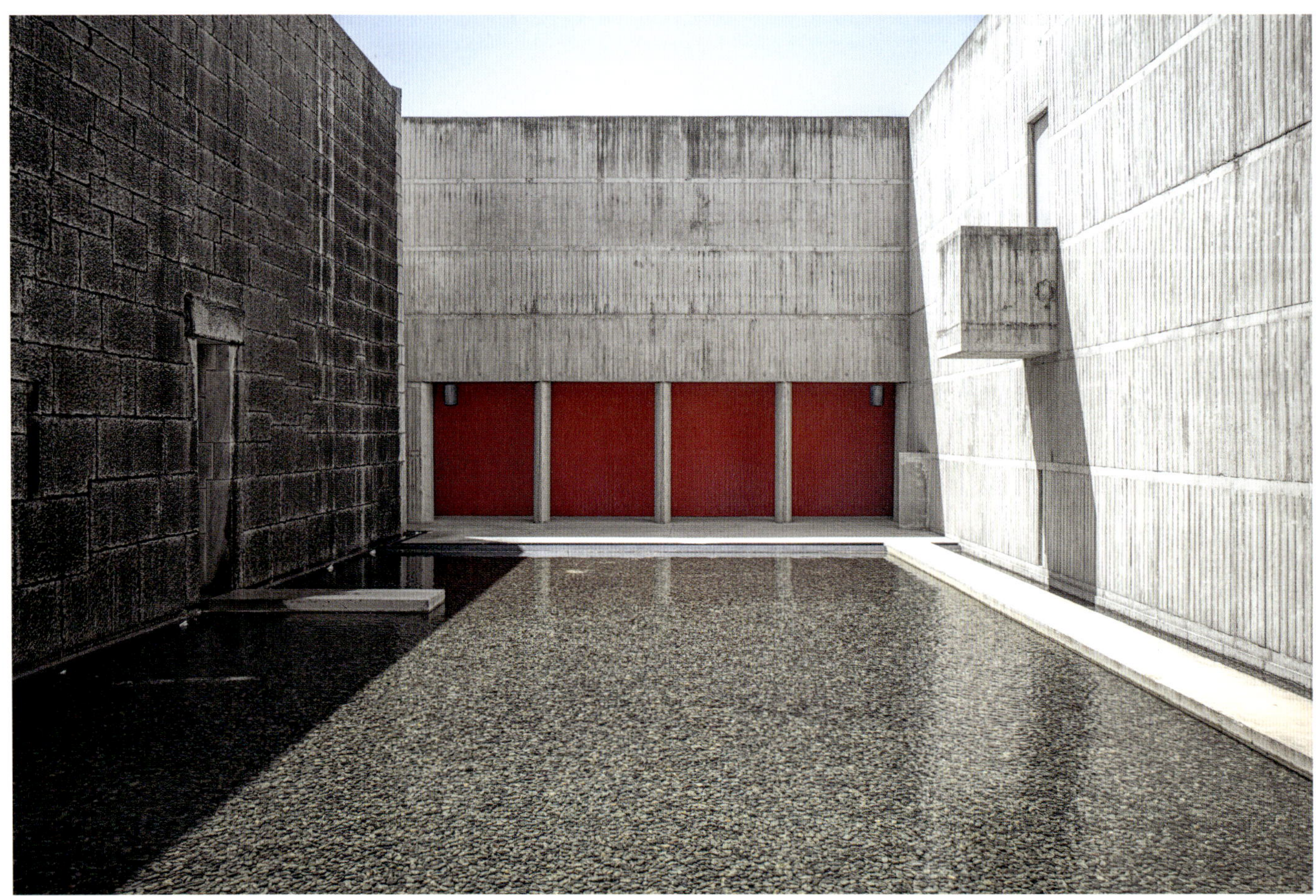

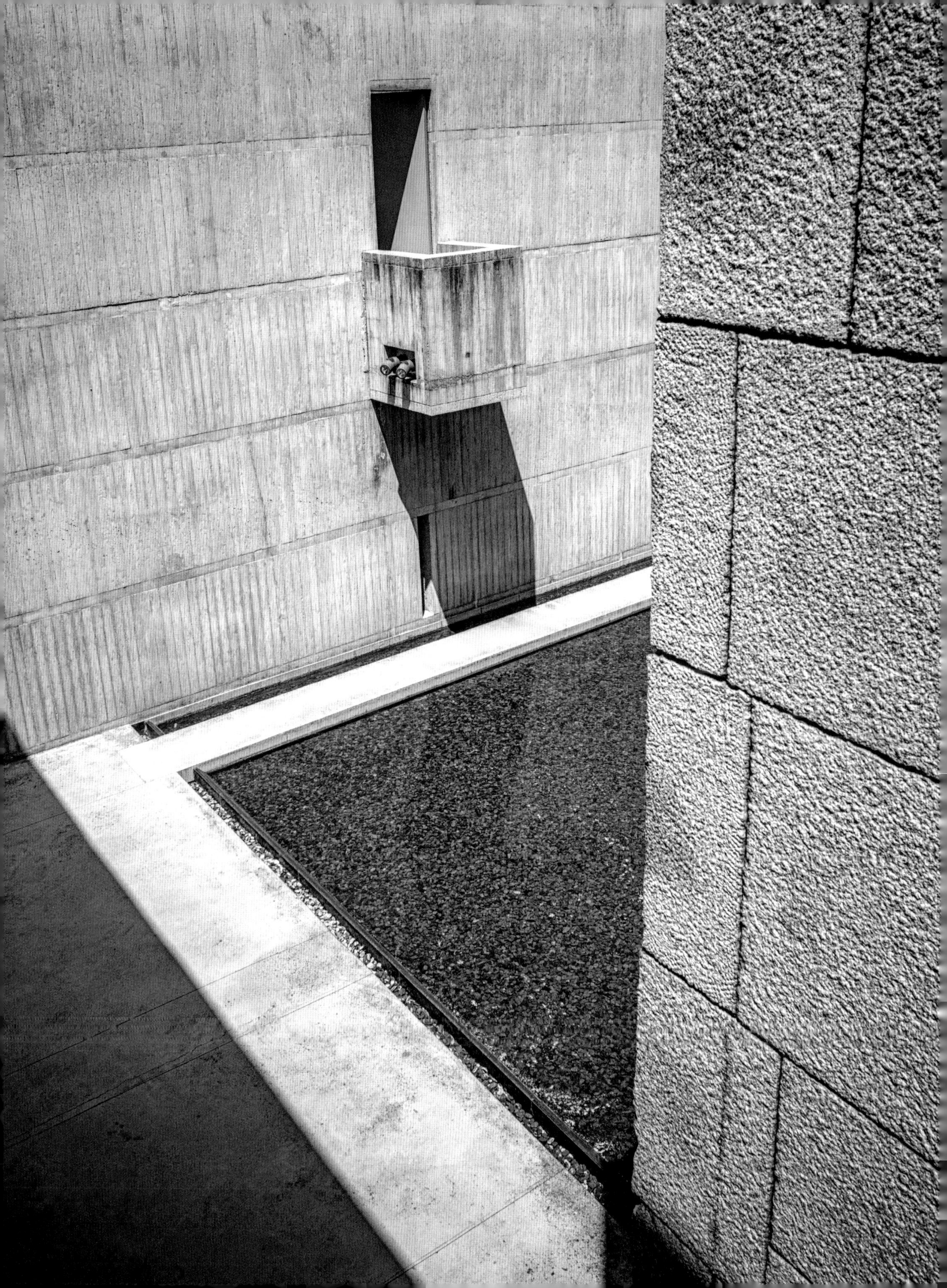

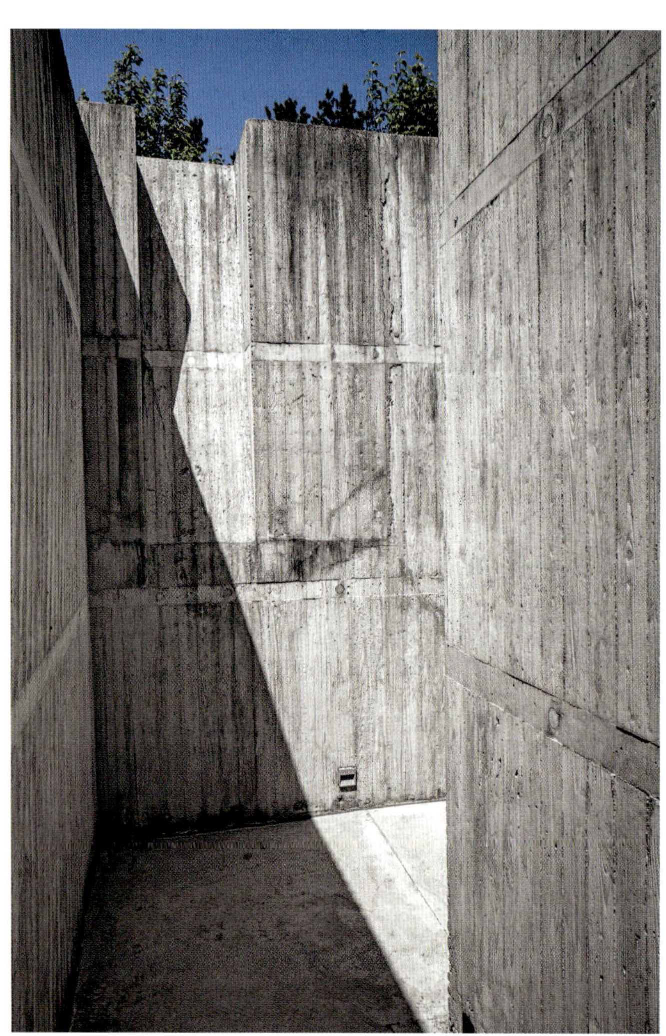

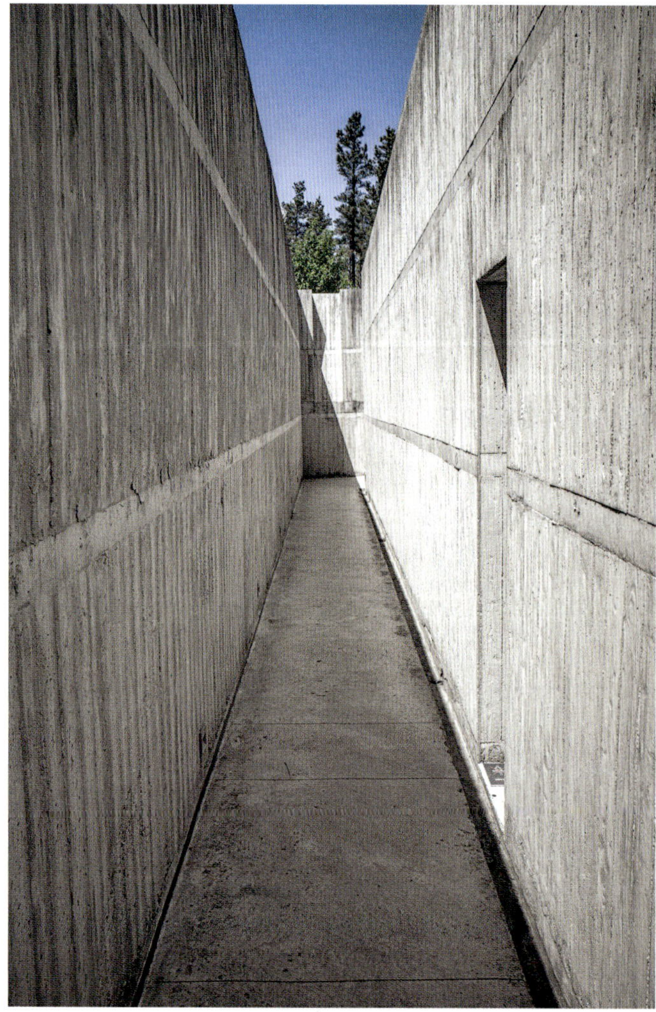

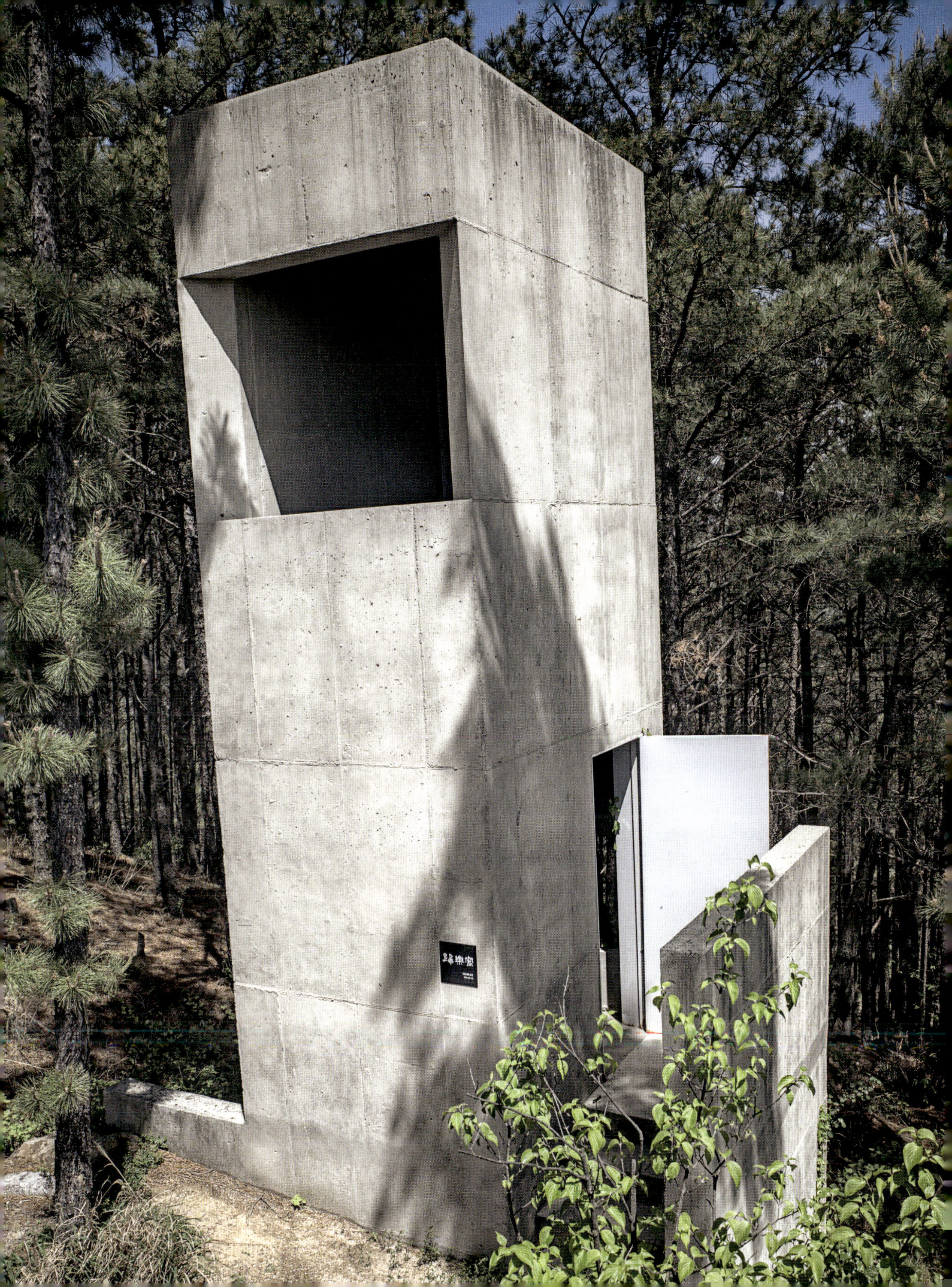

ISABEL MARANT FLAGSHIP STORE

SEOUL · Design Concept: Ciguë · Completed 2012

The Isabel Marant flagship store reimagines luxury retail through a lens of Korean Nu-Bru – that emerging hybrid of neo-Brutalism and urban chic. Its boxy concrete form, coated in a striking acid-yellow render, rejects the gloss of neighbouring boutiques in favour of material honesty – despite the quick facelift. The façade's stark geometry and single deep-set display window create an almost cinematic composition, part minimalist sculpture, part billboard. It is architecture that refuses subtlety yet never slips into excess – confident, youthful, and knowingly raw. Beneath the pigment, the building's concrete body gives it gravity, while the smooth planes and crisp voids lend precision. This interplay of brightness and weight, play and poise, captures Seoul's evolving aesthetic: Brutalism reinterpreted through fashion's eye. In a district defined by polished façades and performative opulence, this cube of yellow concrete is like a rebellious signature – elegant, deliberate, and vivid.

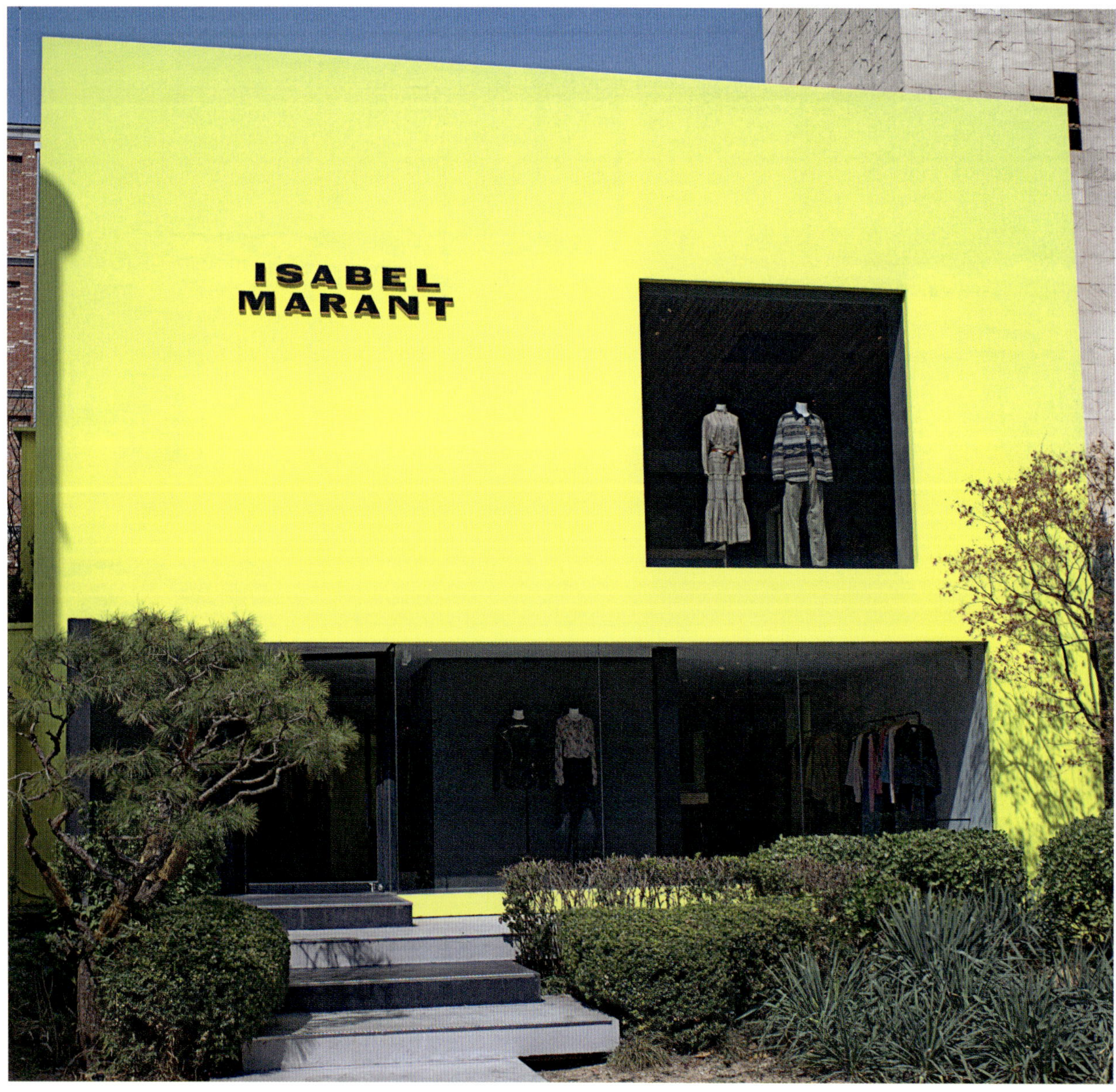

NEW BALANCE FLAGSHIP STORE

SEOUL

The New Balance flagship store in Hongdae, Seoul, takes its stance as a sporting expression of retail modernism rendered in concrete. Its monumental "NB" logo isn't applied branding but architecture itself – cast directly into the building's grey façade, merging identity and structure in one confident gesture. Set along Eoulmadang-ro, in the energetic heart of Mapo-gu's youth district, the building's austere grid and sharp detailing echo the precision of athletic design. The concrete surface, cool and tactile, has a runner's disciplined rhythm. A vivid red annex at street level interrupts the monochrome calm with a splash of colour – a visual dash against the static strength above. In a cityscape crowded with neon and noise, this structure stands firm and unflustered in Seoul's most restless quarter. Brutalist restraint commands attention through poise, proportion, and the quiet endurance of raw material.

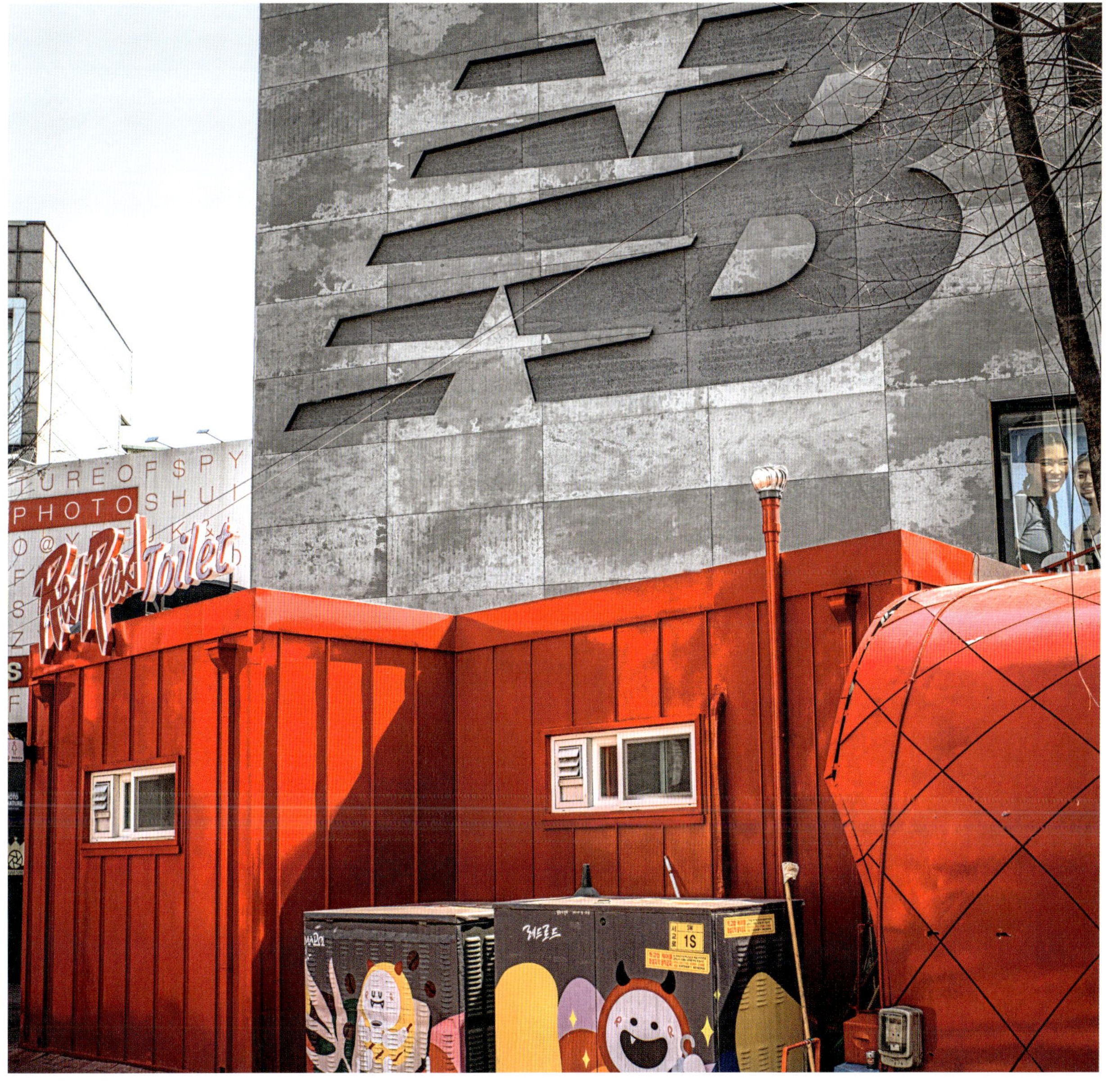

JEJU STADIUM

JEJU ISLAND · Completed 1968

Jeju Stadium grandstands mid-century ambition – an age when concrete was the national muscle and modernism its training regime. Its broad elliptical bowl rises from the island's volcanic plain like a discus mid-flight, its rhythmic supports flexing with the poise of an athlete mid-stride. There's a certain marathon endurance to the structure too: six decades on, it remains active while newer arenas pull hamstrings of obsolescence. The design is all discipline – no frills, no ego – just the clean geometry of purpose. Even its weathered concrete seems to carry the sweat and roar of decades past, each crack a stretch mark of civic pride. Jeju Stadium may not chase Olympic glamour, but it remains a finely balanced performance – part relic, part relay baton – passing on the spirit of post-war optimism, one well-paced lap at a time.

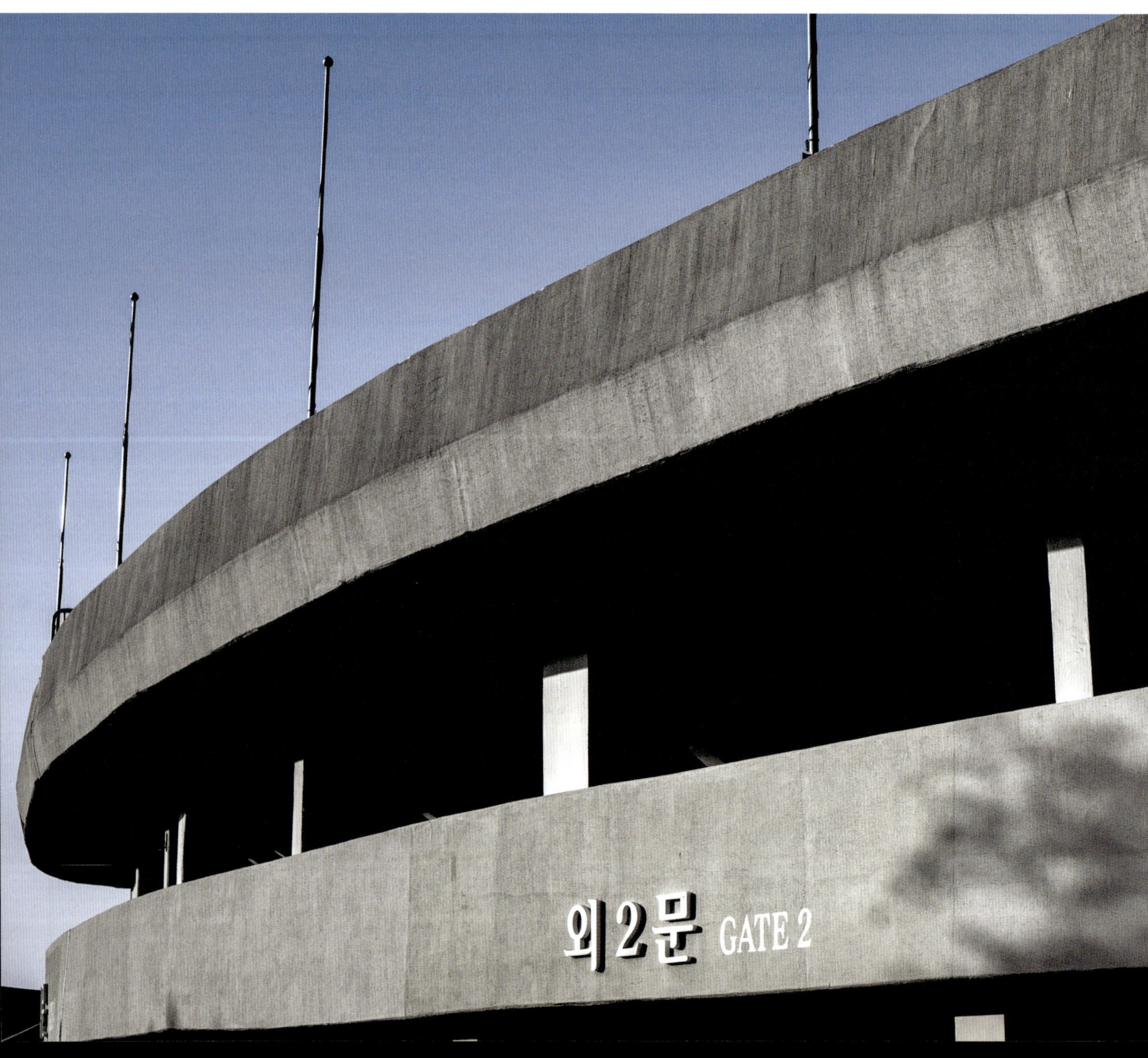

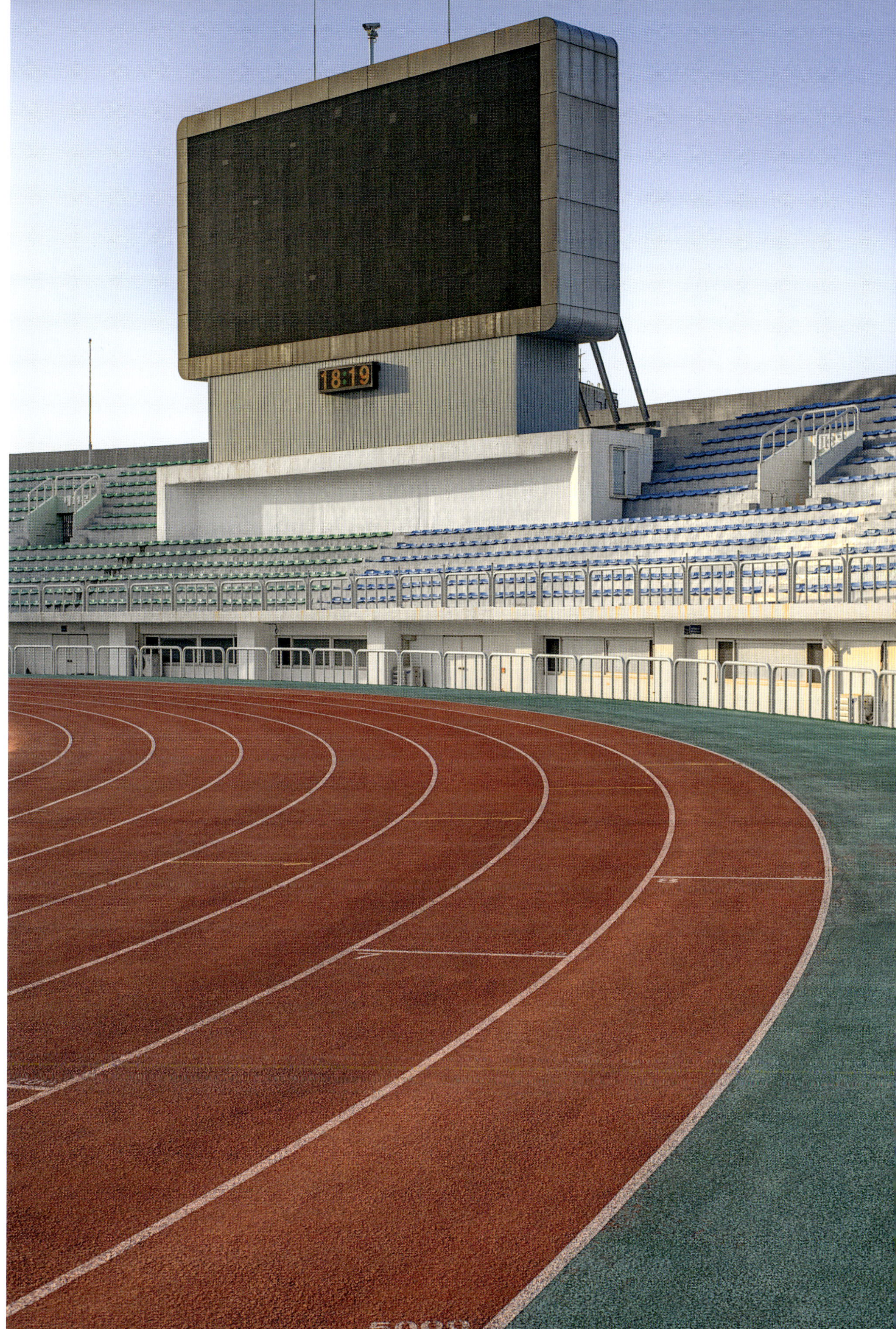
18:19

JEJU GLASS HOUSE

JEJU ISLAND · Architect: ANDO Tadao · Completed 2008

Tadao Ando's Jeju Glass House is where concrete takes a holiday – but refuses to relax. Overlooking a dramatic cliff at the eastern edge of Jeju Island, this architectural poem merges Brutalist gravity with volcanic drama, like a meditative samurai straying into a nature documentary. As always with Ando, concrete holds and contemplates space. Here the material communes with sky, sea, and the lava rock terrain as if they were all equals in a modernist haiku.

The Brutalist DNA is unmistakable: cast-in-place concrete, monumental planar walls, and voids carved with surgical precision. Yet Jeju Glass House is no concrete bunker. Instead it offers tension: between mass and transparency, inside and outside, the man-made and the elemental. The vast glass curtain wall on the ocean-facing side feels almost insolent against the otherwise hermetic concrete – as if the building cracked open to catch its breath.

Inside, spatial sequences unfold with Ando's signature restraint. Light filters in sideways, brushing against rough concrete like an abstract painting in motion. The building is as much about what you feel as what you see – cool shadows, the weight of silence, the awareness of weather passing. It is Brutalism with a soul, shelter with theatrical flair.

And perhaps there's something wry here, too: a glass house by the world's master of concrete? It is Ando's wink at transparency in an era of enclosure. And on Jeju – an island shaped by fire and wind – it's fitting that his fortress of contemplation feels at once ancient and alien, as if unearthed from a future volcanic past.

This isn't just a visitor centre. It's a Brutalist reliquary for light, time, and tide – a structure so still it feels like it's listening. A temple not of gods, but of atmosphere and form.

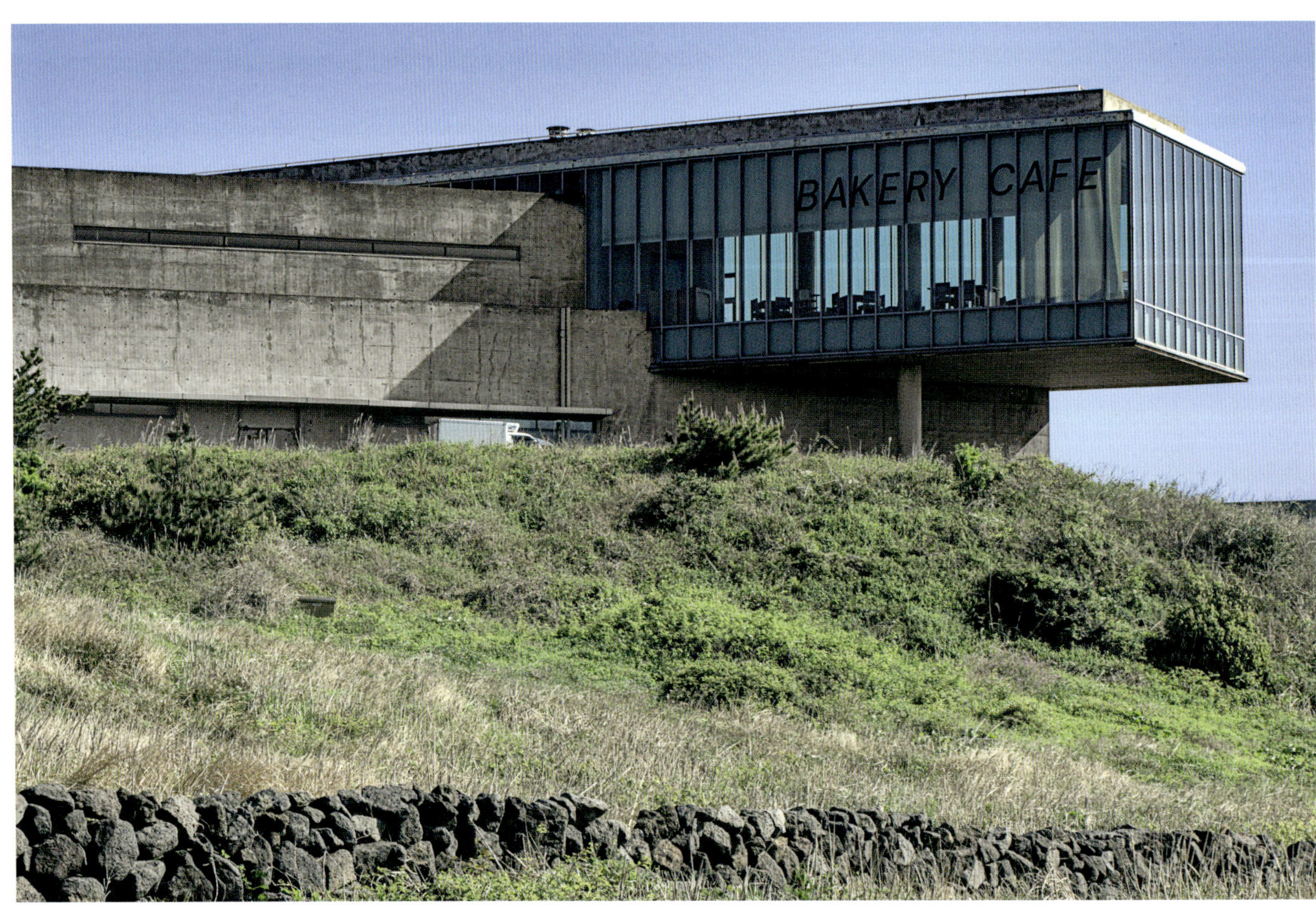

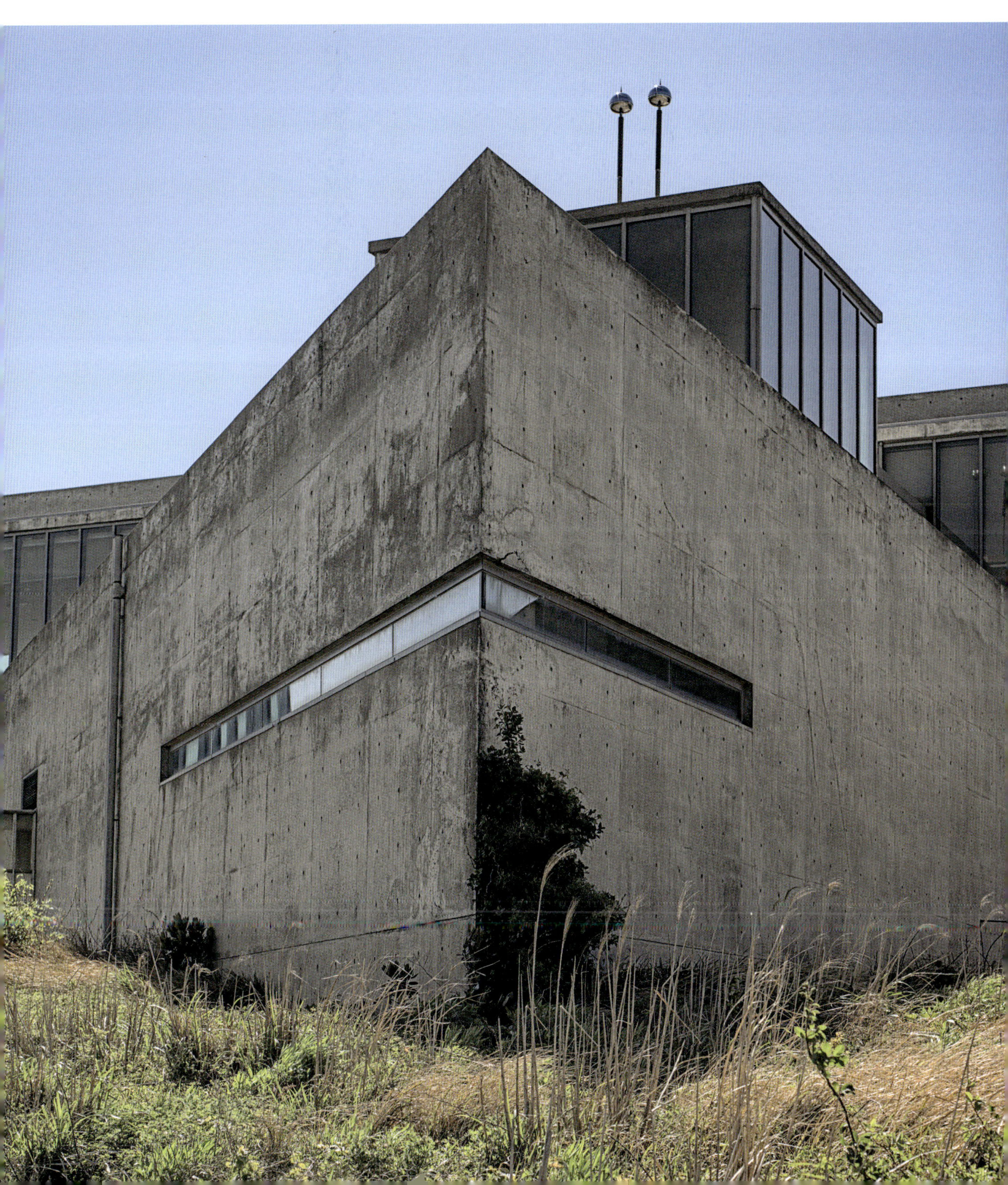

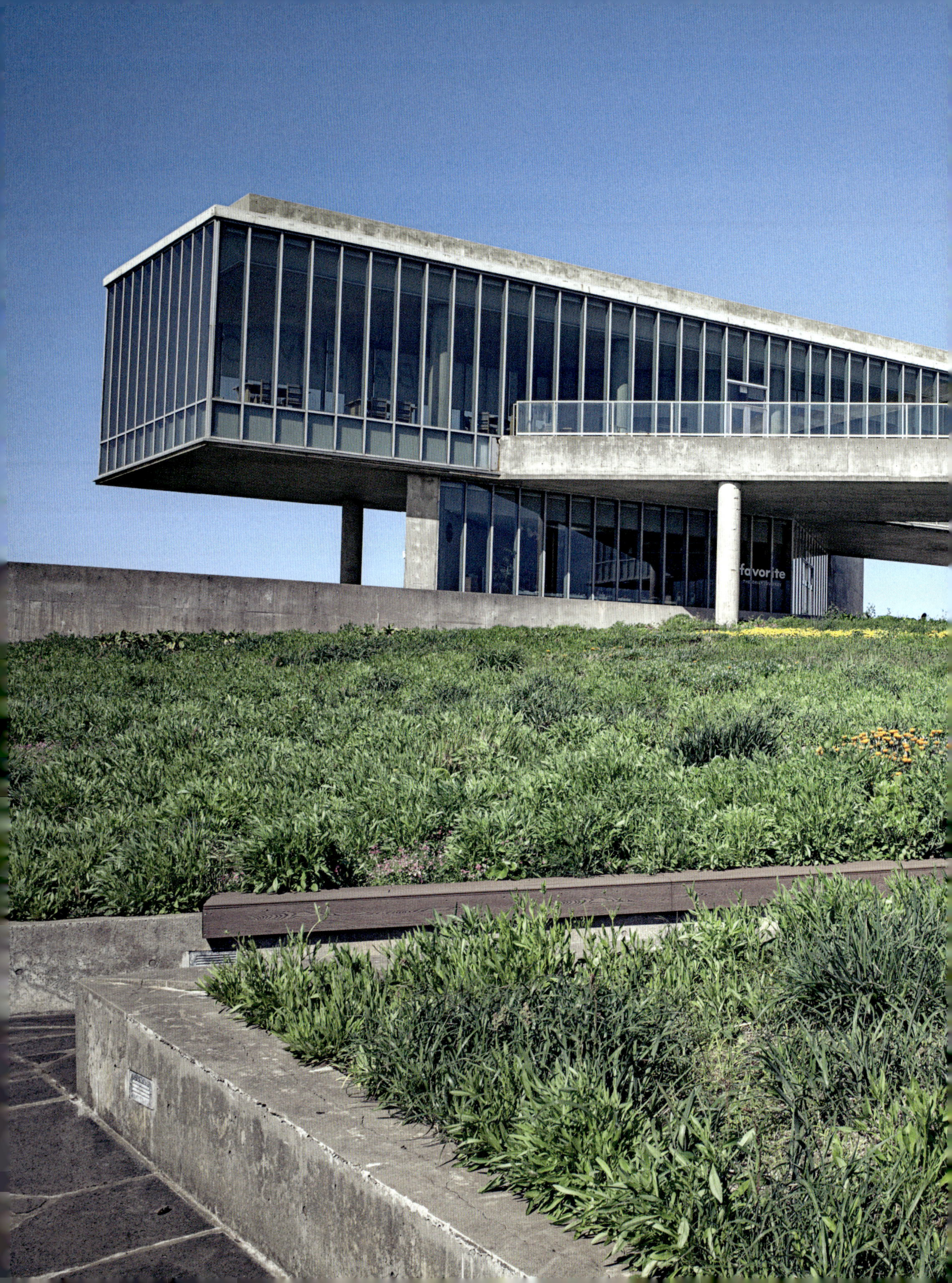
favorite

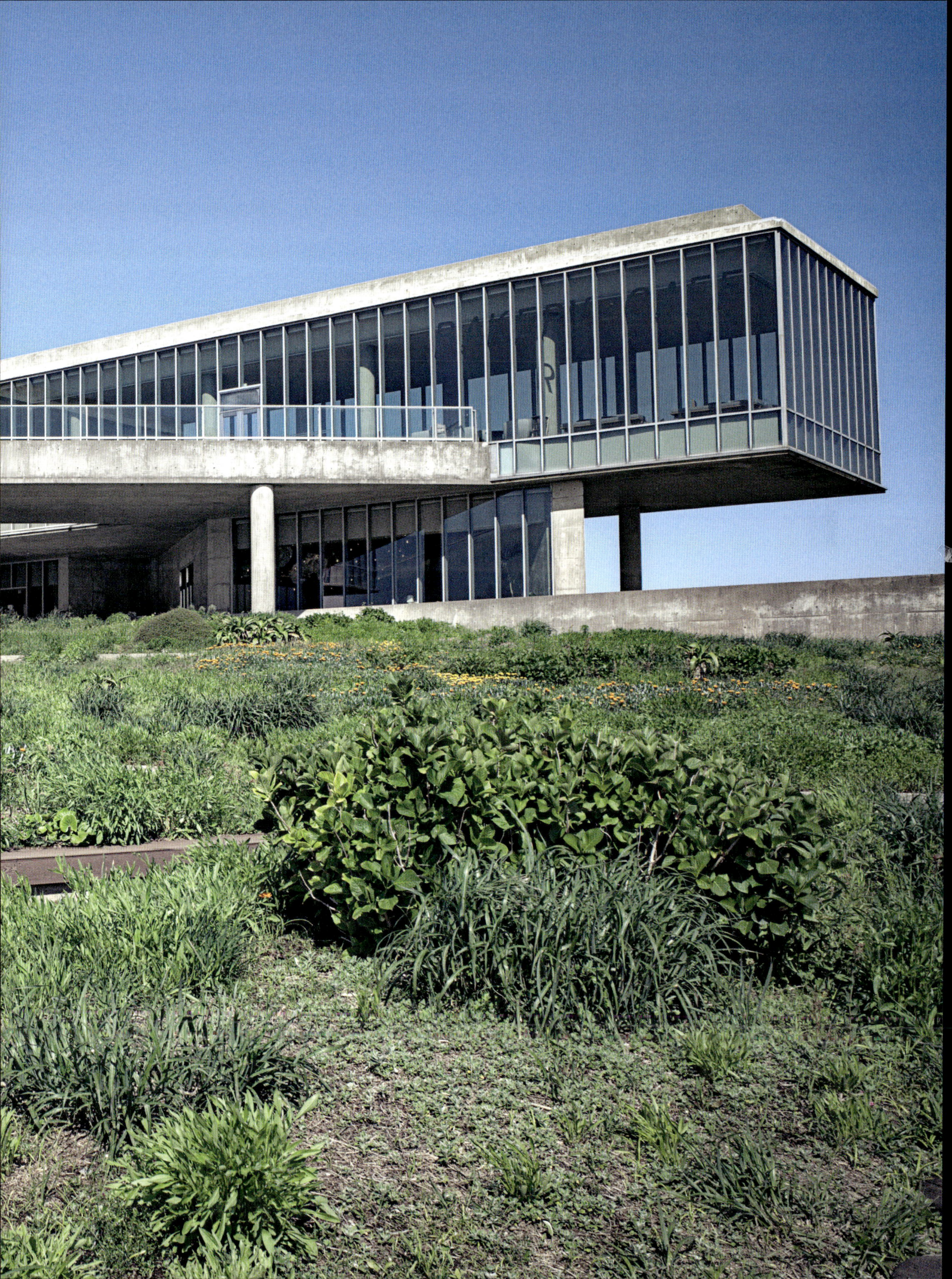

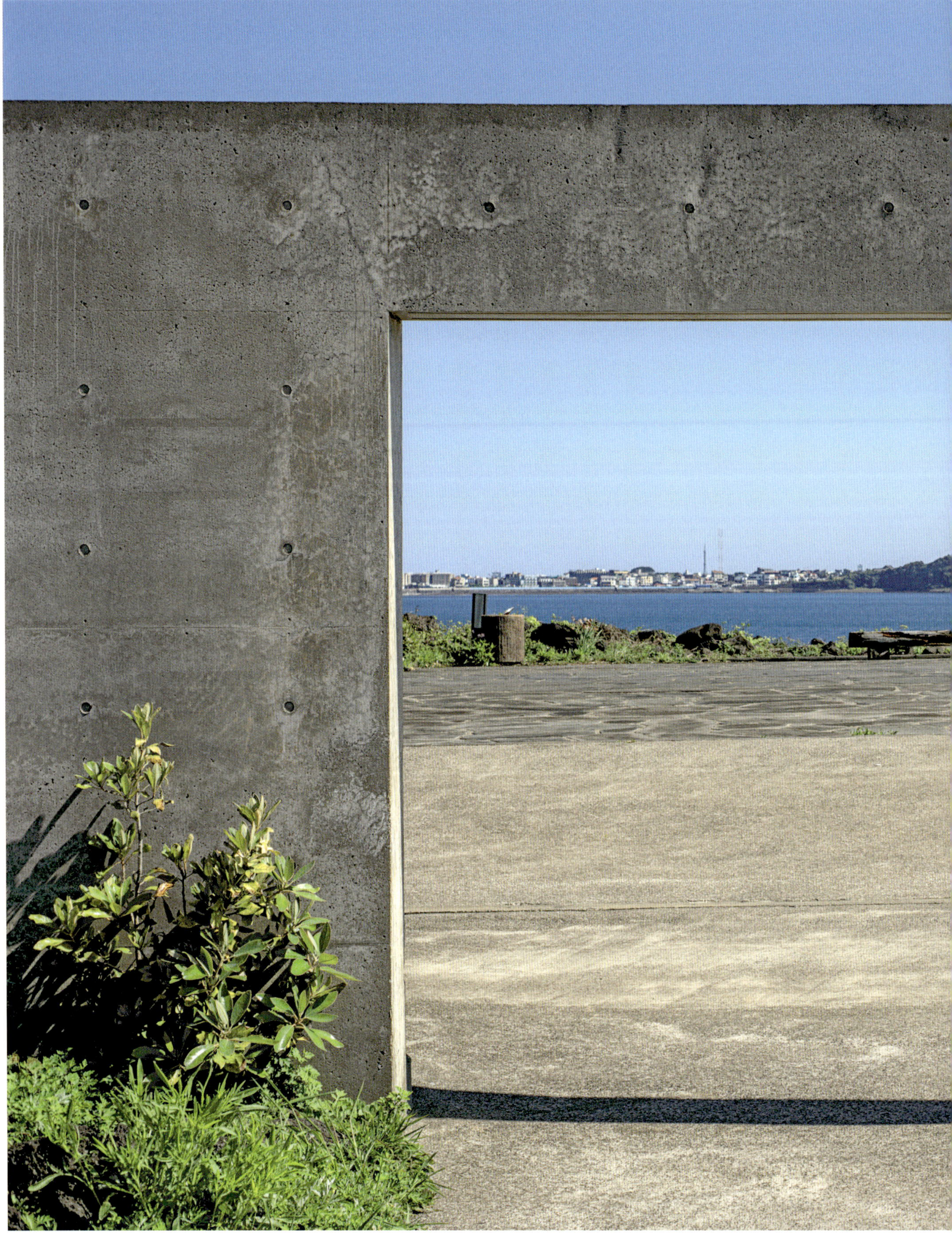

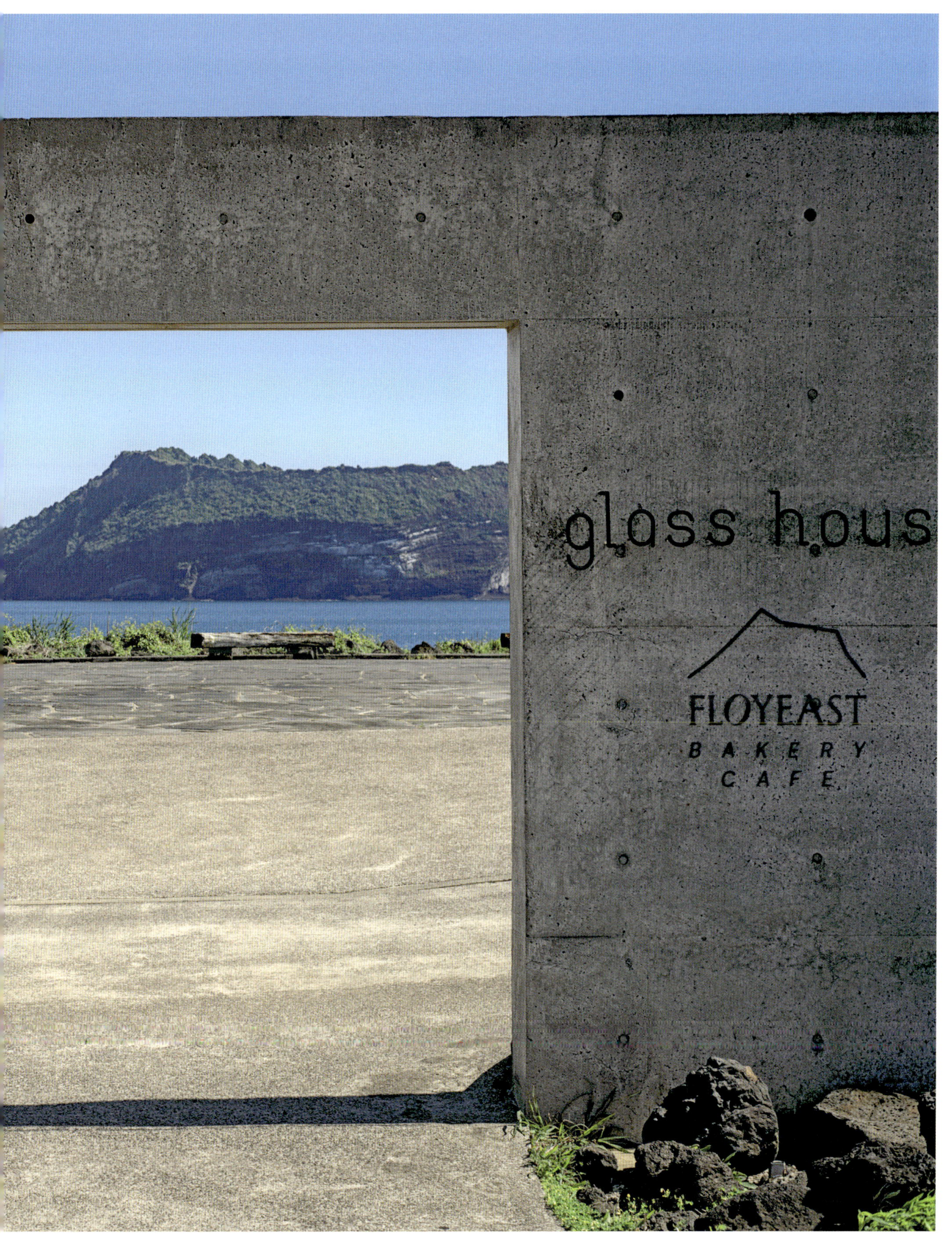
glass hous
FLOYEAST
BAKERY
CAFE

OLYMPIC STADIUM

SEOUL · Architect: KIM Swoo-geun · Completed 1984

The Seoul Olympic Stadium is Brutalism in track shoes – a heavyweight of raw concrete that somehow sprints, vaults, and pirouettes all at once. Built for the 1988 Summer Olympics, it was South Korea's architectural decathlon: part national statement, part myth-making arena, and all muscle.

Inspired by the curves of a traditional Korean celadon vase, the stadium bends Brutalism's usual boxiness into something distinctly Korean – a massive elliptical bowl that embraces both heritage and heroism. From afar, it resembles a titan's fingerprint in the landscape. Up close, it's all imposing concrete ribs and recessed voids – a rhythmic procession of vertical blades that look ready to throw a javelin or deliver a stern lecture, depending on your angle.

Unlike many stadiums, which age into empty hulks, this one still pulses with energy – a relic not of ruin, but of national ascendance. Its enormous cantilevers project confidence, while the exposed structural logic (those thick tapering piers!) gives it a kind of stoic transparency: no frills, just force. It's Brutalism doing lunges.

And yet there's grace in the weight. The asymmetry of the plan, the subtle tapering of the seating bowl, and the floating ring of the roof canopy all show a deftness that sidesteps clumsy bulk. It lifts while it looms.

In true Olympic fashion, the Seoul Stadium is a masterclass in balance – between concrete gravitas and kinetic spirit, between ancient form and modern function. It's a space where marathon runners once wept, boxers bled, and pole-vaulters flirted with flight – all under the watchful gaze of one of the most powerful Brutalist coliseums Asia has ever built. A concrete colossus with gold medal flair.

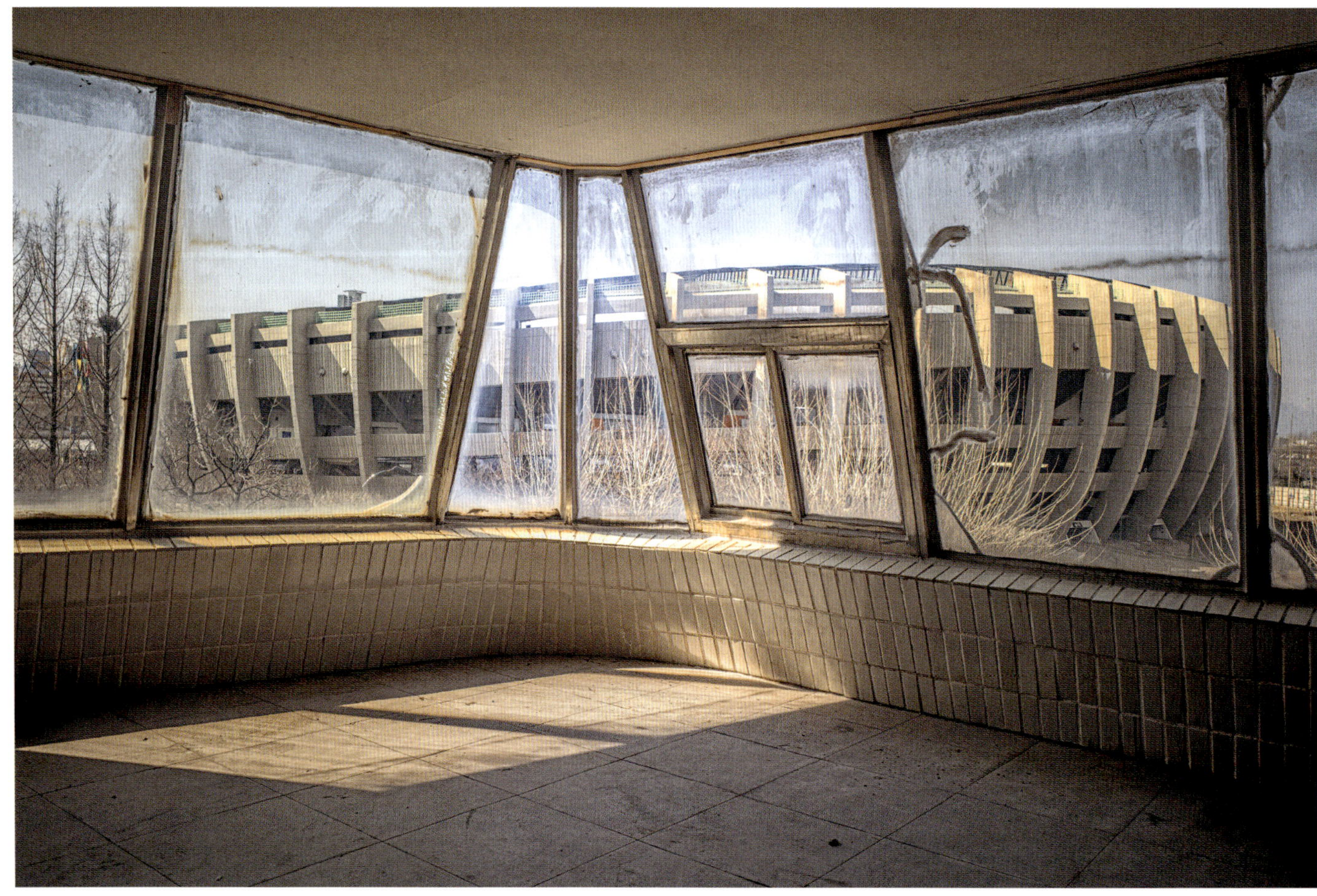

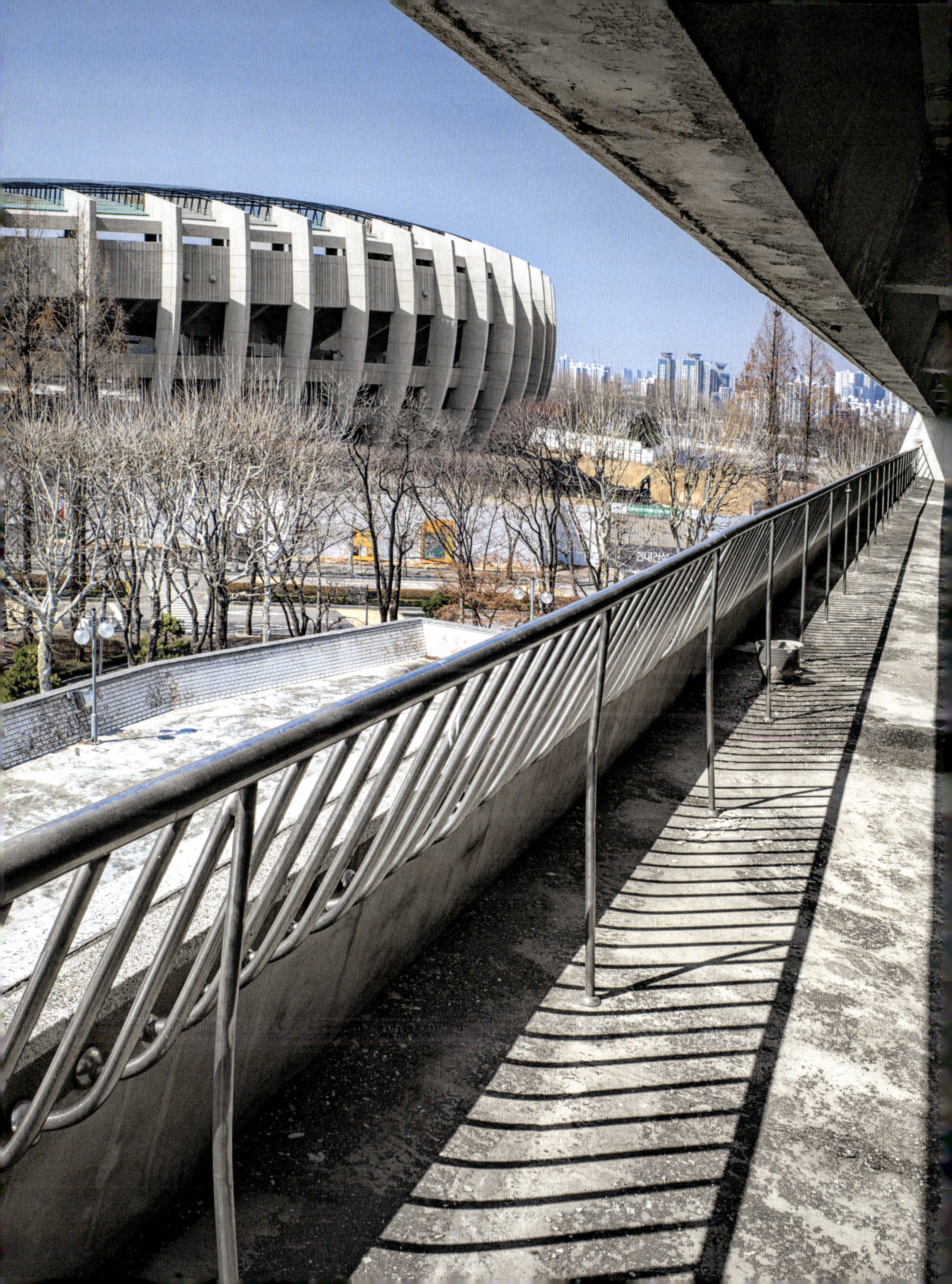

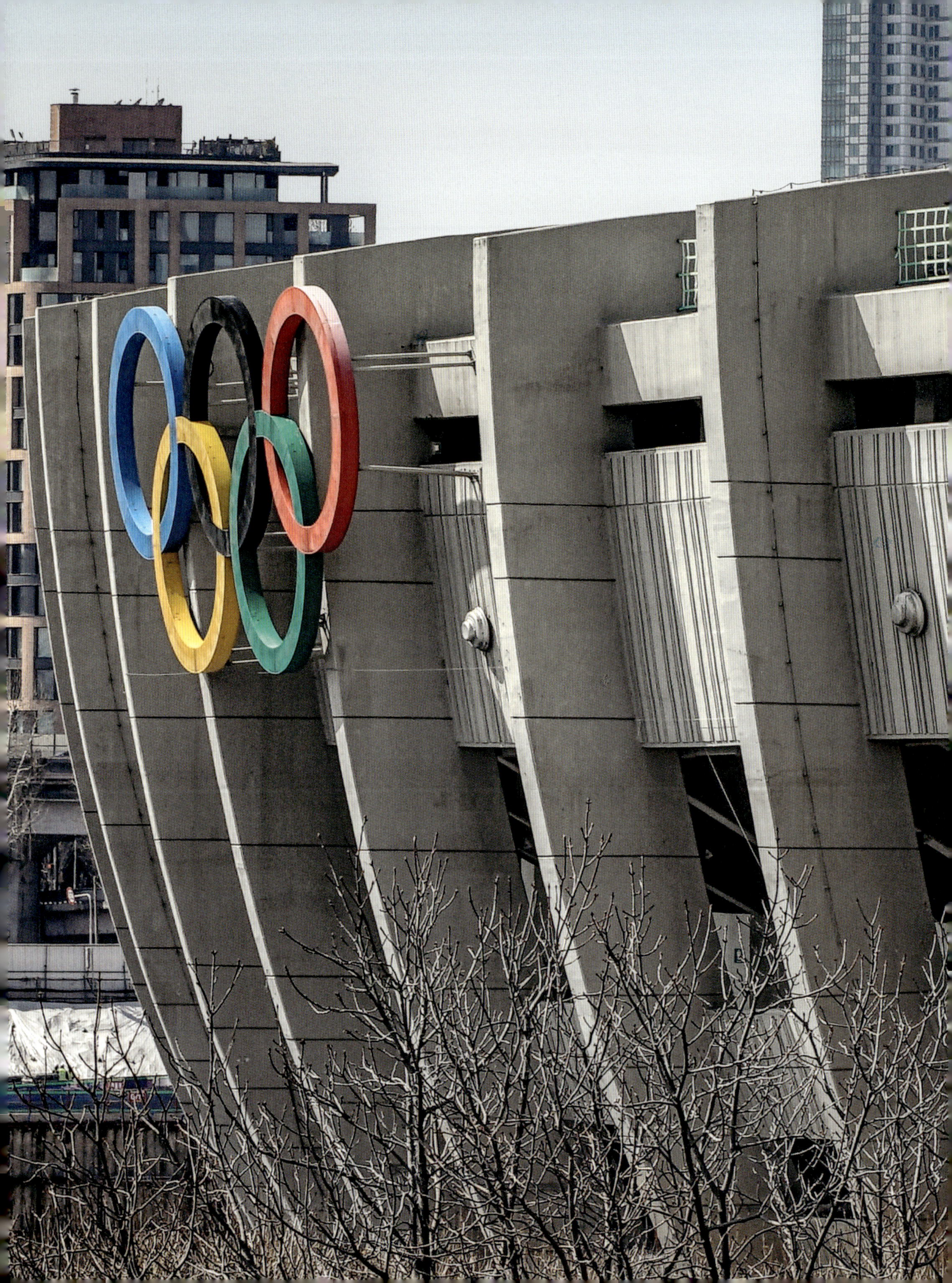

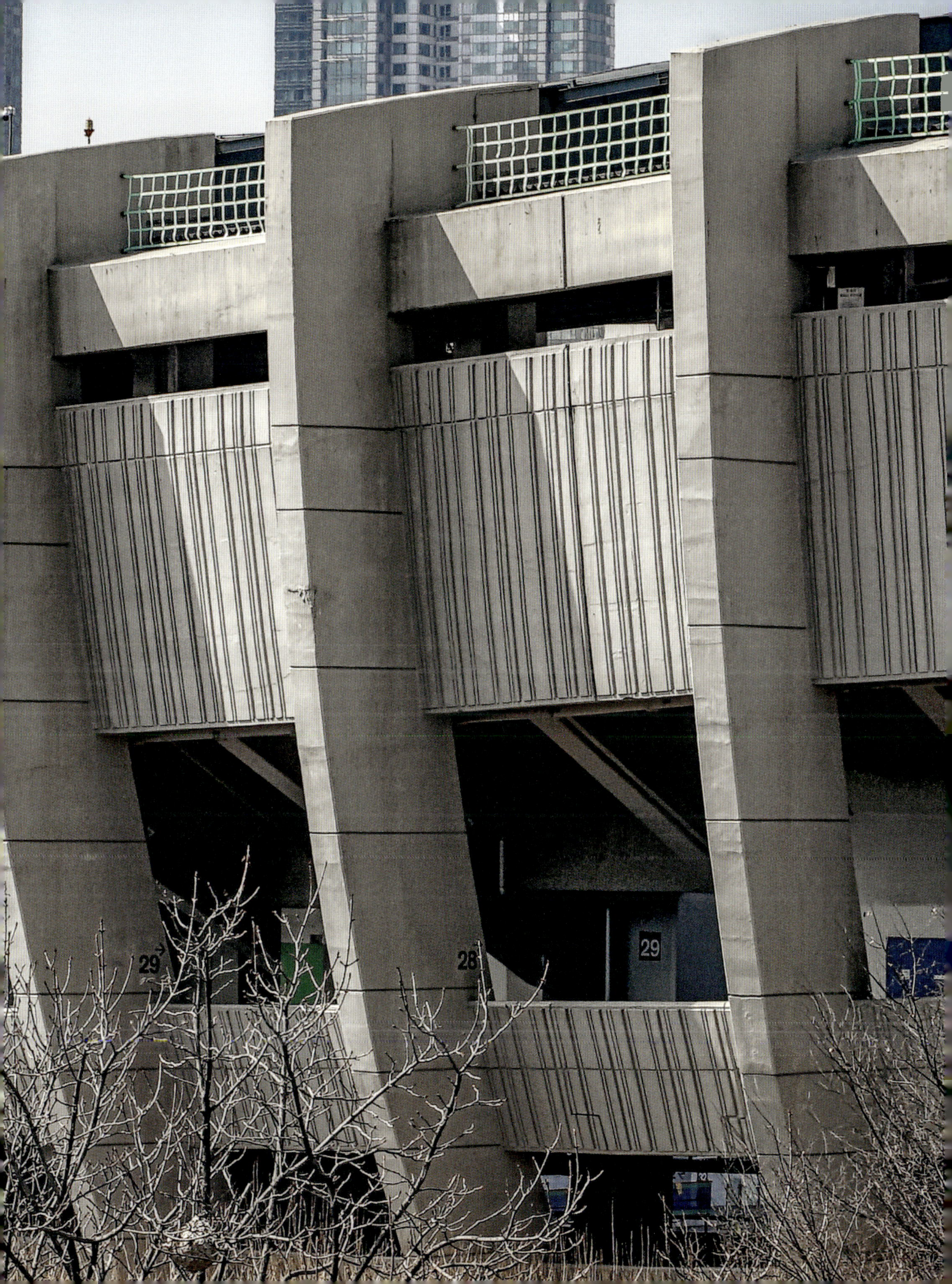
29
28
29

HYEHWA-DONG CATHOLIC CHURCH

SEOUL · Architect: LEE Hui-tae · Completed 1960

The Hyehwa Catholic Church, completed in 1960 and designed by Lee Hui-tae, marks a defining moment in the evolution of modern ecclesiastical architecture in Korea. Set on a hill in Jongno-gu, its monumental granite façade and symmetrical portico reject the drama of Gothic precedent in favour of quiet, grounded faith. The heavy colonnade, carved reliefs, and broad stairway create a ceremonial approach that feels both civic and sacred – religion translated into modern public architecture. The restrained composition and rigorous geometry lend the building a meditative stillness, where every line and surface seems weighed with purpose. The structure's massing and materiality reflect a uniquely Korean response to modernism: solemn, balanced, and deeply introspective. Lee's design replaced decorative flourish with conviction in proportion and weight, producing a church that prays through stone – a work of profound composure and architectural devotion to form, order, and the quiet dignity of belief.

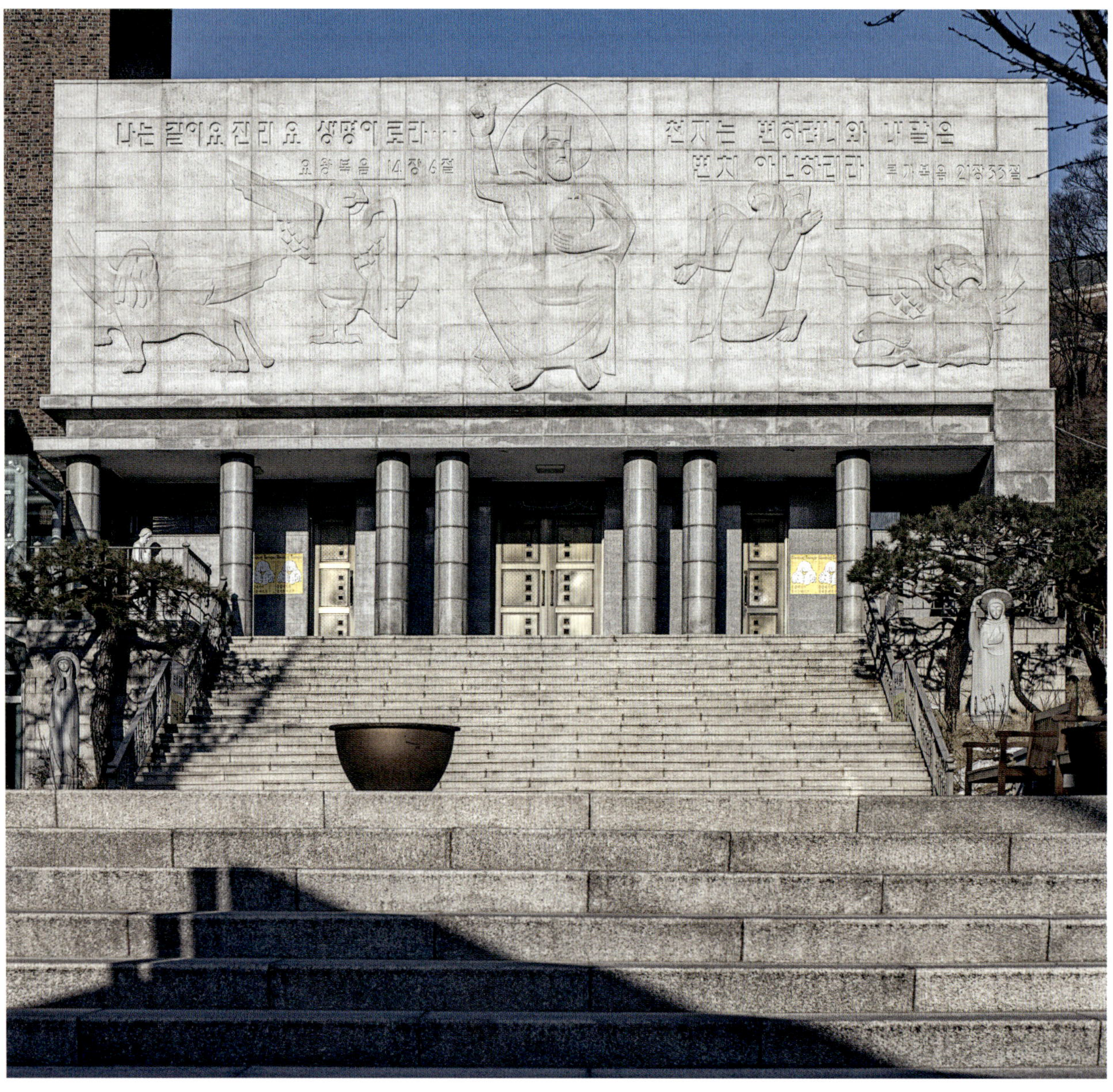

WHANKI MUSEUM

SEOUL · Architect: WOO Kyu-sung · Completed 1993

The Whanki Museum honours the legacy of Kim Whanki (1913–1974), a pioneer of Korean abstract art. Designed by Woo Kyu-sung of Wooksung Architecture and completed in 1993, the structure reflects the painter's meditative approach to form and space. Its restrained concrete geometry and linear clarity evoke a sense of calm. Built into the natural incline of Bugaksan, the museum's layered volumes engage the hillside, allowing architecture and landscape to exist in quiet harmony. The result is both a museum and a spatial reflection of Whanki's philosophy – where emptiness becomes presence and simplicity becomes depth. Subtle, disciplined, and introspective, the Whanki Museum is one of Seoul's most poetic examples of minimalist modernism, translating the spirit of Whanki's art into enduring architectural form. An unfortunate name but nothing onanistic here.

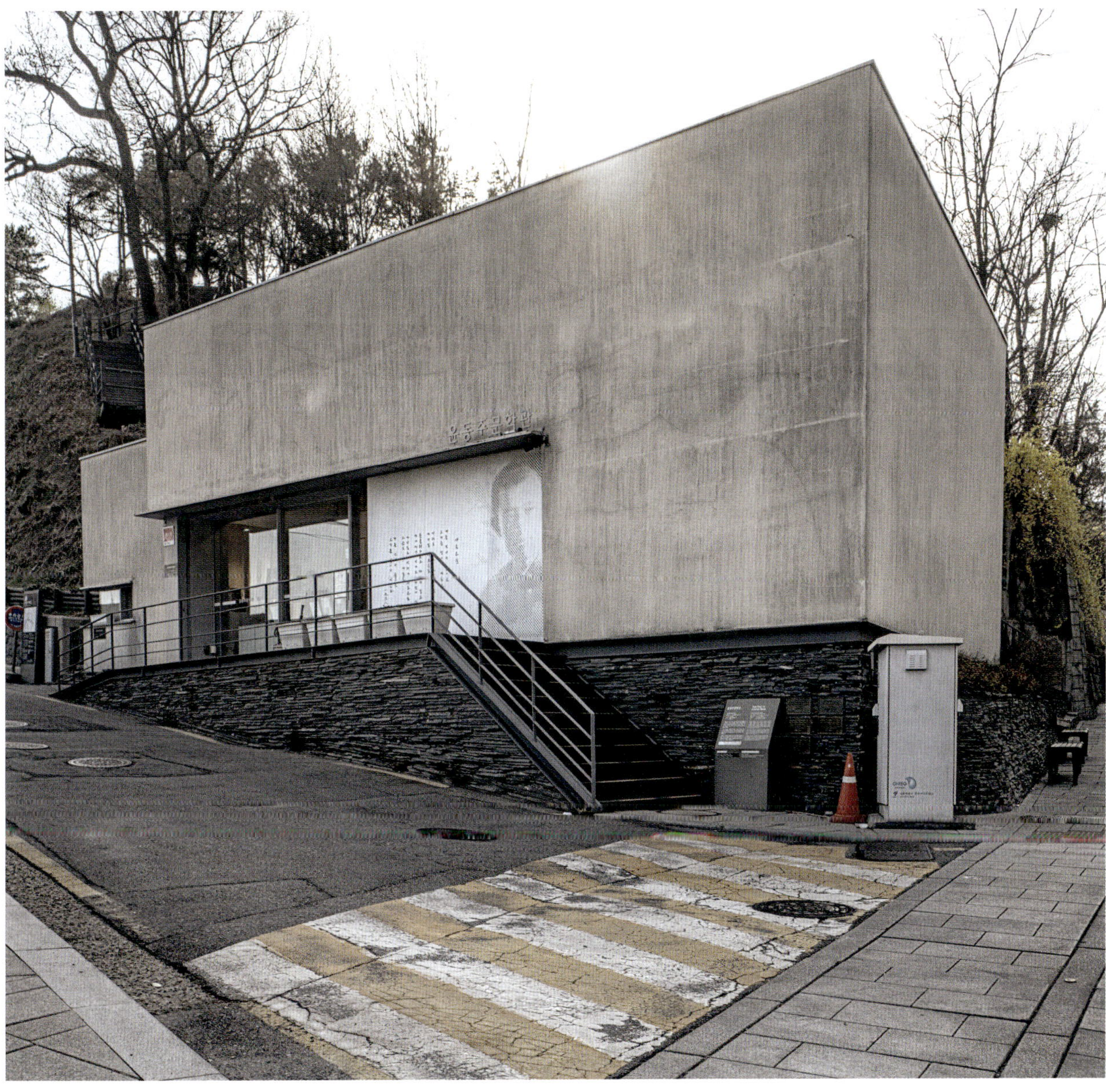

MAPO OIL TANK CULTURE PARK

SEOUL · Architects: HEO Seo-goo and RoA Architects · Completed 1978 / Repurposed 2017

The Mapo Oil Tank Culture Park in Seoul is a rare example of Brutalism reborn through transformation. Originally built between 1976 and 1978 as a fortified oil depot during the global energy crisis, the site stored petroleum in massive reinforced-concrete tanks buried into the hillside of Maebongsan. For decades it was sealed off from public view, an industrial fortress of containment. When Seoul began preparations for the 2002 World Cup and built the nearby World Cup Stadium, safety concerns about the depot's proximity prompted its closure in 2000 – ending one story and making room for another.

Today, the same six tanks hum with new life. Their raw cylindrical forms – thick-walled, weathered, and unashamed – have been reimagined as Seoul's most unconventional cultural park. Each tank plays a different role: one a glass-domed concert hall, another a sunken stage, another preserved in its original state as an educational relic. Others host galleries, studios, cafés, and workshops, all connected by steel walkways and landscaped terraces that weave through the old containment walls.

The architecture's power lies in its restraint. The conversion rejects romanticism – it confronts ruin. Exposed welds, rusting bolts, and unpainted concrete remain visible, testifying to the site's industrial past. Sunlight slices through new apertures; shadows ripple across the tanks like memories in motion. At night, illumination spills from their circular openings, transforming the compound into a glowing sculptural field.

Mapo Oil Tank Culture Park embodies adaptive reuse as cultural alchemy – turning a symbol of resource anxiety into one of creative abundance. What was once a depot of fuel now stores collective energy of a different kind: performance, conversation, community. Its Brutalist bones haven't softened, they've matured – demonstrating that concrete, when given a second life, can channel humanity as powerfully as it once contained oil. This is industry repurposed as empathy, architecture turned into reclamation.

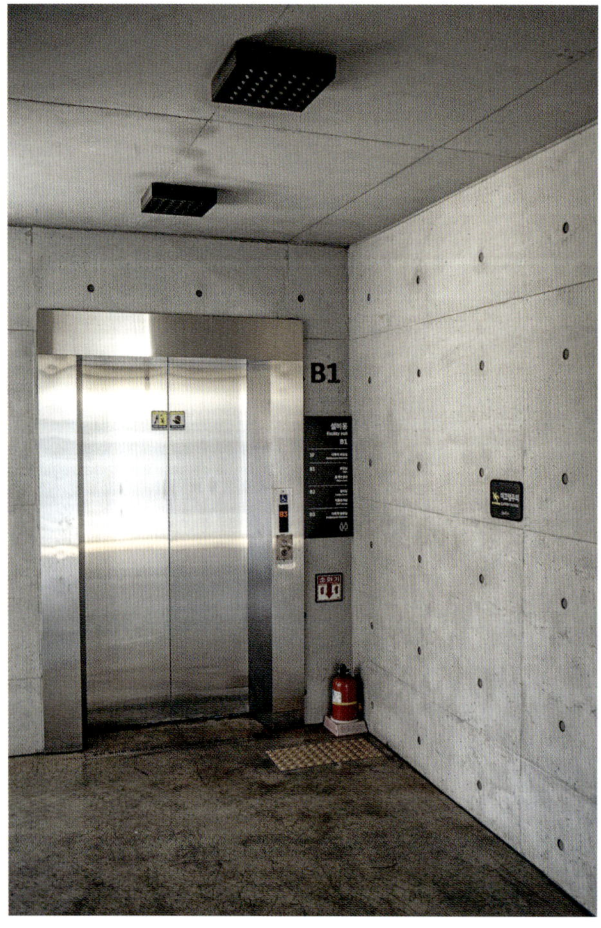

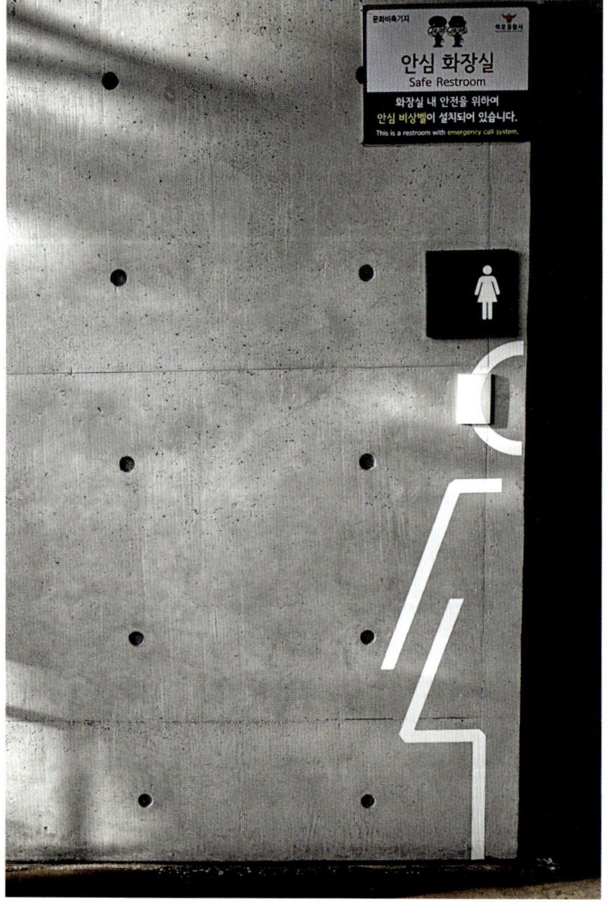

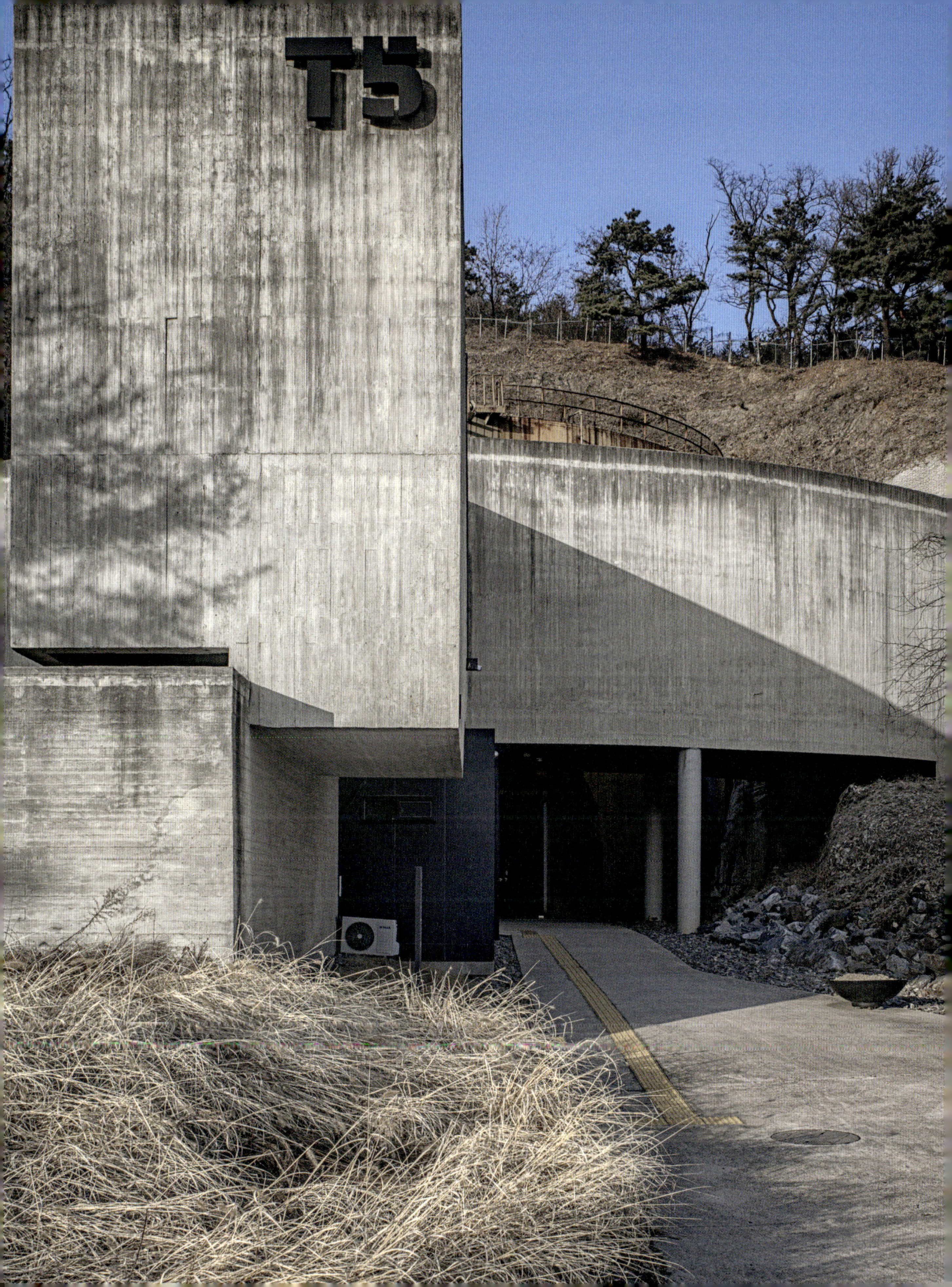
T5

TOILET PAVILION

SAYUWON · Architect: IROJE Architects & Planners · Completed 2016

This toilet block is located opposite the main gallery building known as "Sadam" within Sayuwon – a private cultural and landscape complex where architecture, art, and nature are integrated into a contemplative experience.

The restroom is one of several small architectural interventions scattered throughout the forested site. Its design embraces brutal simplicity – a rectilinear concrete volume pierced by a tall, narrow opening, evoking the spatial austerity of a shrine or gate. The raw material and minimal gesture encourage visitors to perceive it not merely as infrastructure but also as part of the landscape's meditative rhythm. In this way, the Sadam toilet exemplifies Sayuwon's architectural ethos: the elevation of the everyday through restraint, silence, and the quiet communion between human intention and natural surroundings.

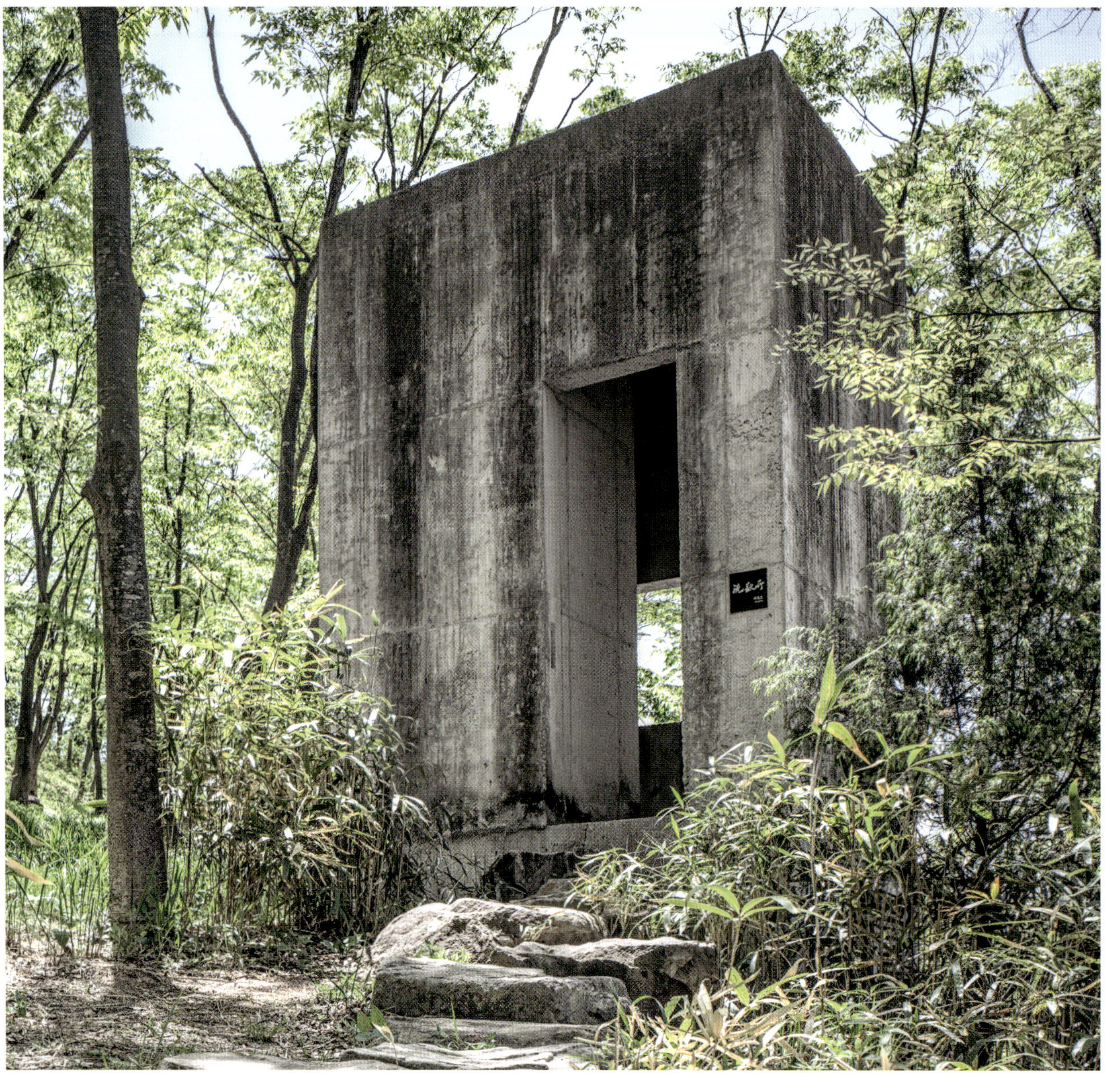

SEOULLO 7017

SEOUL · Architect: MVRDV · Completed 2017

The Seoullo 7017 Skygarden, designed by MVRDV in collaboration with Seoul's city architects, reimagines a 1970 highway overpass near Seoul Station as a 983-metre public park. Completed in 2017, the project turns a relic of the automobile era into a pedestrian sanctuary – a raised botanical walkway lined with more than 24,000 native plants, including trees, shrubs, and flowers, arranged in circular planters that trace the curve of the old road.

Instead of disguising its industrial heritage, Seoullo highlights it. The exposed concrete retains its rawness, while layers of vegetation bring a new-found softness. Seventeen stairways, lifts, and bridges branch from the main route, stitching together districts once cut apart by traffic.

By daylight it is a garden street in the sky; after dark, a luminous ribbon over the city. Seoullo 7017 transforms disused infrastructure into Seoul's elevated green lung – where motion, memory, and renewal intertwine.

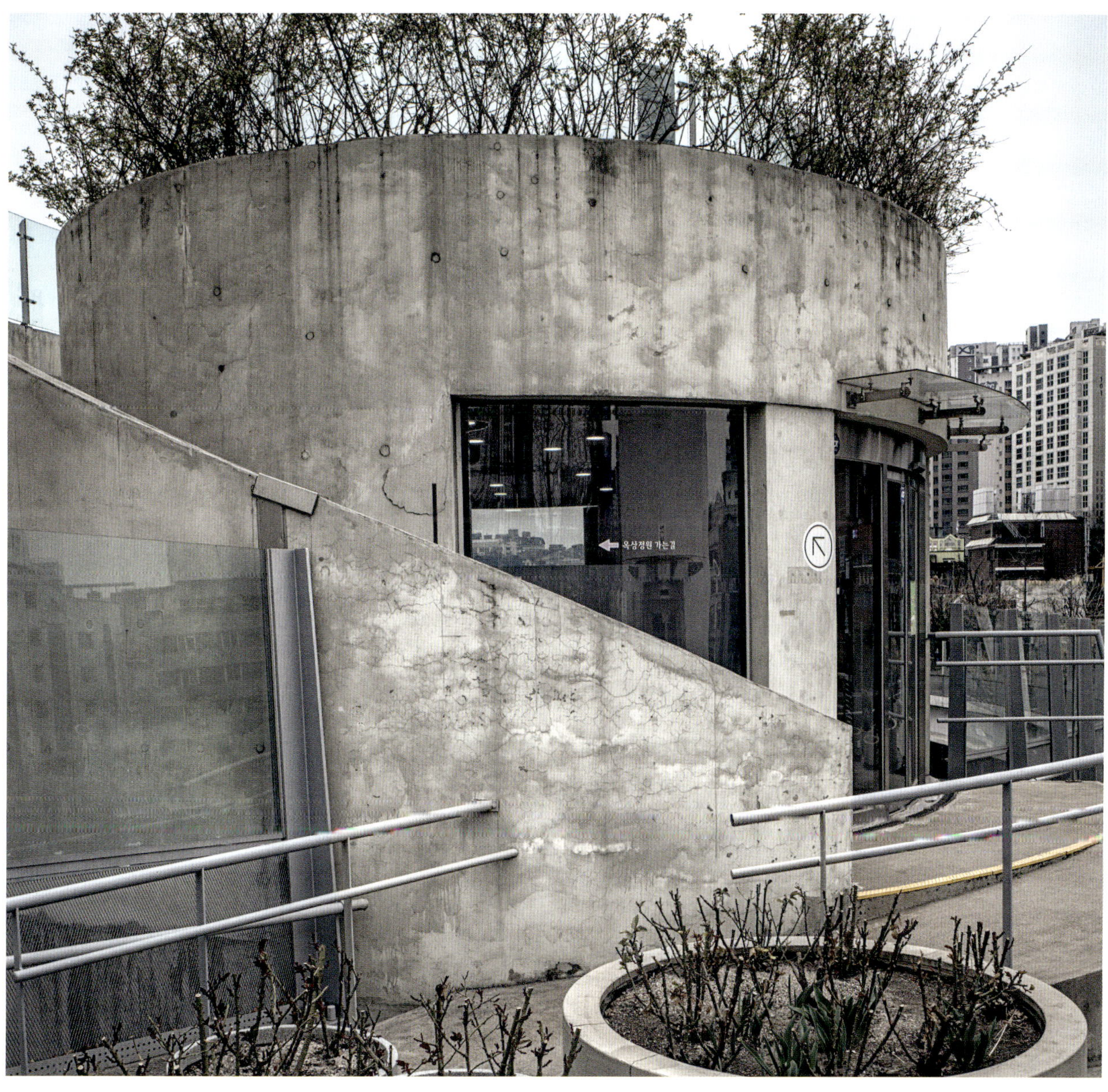

OWL HOUSE

BUSAN · Architect: MOON Hoon · Completed 2015

Perched high in the Busan hills, Moon Hoon's Owl House keeps watch over Korea's southern city. With its twin eye-like windows and beaked geometry, it is Brutalism gone ornithological: concrete plumage, angular feathers, and a stare that could unnerve passing clouds.

The façade juts and folds like origami mid-flight – part bunker, part bird of prey. A vertical slit cuts through the wall like a dilated pupil, turning the structure into a nocturnal observer frozen mid-blink. Inside, rooms stack and twist like an owl's nest assembled from impulse and intuition, not design plans. Corners are abrupt, light is precise, and every aperture feels like a watchful gaze.

Despite its whimsy, this is Brutalism with talons: raw, sculptural, and strange. The concrete gleams under daylight, as if freshly preened. It won't perch quietly – it broods, surveying Busan with amused suspicion. This is architecture that certainly holds parliament.

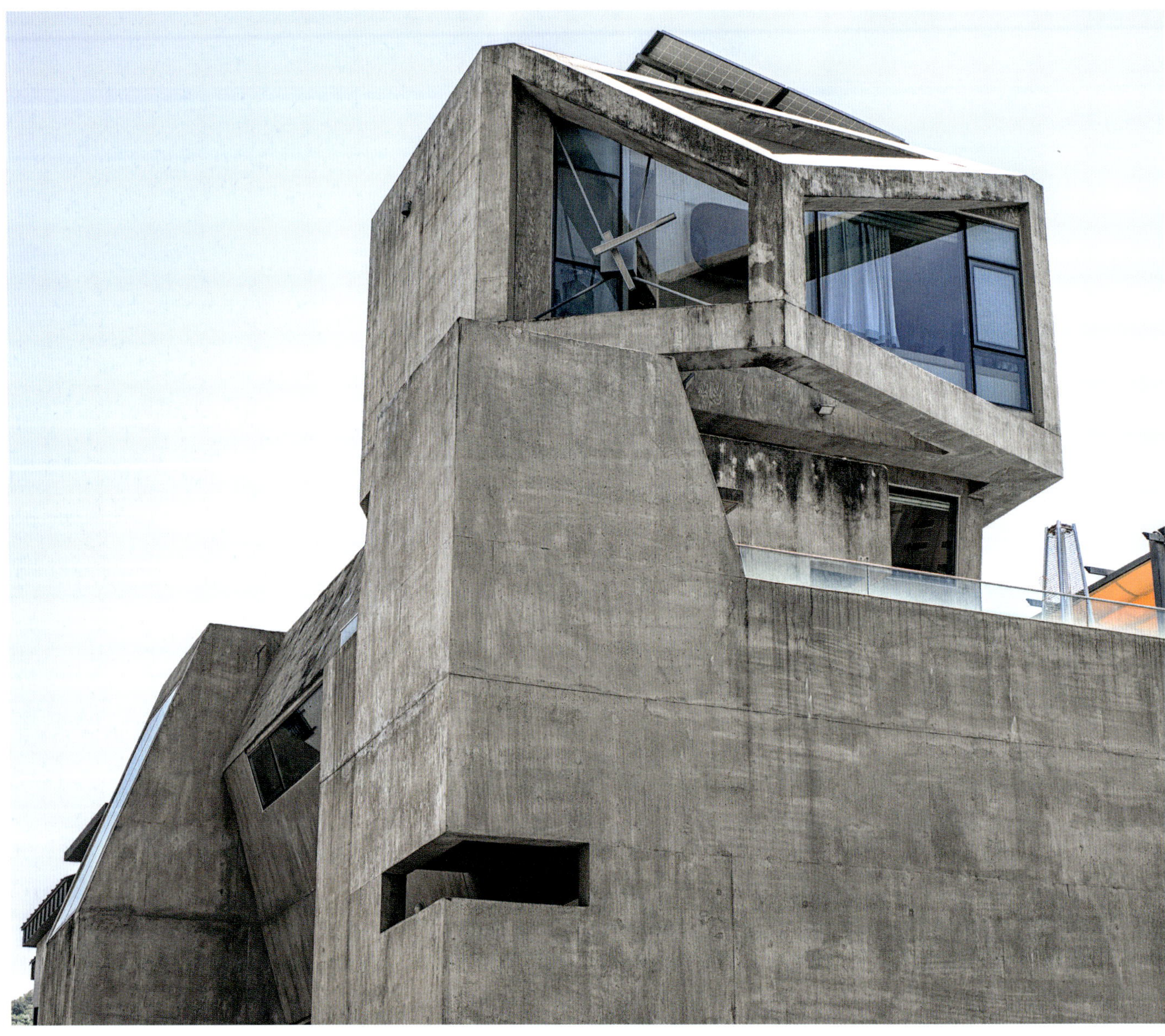

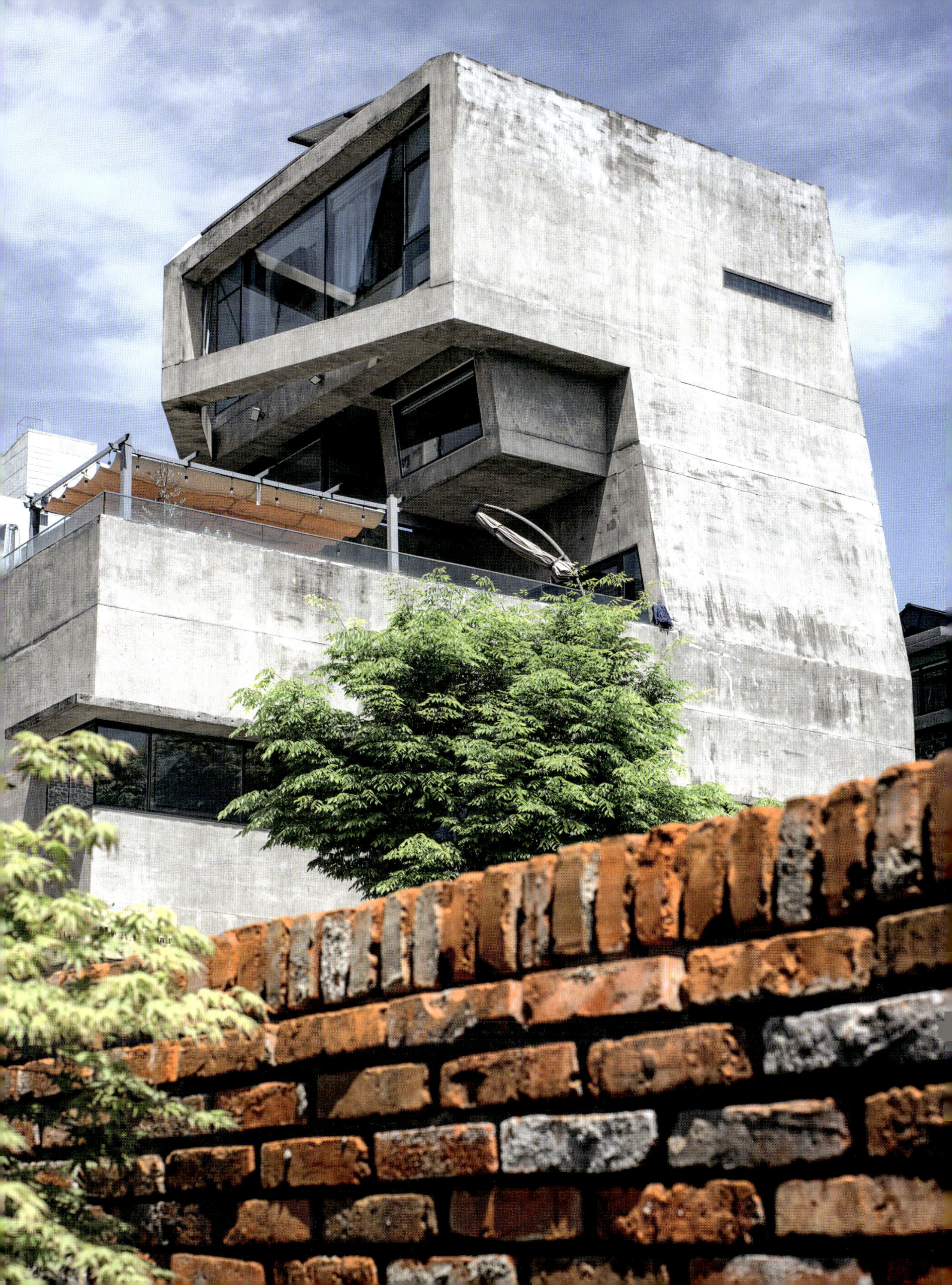

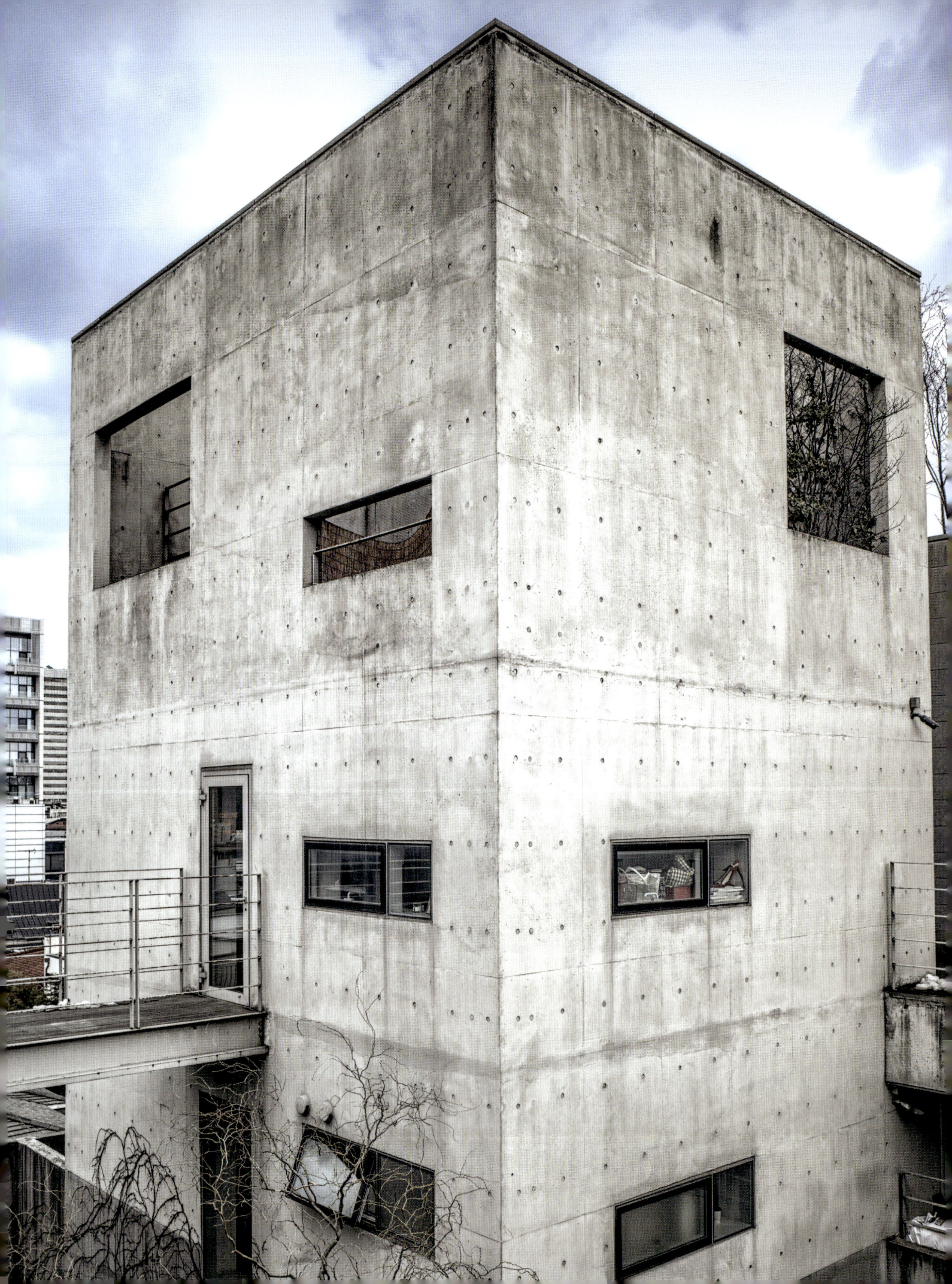

ZWKM BLOCK

SEOUL · Architect: KIM Young-Joon · Completed 2015

ZWKM Block in Nonhyeon-dong, Seoul, isn't so much a building as an experiment in urban negotiation – a quartet of concrete forms learning how to live together. It occupies four adjacent plots that might easily have become four isolated boxes. Instead, the architects turned them into a single living organism, stitched together by shared circulation, underground links, and a quiet architectural empathy rare in Gangnam's hyper-individual skyline.

At street level, ZWKM is all permeability – a series of glassy openings, pedestrian alleys, and shaded recesses that invite passers-by to drift through, not walk past. Above, the four buildings twist and pivot like dancers caught mid-pose. Each has its own silhouette – some taut, others cut by terraces – yet all share a rhythmic sense of mass, proportion, and tone. Reinforced concrete and steel provide the bones, but voids define the personality. Staircases and bridges pierce the façades, creating moments of visual and physical exchange.

This isn't Brutalism in the traditional sense, but it shares the Brutalist virtues of honesty, weight, and structural expression. The exposed materials feel unpolished yet deliberate – concrete surfaces hold light like skin, edges reveal their joints, and shadows fall with architectural precision.

The basement – a hidden artery binding the four structures – connects the ensemble. Mid-levels act as communal lungs, with terraces and platforms that encourage overlap between public and private life. And, at the top, individuality takes over: each roofline breaks free, a celebration of autonomy within unity.

ZWKM Block proposes a horizontal high-rise, a new Seoul typology where collaboration replaces competition. It's an urban quartet composed in concrete – each building a note, distinct yet resonant. Together, they hum with civic intelligence: modest and unmistakably human in scale.

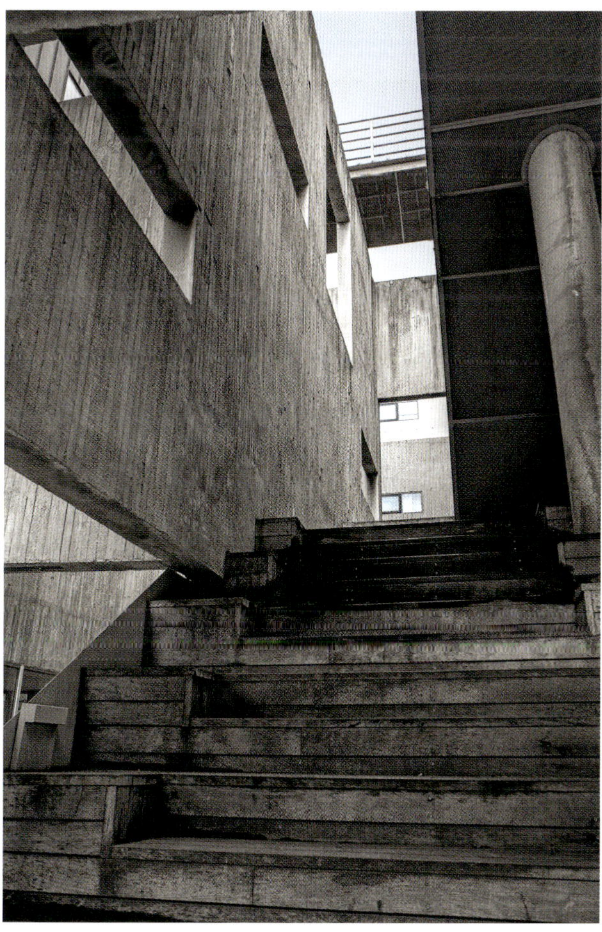

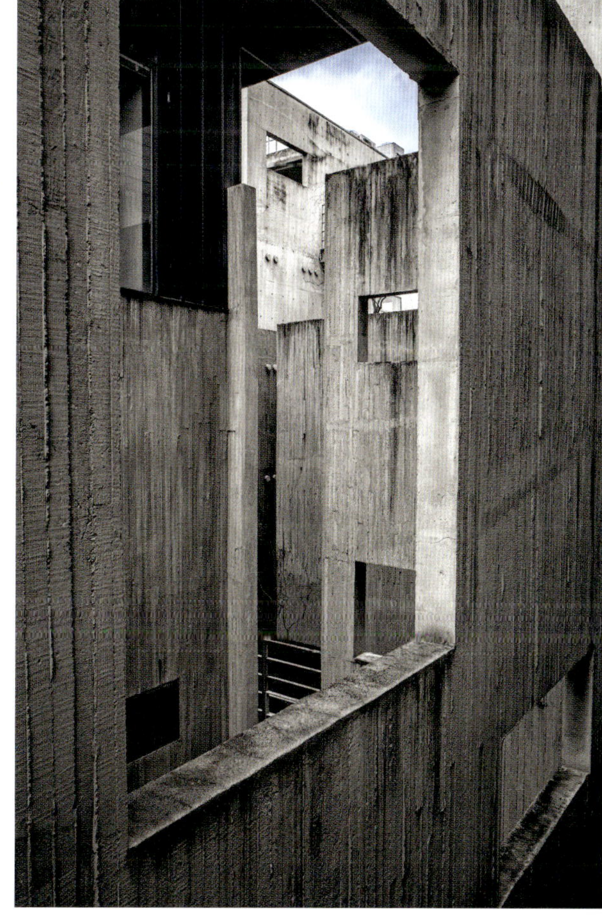

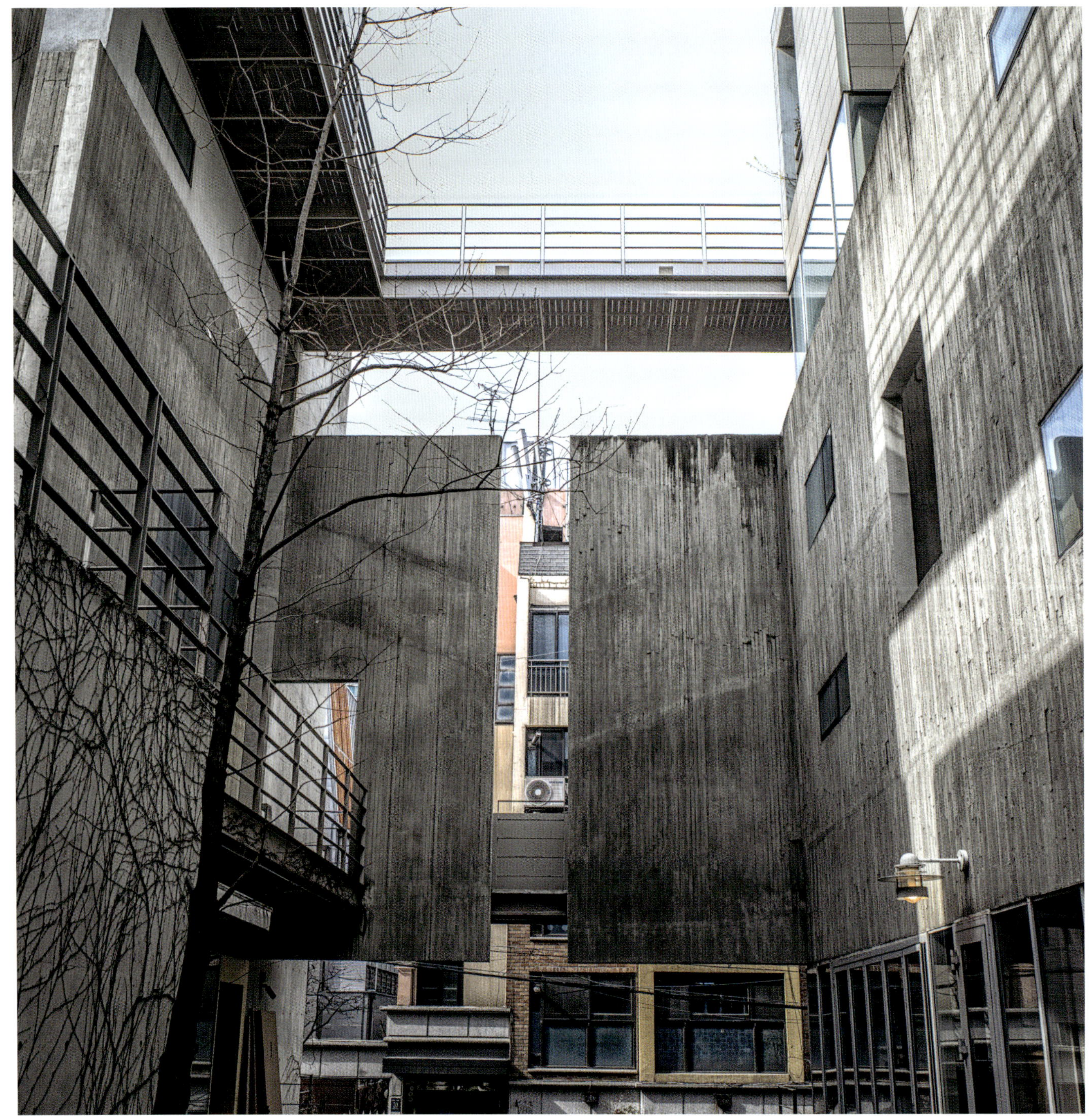

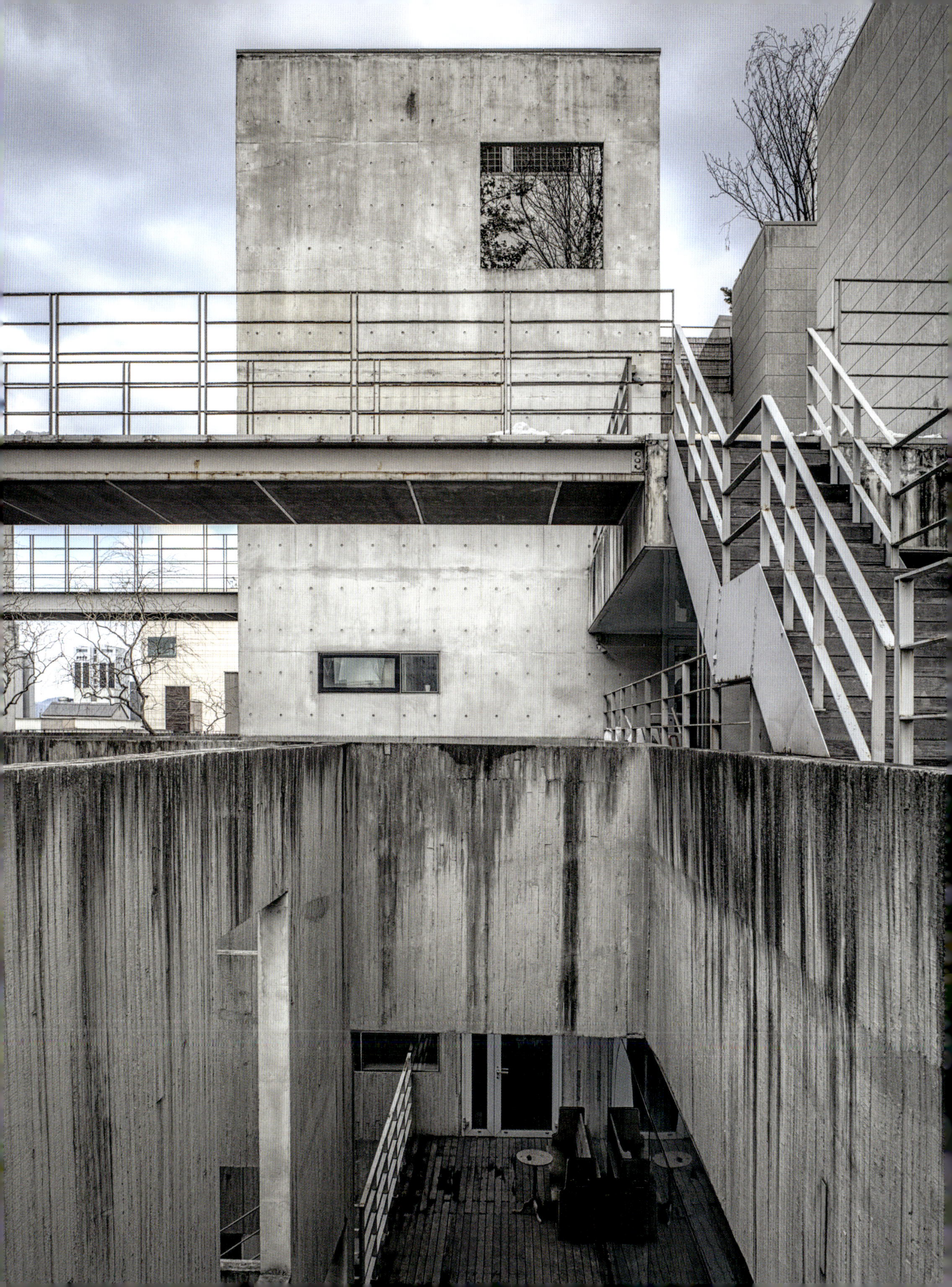

JH BUILDING

SEOUL · Architects: HAN Ji-young and HWANG Su-yong · Completed 2023

This distinctive diamond-grid concrete façade operates as both structure and ornament, framing the building in a rhythmic play of shadow and void. This exoskeletal design gives the compact site a commanding vertical presence, while large inset windows dissolve the boundary between interior and street. The architects employ raw exposed concrete with meticulous precision – its sharp geometries softened only by the passage of light across the surface. Within, open spatial volumes and warm lighting offset the building's exterior austerity, creating an adaptable environment for creative tenants. The JH Building exemplifies the evolving identity of contemporary Seoul – where architectural experimentation and urban density converge to produce structures that are expressive, intelligent, and deeply attuned to the energy of their surroundings.

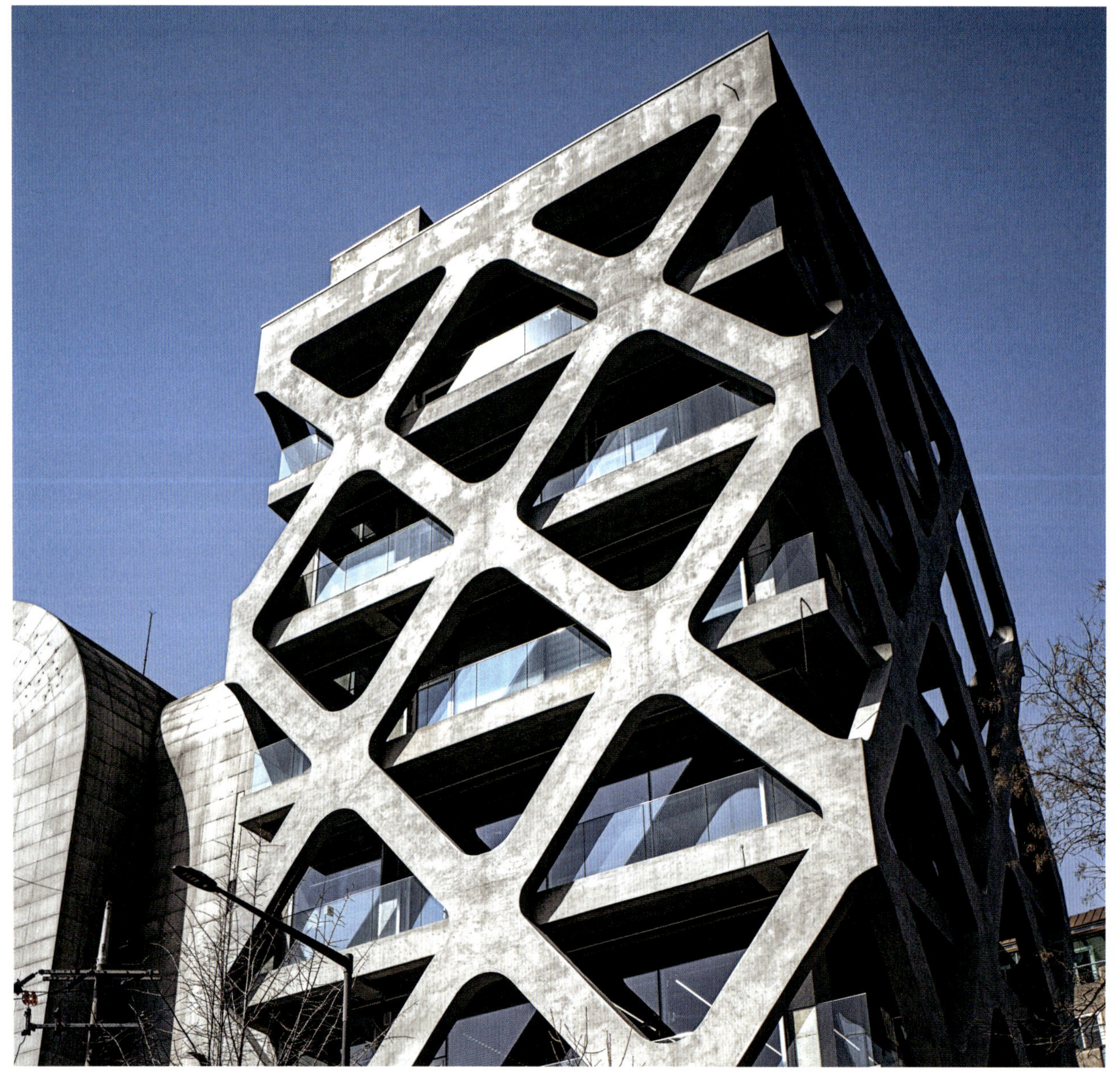

STUDIO EGG

SEOUL · Architect: SHIN Chang-seop (Duga Architects & Engineers) · Completed 2005

The Studio Egg Building echoes elements of Constructivist architecture, though it isn't part of that historical movement. Constructivism, emerging in 1920s Soviet Russia, emphasized expressive geometric abstraction, industrial materials, and the visual celebration of structure and function.

In Studio Egg's façade, the repetitive geometric modules – each a deep circular extrusion within a strict orthogonal grid – evoke the Constructivist fascination with rhythm, structure, and the mechanistic. Its bold frontal composition, use of exposed concrete, and play between mass and void recall the Constructivist pursuit of architecture as a social and visual machine.

However, Shin Chang-seop's design tempers those avant-garde ideals with a more sculptural, postmodern sensibility. The spheres read as playful reliefs mimicking photo studios' cycloramas, not functional components. In short, it's Constructivist in spirit – especially in its geometric rigor and abstraction – but Brutalist in material and urban intent, and ultimately contemporary Korean in execution.

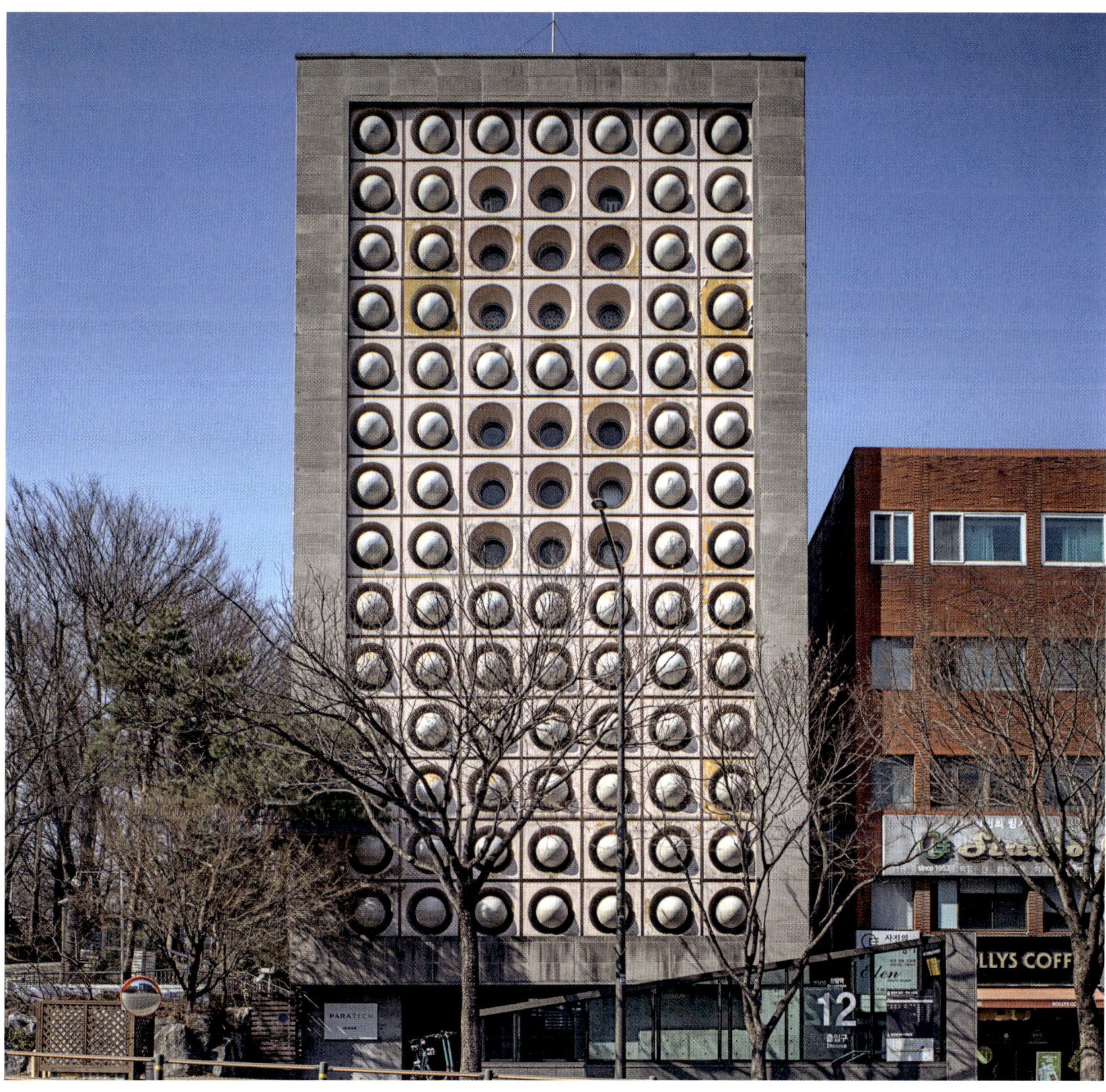

BONTE MUSEUM

JEJU ISLAND · Architect: ANDO Tadao · Completed 2012

Settled into Jeju Island's black lava terrain, the Bonte Museum feels less built than discovered. It pairs austere geometry with the island's quiet vastness – an architecture of breath, not gesture. Concrete, light, and shadow become the materials of contemplation, forming an equilibrium between gravity and grace.

The word *bonte* – Korean for "true essence" – sets the tone. Ando takes it literally. He answers the island not with spectacle but stillness: corridors that stretch like pauses, pools that mirror shifting skies, and monolithic walls that carry the weight of volcanic memory. His concrete is not content merely to contain art – it slows time. Inside, the pace drops to that of a tide. Works spanning Korean crafts to Nam June Paik's electric imagination feel suspended in air, each object held in reverent equilibrium.

This isn't a parachute project by a starchitect but a careful act of listening. Ando engages Korean sensibility with humility, cradling vibrant, handmade objects in a vessel of greyscale quiet. The museum holds opposites in delicate balance – modern and ancient, Japanese and Korean, shadow and illumination.

Even the light behaves differently here. It drifts rather than strikes, tracing the texture of formwork as if reading it. Space unfolds as syntax: a sequence of anticipation, pause, and release. The architecture earns attention through composure, not demand.

Yet serenity, like all things, can be interrupted. Mid-capture, just as the scene settled into focus, a wave of fluorescent-hatted schoolchildren stormed through. The building remained composed, so I followed its lead. Channel the concrete. Breathe.

In the end, Bonte feels less a museum than a reliquary of quietude – a place where architecture meditates on itself, and the world, for a moment, stands still enough to listen.

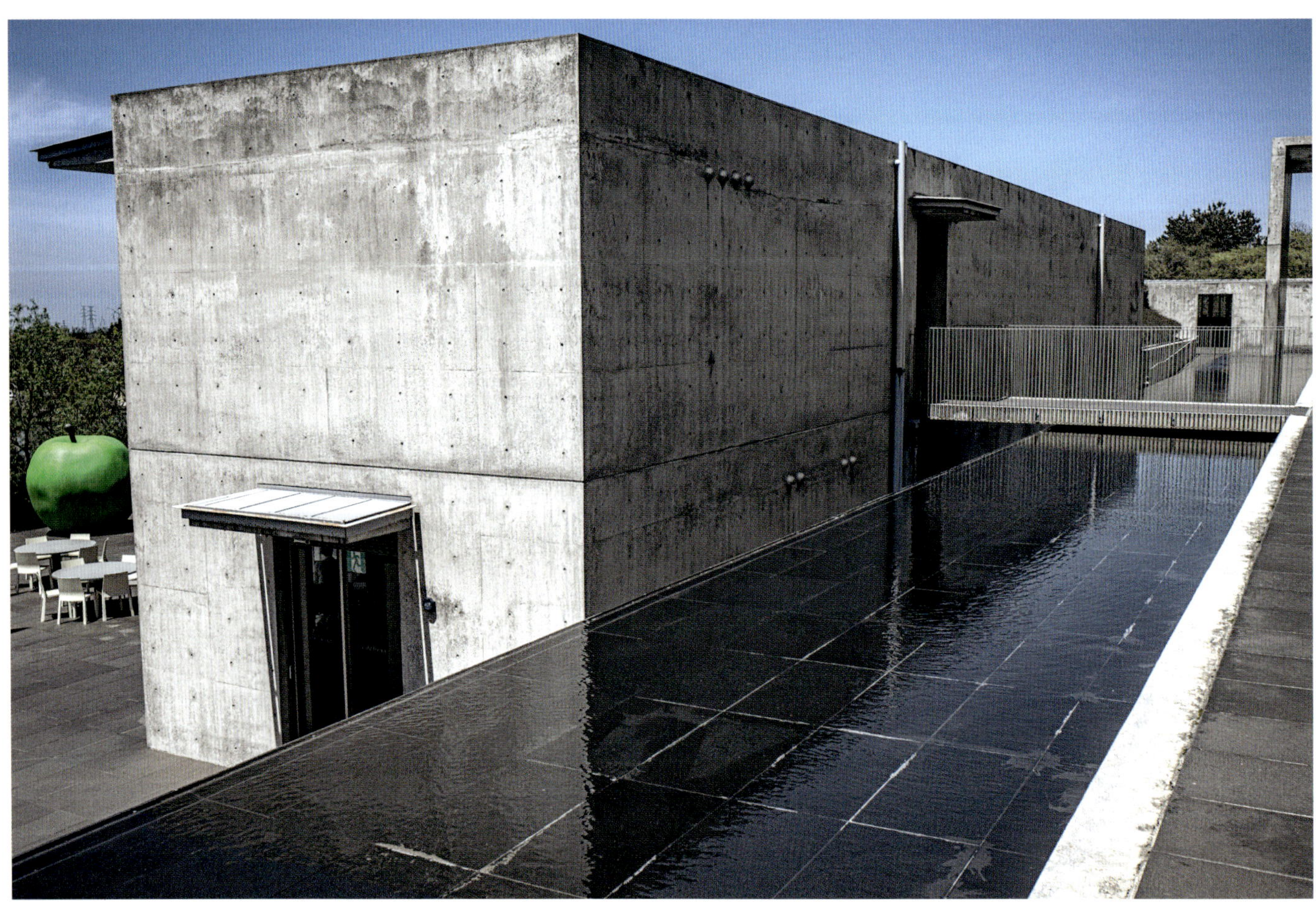

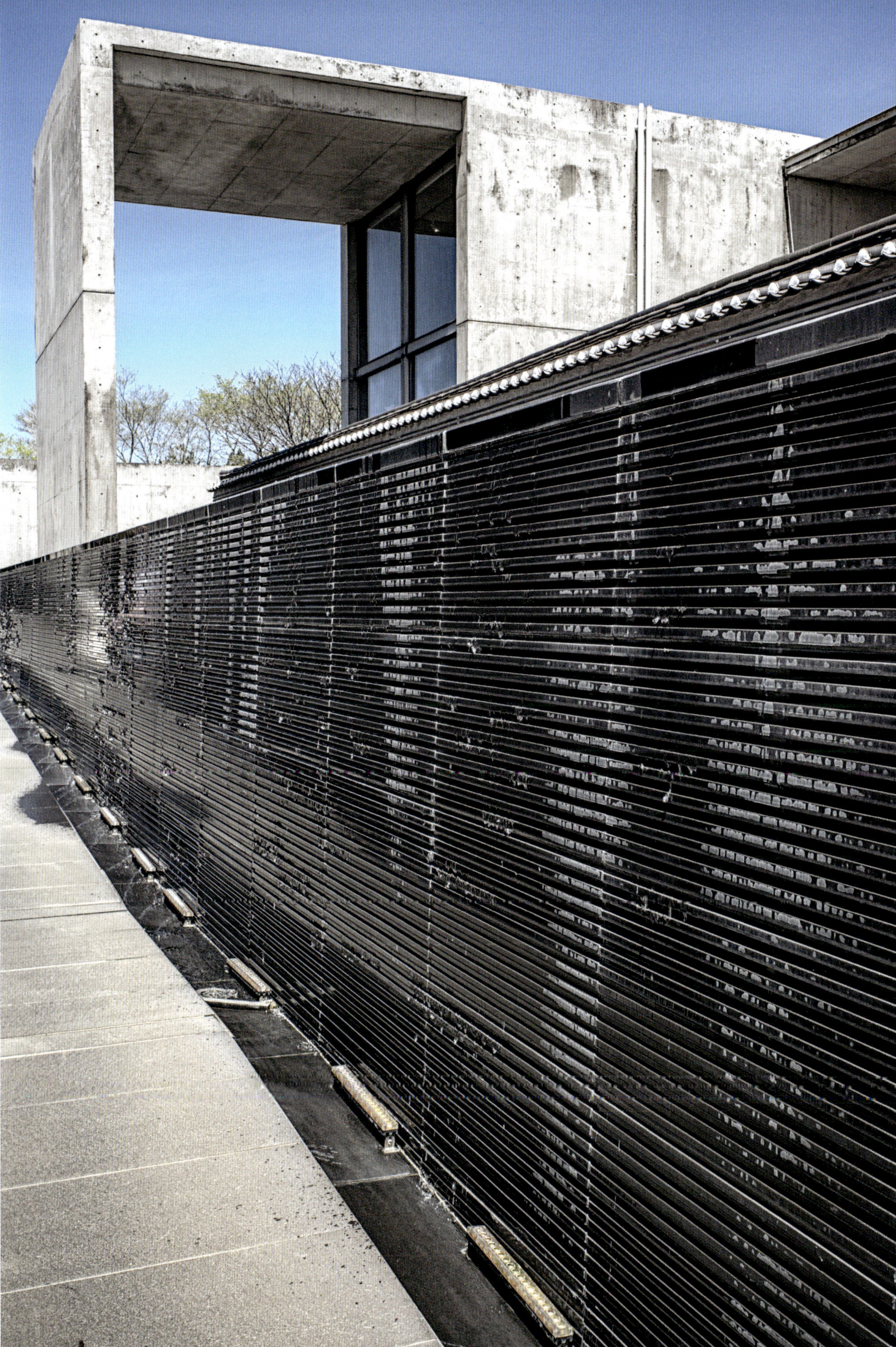

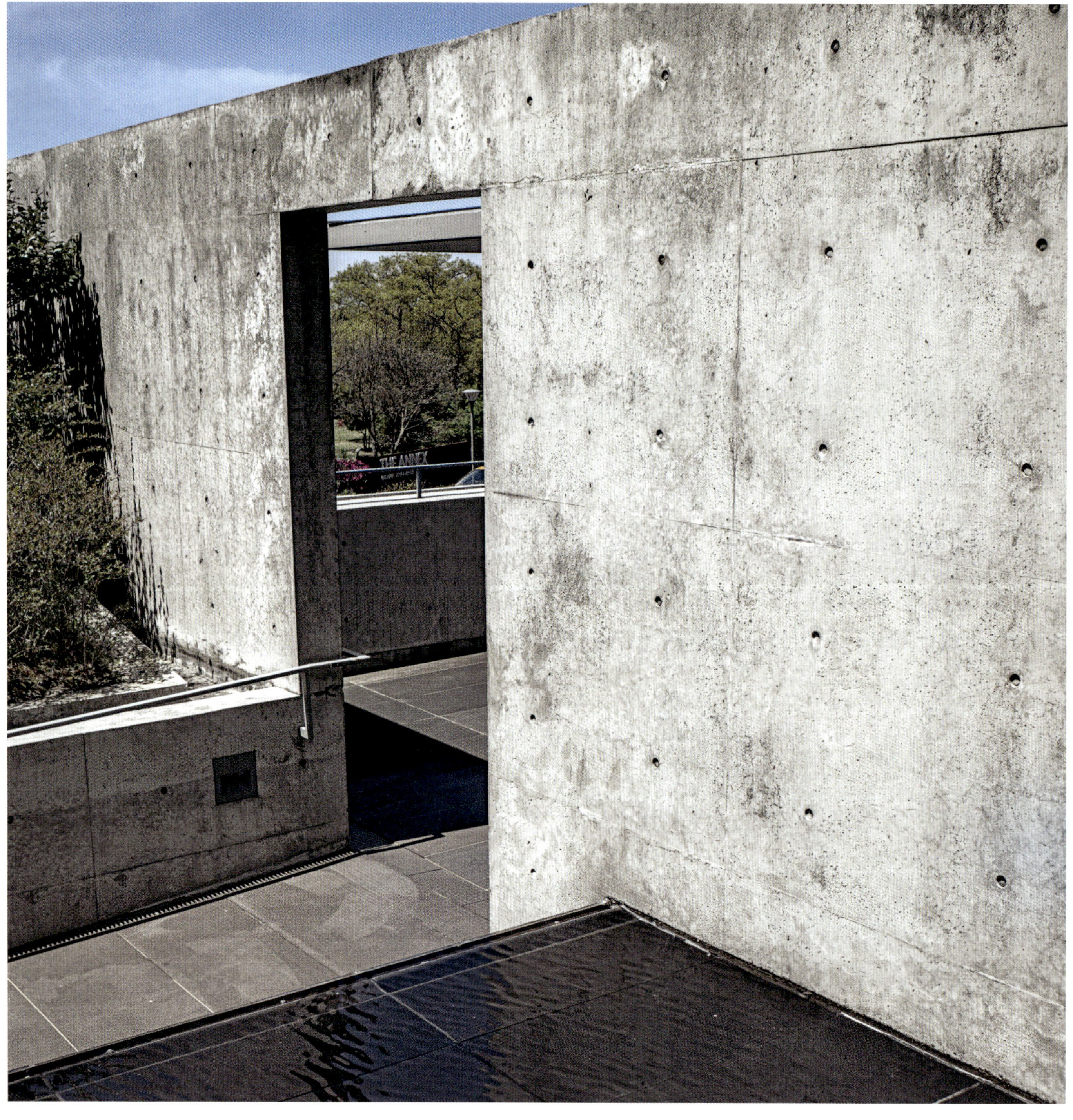
THE ANNEX

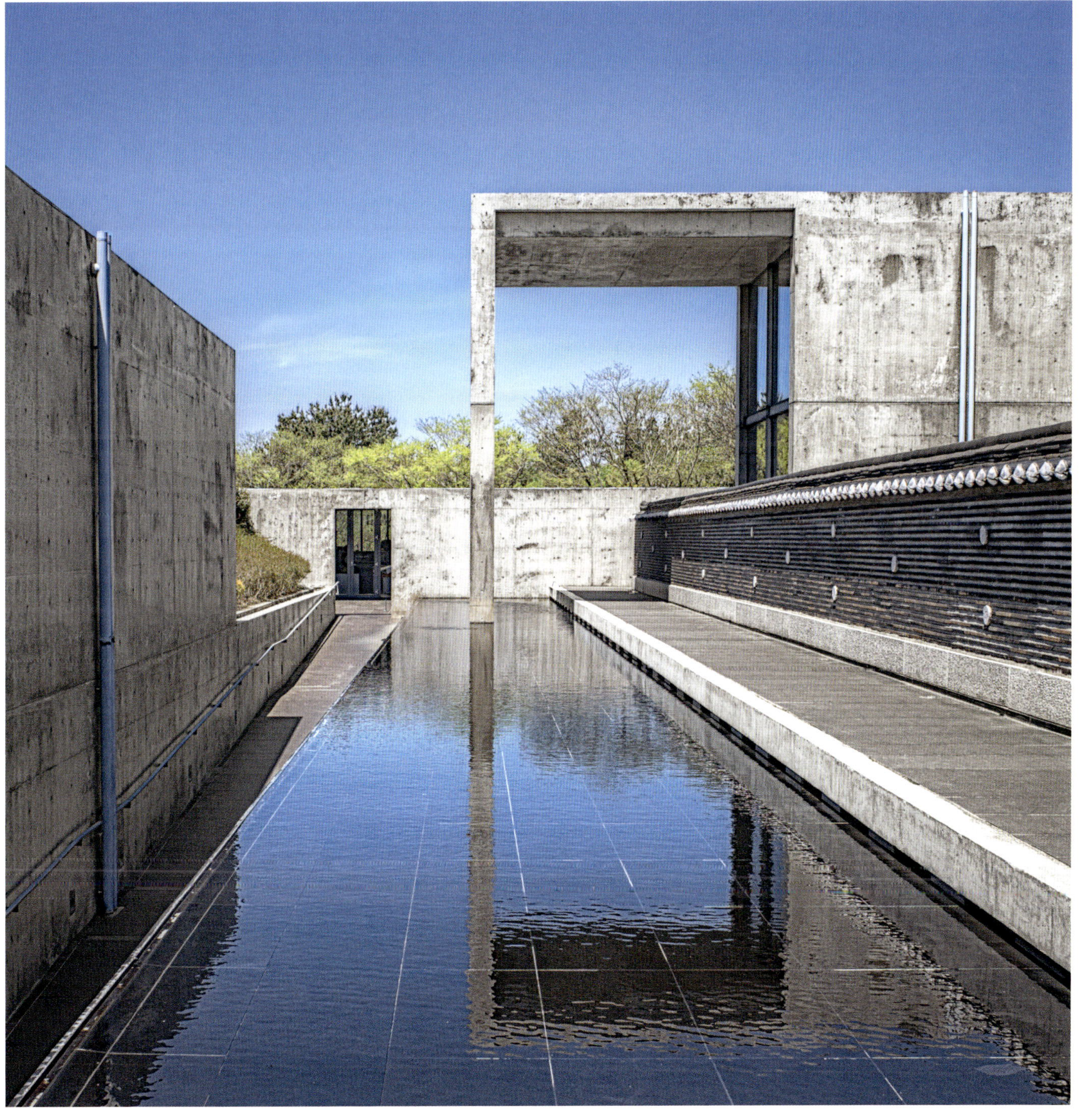

KT&G SANGSANGMADANG

SEOUL · Architect: BAE Dae-yong · Completed 2007

In the feverish heart of Seoul's Mapo district – that restless mix of neon karaoke dens, indie bars, and caffeine-fuelled idealism – KT&G Sangsangmadang looms like a digital relic gone rogue. Its façade, all grids and jutting modules, resembles a circuit board caught mid-surge: part architecture, part motherboard, entirely alive. Every extrusion feels like a thought rendered solid, a sketch that never stopped evolving. Some label it postmodern, others chaotic, but beneath its restless skin lies the spirit of Brutalism – fearless and defiantly material.

Completed in 2007, it's a building that refuses to choose a single identity. It's a gallery, a cinema, a music venue, a studio, a rooftop lookout – a vertical city block for creative misfits. The geometry isn't tidy; it's rhythmic. Boxes jut like ideas interrupting one another, and the stairs seem to wander off mid-sentence. Even the shadows feel curated.

Sangsangmadang, meaning "Square of Imagination", lives up to its name by celebrating disorder as design. It doesn't hide its layers – it parades them. Concrete here isn't oppressive, but conversational: it frames, filters, and dramatizes. You can read its surfaces like a manuscript, each indentation a punctuation mark in the city's ongoing monologue.

And somewhere between the café chatter and the cinema hum, the building becomes its own metaphor for Korean urban culture – contradictory yet coherent, loud yet strangely disciplined.

You don't just enter Sangsangmadang, you plug into it. The place hums with feedback – creative, social, architectural. It's a concrete daydream wired to Seoul's current, a vertical mixtape that never stops looping.

In a city where the youth are addicted to fakeness, Sangsangmadang stays gloriously unfiltered – showcasing that imagination, when given walls, will always find new ways to break through them.

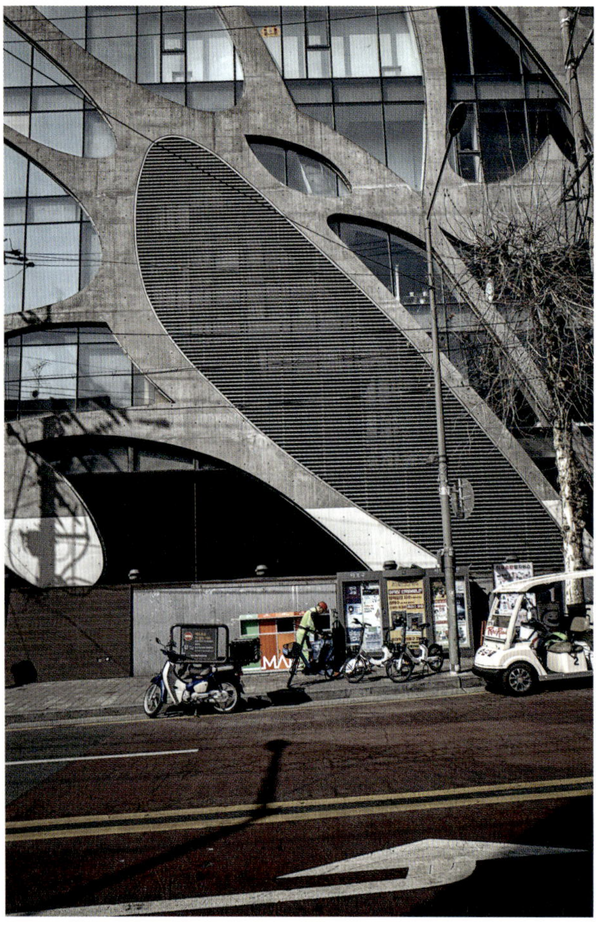

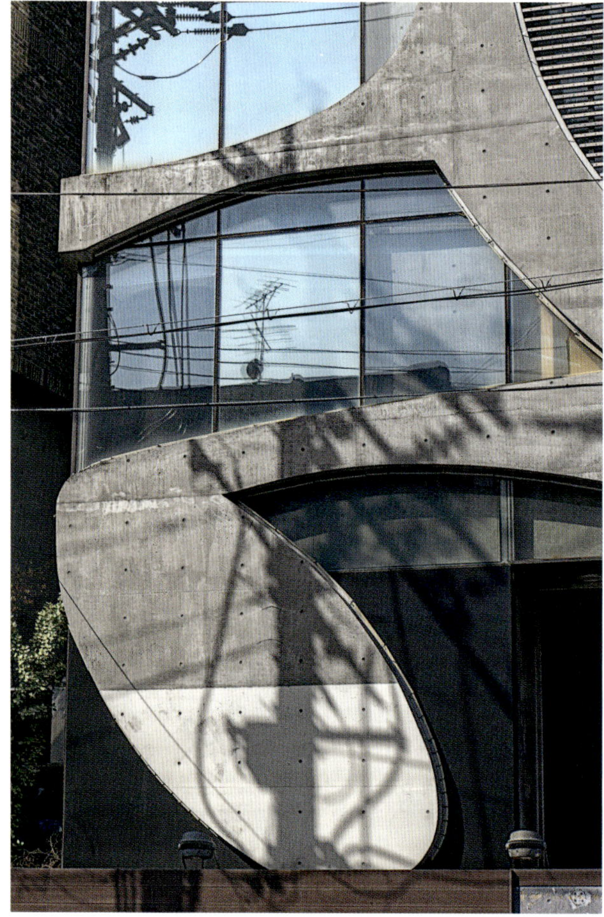

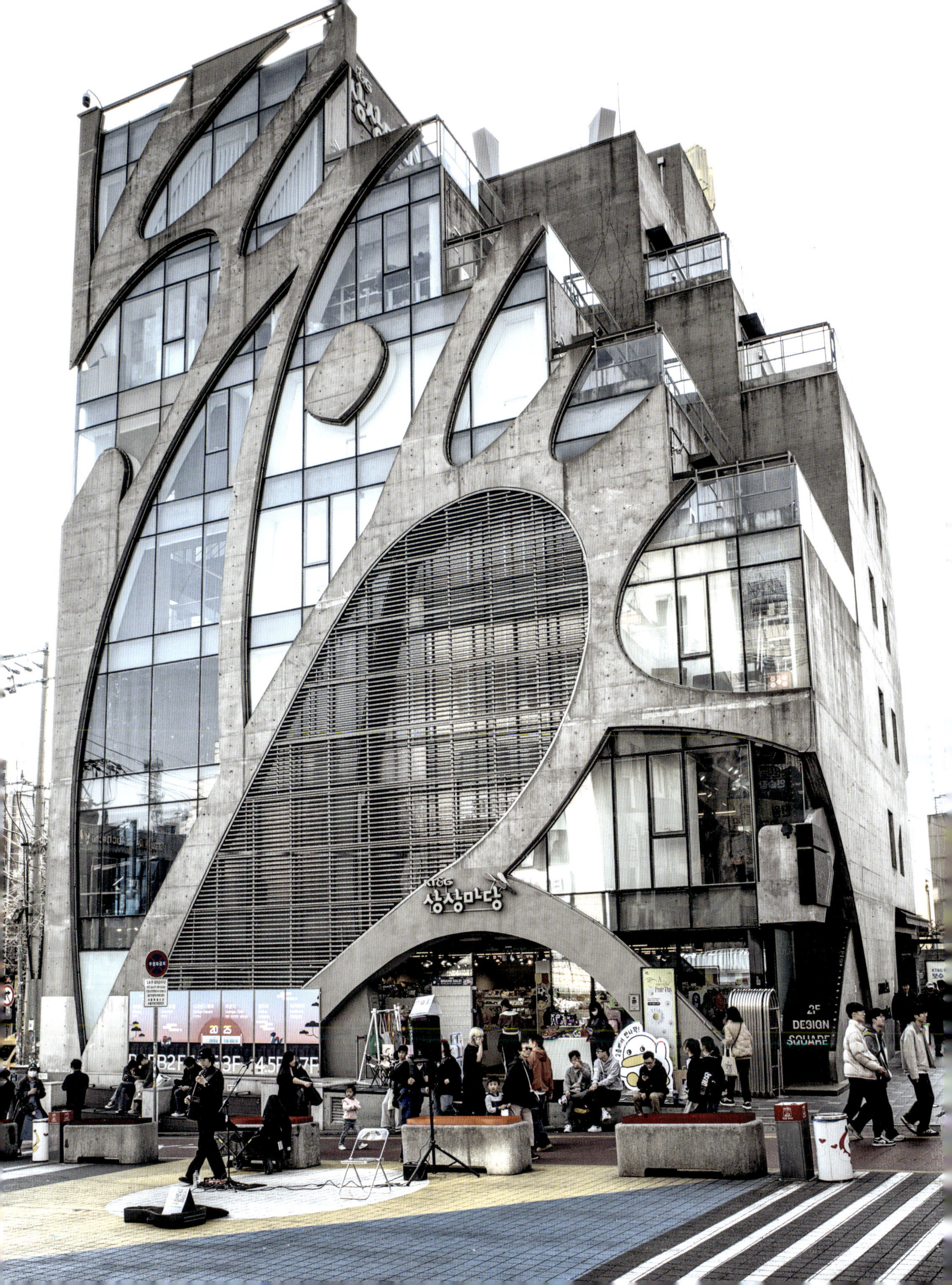
KT&G
상상마당
2F
DESIGN
SQUARE
20 25

SPACE GROUP OF KOREA BUILDING (ARARIO MUSEUM IN SPACE)

SEOUL · Architects: KIM Swoo-geun and CHANG Sea-yang · Completed 1971 and 1977 / Extended 1997

Near to Changdeokgung, one of five grand palaces in Seoul, the Space Group Building – now the Arario Museum in Space – is less an object than an organism. Designed by Kim Swoo-geun as the headquarters of his firm, it remains one of Korea's most intimate conversations between architecture and time.

At first glance, its rough brick façade looks improvised, as if it grew from the earth instead of from a blueprint. Yet within the dense weave of walls, voids, and stairwells lies extraordinary precision. Kim used more than 200,000 hand-pressed bricks, layering them into irregular planes that catch light like shifting soil. Each surface bends and leans, creating a micro-city of recesses and reveals. The result feels both archaic and modern, a sculptural maze that invites wandering.

Inside, space folds into itself. Corridors squeeze and release; stairs climb, double back, and vanish; tiny balconies overlook courtyards barely wide enough for one tree. This labyrinthine sequence reflects Kim's fascination with how architecture can choreograph thought. Even the structure's unfinished quality – its visible pipes, uneven masonry, and exposed concrete – adds to its tactile honesty.

In 1997, architect Chang Sea-yang extended the complex with a crystalline glass tower that rises beside Kim's brick labyrinth like a reflective echo. The juxtaposition of old and new – a Brutalist relic kissing a modernist ghost – gives the ensemble its peculiar electricity. When transformed into Arario Museum in 2014, little was polished or hidden. The patina of decades remained: moss creeping up brick, sunlight leaking through joints. The building endures as both relic and revelation – a porous monument to architectural process.

Kim Swoo-geun didn't design a headquarters, he built a question: What if a building could think? Preservation of ancient traditional architecture on the same plot further provokes reflection.

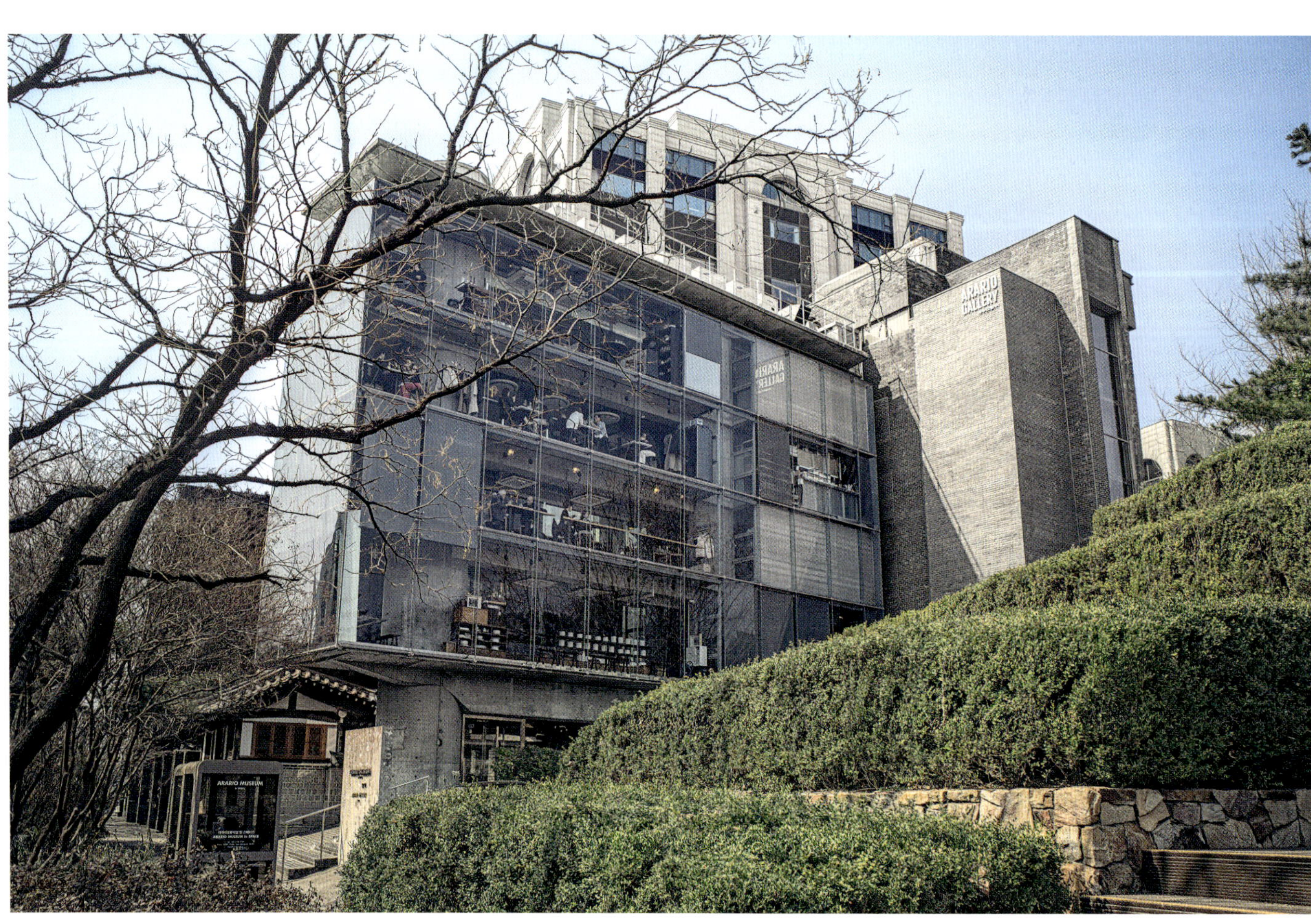

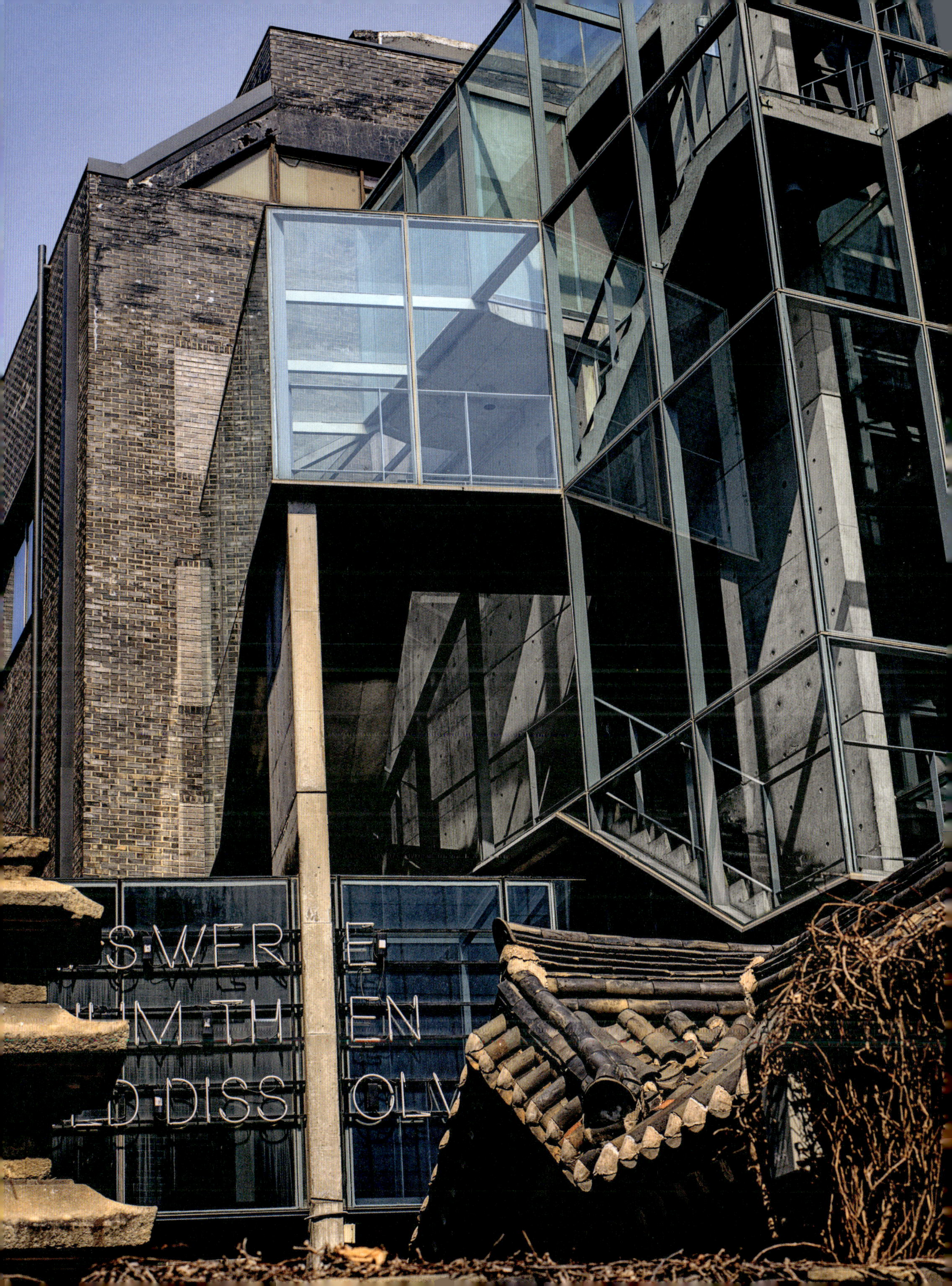

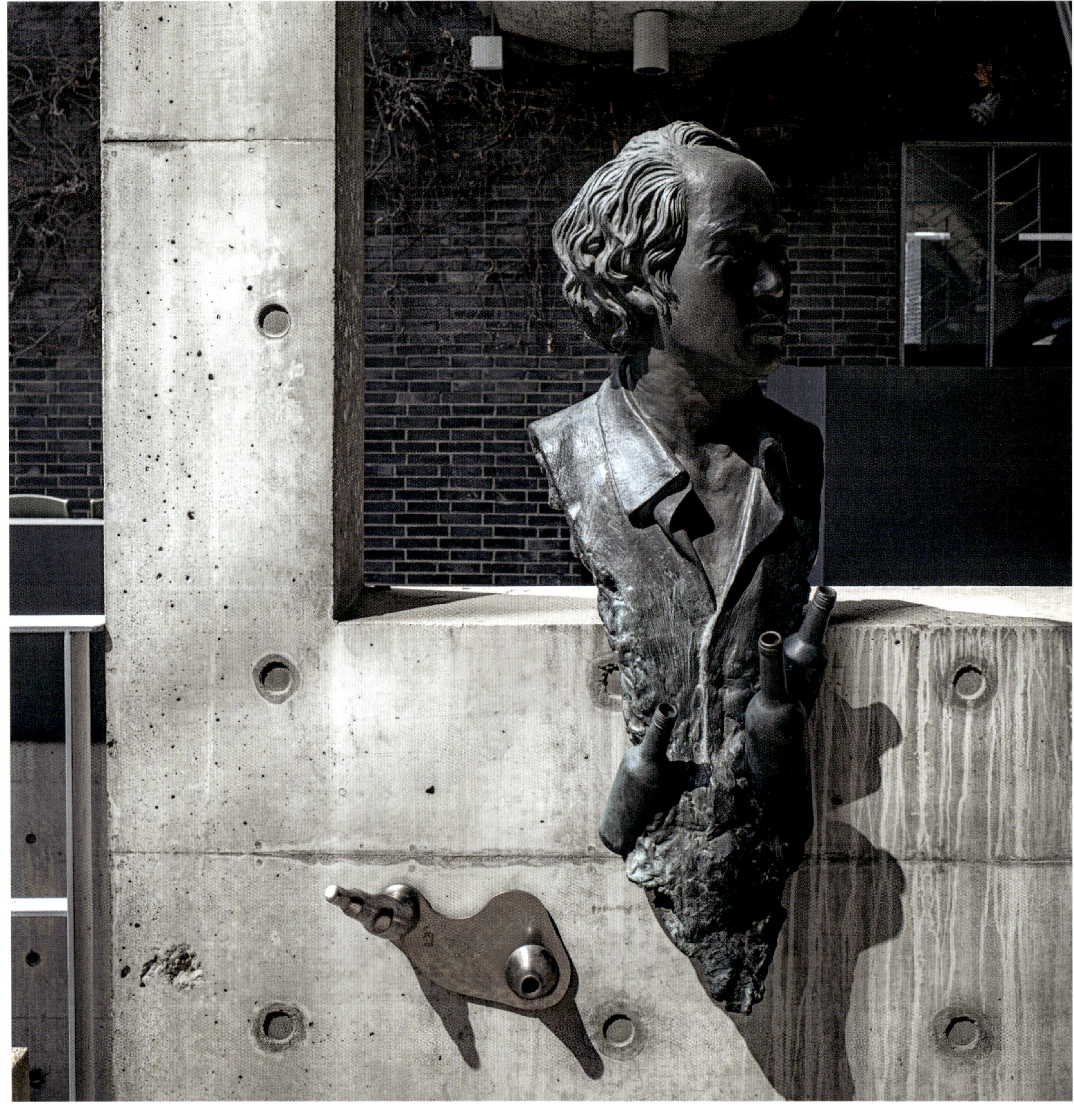

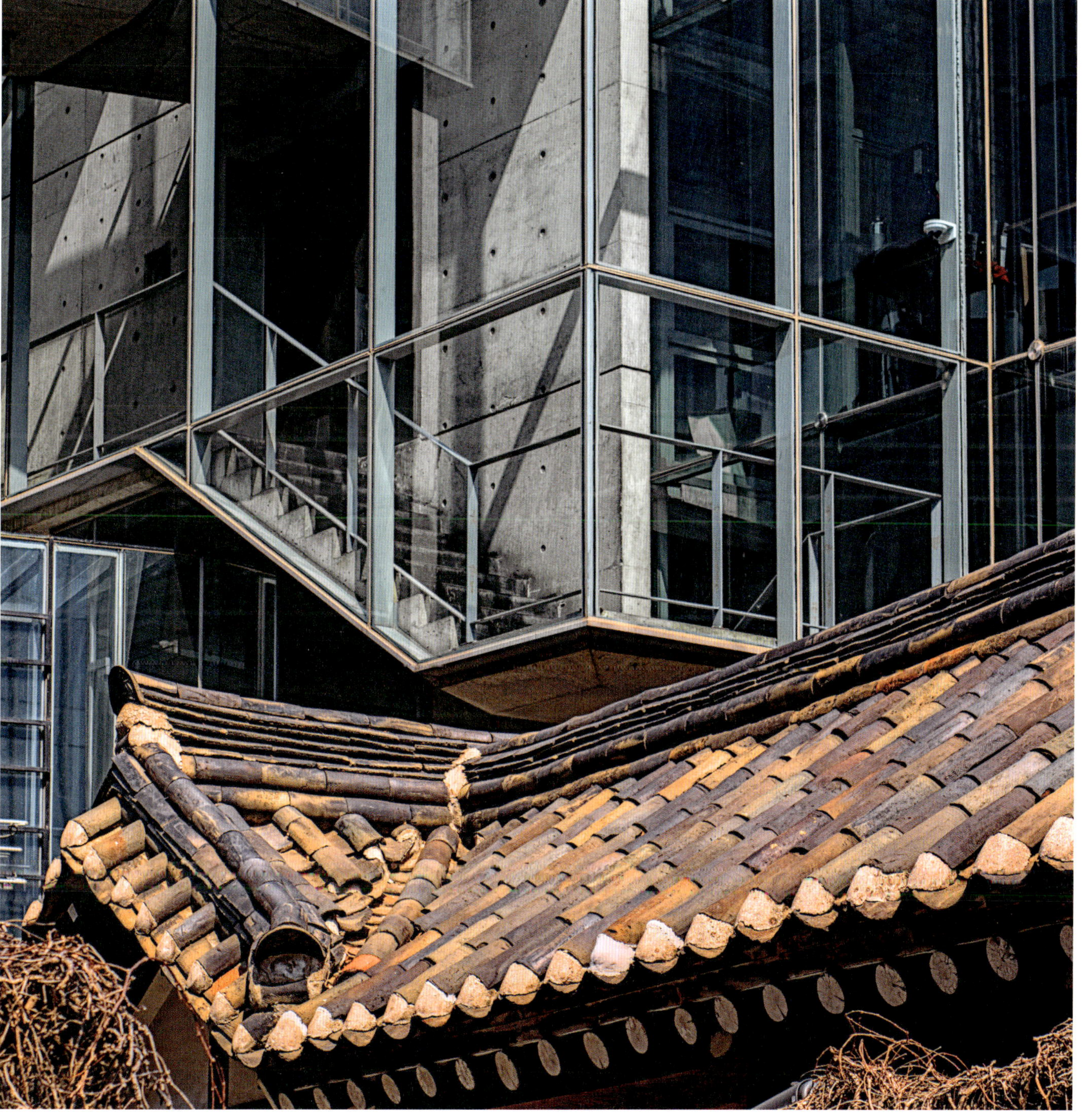

AREUKE SPA

SEOUL · Architect: Chiasmus Partners (lead: LEE Hyunho) · Completed 2021

The Areuke Spa isn't content with serenity – it thrusts it skywards. Rising from a cramped corner of Hongdae like a concrete wave frozen mid-crest, the structure fuses raw materiality with sculptural drama. Its sharply folded form suggests both shelter and motion, a monolith softened by the quiet promise of wellness within. The façade ripples like the surface of disturbed water, as if the building itself exhaled after a long soak.

Windows pierce the concrete skin – not symmetrically, but rhythmically, like breaths in a meditative cycle. Light slides across its rough surface by day, then glows softly from the cutouts by night, turning the mass into a lantern of calm in Seoul's electric tangle. Inside, concrete gives way to warmth, steam, and stillness. It is architecture that cleanses not only the skin but also the palette – a spa rendered in structure, not scent.

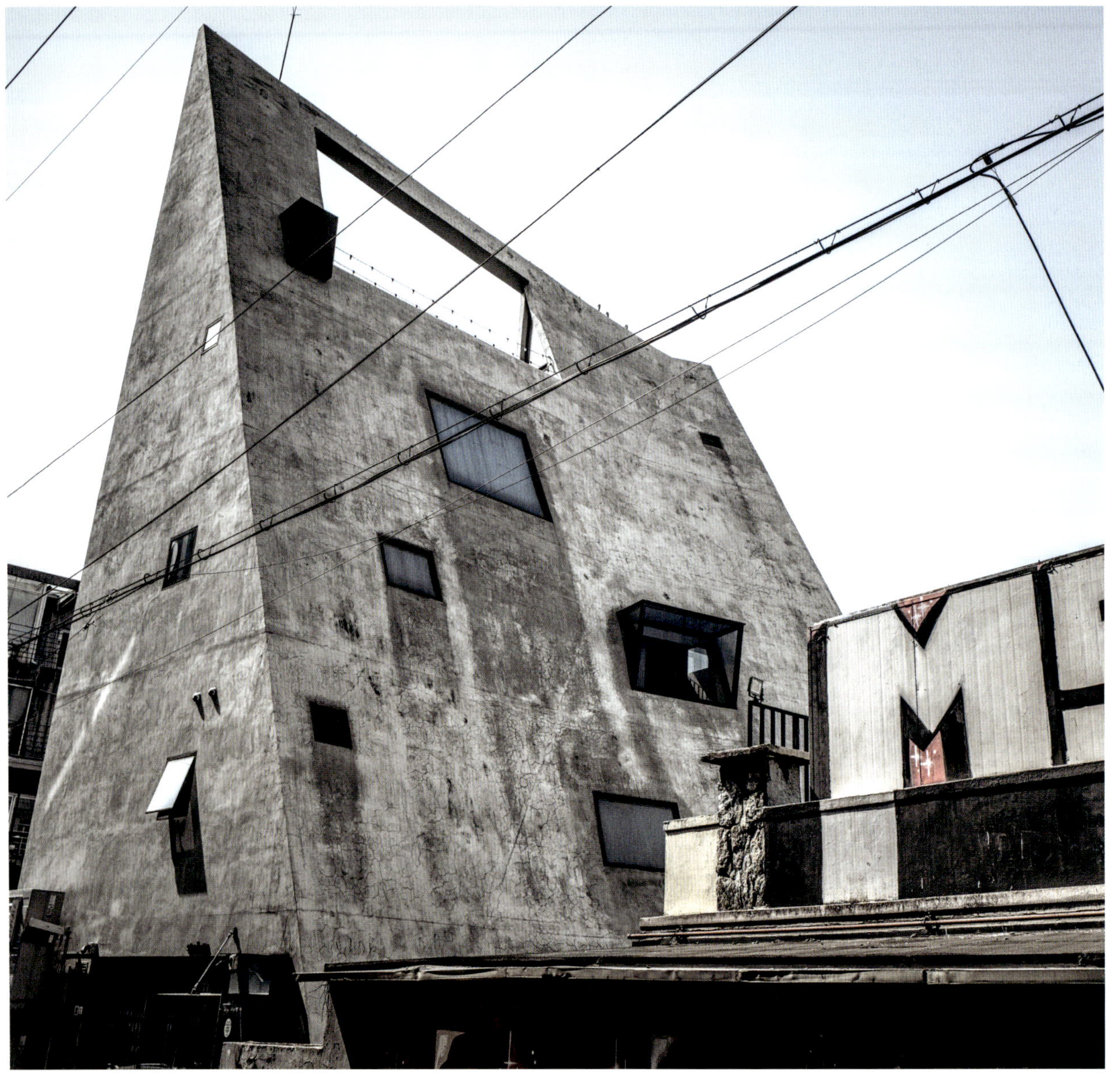

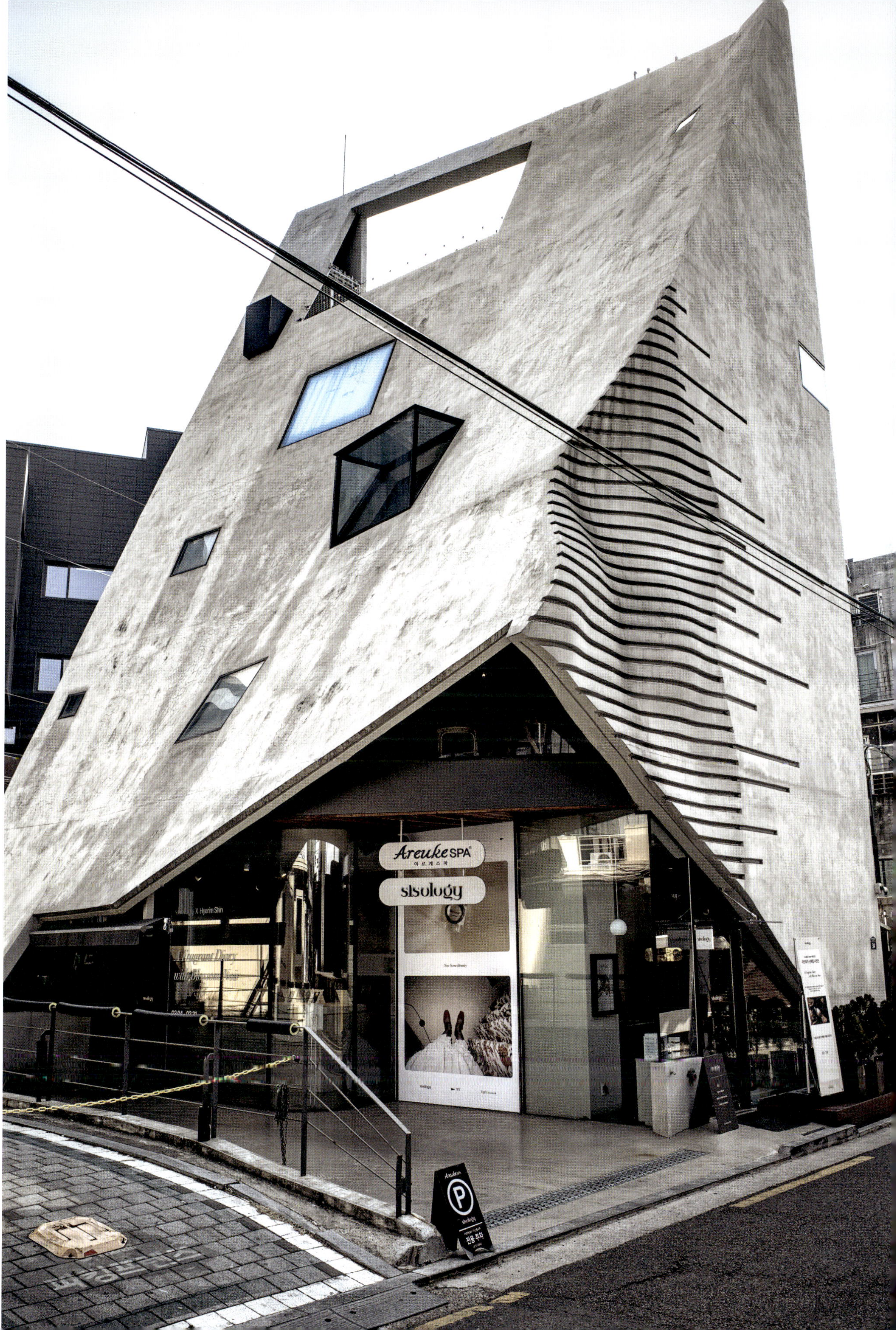
Areuke SPA
sisology

KIM OK-GILL MEMORIAL HALL

SEOUL · Architect: KIM In-cheurl · Completed 1998

Anchored to a quiet slope near Ewha, the Kim Ok-gill Memorial Hall rises low yet feels weightless – a study in vertical poise and material gravity. Its sheer concrete walls, punctuated by narrow slots of glass, create a façade that seems to breathe light in disciplined doses. Built in tribute to the educator and activist Kim Ok-gill, the structure carries memory through its mass, not its symbols.

The architecture is unyielding yet graceful. Planes of exposed concrete form a rhythmic sequence of void and wall, shadow and reflection. Inside, filtered daylight slips down the vertical seams, softening the severity of concrete.

If memory in architecture is too often literal, this is its antithesis: abstract and spatially profound. The Hall resists prettiness, preferring permanence. Like Kim Ok-gill herself, it doesn't seek applause – only understanding. In that way, its Brutalism isn't brutal at all. It is careful, necessary, and quietly radical. A lesson in how to build legacy – one plane of concrete at a time.

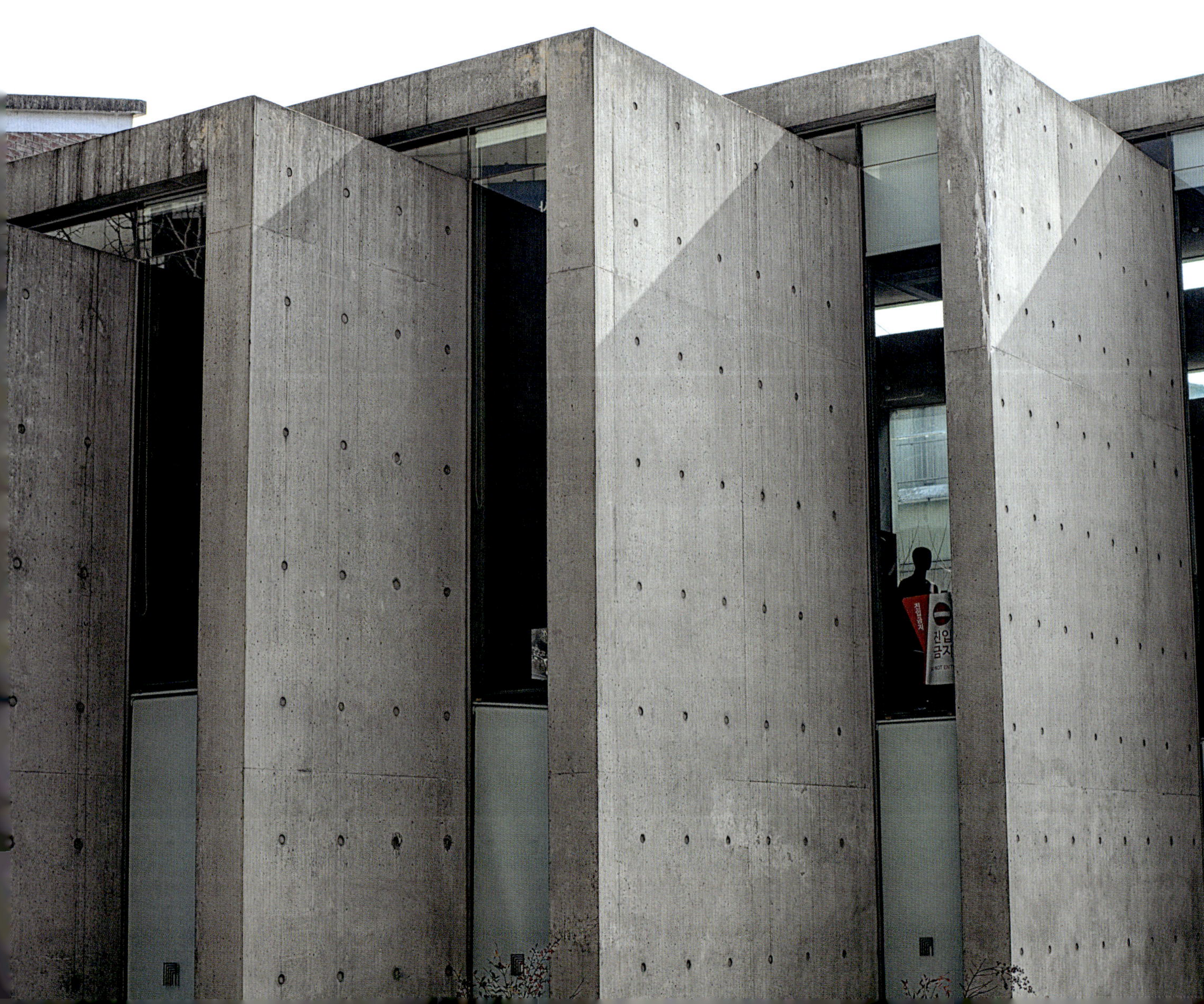

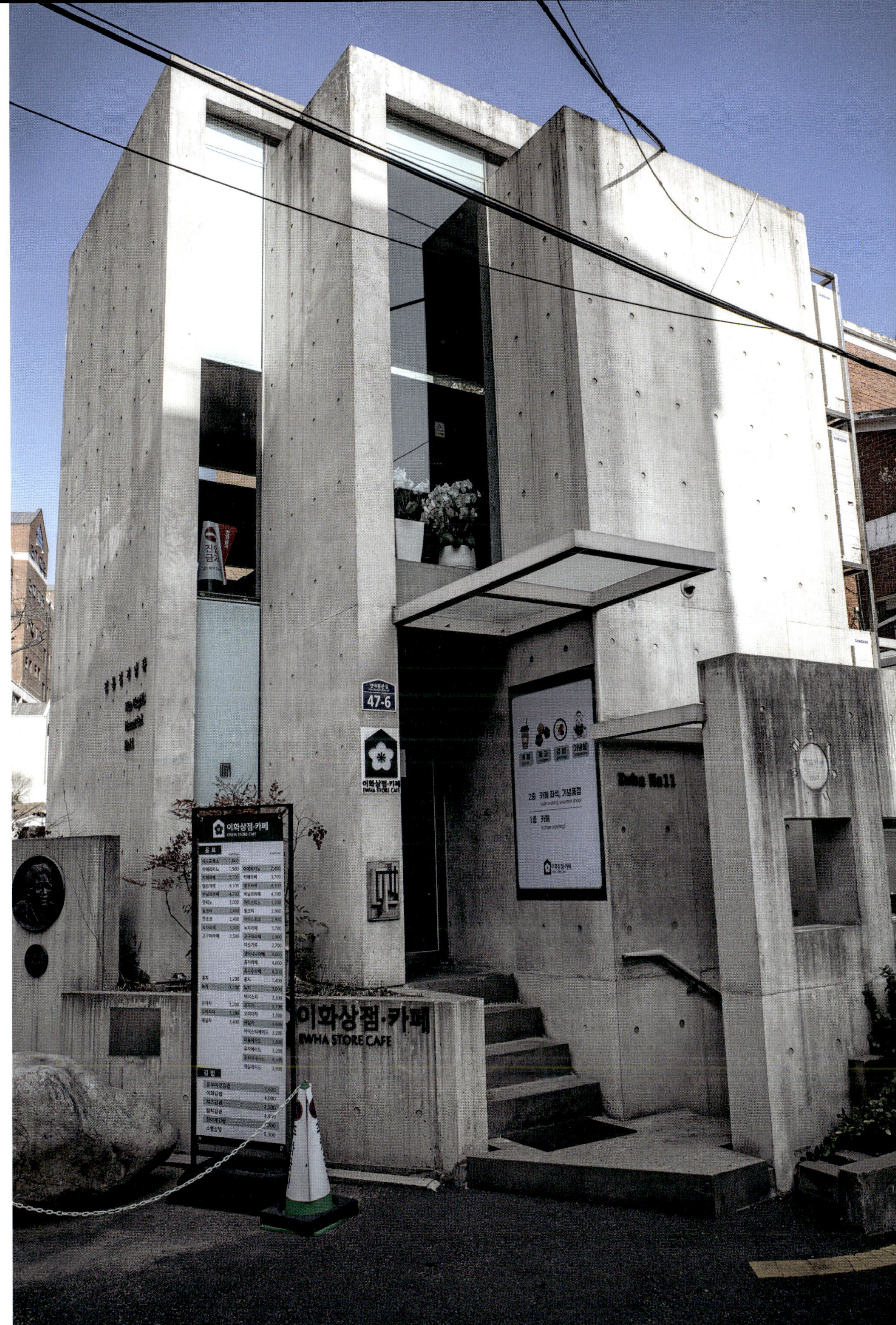
47-6
이화상점·카페
EWHA STORE CAFE
2층 카페 좌석, 기념품점
1층 카페
이화상점·카페
EWHA STORE CAFE

BUSAN PORT INTERNATIONAL PASSENGER TERMINAL

BUSAN · Completed 1978

The original Busan Port International Passenger Terminal was a bold emblem of South Korea's maritime ambitions and post-war modernism. Inspired by the Sydney Opera House, its sweeping shell-like rooflines rose above the harbour as a sculptural celebration of travel, commerce, and the sea. The design translated the optimism of late twentieth-century architecture into concrete form – dynamic, symbolic, and unashamedly monumental.

The terminal's curved roof shells evoked the motion of waves and sails, their rhythmic repetition casting long shadows across the dockside. Beneath these vaults, glass walls opened the interior to natural light and views of the port, linking departing passengers with the ocean they were about to cross. While utilitarian in purpose, the building carried a civic grandeur typical of its era – part transportation hub, part urban sculpture. Though later replaced, the 1978 terminal remains remembered as Busan's most lyrical act of architectural seafaring.

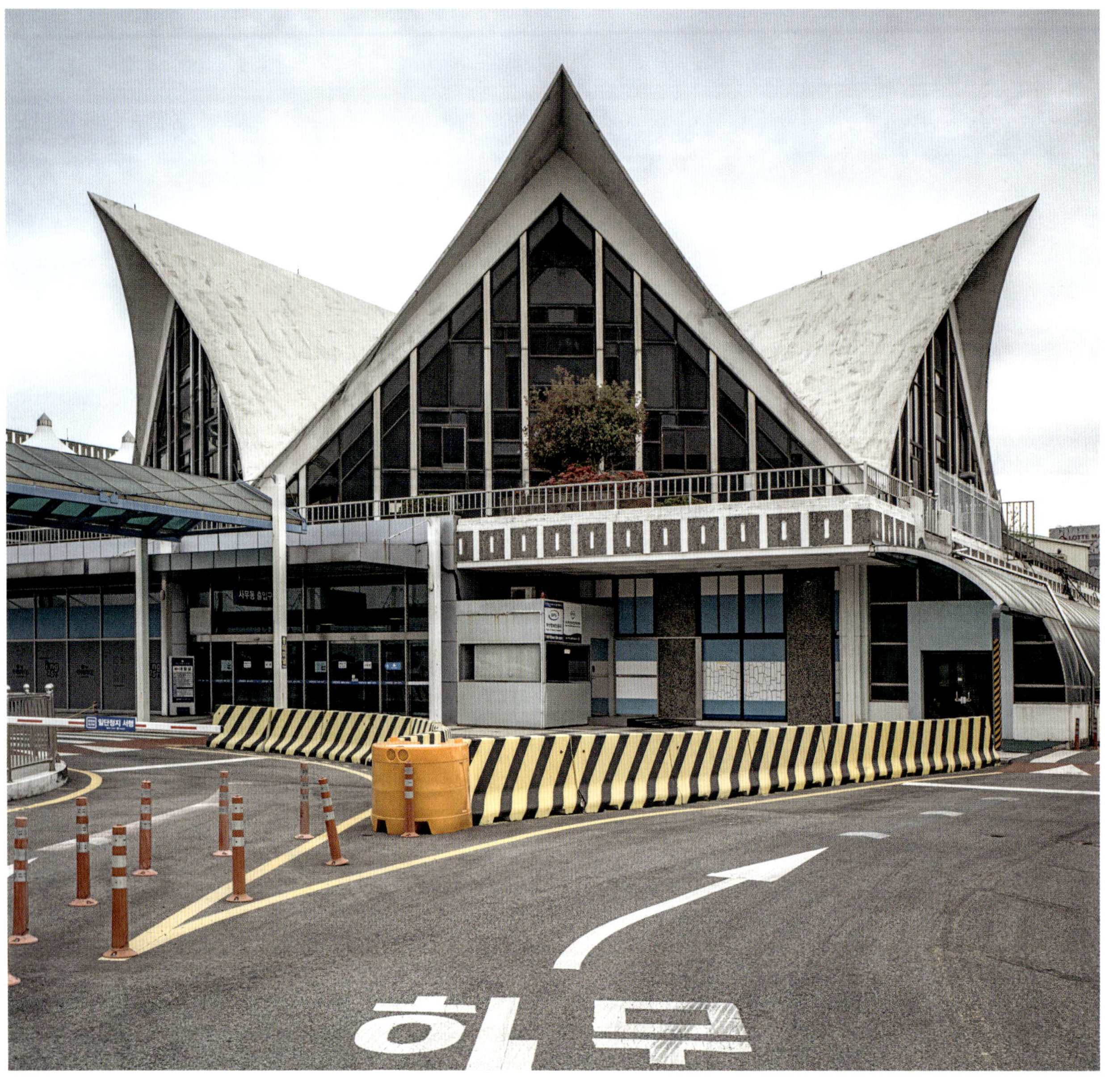

SONGDO HOUSE

BUSAN · Architect: Architect-K · Completed 2014

Rising above the dense streets of Busan's Songdo district, Songdo House by Architect-K is a confident play of mass and balance. Its composition seems to defy gravity: a broad concrete volume cantilevered over a textured brick base, as if pausing mid-motion before tipping into the sea below. The contrast between the cool, smooth concrete and the rough masonry creates a counterpoint between precision and permanence – a material metaphor for the city itself, where raw energy meets coastal calm.

Glass railings and deep-set apertures slice through the weight of the structure, pulling daylight deep into its core and offering cinematic views of the surrounding skyline. There is an architectural swagger here, but it's tempered by restraint – every line, void, and overhang feels measured. Songdo House mimics no high-rise neighbours, it challenges them, standing as an urban sculpture that turns concrete gravity into a quiet dare.

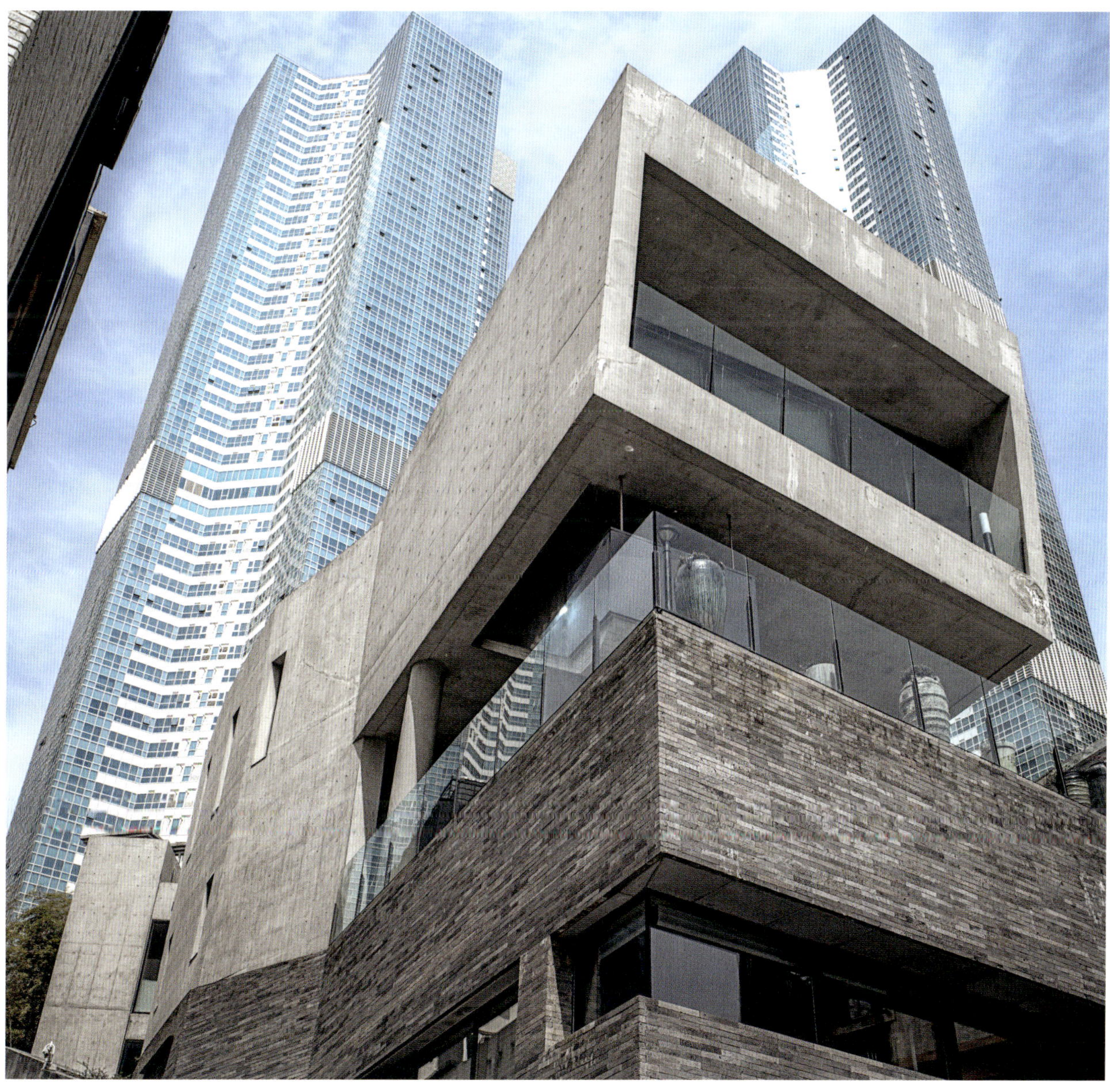

MR KOO'S RESIDENCE (LG SANGNAM LIBRARY)

SEOUL · Architect: KIM Swoo-geun · Completed 1967

Mounted like a concrete mainframe from another age, the LG Sangnam Library began life in 1967 as the private residence of LG founder Koo In-hwoi. Designed by Kim Swoo-geun, it now moonlights as Korea's first digital library – a kind of Brutalist computer housing culture instead of code. What was once a home for an industrial patriarch has become a home for the cloud.

Kim's architecture here predates the digital revolution but somehow predicts it. The structure stacks and interlocks like an early circuit board: balconies jutting out like data ports, vertical fins like cooling towers for an analogue mind. Each concrete module seems to process light, shadow, and air through its own algorithm. The result feels both monumental and strangely intimate – a human-scaled motherboard with impeccable posture.

The façade is punctuated with a sculptural relief of sheep basking in a rising sun – a lyrical flourish amidst the logic that alludes to our unquestioning following of data. Kim loved this tension: rational systems interrupted by poetic impulse. The heavy pilotis and floating terraces give the building a strange levity, as though the concrete were quietly buffering between centuries.

Inside, the former residence has been rewired for the digital age. Bookshelves have given way to screens, and the hum of servers replaces the hush of servants. Yet the bones remain: smooth, cool surfaces that reward touch; light wells that feel more like spiritual search engines than skylights.

In a city awash with glass façades and bandwidth, the LG Sangnam Library is a wry counterpoint – a pre-digital memory stick carved in stone. Its Brutalism never brutalizes; it simply stores information in mass, time, and silence. In Kim Swoo-geun's concrete code, even data may learn patience.

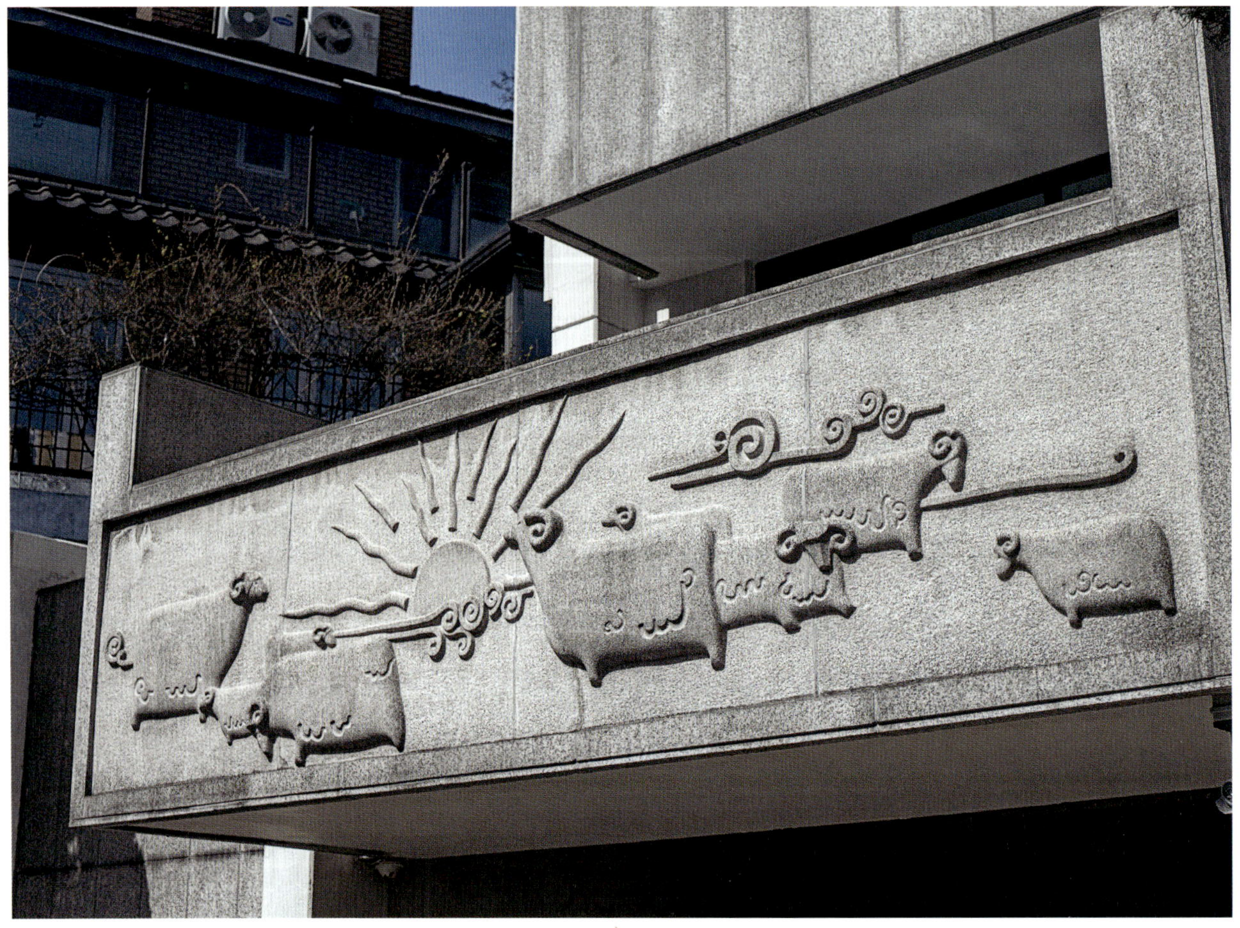

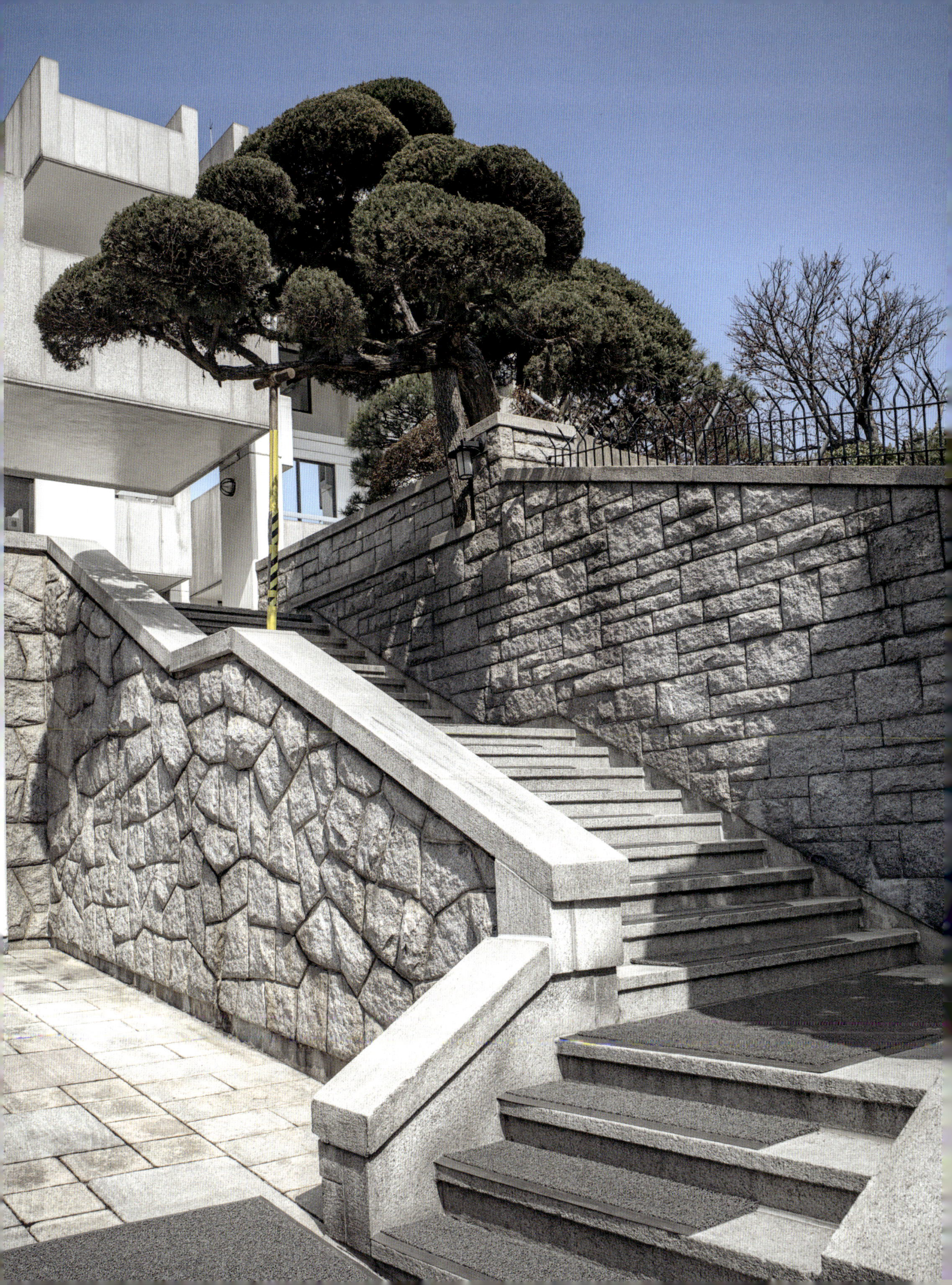

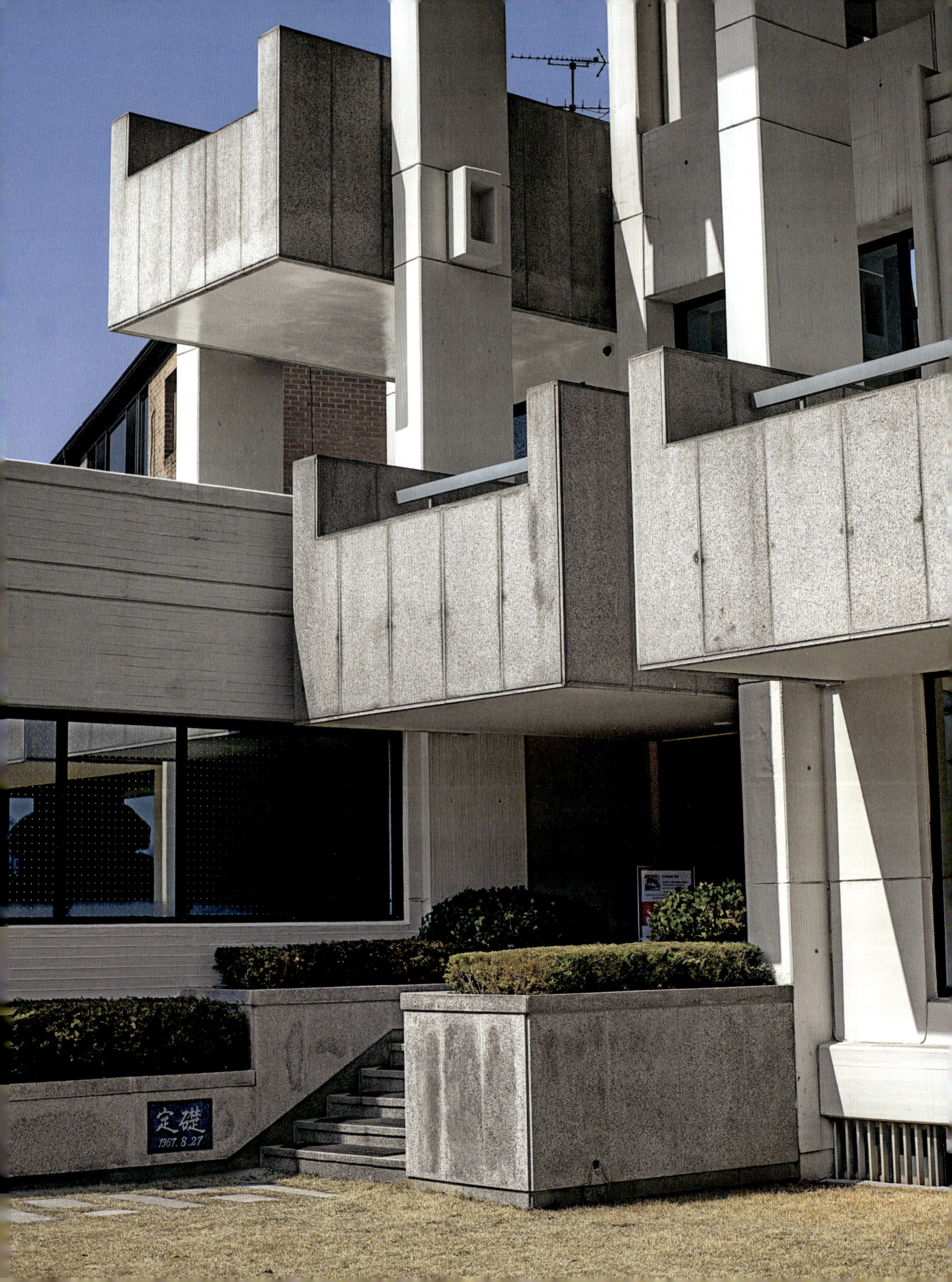
定礎
1967. 8.27

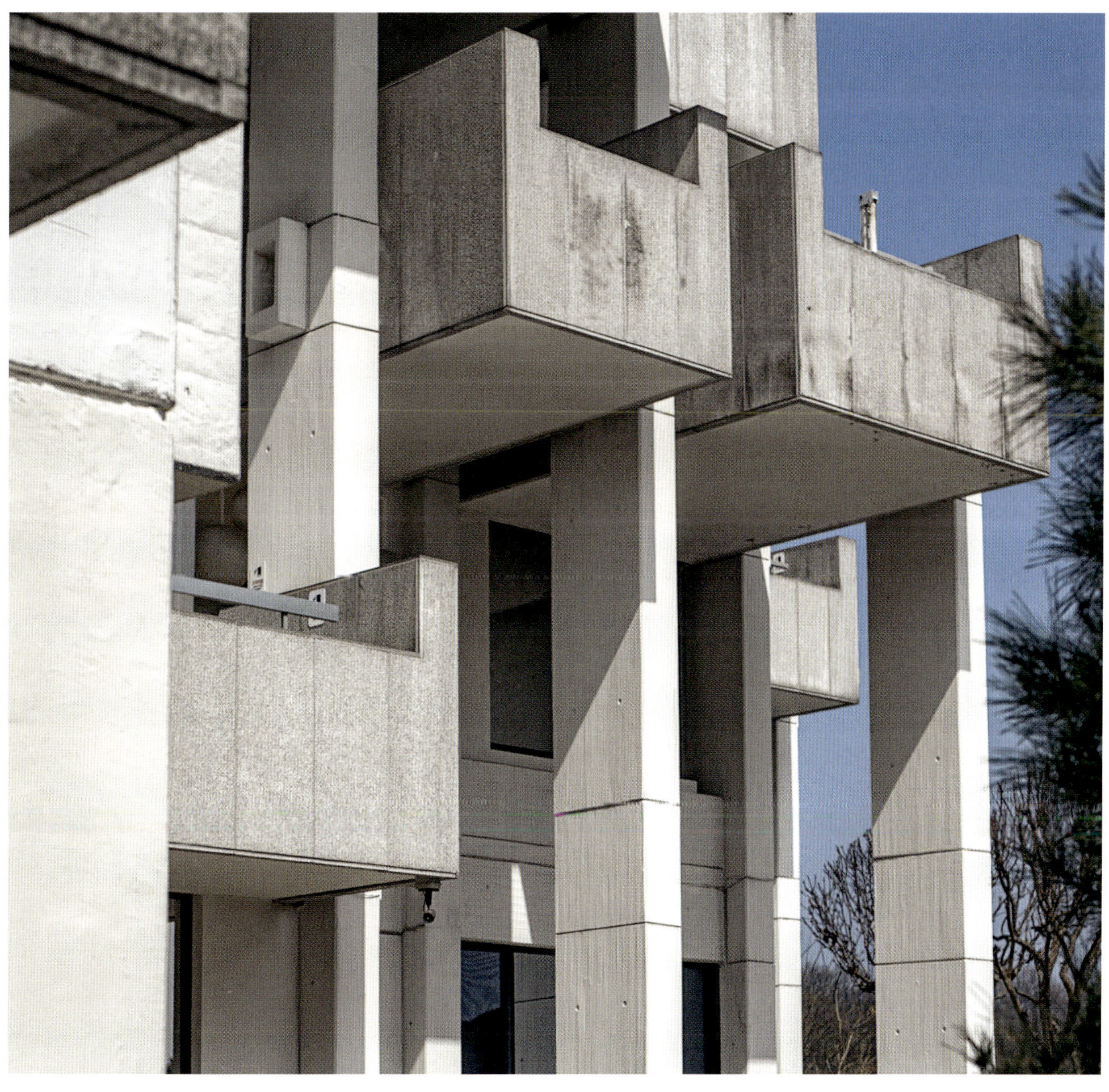

THE CLOSEST CHURCH

GIMPO NEW TOWN · Architect: KWAK Hee-soo · Completed 2015

This is concrete confession whispered through space. Sitting in a modest suburb, it does not shout its presence like megachurches with neon halos. No steeple, no stained glass bombast – just a minimalist slab of raw intent, as if the divine decided to appear not in glory, but in humility.

The exterior reads like a theological *sijo* (succinct traditional Korean poetry): monolithic, precise, and quietly forceful. It's Brutalism in its purest Gospel – not about impressing God, but about confronting man. Kwak trades ornament for honest massing, volume for void. The cross? Subtly carved, not raised – as if heaven's not above, but within.

Inside, you don't ascend – you descend. The journey through this church is not upwards, but inwards. A ramp spirals down around a sunlit void, a concrete reinterpretation of the pilgrimage: every step closer to the sanctuary is a physical metaphor for introspection, repentance, perhaps even doubt. It's part Dante, part Ando, with an extra dose of sobriety.

Light does the preaching here. Slits in concrete walls cast divine geometry across surfaces like a silent sermon, shifting through the day with the patience of a monk. This is a space that avoids emotional manipulation – it just waits for you to meet it halfway.

That's its genius: it constructs holiness rather than performing it. And in doing so, Kwak joins a lineage of architects who understand that Brutalism isn't cold – it's honest. There is faith in its restraint, and grace in its gravity. Here, salvation isn't found in song or spectacle, but in the rough textures of doubt, poured and cured into sacred silence.

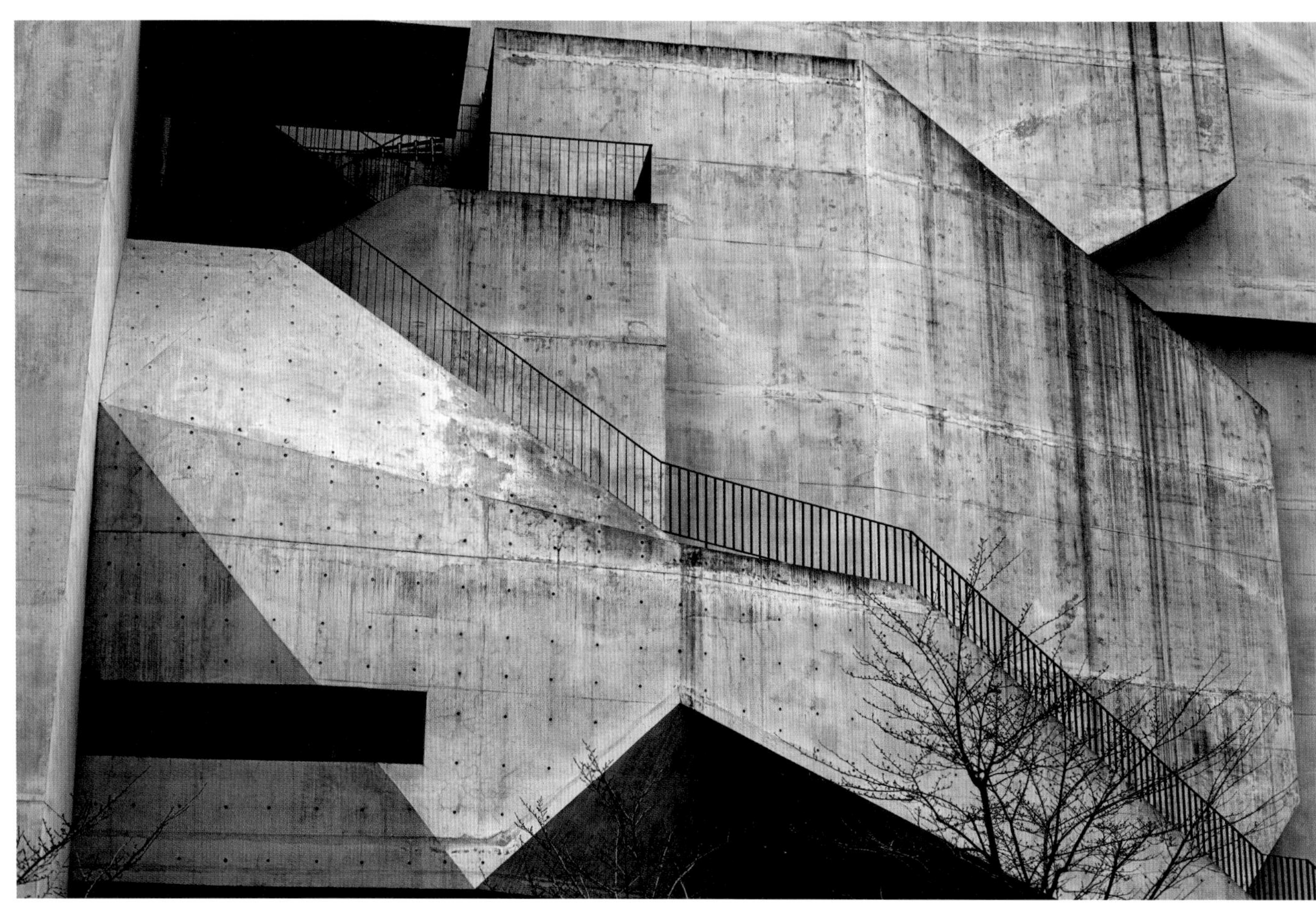

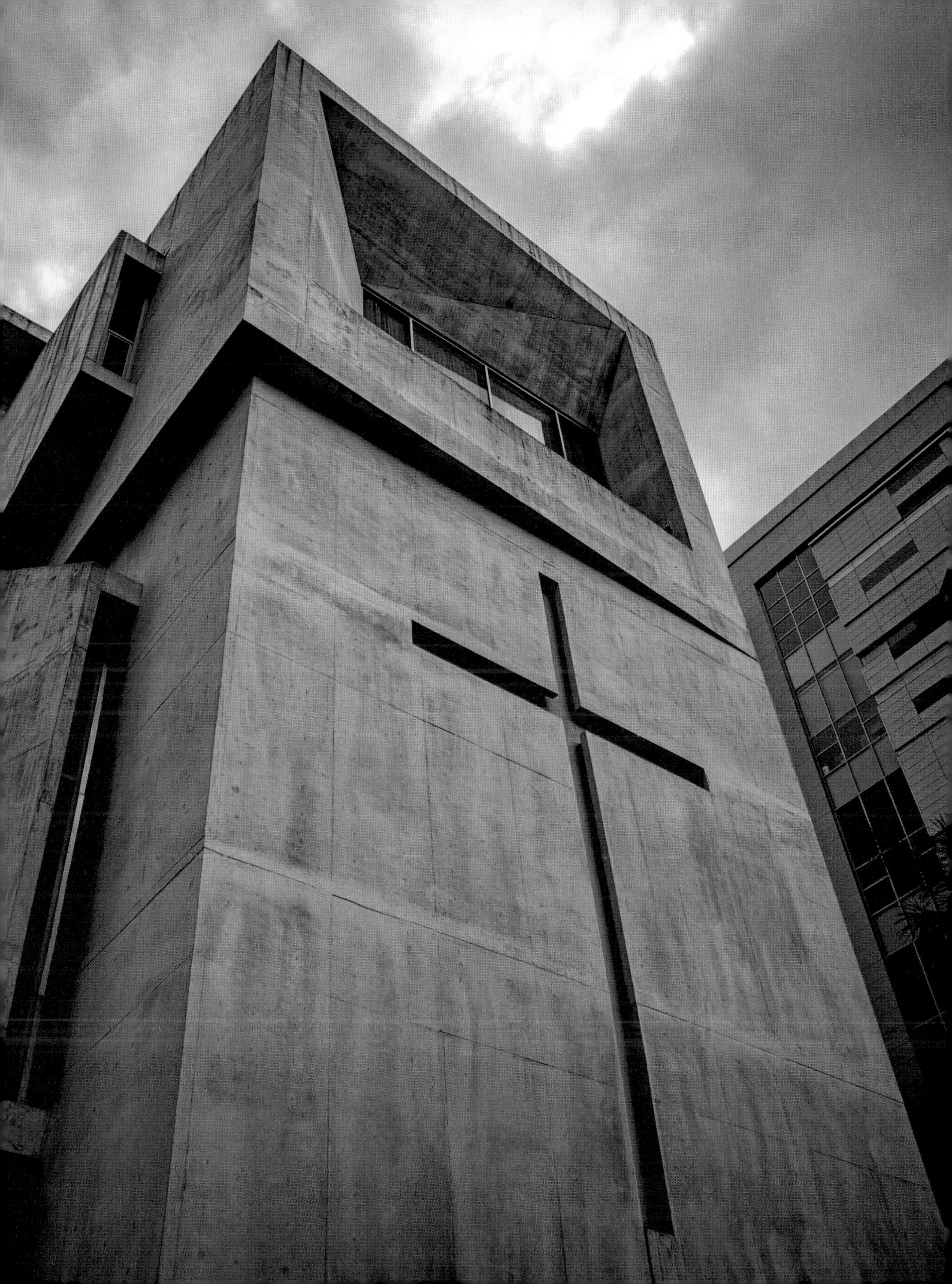

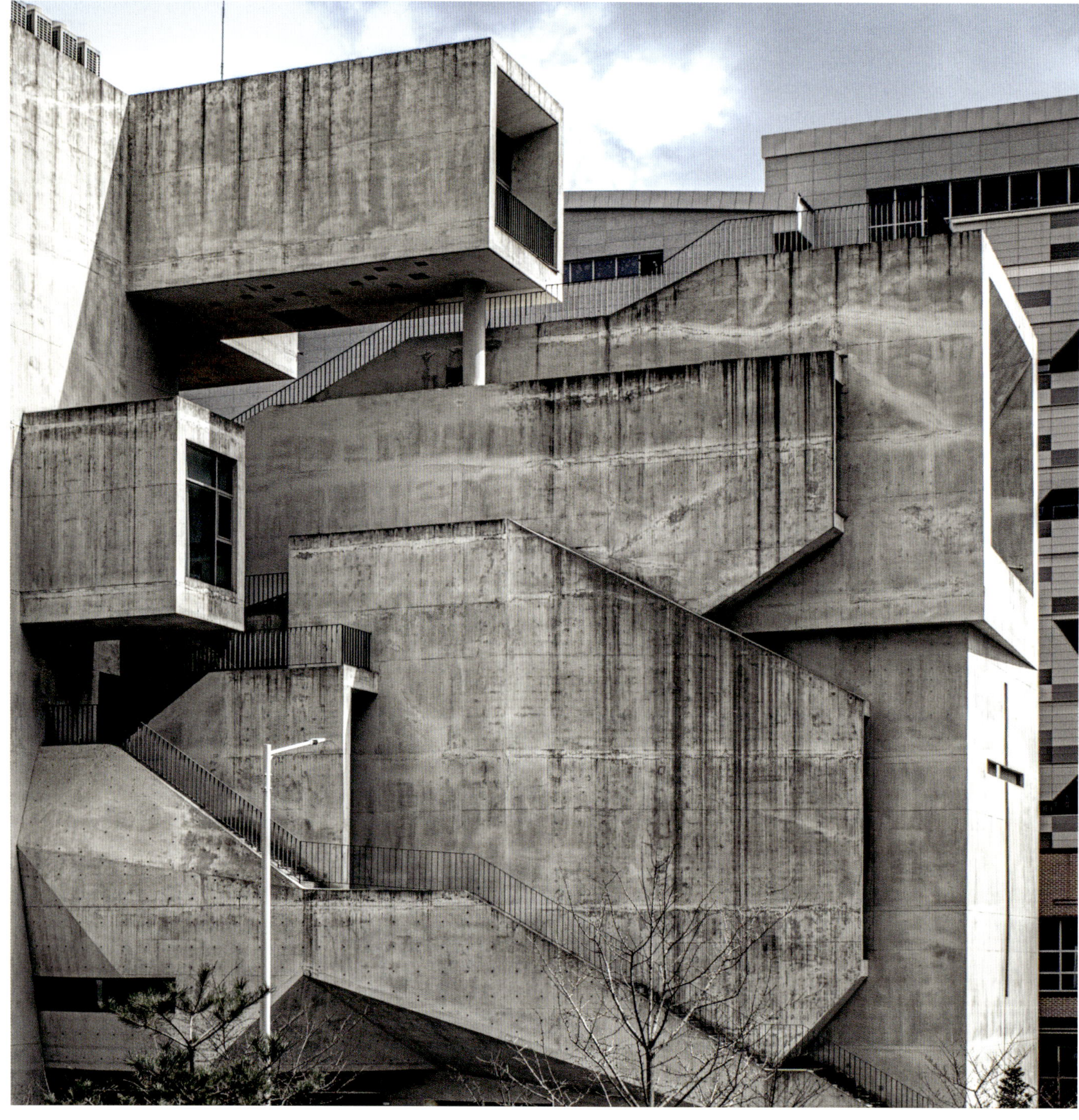

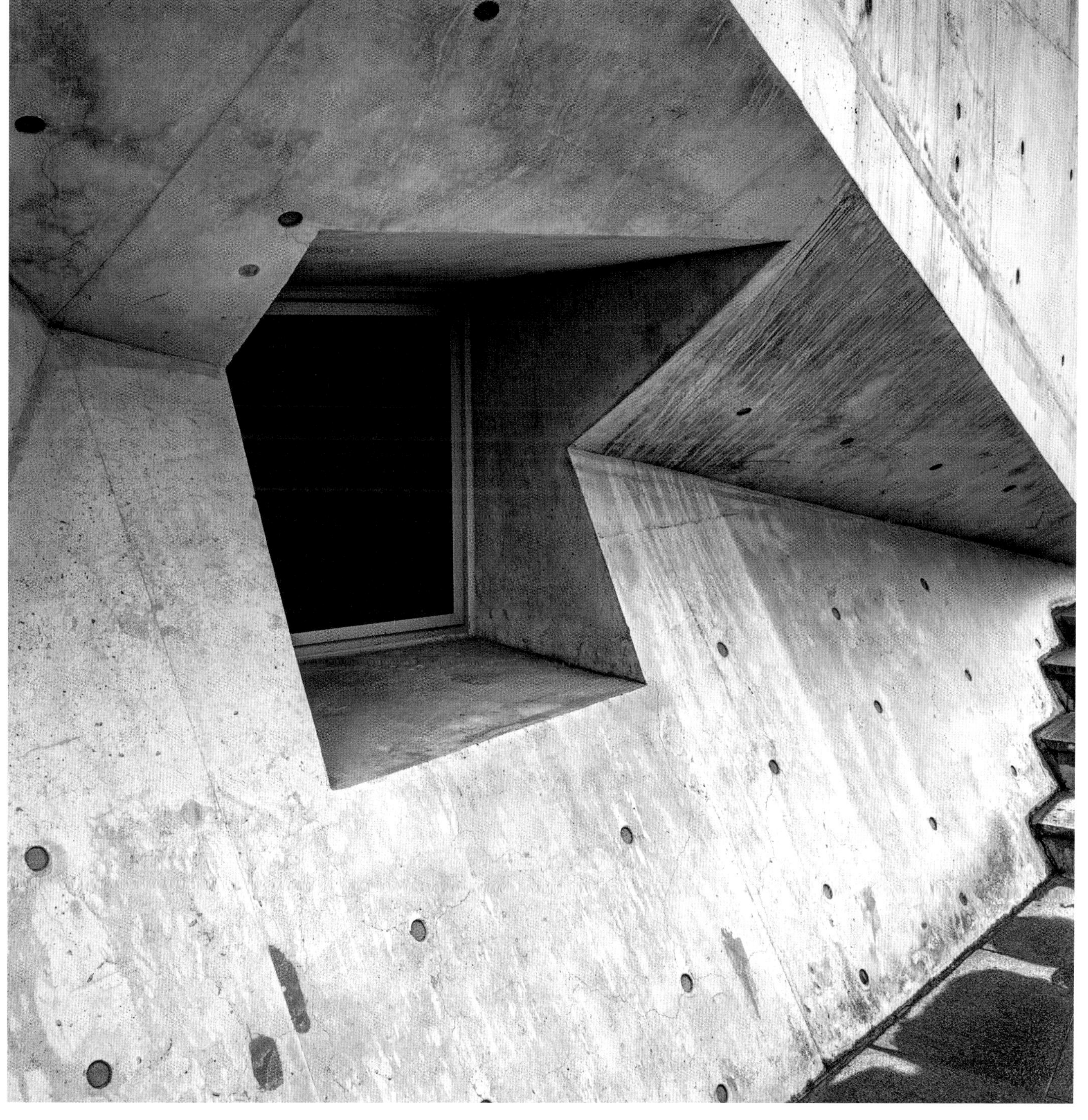

FREEDOM CENTER

SEOUL · Architect: KIM Swoo-geun · Completed 1964

Set along the slopes of Namsan, the Freedom Center displays a kind of architectural defiance. Completed in 1964 by Kim Swoo-geun – one of Korea's post-war visionaries – it was built as the headquarters of the Asia Anti-Communism League, a concrete proclamation at the height of Cold War anxiety. Six decades later, it endures as a paradox: born from ideological rigidity yet designed with striking modern freedom.

The structure itself is pure conviction. An elongated block of concrete hovers above the ground, resting on slender pilotis that make the mass appear both grounded and weightless. A horizontal deck slices through the composition, balancing monumentality with motion. To one side, a tower once blazed with an illuminated map of Asia, a glowing billboard for propaganda's geography. Today, the light is gone but the form still carries presence – a Brutalist relic turned civic landmark.

Kim's architectural language is disciplined but never static. The play of shadow and proportion animates its surfaces, giving the façade a rhythm that feels more measured than militant. Deep-set windows, robust stairs, and clean planes work together like architectural punctuation – each element reinforcing the clarity of the whole. This was concrete as philosophy: honest, unadorned, and built to last longer than politics.

What's compelling now is how the Freedom Center has matured beyond its origins. It no longer preaches, it participates. The site hosts exhibitions and gatherings, transforming from a bastion of ideology into a forum of exchange. The shift feels poetic – architecture outliving its rhetoric.

Time has softened the building's purpose but not its posture. The Freedom Center remains austere, commanding, and quietly human in its endurance. Kim Swoo-geun's design was always about more than concrete and columns – it was about structure as statement. And even now it continues to speak in the firm, unflinching tone of its age.

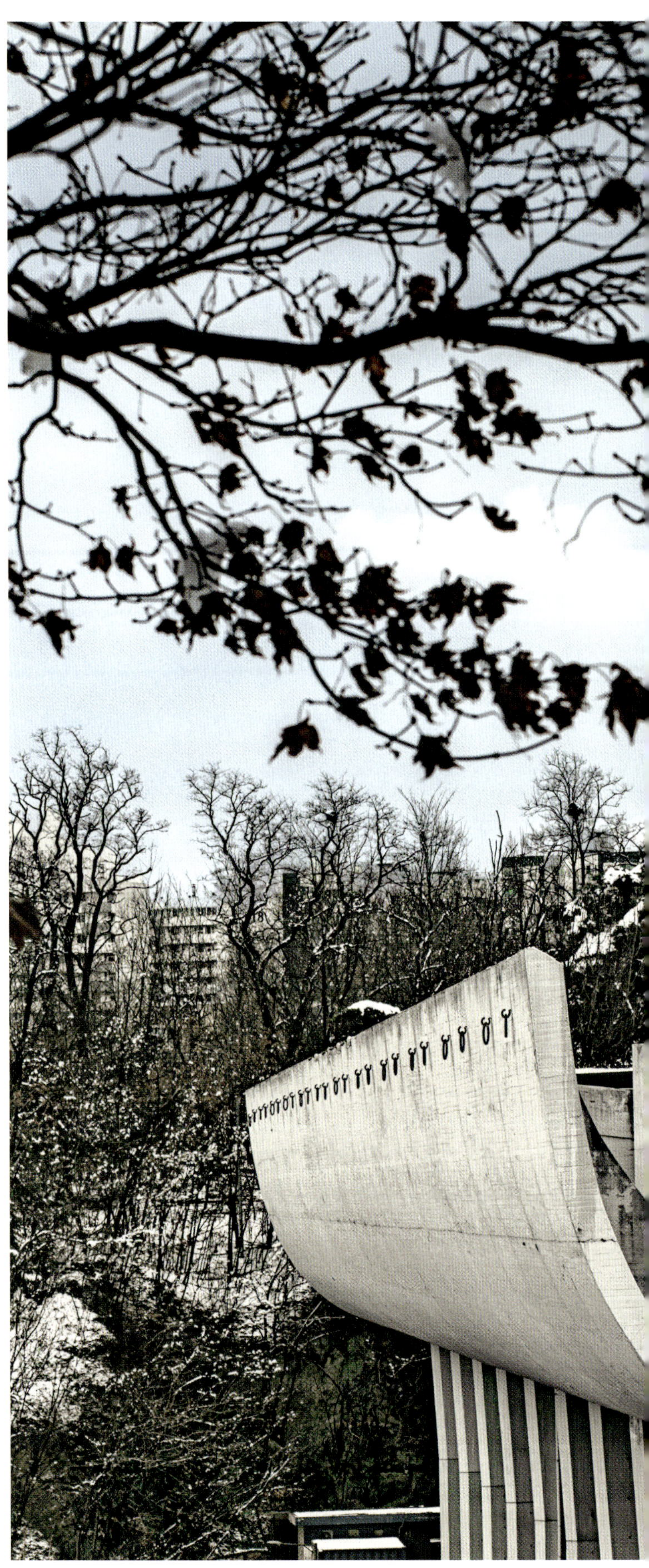

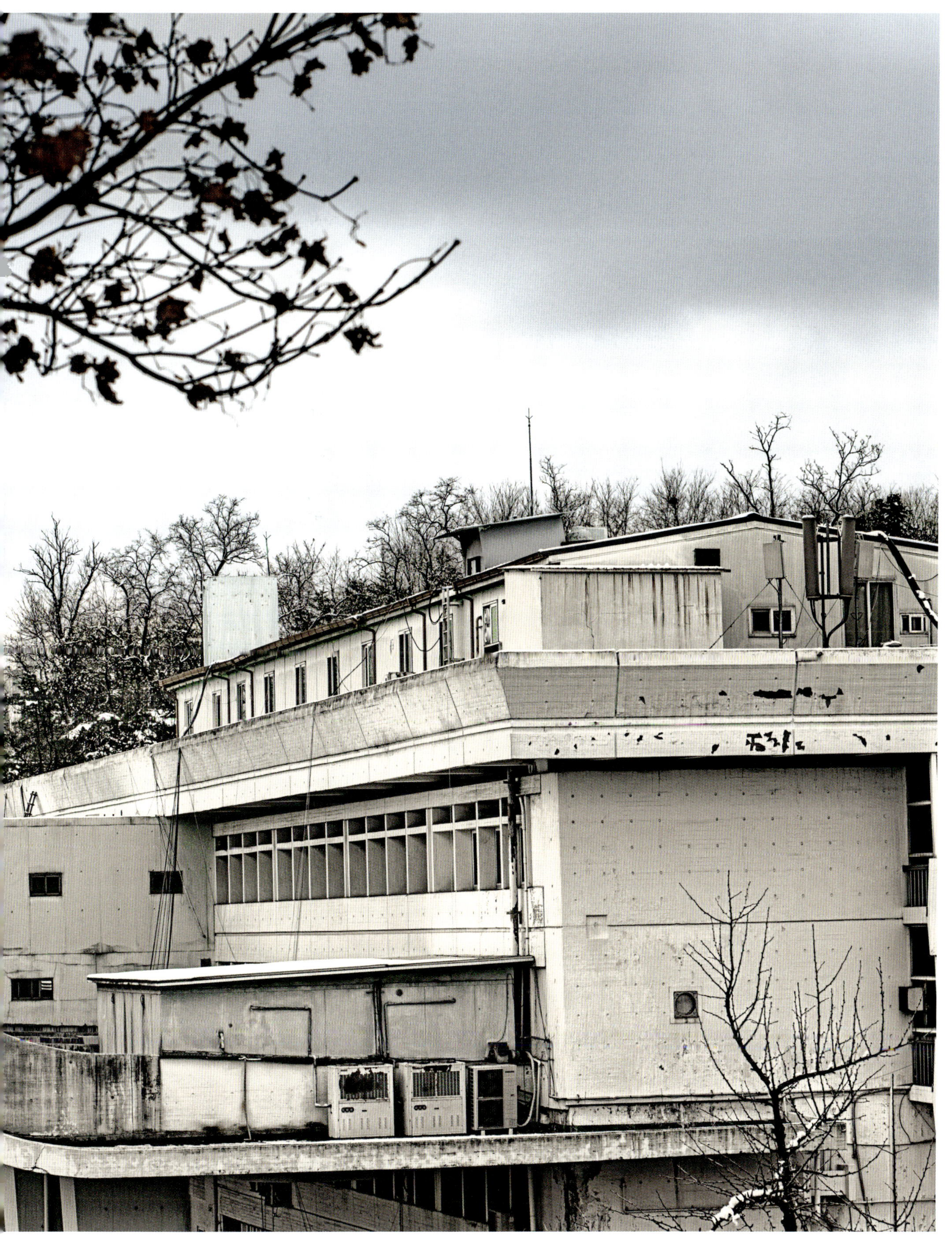

NATIONAL THEATER OF KOREA

SEOUL · Architect: LEE Hee-tae · Completed 1973

The National Theater of Korea, set on the slopes of Mount Namsan, is a concrete performance in its own right. This monumental structure delivers its lines in a deep baritone, each volume and void cast in reinforced drama. If Brutalism were theatre, this would be its epic stage debut – all gravitas, no understudy.

Architecturally, it's a brooding monolith. Not flashy. Not flirtatious. Just a long, slow reveal of weight and mass. Its broad horizontal and narrow vertical planes, a script of concrete and glass co-acted with angular overhangs, evoke a sense of ritual – as if carved from ancient stone to host a civic cult of culture. From certain angles, it resembles a stoic mask – emotion withheld but potent beneath the surface. Call it sombre *talchum* theatre in concrete.

The Brutalist credentials are as clear as a spotlight: form is bold and unornamented, surfaces are textured and raw, and structure is truthfully laid bare. The theatre veils nothing behind curtains – it projects, literally and metaphorically. Its use of *béton brut* and vast open spaces makes it a temple to both art and architecture. This is a building that knows how to command a scene.

Culturally, it marks a key post-war moment when Korea was modernizing rapidly – yet here is a structure that resists the internationalism of the corporate city. Instead, it speaks a heavier, more deliberate language – rooted in land, performance, and presence.

There's even wit in the casting: how fitting that a theatre should be made of concrete, the most rehearsed of materials, poured into formwork like actors into roles. And in this grand production, the National Theater isn't just a stage – it's a star. One that reminds us: sometimes, the heaviest architecture leaves the most lasting applause.

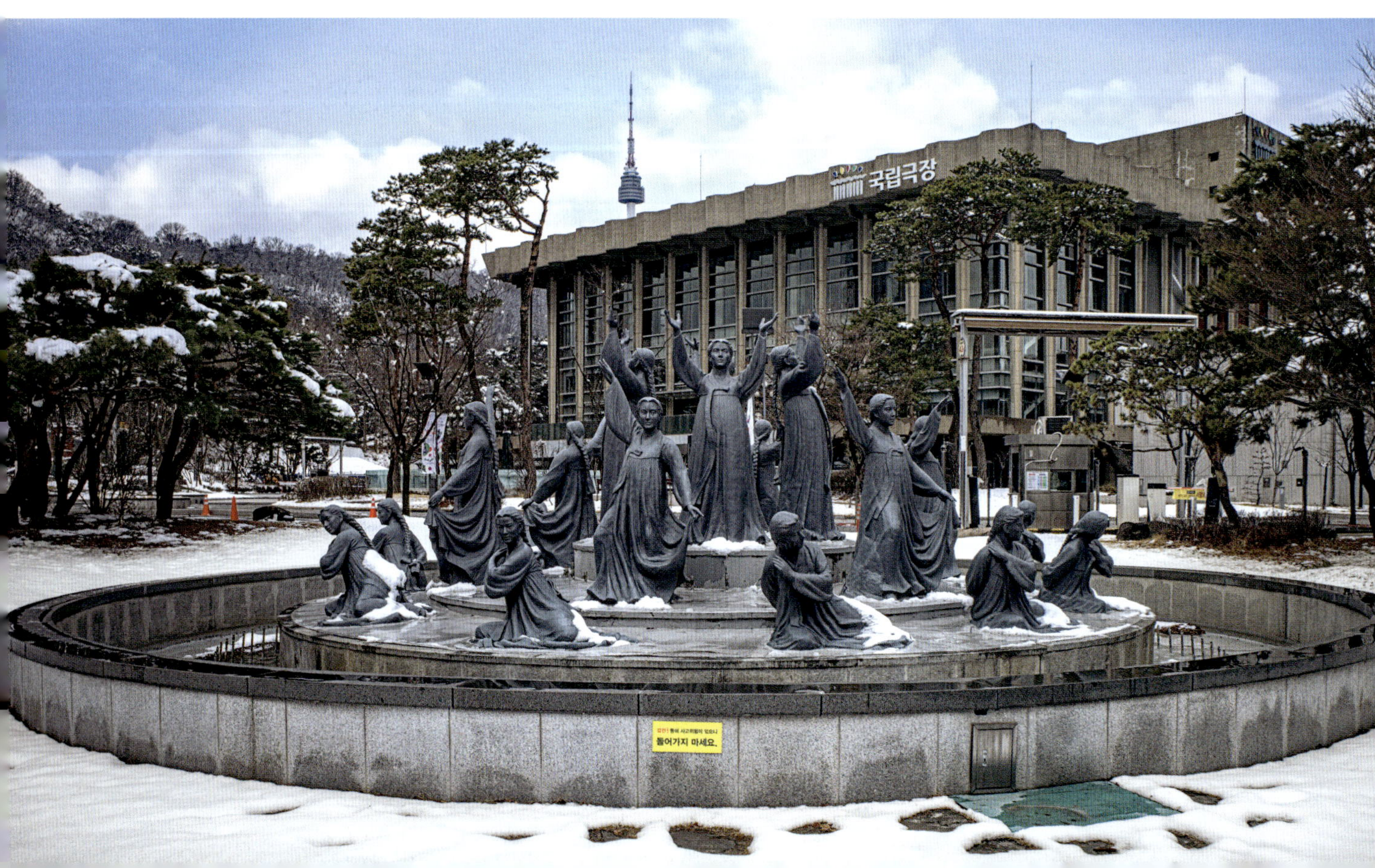

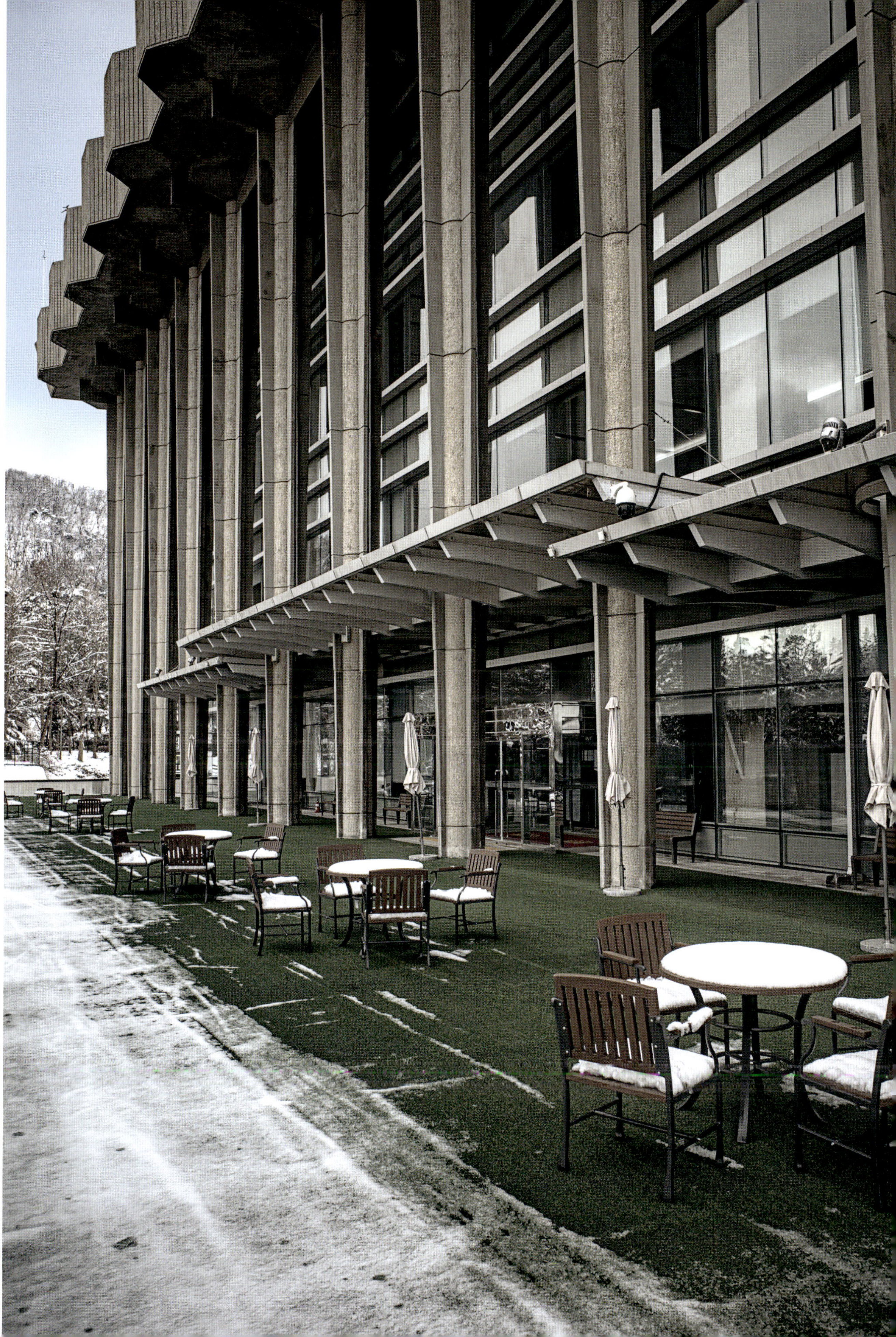

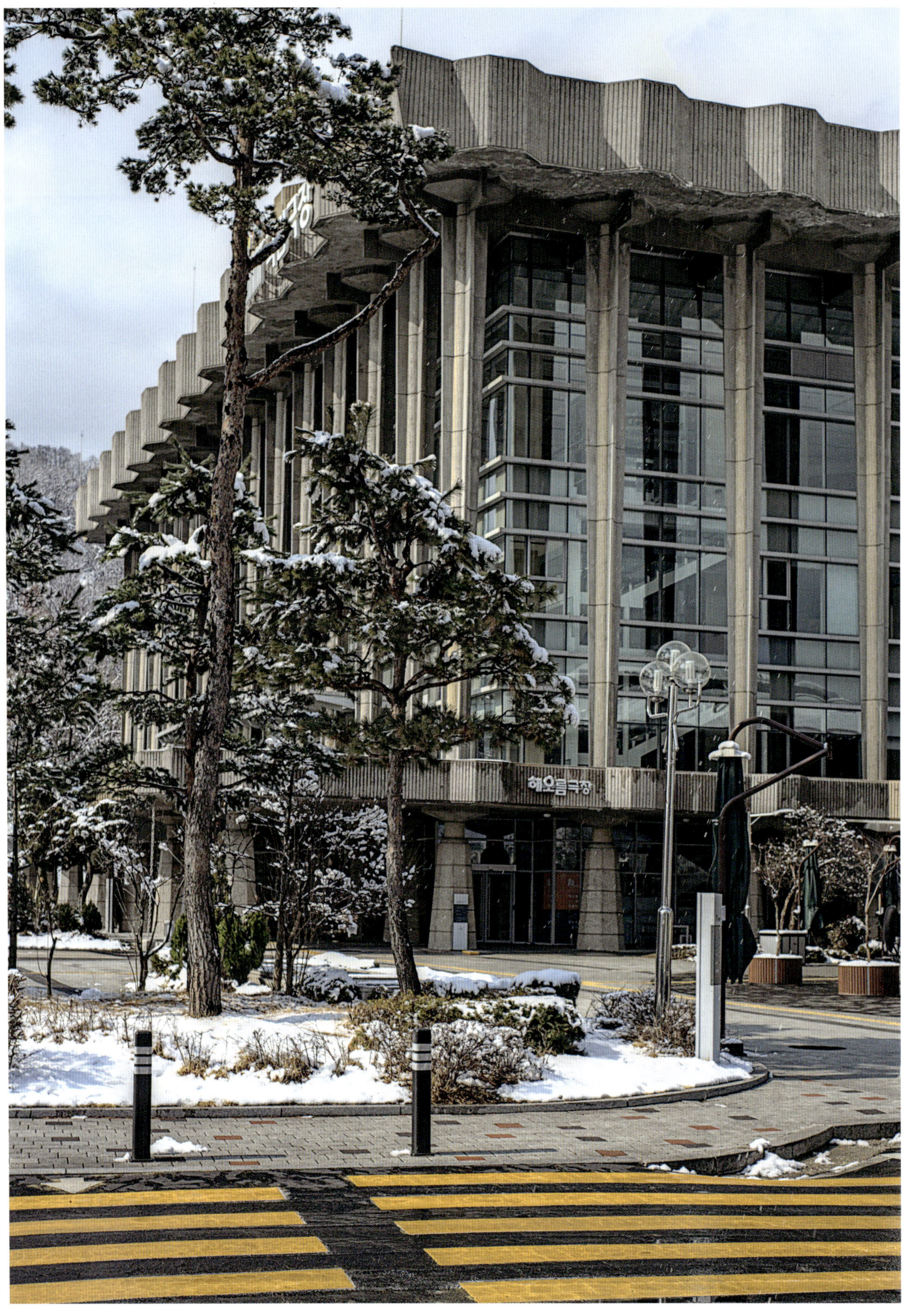
해오름극장

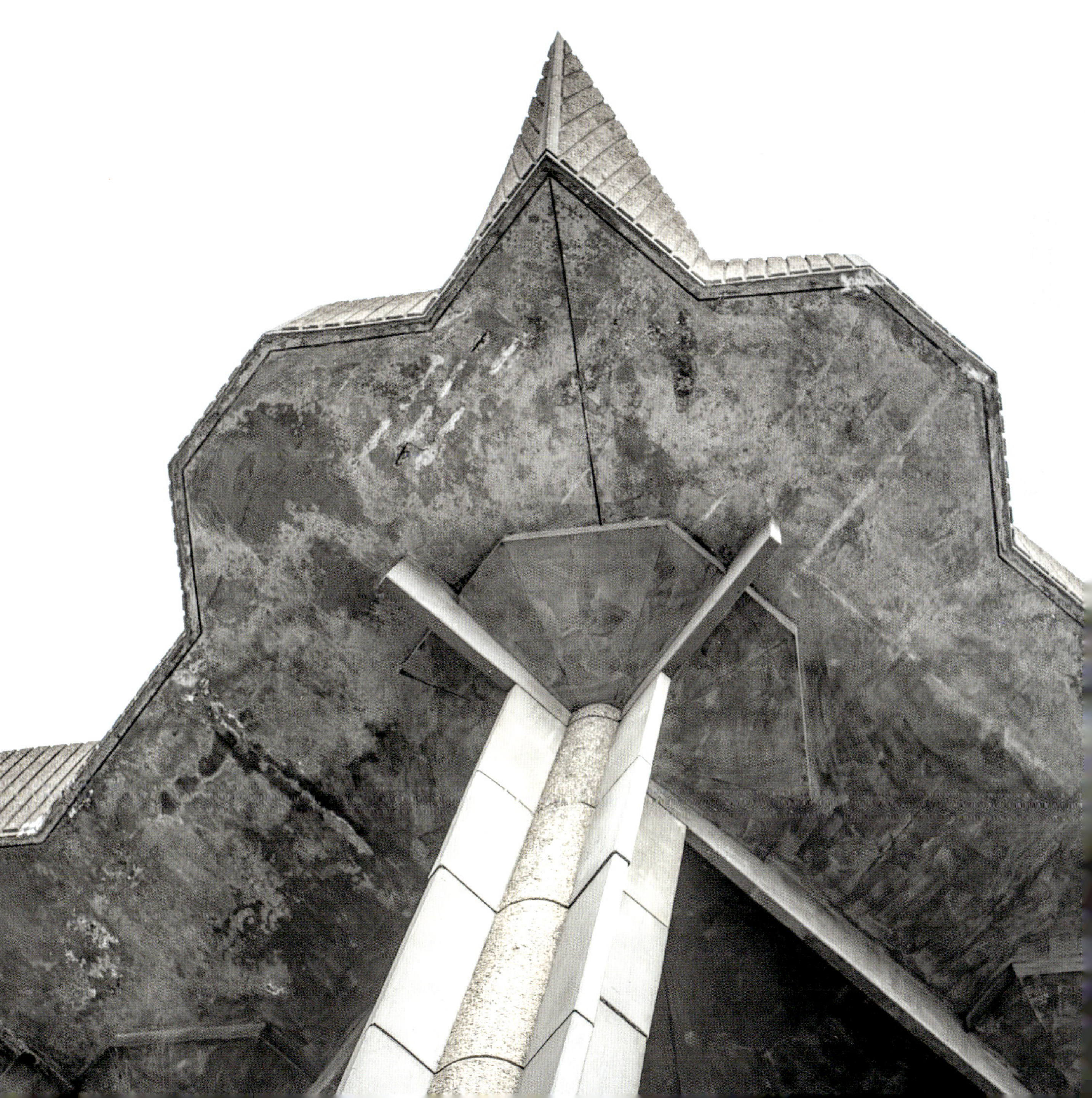

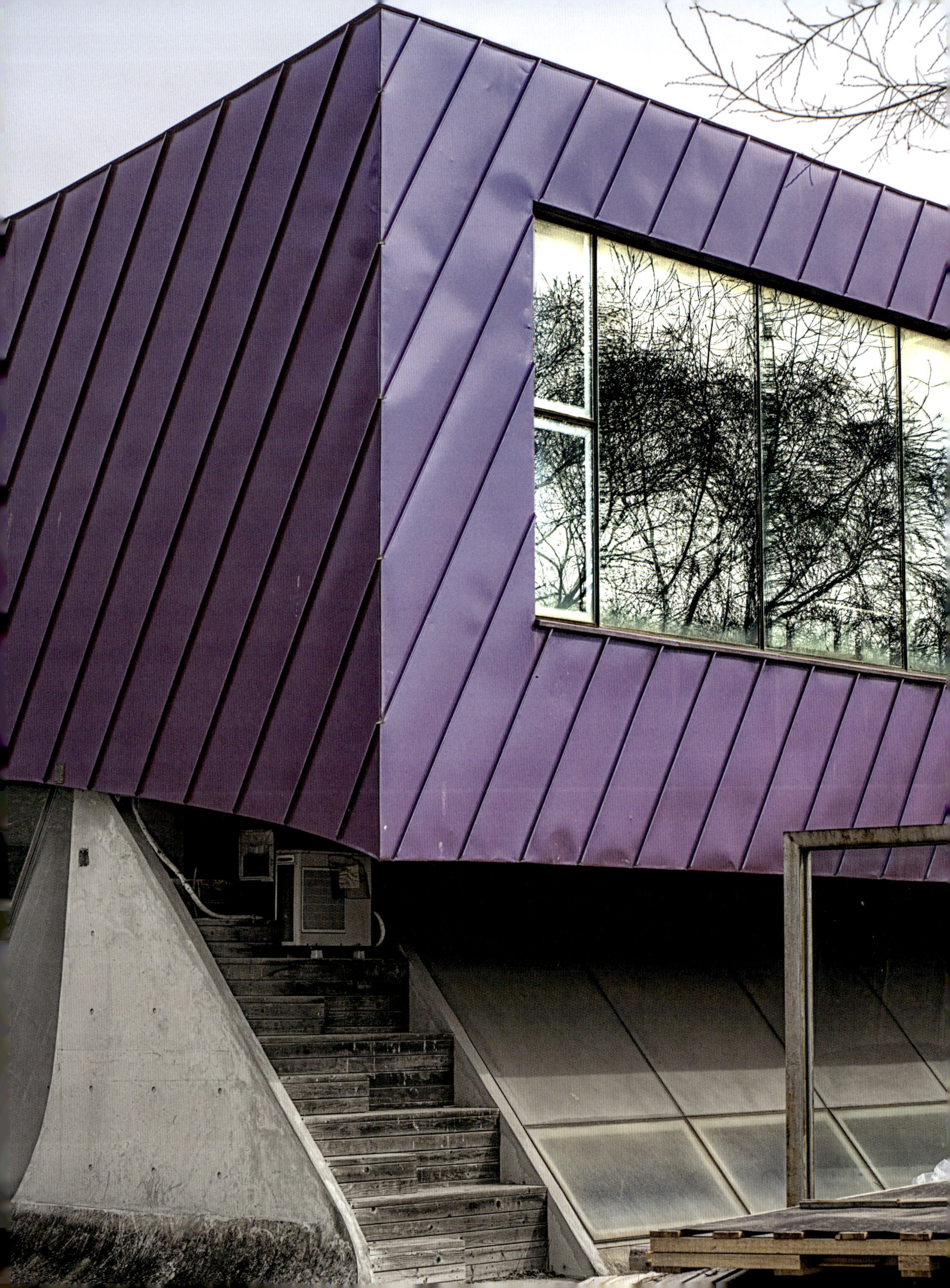

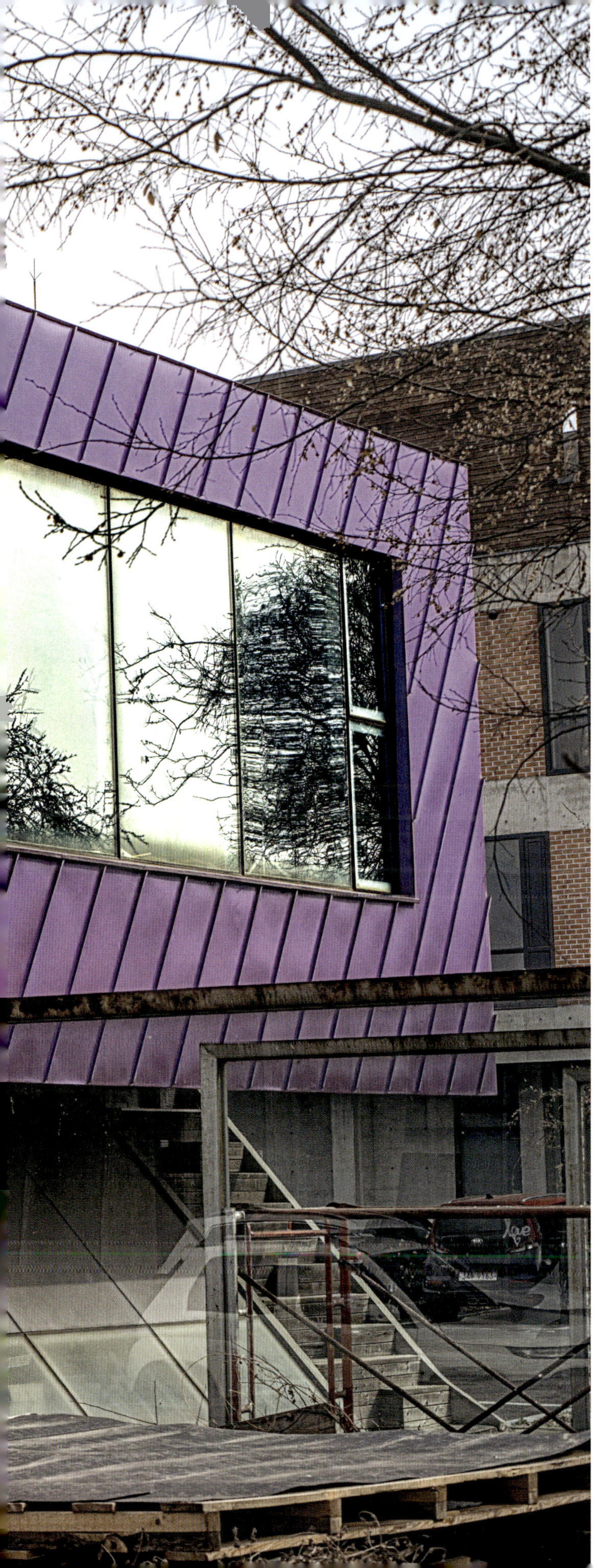

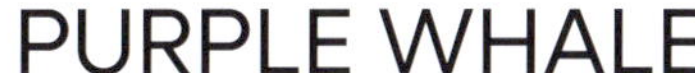

PURPLE WHALE

PAJU BOOK CITY · Architect: KIM Hyo-man / IROJE KHM Architects · Completed 2008

The Purple Whale in Paju Book City is a building that looks as if it has just surfaced from a metallic ocean, shaking off a shimmer of ink. It breaches somewhere between creature and construct – part warehouse, part architectural daydream. The building's body twists and arcs with cetacean poise, a sleek mass of brushed aluminium and exposed concrete that catches the daylight in unpredictable ways. From some angles, it gleams with industrial precision; from others, it sulks in a moody violet haze, as if reflecting both the labour and imagination that drive Paju's publishing world.

The concrete base anchors the structure like a seabed, heavy and dependable, while the metallic upper volume appears to float above it – a fin slicing through air instead of water. It's an oscillation between weight and levity, solidity and reflection, as though the architect wanted to see whether concrete could blush and metal could breathe. The building's purple is more than a colour – it's an attitude, an eccentric self-confidence amid the restrained rectilinearity of its Book City neighbours.

Inside, light filters through the fissures between materials, tracing the contours of ramps and workspaces with liquid precision. The effect is both functional and theatrical – a place for production that performs architecture at every turn. Like its namesake, the Purple Whale never truly rests: it glides between the realms of art and industry, surfacing just long enough to remind us that even in a sea of grey modernism, a bold splash of colour and form can still make waves.

EARTH MUSEUM

JEJU ISLAND

This angular, steel-clad structure feels less built than forged. Rising from the Jeju landscape like a geological shard, its folded planes catch the light in fractured glints – part bunker, part meteorite. The rust-toned ramp slices towards its entrance, an incision through the green hillside that dramatizes arrival. The building's exterior, weathered and irregular, rejects polish; instead, it celebrates corrosion, entropy, and the raw entanglement between artifice and nature.

Inside, the mood shifts to quiet introspection. The dark zinc-lined walls and sharp-edged geometry come together to form a vaulted space that feels simultaneously sacred and industrial. Narrow skylights score the roofline, releasing thin ribbons of light that animate the surfaces like a slow exhale. It's less a gallery than a void of contemplation – architecture as ritual chamber.

I reckon the architect is Itami Jun, though I'm reticent to state this as a result of scant online information. This is probably compounded by the fact that you'll be hunted down by dogged security guards if you haven't booked a tour. Whatever.

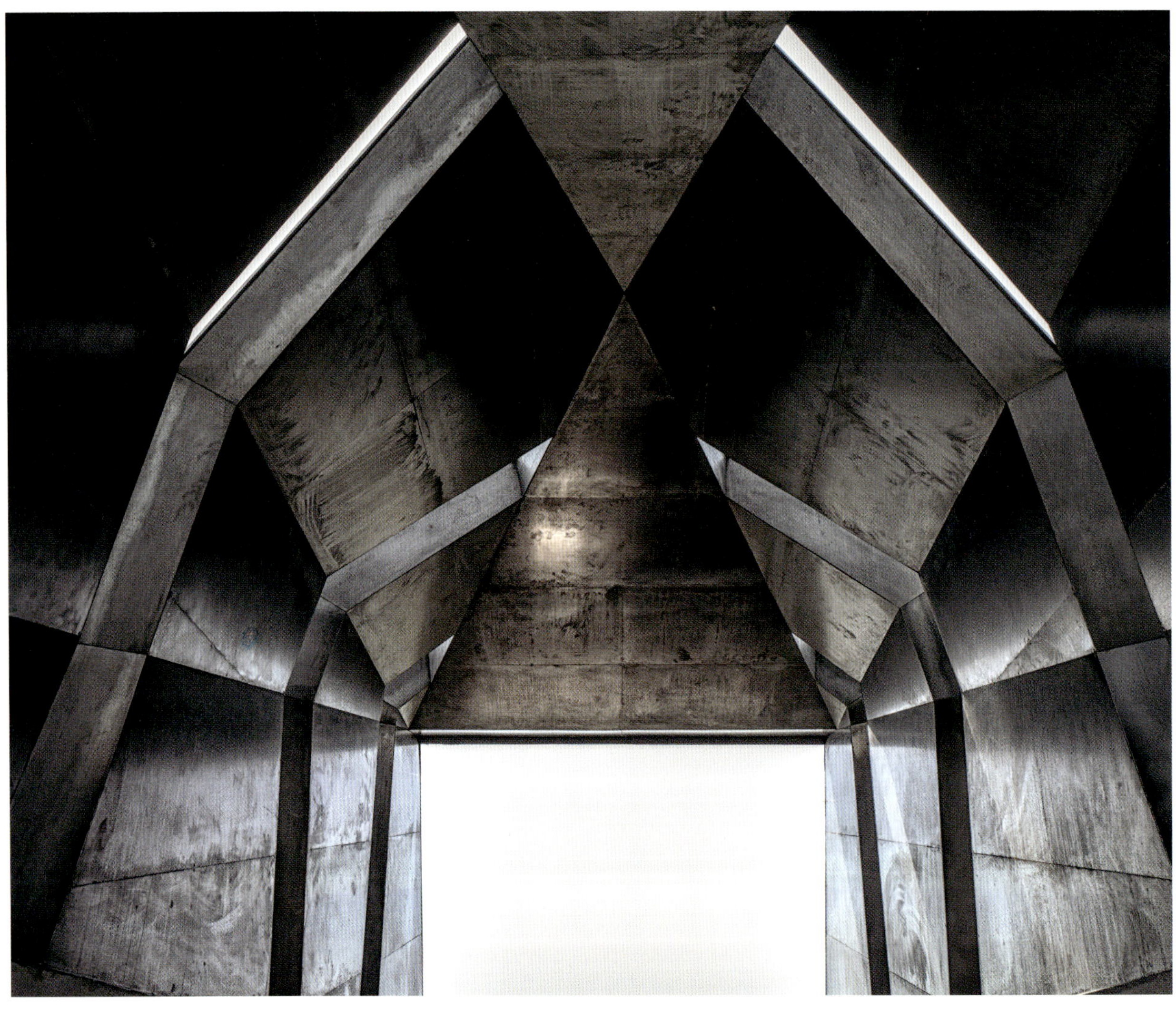

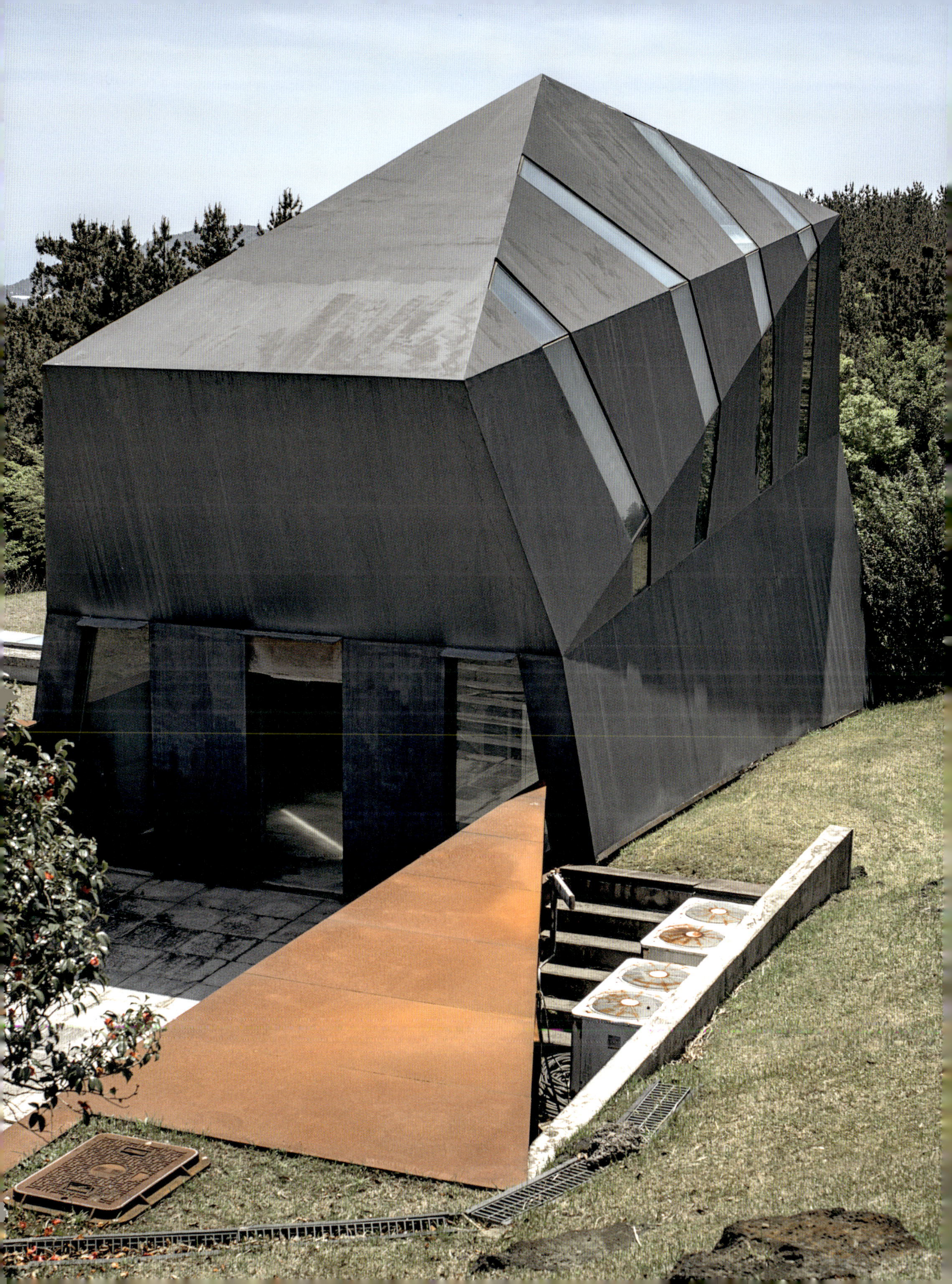

SONGEUN ART AND CULTURAL FOUNDATION

SEOUL · Architect: Herzog & de Meuron · Completed 2021

This wedge rises like a shard of stone caught mid-ascent – a building that seems less constructed than quarried from the city itself. Herzog & de Meuron's 2021 design merges corporate headquarters and cultural space into a single sculptural mass, its sloping façade slicing upwards as if seeking altitude. The surface, clad in rough-textured concrete and stone aggregate, absorbs the city's shifting light, appearing alternately dense, solemn, and weightless.

Within, the narrow vertical apertures and voids form a rhythm of compression and release: corridors tighten like fuselages before opening into vast gallery-like volumes. The tension between heaviness and lift defines the building's atmosphere – a paradox of rooted monumentality and upward motion. This building is both an act of restraint and of defiance, asserting that architecture, like art, need not glitter to soar. It ascends through gravity itself, turning mass into momentum.

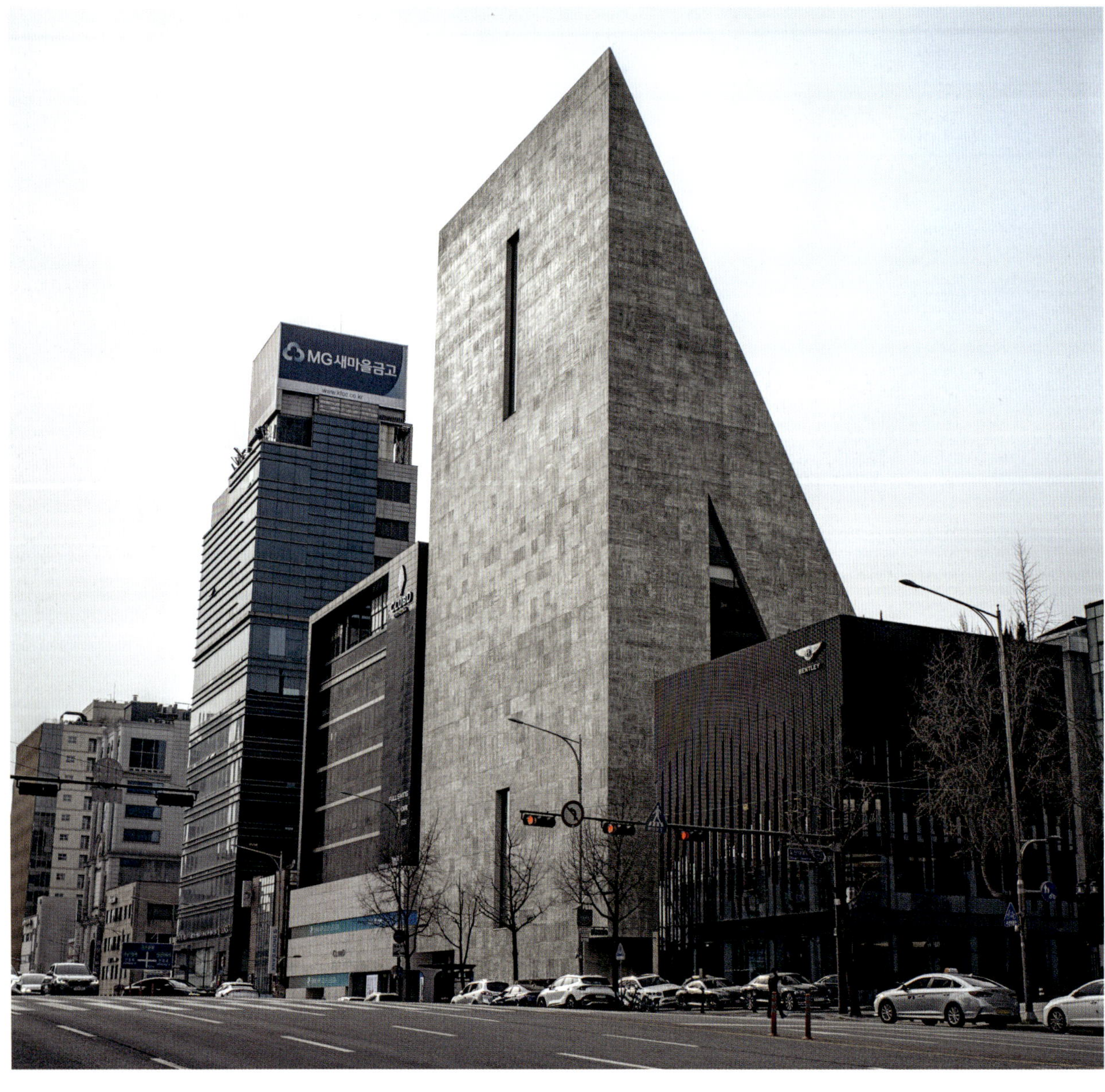

TOILET BLOCK

DAEGU

This public toilet in Mangwoo Park, Daegu, transforms a modest civic utility into an exercise in disciplined geometry and material honesty. The structure employs modern proportion and exposed concrete techniques, achieving an architectural balance between utility and refinement. Each surface and joint expresses clarity – the panelized concrete walls punctuated by precise bolt marks, the recessed entrance framed by vertical fins that lend rhythm and subtle depth. Inside, the sense of order continues through lightweight ceiling panels and a palette of tiles and granite, materials that marry durability with restrained elegance. The relationship between mass, openings, handrails, and colour reveals a thoughtful calibration of parts, where nothing feels accidental. Despite its compact size, the building achieves a quiet completeness: the whole and its elements are bound by a sense of connectedness and perfection, reflecting how even the most ordinary function can embody architectural dignity.

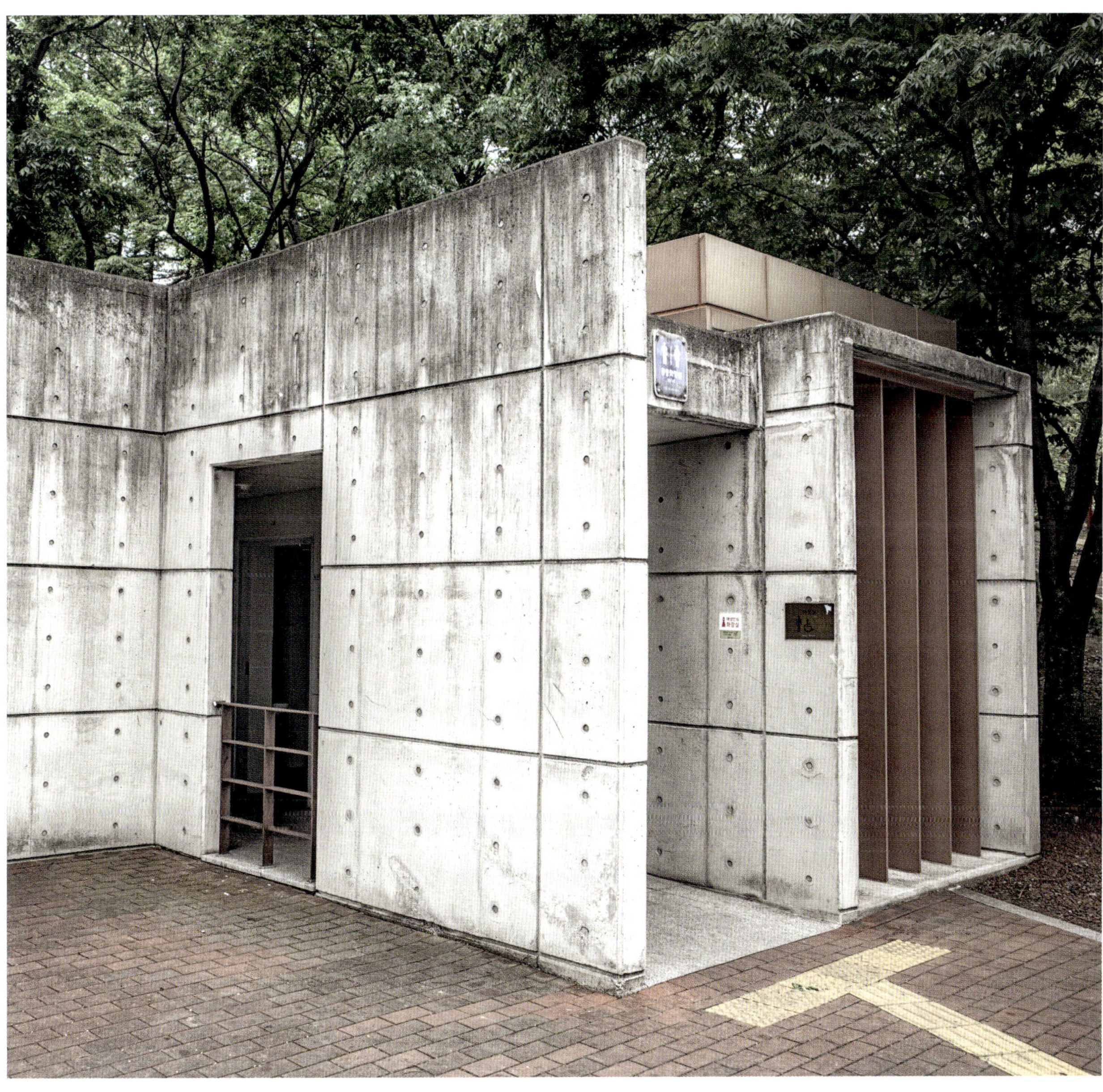

GIMHAE INTERNATIONAL AIRPORT

BUSAN

The gateway is a colossal concrete gesture that seems to mark the border between earth and air. It's part infrastructure, part sculpture – an arch that compresses the sky into a framed departure lounge. Its coarse surface and monumental heft contradict the weightlessness of aviation, as though the building itself is reluctant to let go. Yet as you pass beneath it, the structure begins to feel like a launching pad, a runway turned vertical. The terminal reveals another expression of lift. Its angled supports slice diagonally across the façade like frozen contrails, channelling the motion of aircraft into static form. Where the gateway asserts dominance, the terminal articulates rhythm – gravity countered by geometry. Together, they turn the mundane act of arrival and departure into a study in tension: one structure grounded and stoic, the other forever straining upwards, both caught in that poetic moment just before take-off.

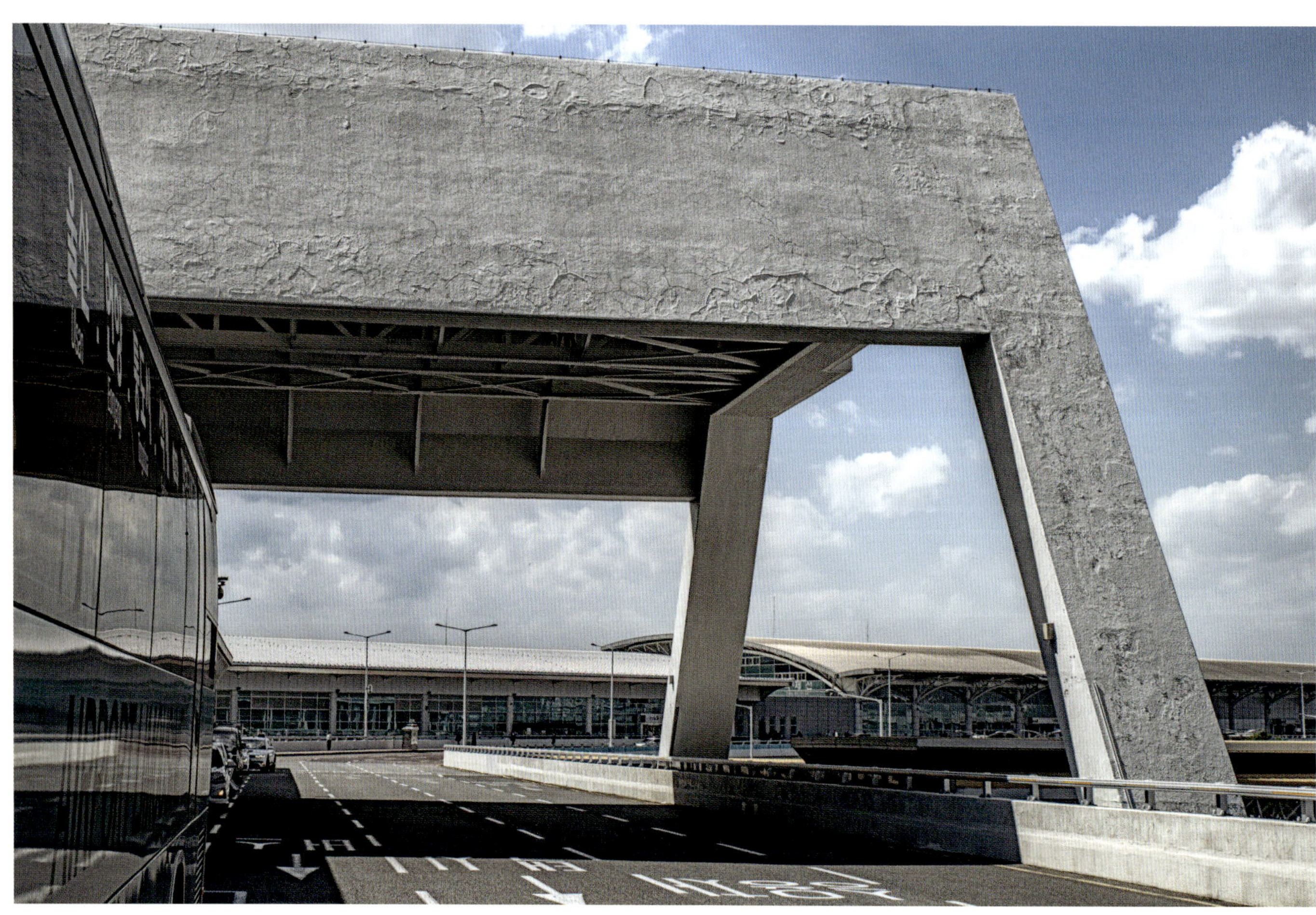

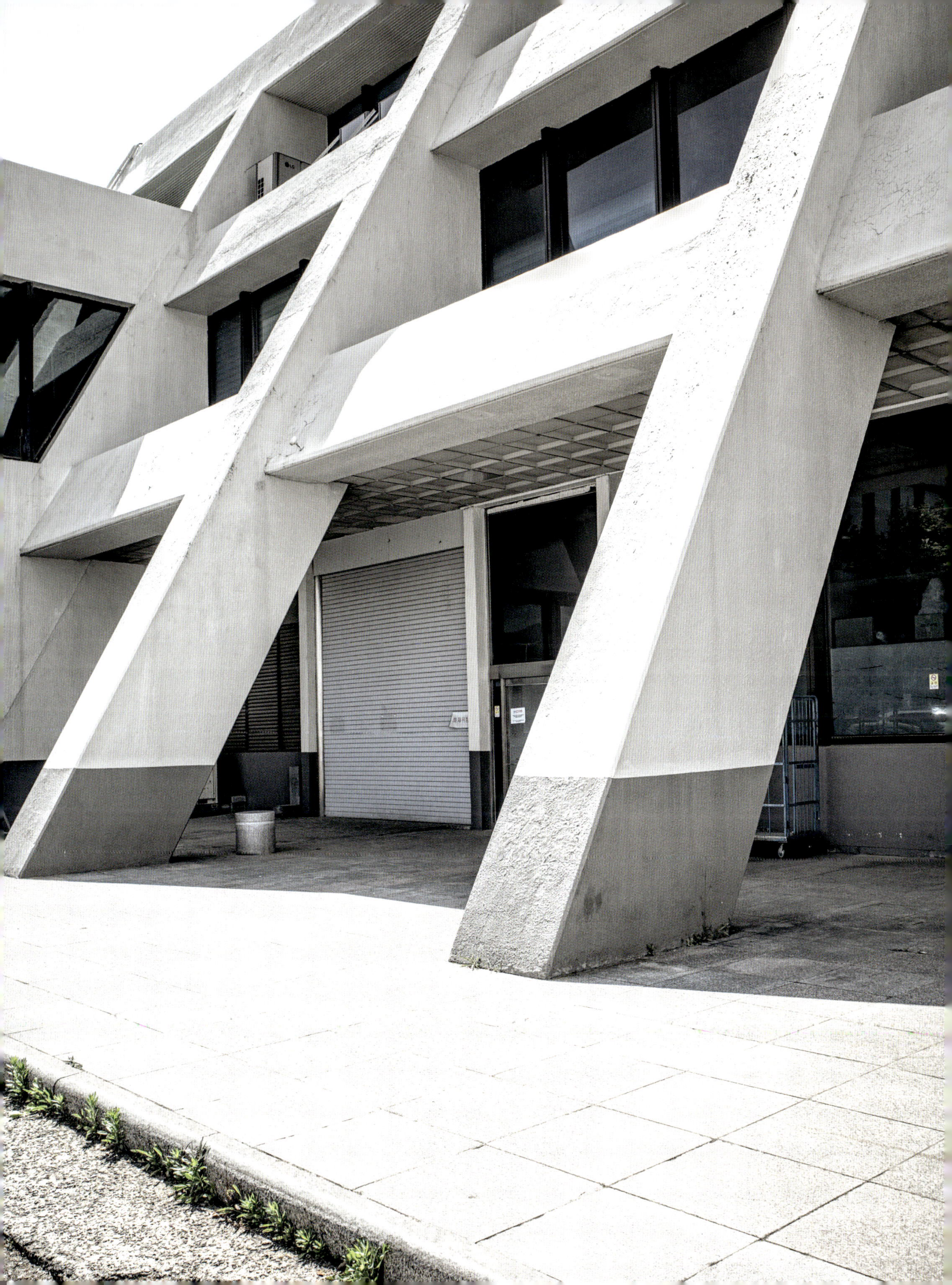

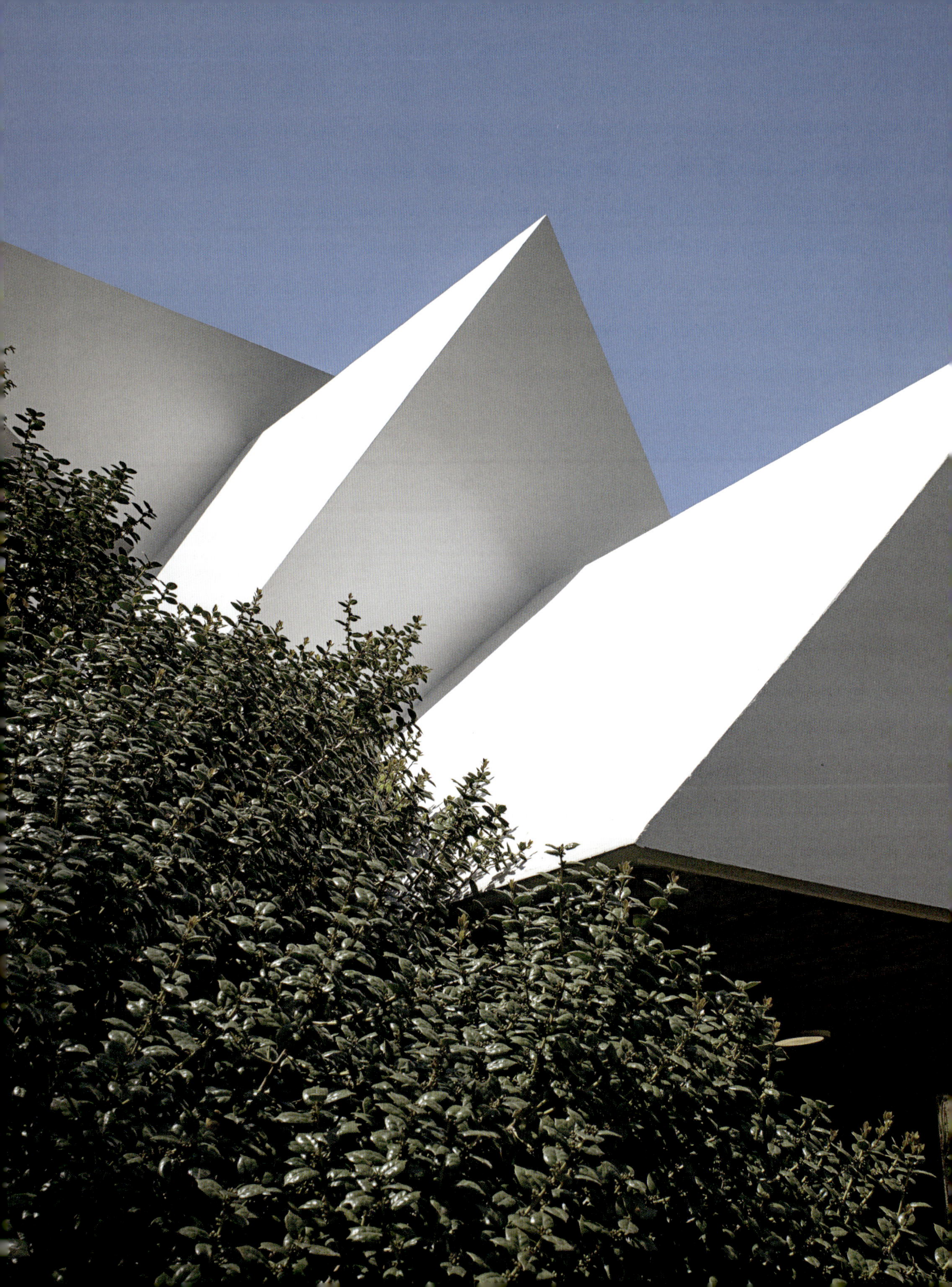

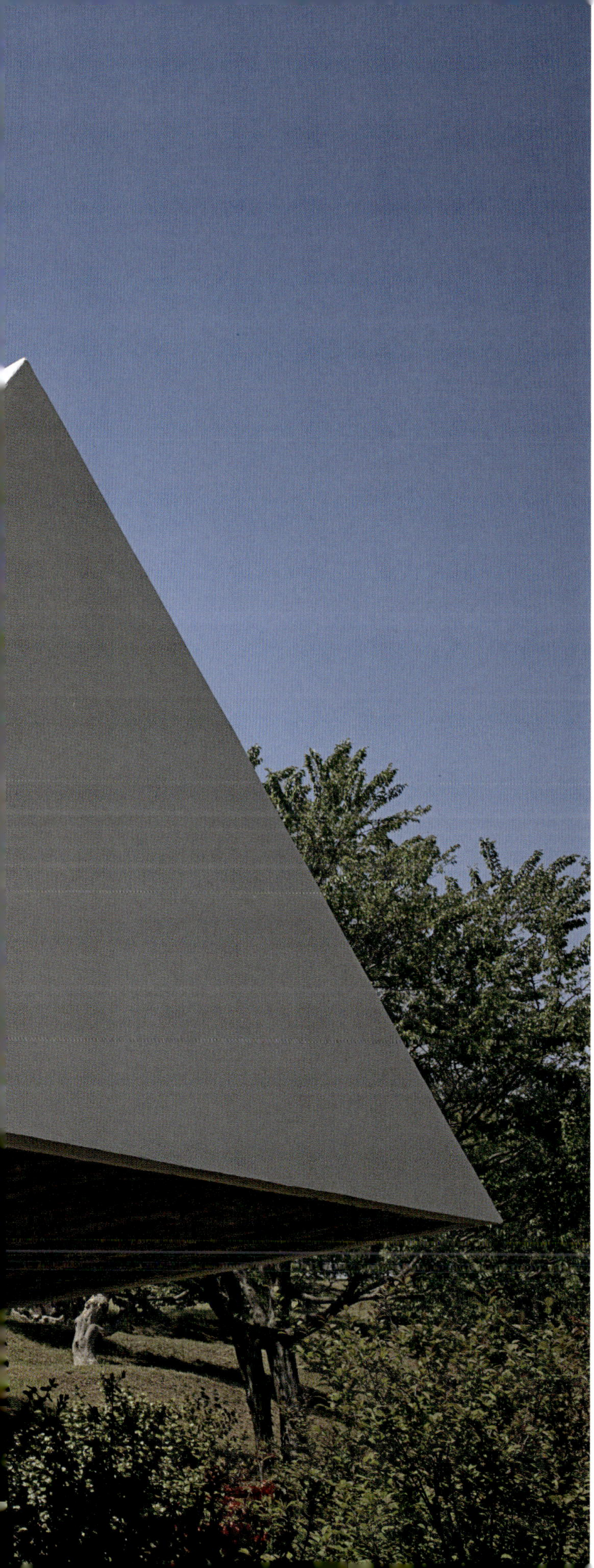

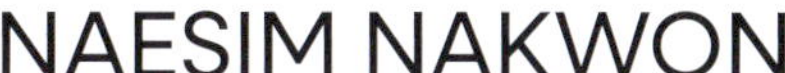

NAESIM NAKWON

SAYUWON · Architects: Álvaro SIZA VIEIRA and Carlos CASTANHEIRA · Completed 2017

This chapel sits quietly within the quince grove at Sayuwon in Gunwi, Gyeongsangbuk-do. Conceived as a place of contemplation and dedication to the philanthropist Kim Ik-jin, it's a structure that speaks in murmurs rather than declarations, a study in stillness rendered in concrete.

Rectilinear and humble, the building holds its ground like a stone set with purpose. Exterior white stucco finishing somewhat undermines Brutalist credentials. The exposed interior concrete is tactile but controlled, bearing the texture of its timber formwork with a gentle rhythm. It reads neither as mausoleum nor church, but rather as something in between – a spatial punctuation mark that leaves the interpretation open.

There is only one opening in the thick concrete shell: a sharply angled, high-cut aperture that lets daylight in but allows no view out. Glazed only with shadow, it resists narrative – more suggestion than spectacle. It denies the typical role of the window, refusing to connect inside and out, and instead casts light as a material in itself.

The result is a space as heavy as it is weightless. One enters by way of a stone slab that sits slightly above the surrounding ground, reinforcing the impression that the building is not placed *on* the landscape but belongs *to* it. There's no ornament, no signage, no skyline gesture. The architecture instead relies on discipline: tight geometry, tight palette, tight control of light.

There are no sermons here, only concrete and time. In its asceticism, Naesim Nakwon recalls both Korean *seowon* and early Christian hermitages – austere, yes, but with a gentleness in the detail. It's not paradise as spectacle, but as withdrawal: a retreat for reflection, built not to inspire awe, but to allow for pause.

MUAE BUILDING

SEOUL · Architect: JEONG Ki-yong · Completed 1994

Jeong Ki-yong's Muae Building in the neighbourhood of Dongsung is seemingly a clear interpretation of Brutalism. Rising from Seoul's dense theatre district, its geometric massing of angled stone planes expresses a textural gravitas and geometric severity uncommon in Korean architecture of the early 1990s. Where much of the city embraced reflective glass and imported postmodern motifs, Jeong's design reasserted the tactile truth of material and the moral weight of structure.

The building's sculpted volumes, sheathed in rough-cut grey granite panels, echo the Brutalist respect for exposed, unadorned surfaces. These stone "skins" serve not as decoration, but as the building's very expression – revealing weather, texture, and the trace of time. Rectangular apertures cut deep into the façades recall Brutalist strategies of light control: voids that carve shadow while allowing no ornament. Seen obliquely, the structure recalls a natural formation – a cleaved mass of stone, severe yet quietly animate.

In a decade defined by economic confidence and architectural spectacle, the Muae Building offered quiet resistance. Its mass and gravity countered the gloss of modernization with the humility of raw matter.

However, the Muae Building may not have been conceived as a Brutalist statement so much as the by-product of Jeong Ki-yong's ethical and spatial philosophy meeting constraint. His belief in architecture that responds to its context merged with the realities of a cramped plot hemmed in by setback rules, height limits, and sightline controls. Instead of imposing formal grandeur, Jeong allowed these pressures to sculpt the building's faceted geometry and dense massing. The resulting severity, its rough granite skin, and the honest exposure of structure arose from necessity and conviction alike. Brutalism's visual language thus emerged here not from ideology, but from responsiveness: a building shaped by constraint, by place, and by Jeong's insistence that architecture remain sincere, grounded, and inseparable from the conditions that produce it.

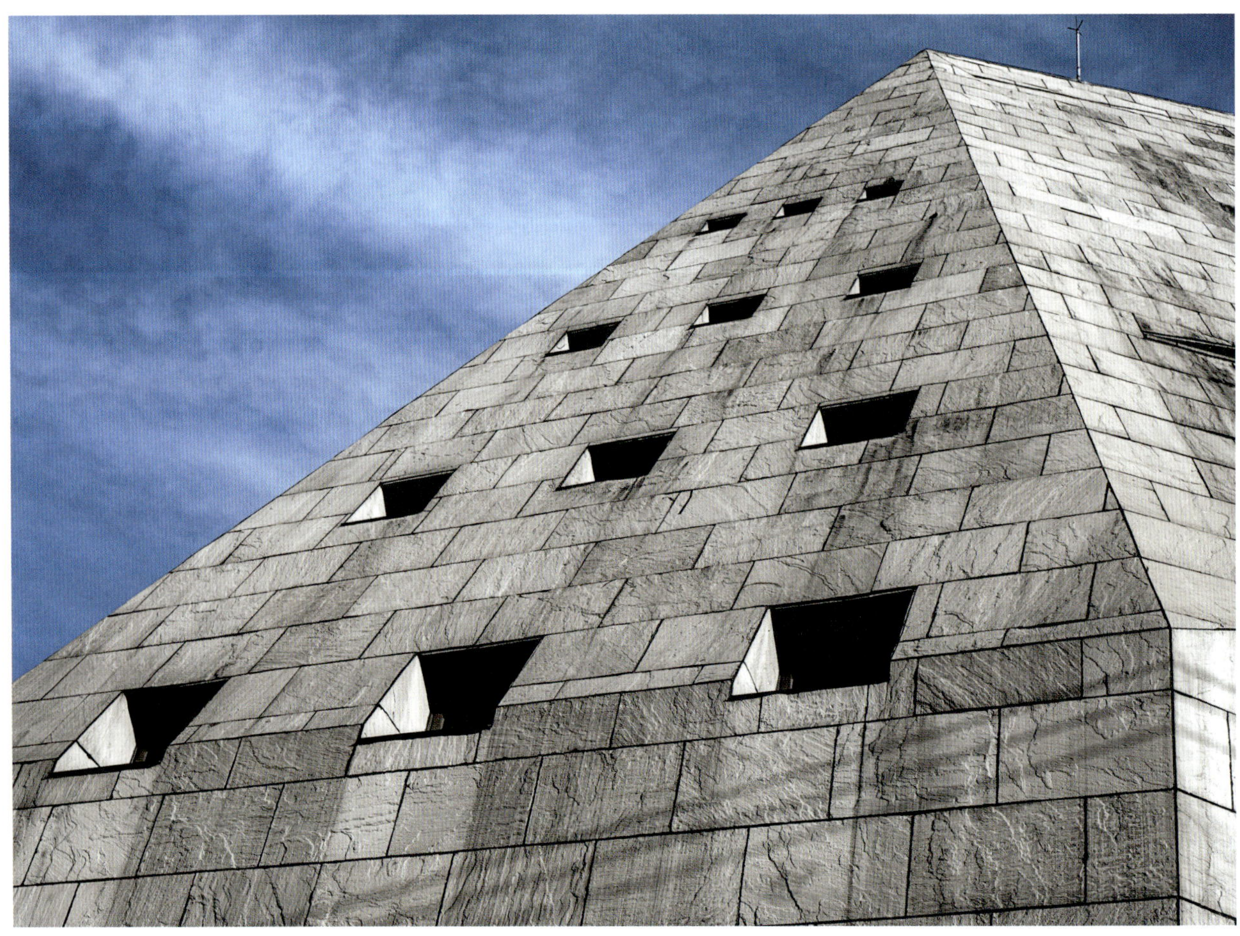

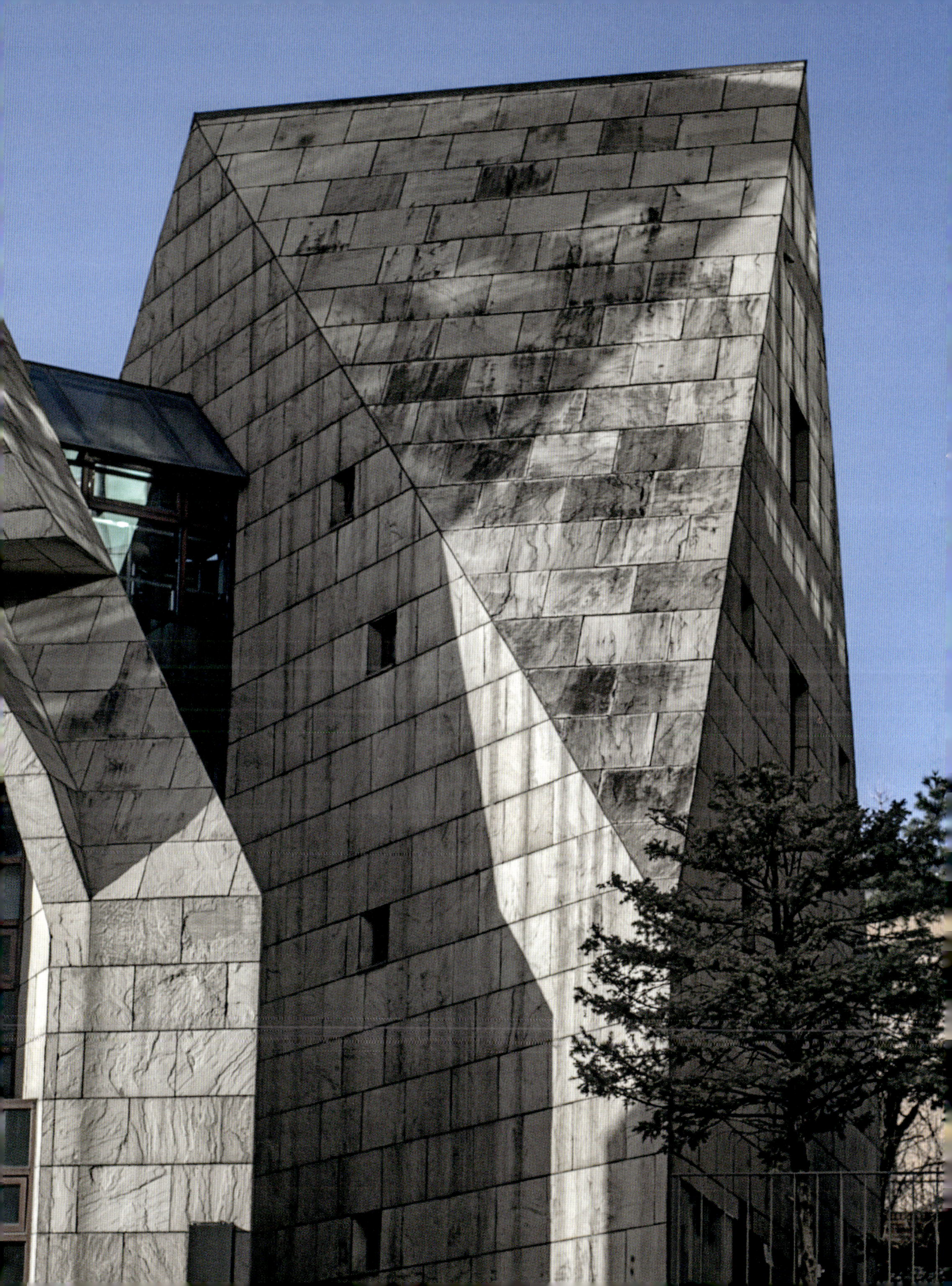

UNESCO WORLD NATURAL HERITAGE CENTER

JEJU ISLAND · Architects: Kyungam Architects and Sun Architects & Engineers · Completed 2012

The Jeju World Natural Heritage Center was conceived as a place for education, research, and reflection on the island's unique environment. Guided by the concept of a "heritage loop", the design expresses the idea that natural treasures must be continuously passed down through generations. The building integrates carefully with its landscape, preserving existing trees and terrain while framing distant views of the volcanic Geomunoreum. Inside, distinct zones serve exhibitions, classrooms, and research spaces; the educational areas feature flexible partitions, while the secluded research wing offers quiet focus with its own terrace. A cafeteria and observatory crown the upper floor, opening towards the surrounding forest and sky. The façade's flowing form, inspired by Jeju's volcanic contours, employs local *hyunmuam* stone, while glass-lined interiors allow light to penetrate deeply, emphasizing openness, sustainability, and the living connection between land and learning.

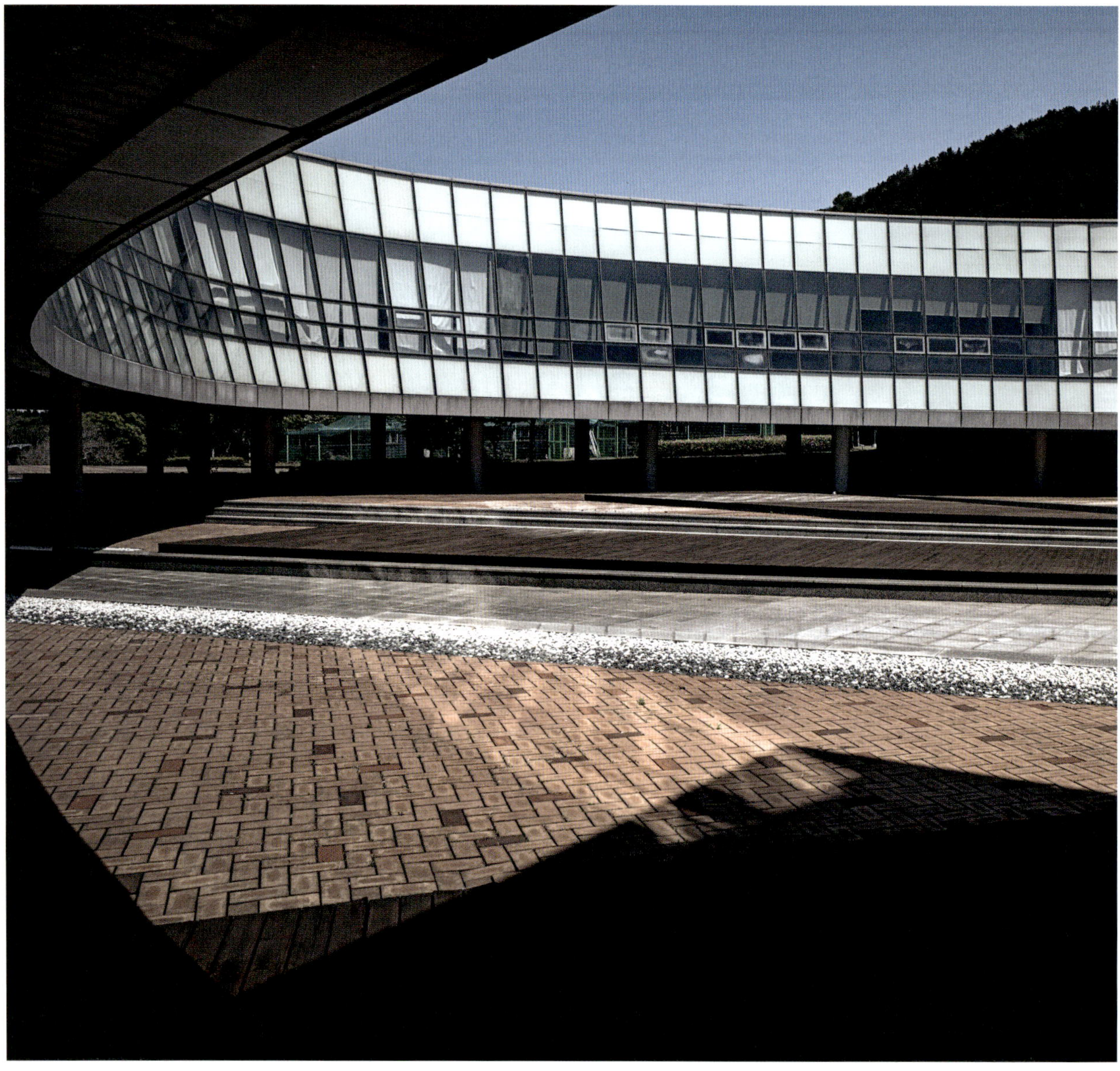

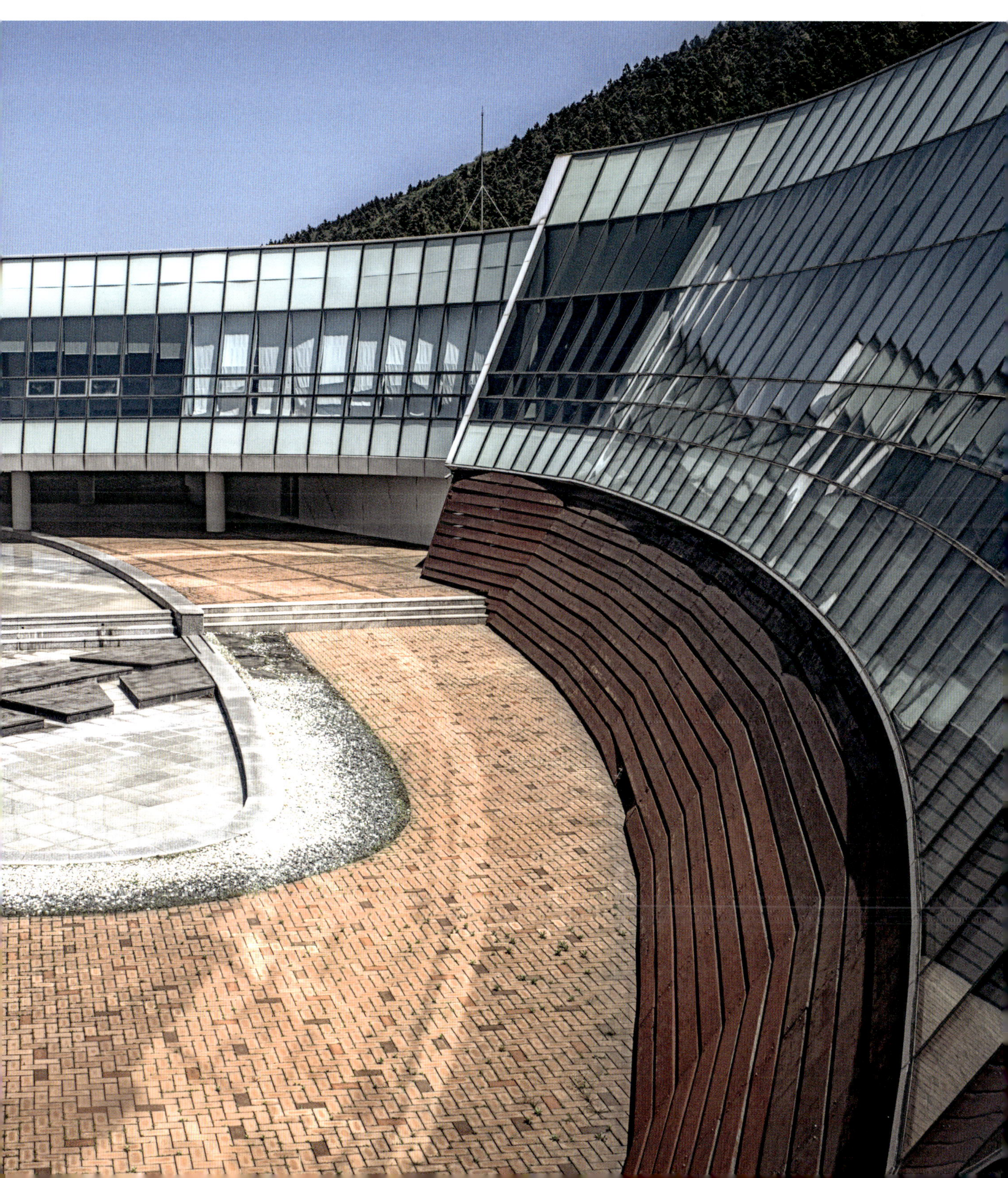

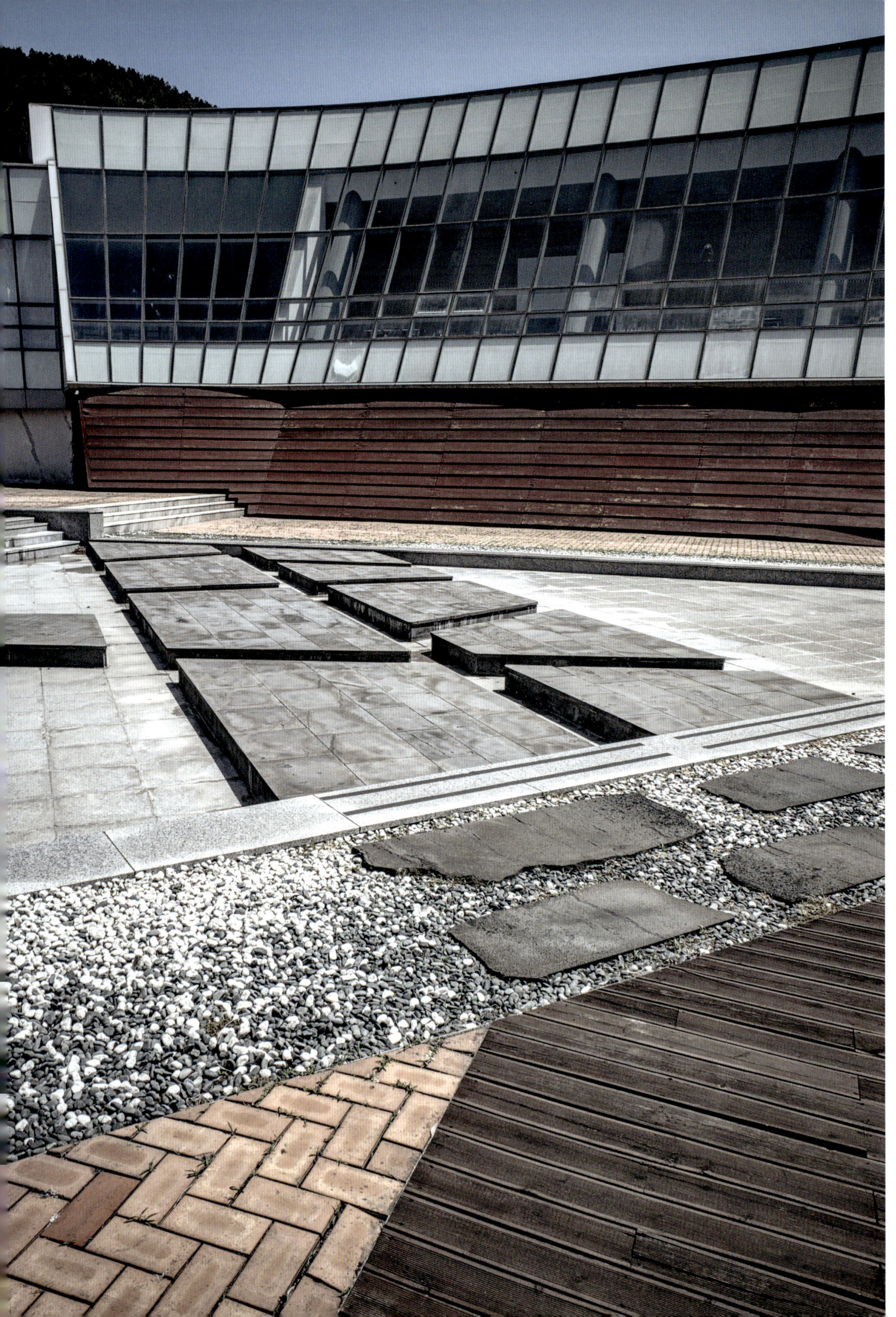

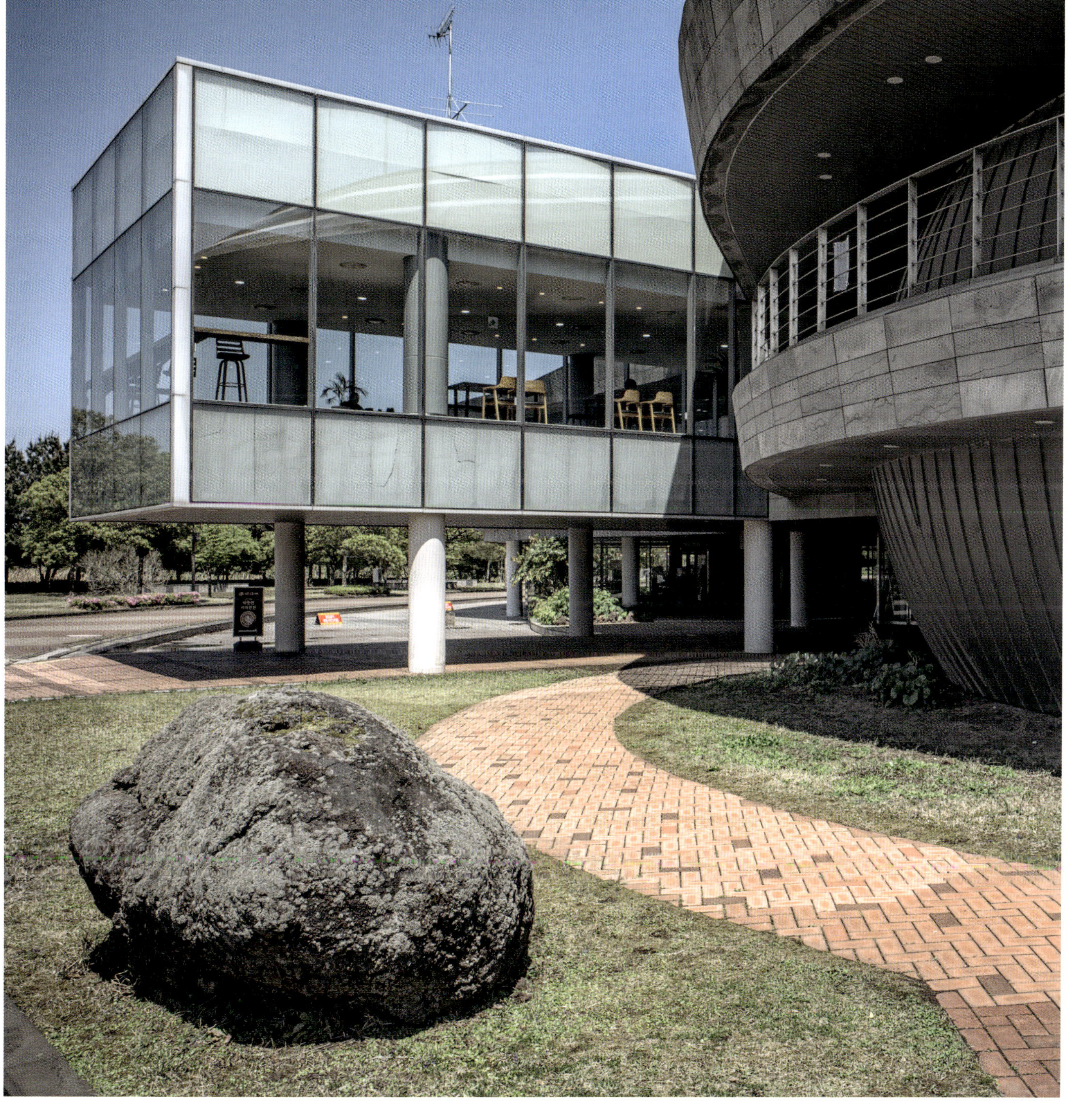

SEWOON SANGGA

SEOUL · Architect: KIM Swoo-geun · Completed 1970

An architectural snake slipping and slicing through central Seoul, Sewoon Sangga is less shopping arcade and more urban megastructure – a proto-smart city cast in concrete. Conceived as the spine of a futuristic utopia, this linear complex stretches like a Brutalist monorail over Jongno's alleys and markets, standing on stilts and stubbornness.

Designed by Kim Swoo-geun, it was Seoul's first mixed-use building, integrating residences, commerce, and technology in one dramatic sweep. Often likened to Le Corbusier's Unité d'Habitation meeting *Blade Runner*, the structure originally connected seven blocks, forming a suspended urban corridor from Jongmyo Shrine to Namsan.

What was once heralded as Korea's answer to Tokyo's Ginza fell into decades of decline, its promise of modern living eclipsed by malls and megaprojects elsewhere. But unlike many of its concrete contemporaries, Sewoon Sangga has dodged the wrecking ball. Recent revivals have polished its raw skin just enough – without sanding off its edge – to reinvigorate it as a hub for electronics tinkerers in a real-world cyberpunk setting.

No-nonsense geometry, deep-set windows, pilotis columns, and its fortress-like massing all mark its Brutalist roots. But the real drama lies in the tension between sky and street: elevated walkways hover over the bustle, while shaded corridors below buzz with soldering irons and second-hand audio gear.

Surviving in a city of the shiny and new, Sewoon Sangga remains an icon of architectural grit: a relic of mid-century ambition refusing to go quietly. Seoulites now picnic on its rooftop garden, sip espresso where resistors were once sold, and stage art festivals beneath its concrete canopy.

In a word? Stubborn. In two? Elton John. Still standing.

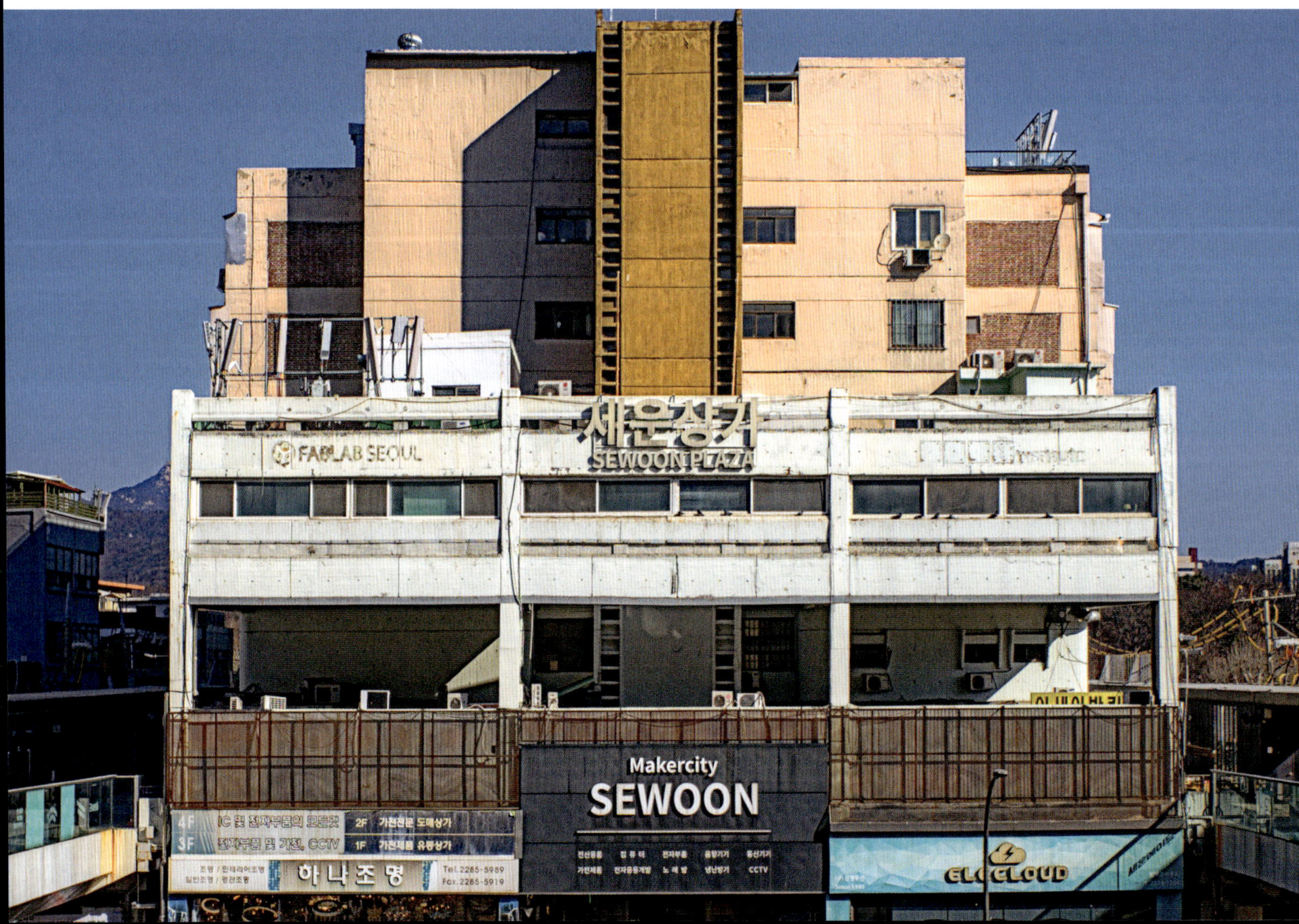

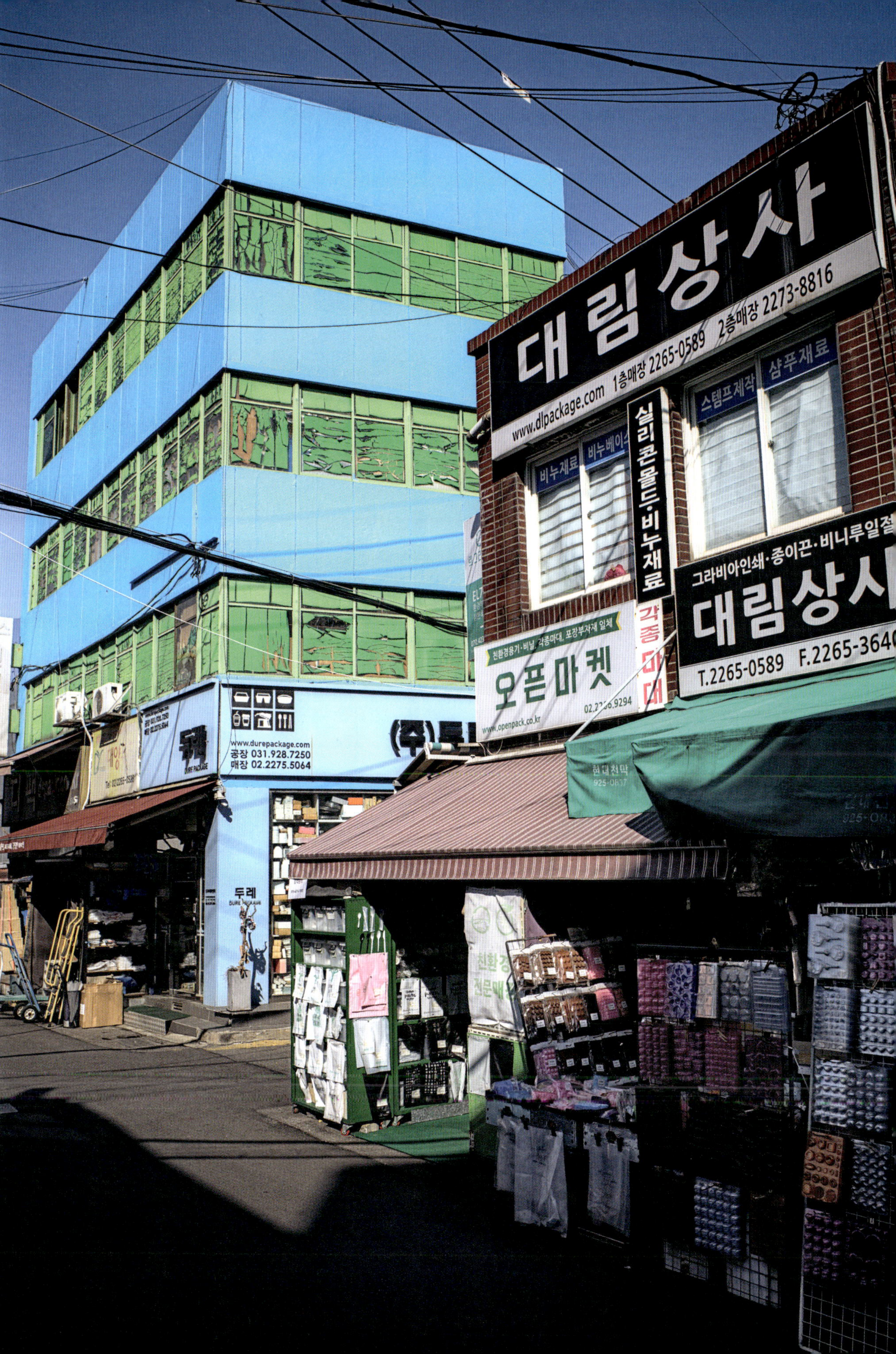
대림상사
www.dlpackage.com 1층매장 2265-0589 2층매장 2273-8816
실리콘몰드·비누재료
비누재료
스탬프제작
샴푸재료
친환경용기·비닐·각종마대, 포장부자재 일체
오픈마켓
www.openpack.co.kr
그라비아인쇄·종이끈·비니루일절
대림상사
T.2265-0589
www.durepackage.com
공장 031.928.7250
매장 02.2275.5064
두레
현대천막
925-0837

SEJONG CENTER

SEOUL · Architect: AUM Duck-moon · Completed 1978

On Seoul's grand thoroughfare Sejong-daero, two great acts face off: the Sejong Center for the Performing Arts and the U.S. Embassy – one built to project culture, the other to manage it. The Sejong Center spreads out like a monumental stage curtain, all rhythm and ceremony. Across the street, the embassy hunches behind its fences, a Brutalist monologue in paranoia. One invites applause; the other awaits clearance.

Inside Sejong, spotlights rise, orchestras tune, and expression spills freely. Inside the Embassy, fluorescent lights hum to the quiet chime of bureaucracy. Both rehearse power – one soft, one hard – but only one knows how to hold an audience.

The Sejong Center plays the better diplomat: fluent in nuance, bold in gesture, and unafraid of drama. Curtain up. Visas pending over the road.

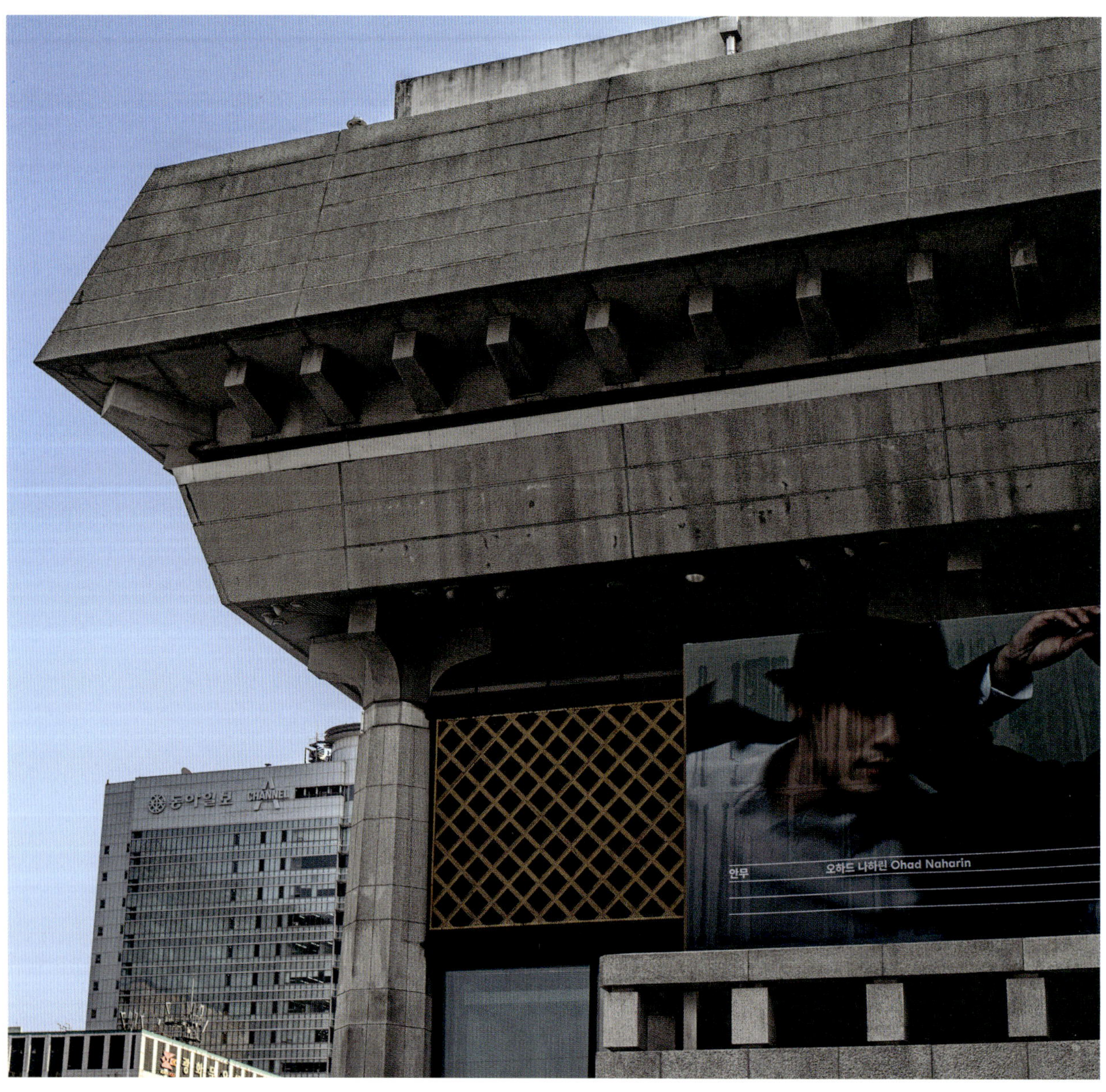

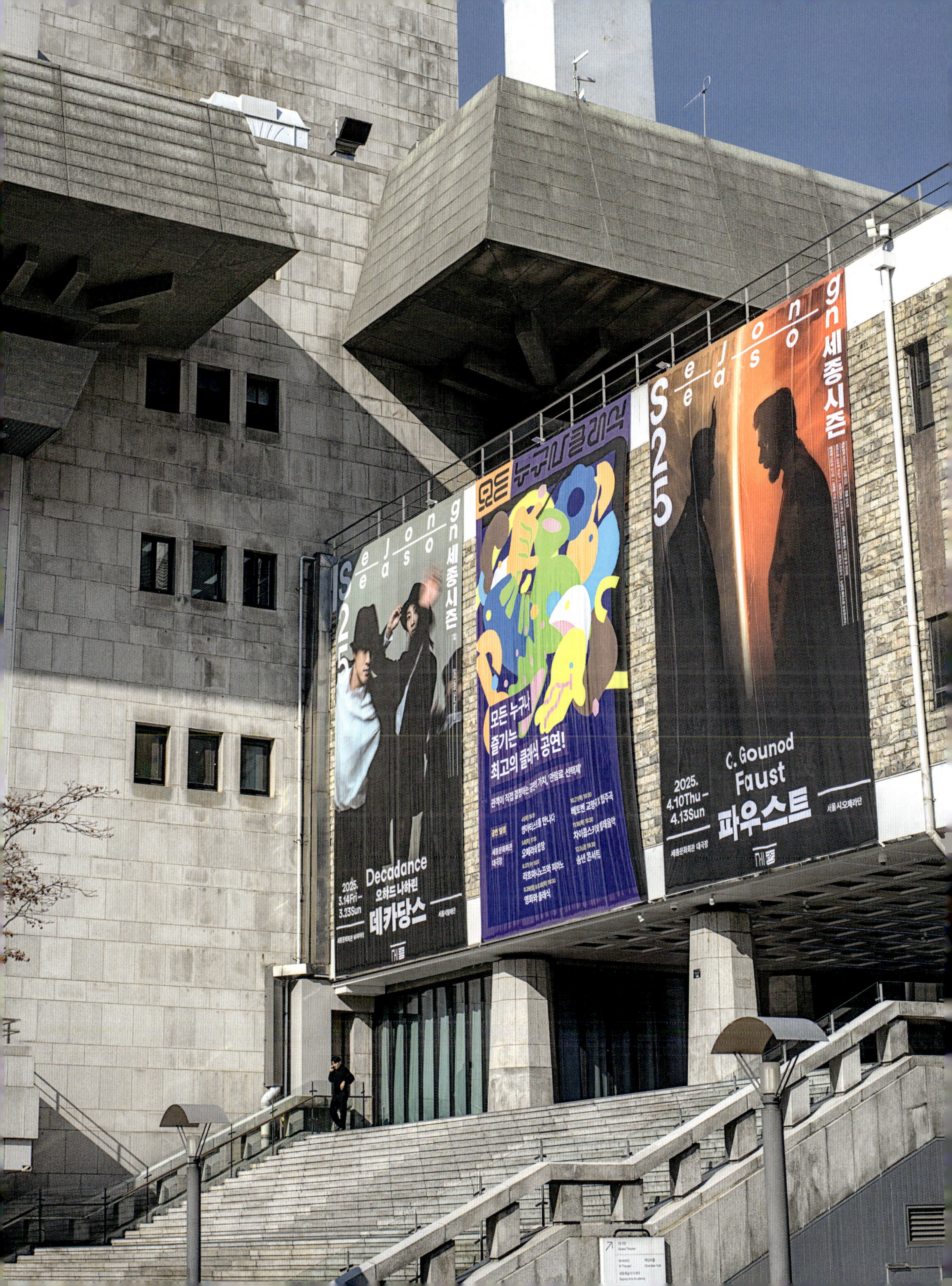
Sejong Season
S25
세종시즌
Decadance
오하드 나하린
데카당스
2025.
3.14Fri –
3.23Sun
모든 누구나 클래식
모든 누구나
즐기는
최고의 클래식 공연!
관객이 직접 결정하는 공연의 가치, '관람료 선택제'
공연 일정
영아티스트를 만나다
베토벤 교향곡X협주곡
차이콥스키와 발레음악
C. Gounod
Faust
파우스트
2025.
4.10Thu –
4.13Sun
세종문화회관 대극장
서울시오페라단

AEKYUNG DESIGN CENTER

SEOUL · Architects: JEONG Hyeon-mi (Jang Hak Design) and MKPL ARCHITECTS · Completed 2007 / Renovated 2023

This building embodies a refined synthesis of material honesty and urban sensitivity. The building's form is dominated by a massive exposed-concrete volume that appears to float above a transparent piloti base, an architectural gesture that elevates the structure both literally and symbolically. This contrast between solidity and transparency mirrors Aekyung's identity as a brand grounded in craftsmanship yet forward-looking in innovation. A full-height glass curtain wall mediates light and reflection, connecting the interior with the lively street below. The addition of a sculpture of a hand at ground level extends the building's narrative – human touch meeting industrial precision – and softens its corporate austerity. When reimagined in 2023, the renovation respected Jeong's original language, refining interior and environmental systems while preserving the building's quietly iconic presence within the Yeonnam district's creative streetscape.

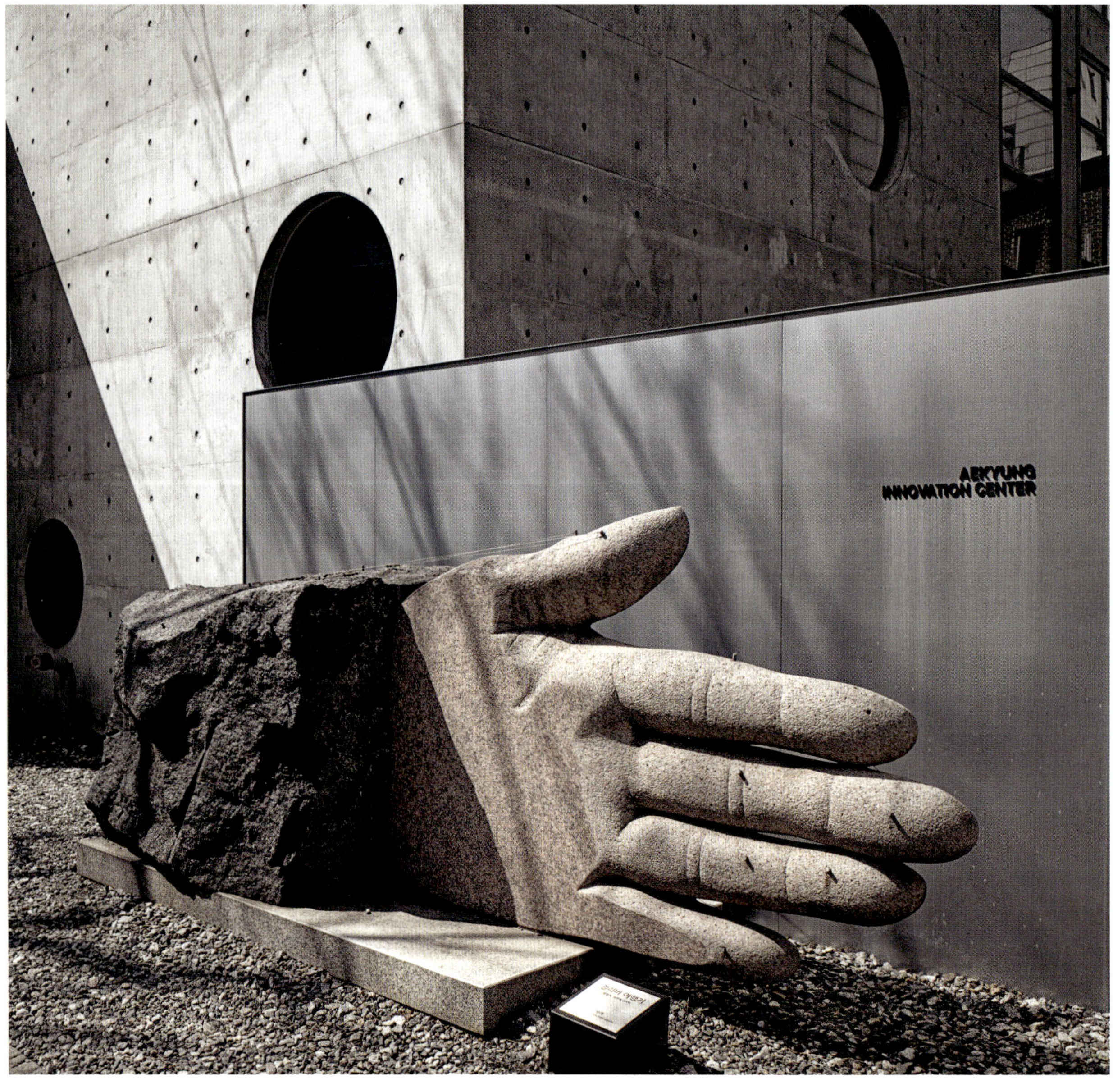

BUSAN MUSEUM OF ART

BUSAN · Architect: LEE Yong-Heum · Completed 2003

The Busan Museum of Art sits with the calm confidence of a building that knows form can be its own exhibition. Its concrete façade – broad, weighty, and rhythmically punctuated – presents a kind of architectural understatement that verges on the sculptural. Light seeps across its surfaces like an artist's wash, revealing the texture of shuttered concrete and the precision of its joints. Inside, the volumes are as deliberate as brushstrokes: voids and planes guiding movement through a sequence of stillness and surprise. There's a Brutalist honesty here – the material is unadorned, the geometry harsh – but it's tempered by the restraint of curation. The museum is less a container for art than an extension of it – a gallery of concrete expressions. It stands as both frame and subject, revealing that architecture shapes not just what we see but also the very act of seeing.

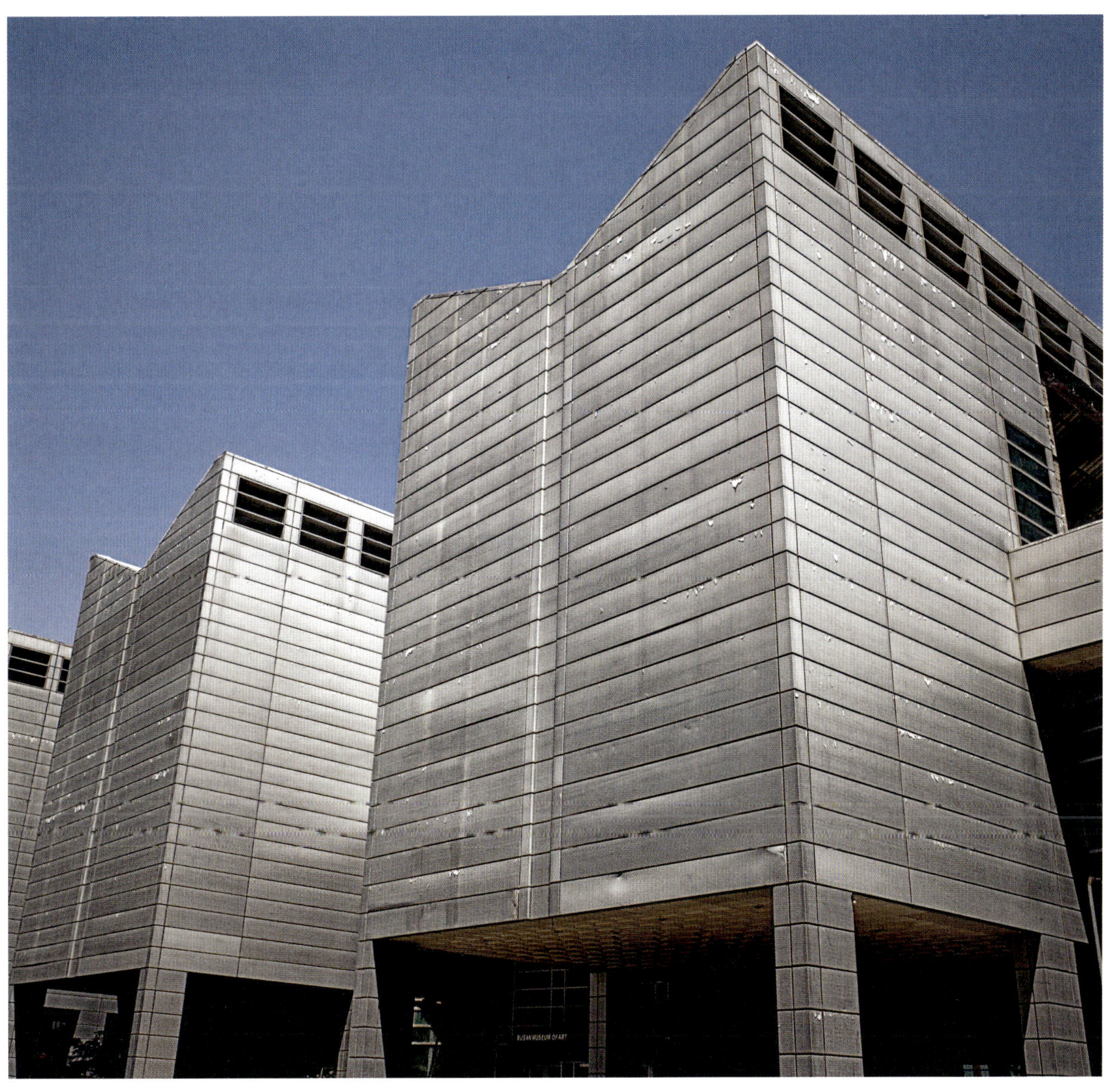

LOGIN HOTEL

JEJU ISLAND

The Login Hotel reimagines the notion of checking in. Its façade – a cheerful stack of cantilevered boxes in turquoise, pink, grey, and violet – turns accommodation into architecture with attitude. Each coloured pod projects from a dark concrete frame like a private thought escaping the building's orderly grid, offering guests both a view and a statement. The playful rhythm of the façade, shifting with light and shadow, suggests movement even in stillness, as if the structure itself were mid-animation. Inside, the protrusions translate into alcoves of intimacy – moments of retreat framed by whimsy. There's Brutalism here, but not the stern kind: the concrete massing is softened by wit, by colour, by the joy of inhabiting something that refuses to take itself too seriously. In a landscape of basalt and restraint, Login Hotel offers a refreshingly human invitation. Sometimes architecture, like a good host, knows how to smile.

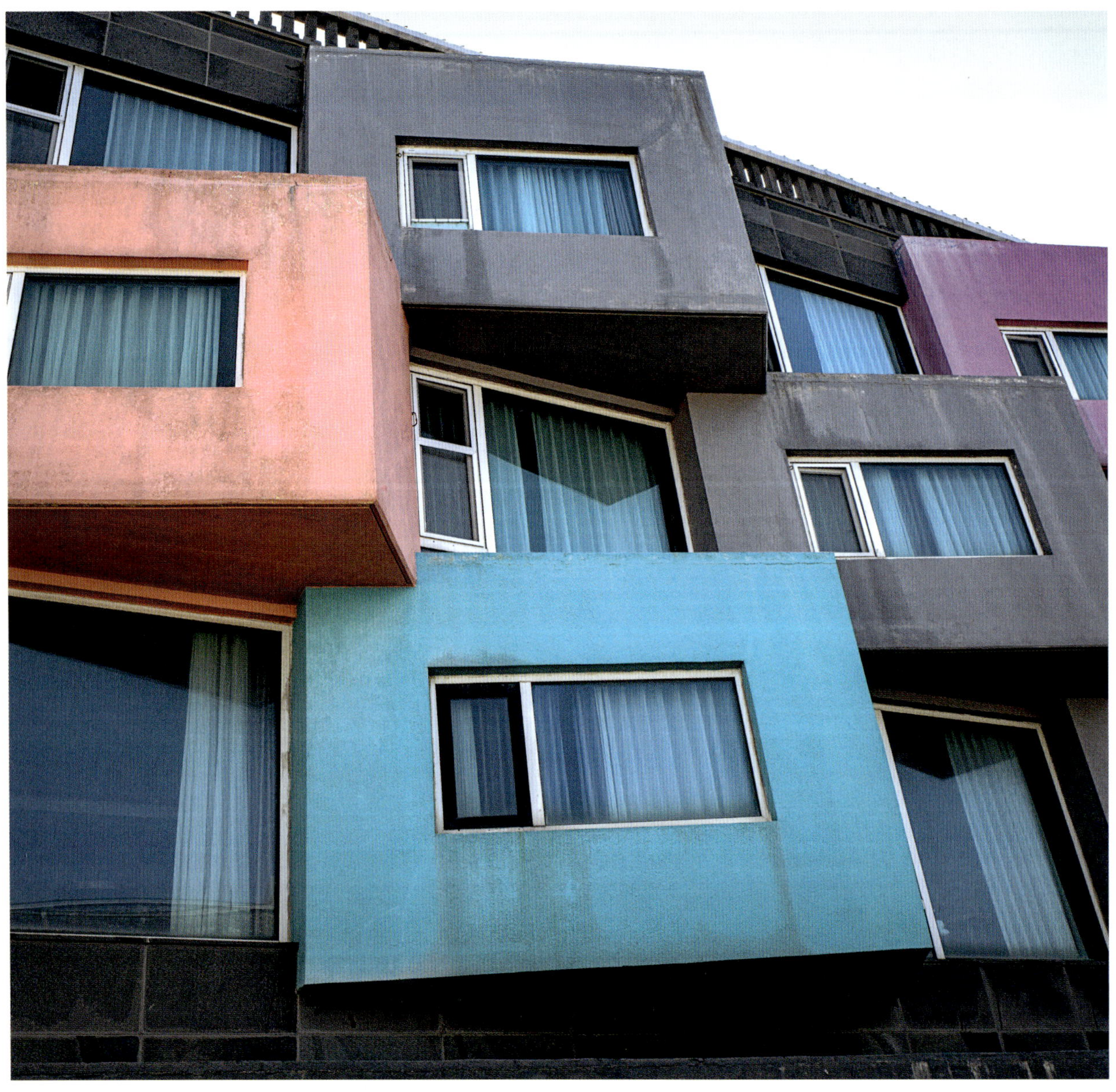

MER BLEUE HOTEL

JEJU ISLAND

This is a seaside hotel fronting the coastal road that runs through Aewol, an area popular for its cafés, sea views, and contemporary concrete-and-glass architecture. The building's façade features a rhythmic grid of recessed balconies and deep window frames – giving it a geometric, Brutalist presence softened by the blue-tinted glazing that mirrors the ocean it faces. The convenience store on the ground floor is part of the structure and typical of Jeju's mixed-use coastal developments.

The hotel's name, Mer Bleue (French for "Blue Sea"), emphasizes the maritime connection, while the bold rectangular composition aligns it with the rationalist concrete-and-frame architecture that defines much of Jeju's recent coastal growth. It's a functional, compact expression of modern Korean coastal urbanism – equal parts hotel, convenience hub, and ocean-view stage. Where convenience meets with concrete.

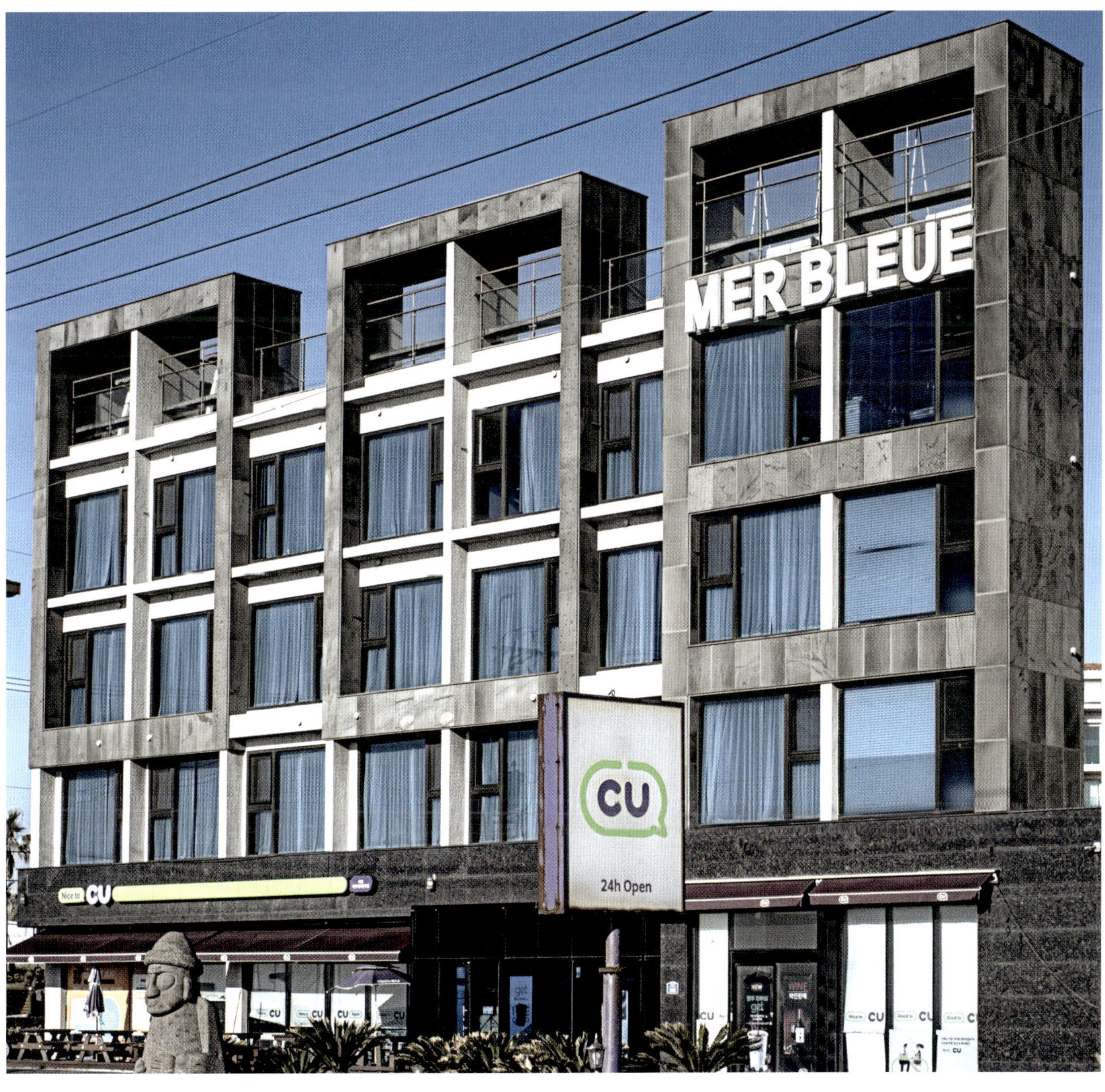

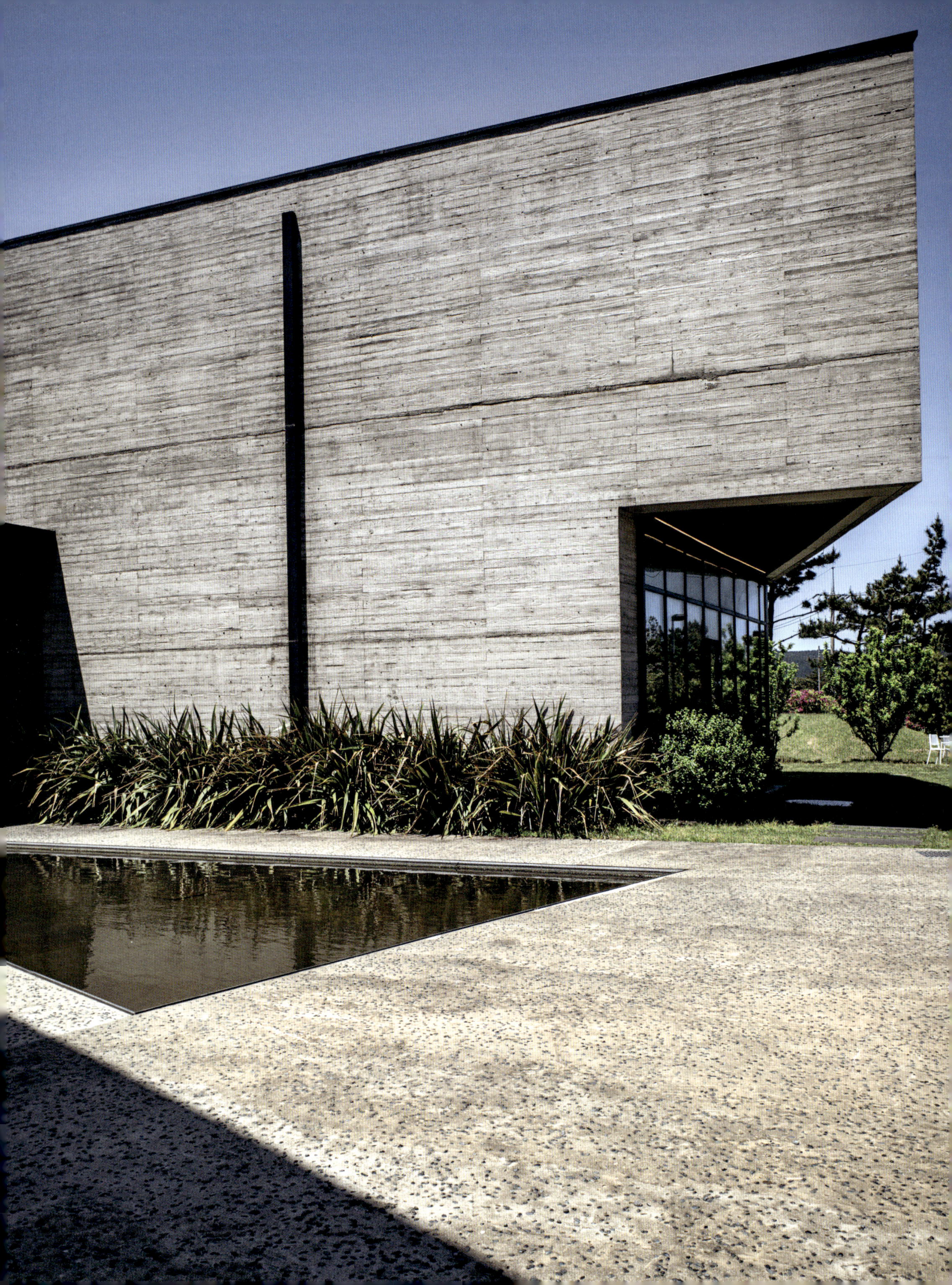

NO BOUNDARY

JEJU ISLAND

The No Boundary café and gallery on Jeju Island wears its name well – a concrete meditation on permeability. Its raw board-formed walls meet sheets of glass in a poised standoff between weight and lightness, opacity and exposure. The two interlocking volumes appear to have been quietly extruded from the volcanic soil, their edges sharp yet humane. One block hovers above the lawn like a held breath, while another folds around a reflective pool, turning water into a partner in the building's curation of light.

Inside, caffeine and contemplation share the same air – a space as comfortable with the chatter of cups as with the hush of art. This is Brutalism with a soft dialect: severe in material, gentle in atmosphere. In a landscape known for wind and stone, No Boundary becomes both shelter and stage – where raw concrete hosts conversation.

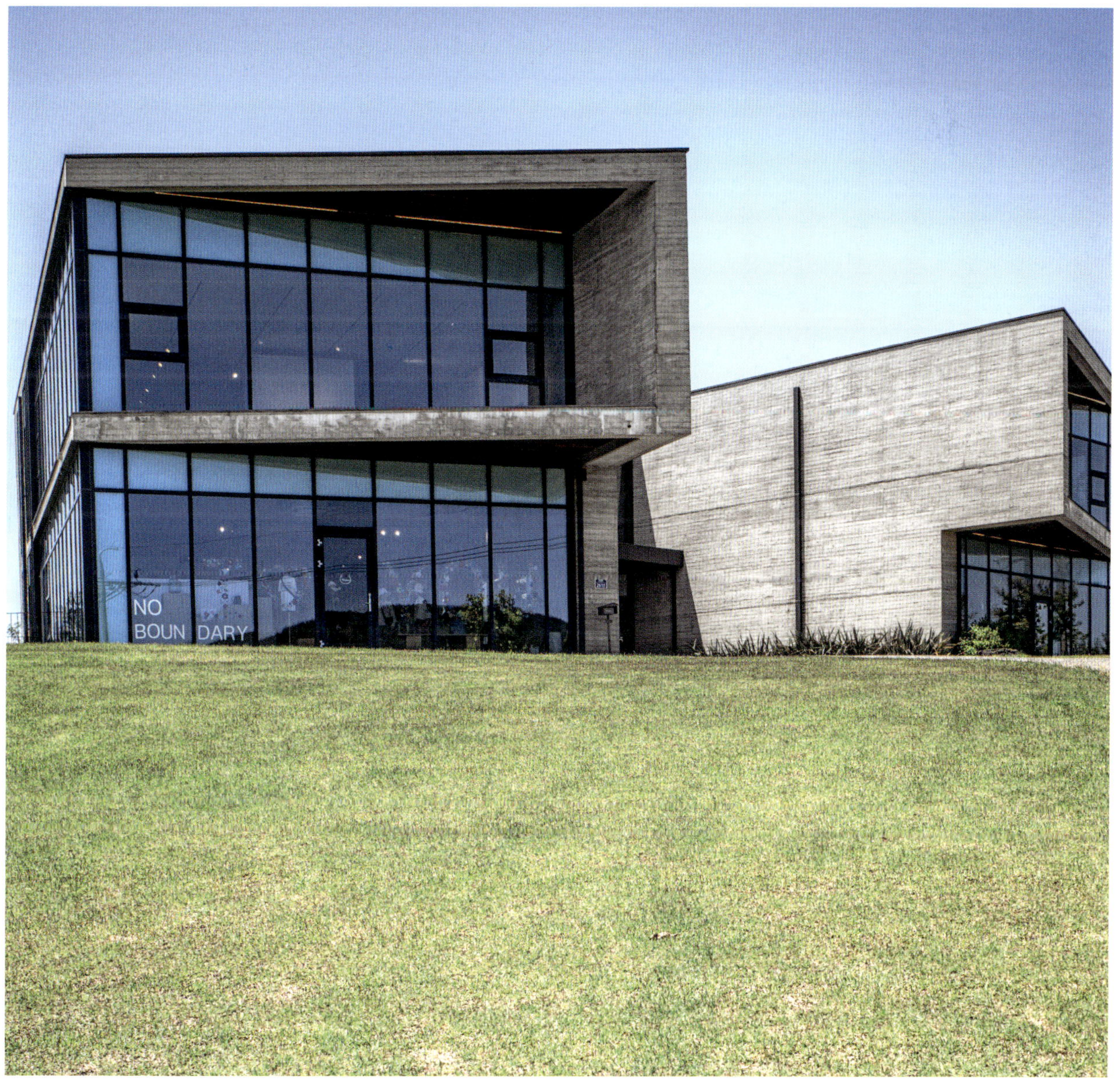

SIMPLE HOUSE

JEJU ISLAND · Architect: MOON Hoon · Completed 2012

For something called "Simple House", Moon Hoon's creation on Jeju Island has a flair for drama and eschews simplicity – it angles, struts, and leans like a piece of geometry caught mid-dance. Cast entirely in exposed concrete, the house looks as if it was poured straight from the imagination of someone who doesn't believe simplicity should mean restraint.

The structure reads like a sketch made solid: an upper box thrust forwards, balanced on diagonals that double as exoskeleton and exclamation mark. The concrete is expressive, rough-grained, and alive with the impressions of its formwork – Moon's favourite medium for turning construction into sculpture. The result is both lofty bunker and praying mantis, part Brutalist sermon, part comic-book insectoid hero spitting out confidence.

Inside, the theatrics settle into rhythm. Angled walls choreograph light; apertures frame fragments of the Jeju landscape with cinematic precision. There's honesty here – no cladding, no pretence – but also wit. The geometry toys with gravity, daring it to object.

Moon once said his buildings are "houses with personalities", and Simple House might be his most extroverted. It has knees, elbows, and a defiant fist. Yet, despite the aggro, there's a curious tenderness: the way the mass lifts to let views flow through, the way sunlight softens its angular armour.

In a landscape of volcanic stone and wind, Simple House makes its own kind of weather – architectural turbulence rendered in concrete. It's a home less in harmony with nature than in negotiation with it – and, somehow, wins. In a submission hold.

This was another one hard to find. Good luck yourself. Imagine taking a few quick sneaky shots and then being welcomed to shoot at will.

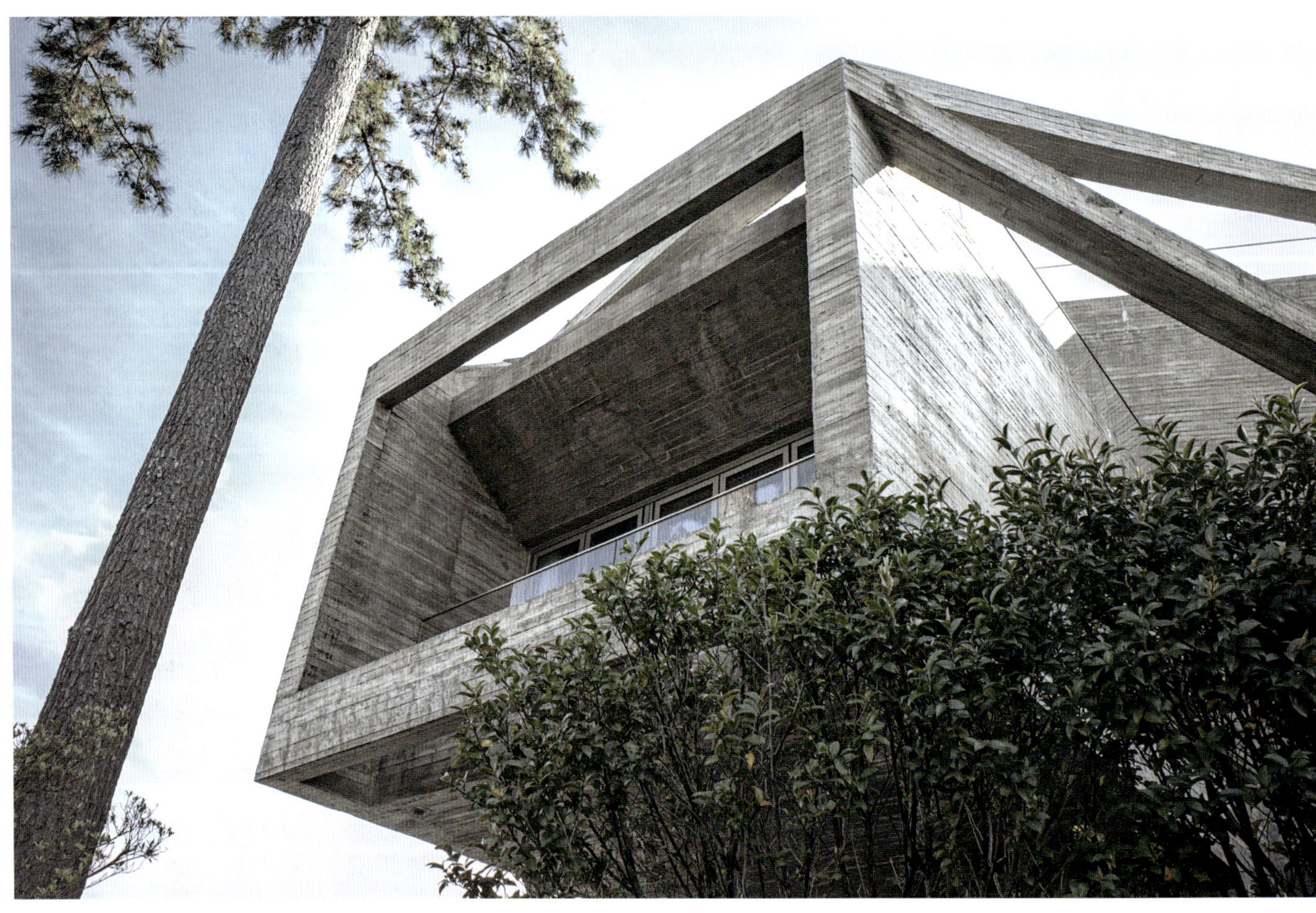

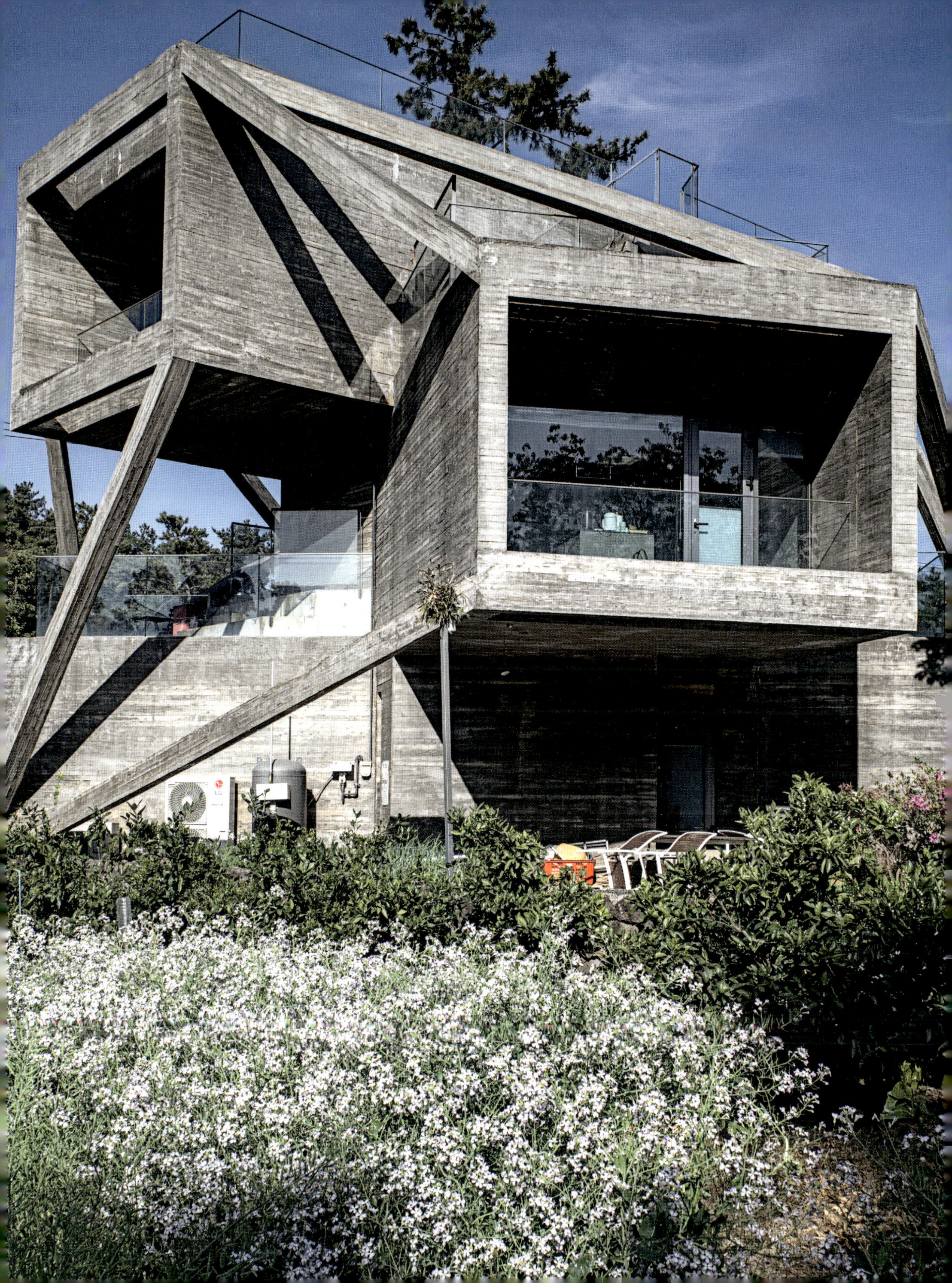

TAMBURINS

SEOUL · Restoration architect: KIM Chan-joong (THE_SYSTEM LAB) · Completed 2023

The Tamburins Seongsu flagship looks, at first glance, like a ruin awaiting rebirth – a skeletal concrete relic left bare against Seoul's electric sky. But that's the point. THE_SYSTEM LAB didn't design a store so much as perform a restoration in reverse. Instead of covering up the old frame, they let it blush through its imperfections – cracked edges, rust stains, scars of time. In a city addicted to cosmetic upgrades, this one dares to go out with its make-up off.

The stripped frame poses like a foundation model mid-photo shoot, all bone structure and confidence. Sunlight catches on the rough aggregate, revealing textures that no cladding could fake. The empty grid becomes perfume without the bottle – form reduced to essence. Each column and beam holds its own quiet fragrance: dust, steel, rain-soaked history.

Tamburins' architectural logic feels distinctly olfactory. Fragrance, after all, is about what remains after everything else has evaporated. The architects chased that same residue – memory in material form. Their intervention is one of restraint: remove the unnecessary, reveal the raw, polish nothing but light.

Cables criss-cross the façade like lines of calligraphy, tracing an urban script that hums with surveillance and electricity. A single digital sign flashes above it, more punctuation than decoration – a reminder that even minimalism in Seoul comes with a current. Yet beneath the wires, the structure feels serene, like the base note in a perfume composition – anchoring, unshakable.

Tamburins' Seongsu project isn't about invention but distillation. It's what happens when architecture trades excess for essence, scaffolding for skeleton, polish for patina. The result is a space that smells of integrity – a building exfoliated to its purest state. In a district characterized by reinvention, this frame stands proudly unfinished, scenting the air with the idea that true beauty doesn't always require a facelift. Sometimes it just needs a little breathing room.

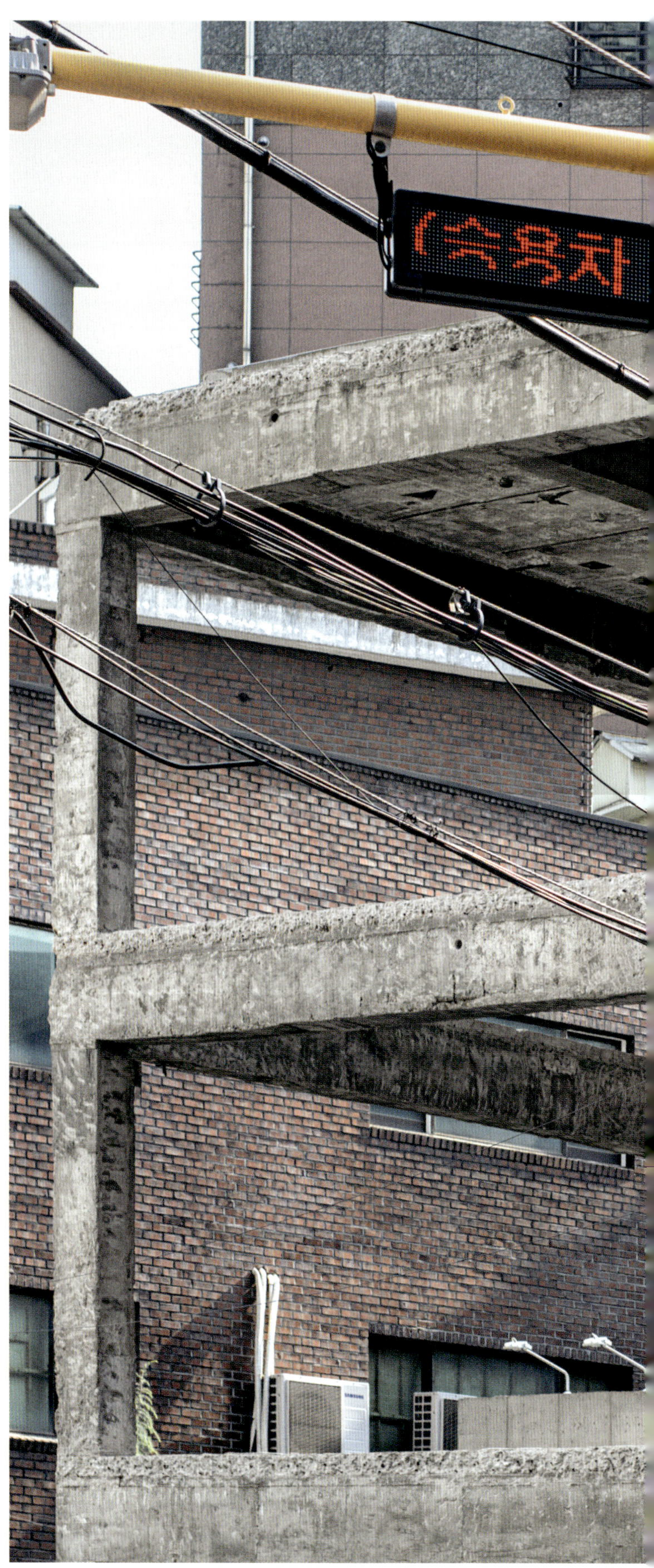

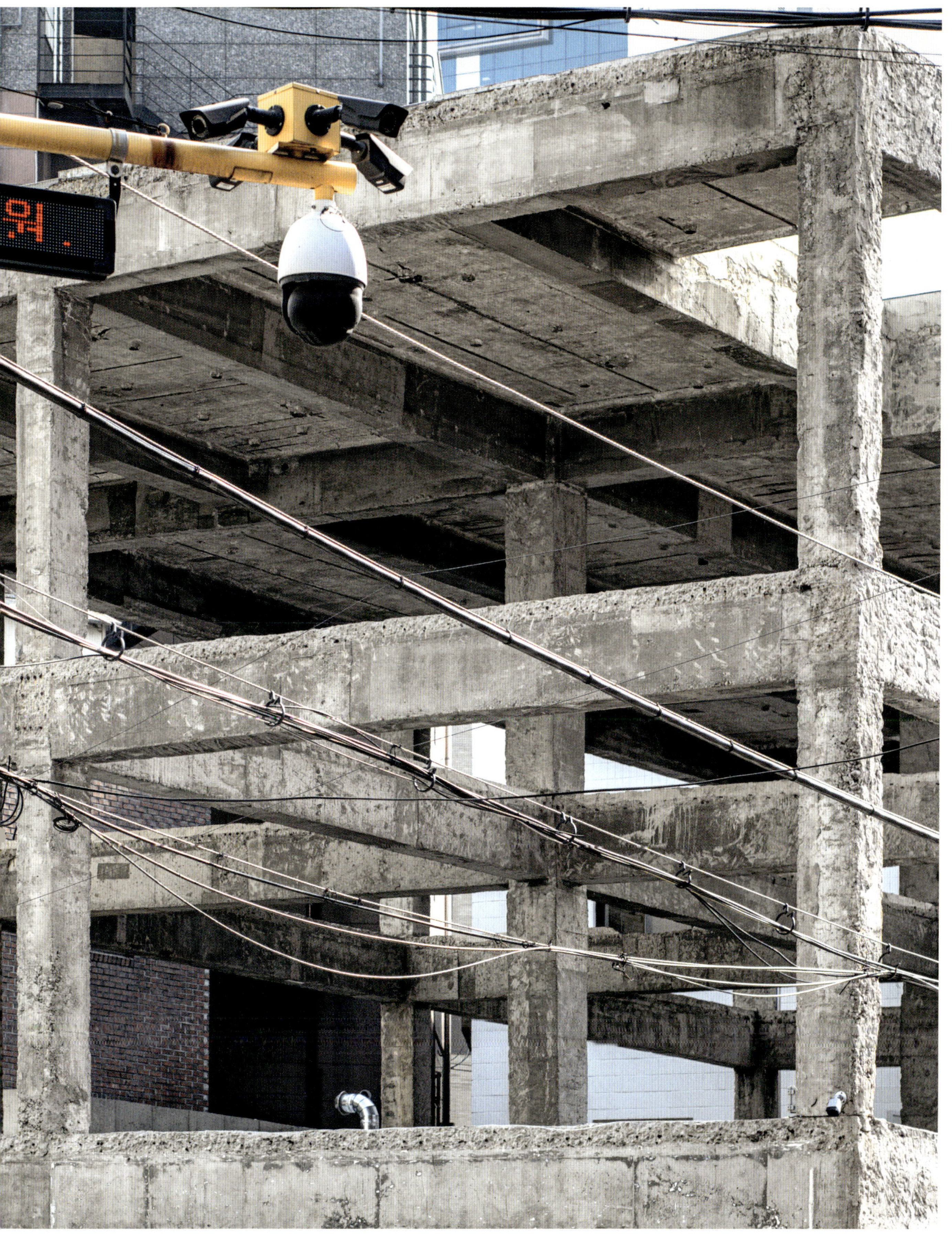

URBAN HIVE

SEOUL · Architect: KIM In-cheurl · Completed 2008

From a distance, Urban Hive looks less like a building and more like something a particularly creative colony of wasps might construct. Located in the heart of Seoul's Gangnam district, this seventeen-storey office block is a masterclass in expressive structuralism – Brutalism not as bunker, but as beehive.

The building's defining feature is its pocked concrete shell, punctuated by 1,318 circular holes that give it the look of a Brutalist apiary. But these aren't just architectural polka dots for visual buzz – they're part of a structural strategy that eliminates internal columns. The result: open, flexible floor plates inside, and a bold, perforated skin outside. Form follows function, sure, but here it also follows honeycomb logic – modular, efficient, and wildly satisfying.

The concrete façade is load-bearing, and proudly so – no cladding, no apologies. It's exposed and swarming with intent. The holes, cast using steel forms, speak to Brutalism's love of imprint and process. You can almost feel the casting; the memory of labour is preserved in concrete.

And if Brutalism has often been accused of coldness, Urban Hive responds with wit. It is playful without being frivolous, poetic without being soft. A honeybee's dream, perhaps – a place where structure, community, and repetition coalesce into an urban ecosystem.

There's a sly cultural sting too: in a district featuring glossy façades and cosmetic polish, Urban Hive embraces its pores. It hides no skin – it revels in it. Concrete here isn't brutal – it's busy, buzzing, bearing weight and meaning.

Kim's vision redefines what Brutalism can mean in a vertical, hyper-dense Korean context. Urban Hive seeks no domination of the skyline – it works it, burrows into it, and proves that, in the right hands, concrete can buzz and fly.

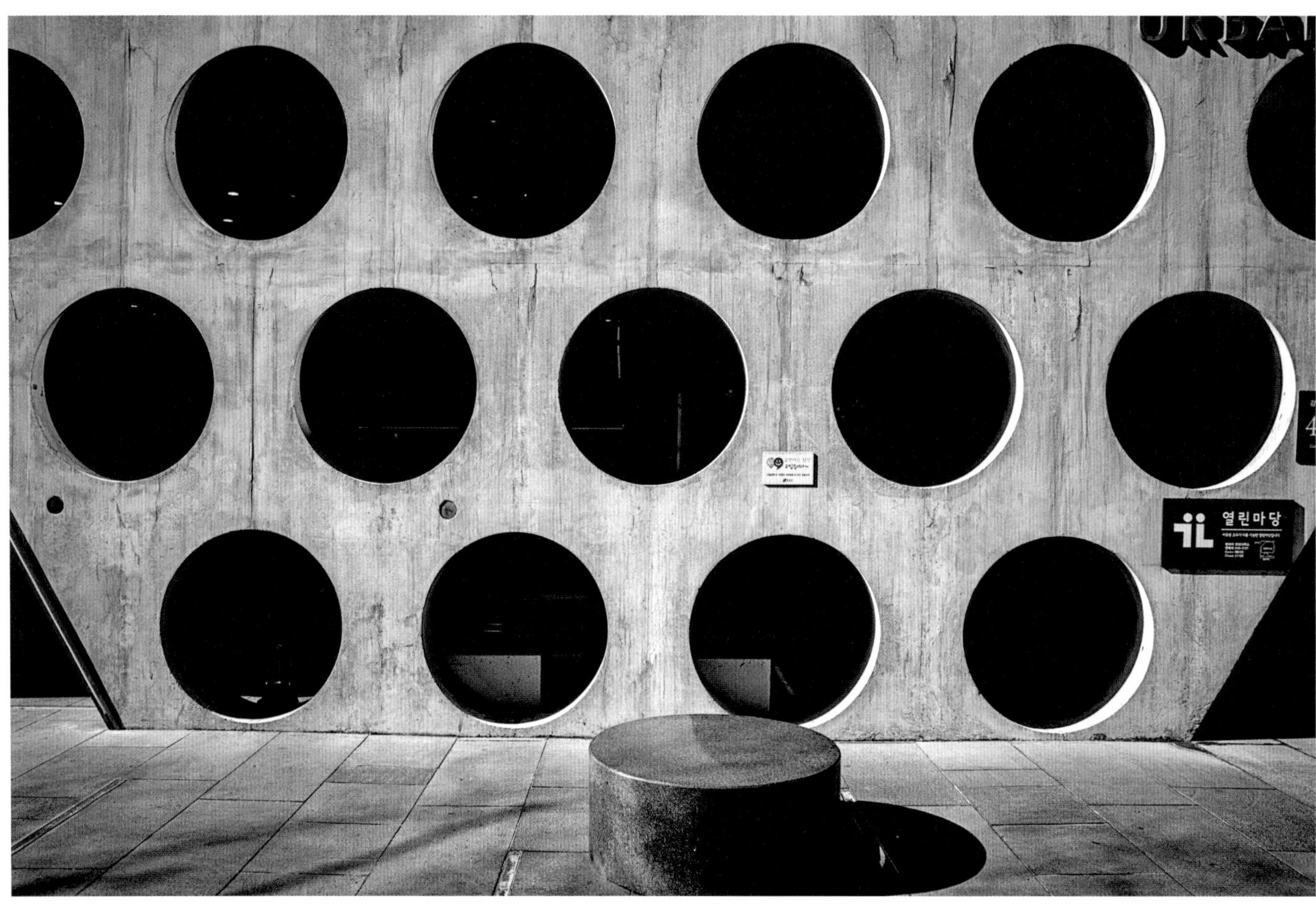

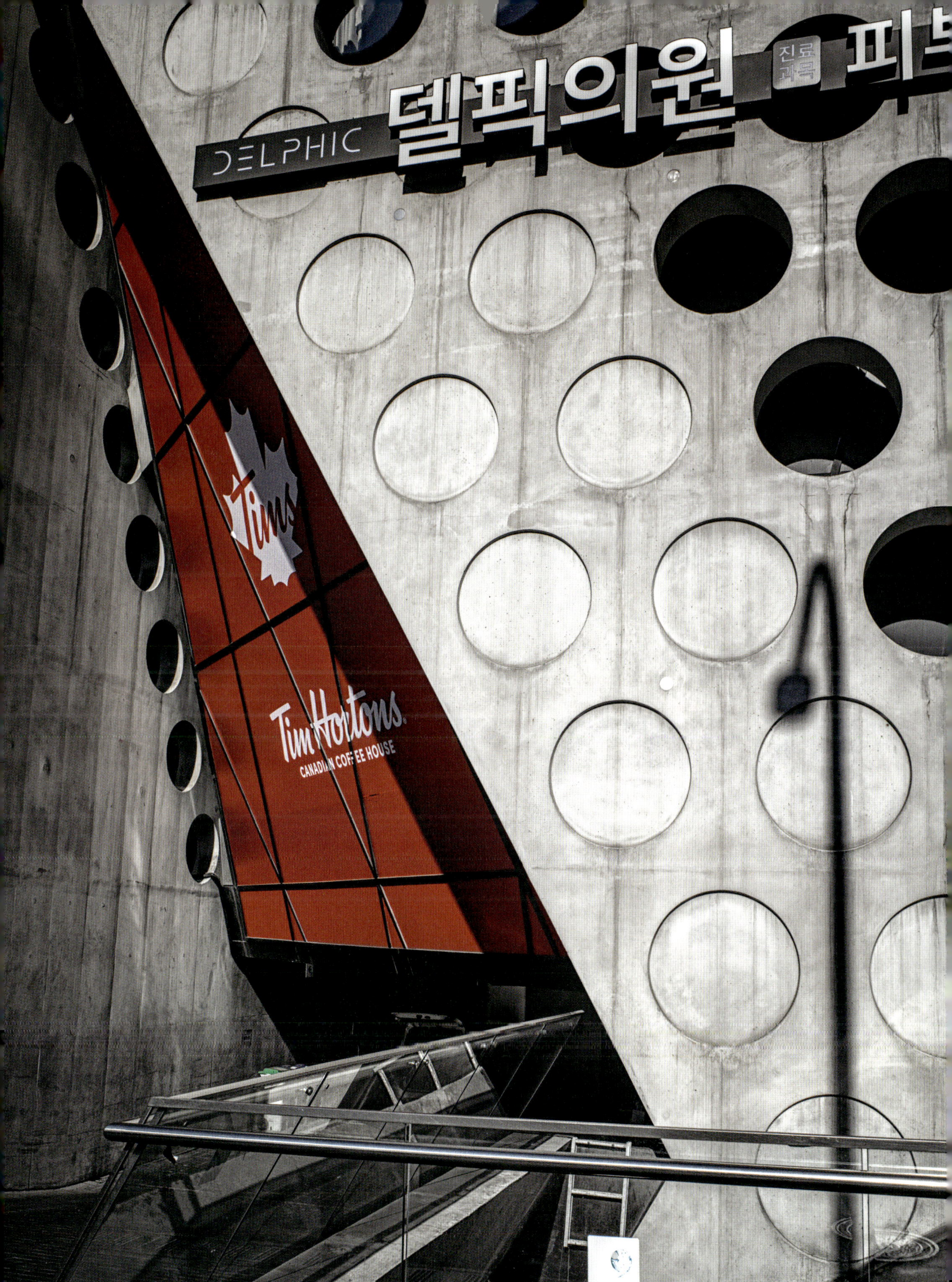
DELPHIC
델픽의원
진료
과목
Tims
Tim Hortons.
CANADIAN COFFEE HOUSE

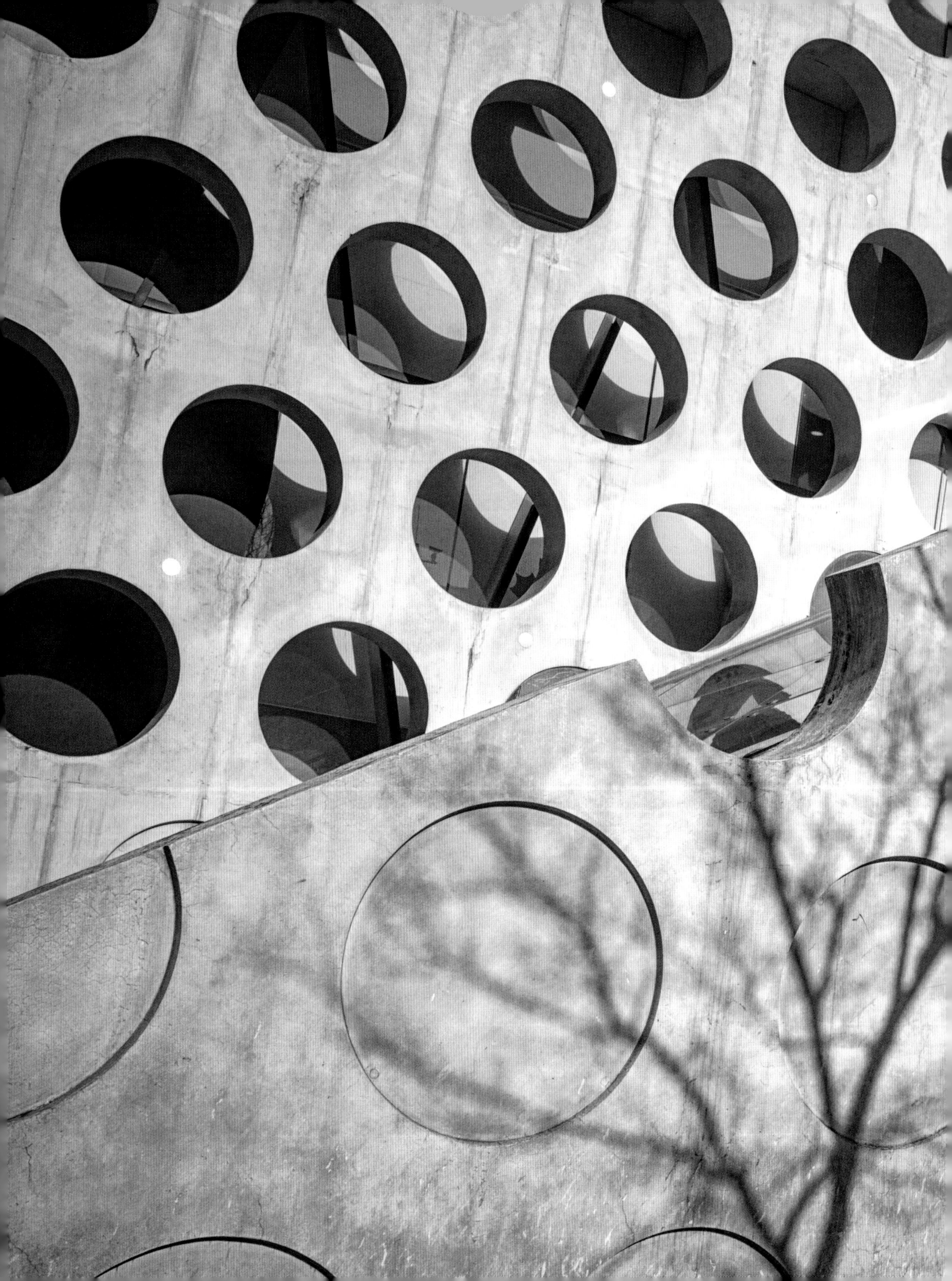

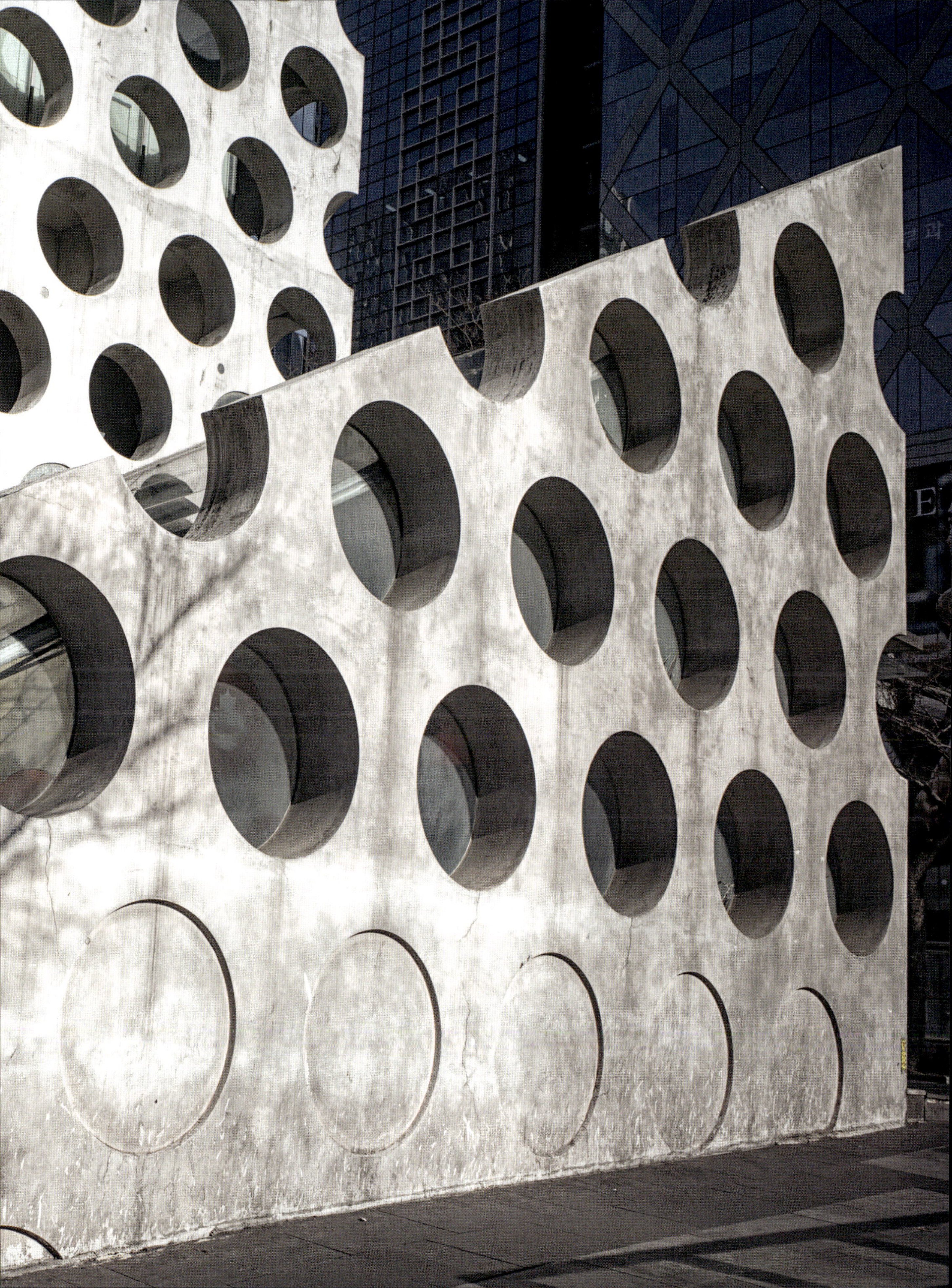

MIRADOURO SODAE

SAYUWON · Architects: Álvaro SIZA VIEIRA and Carlos CASTANHEIRA · Completed 2019

The Sodae observation tower within Sayuwon arboretum rises as a quiet assertion against the sky – a 20.5-metre column of bare concrete that seems to think as much as it offers reflection. Designed by Álvaro Siza and Carlos Castanheira, it doesn't impose on the forest but joins its vertical rhythm, like a man-made tree that forgot to branch.

Inside, a spiral stair coils tightly within the shaft, each pause revealing fragments of pine canopy and slivers of horizon. The climb feels measured, almost meditative – an architectural breath held until release. At the summit, a modest balcony breaks the enclosure, spilling the visitor into a panorama of ridges and light.

Every surface tells its own story: grain marks from formwork, seams left visible, concrete left unvarnished. It is Brutalism stripped of aggression, reduced to patience and precision.

Not just mimicking a pagoda, Sodae Tower distils its spirit – an act of looking upwards through humility. This is architecture without flourish or ego, where material, motion, and meaning are pared to their essence. A tower that seeks not attention, but quietly teaches you to see.

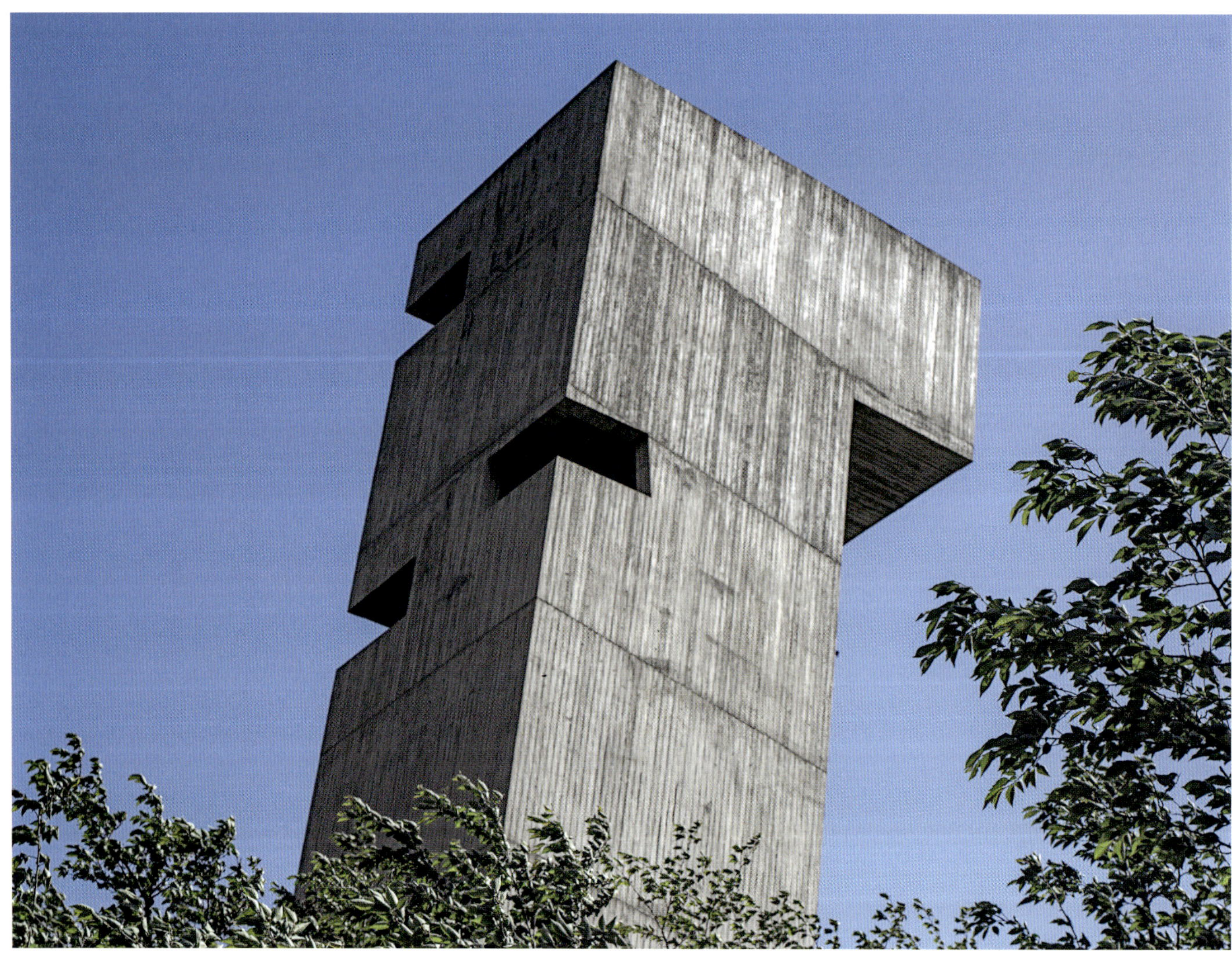

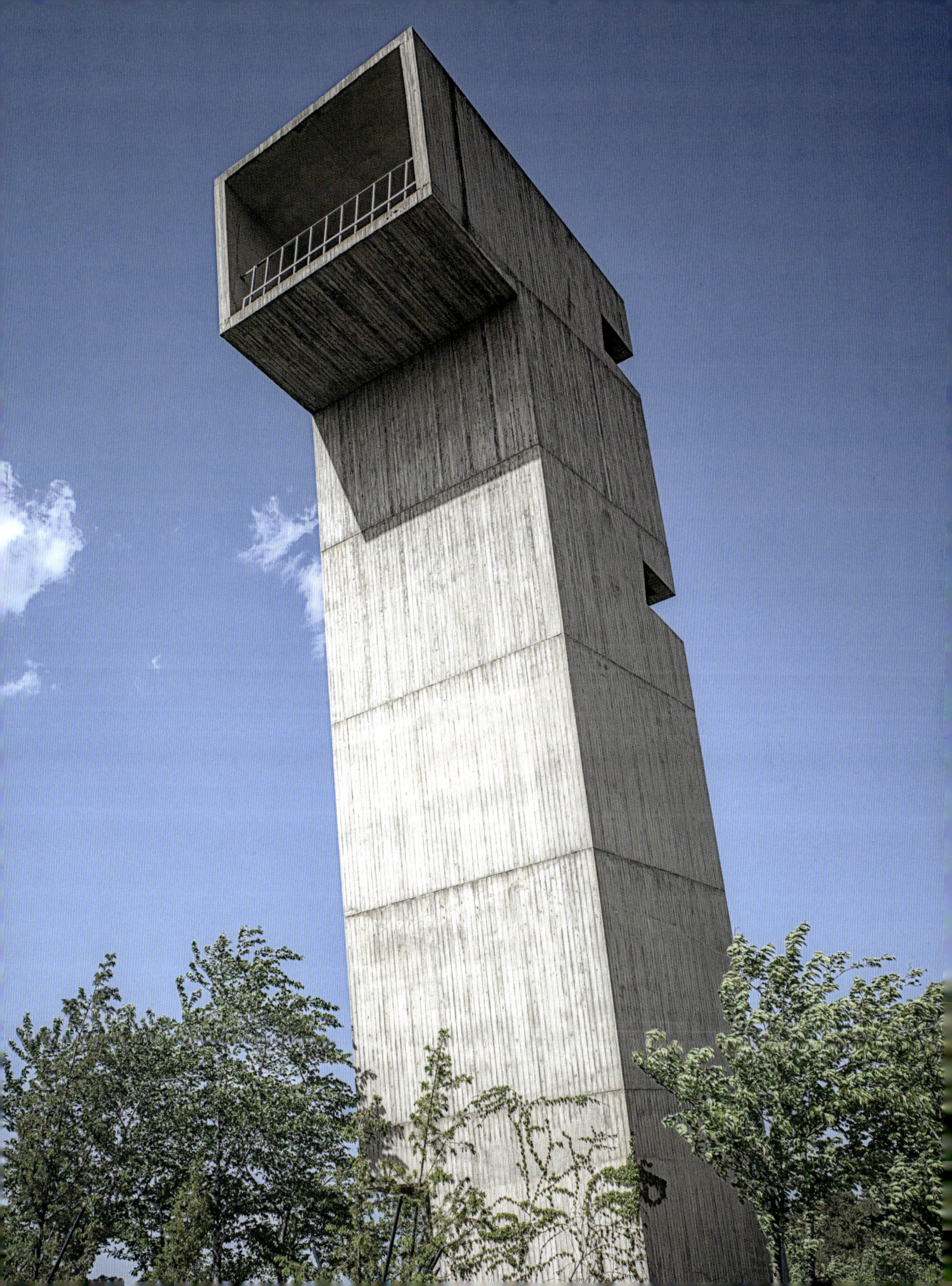

CHURCH OF SKY / BANGJU CHURCH

JEJU ISLAND · Architect: ITAMI Jun · Completed 2009

The Church of Sky feels less like a building and more like an atmosphere with walls. Designed by Itami Jun, it floats above its reflection in quiet defiance of gravity – a glass-and-concrete meditation on stillness. The long, gabled form recalls both chapel and barn, yet it transcends utility, turning simplicity into reverence.

Light here is the true liturgy. It filters through frosted glass like breath through silk, softening every edge until shadow and illumination share equal custody of the space. There's no steeple or stained glass, only a modest arched window – a gentle affirmation that faith can be architectural, not ornamental.

Jun's mastery lies in restraint. Each surface, joint, and reflection contributes to a silence that speaks fluently. The Church of Sky is less an appeal to belief than an invitation to pause – a place where light preaches, glass listens, and architecture remembers to breathe.

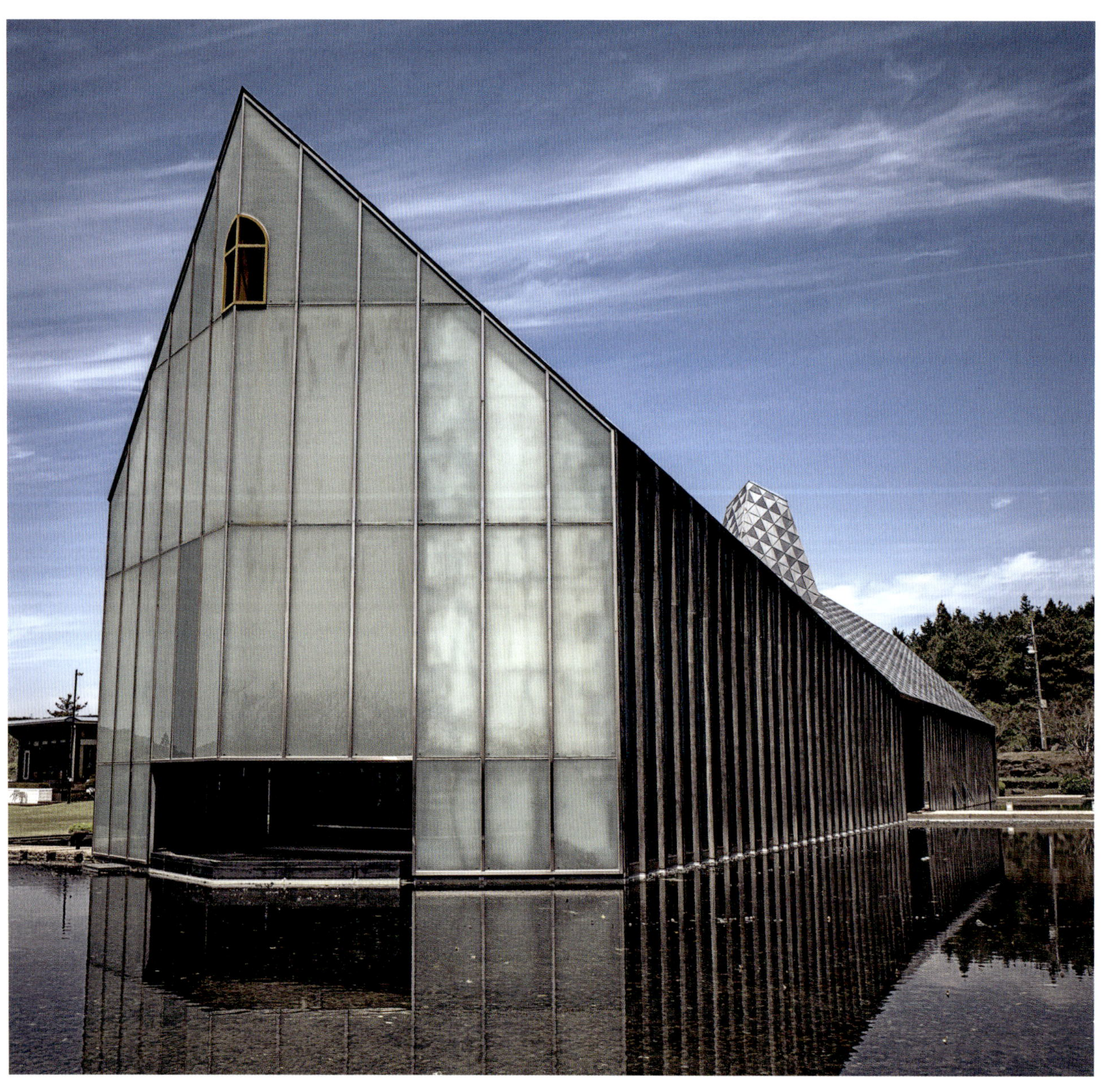

RANDOM CHURCH

JEJU ISLAND

This modest white structure presents a study in restraint and curvature. Its smooth, continuous concrete shell arcs gently from one end to the other, as if shaped by the island's prevailing winds. The exterior is punctuated by an irregular array of square windows, their uneven rhythm softening the otherwise monolithic façade while allowing measured light to filter within. The simplicity of the form belies a sophisticated handling of proportion and mass, the curvature evoking both movement and shelter. A slender cross fixed near the tallest edge quietly declares its ecclesiastical purpose, without indulgence or grandeur. The building's calm, sculptural presence aligns with Jeju's contemplative landscape – an architecture of humility and introspection that fuses modernist clarity with the poetics of local light and stone. My random stumbling across it prays for its anonymity. Apologies if not a confession.

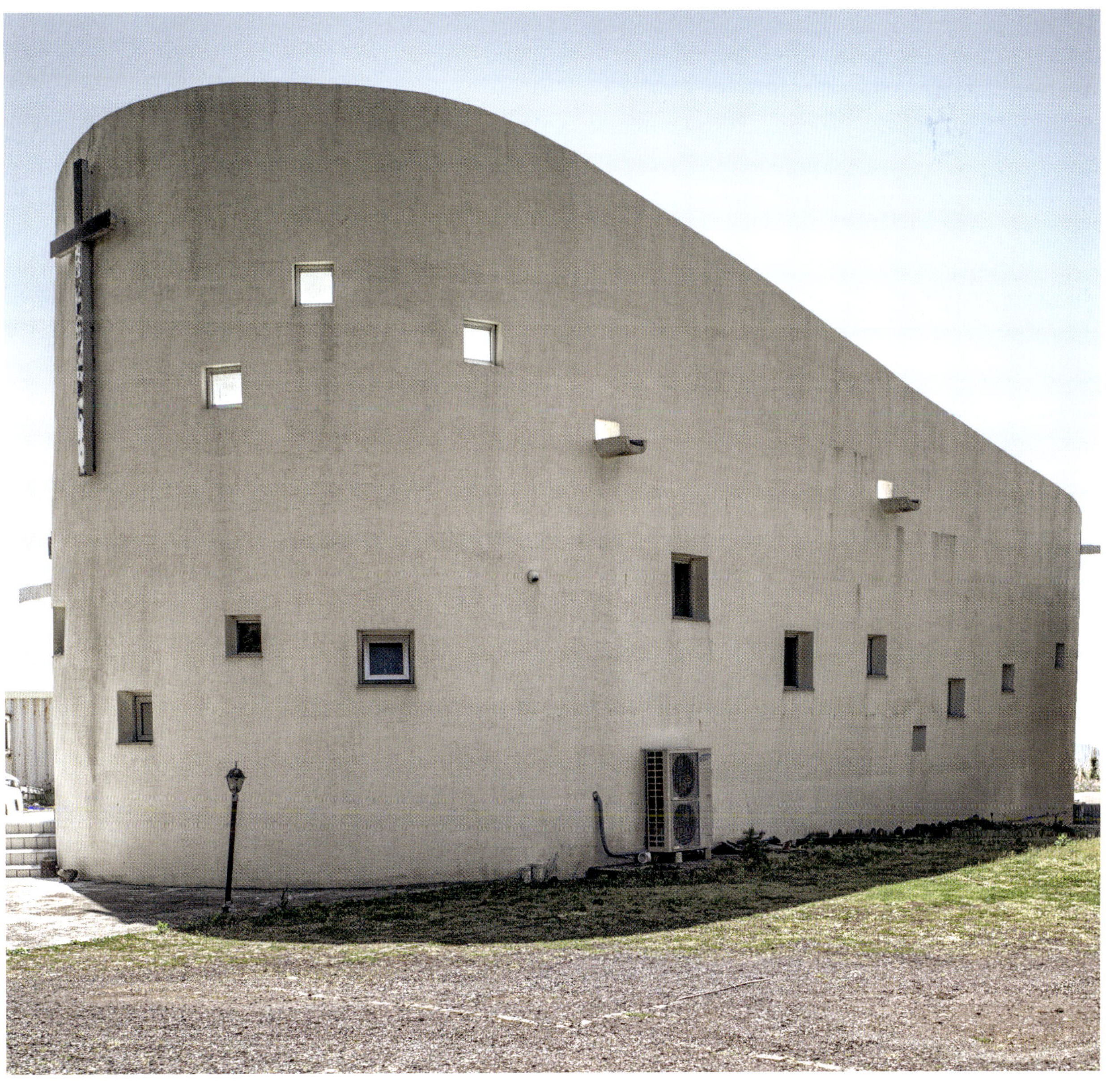

CYBERPUNK SEAWALL

JEJU ISLAND

Concrete and code converge here on the Korean coast – a tableau of Brutalism's endurance refracted through the lens of a cybernetic age. The hulking tetrapods in the foreground are pure utility: mute grey guardians engineered to resist the sea, their fractured geometry shaped by function. They are architecture's most honest expression – unornamented, unsentimental, built to endure. Yet against this landscape of poured defiance rises a façade alive with digital light: a mural flickering with the purple hues of a screen-born world, an avatar presiding over the static architecture of the past.

Together, they form a paradoxical harmony – the tactile and the virtual, the heavy and the ephemeral. The concrete recalls utilitarianism, material honesty as moral virtue; the mural, the synthetic future where identity and image supersede structure. The cracked surfaces of the tetrapods seem almost to absorb and subdue the glow above them, as though the analogue world is learning to dream in pixels.

This juxtaposition feels uniquely Korean – a nation where resilience, reinvention, and restless modernity constantly collide. The tetrapods' utilitarian mass meets the cyberpunk shimmer of the city, evoking a society poised between survival and simulation. Here Brutalism's rough dignity finds its afterlife in a world of networks and colour. The sea defences no longer only hold back the tide, they anchor a visual metaphor – the last bastions of the physical in an age drifting towards the digital.

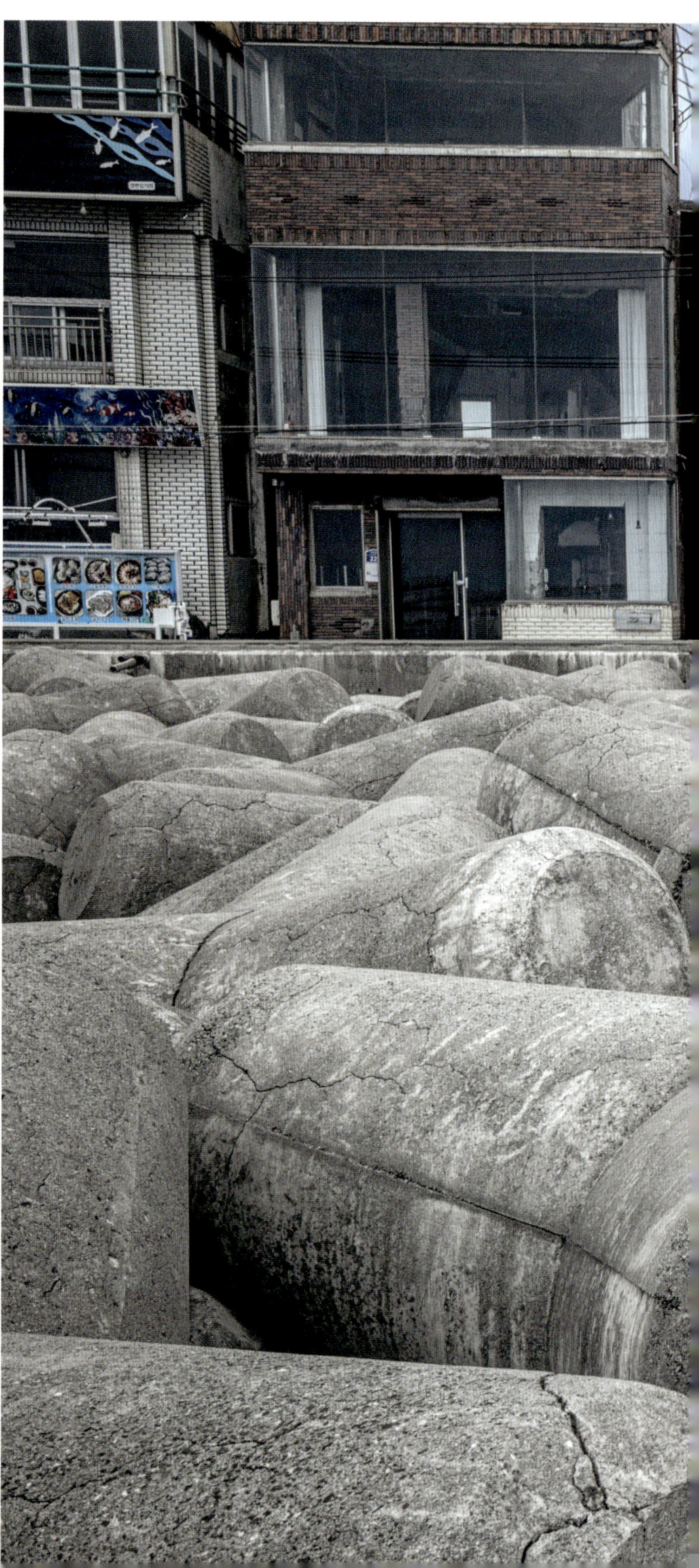

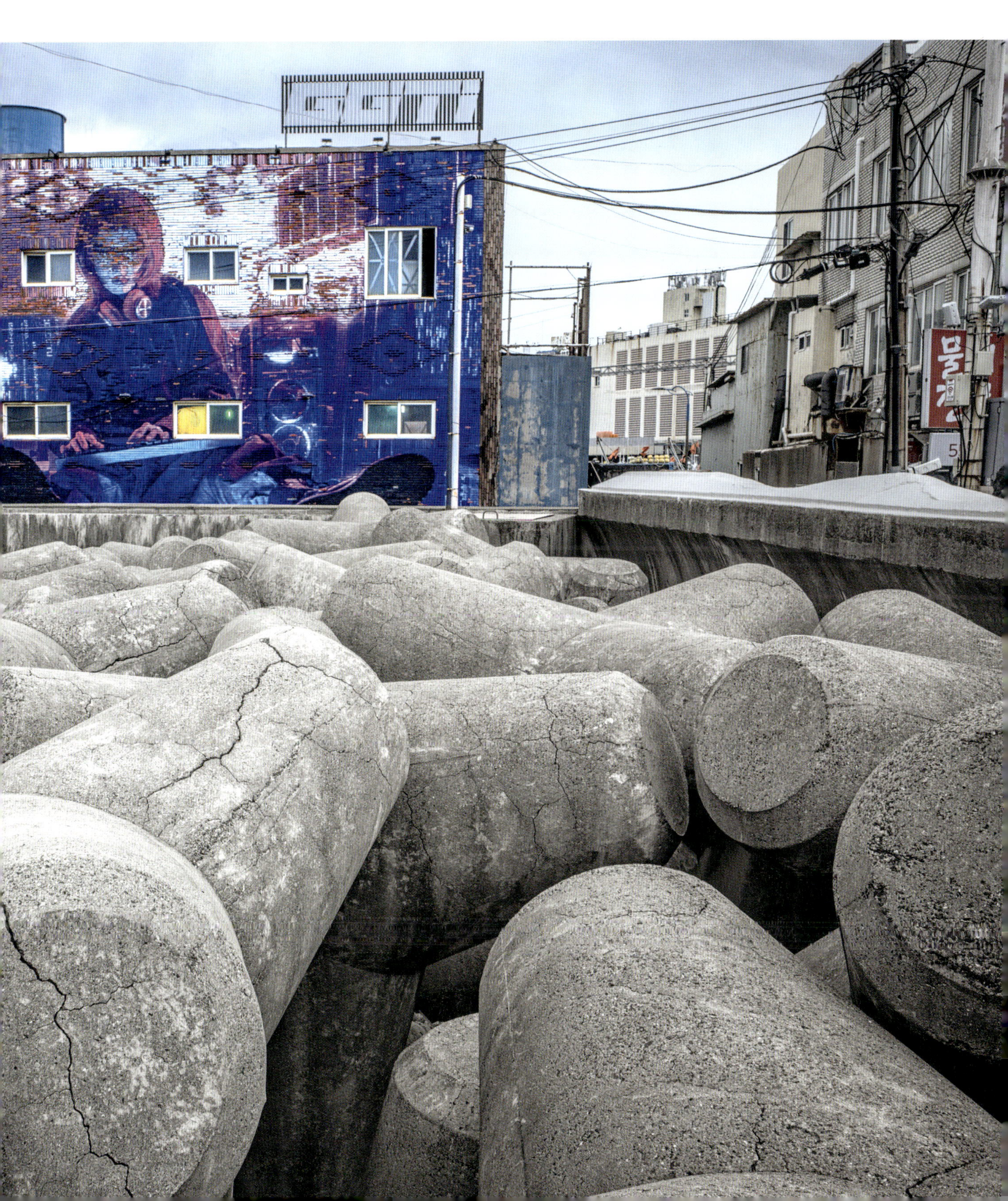

THE NEST OF YELLOW OWL (MU:M BUILDING)

PAJU BOOK CITY · Architect: WISE Architecture · Completed 2015

STUDIO M

PAJU BOOK CITY · Architect: Society of Architecture · Completed 2017

In the quiet order of Paju Book City, the MU:M Education Building (opposite page) composes a lesson in measured expression. Designed by WISE Architecture and completed in 2015, it responds to the region's cold climate with introverted poise. Behind its rectilinear shell lies a carefully orchestrated interior: a T-shaped atrium intersected by a vertical circulation spine, where movement and light choreograph a quiet accord. The building's heart – a terraced garden rising through its levels – turns verticality into social terrain, giving respite and rhythm to the daily routine.

Yet it is the façade that truly instructs. A grid of deep-brown brick folds upwards from the ground as if the earth itself were inhaling. The curvature softens the building's logic, turning a rigid system into tactile sculpture.

If Brutalism is the honest expression of structure and material, then Korea has found its brick vernacular here and in MU:M's fellow Paju resident, Studio M (below) – precise, poetic, and unafraid of warmth. Brutalism, after all, need not always be concrete. Nor must it remain trapped in the mid-century window between the 1950s and 1970s that purists insist upon.

What follows is what I call Nu-Bru: a continuation, not a revival. Brutalism stripped of nostalgia and rebuilt for now – still raw, still candid, but tempered with empathy. A material language that endures because it refuses to pretend.

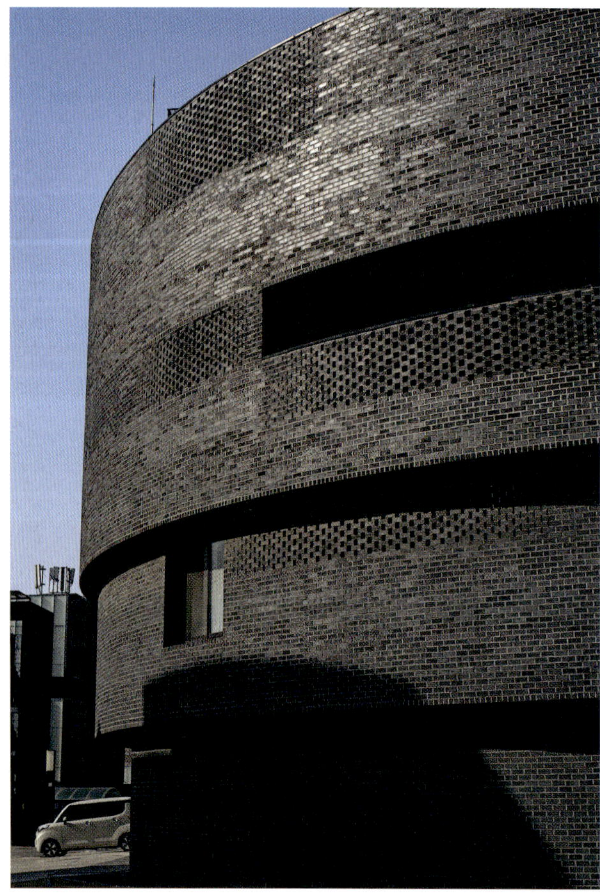

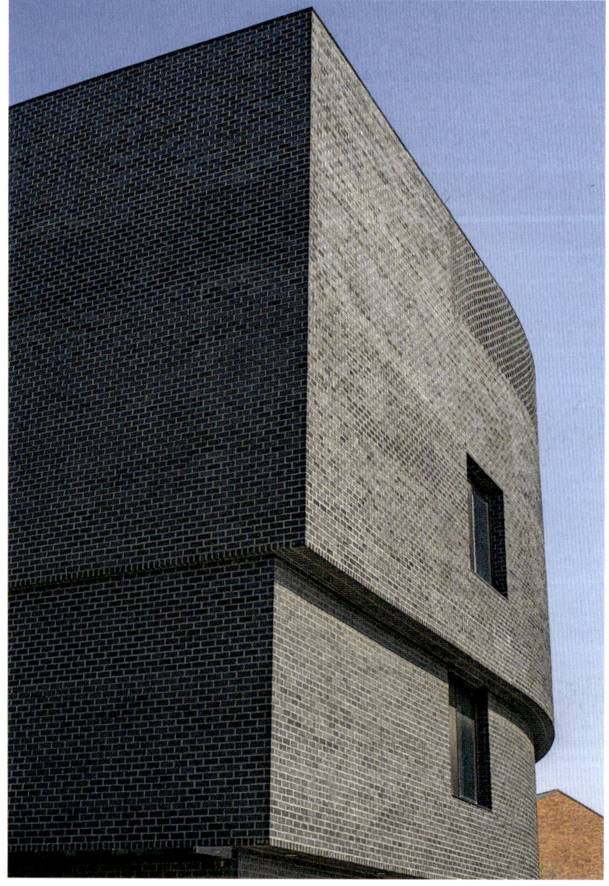

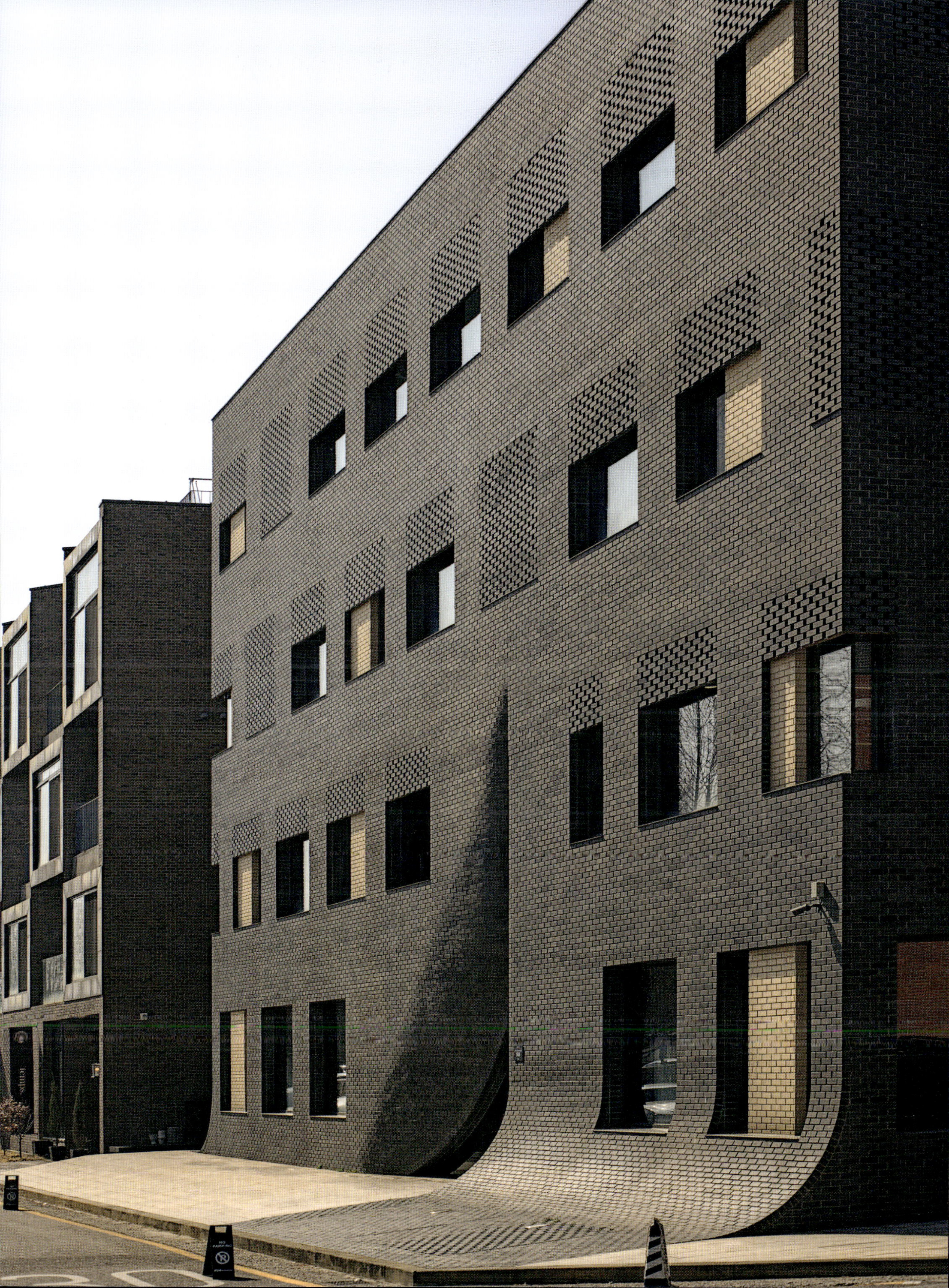

ACKNOWLEDGEMENTS

Immense gratitude to Curt Holtz, whose suggestion, commissioning, and support made this book possible. His enthusiasm, direction, humour, patience, and generosity have been very important, as ever.

Huge thanks again to Jonathan Fox for his incredible hawk-eyed observations as copy-editor.

A big thank you to Saratani Yumi and Oh Woolee for superb location scouting – a task greatly aided by Blue Crow Media's *Concrete Seoul Map*. I am also greatly thankful to Saratani Yumi for some crucial fact-checking.

Massive recognition to Florian Frohnholzer, Lukas Schimpfhauser, and Mirey Aytan for their keen eyes and thoughtful shot selection during the design layout.

Lastly, I wish to thank all those who have supported me in one way or another in completing *Brutalist Korea*. You know who you are. Especially The Rink for being by my feet as I wrote and edited shots. And, of course, Mama and Loon.

AUTHOR BIOGRAPHY

Paul Tulett is an Okinawa-based photographer and writer focused on Brutalist architecture. His interest in Brutalism grew during postgraduate studies in Urban Planning and Environment at RMIT, Australia. Through his Instagram account (@brutal_zen) he aims to promote interest in this previously maligned and misunderstood style. His work has been published in many publications including *The Guardian* and *Design Anthology*. He is also the author and photographer of *Brutalist Japan*, published by Prestel Publishing in 2024.

produktsicherheit@penguinrandomhouse.de
(The above information is mandatory according to GPSR)

First edition

Cover image: Dongdaemun Design Plaza, Seoul; see p. 12
Page 2: Urban Hive, Seoul; see p. 228
Page 6: The Closest Church, Gimpo New Town; see p. 188
Page 10: Dongdaemun Design Plaza, Seoul; see p. 12
Page 62: Diesel Store, Seoul / Architect: Unknown

A Library of Congress Control Number is available. A CIP catalogue record for this book is available from the British Library.

Editorial direction: Curt Holtz
Copy-editing: Jonathan Fox
Design and typesetting: Sofarobotnik, Augsburg/Munich
Production: Cilly Klotz
Origination: Helio Repro GmbH, Munich
Printing and binding: Livonia Print, Riga
Paper: Magno Volume

Penguin Random House Verlagsgruppe FSC® N001967

Printed in Latvia

ISBN 978-3-7913-7655-4
www.prestel.com